THE BEACH BOYS IN CONCERT

THE BEACH BOYS
IN CONCERT

THE ULTIMATE HISTORY OF AMERICA'S BAND ON TOUR AND ONSTAGE

IAN RUSTEN and JON STEBBINS

Backbeat
Books

An Imprint of Hal Leonard Corporation

Published in 2013 by Backbeat Books
An Imprint of Hal Leonard Corporation
7777 West Bluemound Road
Milwaukee, WI 53213

Trade Book Division Editorial Offices
33 Plymouth St., Montclair, NJ 07042

Printed in China through Colorcraft Ltd., Hong Kong

Book design by Damien Castaneda

Library of Congress Cataloging-in-Publication Data

Rusten, Ian.
 The Beach Boys in concert : the ultimate history of America's band on tour and onstage / Ian Rusten and Jon Stebbins.
     p. cm.
 Includes bibliographical references.
 ISBN 978-1-61713-456-2
1. Beach Boys--Performances. 2. Beach Boys--History--Chronology. 3. Rock musicians--United States--Biography. I. Stebbins, Jon. II. Title.
 ML421.B38R87 2013
 782.42166092'2--dc23
 [B]
                          2012040964

www.backbeatbooks.com

CONTENTS

Acknowledgments . . . . *vii*

Opening Act: The Beach Boys'
Pre-Concert History *1*
1961–1962 . . . . *5*
1963 . . . . *17*
1964 . . . . *35*
1965 . . . . *53*
1966 . . . . *69*
1967 . . . . *85*
1968 . . . . *99*
1969 . . . . *117*
1970 . . . . *131*
1971 . . . . *143*
1972 . . . . *159*
1973 . . . . *175*
1974 . . . . *191*
1975 . . . . *205*
1976 . . . . *217*
1977 . . . . *223*
1978 . . . . *231*
1979 . . . . *241*
1980 . . . . *249*
1981 . . . . *257*
1982 . . . . *269*
1983 . . . . *279*
1984 . . . . *289*
1985 . . . . *299*
1986 . . . . *307*
1987 . . . . *313*
1988 . . . . *321*
1989 . . . . *329*
1990 . . . . *335*
1991 . . . . *341*
1992 . . . . *347*
1993 . . . . *351*
1994 . . . . *357*
1995 . . . . *361*
1996 . . . . *367*
1997 . . . . *371*
1998–2011 . . . . *375*
The Beach Boys' Solo Concerts *385*
The 2012 Reunion *399*

Bibliography *405*

ACKNOWLEDGMENTS

We would like to acknowledge the people who helped in the creation of this book, including: Ron Altbach, Bill Allen, Eric Anniversario, Panayiotis Bagdanos, David Beard, Bill Boggie, Russ Bodnar, Alan Boyd, Christian Bremer, Caroline Brenner, Felix Brenner, Ivan Browne, Tracy Bryant, Alex Del Zoppo, Stephen Desper, Mark Dillon, Andrew G. Doe, Daryl Dragon, Dennis Dragon, Doug Dragon, Howie Edelson, Bobby Figueroa, Todd Forman, Jeffrey Foskett, Bill Freedman, Carl Giammarese, George Heon, David Higginbotham, Annie Hinsche, Billy Hinsche, Pete Howard, Martin Johansson, Jesse Karp, Mark Kennedy, Mary Kennedy, Jim Koplik, Peter Kronhagel, Greg Larson, Richard Lazarski, Robert Lecker, Alice Lillie, Jack Lloyd, Tony Loiacano, James Lowe, David and Carrie Marks, Ting Markulin, Steve Mayo, Stephen McParland, Richard Meli, Tom Murphy, Rick Nelson, Gene Oppermann, Michael Osterkamp, Julio Pelayo, Jim Photoglo, Domenic Priore, Chip Rachlin, Dick Ray, Ed and Annie Roach, Lance Robison, Joe Russo, David Salter, John Philip Shenale, Rob Shepherd, Jim Satcher, Craig Slowinski, Sterling Smith, Bruce Snoap, Ron Swallow, Ray Taylor, Fred Vail, Klaas Jelle Veenstra, Justin Waldstein, Jim Waller, Gabriel Witteveen, and Chris Woods.

Special thanks to the Beach Boys for bringing happiness to so many for so long!

IAN'S MESSAGE

I would like to thank the staff at the many universities and libraries that provided me with articles and photographs. I would like to send a personal thanks to my parents and friends for their support. A special thanks to the Witter and Coleman families. This book is dedicated to my beautiful wife Rebekah, who has helped me more than words can say, and my daughters Hannah and Katherine.

JON'S MESSAGE

Thanks to the staff at Backbeat Books and the Hal Leonard Group for believing in this project. A special thanks to Bernadette Malavarca for her patience and understanding. I'd especially like to thank my family and friends for their constant support and good vibrations. To Nadia, Shannon, and Sophie, my little surfer girls . . . I love you!

OPENING ACT:
THE BEACH BOYS'
PRE-CONCERT HISTORY

THE BEACH BOYS story began in Hawthorne, California, nicknamed "The City of Good Neighbors." In the 1940s, Hawthorne was a typical suburban, Southern California town, located five miles from the Pacific Ocean. It was here that Murry Gage Wilson, an employee of the Goodyear Tire and Rubber Company, and his wife Audree Neve Korthof settled at the end of World War II with their young sons, Brian Douglas Wilson (born June 20, 1942) and Dennis Carl Wilson (born December 4, 1944). The birth of Carl Dean Wilson on December 21, 1946, completed the Wilson family. They lived in a modest two-bedroom house at 3701 West 119 Street, right near the border separating Hawthorne from the neighboring town of Inglewood.

Murry was born far from the beach, in Hutchinson, Kansas, in 1917. He came west with his parents and siblings in the 1920s. His father Buddy moved the family to California in the hopes of a better life, but his self-destructive alcoholic ways made life very difficult for his family. Physical abuse was common in the Wilson household, and the children lived in semi-terror of Buddy. Murry was forced, at a young age, to act as protector of his mother and her eight children. At the age of seventeen, he was already working to support them. Murry was determined to be a better provider than his own father had been. He would not let anyone push him around and developed a brash personality, bordering on obnoxiousness. In 1945, he lost an eye in an industrial accident and had to be fitted with a glass replacement. But Murry persevered. After stints at Goodyear and a local Air Research company, he took a major risk, mortgaging his home to finance his own business. His company, A.B.L.E. (Always Better Lasting Equipment), rented heavy industrial equipment like metal lathes and hydraulic presses.

In later years, Murry often repeated a mantra to his children: "You have to fight for success!" He was a bear-like figure with a booming voice. Murry was involved in every aspect of his children's lives and expected them to follow his rules. However, Murry's own parenting skills left much to be desired. Brian frequently suggested that his father was responsible for his deafness in his right ear. In 1971, when writer Tom Nolan asked Brian how he came to lose most of the hearing, he responded, "Ever since I was born, or maybe, when I was two years old, somebody punched me in the ear." Murry was the obvious suspect. Rebellious middle brother Dennis received the worst of Murry's wrath. Dennis received so much physical abuse from his father that by the time he was twelve years old, he made it a point to be out of the house as much as possible. Youngest brother Carl also learned to avoid his father, using his loving mother as a shield.

The one thing that united the family was a love of music. Murry recalled in *Rolling Stone*, "The Wilson boys have always heard music in their home, from my writing songs and friends of ours who came over." Murry was a determined songwriter and spent hours at the piano coming up with polka and easy listening tunes. His proudest moment came when Lawrence Welk performed his own composition, "Two Step, Side Step" on his early 1950s radio show. Murry and Audree often sang duets around the piano at night, and the children were expected to participate. Brian, especially, showed an aptitude for music from a young age and mastered the piano by age ten. He loved the family harmonizing and would often sing with his brothers for fun. In a 1976 *Circus* magazine interview, Dennis recalled, "My dad would take us out to dinner and we used to write tunes. The three of us would sing three-part harmony every Friday night in the back seat." Sometimes, the Wilsons would visit Murry's sister Emily (nicknamed "Glee" by her family) and sing songs with her and her husband Milton Love and their children, Michael, Maureen, Stephen, Stanley, and Stephanie. They lived on the corner of Mt. Vernon and Fairway (later immortalized by Brian in his "Fairytale" on the *Holland* album) in the more prosperous suburb of View Park. The Wilsons and Loves had a competitive relationship, which eldest son Michael Love once referred to as "like the Hatfields and McCoys." Mike recalled in a 1967 *New Musical Express* interview, "Sometimes at Christmas we'd have a tremendous party. All the relatives would come . . . We'd go caroling in a big group—it would sound very impressive."

Michael Love (born 1941) was strawberry blond, athletic, handsome, and confident. He ran track at Dorsey High, a mostly black school, and there he developed a love for the rhythm and blues music that many urban teens listened and danced to. Carl stated, "He was really immersed in doo wop and that music, and I think he influenced Brian to listen to it." Brian, who was a year younger than Mike, loved singing with his cousin. Mike's unique bass voice added a strong element to the vocal blend Brian had developed with his brothers. Brian, who had the ability to sing in a piercing falsetto, would always take the top line, Mike took the bottom parts, and Carl (and sometimes Dennis) filled in the middle register.

It was around 1958 that Brian made one of the most important musical discoveries of his life. His mother took him to a record store where he first heard the music of the modern jazz vocal quartet, the Four Freshmen. Founded in Indianapolis, the group was composed of Ross and Don Barbour, Bob Flanigan, and Ken Errair. Their pioneering style of complex vocal harmony earned them a devoted following and they were signed to Capitol Records, for whom they recorded hit songs such as "Day by Day" and "Graduation Day." As writer Philip Lambert pointed out, their vocal style utilized "wide distances between (vocal) parts, creating a sense of openness not usually found in other vocal groups of the time, and the movement of lower voices while the upper melody holds a note." The Four Freshmen's music had a profound impact on Brian. As he explained to *NME* reporter Ian Dove in 1964, "I heard the Four Freshmen years ago and right away I flipped. They had the most unique harmony, the best arrangements, and a fantastic blend of voices." Carl recalled that his older brother would play the piano for hours, recreating the music that he heard on Four Freshmen records note for note. Brian taught his brothers and his cousin Mike all the parts to their songs, especially "Their Hearts Were Full of Spring" and "Graduation Day," and rehearsed them constantly. Soon Brian began to create his own unique arrangements of the songs. Brian's parents bought a tape recorder and the enthusiastic teenager would record his vocals over and over again, creating harmonies and counter harmonies.

Carl was just as interested in music as Brian. His passion, however, was reserved for the guitar. In a 1966 *Tiger Beat* article, he related, "A friend of my parents, a fantastic guitarist, often dropped by to play . . . Whenever he put down the guitar I'd grab it and start messing around . . . The instrument fascinated me . . . My folks bought me a guitar when I was 12." Soon, young Carl was practicing all the time, eagerly copying the riffs he heard on the records that he loved. Carl recalled in a 1981 TV interview, "I was listening mostly to Chuck Berry. I had Chuck Berry's albums and he was really the main influence on me, musically speaking. The guitar . . . the way he played the boogie guitar and did all those guitar riffs was really thrilling for me to hear." Due to mutual interest in the guitar, Carl befriended a neighbor named David Marks from across the street.

David was born in Pennsylvania in 1948 and had moved to California with his parents Elmer and Jo Ann in 1956. He soon became friends with neighborhood terror Dennis Wilson, and the two often sought trouble together. Though David liked raising hell with Dennis, he had a more serious side. Like Carl, he was fascinated by the guitar and convinced his parents to buy him one when he was only ten years old. He soon began taking lessons from a local boy named John Maus, who would later achieve fame as one of the Walker Brothers. John had impressive credentials, having learned guitar technique from Hispanic rock legend Ritchie Valens. Maus also had the distinction of having recorded a string of singles on the Dore label with his sister Judy. Soon both David and Carl were studying with Maus, who gave them a quick course in Rock Guitar 101. By 1960, David and Carl were spending most of their free time playing guitar together. As David recalled, "We would get together every day in my room and play records by Duane Eddy, Chuck Berry, Dick Dale, and the Ventures." This rock 'n' roll guitar sound would figure prominently in the early Beach Boys records.

Making records, however, was still a distant dream in 1960. That fall, Brian Wilson enrolled at El Camino College with a plan to major in music and psychology. Mike Love had no interest in college and took a job pumping gas. Reality hit Mike hard when his girlfriend Frances St. Martin became pregnant, and his parents reacted by asking him to move out. In early 1961, Mike was married with a young child and working at his father's sheet metal company. Mike continually pestered Brian to form a real musical act to see if they could make some money at it. Brian was intrigued by the idea, but shy as a performer. Brian and Mike would often get together to sing with Mike's sister Maureen or Brian's friends, but this was closer to recreation than ambition. The Wilsons only had to look at their father to see how difficult it was to gain traction in the music business. Still, Brian and Carl would sometimes appear at talent shows or school assemblies. It was at one of these events in 1960 that Brian's classmate Al Jardine first saw them sing.

Alan Jardine was born in Lima, Ohio, in 1942 and moved to California with his family in 1955. He met and became friends with Brian while both played football for the Hawthorne High Cougars. A short compact youth with blond hair, Al was the team's halfback. Besides an interest in football, Al and Brian shared a love for music, though Al's tastes ran more to the Kingston Trio and other folk-styled acts. Al even had his own folk group in high school, called the Islanders. Al was very serious about his music and recorded a demo at the tiny Stereo Masters studio, owned by Hite Morgan. While enrolled in pre-dentistry courses at El Camino College, Al reconnected with Brian, knowing that his old football buddy had quite a talent for music.

Al was so impressed by Brian, Carl, and Mike's singing that he advocated the idea of forming a vocal group with them. They called themselves the Pendletones, after the checkered wool shirts that were popular at the time. Despite his reputation as a troublemaker, Dennis was also included in the group at the behest of Audree Wilson. As Carl recalled in 1966, the five "began practicing vocal harmonies every chance we had. Mostly we sang Coasters songs and Freshmen arrangements, as Brian was high on their style of vocalizing." Soon the new group gave an audition at Hite and Dorinda Morgan's studio with the goal of making a record. The Morgans were happy to oblige but saw little potential in the material that the boys were offering or in their rudimentary musical abilities. Dorinda Morgan recalled to writer Byron Preiss, "They weren't as smooth as the other group Alan had brought, but knowing Murry . . . we figured Brian had talent as a songwriter. We

"We didn't even know we were the Beach Boys until the record came out. It was that kind of thing. We could have said 'No, we're not going to be the Beach Boys,' but it sounded pretty far out."

—Mike Love

asked them if they had any original material and they said they did not." Things might have ended right there, but fate intervened. Dennis yelled out that Brian was writing a song about surfing. The Morgans were intrigued. Surfing was huge in Southern California, and a song about the sport had surefire commercial potential in L.A. Brian and Mike liked the idea and were soon busily writing the song. However, they lacked the instruments to record it. As legend claims, Murry and Audree departed for a Labor Day weekend getaway and left their sons money for food. With this money and/or a $300 loan that Al begged from his mother, the group managed to rent instruments. They spent the weekend perfecting the new song, which they called "Surfin.'" When Murry and Audree returned from Mexico, they, too, were intrigued. On September 15, the group returned to the Morgans, auditioning the song for them. The Morgans loved it and a professional recording session was booked for October 3, 1961.

The first Pendletones recording session was held at World Pacific Studios in Hollywood. They were extremely green. As Carl recalled a few years later, "Not one of us knew an instrument well . . . I played basic chords on the guitar. Al Jardine thrummed bass. Brian took off his shirt, laid it across the drum and beat it with his hand while we all sang into one microphone." Once the record was completed, the Morgans took it to Joe Saraceno, an A&R man with connections in the local music scene. Saraceno believed that the song had commercial potential and took it to the Dix Brothers, who owned a small record label called Candix. In late November, "Surfin'/Luau" was released as Candix single 331. Suddenly, and before they'd played a single gig, Brian and his group were professional musicians. However, when they received their first copy of the record, they found a surprise. Local A&R man Russ Regan suggested to Saraceno that the group needed a catchier name. Without informing them, the label went ahead and pressed the record as by "the Beach Boys." According to Mike in a 1971 *Crawdaddy* interview, "We didn't even know we were the Beach Boys until the record came out. It was that kind of thing. We could have said 'No, we're not going to be the Beach Boys,' but it sounded pretty far out."

"Surfin'" showed off little of the vocal and arranging abilities that Brian would become known for, but it was catchy and original. While surf music was already a popular form of music in California, the bands that were playing it were instrumental groups. Artists like Dick Dale created an aggressive, propulsive guitar-based music that evoked the excitement of riding powerful waves. The Beach Boys, however, were different. From the start they presented themselves as a vocal group. With the opening unison refrain of "Surfing is the only life, the only life for me" and the unusual doo wop–based background parts, the Beach Boys' fundamental style was indeed in primitive evidence. Dennis convinced Brian that the subject matter would be a success because the group was singing about something that the local kids knew and could relate to. He was right. The song was soon in demand across the entire state of California. By December 1961, it began to garner airplay outside California, and by March 1962 the Beach Boys debut single had peaked at number seventy-five on the *Billboard* singles chart. Their wave had arrived.

"Not one of us knew an instrument well . . . I played basic chords on the guitar. Al Jardine thrummed bass. Brian took off his shirt, laid it across the drum and beat it with his hand while we all sang into one microphone."

—Carl Wilson

1961–1962

WITH THE SUCCESS of "Surfin'" as a calling card, the Beach Boys seized the opportunity to develop as a performing entity. The group made their live debut on December 23, 1961, at the Rendezvous Ballroom in Newport Beach, California, during the intermission of a Dick Dale concert. Eyewitnesses described the appearance as eminently forgettable, but it did not matter. Each day seemed to bring more opportunities. The very next week, the group was invited to appear on local television. Wink Martindale, later to achieve national fame as a game show host, hosted a dance show on KHJ TV in Los Angeles. The Beach Boys joined the American Federation of Television and Radio Artists on December 29, so that they could appear on Martindale's *Dance Party* show the next day. The only problem was that not everyone in the group could play an instrument very well. It was decided that Brian would be the onstage bassist and Dennis would be the drummer. Carl remembered in *Tiger Beat*, "Three days before the show my dad bought Brian an amplifier and a bass, which he learned to play in those three days. Meanwhile, Dennis was whipping the drums like there was no tomorrow. Al gave up his bass and bought an electric guitar like mine."

On New Year's Eve the group made another concert appearance at a Ritchie Valens Memorial Dance in Long Beach, sharing a bill with Ike and Tina Turner. In a 1967 *Flip* magazine article, Mike admitted, "I didn't think we were very good. We certainly didn't look great. We wore ochre-colored sports coats, which cost us $30 each, and our slacks, shirts, and ties weren't what we'd have chosen for leisure wear . . . but the thing then was for groups to wear uniforms, so uniforms we wore." Nevertheless, despite his low opinion of their performance, for Mike the show was a major turning point. He recalled in 1975 that the group was paid $300. "My uncle, our manager, didn't take a cut. We each walked up to the box office and got $60 cash . . . no mailing it to us later." Getting paid for making music was a revelation to Mike. Suddenly, he realized that the Beach Boys might actually be his ticket to the American dream.

In January 1962, Mike began missing shifts at his father's sheet metal company and was soon let go. Mike didn't really care about the job anymore. He believed in the Beach Boys. The success of "Surfin'" also changed Brian's life. He happily dropped out of El Camino College to devote himself to music. Murry also became obsessed and was soon spending far more time promoting the group than managing A.B.L.E. Machinery. He set up several weekend concert appearances for the group in early 1962. They played at the intermission of surf movies, at school dances and at other local events.

Mike and Brian were

CONCERTS PLAYED IN
1961-1962

SATURDAY, DECEMBER 23, 1961: Rendezvous Ballroom, Balboa-Newport Beach, CA, with Dick Dale
With "Surfin'" in the California charts, the Beach Boys made their live debut during the intermission of a concert headlined by surf guitar legend Dick Dale. The two-song performance apparently did not go well. Eyewitness Dorinda Morgan later stated that Brian was "humiliated" by the rowdy crowd's disinterest. The Beach Boys had difficulty gaining the support of local surfers who perceived the group as a Hollywood version of surf music.

DECEMBER 30, 1961: Olive Recreation Center, Burbank, CA
Jodi Gable, who ran the Beach Boys' official fan club from 1962 to 1966, recalled that she first saw the group at the Olive Recreation Center in Burbank. She was not particularly impressed by the Beach Boys' rudimentary ability on their instruments, but saw something appealing in them. She talked to Al Jardine about when they would be playing next and he took her phone number. Later he called Gable and asked her if she'd run their fan club. Gable believes that she saw them on December 30, 1961. If this is the case, then perhaps she attended the group's first television appearance on *Dance Party*.

SUNDAY, DECEMBER 31, 1961: Municipal Auditorium, Long Beach, CA, with Ike and Tina Turner, James Darren, Frankie Avalon, Della Reese, Gene McDaniels, and Bobby Rydell
One week after the first short appearance, the Beach Boys took part in a Ritchie Valens Memorial Concert, headlined by Ike and Tina Turner. The other acts are not known with certainty, but Ray Hunt of the Surfmen recalled to writer Robert J. Dalley that they "did a gig in late 1961 at the Long Beach Municipal Auditorium with James Darren, Frankie Avalon, Della Reese, Gene McDaniels, Bobby Rydell, and the Beach Boys." The band performed a few numbers, including "Surfin'" and "Johnny B. Goode."

THURSDAY, JANUARY 25, 1962: "Surf Nite" at the Mesa Presbyterian Church, Hawthorne, CA
This show was a fundraiser for the church. Admission was one dollar and a surfboard was offered as a door prize.

FRIDAY, FEBRUARY 16, AND SATURDAY, FEBRUARY 17, 1962: Rainbow Gardens, Pomona, CA, with the Mixtures
It is generally accepted that Al Jardine left the band following their February 8 recording session and was not present for these shows. Al continued to attend El Camino College full-time and a local paper reported, "while he enjoys working with the group, it takes too much of his time." If the dates of these shows are correct, the group may have played as a four-piece band. Bob Eubanks, who later

$1.00   № 121   № 121

SURF NITE
Featuring
The **BEACHBOY'S**
Presbyterian Church   54 st. & Mullen (w. of crenshaw)
Door Prize: Surfboard
Thurs. January 25   Time: 8:00

Name

Phone

Collection of Chris Woods

The boys in early 1962. Jon Stebbins Collection

achieved fame as host of *The Newlywed Game* on TV, paid the group $150 for the shows. Members of the Mixtures, a popular Chicano band that headlined these shows, recall that the Beach Boys didn't go over very well with the mainly Chicano audience that usually attended concerts at the Gardens.

MONDAY, FEBRUARY 19, AND TUESDAY, FEBRUARY 20, 1962: Academy Fine Arts Theatre, San Diego, CA (Two shows a night at 7:00 and 9:00 p.m.)
In 1966, Carl recalled that the producer of the Ritchie Valens concert was impressed enough to hire them to play these shows for a $500 fee. The band played in between screenings of Bruce Brown's film *Surf Crazy*. A poster for this show is probably the earliest Beach Boys concert poster in existence. Once again, it is possible that the group played as a four-piece. However, in the 1989 *Endless Summer* TV show's "Campfire Segments," Al Jardine recalled playing "Surfer Girl" for the first time at a party the group attended after a San Diego show. It is generally accepted that Al had left the band by this time, but if his memory is correct, then it is possible he played these shows.

FRIDAY, MARCH 2, 1962: Millikan High School Auditorium, Long Beach, CA (8:00 p.m. show)
In addition to a musical performance by the Beach Boys, Don Brown's film *Surf's Up* was screened. This is probably the Beach Boys' first concert appearance with thirteen-year-old David Marks.

encouraged to keep writing songs, and they soon revealed a new tune called "Surfin' Safari." It was much catchier than "Surfin'" and showed that Brian and Mike had quickly improved their songwriting abilities. In addition, Brian arranged a gorgeous ballad, based on the melody of "When You Wish upon a Star," which he called "Surfer Girl." On February 8, the group returned to World Pacific Studios and recorded the two new songs, along with an instrumental called "Karate" and another song by Brian called "Judy," about his then-girlfriend, Judy Bowles. The results were fairly ragged and nothing would ultimately be

released from this session, but
Murry now believed that the
group had real star potential.
He began a concentrated effort
to land the boys a recording
contract from a major label.

Al Jardine, however,
was less sure of the group's
potential. Al had his doubts
that the Beach Boys would ever
amount to anything. Although
"Surfin'" was still on the charts,
the group had yet to make any
significant money. The weekend
gigs were taking too much
time away from his studies.
Al was a folkie at heart, and
performing "Johnny B. Goode"
and "Mr. Moto" seemed like
the wrong direction. A few days
after the February 8 recording
session, Al announced that he
was leaving the group. Brian
was disappointed, and Murry
reacted more angrily. Al later
recalled that it took Murry
many years to forgive him
for leaving. Brian moved on.
He knew the group needed
another guitarist onstage. He
and Carl immediately thought
of their young neighbor David
Marks as the obvious choice.
David recalled that when he
heard "Surfin', " "I was a little
disappointed that I wasn't in on
the actual session, but I was just
so young and I was in school
and everything and there was no
official band yet. Brian was just
going into the studio and trying
out stuff." In February 1962,
opportunity knocked on David's
front door. Brian, Dennis, and
Carl walked across the street
and offered David a place in
the group. With his parents'
permission, David joined and
would be a Beach Boy through
the next two crucial years. He
added a vital element to the
Beach Boys' sound at a critical
time. Unlike Al, David was an
avid rock 'n' roll fan and was

The earliest known photograph of the Beach Boys, taken at the Bel Air Bay Club on March 10, 1962 (left to right: Carl Wilson, Dennis Wilson, Mike Love, David Marks, and Brian Wilson). Marks Family Archive

happy to team with Carl to take the group's instrumental sound in that direction.

By this time, Murry's relations with Hite Morgan had soured. It had become clear that Morgan would not be able to do much for the group. Murry also blamed him for steering the band towards the hapless Candix Records. Due to the Dix brothers' massive debts, the Beach Boys had not received much money for "Surfin.'" Murry decided that new demo sessions should take place away from Morgan's studio. Brian's friend and collaborator Gary Usher had visited Western Recorders in Hollywood and knew the studio had a nice sound. Despite the expense involved, Usher convinced Murry that the group's demos should be recorded there. On April 16, 1962, Brian and Gary held a session with the group to record some of their recent songwriting efforts. Gary sang lead vocals on two songs, "My Only Alibi" and "One Way Road to Love," while Brian took the lead on "Visions" and "Beginning of the End." With the exception of

Marks Family Archive

Let's Go Surfin' —
with the **BEACHBOYS**
and the **VIBRANTS**
SAT. MARCH 31—8 to 12 P.M.
AT THE
Ontario National Guard Armory
JOHN GALVIN PARK
ADMISSION ONLY $1.00

Dance Every Saturday Night

Marks Family Archive

The Beach Boys in March 1962. Marks Family Archive

"Visions," which was retitled "Number One" and released as the B-side of a Rachel and the Revolvers single, these songs remained unreleased. However, three days later the Beach Boys returned to Western and re-recorded "Surfin' Safari," along with the Wilson-Usher tunes "409" and "The Lonely Sea." In addition, Murry had them record the Four Freshmen song "Their Hearts Were Full of Spring" to showcase their impressive vocal blend.

Armed with these new recordings, Murry began visiting record labels. Dot, Decca, and Liberty Records all turned him down, but Russ Regan and Murry's friend Don Podolor helped set up a meeting with Capitol Records. As soon as Capitol A&R man Nik Venet heard "Surfin' Safari" and "409," he knew the label had to sign the group. Usher recalled to writer Steven McParland that Venet "was really 'Mr. Hollywood' with the stylized hair, the fancy shirts and the French cuffs . . . He looked quite impressive. This was Capitol Records, the big time." Venet informed Murry that Capitol wanted to purchase the demo masters for $300 and release a Beach Boys single. He offered them a five percent royalty. Accounts of what happened next differ slightly. Venet told writer Tom Nolan in 1971 that Murry "wanted to

SATURDAY, MARCH 10, 1962: Bel Air Bay Club, Pacific Palisades, CA (8:00 p.m. show)
The Beach Boys appeared at a special Mardi Gras–themed event. Photographs were taken this night, and they are probably the earliest Beach Boys group shots in existence. The band had not yet adopted the red-checkered Pendleton jackets that they sported for much of 1962, but instead performed in identical mustard-colored sportscoats. David Marks recalled in a 1981 interview that this was his first concert appearance with the group, but he has since recanted that recollection: "I don't think that was my very first show. It was the first picture of the band playing live, but I don't believe it was my very first show because in the picture I'm (playing) a Fender Stratocaster, and when I first started playing gigs with them I rented a Rickenbacker solid-body guitar."

FRIDAY, MARCH 16, THROUGH SUNDAY, MARCH 18, 1962: Santa Monica Hotel, Santa Monica, CA, with the Bel-Airs and the Vibrants
The group played from 8 p.m. to 12 a.m. on Friday and Saturday and from 1 p.m. to 5 p.m. on Sunday.

FRIDAY, MARCH 23, 1962: Mira Costa High School Auditorium, Manhattan Beach, CA, with Spencer and Allred, Twin Tones, and Tommy Terry (8:15 p.m. show)
The Beach Boys appeared at a special variety revue to benefit the Manhattan Beach Police. A concert program exists for this show.

SATURDAY, MARCH 31, 1962: Ontario National Guard Armory, Ontario, CA, with the Vibrants (8:00 p.m. to 12:00 a.m. show)
This was the Beach Boys' second known show with the Vibrants, a popular instrumental surf band from Manhattan Beach. A flyer for this show exists.

EARLY SPRING 1962: Harris Department Store Deb Teen Fashion Show, San Bernardino, CA
William F. Williams, a DJ at radio station KMEN in San Bernardino, recalled to writer David Leaf that "Harris had a fashion show/concert each year . . . KMEN was in charge of putting together the talent for Harris's concert, and I remember Murry Wilson came to us and literally begged us to let the Beach Boys be the opening act. As I recall, they barely knew which end of the guitar case was up. They looked very badly, played very badly, and sang very badly."

WEDNESDAY, APRIL 18, 1962: Newport High School Stadium, Los Angeles, CA, with the Bel-Airs, the Vibrants, the Fabulous Biscaines, and Dodie and Dee Dee (7:00 p.m. show)
This was a special Easter week "Stomp."

FRIDAY, APRIL 20, AND SATURDAY, APRIL 21, 1962: Redondo High School, Redondo Beach, CA, with the Vibrants and the Bel-Airs
These shows were originally scheduled for Mira Costa High School, but the venue was changed at the last minute. Posters exist that advertise the appearance as at Mira Costa.

FRIDAY, MAY 4, 1962: Inglewood Women's Club, Inglewood, CA (8:00 p.m. to 12:00 a.m. show)
The concert poster promised "free soft drinks for thirsty stompers." David Marks recalled that at these early shows the Beach Boys often played instrumentals and cover tunes to pad out the set. "We didn't have a string of hits yet, so we just played whatever was on the radio. I sang things like 'Louie, Louie,' 'Kansas City' . . . Carl sang 'What'd I Say.' We did a lot of those hits of the day. I remember when

'Sherry' by the Four Seasons came out. The first time we heard it was on the radio on the way to a gig. I was driving with Brian that day and we started working on the parts in the car. And when we got to the gig, we went in the bathroom and learned the whole song and we did it that night."

FRIDAY, JUNE 8, OR 15, 1962: Wagon Wheels Junction Roller Gardens, Oxnard, CA

A fan recalls seeing the group at this venue soon after her birthday, which was June 5. As the Roller Gardens held dances only on Fridays, the likely dates are either June 8 or 15.

SATURDAY, JULY 14, 1962: "Diaper Derby," Oxnard, CA, with the Surfmen (Afternoon) and "Canteen Dance" Hawthorne High School, Hawthorne, CA (Evening)

These are the Beach Boys' first known appearances after the release of their debut Capitol Records single, "Surfin' Safari" b/w "409." They provided the entertainment at the first annual Diaper Derby, in which babies crawled across a rug while a cheering crowd egged them on. The event was covered by radio station KOXR. A tape featuring a portion of the Beach Boys performance of the Bel-Airs surf classic, "Mr. Moto," and a short radio interview with Brian are in circulation.

Following the Oxnard appearance, the group traveled to Hawthorne for their second performance of the day. All three Wilson brothers and Al Jardine attended school at Hawthorne High. Brian and Al both graduated in the spring of 1960 and Dennis apparently was expelled for fighting, but Carl was still enrolled at the time of this show. The city of Hawthorne created a summer "youth canteen" to curb teenage violence and give students something to do. A gala dance was organized for students from the Centinela Valley and it was held at Hawthorne High School during the summer break. Linda McVeigh was on the committee that was created to plan activities. She recalled that the committee decided to ask the Beach Boys to play the dance despite strenuous objections from many students who felt they were terrible. Although the Beach Boys agreed to play the show for free, some students tried to take up a collection to hire another act instead!

WEDNESDAY, JULY 18, 1962: Jodi Gable's Sixteenth Birthday Party, Burbank, CA

The Beach Boys played a free impromptu performance for fan club president Jodi Gable's sixteenth birthday party.

SATURDAY, JULY 28, 1962: Azuza Canteen, Azuza, CA

According to David Marks, "Azuza was a regular place for us to play . . . It was at the back of a residential area at the end of a street. There was a park and a little building, a little rec center and a little stage. We played there quite a bit." This particular visit turned out to be very memorable for the group. A young man named Dale Smallin was making a short film titled *One Man's Challenge*. "They asked us where we were playing and if they could come down and film us for this documentary they were making," he remembers. Since recordings of all the early local TV appearances that the band made have vanished, this remains the earliest known moving footage of the Beach Boys. For the cameras, they performed "Surfin' Safari" dressed in their Pendleton shirts and white chinos. The footage is shown in its entirety in the 1998 documentary *Endless Harmony*.

SUNDAY, AUGUST ?, 1962: Swing Auditorium, San Bernardino, CA, with Dick Dale

A beautiful poster exists from this concert in a private collector's hands. A photograph of the poster shows the venue, month, and day, but the exact date is cut off. This was one of a handful of concerts that the Beach Boys played with Dick Dale in 1962. David Marks was in awe of Dick Dale, who was "an intimidating figure. He was the king and he knew it . . . I mean when I was a kid and I saw this man up there on stage playing guitar like I was trying to do, I was intimidated. Guitar players all loved Dick Dale . . . When we finally got to play with him on the same stage, we were ecstatic and intimidated at the same time. At least Carl and I were intimidated, the two guitar players." Marks recalled that a riot broke out at this show between the real surfers in the audience and the "hodads." "It was pretty scary. There were thousands of people there, or at least it seemed like it."

MONDAY, AUGUST 20, TO SATURDAY, AUGUST 25, 1962: KFWB "Back to School Jam" at various Broadway Stores

give us the publishing and I had to advise him to open a small company with the boys, with the group, split it between them and keep the publishing." Gary Usher, however, recalled that Venet offered no such advice and intended to acquire the publishing rights for Capitol, as was standard industry practice at the time. Gary and Brian, however, had discussed forming their own publishing company, and Gary boldly announced to Venet and a surprised Murry that the publishing was not available. Aware that he had a surefire hit single on his hands, Venet accepted the unusual situation and had Capitol legal draw up the contract. As a result, the Beach Boys kept control of their own publishing, a rarity at the time.

Gary Usher soon fell out of favor with Murry, who was always very distrustful of outsiders. He thought of Gary as a fast-talking Hollywood type and was suspicious of his motives. Although Gary claimed he'd thought of the idea, Murry shut him out of the Sea of Tunes publishing company that was created. The final straw between Murry and Gary occurred later that summer, when Murry kicked Dennis out of the house for his habitual delinquent behavior. Gary took Dennis in and let him stay with him for the next several months. Murry was enraged. He made it clear that Gary wasn't welcome in the Wilson home and barred him from attending Capitol recording sessions. Murry also tried his best to limit Gary's contact with Brian. Although Brian and Gary continued to occasionally write together, including the beautiful "In My Room," their relationship was never the same.

Meanwhile, the Beach Boys were on the rise. "Surfin' Safari" b/w "409" was released as a single that June. It was soon climbing the *Billboard* national charts, where it peaked at an amazing number fourteen. The Beach Boys had scored a national hit record! Capitol was sufficiently impressed, and by July 16, 1962, the group was back at the tower to sign a seven-year recording contract. It was agreed that each of the five Beach Boys would receive twenty percent of the royalties from album sales. Because David and the Wilson boys were all minors, their parents went to court to approve the contract.

Everyone was very excited. Dennis couldn't wait to show off to the people who had doubted the group. He had been recently suspended from school for fighting and was politely informed that maybe he should just leave Hawthorne High for good. In 1965, he recalled in an interview with Linda McVeigh that right after signing with Capitol he "deliberately loitered in the school parking lot, waiting for my old guidance counselor to come out and give me hell . . . When he did, I just smiled at him and asked him if he wanted to compare checkbooks." Dennis could afford to gloat, for the Beach Boys' success beckoned. With a Capitol Records single near the top of the charts, the Beach Boys were in increasing demand. More concert appearances throughout California were scheduled. On July 14, the group made a live appearance at the annual Oxnard, California, Diaper Derby, which was broadcast on radio station KOXR AM. On July 28, they made their earliest surviving appearance on film in a short

Performing at a Southern California dance in late 1962. Marks Family Archive

The Beach Boys were advertised in the *Los Angeles Times* as one of the Area Code Personalities that would appear at various KWFB events all this week. DJ Roger Christian (who was soon to collaborate with Brian on various songs, including "Shut Down") and other KFWB disc jockeys acted as the event's hosts. The concerts took place at the various Broadway-Hale department store locations in the greater Los Angeles area. Founded in 1896, The Broadway was a dominant retail chain in Southern California. On August 20, events were held at the flagship store in downtown Los Angeles at 2:30 p.m. and at the Del Amo Mall in Torrance at 7:30 p.m. On August 21, events were held at the West Covina branch at 2:30 p.m. and at the Pasadena store at 7:30 p.m. On August 22, the events were at the Orange County location at 2:30 p.m. and at the Whitwood Mall in Whittier at 7:30 p.m. On August 23, there were events at the Westchester store at 2:30 p.m. and the Crenshaw location at 7:30 p.m., while on Friday, August 24 there was an event at the Long Beach store at 2:30 p.m. The final events took place on August 25 at the Hollywood and Vine store at 10:30 a.m. and at the Valley store at 3:30 p.m. It is assumed that the Beach Boys sang a few songs and signed records at each event.

SATURDAY, AUGUST 25, 1962: Reseda Jubilee, Reseda, CA, with Jan and Dean
The Beach Boys received a mention in the *Los Angeles Times* for taking part in this annual community carnival. They were hired to appear on Saturday and shared the bill with another up and coming California act, Jan and Dean. This appears to be the first concert that the two groups played together. As Jan and Dean were strictly a vocal duo, the Beach Boys agreed to back them up during their performance, in addition to playing their own set. Dean Torrence recalled to writer David Leaf that the show "went by pretty quickly. After they did their songs, we did our songs . . . We didn't talk much . . . The total concert was maybe a 30-minute job." The two groups became friendly and

continued to play occasional shows together. Jan and Dean were so impressed by the Beach Boys that they decided to record some of their songs for their next album.

SATURDAY, SEPTEMBER 1, AND SUNDAY, SEPTEMBER 2, 1962: Pandora's Box, Los Angeles, CA
The Beach Boys began a residency at the tiny club situated on the Sunset Strip and owned by Bill Tilden. The exact details are somewhat sketchy, but David Marks recalls that the group played on weekends at the club for approximately three to six weeks. "It seemed like we played at Pandora's Box every weekend, at least in my recollection . . . A lot of hipsters went there. It was small but it was always packed." According to a September 2, 1962, news article, the band was "now playing nightly at Pandora's Box," which suggests that the engagement began no later than this time. Based on their touring schedule, it is possible that the band played every weekend for the month of September. Gary Usher brought his then-girlfriend, fifteen-year-old Ginger Blake, and her cousin Diane Rovell to one of these shows. Blake and Rovell fell in love with the group and promised to return for their next appearance.

EARLY SEPTEMBER 1962: Seventeenth Birthday Party for Milton Berle's daughter Victoria, Los Angeles, CA
Once the Beach Boys became Capitol Records recording artists, they began using the William Morris Agency to book shows for them. Their William Morris agent Marshall Berle got them this gig playing at the party for the daughter of his uncle, comedian Milton Berle. David Marks recalled, "Uncle Milty surprised us with twenty bucks each and told us we did a great job."

SATURDAY, SEPTEMBER 8, AND SUNDAY, SEPTEMBER 9, 1962: Pandora's Box, Los Angeles, CA
The band likely played more shows at Pandora's Box on this weekend. Ginger Blake returned with her fourteen-year-old cousin Marilyn Rovell on one of these nights. Marilyn was born in Chicago and had moved to Los Angeles in 1955 with her parents Irving (a sheet metal worker) and Mae Rovell, and her two sisters Barbara and Diane. Marilyn recalled on BBC Radio that Brian asked her for a sip of her hot chocolate during the show and then spilled it all over her. They began talking and soon hit it off, initiating a romance that led to their marriage two years later. As Brian and Marilyn's relationship solidified, Brian spent much of his time at the Rovell house in the Fairfax district, which became a home away from home for all of the Beach Boys.

FRIDAY, SEPTEMBER 14, 1962: "Surfers Ball," at Morgan Hall, Long Beach, CA, with Lonnie Belmore, the Bonnavills, Russ Storman, and Dean Long
Admission was $1.50 for this 8 p.m. to 12 a.m. event, which featured a "stomp contest." It was around this time that the Beach Boys added the "Monster Mash" by Bobby Pickett into their sets. The song, which had been released in August, became a bit of a comedy routine for Mike in the middle of every show.

SATURDAY, SEPTEMBER 15, 1962: Sixteenth Birthday Party for Helen Lee Stillman, Los Angeles, CA
As a result of their appearance at Victoria Berle's birthday party, the group was invited to perform at this party for a local debutante. The event was actually mentioned in the society column of the September 16 *Los Angeles Times*. According to the article "A Chaperone Learns Ropes," by Wanda Henderson, the Beach Boys arrived late to the event, which was held at the Stillman home, having "locked their drums in the glove compartment or somewhere."

FRIDAY, SEPTEMBER 22, 1962: "Battle of the Bands," Wagon Wheel Junction Roller Gardens, Oxnard, CA, with the Casuals
According to an *Oxnard Press Courier* article dated September 6, 1962, the Beach Boys were booked to play at a "Battle of the Bands" "within two weeks" at the Roller Gardens against the Casuals, a new group that later evolved into the Dartells. The Roller Gardens held dances only on Fridays, thus allowing us to tentatively speculate the date.

SATURDAY, OCTOBER 27, 1962: Hollywood Bowl, Los Angeles, CA, with Doodles Weaver, the Castells, Billy Vaughn, Shelley Fabares, the Lively Ones, Chuck Connors, Bobby Vee, Paul

movie called *One Man's Challenge*, about the effort to found a local teen center. The Beach Boys performed "Surfin' Safari" dressed in matching Pendleton shirts. Not all the group's gigs, however, were so glamorous. David Marks' mother Jo Ann recalled, "They did some awful gigs at that time; there were some scary situations. I even got in between them and a group of surfers who wanted to fight them . . . At the time they started out a lot of people were really jealous of the Beach Boys."

That August, the group strode into the famed Capitol Records studios to record their first long-playing album, *Surfin' Safari*. To this point, there had never really been an albums market for rock groups. Other than Elvis Presley and a few teen idols, rock music only sold on singles, and rock album sales were anemic. Right from the start, the Beach Boys changed the industry. In addition to the title song, "409," and "Surfin'," all of which had been recorded prior to their signing with Capitol, the new album contained six other songs written by Brian with Gary Usher or Mike Love. Although many of the songs, like "Chug-a-Lug," were fairly primitive, the decision to feature so many original songs was a novelty at a time when groups still relied on outside songwriters. Also, right from the start Brian showed a talent for arranging sophisticated vocal harmonies. Of course, Brian gave credit for much of the success to his idols the Four Freshmen. He noted, however, a key difference. For all their vocal abilities, the Freshmen "didn't reach the teenagers. They played and sang at the adult market. All the Beach Boys have done is to incorporate their feeling into a new sound. And direct that sound especially at teenagers." Brian's ability to produce, arrange, write, and perform made him a prodigious talent, and an anomaly in the 1962 music world.

The early Capitol sessions were exciting, but also had their share of tension. On the album covers of the group's first two albums, Nick Venet was given credit as producer, but the group knew that Brian was in charge. Venet, of course, disputed this. He told David Leaf that he played a vital role in the early days by helping "Brian choose which songs to record from the dozens he had written. Also, I was an objective viewpoint. I would say to Brian, 'I don't think you need to do the record over.'" Nevertheless, the group's need for Venet slowly declined, and soon he'd become superfluous. A bigger concern was Murry's attendance at the studio. The group grew to dread his overbearing presence. Brian especially hated when his father was near the mixing console. His booming voice would echo from the intercom in the studio and hurt Brian's ears. On top of that, Murry consistently tried to take over the proceedings from his eldest son, leading to epic arguments. David Marks recalled in 1981 that Murry "tried to horn in on the producing and Brian would get pissed off, storm out of the studio . . ." Although he had little appreciation for rock 'n' roll, Murry believed that he knew how to make good records. The group often had to suppress their laughter when he would suggest old-fashioned ideas. Nick Venet related to Tom Nolan in 1971, " . . . the father did nothing but hinder

THE BEACH BOYS IN CONCERT

Petersen, the Rivingtons, Jackie De Shannon, Soupy Sales, the Leon Russell Quintet, and others (9:00 a.m. show) and National Cystic Fibrosis Parade of Stars Show, Fox Theater, San Francisco, CA, with Joey Bishop, Jayne Mansfield, Troy Donahue, Annette Funicello, Bob Conrad, Donna Loren, Bobby Freeman, Tony Dow, and others (Evening)

The Beach Boys made their first appearance at the famous Hollywood Bowl as part of Y Day, a giant YMCA event attended by 15,000 young people from California, Nevada, and Arizona. This was the first of many appearances by the Beach Boys at the Bowl. The group later expressed mixed feelings about the venue. In 1966, Brian stated that "the sound men at the Bowl are not rock 'n' roll sound men. I would advise people who want to play there and sound good to change their plans or plan their changes."

Following the Y Day show, the Beach Boys flew to San Francisco to play at a National Cystic Fibrosis benefit show with a number of Hollywood stars. Prior to the concert, the Beach Boys attended a dinner for the stars of the show at which Brian chugged an entire bottle of champagne. When the group came out to play that night, Brian was drunk, and, according to David, threw up onstage after the first number. However, Brian remained onstage for the entire performance.

SUNDAY, OCTOBER 28, 1962: Pandora's Box, Los Angeles, CA
The group returned to Pandora's Box on the Sunset Strip for another series of Sunday shows.

THURSDAY, NOVEMBER 1, 1962: Leonard's Department Store, Torrance, CA (7:00 p.m. show)
The *Torrance Herald* reported that the Beach Boys would perform for forty-five minutes and then autograph copies of their album at the grand opening of this Leonard's store. The store was located on the corner of Pacific Coast Highway and Crenshaw.

SATURDAY, NOVEMBER 3, 1962: Leonard's Department Store, Garden Grove, CA (2:00 p.m. show), and "Pickwick Dance Party," Pickwick Recreation Center, Burbank, CA, with Valjean and Maureen Arthur (5:30 to 10:30 p.m. show)
The Beach Boys gave another forty-five-minute appearance at the opening of a second Leonard's store (one of three that opened that week) on Harbor Boulevard in Garden Grove and signed autographs. Following that appearance they headed to Burbank to perform at the Pickwick Recreation Center. This five-hour event was filmed for Bob Eubanks' KTLA TV *Pickwick Dance Party* show. The Beach Boys segment aired locally on Saturday, November 10. They were advertised as playing their second Capitol single "Ten Little Indians."

SUNDAY, NOVEMBER 4, 1962: Pandora's Box, Los Angeles, CA

SUNDAY, NOVEMBER 11, 1962: Pandora's Box, Los Angeles, CA
Following the closing of their engagement at Pandora's Box, the Beach Boys probably did not appear on the Sunset Strip again until 1970.

WEDNESDAY, NOVEMBER 21, 1962: Hermosa Biltmore, Hermosa Beach, CA, with the Journeymen (8:00 p.m. to 1:00 a.m. show)
A "Thanksgiving Eve Dance and Stomp" that was sponsored by the Alpha Omega Fraternity.

THURSDAY, NOVEMBER 22, 1962: William Howard Taft HS, Woodland Hills, CA

FRIDAY, NOVEMBER 30, 1962: Alfred Goode Auditorium, Bakersfield, CA, with the Revlons, Candy Maloney, and Ken and the Ho Daddys (8:00 p.m. show)
In a December 1962 interview, Murry noted that this was the furthest from Los Angeles that the group had yet played.

SATURDAY, DECEMBER 1, 1962: Van Nuys Theatre, Van Nuys, CA, with Dorsey Burnett, the Lively Ones, Dobie Gray, the Crystallets, Cyndy Malone, the Mixtures, Dick Michals, the Pastel 6, and Jimmy Haskell
The Beach Boys were one of the featured performers at this benefit show for the Pacific Lodge Boys

Home. Photographs printed in a local magazine show that they were still wearing their Pendleton shirts onstage.

MONDAY, DECEMBER 3, 1962: USC Pep Rally, Los Angeles, CA, with Ernest Borgnine, Doodles Weaver, and others (3:00 p.m. show)
According to the *Los Angeles Times*, the Beach Boys were scheduled to provide entertainment at a massive pep rally on campus for the USC Trojans.

THURSDAY, DECEMBER 6, 1962: Cinnamon Cinder, Long Beach, CA, with the Challengers, Sandy Nelson and Jan and Dean
Bob Eubanks hired the Beach Boys to perform at the grand opening of his second Cinnamon Cinder nightclub at 4401 Pacific Coast Highway with Jan and Dean, the Challengers, and Sandy Nelson. In addition to the performers, Eubanks convinced numerous recording and TV stars to appear at the opening. Notables included Frankie Avalon, Brian Hyland, Shelly Fabares, Tony Dow, Dobie Gray, and Rod Lauren. David Marks commented that celebrities often turned out for these events. "The disc jockeys had access to all the stars because they wanted to get their records played."

LATE DECEMBER 1962: California Tour
This was the first proper tour undertaken by the group. All that is known about it comes from an interview Murry gave to writer Tom Nolan in 1971, in which he stated that he was told by a twenty-two-year-old William Morris agent, "the Beach Boys would never make more money than Ruby and the Romantics, who were grossing $3,500 for seven days a week . . . I got so mad. It was December 17. I called from my home to key places, and we worked between Christmas Eve and New Year's Eve. We grossed $26,684 . . ." The interview suggests that the tour started on about December 24. Keith Badman's book *The Beach Boys: The Definitive Diary of America's Greatest Band, on Stage and in the Studio* states that the tour started in Santa Barbara on December 17. But there were no ads for any Beach Boys show in the Santa Barbara papers, and none of Badman's dates could be verified by actual evidence.

LATE DECEMBER 1962: Unknown Venue, Santa Cruz, CA
Ron Swallow, the Beach Boys' friend and longtime roadie, recalled that following the show the group had a party in their rooms, which attracted many young people. Some local boys became jealous of the attention their girlfriends were paying to the group, stormed the hotel, and challenged the group to a fight. Dennis allegedly attempted to intervene on behalf of the group and got into an altercation resulting in serious injury to one of the local boys. The case later went to court, but Dennis was cleared of any charges as it was ruled he had acted in self-defense.

THURSDAY, DECEMBER 27, AND FRIDAY, DECEMBER 28, 1962: "Surf Fair" Santa Monica Civic Auditorium, Santa Monica, CA, with the Shenandoah Singers, the Surfaris, Surf-Tones, and the Surf Side Four
A program exists for this two-day event. The group reportedly played both days, though the program lists them as appearing only on Friday.

OTHER 1961–1962 CONCERTS

When the Beach Boys began performing live, newspapers rarely advertised rock shows. The Beach Boys undoubtedly played a number of shows in this period that remain undocumented. I have chosen to list other known appearances here. Obviously, this list is not complete and most likely no definitive list of 1962 shows will ever be possible.

The group played at a Sigma Chi fraternity party at UCLA in the summer of 1962, at which Brian met Bob Norberg. As Brian produced a record of Bob and his girlfriend Cheryl Pomeroy singing Brian's composition "The Surfer Moon" in September 1962, the concert must have been before that date. Brian and Bob were roommates in 1963, after Brian left the Wilson home. Although it could not be confirmed, some fans have stated that the appearance was in June at the Dykstra Hall student dormitory.

them, but I think he assumed a lot of credit. If he heard them doing something good, he'd say 'right' . . . Brian would say, 'Let's do that again.' He (Murry) would say, 'Let's do that again.' Got to the point where Brian would say 'Le—' and he would say 'Let's do that again.'"

If Murry was difficult to deal with in the studio, he was even more of a headache as the group's manager on the road. At meetings before concerts, it was asserted by Murry that they were in a business and must act professionally. David Marks remembered, "He would give us an orientation before every gig . . . he'd give us a pep talk." Murry insisted the group set a proper example in public and created a system of fines for infractions, like swearing or drinking. David Marks loved to flaunt such rules and paid the price. "Murry gave Carl instructions to document when I used dirty lyrics in the shows. I shared a microphone with Carl and on a dare I would lean over and shout some profanities and Carl would get all mad and yell 'Fifty dollars! That's fifty dollars!' which was a helluva lot of fucking money back then." The fines were intolerable to Brian, now twenty, and Mike, who was married with a child. As Jo Ann Marks recalled, "What should have been a joyous time, when the boys became so successful, was not, thanks to Murry. He just had a way of taking the fun out of everything."

On the other hand, Murry fiercely believed in the group and was a loyal promoter of their interests. He always made sure to follow up with thank-you letters and advertisements in trade papers for any promotional help given to the group. In 1962 he aggressively toured California radio stations and offered the services of the group for station-sponsored dances, in exchange for airplay. Promoter Fred Vail recalled that "Murry would go to the station, and when he'd see the DJs, he would ask them about their families. He would even remember their wives' names. And then he would give the guy some French perfume to give his wife." As a result of Murry's and Capitol's vigorous promotion, the group began to achieve greater notice. Their August 25 appearance at the Reseda Jubilee earned them their first mention in the *Los Angeles Times*. There were long lines to see them when they performed at the Pandora's Box nightclub on the Sunset Strip. When the group performed at the "Surfer's Ball" at the Morgan Hall in Long Beach on September 14, they headlined the bill. On October 27 they were even invited to take part in a star-studded event at the prestigious Hollywood Bowl. When DJ and TV host Bob Eubanks opened his Cinnamon Cinder nightclub in Long Beach, the group performed at the gala opening on December 6. The Beach Boys also made many local television appearances. That same December, Murry booked them on their first real tour, a week of one-nighters across California during the Christmas break. For the group, it was very exciting, but still relatively modest. By the end of 1962, the Beach Boys had one national hit and still had not performed outside of California. However, within a few months they would become the most popular rock and roll group in America.

The Beach Boys played at many local high school dances, which are difficult to trace because they were not advertised in newspapers. For example: A California fan recalls seeing the group perform in 1962 in the auditorium of Morningside High School.

Murry Wilson had the boys play for free at numerous radio-sponsored promotions and dances in the hopes of gaining airplay for the group. He referred to these shows as "the forty freebies," suggesting that the band played quite a number of them. Jim Waller of the popular Fresno band Jim Waller and the Deltas witnessed one such show. "The first time I saw the Beach Boys perform was on top of the roof of the KMAK radio station in Fresno during the summer when their first record 'Surfin'' was out. I heard they played for free in the hopes of getting some good airplay. It was a one-story building with a tar roof and Fresno is always hot in the summer."

Jodi Gable also recalled that the group played for free all over the Centinela Valley, hitting parking lots, shopping malls, radio stations, and sock hops.

Writer Dominic Priore, who grew up in Southern California, recalls that the group played at Barnes Park Community Center in Monterey Park and at Mark Keppel High School in Alhambra with Dick Dale. These shows most likely took place in the summer or fall of 1962.

Many local bands have shared stories about playing with the Beach Boys. Members of the Mixtures, a popular Chicano band in the late '50s and early '60s, recall playing with the Beach Boys numerous times at Pop Leuder's Park in Compton, California. Randy Nauert of the Challengers recalls playing a show with the Beach Boys at the Hermosa Biltmore in the fall of 1962. This appearance was probably in September or October 1962. It's possible that the Challengers were also on the bill on November 21, though they are not mentioned on the surviving poster. The Beach Boys also played at the Arrowhead Pavilion with the Tornadoes at some point in 1962, according to sax player George White.

Carl's best friend Ron Swallow, who often traveled with the group, recalled that the band played at the Rendezvous Ballroom in Balboa on a number of occasions. In addition to their well-known appearance in 1961, it is likely the Beach Boys played there several times in 1962.

Swallow also recalls the group playing numerous shows at the Cinnamon Cinder in Los Angeles, which was located near Universal City. Keith Badman's book *The Beach Boys* lists the band as playing two shows at the Cinnamon Cinder in February 1962. He clearly erred, as according to a contemporary article in the *Long Beach Independent*, Bob Eubanks and his partners "started the original Cinnamon Cinder in North Hollywood in July of 1962," making it impossible for the Beach Boys to have performed there as early as February. Another article in the *Van Nuys News* from July 1963 states, "This month marks the first anniversary of the Cinnamon Cinders, young adult night clubs . . . " However, while Badman erred on the dates of the shows, the group clearly played there on numerous occasions. David Marks also recalls playing there "a lot in the real early days." Hence the group most likely played there soon after the club opened and throughout the summer months of 1962. No advertisements confirming this have been found.

Marks also recalls playing at the Avalon Ballroom at Pacific Ocean Park a number of times. He vividly remembers one occasion where the Beach Boys took part in a "battle of the bands" with an act called the Crossfires. This band later became the Turtles.

One woman from Hancock Park (an affluent L.A. suburb), whose father was a prominent radio and TV producer, recalled the Beach Boys playing at a party for her older sister in the family's backyard in the summer of 1962. They were members of the Bel Air Bay Club and had seen the Beach Boys perform there that spring.

CONCERTS NOT PLAYED

The Beach Boys did not play at the Hollywood Palladium on November 12 with Dick Dale, as reported in Keith Badman's book. An examination of the poster shows that a group called "The Latin Beach Boys" played that night instead.

The Beach Boys did not play a two-week tour of the U.S. Midwest in 1962 as was erroneously reported in several Beach Boys books.

1963

THE YEAR 1963 was when the Beach Boys went from modest local band to American phenomenon. The song that catapulted them to national success was "Surfin' USA," recorded in late January 1963. Brian hit upon the idea of adding new surfing lyrics to the melody of Chuck Berry's "Sweet Little Sixteen." It was a masterstroke. The song had national appeal and a dynamic rock arrangement. Carl recalled, "When we heard 'Surfin' USA' we just knew it was going to be an undeniably big hit. It was the first time we were aware we could make a powerful record." The song featured a scorching lead guitar flurry by Carl and a snappy lead vocal from Mike. It was released in March 1963 and rocketed all the way to number three on the national charts. The Beach Boys helped create a new fad, the surf music craze. A wave of influence engulfed the entire U.S. to the point where even teens that lived in the landlocked Midwest became "surfers." The Beach Boys almost single-handedly created what would later be called "the California Myth." Brian's songs projected a California that was a teen paradise where, as Brian immortalized in a song he wrote with Jan Berry, there were "two girls for every boy." As Carl recalled, "People were mad to get to

CONCERTS PLAYED IN
1963

California. There was an awe connected to California and the beach and the way we lived. Those were the people who were really cool. But it wasn't the real California so much as the California in Brian's songs." "Surfin' USA" turned the group into cultural icons and California's number one export.

There was only one problem with "Surfin' USA." Brian liked Chuck Berry's melody so much that he basically left it unchanged and Capitol initially did not credit Berry as co-composer on the record. Berry's music publishers, Arc Music, however, quickly noticed the similarity and their lawyers launched a lawsuit for a share of royalties. As a result, the songwriting credit later had to be amended to include Berry's name as composer and Brian lost all rights to its lucrative songwriting royalties. Many in the Beach Boys inner circle were amazed that Brian had not bothered to alter the melody slightly to avoid such

WEDNESDAY, JANUARY 2, 1963: Unknown Venue, CA
David Marks' mother Jo Ann began keeping a journal at this time that listed shows that the group played. According to her journal, the group played in California on this date.

WEDNESDAY, JANUARY 9, 1963: Unknown Venue, CA
Another show listed in the journal with no other info.

LATE JANUARY 1963: Zeta Beta Tau Frat Party, University of Arizona, Tucson, AZ
The Beach Boys made their first trip outside of California at the end of January 1963. Murry Wilson apparently did not make the trip, giving the young group the opportunity to let loose away from home. David Marks recalled that "it was just really awesome to be able to do that at that young age and we were just very excited and having lots of fun." Although the group was hired to play this fraternity dance party, they ended up enjoying a marathon party weekend. As Mike Love recalled, "We went there for one show and we stayed there for three days."

WEDNESDAY, JANUARY 30, 1963: Navajo Nations Fairgrounds, Window Rock, AZ
Before returning home for a recording session, the group played one last show in Arizona.

SATURDAY, FEBRUARY 2, 1963: March of Dimes Show, Swing Auditorium, National Orange Show Grounds, San Bernardino, CA, with Jan and Dean, Eddie Hodges, April Stevens, Nino Tempo, and Dick and Dee Dee (8:00 p.m. show)

SATURDAY, FEBRUARY 9, AND SUNDAY, FEBRUARY 10, 1963: Rod and Custom Car Show, Great Western Exhibit Center, Los Angeles, CA, with the Royal Monarchs (One show each day at 2:00 p.m.)
The group played for hot rod enthusiasts in L.A. A program exists for this appearance. According to Jack Schaefer of the Royal Monarchs car club, it was raining at one of the shows and the "rain came down so hard on the gigantic tin roof that it all but drowned out the vocals and Mike Love was pissed at the sound guy!"

FRIDAY, FEBRUARY 15, 1963: Hawthorne High School, Hawthorne, CA (8:00 p.m. to 12:00 a.m. show)
The Beach Boys provided the entertainment for a Valentine's Day dance at the Wilsons' alma mater. Carl was the only Beach Boy still attending classes there, though he would soon switch to Hollywood Professional School. Prior to this show, Dennis drove his car into a cement wall and damaged his legs. As a result, Mark Groseclose was recruited to fill in as drummer for four concerts, probably starting with this one. According to David Marks, Groseclose "was a friend of Carl's at Hawthorne High. He was a great drummer, a great artist, and a funny guy."

SATURDAY, FEBRUARY 16, 1963: KFWB Charity Show, Los Angeles Sports Arena, Los Angeles, CA, with Fabian, Bobby Vinton, Ann Margaret, Jayne Mansfield, and others (8:00 p.m. show)
Mark Groseclose again took Dennis's place on the drums at this charity show advertised in the *Los Angeles Times*. DJ Roger Christian, a regular songwriting collaborator with Brian, hosted the show.

FRIDAY, MARCH 8, 1963: Unknown California Show
As a result of the journal kept by Jo Ann Marks, we know that David Marks received $217.50 for a show on this date.

Carl with Mark Groseclose on drums at Hawthorne High School. Courtesy of Kathy Groseclose

1963

SUNDAY, MARCH 10, 1963: KMEN Party, San Bernardino, CA
According to a KMEN radio survey, the Beach Boys entertained KMEN listeners as part of the radio station's first anniversary celebration.

SATURDAY, MARCH 16, 1963: Hemet Armory, Hemet, CA
Jo Ann Marks listed a show in Hemet, California, on this date, and a fan that attended the show supplied the venue information.

MONDAY, MARCH 18, 1963: Unknown California Show

FRIDAY, APRIL 5, THROUGH SUNDAY, APRIL 14, 1963: Los Angeles Teenage Fair, Pickwick Recreation Center, Burbank, CA
The Beach Boys played at this annual teenage event, which ran from April 5 to April 14. It is not known how many performances the group gave. There is confirmation of their presence on April 5, when they signed autographs by the pool at 5:30 p.m. It's likely that they performed that night as well. They were photographed at the event with their fan club president Jodi Gable. The band had abandoned their signature Pendleton shirts in favor of a uniform of green sweaters, skinny ties, and Hush Puppies. David Marks recalled, "That was Carl's idea. All of a sudden when we got successful he got all fashion conscious. He would take us shopping for clothes and tell us to get our hair done by (Jay) Sebring and all that crap . . . I loved it for a second and then I hated it. Dennis really hated it . . . all that hairspray and stuff."

FRIDAY, APRIL 12, 1963: Rendezvous Ballroom, Balboa-Newport Beach, CA
According to Dennis Rose, of the surf band the Centurions, hardly anyone showed up for the Beach Boys' appearance, since it was the first night of Easter. David Marks recalled, "It was common to have a night like that once in awhile. You got a thin crowd every now and again."

MONDAY, APRIL 15, 1963: Unknown Venue, Bakersfield, CA
With "Surfin' USA" in the charts, the group was able to charge more money for personal appearances. David Marks recalls receiving $300 for this show. It is possible that Al Jardine played this show in place of Brian.

SATURDAY, APRIL 20, 1963: Felton Intermediate School Dance, Lennox, CA (7:00 p.m. show)
A ticket stub exists for this show, which was sponsored by the school's PTA. This was a momentous weekend for the group. On the day following this concert, Sunday, April 21, 1963, the Beach Boys taped their first national television appearance on the CBS variety program *The Red Skelton Show*. The appearance aired as the 1963 season premiere on September 24, 1963. Shirley Temple Black was also a featured guest on the program. The shooting schedule for the day reveals that Brian, Dennis, and Mike came to the studio two hours earlier than David Marks and Carl. This was so they could pre-record their vocals for their a cappella version of the Four Freshmen song, "Things We Did Last Summer." Later, the whole group mimed to their hit song "Surfin' USA." This footage survives and can be seen in its entirety as a bonus feature on the *Endless Harmony* DVD.

THURSDAY, APRIL 25, 1963: Val-Air Ballroom, Des Moines, IA
This was the opening date of the Beach Boys' first extensive tour outside California. Brian did not make the trip. Al accompanied the group in his place. David Marks recalled that the group was nervous about going without their leader, especially since Brian's high falsetto was absolutely crucial to their sound. "To be honest, we were freaked! We thought we were finished because Brian didn't want to go on the road with us. So Brian gave Al a call. And we were so happy because he sounded exactly like Brian, sang exactly like Brian, and played the bass beautifully. We were real happy that Al came in and saved the day."

David Marks' father Elmer acted as road manager on this tour. He recorded in his tour journal that the group attracted 1,870 fans to the Val Air Ballroom, a 1930s jazz dance hall. The band received a $450 guarantee and half the gate, for a total of $1,385.

Ian Rusten Collection

an outcome. Gary Usher, however, was not surprised. He noted to writer Stephen McParland, "The episode was a perfect example of Brian being Brian. He never . . . thought in business terms."

Brian even gave away his first number one song to Jan and Dean. The Beach Boys had met the recording duo the previous year, when they played together at the Reseda Jubilee. Jan Berry and Dean Torrence were fun California guys, close in age to the Beach Boys and with a similar musical sensibility. The two groups quickly hit it off. In March 1963, they decided to record two Beach Boys songs for inclusion on an upcoming Jan and Dean album. The Beach Boys came to the studio to sing backing vocals and provide some of the instrumental backing. Brian also played Jan some songs he was working on. Although he declined to give Jan "Surfin' USA," Brian did offer up a new song he hadn't quite finished. Jan and Brian completed the song, and on March 20, 1963, Brian, Carl, and David returned to the studio to help them record it. "Surf City" was clearly a hit song, but Brian was stunned when it catapulted all the way to number one on

Concert poster for the Beach Boys' first appearance in Cedar Rapids, Iowa. Jon Stebbins Collection

the *Billboard* national charts. Brian's dad Murry was disgusted that Brian had disregarded the interests of the family and given away a hit. Murry labled Jan Berry "a pirate" and tried to prevent Brian from collaborating with him.

One person Murry encouraged his son to write with was Roger Christian, a prominent DJ at KFWB in Los Angeles. Brian was introduced to Christian by Gary Usher one night and was impressed by the DJ's great knowledge of hot rods and car culture. Although Roger (born 1924) was much older than Brian, the two became friends and began collaborating. As Gary Usher recalled to Stephen McParland, "I became more involved in other things and, with Murry driving a wedge between Brian and me, Roger eventually took my place with Brian. He had good ideas and just happened to be in the right place at the right time." One of Brian and Roger's first collaborations

FRIDAY, APRIL 26, 1963: YWCA Teen Canteen, Rockford, IL (8:00 to 12:00 p.m.)
The group provided entertainment for dancing. The band did not play for four hours straight, but they were kept busy. David Marks remembered, "We usually played three forty-five-minute sets a night on that tour." According to Elmer Marks' tour diary, the group was paid $650 for the night's work.

SATURDAY, APRIL 27, 1963: Danceland Ballroom, Cedar Rapids, IA
Elmer Marks recorded that the band took home $1,403 for the night.

SUNDAY, APRIL 28, 1963: Terp Ballroom, Austin, MN (8:00 p.m. to 12:00 a.m. show)
The group played to a small audience of 500 people.

TUESDAY, APRIL 30, 1963: Arkota Ballroom, Sioux Falls, SD
The group was booked to provide entertainment for dancing from 8:30 p.m. to 12:30 a.m. Admission was $1.50.

WEDNESDAY, MAY 1, 1963: Kiddieland Roller Rink, Wichita, KS (8:00 to 12:00 p.m.)
According to Elmer Marks' diary, 1,783 fans saw the group play at the roller rink.

FRIDAY, MAY 3, 1963: Excelsior Amusement Park and Big Reggie's Danceland, Excelsior Park, MN
Radio station WDGY sponsored a "Twin City High Night," in which the Beach Boys played one free show at the amusement park and a paid concert at Big Reggie's hall. Located next to the Excelsior Amusement Park on Lake Minnetonka, Big Reggie's had a capacity of over 1,700. Ray Colihan, known as Big Reggie, booked the group in February, when they were fairly unknown, and was not expecting the huge crowd that turned out to see the group. The hall was filled to capacity and over 1,000 fans had to be turned away.

Mike often referred to this show in later interviews as the moment that he knew the group was becoming a phenomenon. He recalled to writer Marilyn Beck in 1976, "The gig was sold out . . . but what we didn't know 'til later was that cars were jamming up the roads to the ballroom for miles around. It got so heavy that the mob outside started throwing rocks at the windows to try and get in."

SATURDAY, MAY 4, 1963: Duluth Armory, Duluth, MN, with Chet Orr and the Rumbles
There is some debate as to whether this show was actually May 2, as remembered by Chet Orr, whose band opened the show. David Marks recalled that the teenage fans at this show rushed the stage, knocking Dennis off of his drums.

SUNDAY, MAY 5, 1963: Surf Ballroom, Clear Lake, IA (8:00 p.m. to 12:00 a.m.)
The group finished their first Midwest tour with a show at this infamous balllroom, where Buddy Holly played his last show before his tragic death in 1959. All of the members of the band were aware of this significance. David Marks commented: "I recall that show vividly. Certain things just stick out in your mind. I remember that there were puddles outside, because it had just stopped raining, and we were all talking about Ritchie Valens, Buddy Holly, and the Big Bopper."

MONDAY, MAY 13, 1963: Unknown Venue, CA
According to Jo Ann Marks' journal, the group played an otherwise undocumented show in California.

FRIDAY, MAY 17, 1963: Santa Fe Springs, CA
According to Jo Ann Marks' journal, the group played an otherwise undocumented show in California.

SATURDAY, MAY 18, 1963: Southern California Hot Rod Show, Los Angeles, CA
The group was advertised as appearing at such a show on May 24. Since they played in Sacramento that day, it is possible that the car show appearance was rescheduled to the May 18.

SUNDAY, MAY 19, 1963: Long Beach, CA
According to Jo Ann Marks' journal, the group played an otherwise undocumented show in California.

FRIDAY, MAY 24, 1963: Memorial Auditorium, Sacramento, CA
This show marked the group's first encounter with nineteen-year-old promoter Fred Vail, who would form a long-lasting relationship with the group. Vail began in radio as a gofer when he was twelve and became a local DJ by the time he was fifteen. He was also involved in student activities at El Camino High School. The Beach Boys concert came about because in the spring of 1963, the senior class at El Camino asked Vail to help obtain entertainment for their grad party. Vail suggested, "'Why don't we take the $750 that you've raised and buy an act and put on a public show to raise the money that you'll need to put on the grad party?' . . . It was 1963 and it was during the surf craze. I was aware of all the surf groups . . . but there was this group called the Beach Boys that not only did surf music but also wrote a lot of their own songs and they had these great harmonies. I said, 'We ought to get the Beach Boys.'"

"I called all around trying to find the Beach Boys and I finally talked to this promoter from Southern California that had once booked them . . . and he said he could get me the Beach Boys for a weekend date and it would be $800. That was more than we could afford because we had other expenses . . . so I decided I'd call Capitol Records." Vail was put in touch with Marshall Berle, the Beach Boys' William Morris agent. "He said, 'You can either have them for $750, or you can have them for $500 but you'll have to pay for six round-trip airline tickets.' Well, airplane tickets to Sacramento were about $65 in those days and that would bring the total to over $800, so I just said 'I'll take them for the $750 flat. Issue the contracts.' And that's basically how the whole first show came about."

was on "Shut Down," a cool song about drag racing that was enlivened by great guitar interplay between Carl and David, and Dennis' rocking beat. "Shut Down" was released as the flip side of "Surfin' USA" and was so popular that it charted on its own.

Both songs appeared on the *Surfin' USA* album, which was released in March 1963. The record marked a transitional phase for Brian and the group. They were at last becoming comfortable in the studio. A year later Brian remarked, "with *Surfin' USA* we developed grace and style. For the first time we used modern techniques, singing twice, the second time exactly on top of the first, perfectly synchronized. This gives a rather shrill and magical, much brighter, more gutsy, and spectacular sound." While the vocals had certainly improved, the album was still very much in the surf music genre of the time and included five instrumentals. More than any other Beach Boys album, *Surfin' USA* was a guitar record. While the Beach Boys were not the first group to record surf instrumentals, they were the band that made them popular nationwide.

Although Brian actually produced the songs on *Surfin' USA*, the label once again read "Produced by Nick Venet." Brian announced to Capitol, however, that in the future he would produce the records without Nick and that he would no longer record at the Capitol Tower. As Carl recalled in an interview with Geoffrey Himes, "He wouldn't work at Capitol, because it was a crappy-sounding studio. It had a fabulous string sound, and it was great for those records that Nat King Cole made, but not for rock 'n' roll guitar." Brian had recorded the "Surfin' USA" single at Western with engineer Chuck Britz, and he decided that this was the place where he wanted to record from now on. As Britz explained to David Leaf, a studio like Western was a far better environment for sparking creativity than Capitol, where "it's easy for people to walk in and out and destroy the process that gets you going. If you're in a groove, there's nothing worse than somebody coming in and asking a political or financial question." Although the label was unhappy about giving the group so much creative freedom, the Beach Boys were becoming one of their biggest moneymakers, and they reluctantly agreed.

On the day of the show, Vail drove his folks' '54 Chevy station wagon to pick up the Beach Boys and their manager Murry Wilson at the airport. When the group arrived, with Al Jardine in place of Brian, they loaded their gear into the wagon and left for the hotel. During the car ride Vail informed the group that they were the sole act on the bill. Vail recalled, "Carl said they hadn't done that too much and I said, 'Well you're doing it tonight.' He said, 'Oh man, I hope the promoter comes out OK!' So I said, 'Carl, I'm the promoter.' And he looked at me kind of funny and said, 'But you're a kid like us!' I said, 'Yeah, but I'm the guy that hired you.' . . . Anyways, that night I introduced them, 'And now here's America's number one surfing group, the Beach Boys' and they came out. The timing couldn't have been better, because only the week before, 'Surfin' USA' had peaked at number one on KXOA radio in Sacramento. So they did 'Surfin' Safari' and 'Surfin' USA' but they also did a lot of covers. Al did 'Runaway' and Dennis did 'The Wanderer' and Carl did 'Misirlou' and Mike did 'Long Tall Texan.' There were a lot of cover tunes."

After the shows, the Beach Boys went back to the Mansion Inn with Vail and had dinner at the hotel restaurant. "We were sitting at a long table and Carl said to Murry, 'Hey Pop! How did we do tonight?' And Murry pulled out an envelope and start sketching some numbers and said, 'Well, Mr. Vail paid the William Morris Agency $750, so we have to give them their commission and we have to pay for the airline tickets and the rental car and a couple of meals. I think by the time everything is said and done you guys will make between $50 and $55 apiece.' . . . So Carl said, 'Well how did you do tonight Fred?' And I said, 'After everything is said and done, the class and I made $4000.' Their mouths dropped. Murry couldn't believe it." Vail was sympathetic and gave Murry some advice. "I said, 'The William Morris Agency doesn't know what they have here. You went over great tonight and there are going to be a lot of promoters like me that are going to buy you guys for a night for $500 or $600 and they're going to make a lot of money off you because I don't think William Morris realizes your potential . . . So why don't you do what I did? Why don't you start promoting your own concerts? . . . So Murry said, 'Well, that's a great idea but I have my machinery company A.B.L.E. I am pretty much tied up with that during the day . . . I have to keep my business. I can't do it.' So I said, 'Well I'll do it!' And that was the beginnings of what ultimately became American Productions." By the fall of 1963 Vail was working for the Beach Boys.

SUNDAY, MAY 26, 1963: Inglewood High School, Inglewood, CA

WEDNESDAY, MAY 29, 1963: Buc's Gym, Bellflower High School, Bellflower, CA, with Jan and Dean (Afternoon) and Unknown Venue, San Bernardino, CA, with Jan and Dean
These were the first two dates of a short tour with Jan and Dean. Jo Ann Marks' journal mentions both shows. In addition to listing the cities that David played, Marks also recorded how much David received. According to her journal, these were the last shows that he was paid for. Next to all show dates from this date forward, she wrote "did not receive" in the pay column. According to David Marks, "Murry insisted that to cover growing expenses, the band's profits from concert appearances had to be recycled back into the Beach Boys franchise . . ."

THURSDAY, MAY 30, AND FRIDAY, MAY 31, 1963: San Francisco, CA, with Jan and Dean

---

FRIDAY, MAY 31, 1963: Oxnard, CA, with Jan and Dean

CIRCA SATURDAY, JUNE 1, 1963: Rio Nido, CA
A California fan named Mark Westbury recalls a Beach Boy appearance at the town of Rio Nido, on the Russian River, being advertised on radio. Singer Sharon Marie recalled that she first met the Beach Boys at this appearance, which she remembered as August 1963 in one interview and Memorial Day weekend in another. Since the group was touring outside of California the entire month of August, Memorial Day weekend is the logical date.

WEDNESDAY, JUNE 5, 1963: Municipal Auditorium, Modesto, CA

FRIDAY, JUNE 7, 1963: Veterans Hall, Bakersfield, CA, with Jan and Dean and Sam Cooke (with

Performing in Hawaii with Al Jardine in place of Brian Wilson, June 1963.
Jon Stebbins Collection

Lou Rawls), "Grad Night Dinner Dance," Bakersfield College, Bakersfield, CA, and "Grad Night Dinner Dance," Albert S. Goode Auditorium, Bakersfield, CA, with the Cherry Creek Singers
The group played at three separate Bakersfield venues. This was grad night at a number of Bakersfield high schools and they agreed to share the talent. David Marks fondly recalled backing up Sam Cooke and Lou Rawls on this night, though he had his doubts about how memorable it was for them. "Because we had instruments, the DJs would have us back the other artists. Backing Sam Cooke was wild! They had a little trouble comprehending it. 'These guys are gonna back us?' You know . . . but it went all right. I remember backing them on the one with the call-and-response vocals ['Bring It on Home to Me']."

SATURDAY, JUNE 8, 1963: Unknown Venue, Palmdale, CA
This show is mentioned in Jo Ann Marks' diary. DJ Chris Charles of KUTY recalled that the Beach Boys were paid $500 to appear at the four-hour concert event.

WEDNESDAY, JUNE 12, 1963: Unknown Venue, Houston, TX, with Jan and Dean and Jimmy Reed
The group made their first Texas appearance with this show in Houston. If the date as recorded by Jo Ann Marks is correct, then the group must have flown there after their recording session that day. According to David Marks, the group backed blues legend Jimmy Reed, before playing their own set.

FRIDAY, JUNE 14, TO SUNDAY, JUNE 16, 1963: "Show of Stars," Civic Auditorium, Honolulu, HI, with Dee Dee Sharp, the Treniers, and Jackie De Shannon (One show at 8:00 p.m. on Friday; three shows at 2:30, 7:00, and 8:45 p.m. on Saturday; and one show at 2:30 p.m. on Sunday)
On June 13 the group embarked on their first tour of Hawaii, where they played sixteen shows in

The Beach Boys were now a major act. However, as a result of Carl and David's need to attend school regularly, they mostly played weekend gigs in early 1963. It was not until April that they finally embarked on their first major tour outside of California. Increasing demand for the group as live performers meant Brian had little time to concentrate on songwriting. David Marks recalled that "Brian loved to perform, but he didn't like touring because he was really driven to write songs and produce records, and he couldn't do that when he was traveling around on the road all the time with us." Brian's solution was to contact Al Jardine and ask him if he would take his place at some shows. Since leaving the band Al had taken a job at a local aerospace company, but he remained in touch with Brian and Dennis. That spring, Brian sent Al a copy of the *Surfin' USA* album and invited him to begin attending some of the group's rehearsals. Brian did not bother to tell his father about his plans and Murry reacted predictably when he attended a show and saw Al subbing for Brian. As Al recalled in a BBC interview, "It affected his father intensely. His dad was really uptight about it. He felt that (Brian) was copping

> "People were mad to get to California. There was an awe connected to California and the beach and the way we lived."

out . . . dodging responsibilities and gave him a pretty rough time." Carl remembered that Brian "just said 'I don't want to tour. I want to stay home and I want to make music.' And I remember my dad was upset because he thought it wasn't fair for him not to go and play for the people, because they bought the records and they want to see you and so forth. Anyways, he just wouldn't do it because he wanted to write, and then Alan came in the group to take Brian's place." Al accompanied the group on their first Midwest tour, while Brian stayed home.

nine days. Brian opted to stay home and Al Jardine again took his place. The Beach Boys shared a bill with Dee Dee Sharp, the Treniers, and Jackie De Shannon that was advertised as the "Show of Stars." David Marks recalled that since the Beach Boys were a self- contained unit, "we played backup musicians for Dee Dee Sharp and Jackie De Shannon. The Treniers were kind of a Vegas act and we became good friends with them as well." Elmer Marks and Audree Wilson served as tour managers and chaperones. Elmer shot home movies of the group onstage and at the beach, portions of which were used in the 1985 Malcolm Leo documentary *The Beach Boys: An American Band*.

The group obviously had a fantastic time in Hawaii, especially with Murry remaining in L.A. As David Marks recalled, "we drove around the island in convertibles, we rented surfboards, sailboats, and motorbikes, and we annoyed all the women on the beach." Bruce Johnston, who would join the group in 1965, recalled that he was in Hawaii for a vacation at this time. He told *Time Barrier Express* that he "heard them back up Jackie De Shannon, who was doing very complicated songs at that time, and I thought 'Whooaahh, not bad.' Then I got to know the guys a little bit."

SUNDAY, JUNE 16, 1963: "Show of Stars," Schoefield Barracks, Honolulu, Hawaii, with Dee Dee Sharp, the Treniers, and Jackie De Shannon
For the next seven days, the group mainly played to military personnel stationed in Hawaii. David Marks recalled, "The tour was set up mainly for us to play to servicemen. They were some of the best audiences we ever had. Those guys and girls really received us well. The military really appreciated the entertainment."

MONDAY, JUNE 17, 1963: "Show of Stars," Hickam Theater, Honolulu, HI, with Dee Dee Sharp, the Treniers, and Jackie De Shannon (Two shows at 7:00 and 9:00 p.m.)
The group played two shows at this theater on Hickam Air Force Base.

TUESDAY, JUNE 18, 1963: "Show of Stars," Barber's Point, Oahu, HI, with Dee Dee Sharp, the Treniers, and Jackie De Shannon (7:30 p.m. show)
A show played for the Coast Guard stationed at Barber's Point.

WEDNESDAY, JUNE 19, 1963: "Show of Stars," Kaneohe Marine Corps Air Station, Oahu, HI, with Dee Dee Sharp, the Treniers, and Jackie De Shannon (Two shows at 6:30 and 8:30 p.m.)

THURSDAY, JUNE 20, 1963: "Show of Stars," Baldwin High School Auditorium, Honolulu, HI, with Dee Dee Sharp, the Treniers, and Jackie De Shannon (Two shows at 7:00 and 8:45 p.m.)

FRIDAY, JUNE 21, 1963: "Show of Stars," Hilo Civic Auditorium, Hilo, HI, with Dee Dee Sharp, the Treniers, and Jackie De Shannon (Two shows at 2:30 and 7:30 p.m.)

SATURDAY, JUNE 22, 1963: "Show of Stars," Bloch Arena, Pearl Harbor, HI, with Dee Dee Sharp, the Treniers, and Jackie De Shannon (7:30 p.m. show)
This was the final show of the tour.

SATURDAY, JUNE 29, 1963: Convention Center, Las Vegas, NV, with the Teen Beats (8:00 p.m. show)

FRIDAY, JULY 5, AND SATURDAY, JULY 6, 1963: Phoenix, AZ
According to Jo Ann Mark's journal, the Beach Boys played in Arizona for the second time on these days.

THURSDAY, JULY 11, 1963: Retail Clerks Hall, Buena Park, CA, with the Astronauts
This was an extremely popular California venue for surf bands. To underline the wide impact of surf music, opening act the Astronauts were a Colorado, rather than California, surf band! Apparently, the Beach Boys did not play very well at this show. According to Astronauts leader Bob Demmon,

"We got on stage and blasted the kids and they loved us. After our set, we stayed to listen to the Beach Boys. They were so bad vocally and musically that we left. Brian Wilson later told me that it was that gig that became the turning point in the Beach Boys' career because they realized that they had to get it together for live appearances."

CIRCA FRIDAY, JULY 12, 1963: Orange County Fair, Costa Mesa, CA, with Adrian and the Sunsets
Adrian and the Sunsets recalled playing this show with the Beach Boys, but the exact date is unknown. As the fair opened on Tuesday, July 9, and ran for only six days, Friday, July 12, is the likely date.

SATURDAY, JULY 13, 1963: Veteran's Memorial Stadium, Santa Maria, CA, with the Honeys and the Four Speeds
Gary Usher led the Four Speeds, who opened the show. Usher recalled the show as one of the highlights of his life and bragged to writer Stephen McParland, "On that particular night we blew the Beach Boys off the stage." Apparently, the Four Speeds learned that the audience would be predominantly Mexican and prepared a set of songs geared to them. The Beach Boys, "dressed in their surfer shirts and sporting short hair, died! They didn't go over well at all."

FRIDAY, JULY 19, 1963: Indiana Beach, Shafer Lake, Monticello, IN (8:45 to 12:45 p.m.)
This was the opening gig of the Beach Boys' first summer tour. They flew to Chicago and then drove to Monticello. Brian accompanied the group on this tour. The only other people on the road with the group were a friend of Dennis's named Bob Chambers and manager John Hamilton. Unlike the first tour, the group now traveled in two separate cars. After the craziness of the first tour, Mike said, "Never again. So I bought a Jaguar—my first real nifty car—and I took out the right-hand seat and made a bed in it. So if there were three of us in the car, one guy would be able to sleep; one guy would be resting, sitting in back; and one guy would be driving, and it worked out really well." David Marks recalled that "Mike was the oldest and I don't think he really enjoyed some of the things that Dennis and I were up to . . . One of our buddies, Bob, drove Mike's car around. It was just he and Mike and the rest of us had a station wagon that we had to cram into. And then we had a U-Haul trailer with our equipment in it. We would have to pack up right after the gigs and then drive 400 or 500 miles to the next town."

SATURDAY, JULY 20, 1963: Danceland Ballroom, Cedar Rapids, IA
As David Marks recalled, the Everly Brothers were on the road at the same time and earned a reputation for raising hell and wrecking hotels. Every time the Beach Boys pulled into a town that the Everlys had recently visited, they found themselves being scrutinized for any potential Everly-esque havoc they might cause. For example, the Everlys played Danceland on Friday, July 12, a week before the Beach Boys.

SUNDAY, JULY 21, 1963: Cobblestone Ballroom, Storm Lake, IA

TUESDAY, JULY 23, 1963: Roof Garden Ballroom, Arnold's Park, IA (8:00 to 11:00 p.m. show)
David Marks recalled frequently playing four sets because "if we took too long a break, the kids would get bored and leave. We had to really dig deep and play more instrumentals by the last set. In fact Carl and I started making up instrumentals on the spot that we played on stage."

WEDNESDAY, JULY 24, 1963: Shore Acres Ballroom, Sioux City, IA (8:00 to 11:00 p.m. show)
According to an AFM sheet, Brian was in California on this day, producing a Honeys session. If the sheet is correct, than he briefly left the tour. It is not known how long he was absent or if Al replaced him.

THURSDAY, JULY 25, 1963: Val Air Ballroom, Des Moines, IA
Most likely, the group once again played at the Val-Air Ballroom, but no ad for the show has been found. However, Jo Ann Marks' journal records that they played there.

On April 24 the band flew to Chicago, rented a Chevy station wagon and a U-Haul trailer, and drove to Des Moines, Iowa, for the first date of the tour. The group was giddy with excitement about at last being on the road like real rock stars. David Marks recalled, "The five of us strutted around like kings of the world." Touring in 1963, however, was far from glamorous. As Mike later recalled on BBC Radio, "The first tour we went out with like a station wagon . . . There were five of us and a driver and we all lugged our own instruments, you know, and we'd drive sometimes 500 miles to the next date because the routing wasn't that great. We'd be in Fargo, North Dakota, and then we'd go somewhere in Minneapolis, Minnesota." The Beach Boys were all quite young and driving around together in one station wagon for hours and hours was tedious. To relieve the boredom, the group engaged in a lot of silly behavior. Mike recalled one incident amongst many: "We said, 'OK you guys, let's all jump in the back and freak this gas station attendant out.' So we all jumped in the back of the station wagon and all five or six of us were piled up together writhing and squirming around with legs and arms hanging everywhere and the guy comes up with the hose in the gas place . . . and he just blew his mind. Here were five guys just crawling over each other in the back of a station wagon, but that's how crazy we got on that first tour."

It was soon after the Midwest tour that the group began recording their third album, *Surfer Girl*. The album was the first on which Brian

THE BEACH BOYS IN CONCERT

had complete control with no interference and was listed as producer on the album's cover. The move to Western allowed Brian to keep working on a song until he was satisfied. Late nights in the studio became the norm. As Nick Venet related to writer Tom Nolan, Brian "was the first guy to do it until it was right. He damned everyone till it was right and then he gave them the record; he took his chances. A lot of us would get chicken after four hours, and say, 'We'd better get off the tune.' Brian would hang in there for nine hours, no matter what the cost. I used to think he was crazy, but he

Ian Rusten Collection

Poster advertising a 1963 concert in Michigan. Courtesy of Bruce Snoap

SATURDAY, JULY 27, 1963: Unknown Venue
The group apparently played on this night, but there is no further info.

SUNDAY, JULY 28, 1963: Peony Park Ballroom, Omaha, NE (8:00 to 12:00 p.m. show)
Peony Park was an amusement park founded in 1919 that hosted occasional dance concerts. Although Jo Ann Marks' diary records a Monday show as well, the advertisement suggests that the show was only on Sunday.

TUESDAY, JULY 30, 1963: Coliseum Ballroom, Davenport, IA (8:00 to 11:00 p.m. show)
This was the Beach Boys' only appearance at this legendary Midwest landmark, built in 1914, which has hosted virtually every famous musician that played in the area.

WEDNESDAY, JULY 31, 1963: Indian Crossing Casino, Waupaca, WI
The promoter of this show allegedly called Murry Wilson to complain about the band's unprofessional behavior and alcohol consumption.

THURSDAY, AUGUST 1, 1963: Surf Ballroom, Clear Lake, IA

FRIDAY, AUGUST 2, 1963: Prom Ballroom, St. Paul, MN
This ballroom, built in the 1940s, was located on University Avenue. It was torn down in 1987.

SATURDAY, AUGUST 3, 1963: Terp Ballroom, Austin, MN

SUNDAY, AUGUST 4, 1963: Kato Ballroom, Mankato, MN
Brian Wilson apparently was in Los Angeles for a recording session on this date. It is possible Brian left the tour and did not return until August 9 or later. As none of these shows were reviewed (with only one or two exceptions), it is impossible to be more precise about what shows Brian played or did not play. David Marks recalls him being at most shows, but has distinct memories of Brian's unhappiness at being away from home and of his frequent phone calls to Murry, requesting permission to return to California.

TUESDAY, AUGUST 6, 1963: Electric Park Ballroom, Waterloo, IA (8:00 to 11:30 p.m.)

WEDNESDAY, AUGUST 7, 1963: Ithaca, MI

THURSDAY, AUGUST 8, 1963: Club Ponytail, Harbor Springs, MI, with the King Tones (Two shows)
Although Jo Ann Marks' journal dated these shows as August 5, a newspaper article confirms they took place on this date. The earliest known concert review of a Beach Boys show, the article in the *Petoskey News Review* by Bob Shephard states, "At first the Beach Boys seemed to be the biggest disappointment of the season. Without their echo chambers the sound they produced was far below par. They were lacking in organization and harmony all during their first performance. However they did seem to improve with time and by the end of the evening were sounding more like everyone expected them to . . . they really packed the house; in my estimation, there were probably 1,500 people at the Tail, give or take a few hundred." A blurry photograph that accompanies the article clearly shows Carl on guitar, Mike playing sax, and David on guitar. The bassist is obscured by Mike's sax, but is clearly shorter and has what looks like a crew cut. Thus, it appears to be Al, rather than Brian.

FRIDAY, AUGUST 9, 1963: Cold Springs Resort, Hamilton, IN
The group played for about 3,000 teenagers.

SUNDAY, AUGUST 11, 1963: Auditorium Theater, Chicago, IL
The Beach Boys' first Chicago appearance took place at this legendary venue, in operation since 1889 and located on the corner of East Congress and Michigan Avenue.

TUESDAY, AUGUST 13, 1963: Music Hall, Boston, MA, with Jan and Dean, Tony and the Del Fi's, Myles Connor and the Ravens, and Mary Ann Mobley (9:30 a.m. show)
The Beach Boys' first New England appearance was at the "Fifth Annual Back to School Fashion Hop and Surf-Sing Show" sponsored by Gilchrist's Department store, and hosted by Arnie "Woo Woo" Ginsburg of radio station WMEX. In addition to the morning concert, there was also a beauty pageant and a film shown.

WEDNESDAY, AUGUST 14, 1963: Palace Ballroom, Old Orchard, ME
This concert was billed as the Beach Boys' "first and only Maine appearance."

THURSDAY, AUGUST 15, 1963: Surf Auditorium, Hill, NH

FRIDAY, AUGUST 16, 1963: Mountain Top Ballroom, Holyoke, MA

SATURDAY, AUGUST 17, 1963: Wayne County Fair, Homedale, PA (Two shows)
The set list for these shows was saved by David Marks and gives us an idea of the songs played by the group on this tour. Songs played were "Surfin' Safari," "409," "Little Deuce Coupe," "Runaway," "Blue City" (a Carl and David guitar instrumental), "Farmer's Daughter," "Monster Mash," "Movin 'n' Groovin" (a 1958 song by Duane Eddy), "Silly Boy" (a 1962 song by the Lettermen), "Papa-Oom-Mow-Mow," "Honky Tonk," "Shut Down," "Louie, Louie," "Surfer Girl," "Let's Go Trippin'," "Surfin' USA," "Johnny B. Goode," and "What'd I Say."

SUNDAY, AUGUST 18, 1963: Lakewood Park, Mahanoy, PA

TUESDAY, AUGUST 20, 1963: Reimold Brothers Hall, Sharon, PA

WEDNESDAY, AUGUST 21, 1963: West View Park Danceland, Pittsburgh, PA (9:00 p.m. to 1:00 a.m.)
This venue was located at the West View Amusement Park, just north of Pittsburgh. The Rolling Stones appeared here on their 1964 tour.

THURSDAY, AUGUST 22, 1963: Wheeling Downs Roller Rink, Wheeling, WV
Tickets to this show cost one dollar. David Marks celebrated his fifteenth birthday with a prostitute.

FRIDAY, AUGUST 23, 1963: Le Sourdsville Lake Amusement Park, Middletown, OH
Le Sourdsville Lake Amusement Park, located thirty miles north of Cincinnati, was a huge tourist attraction and hosted many concerts from the 1930s to the 1970s, when it was eclipsed by the opening of King's Island nearby.

SATURDAY, AUGUST 24, 1963: Midway Ballroom, Cedar Lake, IN, with the Exports
The Beach Boys played three sets at this picturesque dancehall located on a pier overlooking the water on the edge of town. According to one Indiana fan, his father ended up playing with the Beach Boys on this night. Dennis Wilson allegedly had not been informed that they would be playing a third set and had made other plans. He disappeared and Mike was forced to ask from the stage if there was a drummer in the house. An audience member from a local band called the Surfs volunteered to play the final set. The band liked his playing so much that they took his phone number and ended up using him again on another night.

SUNDAY, AUGUST 25, 1963: Melody Mill, Sageville, IA (7:30 to 11:30 p.m.)
This was a popular dancehall near Dubuque that was torn down in 1964. The Beach Boys probably played three sets.

MONDAY, AUGUST 26, TO TUESDAY, AUGUST 27, 1963: Venues and states unknown
Brian is reported to have been in Los Angeles at this time recording the Survivors. He likely had left

PALACE
Showplace Of Stars
Old Orchard

In Person — **WEDNESDAY** — Only Maine Appearance

BEACH BOYS

ADVANCE ADM. $1.25—ADM. AT DOOR $1.50

Advance Adm. Tickets Now On Sale At
Murphy's Music and Palace

Ian Rusten Collection

IN PERSON
THE BEACH BOYS
(TOP RECORDING "SHUT-DOWN")
THURSDAY, AUG. 22
8 to 11
DANCE and SHOW!
WHEELING DOWNS
ROLLER RINK
— INSIDE —
TICKETS NOW AT
Slater's—Roller Rink—
Yacht Club
$1.00 LIMITED TO 3,000 PERSONS

Ad for an appearance in Wheeling, West Virginia, on August 22, 1963. Ian Rusten Collection

was right." As a result of his growing perfectionism, the *Surfer Girl* LP also marked the first album on which Brian used outside musicians on several of the tracks. Al Jardine, still not an "official" Beach Boy again, played bass on a few tracks, freeing Brian to play piano. More importantly, Brian had session musician Hal Blaine come in to add drums to "Our Car Club."

Blaine was a member of the famous Wrecking Crew that "boy genius" Phil Spector used to create his famous Wall of Sound. If the Four Freshmen were the biggest influence on the development of the Beach Boys' vocal style, Phil Spector was the most important influence on Brian as a producer. Spector developed his Wall of Sound by combining large numbers of instruments all playing together to create a dense, layered sound. Just as Brian double-tracked vocals, Phil would often double or triple a bass part or electric guitar line. As a result, he created an enormous, thunderous sound that overwhelmed the listener. Songs like the Crystals' "There's No Other Like My Baby" and "He's a Rebel" were productions, as writer Timothy White described, "with an almost preternatural sensory impact . . ." Spector's productions fascinated Brian. When he met Hal Blaine, he pumped him for information about the reclusive "Tycoon of Teen." Soon, Brian was attending Spector sessions, soaking up how he achieved the dynamic sound on his records. As Brian recalled to David Leaf, "I was unable to really think as a producer up until the time where I really got familiar with Phil Spector's work . . . then I started to see the point of making records . . . You design the experience to be a record rather than just a song . . . It's the overall sound, what they're going to hear and experience in two and a half minutes, that counts." When Spector released the Ronettes' "Be My Baby" that summer, Brian became obsessed with the song, playing it over and over again on his turntable, until he knew how every bit of sound on it was made. Brian applied the Spector influence to his own productions, but with a one-of-a-kind Wilson twist, and in the process produced something uniquely his own.

The group (left to right: Al, Dennis, Carl, David, and Mike) pose at the Melody Mill on their first big summer tour, August 25, 1963. Courtesy of Dick McGrane

the tour again for a few days. Brian more than likely rejoined the group after a flight to Chicago with his father on August 29. It is conceivable that the Beach Boys played at the Hammond Civic Center, Hammond, Indiana, on one of these nights, as recalled by the Surfs' drummer.

THURSDAY, AUGUST 29, 1963: Avalon Ballroom, La Crosse, WI

FRIDAY, AUGUST 30, 1963: Fox Theater, Brooklyn, NY, with Little Stevie Wonder, Ben E. King, Gene Pitney, the Miracles, the Shirelles, the Drifters, the Dovells, Jay and the Americans, the Tymes, the Chiffons, the Angels, and Randy and the Rainbows

A "Murray the K" package show, with the Beach Boys listed on the program as special guests, this marked the group's first New York appearance. It was on the drive from Chicago to this New

York gig that a major argument broke out between Murry and the band, causing David Marks to announce he was quitting the Beach Boys. He would remain with the band for another five weeks. After the show, the group caught a late-night flight back to Los Angeles, ending their first big summer tour.

SATURDAY, AUGUST 31, 1963: "Show of Stars Spectacular," Los Angeles Sports Arena, Los Angeles, CA, with the Orlons, Jan and Dean, Andrea Carroll, Steve Alaimo, Johnny Fortune, Ray Sharpe, Marvin Gaye, the Righteous Brothers, the Olympics, Darlene Love, Wayne Newton, Little Eva, the Cookies, Mel Carter, Paul Peterson, Dee Dee Sharp, the Challengers, Dick and Dee Dee, Donna Loren, and Jackie De Shannon (8:00 p.m. show)

The Beach Boys returned to Los Angeles just in time to take part in this massive star-studded event. David Marks recalled, "Things started getting really hectic at that time and we started getting really, really busy . . . Carl and I always got a little starstruck when we played those kind of shows."

WEDNESDAY, SEPTEMBER 4, 1963: Moonlight Ballroom, Denver, CO

This show was a benefit for the Jefferson County Association for Retarded Children. Following the show, the group judged a "Miss Denver Surfer" contest.

SATURDAY, SEPTEMBER 7, 1963: Lagoon, Farmington, UT

The Beach Boys made their first appearances at this famous venue near Salt Lake City. The group was extremely popular in Utah and over 4,500 fans attended this show. The audience response was so strong that the group was hastily booked for more Salt Lake shows that December. The Beach Boys proved so popular in the Salt Lake City area that they performed over a dozen shows there from 1963 to 1970.

According to David Marks, Brian and Mike composed the song "Fun, Fun, Fun" at the hotel room after this concert. In a humorous interview segment seen in the *Endless Harmony* film, Mike Love also recalled writing the song here, while Brian Wilson swore they wrote it in Australia. As the song was recorded before they went to Australia, Brian's memory was at fault.

MONDAY, SEPTEMBER 9, 1963: Helix High School, San Diego, CA

The show was advertised in the papers as a "Back to School-O-Rama."

The improvements in production and arrangement were quite noticeable on the *Surfer Girl* LP. If the *Surfin' USA* album suggested that the Beach Boys might have a future as a surf garage band, the *Surfer Girl* LP gave notice that the Beach Boys were a fantastic vocal group. The title track contained an incredibly lush aural appeal, soon becoming an evergreen classic. "Catch a Wave," a new composition written by Brian and Mike, spotlighted Brian's swooping falsetto, the group's dynamic harmonies, and Dennis' thumping drums. As writer Philip Lambert stated, Brian was finally confident enough to place "total faith in the sound and force of the vocal presentation." It was clear that Brian's time listening to the sophisticated jazzy vocals of the Four Freshmen had not been wasted. Carl believed that an important element of their vocal style was the fact that "vocals were voiced like horn parts, the way those R&B records made background vocals sound

Performing in Sacramento, California, on September 14, 1963, with Al standing in for Brian. Courtesy of Kathy Groseclose

Poster for the band's second appearance in Sacramento, September 1963. Courtesy of Fred Vail

like a sax section. They're all within the same octave; that's really the secret to it. We didn't just duplicate parts; we used a lot of counterpoint, a lot of layered sound." The Beach Boys' vocal style blended especially beautifully on the melancholy "In My Room," one of Brian's last collaborations with Gary Usher. The song was one of the first to highlight Brian's amazing ability to express his deepest feelings within a pop song. With lines like "Now it's dark and I'm alone, but I won't be afraid," the song expressed a naked vulnerability that was rare in pop music. Brian's aching voice seemed tailor-made to express such sentiments, and his introspective ballads were often the creative highlight of Beach Boys albums.

If Brian was growing as a musician and producer, his growth was tempered by the demands of the music business. The *Surfer Girl* album sessions were squeezed in between dates on the group's increasingly hectic touring schedule. As soon as the album was completed in July, the group embarked on the biggest tour of their career to date: a forty-three-day swing from California all the way to New York, with a concentration of dates in the Midwest, where the group's popularity continued to swell. Their William Morris agent Ira Okun recalled, "Those really early days were really not that difficult, because they seemed to catch on quite a bit all over the country. The one place we did have a problem booking them at the very beginning was the Southeast. They didn't want any part of the Beach Boys, but we had a lot of dates in the Midwest and a lot of dates on the West Coast." Although Al

David Marks in September 1963.
Jon Stebbins Collection

SATURDAY, SEPTEMBER 14, 1963: Memorial Auditorium, Sacramento, CA (two shows at 2:15 and 8:00 p.m.)

Brian was not present at these shows and was replaced by Al. These two Sacramento shows were very successful and sold the group completely on the merits of hiring Fred Vail to promote their dates. At the time of these concerts, the William Morris Agency was only charging promoters about $1200 to book the group. According to Vail's recollections, the band made over $6,000 on this day by co-promoting the shows with him.

1963

FRIDAY, SEPTEMBER 20, 1963: Long Beach, CA
This show is listed by Jo Ann Marks in her journal. The venue is not known.

SATURDAY, SEPTEMBER 21, 1963: Memorial Coliseum, Portland, OR, with Jan and Dean (8:00 p.m. show)
The Beach Boys were now routinely playing much larger venues then they had in the past. This arena held more than 10,000 fans. David Marks recalled, "It was a spectacular rush to play them. I just remember all those cheering people. It was like the Beatles! Chicks were going nuts! When we were at one of those gigs I happened to be next to Dennis and got pushed up against a chain link fence and had my clothes ripped off."

KISN radio sponsored the Beach Boys first concert in Portland at the Coliseum. Al played the show in place of Brian, who stayed home. David Higginbotham, a fourteen-year-old surf music fan, attended the show and later recalled, "What I remember most about it was that it was very, very loud . . . low-tech loud, with Fender amps turned up full blast. This was the surfing era. This was surf music. It wasn't like, hey this is Brian Wilson's band and we're going to do some incredible vocals, harmony and stuff. It was just the Beach Boys blasting out rock 'n' roll. All my friends and I were waiting for them to play our favorite songs, which were 'Surf Jam' and the other instrumentals (on their early albums). I recall not even liking 'Surfer Girl' because to me it was just a ballad. We were there to here surf music! . . . I do recall that they played 'Surf Jam,' which was my favorite song. Of course they played 'Surfin' USA' and it was really loud and really strong. Dennis Wilson was pounding the drums! The stage was just shaking! Dennis also came up front to sing a song at one point and David Marks played drums. . . . I recall that Mike played a lot of saxophone."

SATURDAY, SEPTEMBER 28, 1963: Cow Palace, San Francisco, CA, with Jan and Dean, the Ronettes, Little Stevie Wonder, Dionne Warwick, the Righteous Brothers, Nino Tempo, Trini Lopez, Dee Dee Sharp, Freddie Cannon, the Coasters, Donna Loren, Ray Stevens, the Original Drifters, Bobby Freeman, the Pyramids, April Stevens, and others
The Beach Boys' first appearance at the Cow Palace was a massive star-studded concert sponsored by KYA and Tempo Productions that was billed as the "Surf Party." The Beach Boys' popularity was reaching a peak and many people came to this show especially to see them and to scream at "the sex symbol of the group," Dennis Wilson. Disc jockey Jim Satcher recalled one hair-raising moment backstage that illustrates how popular Dennis had become: "At the end of the show Dennis came out of the dressing room door and was seen by fans exiting the building. The crowd surged toward Dennis, pushing him against the door and then down on the floor. The people closest to Dennis fell on top of him. I was guarding the pay room door and I told people inside to call the police and to secure the door. I then went into the crowd pulling people off Dennis. I remember covering his head with my jacket as we made our way outside. . . . we ran toward the cars and . . . we jumped on top of one car. I told the crowd that Dennis was hurt and to back off so we could go back inside the building. At the cast party afterwards, Dennis introduced me as the person who saved his life. Dennis was overly grateful to me."

Though he didn't promote it, Fred Vail was also at this show and recalled, "Cassius Clay (the future champ Muhammad Ali) was there, backstage reciting his poetry and stuff. After the show, we all went down to the Hilton Hotel to see the Treniers play, so I got to hang out with Cassius Clay at the Treniers show . . . "

SUNDAY, SEPTEMBER 29, 1963: Fresno, CA (early afternoon), and Seattle Opera House, Seattle WA, with Freddie Cannon, Ray Stevens, the Wailers, the Viceroys, the Lancers, April Stevens, Nino Tempo, Gail Harris, Billy Saint, Little Stevie Wonder, Dee Dee Sharp, and others (Two shows at 3:00 and 7:00 p.m.)
David Marks' mother lists the Fresno appearance in her diary. The Beach Boys likely made a daytime promotional appearance. They then flew to Seattle for two big concerts. The Seattle shows were advertised as the "63 Hit Parade of Stars" and featured twenty-six acts.

SATURDAY, OCTOBER 5, 1963: "Surfin' at the Bowl," Balboa Park Bowl, San Diego, CA, with the Honeys and Eddie and the Showmen

had been playing many shows with the group, when they set off from California for the first date in Indiana, Brian was back on the road with them. Murry had continued to hound Brian, saying that he owed it to his fans to appear onstage. He felt it was dishonest to advertise a Beach Boys show at which the group's leader would be absent. Brian reluctantly caved in and agreed to go on tour. Since Murry had booked the tour months in advance, the group revisited many of the small venues and clubs that they had played on their first Midwest tour. The popularity of their records was such that they could easily have sold out far larger venues by the summer of 1963, but a commitment was a commitment.

The group was pleased to learn that Murry was too busy with his business interests to travel with the group. Instead, he hired professional road manager John Hamilton to chaperone them. By Murry's

This appearance in San Diego was David Marks' last concert as a Beach Boy until 1997. Ian Rusten Collection

The Beach Boys perform at the Hollywood Bowl on October 19, 1963. Al Jardine replaces David Marks as a full-time Beach Boy.
Jon Stebbins Collection

standards, Hamilton turned out to be a woefully poor choice, indulging the group's whims and allegedly even helping young Carl and David lose their virginity. Inevitably, Murry learned of their wild behavior on the road and flew to Chicago on August 29, following a show in Wisconsin, to read them the riot act and fire Hamilton personally. Murry's return led to one of the more momentous events of the Beach Boys' career. That fateful August night, Murry drove with the group to New York, lecturing them for the entire ride. Tempers flared and a fed-up David announced he was quitting the group. The others did not take his resignation seriously at first: "All the other guys thought it was too absurd to leave while the band was at the top, so they just dismissed the whole

Once Upon a Wave, a surfing movie by Walt Phillips, was shown at this concert. This was David Marks' last performance as a Beach Boy until his return to the band in the 1990s. With his contractual obligations fulfilled, he left to form his own band, the Marksmen, with his friend Mark Groseclose. According to David, he felt no regrets at the time. "You may not believe this but I kept pestering Murry all the time, 'When can I leave? When can I leave?' We were booked so far in advance that I had to ride it out, but I was anxious to leave. I had my own band and I wanted to record with my own band because I was sure they were going to be a hit. And so when I finally got to my last job at Balboa Park I was very happy to be free of that so I could concentrate on my own band . . . I didn't start feeling remorseful until I was feeling the financial pinch later on in life."

SATURDAY, OCTOBER 19, 1963: "Y Day Concert," Hollywood Bowl, Los Angeles CA, with the Routers, Mike Clifford, the Cornells, Soupy Sales, the Mixtures, Keith Colley, Eddie and the Showmen, the Fleetwoods, Vic Dana, the Honeys, the Challengers, the Surfaris, Bobby Rydell, Jan and Dean, Duane Eddy, Dodie Stevens, and Paul Peterson
This is the first known Beach Boys show with Al Jardine on guitar in place of David Marks. The Beach Boys' short appearance aired on KFWB radio on November 1 and a tape of it exists. They performed "Little Deuce Coupe," "Be True to Your School," and "Surfer Girl," as well as the KFWB theme.

WEDNESDAY, OCTOBER 23, 1963: Santa Maria HS Gym, Santa Maria, CA, with Jan and Dean and the Honeys

THURSDAY, OCTOBER 31, 1963: "Loyola Carnival," Loyola University, Loyola, CA (Two shows)
The audience at these shows was particularly rowdy, and Al was beaned in the head by an egg. The Beach Boys swore to never play on Halloween night again. They broke their oath in 1966.

FRIDAY, NOVEMBER 15, 1963: Wallich's Music City, South Bay Center, Los Angeles, CA, with host

Bob Crane, Jan and Dean, Dodie Stevens, the Lennon Sisters, Johnny Prophet, Dick Dale, Wayne Newton, Rose Marie, Jack Jones, Bud and Travis, Tony Jerome, Tim Morgan, Trini Lopez, Vic Dana, Gene McDaniels, the Righteous Brothers, the Surfaris, the Ventures, and Kay Starr (7:00 p.m. show)

The group appeared at the grand opening of this branch of the famous store. The *Torrance Herald* announced, "Dancing in the parking lot of the South Bay Shopping Center will highlight the grand opening of the new Music City store." The paper also stated that the opening was being treated like a Hollywood premiere party and that DJ (and future *Hogan's Heroes* star) Bob Crane would emcee the event.

FRIDAY, NOVEMBER 22, 1963: Memorial Auditorium, Marysville, CA, with Freddie and the Statics (8:30 p.m. show)

The group performed on the same day that President Kennedy was assassinated. Fred Vail promoted the show and made the decision to go on despite the tragedy. Vail recalled on BBC Radio that "we came back to the hotel and we just dumped all this money on a big bed in the hotel room and the boys were just totally in shock and bewildered to see three or four thousand dollars in cash and it was all theirs and they were excited."

SATURDAY, NOVEMBER 23, 1963: Memorial Auditorium, Sacramento, CA (postponed)

Radio station KXOA arranged for the six high schools in Sacramento County that had the best attendance to see the show for free. The concert was canceled in the wake of President Kennedy's death and rescheduled for December 21.

FRIDAY, NOVEMBER 29, 1963: National Guard Armory, Indio CA

A poster exists for this show, which advertises the concert as the Beach Boys' "one and only Central Valley appearance."

SATURDAY, NOVEMBER 30, 1963: Municipal Auditorium, San Bernardino, CA, with the Torquays, the Astronauts, and the Dave Pell Octet (8:30 p.m. to 12 a.m.)

From 9:30 to 10:30 p.m., channel 18 TV aired a telecast live from the auditorium. This was the first of many Saturday Night Bandstand Dances that aired locally. Considering their popularity, the TV cameras undoubtedly captured the Beach Boys' performance.

FRIDAY, DECEMBER 20, 1963: Civic Auditorium, Stockton, CA

SATURDAY, DECEMBER 21, 1963: Memorial Auditorium, Sacramento, CA (8:00 p.m. show)

This show marked Brian's first appearance with the group in Sacramento. It was also Carl's seventeenth birthday and the band sang happy birthday to him at the gig. Capitol Records recorded the show for a proposed live album. Fred Vail recalled, "That was my idea. I went to Murry and Brian in late October or early November and I said, 'you know we ought to record one of these concerts. We ought to record Sacramento when you come in December.' Brian and Murry looked at me like, 'Number one why would we do that? Number two who would buy a concert album of a concert?' I said, 'Well every kid that's ever been to one of your concerts will buy it so he can relive the experience and every kid that you've never played before because you've never been to their city will buy it because they want to know what it's like to go to a concert.' . . . So I convinced them to do that and they brought some equipment up in a truck . . . and we set up a control room in the janitor's supply room. We ran cable out to the stage. I think we had three or four microphones.'" Fred Vail's iconic introduction can be heard on the 1964 album. "I wasn't supposed to emcee that show. There was a DJ from KXOA named Bob Early who was supposed to emcee it, but he never showed up. It got to be about ten minutes after eight and the kids were starting to stomp their feet and I said, 'Murry, we have to get going here. The kids are getting restless.' And he said, 'Well, you introduce them! You've done it before.' So then I went out there and just ad-libbed it. 'And now from Hawthorne, California, here to entertain you tonight with a gala Christmas concert and recording session, the fabulous Beach Boys!'"

thing . . . since they kind of dismissed me, it made me want to leave even more." As a result of growing tension between Murry and the Marks family over management decisions and money, Murry was happy to let David go. With the Beach Boys becoming more popular by the day, David took part in concerts and recordings with the group until October 5, at

> "Murray said, 'Bill, go back and tell Dennis he's fined $50 because he's playing too loud.' I found Dennis and told him about the fine and he said 'I know I'm playing too loud.' Then . . . Dennis played even louder at the next show."

which time he departed to lead his own band, Dave and the Marksmen.

With David leaving, it was only natural that the Beach Boys would offer Al Jardine a permanent spot in the group again. The turmoil with David occurred just as the Beach Boys were going back into the studio to record their next album, *Little Deuce Coupe*, and both he and Al performed on the record.

Today it is not uncommon for a band to release only one album in three years, but in 1963 the Beach Boys released three albums of new material in one year. This illustrates the relentless pressure that Brian was under to create new material. Four of the songs on the new record ("409," "Little Deuce Coupe," "Our Car Club," and "Shut Down") had already appeared on previous Beach Boys albums. Nevertheless, the album still showed signs that Brian was continuing to grow as a producer. "Be True to Your School" and "No Go Showboat" were both classics.

That Brian found any time to write in late 1963 was rather incredible. The Beach Boys were in great demand for personal appearances, and by the time Al returned they were already booked for a tour of Australia and New Zealand. By the end of 1963, the Beach Boys were national stars that attracted huge crowds wherever they played. Although Murry Wilson was still managing them, they realized that the situation could not go on forever. He continued to impose his ridiculous rules and to fine them for cursing or playing too loud. Not that they all listened to him. Bill Hesterman of KNAK in Salt Lake City recalled that in December 1963, "when the Beach Boys were playing at the Terrace, Murry said, 'Bill, go back and tell Dennis he's fined $50 because he's playing too loud.' I found Dennis and told him about the fine and he said 'I know I'm playing too loud.' Then . . . Dennis played even louder at the next show." It was clear that the Beach Boys had outgrown the need for a father figure. Big changes would happen in 1964.

Brian took the tapes back to Los Angeles, but decided against releasing the album right away. Vail recalled, "He wanted to try to get better quality recordings and he wanted to record another show so he could choose between the two, and also at the time of the Sacramento concert (in '63) they had yet to record 'Fun, Fun, Fun' and they wanted to include that on the album because it would be coming out in 1964." The LP was released in October 1964 and became the Beach Boys' first number one album on the *Billboard* charts.

FRIDAY, DECEMBER 27, AND SATURDAY, DECEMBER 28, 1963: Terrace Ballroom, Salt Lake City, UT
The Beach Boys were scheduled to play only one night, but a second show was added due to demand. The *Davis County Clipper* noted "the crowds were enormous" at these shows and that a new dance fad, "surfing," was all the rage in Utah. The frequency of visits to Utah in the 1960s attests to the Beach Boys' popularity in the state.

TUESDAY, DECEMBER 31, 1963: Cinnamon Cinder, San Bernardino, CA
Fred Vail attended this gig. He recalled, "There were other acts on the bill and we were done before midnight and Carl had a new Grand Prix. He and I got in the Grand Prix to go back home. He was still living with Murry at the time. KFWB was counting down the hits of 1963 and they played the number one hit of 1963 at midnight and it was 'Surfin' USA' and Carl and I just screamed. It doesn't get much better than that!" The next day, Vail attended the Beach Boys' January 1, 1964, recording session for "Fun, Fun, Fun."

OTHER 1963 CONCERTS

The group is known to have played a number of local California shows that are impossible to precisely date, as they relied only on radio for promotion.

The Beach Boys appeared at the Score in Alhambra, with the Rumblers, in February 1963.

According to Patrick Willford of the Whittier, California band the Hustlers, they opened for the Beach Boys in 1963 at the Downey Skate-O-Rama, a popular venue for surf bands.

Dennis McClelland of the Reverbs recalls opening up for the Beach Boys at the Pasadena Civic Auditorium during the summer. If this is true, the show must have been in either early June or early July. The Beach Boys headlined a "Stars of the Century Show" at the Orange Show Stadium in San Bernardino in the fall of 1963. Also on the bill were the Surfaris, the Tornadoes, the Truants, and the Coasters.

The Beach Boys also appeared at a Hawthorne High School Senior breakfast in early 1963. A photo of Brian, Carl, and David performing at this event appears in that year's yearbook.

According to a January 30, 1965, concert program, the Beach Boys played at the Spanish Castle in Seattle, Washington, in the summer of 1962. When contacted, promoter Pat O'Day confirmed that the group did indeed play there, but stated it was actually on a Friday in "early 1963," not 1962. O'Day recalled that they played at his nightclub, the Pat O'Day Party Line Club, the next day (Saturday) as well. O'Day knew Murry and agreed to fly the band to Seattle and give them some exposure to Pacific Northwest audiences. The shows lost money because, according to O'Day, the Seattle audiences were not ready for surf music yet. The most likely dates are late February or mid-March 1963. No mention of any Beach Boys concerts appeared in the *Seattle Times*. David Marks recalled the Party Line engagement: "It was a nightclub and they had phones at all the tables. I remember that well. You could call other tables on their phones. The phones only reached other tables. It was cute idea. Dennis was calling all the chicks, of course, at all the other tables!"

CONCERTS NOT PLAYED

Although Keith Badman's book, *The Beach Boys*, listed a February 14 concert at Hermosa Beach High School, there is no high school in Hermosa Beach.

1964

NINETEEN SIXTY-FOUR was an incredible whirlwind year for the Beach Boys, filled with numerous highs and lows. They began the year in a strong position, having established themselves as the top American rock group. The Beatles-led British Invasion would challenge them, but unlike many other American groups, the Beach Boys would survive the onslaught and finish the year in an even stronger position of popularity. This year was also the year in which they would fire their father as manager and witness their creative leader Brian Wilson suffering a nervous breakdown.

The year began with studio sessions for their latest album, *Shut Down Volume 2*. Though it was recorded in haste, *Shut Down Volume 2* contained three of Brian's all-time greatest compositions. The opening track, "Fun, Fun, Fun," was a top-five hit and found a permanent place in their concert act. Co-composer Mike Love later called it "one of the greatest 'roll down the windows and cruise to' type songs ever recorded." "Don't Worry Baby" was a gorgeous ballad and featured one of Brian's best lead vocals. It also signaled a shift in his composing style. As writers Andrew Doe and John Tobler have pointed out, though disguised as a song about a drag race, it may actually be viewed as a move towards more adult themes. "The Warmth of the Sun," written by Brian and Mike in the wake of John F. Kennedy's late-1963 assassination, is perhaps an even better example of Brian's shifting style. The song projects an aura of bittersweet loss that lingers with the listener long after the record ends.

In the midst of recording the album, the Beach Boys departed for their first international performances. The tour of Australia and New Zealand with support acts Roy Orbison, the Surfaris, Paul and Paula, and the Joy Boys was a major success. Much to the group's chagrin, father/manager Murry Wilson accompanied them on the tour. He told a reporter for the *Melbourne Age*, "When they are traveling, they find a father comes in handy, and I can also keep an eye on them." Murry's presence resulted in a great deal of strife as the group simply could not stand traveling with him anymore. As Carl explained to writer David Felton in 1976, "Brian and Michael especially, wanted to not have my father involved because he screwed them up with chicks, you know? We'd want to find a girl to be with, the thing on the road, and he was really kind of prudish about it."

Ian Rusten Collection

Ian Rusten Collection

CONCERTS PLAYED IN
1964

WEDNESDAY, JANUARY 15, 1964: Festival Hall, Brisbane, Queensland, Australia, with Roy Orbison, the Joy Boys, Paul and Paula, and the Surfaris (Two shows at 6:00 and 8:45 p.m.)
These were the first dates of a two-week tour of Australia and New Zealand, the Beach Boys' first trip outside of the United States. The legendary Roy Orbison, who had recently toured with the Beatles and was known for hits like "Crying" and "In Dreams," was the headliner. Rounding out the bill were the Surfaris, a mainly instrumental surf band famous for their hit recording "Wipe Out;" Paul and Paula, a duo from Texas known for their hit "Hey Paula;" and the Joy Boys, an Australian surf music group who had scored on the local charts with "Murphie the Surfie." Surf music was extremely popular in Australia and most of the shows were sold out.

The touring party landed in Sydney on January 13 and was greeted by hundreds of frenzied local teenagers at the airport. *The Brisbane Telegraph* reported that "the teenagers, mostly girls, many of them barefooted, forced their way into a private lounge, trampled gardens, knocked over chairs, and clambered over a 10 ft. high partition to obtain autographs from the entertainers." The Beach Boys remained in Sydney for two days of promotion before flying to Brisbane for what was reported as a very wild pair of concerts. *The Brisbane Courier Mail* noted that, "Festival Hall last night nearly lost its roof . . . after what was the wildest show it has ever had."

FRIDAY, JANUARY 17, AND SATURDAY, JANUARY 18, 1964: Sydney Stadium, Sydney, New South Wales, Australia, with Roy Orbison, the Joy Boys, Paul and Paula, and the Surfaris (Two shows on Friday at 6:00 and 8:45 p.m. and three shows on Saturday at 2:30, 6:00, and 8:45 p.m.)
Promoter Harry M. Miller claimed with obvious exaggeration that over 50,000 fans attended these shows. There were two performances on Friday and three on Saturday, including an added 2:30 p.m. matinee. The local radio station recorded three songs performed by the Beach Boys on Friday night: "Papa-Oom-Mow-Mow," "Little Deuce Coupe," and "What'd I Say." This incredible live version of "What'd I Say" was released in 1981 on the Australian *Rarities* album.

MONDAY, JANUARY 20, 1964: Centennial Hall, Adelaide, South Australia, with Roy Orbison, the Joy Boys, Paul and Paula, and the Surfaris (Two shows at 6:00 and 8:45 p.m.)
The touring party flew to Melbourne on Sunday morning, arriving at about 12:30 p.m., where 3,000 teenagers greeted them. The Beach Boys, stunned by the Beatles-like airport reception, asked a reporter, "Is it always like this?" After an hour, they made a connecting flight to Adelaide. *The Advertiser* reported, "close to 6,000 clapping, stomping, whistling, screaming teenagers in the seats rocked Centennial Hall, Wayville, last night."

TUESDAY, JANUARY 21, AND WEDNESDAY, JANUARY 22, 1964: Festival Hall, Melbourne, Victoria, Australia, with Roy Orbison, the Joy Boys, Paul and Paula, and the Surfaris (Two shows each night at 6:00 and 8:45 p.m.)
The Beach Boys returned to Melbourne for two sold-out concerts. The *Melbourne Herald* reported that "the Surfies were in full swing as the top American guitar and vocal groups, the Surfaris and the Beach Boys, followed suit. The Surfaris, surprisingly un-bronzed under the bright lights, tested our eardrums with their guitars and cymbals; the Beach Boys, looking less beachy than even the Surfaris, presented surf songs that reached top notch on the American charts."

THURSDAY, JANUARY 23, 1964: Town Hall, Hobart, Tasmania, Australia, with Roy Orbison, the Joy Boys, Paul and Paula, and the Surfaris (Two shows at 6:00 and 8:45 p.m.)
This was the Beach Boys' last Australian date, as they returned to Melbourne and then flew to Wellington, New Zealand, landing at Rongotai airport around 7:00 p.m. The tour party spent the night at the Mutual Motor Lodge before flying on to Invercargill the next morning.

SATURDAY, JANUARY 25, 1964: Civic Theatre, Invercargill, South Island, New Zealand, with Roy Orbison, the Joy Boys, Paul and Paula, and the Surfaris (Three shows at 2:15, 5:00, and 8:30 p.m.) The entourage landed at Invercargill on Saturday morning and held a meet and greet at the airport at 11:30 a.m. The tour proved just as popular in New Zealand, with sold-out shows prompting an added matinee. The *Southland Daily News* reported that "the Beach Boys were quite an entertaining group and their surfin' numbers went across well. Even though they were an almost identical combination to the Surfaris, they overshadowed them somewhat. The group's saxophonist was humorous and during his version of 'The Monster Mash' he had the audience rollicking."

MONDAY, JANUARY 27, AND TUESDAY, JANUARY 28, 1964: Theatre Royal, Christchurch, South Island, New Zealand, with Roy Orbison, the Joy Boys, Paul and Paula, and the Surfaris (Two shows each night at 6:00 and 8:30 p.m.) The tour arrived at Harewood Airport in Christchurch on Sunday, January 26 at 11:45 a.m. On Monday morning, Al gave an interview over breakfast to a reporter from The *Christchurch Star*. He declared that he got a "terrific kick from success . . . it's good to be able to go around the world without having to be in the army." A reporter commented that "the Beach Boys proved the funny men, carrying off their 'act' with a mild degree of polish. They . . . had a fairly wide range of style, harmony, and rhythm." The *Christchurch Press* panned most of the acts on the bill, suggesting that only Roy Orbison had real stage presence. However, it threw some faint praise at Mike, noting, "he danced and jigged in stocking feet, and achieved some strange contortions in an offbeat number called 'Monster Mash.' No doubt the audience wondered what the submerged words were, because the guitars drowned out every one. It may have been just as well, because the group hit a high proportion of wrong notes when they tried to harmonize a slow song about graduation day."

WEDNESDAY, JANUARY 29, 1964: Town Hall, Wellington, North Island, New Zealand, with Roy Orbison, the Joy Boys, Paul and Paula, and the Surfaris (Two shows at 6:00 and 8:30 p.m.) The two concerts in Wellington again drew huge crowds and rave reviews from the local papers. The *Dominion* reviewer wrote, "Harry M. Miller's Surfside '64 Show drew two capacity audiences to the Wellington Town Hall last night. Right through the show an audience of all ages, from sub-teens to grandparents, stomped, clapped, whistled, and screamed for more." The *Wellington Evening Post* reviewer stated that "the longest surfie spot went to the Beach Boys, wearing open-neck blue shirts and slacks and with longish hair which added to their wind-swept look . . . They are an exceptionally young group and are led by the big brother of three of the members whose high spiritedness infects the others. 'Surfin' USA' went over well, like all the other numbers, and the audience was in no mood to let them go."

THURSDAY, JANUARY 30, 1964: Founders Hall, Hamilton, North Island, New Zealand, with Roy Orbison, the Joy Boys, Paul and Paula, and the Surfaris (Two shows at 6:00 and 8:30 p.m.)

FRIDAY, JANUARY 31, AND SATURDAY, FEBRUARY 1, 1964: Town Hall, Auckland, North Island, New Zealand, with Roy Orbison, the Joy Boys, Paul and Paula, and the Surfaris (Two shows at 6:00 and 8:30 p.m. on Friday and three shows on Saturday at 2:00, 6:00 and 8:30 p.m.) Due to demand, five shows in two days were performed in Auckland. The *New Zealand Herald* noted, "The Beach Boys contributed an element of comedy and some slow-beat surfing songs which were very easy to listen to." The *Auckland Star* enthused that "musically, the Beach Boys provided the best material of the night with some surprisingly smooth harmony, particularly in the tuneful 'Graduation Day.'" The three shows on Saturday concluded the group's Australia/New Zealand tour. On their return to California, Alan married Lynda Sperry on February 4.

SATURDAY, FEBRUARY 8, 1964: Pavalon Skating Rink, Huntington Beach, CA, with the Surf Riders According to a fan who saved his ticket stub from this concert, the Beach Boys were not the headliners at this concert promoted by KRLA disc jockey Casey Kasem. The small venue, with room for about 600, catered to a tough surfing crowd that had little love for the "Hollywood" Beach Boys.

Back at home Murry was a continual distractive presence in the studio. Although he believed that Brian was a genius and praised him in interviews, he continued to second-guess him in the studio. Carl recalled, "He and Brian drove each other nuts. You know, here Brian is really growing massively musically right? And his old man's telling him how the records should sound." Things reached such an impasse that the group would sometimes pretend to record while Murry was there, but wait until he left to actually make the record. Brian was horribly conflicted. On one hand, Murry's presence in the studio unnerved him, but on the other hand, he was his father and a ferocious defender of the group's interests. Indeed, Roger Christian believed that "if it weren't for Murry in the early days, pushing, the royalties wouldn't have been what they were. Murry fought hard to get things straight."

In April 1964, matters came to a head at a recording session for a new song called "I Get Around." Brian was certain it was a number-one record, while Murry insisted on questioning his son's artistic instinct. He interrupted the session and criticized the group's singing. Brian reportedly grabbed his father by the collar and threw him against the wall. "You're fired," he screamed. "Do you understand me, you're fired!" A shell-shocked Murry stayed in bed for a week. Meanwhile, the Beach Boys signed with the management firm of Cummins and Currant, with whom they remained until 1966. Brian later explained to reporter Ian

Dove that the group "changed from our father to outside management basically because of the emotional strain we were under. We didn't feel that we were driving for the things we should have been since we are in a golden position to progress and become possibly more successful."

"I Get Around" was a tremendous success, and just as Brian hoped, it hit number one on the U.S. charts. It came at a critically important time

> Brian reportedly grabbed his father by the collar and threw him against the wall. "You're fired," he screamed. "Do you understand me, you're fired!"

for the band. The Beatles' appearance on *The Ed Sullivan Show* in February 1964 had created a sensation in the music industry. Overnight, the U.S. charts were full of English artists like the Dave Clark Five, the Animals, and Gerry and the Pacemakers. The British Invasion knocked many of the top American artists permanently off the charts. As Brian said at the time, "I know the competition is strong, with

FRIDAY, FEBRUARY 21, 1964: Hoquiam High School, Hoquiam, WA, with the Beachcombers and Shirley Owens, the Capris with Gail Harris, and the Chandells (10:00 p.m. show)
The Beach Boys headed to the Pacific Northwest for three nights.

SATURDAY, FEBRUARY 22, 1964: "1964 All Star Revue," Seattle Opera House, Seattle WA, with Bobby Vinton, Trini Lopez, Jimmy Gilmer, Mel Carter, and the Cascades (Three shows at 2:00, 6:00, and 9:00 p.m.)

SUNDAY, FEBRUARY 23, 1964: Spokane Coliseum, Spokane, WA, with Jimmy Gilmer and the Cascades (8:00 p.m. show)

FRIDAY, FEBRUARY 28, 1964: Cupertino High School, Cupertino, CA (afternoon show), and Santa Clara County Fairgrounds, San Jose, CA
Played prior to their scheduled San Jose concert, the group's Cupertino High School appearance was a last-minute decision. According to Bill Boggie, a teacher at the school, the concert came about because "one day a very popular disc jockey decided to run his morning show jumping around from paid phone booths in the greater San Jose area. One of these phone booths was very close to Cupertino High. Fifty or sixty kids decided to skip classes and watch him do his thing. The dean of student activities and the dean of boys descended on the phone booth too, and got the students back in class. To smooth things over, the disc jockey prevailed on the Beach Boys, who happened to be in the area, to do their short brunch concert at CHS."

The concert was a complete surprise to students and staff. Boggie recalled that as they were about to go for brunch, "the principal came on the PA and welcomed all students to come to the rally court for a special musical treat. As I left my classroom I heard the distinctive beginning of 'Fun, Fun, Fun' [and] I, along with the students and fellow teachers, raced to see if it could possibly be the Beach Boys in person. To our amazement, it really was America's number one band. They played three other songs, with Mike Love adding clever banter in between." According to the 1964 Cupertino yearbook, two of the other songs performed were "Long Tall Texan" and "Monster Mash." After the short show, the band signed autographs for the students. Brian skipped the afternoon show but was present for the evening show in San Jose.

FRIDAY, MARCH 6, 1964: Bellflower Rollerena, Bellflower, CA
Soon after this show, the Beach Boys taped an appearance on the NBC TV *Steve Allen Show* in San Diego. Dressed in their matching striped shirts, they performed "Fun, Fun, Fun" and "Surfin' USA" before a live audience. This show (which aired on March 27) survives in its entirety and portions of the Beach Boys performance were used in the 1998 documentary *Endless Harmony.*

SATURDAY, MARCH 14, 1964 "The Lost Concert," NBC TV Studios, Burbank, CA
The Beach Boys taped a special concert before a live audience for the National General Corporation. The footage was shown in theaters with a film of the Beatles' recent concert in Washington, DC, and live footage of Leslie Gore. The Beach Boys performed "Fun, Fun, Fun," "Long Tall Texan," "Little Deuce Coupe," "Surfer Girl," "Monster Mash," "Surfin' USA," "Shut Down," "In My Room," "Papa-Oom-Mow-Mow," and "Hawaii." Among the people visible in the audience are Fred Vail, Marilyn Rovell (who can clearly be seen attempting to communicate with her boyfriend Brian onstage), and Beach Boys Fan Club president Jodi Gable. The footage, believed lost for many years, was eventually located and released on home video in 1998, hence the title.

The Beach Boys also taped an appearance on ABC TV's *American Bandstand* the same day (which aired in April). The Beach Boys mimed to "Don't Worry Baby" and gave a brief interview to host Dick Clark, in which they discussed their recent Australian tour. The Beach Boys, however, were less than thrilled when they arrived on the set and discovered that they were expected to stand in front of a curtain without their instruments and lip-synch. Carl later told Earl Leaf, "Once we went on a filmed Dick Clark TV show without our instruments, dong a lip-synch to records. Later when we saw how we looked, we each died a thousand deaths. It was awful. We'll never do that again."

1964

SATURDAY, MARCH 28, 1964: Civic Auditorium, Santa Cruz, CA (Two shows at 7:30 and 9:30 p.m.)

FRIDAY, APRIL 3, 1964: Whittier HS Auditorium, Whittier CA, with Mahalia Jackson, Andre Previn, Andy Williams, and Pat Boone
This was a special benefit concert with proceeds going to the Metabolic Unit of UCLA Medical School and to the Susan Townsend Scholarship Fund.

FRIDAY, MAY 8, 1964: Centennial Coliseum, Reno NV (Two shows)
Over 5,000 fans attended these two wild shows, which were promoted by Fred Vail. The Reno fans screamed so loud, that reportedly they could be heard over two blocks away. According to the reviewer from the *Reno Evening Gazette*, "While the Beach Boys . . . sang and danced, police noted at least three teenage girls fainted . . . The youngsters yelled themselves hoarse. The second show was comparatively quiet until final numbers. Then the kids went wild . . . They danced in the aisles atop chairs, and even on the stage with the Beach Boys."

SATURDAY, MAY 9, 1964: Memorial Auditorium, Sacramento, CA (Two shows at 7:00 and 9:30 p.m.)
The group played two benefit shows for the Sacramento Easter Seals Society. Arriving in Sacramento at 10:30 a.m., the boys were presented with the key to the city by Mayor James B. McKinney at the Municipal Airport. Fred Vail, who was still promoting occasional shows on their behalf, recalled, "I was doing some shows but I couldn't do a whole lot because I'm only one guy and I am doing all the leg work myself, finding the hall, booking PAs, setting up box office, etc. . . . So I only did a few shows a month if that. . . . William Morris was still booking them. It's just that every time they did a show with me they made more money than with other promoters."

THURSDAY, MAY 14, 1964: Houston, TX

FRIDAY, MAY 15, 1964: Southern Methodist University Coliseum, Dallas, TX, with the Jades, Bob Hayden and the Marksmen, Kirby St. Romaine, and Scotty McKay (8 p.m. show)
Prior to the 8 p.m. show, billed as a "School's End Spectacular," the Beach Boys made a 4:30 p.m. appearance at the Sanger-Harris Preston Center store, where they signed autographs.

SATURDAY, MAY 16, 1964: Municipal Auditorium, San Antonio, TX, with Barbara Lynn, Little Johnny Taylor, Bob Hayden and the Marksmen, Dawn Six and the Rel-Yeas (8 p.m. show)
Before the show, the Beach Boys made a personal appearance at the North Star Mall in the Grand Court at 2 p.m. to sign autographs.

SATURDAY, MAY 23, 1964: Memorial Coliseum, Portland, OR, with the Viceroys, Nino Tempo and April Stevens, and Ray Stevens (8:00 p.m. show)
KISN radio sponsored this show, billed as "The All Star Revue," with the Beach Boys as headliners. Fan David Higginbotham, who'd also attended the band's 1963 Portland appearance, recalled, "The big distinction between the 1963 appearance and this one, besides the fact that this time Brian was there, was that they were obviously much more polished. They weren't quite as loud and brash. . . . They obviously had a backlog of hits and great songs that they'd worked up . . . When they came onstage for their encore . . . Mike said, 'Ladies and gentlemen, we have a special treat for you. We're going to debut our new single, which just came out.' And then they sang 'I Get Around' and 'Don't Worry Baby.'"

the Beatles and Dave Clark, but this only makes us work harder . . . Anybody singing today who says they're not afraid of the Beatles is a liar!" The "I Get Around" single gave the band confidence that they would survive if they kept growing and moving forward.

Success created a constant need for more and better material. The Beach Boys relied on one man to write, arrange, and produce

Program for a May 9, 1964, concert in Sacramento. Collection of Chris Woods

Mike with his sax in Portland, Oregon, on May 23, 1964. Collection of David Lee Higginbotham

THE BEACH BOYS IN CONCERT

Performing in Portland, Oregon, on May 23, 1964. Collection of David Lee Higginbotham

their recordings—Brian Wilson. Brian was finding it increasingly hard to find the time to do it all because of the Beach Boys' punishing schedule. No sooner was the *Shut Down, Volume 2* LP finished than Capitol was demanding another album for summer release. They also wanted a Christmas LP prepared for the holidays. While trying to satisfy these recording commitments, Brian and the Beach Boys had to find time to film appearances in two movies and several TV shows, appear at dozens of concerts scattered all over the U.S., and satisfy neverending demands for press and radio promotion.

Despite the frenetic pace, Brian managed to create the strongest Beach Boys album yet. *All Summer Long* (released in July 1964) featured a fantastic collection of songs including the hit "I Get Around," a lush cover of the Mystic's 1959 hit "Hushabye," the deftly arranged ballad "The Girls on the Beach," the pounding surf tune "Don't Back Down," the

FRIDAY, JUNE 12, AND SATURDAY, JUNE 13, 1964: Lagoon, Farmington, UT
Over 5,500 fans attended the Saturday show underlining the Beach Boys' strong popularity in this area.

FRIDAY, JUNE 26, 1964: Civic Auditorium, San Jose, CA, with Bobby Freeman, Rene and Rene, and the Paris Sisters
While recording their Christmas album, the group took a day off to play their second concert of the year in San Jose.

FRIDAY, JULY 3, AND SATURDAY, JULY 4, 1964: "Million Dollar Party," HIC International Arena, Honolulu, HI, with Bruce and Terry, Jan and Dean, the Righteous Brothers, the Kingsmen, Freddy Cannon, Jimmy Griffin, the Rivingtons, Ray Peterson, Jody Miller, Jimmy Clanton, and Peter and Gordon (One show at 7:30 p.m. on Friday and three shows at 2:00, 6:30, and 9:00 p.m. on Saturday)
Future Beach Boy Bruce Johnston, who performed with friend Terry Melcher, recalled these shows during the campfire sequences of the Beach Boys' 1989 *Endless Summer* TV show. Bruce related that the British act Peter and Gordon were unprepared for the heat of Hawaii and quickly turned as red as lobsters. During the same segment, Mike Love noted that Jan and Dean ran onstage during one of these shows shooting fire extinguishers at the group. Al Jardine recalled that he walked backstage and found Jan tied up "like a mummy" with surgical gauze.

Wayne Harada of the *Honolulu Star Bulletin*, who attended the Friday night concert along with 7,000 screaming fans, reported, "the Beach Boys, who originated the surfing and hot rod trends in music last year, offered thirteen hit tunes, including 'Hawaii,' '409,' 'Surfin' Safari,' and 'I Get Around.' The headliners showed they were capable of handling ballads, singing 'Surfer Girl,' 'In My Room,' and 'Don't Worry Baby' à la Four Freshmen."

SUNDAY, JULY 5, 1964: "Million Dollar Party," Bloch Arena, Honolulu, HI, with Bruce and Terry, Jan and Dean, the Righteous Brothers, the Kingsmen, Freddy Cannon, Jimmy Griffin, the Rivingtons, Ray Peterson, Jody Miller, Jimmy Clanton, and Peter and Gordon (2:00 p.m. show) and Schofield Barracks, Honolulu, HI, with Bruce and Terry, Jan and Dean, the Righteous Brothers, the Kingsmen, Freddy Cannon, Jimmy Griffin, the Rivingtons, Ray Peterson, Jody Miller, Jimmy Clanton, and Peter and Gordon (7:30 p.m. show)

MONDAY, JULY 6, 1964: University of Arizona, Tucson, AZ, with Freddy Cannon, Jimmy Griffin and Lynne Easton and the Kingsmen (8 p.m. show)
This was the opening show of the "Summer Safari Tour," a thirty-three-day trek across the United States in a rented Greyhound bus. Other acts on the tour included Lynn Easton's Kingsmen, Jimmy Griffin, and Freddy Cannon. Cannon became ill halfway through the tour and was replaced by Eddie Hodges. The Beach Boys were accompanied on the tour by Ron Swallow, their main roadie and assistant, who carried the instruments, manned the sound boards, handled tour logistics, did some of the driving, and even saw to the lighting. He also assisted new road manager Don Rice, who was hired by Cummins and Currant. Rice's number one job was to make sure that the Beach Boys weren't cheated and got an accurate percentage of the gate.

Promoter Irving Granz began a long relationship with the group on the "Summer Safari Tour." He recalled to the BBC in 1974 that Brian had balked at the prospect of driving all the way to Oklahoma City, where the tour was originally scheduled to begin on July 9, so Granz was hired by the William Morris Agency to book some last-minute shows that the band could play on the way. Granz recalled that he "booked them in a college, who thought they were a folk act, because I played folk groups there before . . . and the ceiling fell down from the vibrations of the guitar, because they'd never had anything like that before. It was really wild."

Dan Pavillard of the *Tucson Daily Citizen* wrote that "the decibel level in the auditorium was sky high. Only with difficulty could one catch enough of the words from amidst the amplified whanging of steel guitars even to fit a song with a title, as if that mattered. BB fans made the first concert of a five-month U.S. tour for the group sound like a high-school pep rally. Shrieks, squeals, and whinnies greeted the initial chord of every number . . . Dennis Wilson, whose every toss of his blond mop brought a groundswell of sighs from the girls, drummed and tossed unremittingly throughout the evening . . . Mike Love, spokesman, sometime vocalist, and sax player, danced all over the stage and his enthusiasm was wildly contagious."

TUESDAY, JULY 7, 1964: Civic Auditorium, Albuquerque, NM, with Freddy Cannon, Jimmy Griffin, and Lynne Easton and the Kingsmen (8 p.m. show)

WEDNESDAY, JULY 8, 1964: Memorial Auditorium, Amarillo, TX, with Freddy Cannon, Jimmy Griffin, and Lynne Easton and the Kingsmen
The group apparently did not enjoy playing this show. They remarked to writer Earl Leaf that the audiences in Amarillo (and San Antonio, where they played in May) were "the coldest they've ever seen. The kids there seem to be saying, 'We dare you to entertain us!'"

THURSDAY, JULY 9, 1964: Spring Lake Amusement Park, Oklahoma City, OK, with Freddy Cannon, Jimmy Griffin, and Lynne Easton and the Kingsmen (Two shows at 8:00 and 10:00 p.m.)
In the book *Springlake Amusement Park*, one fan recalled that a fistfight broke out at one of these concerts between boys from two rival schools. "Every member of the Beach Boys, except the drummer, moved to the edge of the stage and looked down with glee at the melee below. And they never missed a note: true professionals."

FRIDAY, JULY 10, 1964: Tulsa Assembly Center, Tulsa, OK, with Freddy Cannon, Jimmy Griffin, and Lynne Easton and the Kingsmen (8:30 p.m. show)

SATURDAY, JULY 11, 1964: Rosenblatt Stadium, Omaha, NE, with Freddy Cannon, Jimmy Griffin, and Lynne Easton and the Kingsmen (8:00 p.m. show)
Ron Swallow recalled that Brian could be moody and introverted before shows, but that at other times on the road he was a wild, practical joker. His favorite routine, frequently repeated on the tour, was to walk onto a crowded hotel elevator and pretend to suffer a heart attack. Ron would then push the emergency button and everyone would scurry off the elevator. Brian found this hysterical.

SUNDAY, JULY 12, 1964: Municipal Auditorium, Kansas City, MO, with Freddy Cannon, Jimmy Griffin, and Lynne Easton and the Kingsmen (8:30 p.m. show)
Although the show was not reviewed, a fan that attended the concert wrote a letter to the *Kansas City Star* to complain about the audience's unruly behavior. She wrote, "Someone had to throw something on the stage. It hit Dennis Wilson, the drummer, on the face and he could not continue in the show. One of them said that something like that had never happened before—but it happened in Kansas City." The drummer from the Kingsmen sat in for Dennis.

MONDAY, JULY 13, 1964: Veteran's Memorial Auditorium, Des Moines, IA, with Freddy Cannon, Jimmy Griffin, and Lynne Easton and the Kingsmen (8:00 p.m. show)
According to *Des Moines Register* reviewer Donald Kaul, "more than 5,000 youngsters turned out to hear the Beach Boys and assorted other 'singing' groups in concert . . . Wearing tight white pants and yellow shirts open at the throat, they (the Beach Boys) bounded onto the stage and promptly gave imitations of pots and pans falling downstairs (although they called it something else) . . . Several hundred of the younger children in the young audience immediately rushed to the edge of the stage and tried to touch their heroes. One felt pity for the policemen who attempted to keep order around the stage area."

TUESDAY, JULY 14, 1964: RKO Orpheum Theater, Davenport, IA, with Freddy Cannon, Jimmy

Dennis pounds the drums in May 1964. Collection of David Lee Higginbotham

catchy pop classic "Wendy," the iconic scooter tune "Little Honda," and the charming title song. The album was, in a way, one last breath of innocence. Brian was feeling more and more restrained by the sunny themes that had become the group's brand and was preparing to move on. He told *Record Mirror* that "the surfing theme has run its course. Cars are finished now, too, and even the Hondas are over. We're just gonna stay on the life of the social teenager."

All Summer Long became an absolute smash, rising to a lofty number four on the *Billboard* LP charts. There was little time to enjoy the success. The Beach Boys flew to Hawaii at the beginning of July to begin another summer tour. There were screaming crowds at every stop along the way and reporters and photographers

Poster for a 1964 concert in Urbana, Ohio.
Ian Rusten Collection

Poster for a summer 1964 concert in Hawaii.
Courtesy of PosterCentral.Com

Griffin, and Lynne Easton and the Kingsmen (Two shows at 6:00 and 8:30 p.m.)
This concert reportedly caused a near-riot in downtown Davenport.

WEDNESDAY, JULY 15, 1964: Kiel Auditorium, St. Louis, MO, with Freddy Cannon, Jimmy Griffin, and Lynne Easton and the Kingsmen (Two shows at 6:30 and 9:00 p.m.)
During this time, Beach Boys concerts continued to feature at least one song featuring Mike on saxophone. Mike later alleged that his saxophone playing came to an end when Ron Swallow left the instrument at a venue after a show. Ron recalled, "Mike's saxophone story was just ridiculous. He couldn't play the instrument very well anyways so if he wants to credit me with losing it, I am happy to take the blame."

THURSDAY, JULY 16, 1964: Kentucky State Fairgrounds, Louisville, KY, with Freddy Cannon, Jimmy Griffin, and Lynne Easton and the Kingsmen (8:30 p.m. show)
Dennis was attacked by a mob of female fans after this show. He was knocked out, and needed stitches.

FRIDAY, JULY 17, 1964: Indiana Beach, Shafer Lake, Monticello, IN, with Freddy Cannon, Jimmy Griffin, and Lynne Easton and the Kingsmen (Two shows between 8:45 p.m. and 12:45 a.m.)

SATURDAY, JULY 18, 1964: Indiana State Fairgrounds Coliseum, Indianapolis, IN, with Freddy Cannon, Jimmy Griffin, and Lynne Easton and the Kingsmen (8:00 p.m. show)

SUNDAY, JULY 19, 1964: Milwaukee Auditorium, Milwaukee, WI, with Eddie Hodges, Freddy Cannon, Jimmy Griffin, and Lynne Easton and the Kingsmen (Two shows at 3:00 and 8:00 p.m.)
Dressed in gray slacks and striped shirts, the group performed before 6,231 people, most of them screaming teenage girls. Brian told Earl Leaf, "Milwaukee is the wildest. Those Milwaukee gals are like hungry tigresses. They grabbed our feet while we were performing on stage and tore at our clothes on the street. If many other cities were like Milwaukee, we'd have to buy a wardrobe of breakaway suits." According to the *Milwaukee Sentinel*, "At times, the boys, who had numerous amplifiers to aid them, were nearly drowned out by the audience." When the band headed offstage, "moaning youngsters found all the doors leading backstage. A couple of the fellows were stripping off their perspiration-soaked shirts when a small group of girls discovered them. 'I'm going to faint,' one screeched, putting her hands over her eyes but peeking between her fingers."

TUESDAY, JULY 21, 1964: Coconut Lounge, Urbana, OH, with Freddie Cannon, Jimmy Griffin, and Lynne Easton and the Kingsmen (Two shows at 7:30 and 10:00 p.m.)
The Beach Boys performed at the legendary venue on Lakewood Beach, a few miles from Urbana, Ohio. The Lounge closed in 1965.

JULY 20 TO JULY 22, 1964: Flint, MI, and Fort Wayne, IN
These cities are listed on the tour itinerary printed in the August 26 *Billboard* magazine.

THURSDAY, JULY 23, 1964: Capitol Theater, Madison, WI, with Eddie Hodges, Jimmy Griffin, Lynne Easton and the Kingsmen, the Dynastics, and the Novells (Two shows at 7:00 and 9:30 p.m.)
For this show only, the band was preceded by two local acts, the Novells from Madison and the Dynastics from Milwaukee. The overwhelmingly female audience gave the Beach Boys a rousing welcome, especially Dennis. The *Daily Cardinal* reviewer exclaimed, "Have you ever heard an air raid siren? It's nothing compared to the shrieks which went through the young ladies lips and reverberated throughout the theatre. The five 'Surfer Kings' acknowledged the noise, but for a moment they seemed a little perplexed, because everybody kept screaming for the drummer, Denny. He had his blond hair flopping in front of his forehead, much like his English counterpart Ringo. Finally Denny came down from his stand and sang a song. Have you ever heard an air raid siren?"

FRIDAY, JULY 24, 1964: Arie Crown Theater, Chicago, IL, with Eddie Hodges, Jimmy Griffin, and Lynne Easton and the Kingsmen (8:30 p.m. show)

SATURDAY, JULY 25, 1964: Mary E. Sawyer Auditorium, La Crosse, WI, with Eddie Hodges, Jimmy Griffin, and Lynne Easton and the Kingsmen (Two shows at 7:30 and 9:30 p.m.)
Reviewing the show in his column, Lindy Shannon wrote, "As they strolled on stage, 1,500 teens grabbed the neatly arranged chairs in the auditorium, and went scrambling for the front of the stage. For a few moments it was pandemonium. Then they settled down to the normal crowd noises that seemed to engulf the entire evening, as they clapped their hands, stomped their feet, and sang along to the familiar songs of their times, 'Little Deuce Coupe,' 'Shut Down,' 'Surfer Girl.' Even when three of the members had a disagreement on stage during their finale of 'I Get Around,' the audience didn't seem to mind, because that was a precious night to the young folk of the area. The idols of millions of teens around the world were performing within reaching distance."

TUESDAY, JULY 28, 1964: Auditorium Theater, Denver, CO, with Eddie Hodges, Jimmy Griffin, and Lynne Easton and the Kingsmen (8:15 p.m. show)
This show was originally scheduled for Red Rocks, but the venue was changed at the last minute.

WEDNESDAY, JULY 29, 1964: Lagoon, Farmington, UT, with Eddie Hodges, Jimmy Griffin, and Lynne Easton and the Kingsmen (8:00 p.m. show)
Over 3,500 teenagers attended this show, breaking the Lagoon's weekday attendance record.

THURSDAY, JULY 30, 1964: State Building Auditorium, Reno, NV, with Eddie Hodges, Jimmy Griffin, and Lynne Easton and the Kingsmen (Two shows at 7:00 and 9:30 p.m.)
Fred Vail promoted these two shows on the Beach Boys' behalf.

FRIDAY, JULY 31, 1964: Oakland Civic Auditorium, Oakland, CA, with Eddie Hodges, Jimmy Griffin, Rene and Rene, and Lynne Easton and the Kingsmen (8:30 p.m. show)
The Beach Boys' sole Bay Area appearance on the tour attracted thousands of fans. The *Oakland Tribune* reported that the Beach Boys had kids "squealing, screaming, and dancing in the aisles. Girls jumped out of their chairs and began to dance, and several boys tried to get on stage and demonstrate their surfing steps . . . Although the Beach Boys have their devoted followers who think they outclass the Beatles, the most popular member of the group was the drummer, the only one with a Beatles haircut."

DJ Jim Satcher, who had become friendly with Dennis while hosting dances in San Francisco, was now a soldier on leave and met up with the group at this show. The Beach Boys were now huge stars and crowds surrounded their tour bus wherever they went. Satcher recalled that "Dennis told me to get on the bus and wait while they tried to lose the crowd before running to get on the bus. They didn't want the fans to follow and get hurt by jumping in front of the bus. I remember others already on the bus—maybe Eddie Hodges . . . They thought I was a soldier who got on the wrong bus. They commented to themselves, 'Was I in for a surprise.' But a moment later Dennis got on the bus and introduced me to the others."

SATURDAY, AUGUST 1, 1964: Memorial Auditorium, Sacramento, CA, with Eddie Hodges, Jimmy Griffin, and Lynne Easton and the Kingsmen (Two shows at 7:00 and 9:30 p.m.)
Jim Satcher recalled that "Brian had brought a full studio worth of recording equipment and had it installed backstage. Brian was calm and in control of the rehearsal and both shows. The best part of the show in Sacramento was watching Brian work." The two shows were being recorded because Capitol Records was intent on releasing a live album. The LP that ultimately appeared is a combination of recordings from the December 1963 Sacramento appearance and this one. The version of "Little Old Lady From Pasadena" heard on that album, as well as an outtake of "Don't Worry Baby" included as a bonus track on the CD reissue, clearly come from these 1964 concerts.

SUNDAY, AUGUST 2, 1964: Veterans Memorial Building, Santa Rosa, CA, with Eddie Hodges, Jimmy Griffin, and Lynne Easton and the Kingsmen (Two shows at 4:00 and 8:00 p.m.)

Brian performing in Portland, Oregon, on May 23, 1964.
Collection of David Lee Higginbotham

demanding attention. There were no breaks. The day the Hawaii tour ended, the group began a string of Midwest and East Coast concert dates that culminated with their first appearance on the highly influential TV show *The Ed Sullivan Show* on September 27, 1964.

In October, the Beach Boys took part in the massive Teenage Music International Awards concert in Santa

Monica, California, that was filmed for movie release. There they shared the bill with an incredible roster of talent, including the Rolling Stones, James Brown, and the Supremes. The footage is the best surviving document of the 1964 group onstage. The Beach Boys blazed through high-spirited versions of "Surfin' USA," "Surfer Girl," "I Get Around," and their new single, "Dance, Dance, Dance." They were clearly the stars of the show and were paid $50,000 for their appearance—a huge sum in 1964 dollars, and more than double what the Rolling Stones received. They also received star billing in the advertisements for the film. After filming the show, the Beach Boys headed to the East Coast for a wild show in Worcester, Massachusetts, and then boarded a flight to the U.K. to begin their first European tour. The group was in Europe for twenty-three days, mainly making promotional appearances, though they did find time to play two concerts in Paris and Stockholm. Upon their return to the U.S. they immediately performed several more concerts on the East Coast before finally heading home to L.A. to work on their next album.

In the midst of this tornado of success, Brian complained to writer Sidney Scoop that "the Beach Boys is a big business; not as big business as the Beatles, mind you, but big business nevertheless. We're the top-selling group in this country (at the moment anyway) and the more popular we get, the less freedom we have."

THE BEACH BOYS IN CONCERT

MONDAY, AUGUST 3, 1964: Memorial Auditorium, Fresno, CA, with Eddie Hodges, Jimmy Griffin, and Lynne Easton and the Kingsmen (8:00 p.m. show)
Over 2,800 local teenagers attended this wild show, and over a hundred girls chased the group when they left the auditorium that night. The *Fresno Bee* reported, "The pitch in complicated five-part harmony was true and in quiet moments such as 'Surfer Girl' . . . with lead man Brian Wilson contributing a soft banshee-like wail, the sound was audibly 'different' and pleasant . . . Shaggy-haired drummer Dennis Wilson . . . brought girls scrambling to the barriers with 'The Wanderer.' 'The Monster Mash' and 'Ooh Mau Mau' [Papa-Oom-Mow-Mow] drew sighs and squeaks of appreciation. The crowd found the antics as delightful as the music. Especially those of Mike Love who meandered about crouched in steps called the Slauson Shuffle, The Monkey, and The Dog, Southern California calisthenics which, off the reception for Love, should signal a new fad here."

TUESDAY, AUGUST 4, 1964: Earl Warren Showgrounds, Santa Barbara, CA, with Eddie Hodges, Jimmy Griffin, and Lynne Easton and the Kingsmen (8:15 p.m. show)
The *Santa Barbara News Press* reported that "The headliners of the evening, the Beach Boys, received the warmest reception of the evening . . . Wearing sun yellow shirts and gray pants, the number one singing group in the nation sang their current hits, 'I Get Around' and 'Don't Worry Baby,' along with a variety of other tunes including 'The Monster Mash,' 'Graduation Day,' and surfing sounds."

WEDNESDAY, AUGUST 5, 1964: Starlight Bowl, Burbank, CA, with Eddie Hodges, Jimmy Griffin, and Lynne Easton and the Kingsmen (8:15 p.m. show)

THURSDAY, AUGUST 6, 1964: Convention Center, Las Vegas, NV, with Eddie Hodges, Jimmy Griffin, and Lynne Easton and the Kingsmen (7:30 p.m. show)

FRIDAY, AUGUST 7, 1964: Arizona State Fairgrounds, Phoenix, AZ, with Eddie Hodges, Jimmy Griffin, and Lynne Easton and the Kingsmen (8:30 p.m. show)

SATURDAY, AUGUST 8, 1964: Russ Auditorium, San Diego HS, San Diego, CA, with Eddie Hodges, Jimmy Griffin, and Lynne Easton and the Kingsmen (Two shows at 7:30 and 9:45 p.m.)
These were the final shows of the exhausting "Summer Safari" tour. The *San Diego Evening Tribune* writer, who was obviously of the previous generation, complained about the loud volumes, but conceded that "The quintet . . . is more melodic than most of its contemporaries. The boys performed many of their million-selling hits like 'Surfing USA,' 'Little Deuce Coupe,' 'Don't Worry Baby,' and a newer hit, 'Wendy.' A highlight of the evening was Mike Love, one of the members, doing the 'Monster Mash,' bathed in an eerie, green light. The predominantly youthful audience responded enthusiastically as expected. A few elders in the crowd, though, had more of a blank, glazed expression on their faces."

FRIDAY, AUGUST 21, 1964: Euclid Beach Amusement Park, Cleveland, OH (Two shows at 4:00 and 7:00 p.m.)
Less than two weeks after the conclusion of the "Summer Safari" tour, the group was back on the road. The group's first appearance in the Cleveland area at Euclid Beach was very memorable for them, though not because of the concert itself. In June 1974 Dennis told a reporter that the group still "talked a lot about Euclid Beach . . . We've always remembered that apple pie that the nice lady (Mrs. Doris Mackey) made for us." Clearly the apple pie was delicious, because Al Jardine also rhapsodized about it in 1983, telling a reporter, "I remember the Flying Turns. And that's where I had the best apple pie I've ever eaten." The concerts were broadcast live on KYW radio.

SATURDAY, AUGUST 22, 1964: Syria Mosque, Pittsburgh, PA (Two shows at 7:30 and 9:30 p.m.)

MONDAY, AUGUST 24, 1964: Agricultural Hall, Allentown Fairgrounds, Allentown, PA (10:00 p.m. show)
Advertisements erroneously listed this concert as "The Beach Boys' first East Coast appearance."

According to the ad, the Beach Boys were scheduled to play from 10 to 12 p.m. Most likely other acts were on the bill, though none are listed in the ads.

FRIDAY, AUGUST 28, AND SATURDAY, AUGUST 29, 1964: Spring Lake Amusement Park, Oklahoma City, OH (Three shows each day at 7:00, 8:30, and 10:00 p.m.)
The Beach Boys were clearly popular in the Oklahoma City area, since they returned for six more shows only a month and a half after their previous appearance here. The two 7:00 p.m. shows were broadcast live on WKY radio.

WEDNESDAY, SEPTEMBER 2, 1964: Kleinhan's Music Hall, Buffalo, NY
After a few days in California, the group set out on the first leg of their first extensive east coast tour. *Buffalo News* reviewer Nell Lawson wrote, "They invited and got roaring audience participation for 'Let's Go Trippin',' [and] scared the girls into near hysteria with 'The Monster Mash.' The coup de grace was a fast beat, 'Wanderin.'' What would Sigmund Freud have made of it all?"

THURSDAY, SEPTEMBER 3, 1964: MacArthur Stadium, Syracuse, NY, with Carmen and the Vikings and the Treblemen (8:00 p.m. show)

FRIDAY, SEPTEMBER 4, 1964: Rensselaer Polytechnic Institute Fieldhouse, Troy, NY
Andy Paley, who worked with Brian in the 1980s and '90s, recalled seeing the group at the RPI Fieldhouse in Troy as a youngster. The concert was mentioned in a December 1964 Schenectady newspaper as having taken place "in September." This is the likely date, but it is not 100 percent certain.

SATURDAY, SEPTEMBER 5, 1964: Bushnell Memorial, Hartford, CT (8:00 p.m. show)
The advertisement announced "America's Foremost Recording Stars in their First and Only Connecticut Appearance."

SUNDAY, SEPTEMBER 6, 1964: Boston Garden, Boston, MA
Dennis told Earl Leaf that at this Boston show, "we were drowned in a surging sea of 4,000 hysterical girls. About 1,000 waited at the stage door when we came out and wrecked the taxi to get at us." Following this appearance, the group returned to L.A. for recording sessions.

FRIDAY, SEPTEMBER 11, AND SATURDAY, SEPTEMBER 12, 1964: Lagoon, Farmington, UT
This was the group's third appearance in the Salt Lake City area in 1964.

SUNDAY, SEPTEMBER 13, 1964: Grand Central Store, Boise, ID, with Dick Cates and the Chessmen and Boise High School Auditorium, Boise, ID (Two shows at 6:30 and 9:00 p.m.)
John Arant, a member of the Idaho group Dick Cates and the Chessmen, recalled opening for the group at a personal appearance at the Grand Central Store in Boise, prior to the evening concerts.

THURSDAY, SEPTEMBER 17, 1964: Cameo Theater, Miami, FL
The group began the second leg of their East Coast tour with their first Florida appearance.

FRIDAY, SEPTEMBER 18, 1964: Alabama State Coliseum, Montgomery, AL, with Jan and Dean, Ronnie and the Daytonas, Bobby Wood, Don Gibson, Ace Cannon, Norma Jean, Jerry Wallace, Travis Wommack, Porter Waggoner, and the Chartbusters (8:00 p.m. show)
The set list for this show was "Fun, Fun, Fun," "Surfin' USA," "Little Deuce Coupe," "Surfer Girl," "Shut Down," "I Get Around," "Johnny B. Goode," "Monster Mash," "In My Room," "Be True To Your School," "Don't Worry Baby," and "Little Honda."

SATURDAY, SEPTEMBER 19, 1964: Municipal Auditorium, Birmingham, AL, with Jan and Dean, Ronnie and the Daytonas, Bobby Wood, Don Gibson, Ace Cannon, Norma Jean, Jerry Wallace, Travis Wommack, and the Chartbusters (Three shows at 2:00, 6:00, and 9:30 p.m.)

Ian Rusten Collection

Collection of Chris Woods

The Beach Boys perform "I Get Around" on *The Ed Sullivan Show*, September 27, 1964.
Jon Stebbins Collection

SUNDAY, SEPTEMBER 20, 1964: City Auditorium, Atlanta, GA (3:00 p.m. show)

MONDAY, SEPTEMBER 21, 1964: Civic Coliseum, Knoxville, TN (8:00 p.m. show)

Brian was interviewed backstage by a reporter from the *Nashville Tennessean* and told him that because of their frenzied fans, "After we finish a performance, we usually grab everything and run out the back door to a car . . . Sometimes we don't make it."

TUESDAY, SEPTEMBER 22, 1964: Municipal Auditorium, Nashville, TN (8:00 p.m. show)

Brian Wilson was hot to record a new song he'd written titled "Dance, Dance, Dance," so the Beach Boys held a recording session at the Columbia Studios in Nashville prior to this show. This alternate version of the song appeared on the 1990 CD release of *Today/Summer Days* as a bonus track. A photo from the session appeared in the October 17 edition of *Billboard* magazine.

WEDNESDAY, SEPTEMBER 23, 1964: Alexandria Roller Rink, Alexandria, VA (7:00 p.m. show)

Over 3,500 fans attended the Beach Boys' first Washington, DC, area performance. It was fairly common at concerts during this period for fans to throw presents onstage for groups. After finding out that the Beatles liked candy, fans threw tons of it onstage throughout their 1964 tour. The Beach Boys had similar experiences with their fans on this tour. Carl told a reporter that "in Alexandria, Virginia . . . you couldn't see the floor for the candy." To which Al added, "You're always trying to protect your eyes. You get the candy right in the face." Ronnie Oberman from the *Washington Star* interviewed the Beach Boys after this show. Brian told Oberman that the group was finished singing about surf and cars: "It's served its purpose to help create our image. It's now a thing of the past. As far as crazes are concerned, if you base overall existence too much on the craze, pretty soon the emphasis is on the craze rather than on the group. Since we moved out of the craze thing, more emphasis can be put on us as a group . . . We now want to go in the direction of the big beat and hard rock with lyrics that don't limit themselves to one specific thing."

Performing "Wendy" on *The Ed Sullivan Show*, September 27, 1964. Collection of Joe Russo

THURSDAY, SEPTEMBER 24, 1964: Loew's State Theater, Providence, RI (8:15 p.m. show)

The reporter from the *Providence Journal* seemed at a loss to understand what he saw. "I suspect these concerts should be reviewed by our resident psychiatrist. In their public form they aren't music: they're a social phenomenon, far less explicable than a Labor Day riot . . . but it can send the little girls. One, utterly hysterical, was carried out kicking and screaming by the gendarmes hired to guard the stage against forays by the uncontrollably enthusiastic and another had to be hauled off the stage bodily. The concert, incidentally, was a dead sell-out." Following this show, the group headed to New York, where they took part in rehearsals at CBS Television Studios for their September twenty-seventh appearance on *The Ed Sullivan Show*. The group also attended a luncheon in their honor, thrown by Capitol Records, at the Gaslight Club.

1964

SATURDAY, SEPTEMBER 26, 1964: West Orange National Guard Armory, West Orange, NJ, with the Ubans, the Fairlanes, the Creations, and Carol Summers (8:30 p.m. show)

In between Friday rehearsals and the Sunday night live appearance on *The Ed Sullivan Show*, the group squeezed in one more concert appearance, their last of the tour. According to AP reporter Mary Campbell, "the audience was nearly as frenzied as a Beatles audience. Dennis, shaking his long hair while drumming, was clearly the favorite."

FRIDAY, OCTOBER 16, 1964: Civic Auditorium, San Jose, CA (8:30 p.m. show)

A flyer for this show, presented by KLIV radio, stated that "Other Big Acts" would be on the bill as well, but did not name them.

SATURDAY, OCTOBER 17, 1964: Long Beach Arena, Long Beach, CA

SUNDAY, OCTOBER 18, 1964: Mountain Home Air Force Base, Mountain Home, ID (Two shows at 2:00 and 8:00 p.m.)

The Beach Boys flew to Boise and drove to the MHAFB near Mountain Home to play for the members of the Air Force. Photos taken that evening show that the group tuned in to *The Ed Sullivan Show* to catch the American TV debut of the Animals.

WEDNESDAY, OCTOBER 28, AND THURSDAY, OCTOBER 29, 1964: The *T.A.M.I. Show*, Santa Monica Civic Auditorium, Santa Monica, CA, with Jan and Dean, Chuck Berry, Gerry and the Pacemakers, Smokey Robinson and the Miracles, Marvin Gaye, Lesley Gore, Billy J. Kramer and the Dakotas, the Supremes, James Brown, and the Rolling Stones (Rehearsals on Wednesday and 6:00 to 10:00 p.m. show on Thursday)

Bill Sargent, who had achieved success offering closed-circuit screenings of major sports events to theaters, organized the Teenage Music International (T.A.M.I.) Show. The idea was to film a major rock concert and release it as a theatrical film. The show was filmed in Electronovision, a new camera process created by Joseph Bluth that offered higher resolution than regular television cameras.

Artists from all different genres of pop music, including rock, soul, R&B and British invasion were invited to appear. The Beach Boys' friends Jan and Dean hosted the show. Steve Binder, who later directed the *Elvis 68 Comeback* Special, was the film's director and Jack Nietzsche, who had worked with Phil Spector, was hired as the show's music arranger. Members of Spector's Wrecking Crew made up the house band.

The acts rehearsed for two days. On the first night they stayed at a local hotel, but huge crowds swarmed outside and most of the musicians chose to sleep at the Auditorium on the second night. The producers insisted that the performers play three shows (one concert each night in front of a live audience and one additional show with no audience) so that they would have multiple takes to choose from. Ultimately only the footage shot at the live concert on October 29 was used in the finished film. The Beach Boys performed four songs: "Surfin' USA," "Surfer Girl," "I Get Around," and "Dance, Dance, Dance." They also took part in the finale "Get Together," for which all the acts crowded onto the stage.

The finished film was screened in California starting in mid-November and released nationally on December 29, 1964. It proved to be highly successful and remained in theaters through the first half of 1965. After its initial run, the Beach Boys footage was cut from the film due to contractual issues. When Dick Clark Productions acquired rights to the film and released it on home video, the Beach Boys footage was missing. It was not re-inserted until the film's DVD release in 2010.

FRIDAY, OCTOBER 30, 1964: Memorial Auditorium, Worcester, MA (8:30 p.m. show)

The Beach Boys traveled to Boston on Friday afternoon to play one more show, before flying to Europe on Saturday night. The Boston-area concert ended up being one of the wildest and most memorable in their career. Fans rioted and police stopped the show after fourteen minutes. The Beach Boys went onstage around 9:45 p.m. Jack Tubert of the *Worcester Telegram* reported, "After only two bars of 'Fun, Fun, Fun,' two girls were out of their seats. Then six, eight, and finally a wave of girls

Always more comfortable at home, Brian was dreading the pressure of the relentless touring. As Fred Vail remarked, "Brian was an introvert in an extroverted industry. Brian never got a charge out of doing live events. I don't think Brian ever really appreciated the adulation and the roar of the crowd . . . Brian hated to fly and he wasn't an extroverted guy." He began suffering panic attacks before showtime. Ron Swallow recalled a number of occasions when he had to track down Brian to coax him onstage at curtain time. On one such occasion, Ron found him hiding in a bathroom stall, shaking and saying, "I can't do it." Ron would guide him onto the stage, where Carl was waiting to help him strap on his bass. Once onstage Brian was professional, but it was evident to those around him that he was not happy.

On December 23, 1964, the group boarded a flight from Los Angeles to Houston to start another tour. Problems developed soon after takeoff. An overworked and emotionally exhausted Brian finally snapped. He suffered his first nervous breakdown. When the band finally made it to Houston, tour manager Ron Swallow recalled Brian crying uncontrollably in his hotel room. The next day, Brian flew back to California. Carl told the BBC in 1974 that "he just really got upset and he just had to leave. I think that's what people call his first nervous breakdown. He was just holding it in and it just came out and he said 'No, I can't do it and I'm stopping.' And that was it. It was a thing where it hurt his ears because he can only hear

Performing at the *T.A.M.I. Show* in Santa Monica, California, on October 29, 1964. Jon Stebbins Collection

in his left ear. The high sound pressure level was just too much." While the amplifiers' effect on his ears certainly contributed to the decision, Marilyn Wilson believed that the main reason Brian left the road "at the beginning was because he couldn't write and tour at the same time. Touring is a hectic life. It's really hard for Brian, that's not his makeup. He had to

surged to the stage. The eleven policemen were powerless to stop them . . . the show was stopped at 9:54 p.m. Dick Smith, the master of ceremonies, urged the youngsters to return to their seats so the show could continue. At 10:11, the Beach Boys took off again and within seconds the area in front of the stage was more crowded than it had been before. At 10:16 the curtain came down for good."

During the show, hundreds of teenagers without tickets rioted outside. They broke windows and kicked in doors. The newspapers reported, "Most of the damage was done by a roving gang of 200 to 300 boys outside the hall, police said. Youngsters inside the hall broke the window in the ground floor men's room and handed ticket stubs out to friends . . . Police reported using clubs to keep the crowd from surging into the hall when throngs broke through the outside door." The Beach Boys retreated backstage, but insisted that the show should have gone on. Mike argued, "We were just getting started . . . We didn't give the kids their money worth." The promoter of the show was furious at the police for stopping the show and claimed that the Beach Boys would never play there again, but the group returned in February 1965.

EUROPEAN TOUR (NOVEMBER 1 TO NOVEMBER 24, 1964)

The Beach Boys boarded a flight to London on October 31 for a twenty-three-day promotional tour of Europe. Five people, including road manager Don Rice, friend/roadie Ron Swallow, and writer Earl Leaf accompanied them. Their plane was forced to land at Shannon Airport in western Ireland because London was shrouded in fog, and the group spent three hours in a transit lounge. While there, they met and talked with Brian Epstein, the Beatles manager, who was also on his way to London. The group finally arrived in London on November 1, where hundreds of British teens welcomed them. Ron Swallow recalled that the band was elated by their reception in London, where they were treated "like the Beatles. We did not expect it."

On November 2, the group held a press conference and photo op at EMI Records' main headquarters in London. Brian told a reporter from *Record Mirror* that he hoped to record a song in London "because everybody comes here to record. We think we may get a better sound in one of your studios." The group ultimately did no recording in London. A proposed meeting with the Beatles, who were touring throughout the UK during the Beach Boys' visit, also failed to happen. The two supergroups had arranged to convene at the Ad Lib Club one night, but a fire at the club prevented the meeting.

The Beach Boys spent eight days in the United Kingdom, making promotional appearances, TV and radio appearances, and giving interviews; however, they performed no concerts on UK soil. Carl told reporter Penny Valentine that he was disappointed but explained, "There is some musician exchange trouble because we are musicians as well as singers and this raises some difficulty. But we're hoping to come back next year. People often ask us if our sound is difficult to recreate on stage but really it isn't, because a sound is a sound."

On November 2, the group taped an appearance on the Radio Luxembourg program *Friday Spectacular* in front of a live audience. The group mimed to both sides of their latest single, "When I Grow Up (to Be a Man)"/"I Get Around" and were interviewed by host Muriel Young. On November 4, they taped an appearance on the ITV show *Discs a Go-Go* in Bristol. The following night, they taped an appearance on the BBC TV show *The Beat Room*. On November 6, they appeared on the ARTV show *Ready Steady Go*. On the night of November 6, they recorded an appearance for the BBC's *Top Gear* radio program at the Playhouse Theatre in London. They performed live versions of "I Get Around," "Hushabye," "Surfin' USA," "Graduation Day," "Wendy," "Little Old Lady (from Pasadena)," and "When I Grow Up (to Be a Man)." The program aired on November 19. The group also taped TV appearances on *Open House* (November 7) and *Thank Your Lucky Stars* (November 8) before heading to Paris.

On November 9, the group flew to Paris, where they taped television appearances on November 10 and posed for the camera of Earl Leaf at various Parisian landmarks. Leaf, who considered himself a man of the world, took the group to museums, restaurants, and clubs, including the famous Follies Bergere. After leaving Paris, the group headed to Italy, where they spent a few days in Rome. Although they made no concert appearances, they taped an appearance on RAI TV on November 11 and posed for numerous photographs at the Coliseum and other locations the next day. According to Leaf, "they took off on a mad shopping spree until nearly three. Bribing our drivers (there were ten in our party), we shattered speed laws and traffic rules, tore through shortcut passageways, careened around corners, and lunged about to the Coliseum, Roman Forum, Vatican City, and other historic points of interest, staying only long enough to grab a few shots before charging on. 'How to see 2,000 years of Roman history in thirty-seven minutes' cried Mike Love, cracking us up. We screeched to the airport a few minutes before four—only to be told the plane would depart two hours late. Once again we had hurried-hurried to stand around and wait-wait."

The group then traveled to Munich, Germany, where they taped an appearance on Second Program Television on November 13. Possibly the wildest event of the tour occurred in Munich when Mike was briefly arrested. According to Leaf's 1965 account, "One 4 a.m., Mike and Don Rice, the BB's road manager, were closing up a club in Munich, Germany . . . In the parking lot they witnessed a mean scene: a husky nasty dragging a frail fraulein into a Mercedes 300SL. So now Mike makes like Sir Galahad to the rescue of the damsel fair, charging the hulking brute . . . With that the fighting female turns on her rescuer, scratching, clawing, and screaming to lay off her husband. Foiled and frustrated in his big Galahad scene, Mike was so mad he slammed his fist through the car's windshield . . . When Mike turned around to apologize he found himself looking into the barrel of a Luger pistol held by the husband who was now telling his wife to call the police. Three hours in the clink, a bruised hand, and a $250 fine taught Mike a lesson." The band also visited Frankfurt and Berlin, while in Germany. While at the Berlin Wall, an impetuous Dennis attempted to climb over it and had to be pulled back by the group before he was shot by East German soldiers. Dennis later said, "I just wanted to talk to that little Russian girl."

Late 1964 tour program. Jon Stebbins Collection

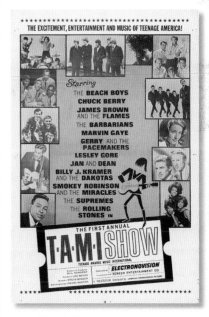

Jon Stebbins Collection

be home and he had to write and get all the vibrations from everywhere in order to, you know, do his thing . . . and we'd just got married which also helped, you know." Brian made the decision to permanently stop appearing with the group onstage. He filled in a bit in early 1965 and occasionally

THE BEACH BOYS IN CONCERT

The Beach Boys performing in Rochester, New York, on November 25, 1964.
Dick Hollaert/Joe Russo (www.therascalsarchives.com)

Brian and Mike onstage in Rochester, New York, on November 25, 1964.
Dick Hollaert/Joe Russo (www.therascalsarchives.com)

WEDNESDAY, NOVEMBER 18, 1964: Olympia, Paris, France, with Dick Rivers
The group returned to Paris, where they played their first European concert. Parisian audiences were legendary for being difficult to please and even the Beatles had trouble eliciting enthusiasm when they performed at the Olympia earlier in the year, so the Beach Boys were nervous. According to Earl Leaf, when the show began, "The curtains parted and they saw five front rows of stony faced over-agers with folded arms and cold eyes—the press critics and reviewers . . . The Boys began to play and sing their hearts out. . . . the BBs spurted sixteen great power-packed swing songs at the huge Olympia Hall audience . . . excitement mounting with each song. Soon the customers were dancing in the aisles and standing in their seats writhing and wriggling to the beat. By the end of the show, the throng was out of their gourds. Even the uncool press corps was standing, shouting, and pounding their palms to a din."

SATURDAY, NOVEMBER 21, 1964: Koncerthuset, Stockholm, Sweden, with Jackie DeShannon, Jan Rohde and the Wild Ones, and the Mascots (8:00 p.m. show)
The Beach Boys headed to Sweden for more promotion and more hysteria. The group was surprised to learn how popular they were there. According to Leaf, "The zero temperatures did not stop hundreds of fur-bundled girls from waiting day and night outside the Foresta Hotel to see their idols. Some of the sneaky ones got upstairs and into the Beach Boys' rooms. On arrival, the boys had to change clothes quickly and go down to the lobby for a press interview. Carl Wilson changed—then flung open the curtains of his room to find four cute little Swedes on his balcony peeking in."

While in Stockholm, the Beach Boys were interviewed on the radio by Klaus Burling. During the interview, Burling asked Carl if he knew anything about Sweden and Carl replied, "I know that, like, uh, my grandparents are from Sweden and I don't really know that much about the family background except that my grandparents were full-blood Swedish people, and that . . . You know, on the way from the airport we were noticing that it looks a lot like the States." Burling also asked Brian about songwriting and Brian stated "I do quite a bit of composing as I spend most of my time creating songs and trying to think of new ideas for the group and planning our records, and . . . I don't really have much time for leisure at home like the other guys, like surfing and things, but . . . But I have a lot of fun, I love what I do."

On November 21, the group performed their second and last live concert of the tour at the Koncerthuset. The show was simulcast on radio as well. Earl Leaf reported, "During the performance, gaggles of girls ran up on the stage to grab their favorite, wrenching Carl Wilson's neck, tearing Brian Wilson's shirt, biting Alan Jardine's cheek and grabbing Mike's legs, almost toppling him to the floor. When one Swede-heart hurled herself at Dennis Wilson and sent his drum sticks flying, he has to finish the show beating the skins with his bare hands."

The next day, the Beach Boys headed to Copenhagen, Denmark for a "quickie holiday." One famous incident from this short visit occurred when Brian and Earl Leaf were wandering around the Nieu Haven district and heard someone playing the piano nearby. According to Leaf's account a few months later, Brian "dashed into this dancehall-opium den-chop suey joint . . . Edged the piano player off the stool and started whomping the keys in a creative frenzy. The piano player yanked the stool away. Brian continued to bang the piano sitting on the floor . . . a bruiser-bouncer with Samson muscles and Frankenstein eyebrows broke his trance by slamming down the keyboard cover. Brian darted out into the roaring slum street, whistled up a Danish cab and raced back to the Royal Hotel. He spent the night composing at the piano in a shut down hotel café. The song, 'Kiss Me Baby' will be heard on the next BB LP."

WEDNESDAY, NOVEMBER 25, 1964: Auditorium Theater, Rochester, NY (Two shows at 7:30 and 9:30 p.m.)
Rather than returning home for some rest, the Beach Boys flew from Denmark to New York for more concert dates. The two Rochester shows were rather nostalgic for Al Jardine, who had briefly lived in the city in 1950 and 1951 while his father was teaching at the Rochester Institute of Technology.

In between shows, the group was interviewed by local DJs. Asked about the European tour, Dennis commented, "I'm glad to be back. I can't make it in other countries. I dig America. I don't dig their food, their weather. I don't dig girls that don't shave their underarms. I don't dig the milk—it's rancid. I don't dig wine. So I'm lost. They have Coke, which is warm. They don't serve beer cold, unless you're in a good place. They pull it off a shelf! I don't dig their television shows. They take too long, like six hours for a thirty-minute TV show. I don't like Germany. But I love Europe!"

THURSDAY, NOVEMBER 26, 1964: New Haven Arena, New Haven, CT

FRIDAY, NOVEMBER 27, 1964: Cleveland Arena, Cleveland, OH, with the Shangri-Las, Jay and the Americans, Ivan and the Sabers, the Grasshoppers, Joey and the Continentals, Rocky and the Visions, the Tulu Babies, the Uniques, and the Sensations (2:00 p.m. show)
The Beach Boys returned to Cleveland for the second time that year. Ivan Browne of opening act Ivan and the Sabers recalled, "The tour occupied a floor in a hotel in Cleveland. It was very exciting. I played Carl Wilson's 12-string Rickenbacker in one of the rooms." Ivan and the Sabers were one of the many acts preceding the Beach Boys on the impressive bill. Another act, the Grasshoppers, included a young Ben Orr, later to achieve fame in the Cars.

Despite the star-studded bill, only 2,568 tickets sold. Fans blamed high ticket prices for the small crowd (tickets ranged from $2.50 to $4.50). The promoters were forced to charge more for tickets because of the 71 policemen hired for security. The *Plains Dealer* reported, "Nine patrolmen made a living barrier across the front of the floor to keep overeager photographers back during the Beach Boys' act."

SATURDAY, NOVEMBER 28, 1964: Olympia Stadium, Detroit, MI, with the Shangri-Las, Jay and the Americans, and Gino Washington
The Beach Boys first visit to Detroit was not altogether pleasant. As Brian related to Earl Leaf a few months later, "We finally got to Detroit and were at the airport and about 16 people in different cars came to help us take our luggage to the hotel and we get to the hotel and it was time to take our luggage out of the cars and put it in, and about six of the suitcases were gone . . . The ones with all the gifts we brought back from Europe. I lost about 1,500 dollars . . . There was nobody to hit. Somebody had a good Christmas."

SUNDAY, NOVEMBER 29, 1964: Cincinnati Gardens, Cincinnati, OH, with Jan and Dean, Jay and the Americans, the Shangri-Las, and Ron Britain (2:00 p.m. show)
This was the first of many appearances by the Beach Boys in Cincinnati. The group flew home afterwards. Brian was married to Marilyn Rovell on December 7 in Los Angeles.

SATURDAY, DECEMBER 19, 1964: Assembly Center Arena, Tulsa, OK (8:30 p.m. show)
The group flew to Oklahoma for a one-night stand in the midst of promotional activities for their new single "Dance, Dance, Dance." This show is noteworthy as it was the last before Brian's famous airplane breakdown.

WEDNESDAY, DECEMBER 23, 1964: Music Hall, Houston, TX, with the Dynamics
With their new single "Dance, Dance, Dance" on the charts, the Beach Boys launched another ten-day tour. Their grand plans suddenly became meaningless when Brian suffered an apparent nervous breakdown on the flight to Texas. The group was understandably concerned, and there was a state of high anxiety in their hotel room. Brian related a few months later to writer Earl Leaf, "That night I cooled off and I played that show. Next morning I woke up with the biggest knot in my stomach and I felt like I was going out of my mind. In other words it was a breakdown period." Rather than continue the tour, Brian flew home on Christmas Eve, accompanied by Ron Swallow. The Beach Boys had no concerts scheduled for Christmas Eve, but a planned show on Christmas Day in Mississippi was canceled.

SATURDAY, DECEMBER 26, 1964: Memorial Auditorium, Dallas, TX
This show marked the first concert appearance of Glen Campbell in place of Brian. Glen recalled

Ian Rusten Collection

played an important concert or two after that, but he would not return to full-time touring until 1976.

Brian's sudden departure placed the group in a panic. Although they had no shows scheduled for Christmas Eve, they had no choice but to cancel a planned Christmas Day show in Jackson, Mississippi. In need of a bassist who could sing Brian's parts, the group placed a call to Glen Campbell (born in 1936 in Arkansas), a talented guitarist/performer who was then making a living as a session musician and

Dennis leaving his drums to sing in 1964. Jon Stebbins Collection

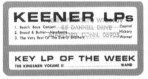

THE BEACH BOYS
First Detroit Show!

Radio survey picturing the group's first concert in Detroit, Michigan, on November 28, 1964. Ian Rusten Collection

to reporter Hy Gardner in 1975, "I first played with the group in Dallas and made two million mistakes. But there was so much screaming and hollering by 17,000 kids, nobody noticed it. After the concert the Beach Boys made a dash for their cars. Not being a Beach Boy, really, I didn't care about rushing. But the fans jumped on me anyway, started yanking my hair, stealing my watch, tearing off my shirt. From then on I was the first one in the car."

SUNDAY, DECEMBER 27, 1964: City Auditorium, Omaha, NE, with the Megatones and the Royal Flairs (4:00 p.m. show)

Fans that attended the Beach Boys Omaha concert were informed that Brian was suffering from "a sore throat." Steve Jordon and his band the Megatones were one of the local bands that opened for the Beach Boys at this concert. He later recalled in the *Omaha World Herald*, "There were no special arrangements for the stars in those days. No bottles of imported beer or luxuries. The locker room was just a locker room with benches to sit on and wait. So the Beach Boys . . . were sitting on the benches and waiting with the rest of us. Carl Wilson was the personable member of the group that night, strumming a guitar while he chatted with inquisitive musicians from the local bands." Jordon noted that when the Beach Boys went onstage, "From behind the music was very simple. Drummer Dennis Wilson didn't seem any great shakes and it was hard to hear the singing. But it was easy to hear the audience. They went wild. The atmosphere was like a party." Unfortunately, the party was spoiled when two of Carl's guitars were stolen from the Beach Boys' rented car.

MONDAY, DECEMBER 28, 1964, KRNT Theater, Des Moines, IA (8:30 p.m. show)

This was the first of two 1960s appearances by the Beach Boys at this 4,200-seat Iowa venue that was at one time one of the largest in the Midwest. It was demolished in 1982.

TUESDAY, DECEMBER 29, 1964, Indiana State Fairgrounds Coliseum, Indianapolis, IN, with the Fantastic Four Wheels and Sir Richard and the Mark IV's

WEDNESDAY, DECEMBER 30, 1964, Kentucky State Fairgrounds Coliseum, Louisville, KY, with Lonnie Mack, the Newbeats, and the Monarchs (8:00 p.m. show)

Jay and the Americans were initially advertised as appearing with the Beach Boys, but Jay Black was involved in an automobile accident, so the group canceled. The Beach Boys were promised $3,500 for the night plus a percentage of the gate.

THURSDAY, DECEMBER 31, 1964, Coliseum, Charlotte, NC

OTHER 1964 CONCERTS

It is likely that the group played a few more California shows early in the year. Many newspapers continued to adopt a rather snobbish attitude towards "pop" concerts and not all shows received a mention, making them difficult to trace. On top of that, some shows sold out based solely on radio advertisements.

CONCERTS NOT PLAYED

The Beach Boys were scheduled to appear at the Seattle Teenage Fair from September 3 to 5 with the Kingsmen. The group ultimately canceled, and Paul Revere and the Raiders took their place.

The group was scheduled to appear in Jackson, Mississippi on December 25, but canceled due to Brian's breakdown.

Although listed by author Keith Badman in his book, the Beach Boys did not play a Christmas Eve show in Houston. They were only booked for December 23.

as a member of the *Shindig* television show band. In a BBC Radio interview, Al recalled, "hearing it come up: 'Hey what about Glen?' And I said, 'Hey yeah he can sing. I think he can sing high as well, and I know he can play the guitar because he did a lot of our sessions. He looked nice, he was a nice-looking guy, and just seemed to fit in for that period of time." Glen agreed to join the group on the road and flew to Texas to continue the tour. He continued to perform with the group until mid-May 1965.

THE BEACH BOYS saw continued commercial success in 1965, while they also demonstrated an ability to grow artistically. They recorded three albums and a number of singles that highlighted Brian Wilson's progression as a composer and producer. By the end of the year he had essentially eclipsed Phil Spector as the king of the L.A. music scene.

The year began with major drama. The Beach Boys initially hoped Brian's breakdown was a temporary setback and that he'd continue as before once he was rested. But in early January, Brian informed the group that he was done with touring and would now solely concentrate on writing and recording music. After their initial shock and dismay, the Beach Boys reluctantly accepted Brian's wishes. Glen Campbell, who had filled in for Brian at the end of 1964, was only a temporary solution. From the start he saw being a Beach Boy as a part-time gig. Ron Swallow, who roomed with him on tours, recalled, "Glen was always interested in a solo career and never seriously considered becoming a permanent Beach Boy." Campbell himself told the BBC in 1974, "I was probably too much of an individual. I was with the Champs for a while. I enjoyed it for a time but I didn't really like being responsible for something that a group did, and that's the way I felt when I was with the Beach Boys. If the Beach Boys did something, then I did it, and I didn't like that at all. I wanted to do what I wanted to do and that was the goal that I shot for."

Campbell had numerous other commitments, including his regular gig as a member of the *Shindig* house band and studio session work. In early 1965, Brian found himself back on the road with the Beach Boys multiple

CONCERTS PLAYED IN
1965

BEACH BOY'S BIG BLAST BREAKS ALL RECORDS!
Makin' it for the first time in Virginia, THE BEACH BOYS had Virginia Beach SWINGIN' for good ole WGH RADIO. By the time these five WEST COAST-ERS hit the area ALL TICKETS FOR BOTH SHOWS WERE GONE, GONE, GONE! 'Tis possible that maybe WGH can swing a return engagement during the next couple of months. YOU LIKE? Drop us a card and let us know . . . . .

WGH radio flyer picturing the group in Virginia Beach on January 2, 1965, with Glen Campbell on bass. Ian Rusten Collection

times when Glen was too busy to make a gig. Brian made it clear that the situation would have to be remedied and as a result, the group began searching for a permanent replacement.

That April the Beach Boys turned to twenty-year-old Bruce Arthur Johnston (born June 27, 1944, in Chicago). Bruce had been involved in the California music scene since high school and had worked with Phil Spector, among others. Bruce recalled in *Record Mirror,* "I was producing records at Columbia and Mike called me and said he'd like me to stand in for two weekend concerts because Brian was sick." Bruce flew to New Orleans on April 9, 1965, to play the opening show of the tour. Since he did not know how to play bass yet, Al temporarily took over the instrument, while Bruce played electric piano and sang Brian's parts. Glen Campbell returned to the lineup two days later, but made it clear that his days as a Beach Boy were numbered.

FRIDAY, JANUARY 1, 1965: Greensboro Coliseum, Greensboro, NC (8:00 p.m. show)

SATURDAY, JANUARY 2, 1965: Alan B. Shepard Civic Center ("The Dome"), Virginia Beach, VA (Two shows)
Over 4,000 Virginia teens attended these two shows. The Beach Boys were so well received that promoters immediately made plans to bring the group back for a return appearance in May. According to John Moreau of the *Virginia Beach Pilot,* "Brian, who writes ninety percent of the Beach Boys' music, wasn't there. Glen Campbell, 23, filled in for him." The reporter and a slew of fans greeted the group at Norfolk Airport that afternoon. Asked why he wore his hair long, Dennis pointed at the fans, "They like it, it's exciting on stage." Discussing the British invasion, the group expressed admiration for the Beatles, but Mike stated, "The others . . . sound awful and they're lousy musicians. They don't have any talent . . . they just don't cut the mustard."

SUNDAY, JANUARY 3, 1965: Mosque, Richmond, VA (8:00 p.m. show)

WEDNESDAY, JANUARY 27, 1965: Memorial Coliseum, Portland, OR, with Don and the Goodtimes and the Sonics
This concert, sponsored by KISN radio and promoted by Irving Granz, generated $17,000 in revenues and the Beach Boys received sixty percent of the profits. Glen Campbell was unable to play this show (he rejoined the tour in Vancouver) and Brian Wilson, making his first appearance since his Houston breakdown, took his place. One unusual aspect of this show saw the Beach Boys perform the concert dressed in yellow KISN cotton sweatshirts. Longtime fan David Higginbotham was in attendance and recalled, "They had even more hits than the last time I saw them (in May 1964) so the show was even bigger . . . It was more colorful too, because they were on a stage that had brighter lighting and they had on those yellow sweatshirts which made them much more colorful . . . They had brand new Showman amps and JBL speakers. . . . Carl had the 12-string guitar, which was kind of impressive. We didn't know quite what to make of that, because we'd never seen one before . . . The show was more intense and fever-pitched (than previous Portland shows), with lots of girls screaming . . . It was kind of like the *T.A.M.I. Show* scene."

One bizarre incident at this show occurred when it was time for Dennis to sing "The Wanderer." Brian usually played drums on this song, while Al played bass. Higginbotham recalled, "When Brian removed the bass strap to go and play drums, he decided to hand the bass to Mike, so he could hand it to Al. Mike was holding a microphone and Brian was holding the bass with his hands on the strings. There was a ground problem between the PA and the amplifiers and when Mike grabbed the bass, they got shocked. Brian and Mike both jumped out of their pants practically, and they dropped the bass. When it fell to the stage floor it just made this horrible super loud crashing sound. They did their best to just kind of laugh it off." In his June 1965 column, *Beach Boys Scene,* writer Earl Leaf exaggerated the story to include Mike falling to the ground and nearly being killed!

FRIDAY, JANUARY 29, 1965: Exhibition Forum, Vancouver, BC, Canada
This show marked the group's first ever appearance in Canada. They quickly discovered that Canadian fans were just as wild as Americans. The *Vancouver Sun* reported, "Hysterical fans attempted to climb on stage at the Forum where a Hollywood group called the Beach Boys was performing. Five police officers holding barricades against the pressing crowd lost their uniform hats to youths who snatched them off their heads."

SATURDAY, JANUARY 30, 1965: Seattle Coliseum, Seattle, WA, with the Sonics, the Dynamics, the Viceroys, Sir Raleigh and the Coupons, Terry Black, Jimmy Hanna, the Astronauts, and Jan and Dean (8:00 p.m. show)

The Beach Boys flew from Vancouver to Seattle-Tacoma International Airport and were greeted by 800 frenzied fans that after them as they left for their hotel. One female fan crashed her father's car into the back of their rented limousine in an effort to catch up with them. A nonchalant Mike told a reporter, "It's a great life. [We] have our cake and eat it too. Most people over twenty-five never heard of us and when we go out in the evening with adults nobody bothers us at all."

SATURDAY, FEBRUARY 6, 1965: Wichita Forum, Wichita, KS, with the Profits, Dick and Dee-Dee, and the Singing Conners (8:30 p.m. show)

The Beach Boys perform in Portland on January 27, 1965, with Brian front and center. Collection of David Lee Higginbotham

FRIDAY, FEBRUARY 12, 1965: Convention Hall, Philadelphia, PA (8:30 p.m. show)
The Beach Boys embarked on a ten-day east coast tour. Glen Campbell had other commitments, so Brian took his place for a week. Ron Swallow, who accompanied the group, recalled, "Brian agreed to tour again because the East Coast dates, especially Philadelphia and New York, were important for the group, as those markets attracted a lot of press." Geoffrey James of the *Evening Bulletin* was one of the reporters at the concert, which attracted 12,000 fans. James noted that the group "opened and closed their mouths, swung their guitars from the hip, and even smiled occasionally. But their singing was as audible as a man gargling in a hurricane. It didn't seem to matter. The teens jumped on their chairs, beat their hands against their heads, flailed their arms in the ritual motions of the Jerk, the Slop, and the Crossfire . . . Others threw notes to Dennis Wilson, the group's lank haired drummer. He in return tossed drumsticks into the crowd, causing chaos wherever they landed."

Collection of David Lee Higginbotham

SATURDAY, FEBRUARY 13, 1965: Academy of Music, New York, NY (Two shows at 2:00 and 4:00 p.m.)
The Beach Boys made their second New York City appearance at this now demolished venue on Fourteenth Street and Third Avenue. Don Paulsen photographed the group for *Hit Parader* magazine. He reported on backstage happenings and a press conference, at which most of the questions were directed to Brian.

When asked what his criterion for success was, Brian stated, "Record sales and screams." Responding to a question about his music, he said, "When I write a song, I believe in it . . . I'm usually happy with the songs I write." Brian also stated, "Each successive record should have more polish. We don't want to get too complex, but we'd like to improve harmonically. The lyrics are part of American teen culture." When asked if he considered his records artistic or commercial, Brian answered "Five years ago, there may have been a gap between the two, but not today. Take Dionne Warwick. Her records are obviously commercial because they sell, but they're also very lovely. Phil Spector is great. It's much easier to be expressive in a record nowadays." Speaking about New York City, Brian said, "I don't think I could live here" and quoted from a then popular song: "New York's a lonely place when you're the only surfer boy around."

The *Hit Parader* article mentioned that a German TV company was present, filming backstage sequences for a documentary. The television crew was making a film about American teenagers, specifically focusing on the Rock 'n' Rods Auto Club of Yonkers, New York. Members of the club attended the concert and met the Beach Boys backstage, all of which was filmed. This footage has not surfaced.

Eighteen year-old Carl Wilson onstage in Portland on January 27, 1965. Collection of David Lee Higginbotham

SUNDAY, FEBRUARY 14, 1965: Mosque Theatre, Newark, NJ, with the Magnificent Seven (3:00 p.m. show)

Promoter Pat O'Day (far left) poses with the group, including Glen Campbell (far right), in Seattle on January 30, 1965. Ian Rusten Collection

Brian helped Glen get his solo career started by producing a single for him called "Guess I'm Dumb." As far as can be determined, Glen Campbell's last concert with the Beach Boys was May 15, 1965, in New Haven. By May 19 Bruce Johnston had become a full-time member of the group, playing bass and keyboards with them until April 1972.

WEDNESDAY, FEBRUARY 17, 1965: Rhodes Ballroom, Cranston, RI, with Joey Major and the Minors and Dipsey (8:00 p.m. show)

Over 3,000 teens attended this concert. The group came onstage just after 9 p.m., but for unexplained reasons played for twenty-five minutes instead of the scheduled 50. According to the *Providence Journal*, "Cranston Police were displeased with the Beach Boys, particularly one who several times jumped off the stage and was smothered by young girls in the front row. After their last number, the Beach Boys dropped their instruments, ran out a backstage door, and out the front door of the building into a waiting cab. They were pursued by several hundred youngsters, but drove away with only 30 hanging on to the cab as it left." The show was marred by an odd incident. As the Beach Boys were exiting the venue, a young man grabbed Dennis, tearing his shirt. According to Earl Leaf, "He nabbed the boy and started a hay-maker swing. 'Don't you hit him,' yelled a cop in the nick of time. Denny turned the offender loose."

THURSDAY, FEBRUARY 18, 1965: Memorial Auditorium, Worcester, MA

Three and a half months after their first appearance at Worcester ended in a riot, the Beach Boys returned to play for their fans. Security, which included thirty police officers, was so tight at the venue that the group had trouble getting in. Fortunately, there were several fans outside who eventually convinced the guards that the boys trying to gain entry were the Beach Boys. Gerard Goggins of the *Worcester Evening Gazette* described the scene backstage: "One of the Beach Boys, Brian Wilson, sat down at an upright piano and played part of his repertoire while another, Mike Love, wrote down the songs they were to play on a few pieces of borrowed paper. The program didn't help much because most of them didn't know the order of songs anyway, even though Carl Wilson had duplicated a high school crib sheet by writing the songs down on the palm of his hand."

The concert itself was a success, unlike the group's last visit to Worcester. The *Worcester Telegram* reported, "There were screams, screams, and more screams, supplied mostly by adoring and excited young females, but there was no repetition of last October's near-riot . . . The closest thing to an incident came after the show was over, as the five singers, clad in short-sleeved shirts and tight chino pants, sprinted through a side exit to escape the crowd. A swarm of frantic teenagers tried to follow their idols, but a police line, bulwarked by two long aisle-blocking tables, held firm and the crisis passed."

FRIDAY, FEBRUARY 19, 1965: Maurice Richard Arena, Montreal, QB, Canada, with M.G. and the Escorts and J.B. and the Playboys

Glen Campbell returned to replace Brian for this show. Over 5,000 teenagers attended this concert, the Beach Boys' second appearance in Canada. The concert was a wild one and was briefly stopped by the Montreal police when a riot broke out. Glen Campbell recalled, "We came out and sang the opening notes of 'Round, round, get around, I get around' and man you couldn't even see the cops under the mob that was charging the stage. We lit out for the dressing rooms until reinforcements came." According to the *Montreal Gazette*, one female fan broke through the tight security and grabbed Dennis, who barely escaped to the dressing room with his hair intact. The maniacal crowds that the group continually encountered bothered Carl. He told Earl Leaf that "after awhile it gets to you. We don't mind the screaming, jumping, throwing harmless objects, and pushing for autographs. That's part of our job. But we don't like hoodlums pulling our hair, tearing our clothes, pitching bottles and rocks, or stealing our instruments."

SATURDAY, FEBRUARY 20, 1965: YM/YWCA Auditorium, Ottawa, ON, Canada, with the Big Town Boys, the Girl Friends, and the Staccatos (8:30 p.m. show)

According to the *Ottawa Citizen*, 5,000 fans all but drowned out the group and near-riots broke out as fans tried to storm the stage. Three girls had to be carried out in stretchers and police had to remove a girl who was hiding in the shower of the group's dressing room. Earl Leaf noted that towards the end of the concert, "so many chicks charged on stage that the city police and security guards stood shoulder to shoulder on the stage itself in front of the Beach Boys. It was a laugh to see the guys playing and singing their hearts out to the backs of the fuzz."

SUNDAY, FEBRUARY 21, 1965: Maple Leaf Gardens, Toronto, ON, Canada, with the Esquires, the Big Town Boys, and the Girl Friends (7:00 p.m. show)
Over 8,000 teenagers turned out for the group's first show in Toronto. Gerald Utting of the *Toronto Star* described the performance as "a cacophonous blend of staccato chords; massed wailing; thundering, meaningless shouts; uniforms of yellow shirts and tight, tight pants; semi-erotic gyrations; blinding and ceaseless barrages of flashbulbs; thousands of straining youngsters raising arms high in triumph."

MONDAY, FEBRUARY 22, 1965: Kleinhan's Music Hall, Buffalo, NY, with the Frontiersmen
The group wrapped up their tour with their second appearance in Buffalo. Dressed in lemon yellow shirts and white pants, they performed to more than 3,000 fans. Susan Dormady of the *Dunkirk Observer* reported, "Buffalo was the last stop on their six-day one-nighter tour of the States. . . . The group lived up to its high standards and gave a marvelous performance filled with liveliness, humor, vigor, and enthusiasm." The *Courier Express* reported, "Policemen were able to keep the 3,000 young people under control until the end of the program. At that point, teenagers, reluctant to allow their idols to leave, clambered on stage and attempted to storm the backstage area." As a result of this riot, the city banned concerts at the venue for a number of years.

The Beach Boys with Glen Campbell (second from left) perform in Buffalo, New York, on February 22, 1965. Dick Hollaert/Joe Russo (www. therascalsarchives.com)

FRIDAY, FEBRUARY 26, 1965: Civic Auditorium, San Jose, CA, with Paul Revere and the Raiders, the Preps, the Tikis, and the Beau Brummels (8:30 p.m. show)

SATURDAY, FEBRUARY 27, 1965: Memorial Auditorium, Sacramento, CA, with Paul Revere and the Raiders and the Marauders (Two shows at 7:00 and 9:30 p.m.)
The show was advertised as the group's "Sixth Smash Sacramento Appearance."

FRIDAY, MARCH 26, AND SATURDAY, MARCH 27, 1965: Arie Crown Theatre, Chicago, IL
Brian rejoined the group for these shows, both of which were recorded for a possible live album. On March 26 the full set list was: "Do You Wanna Dance," "Little Honda," "Surfin' USA," "Don't Worry Baby," "Papa-Oom-Mow-Mow," "Monster Mash," "Louie Louie," "Hawaii," "Surfer Girl," "Runaway," "Shut Down," "Wendy," "Please Let Me Wonder," "Fun, Fun, Fun," "I Get Around," and "Johnny B Goode." On March 27 it was: "Do You Wanna Dance," "Hawaii," "Please Let Me Wonder," "Surfer Girl," "Runaway," "Louie Louie," "Fun, Fun, Fun," "409," "Shut Down," "Monster Mash," "Surfin' USA," "Little Honda," "Wendy," "In My Room," "Don't Worry Baby," "I Get Around," "Johnny B. Goode," and "Papa-Oom-Mow-Mow." The album was ultimately scrapped, but the tapes are still in the Beach Boys' vault. A live version of "Shut Down" from the March 26 show was officially released on the 2001 *Hawthorne, CA* CD.

SUNDAY, MARCH 28, 1965: Cincinnati Gardens, Cincinnati, OH, with Billy Joe Royal, Avo and Ray, the Driving Winds, Kenny Price, Geri Diamond, the Casinos, the Teardrops, the Cincy Singers, and the Contenders (7:30 p.m. show)
With Brian in the lineup, the group played one more Midwest show, attended by 7,507 fans. Dale Stevens of the *Cincinnati Post* and *Times Star* noted that the crowd was almost as wild as the audience at a recent Beatles concert. Stevens commented that the Beach Boys "played to the crowd to keep things at a fever pitch, in a manner calculated to make the girls leap at the five guys.

Dennis pounds the drums in Buffalo, New York, February 22, 1965. Dick Hollaert/Joe Russo (www.therascalsarchives.com)

This allowed an incredibly fertile period for Brian Wilson to begin. The decision to stop touring gave Brian the time to reach his creative potential. As he told writer

"The Beach Boys concert literally left the huge audience breathless. The boys chewed them up, swallowed them, and spit them out and they came up yelling for more. Getting most of the loud screams was Dennis, who received an ovation with every shake of his long, blonde hair."

Jamake Hightower in 1968, "A revitalization of total life energy is what happened to me. I was able to express myself in such complete terms. I could take all the time I wanted. I had no chains. I

The poor drummer was assaulted with love three times. The first time he went over backwards. The next two he didn't miss a beat. Just like vaudeville. Stage style of the Beach Boys is wacky. One wears a Rex Harrison hat at all times and roams all over the stage. They have adopted the general devil-may-care approach of the Beatles and to give them their dues, they sing quite well."

Following this concert, the Beach Boys returned to L.A. for recording sessions and an appearance on the TV show *Shindig*. The group (including Brian) performed live versions of "Do You Wanna Dance," "Fun, Fun, Fun," "Long Tall Texan," "Please, Let Me Wonder," and "Help Me Rhonda" before a studio audience. They also sang "Their Hearts Were Full of Spring" without instruments. The show aired on April 21, 1965.

MONDAY, APRIL 5, 1965: Melodyland, Anaheim, CA, with the Munsters and the Pat and Lolly Vegas Trio (Two shows at 5:00 and 9:00 p.m.)
Future Beach Boys percussionist Mike Kowalski was then a member of the Pat and Lolly Vegas Trio, who opened for the group on this day.

FRIDAY, APRIL 9, 1965: Municipal Auditorium, New Orleans, LA, with the Aubry Twins, the Fabulieres, and Bobby Goldsboro (8:30 p.m. show)
This concert marked Bruce Johnston's debut with the Beach Boys. An eight-person entourage, including Al's wife Lynda, Ron Swallow, the Wilson's cousin Steve Korthof, and new road manager Richard Duryea (son of actor Dan Duryea) accompanied the group. Duryea had entered the picture in early 1965 as a partner for then-manager Don Rice, but according to Ron Swallow, "Duryea didn't get along with Don Rice and he quickly forced him out of the picture." He would remain with the group until June 1969. Carl Giammarese of the Buckinghams, who toured with the Beach Boys, recalled that Duryea was very protective of the group, saying, "Duryea was pretty hard-ass. He was looking out for the Beach Boys and was pretty hard on everybody else. Duryea was good at keeping a wall up between you and the Beach Boys."

SATURDAY, APRIL 10, 1965: Ellis Auditorium Amphitheater, Memphis, TN, with Sam the Sham and the Pharaohs, Bobby Woods, and Bobby Goldsboro (8:30 p.m. show)

SUNDAY, APRIL 11, 1965: Municipal Auditorium, Atlanta, GA, with Sam the Sham and the Pharaohs, Bobby Woods, and Bobby Goldsboro (3:30 p.m. show)
Glen Campbell returned to the road and replaced Bruce Johnston, who headed to Miami, where he holed up in a hotel room learning the bass.

MONDAY, APRIL 12, 1965: Jack Russell Stadium, Clearwater, FL, with the Roemans and Pam Hall and the Catalinas (7:00 p.m. show)
The Beach Boys made a memorable entrance to this show, riding into the stadium atop a white MG sports car. Sallie Elmore of the *Clearwater Sun* reported, "Halfway through their first song, a dozen or more girls jumped the railings and ran for the stage. What they planned to do once they got there we'll never know. After that it was something of a free for all—kids in surfer shirts dancing on the dugout roof, young boys running after drum sticks thrown by Dennis Wilson, and always the screaming, clapping, and whistling." The reviewer met the group later that night at their motel and reported, "Despite their popularity, the Beach Boys remain nice guys. At the motel, Dennis had filled his bathtub with fish and was scuba diving in the swimming pool, (while) Carl Wilson, Mike Love, and Glen Campbell (substituting for Brian Wilson) were sitting around eating hamburgers and talking about the show."

WEDNESDAY, APRIL 14, 1965: Yankee Stadium, Fort Lauderdale, FL (8:00 p.m. show)
This show was a benefit for the Campfire Girls, Inc.

THURSDAY, APRIL 15, 1965: Convention Hall, Miami, FL (8:30 p.m. show)

SATURDAY, APRIL 17, 1965: City Island Ball Park, Daytona Beach, FL, with the Escorts (8:00 p.m. show)

The Beach Boys performed for an enthusiastic crowd of 7,000 college students on their spring break. Photographs show that Glen Campbell was playing bass that night.

MONDAY, APRIL 19, 1965: Tinker Field Stadium, Orlando, FL (8:00 p.m. show)
Bruce Johnston, having adequately learned bass guitar, replaced Glen Campbell for this show.

TUESDAY, APRIL 20, 1965: State Armory, Wilmington, DE, with the Sonics and the Nebulas (8:00 p.m. show)
The Beach Boys flew from Orlando to Washington and then switched planes for the short flight to Wilmington. Dennis's drums, however, didn't make the second flight and the group had to borrow a set of drums from another act.

About 3,500 teenagers attended the concert that night. Judith M. Roales of the *Wilmington Evening Journal* reported, "As Dennis Wilson, on the borrowed drums, led into the song 'Do You Wanna Dance' tears streamed down the cheeks of infatuated females yelling 'Yes, yes.' There was one other substitute on the program, Brian Wilson . . . missed the tour because of illness and was replaced by Bruce Johnston. No one seemed to mind that either." The group's contract for this show promised a sum equal to fifty percent of the gross box office receipts with a minimum guarantee of $4,000. With tickets priced at $3.00, $4.00, and $5.00 and 3,500 fans in attendance, the group did considerably better than that minimum.

WEDNESDAY, APRIL 21, 1965: JFK Coliseum, Manchester, NH, with the Knights
Glen Campbell returned to the lineup for the remainder of this tour, though Bruce toured with the group as well, reportedly in charge of the lighting!

THURSDAY, APRIL 22, 1965: Memorial Auditorium, Lowell, MA, with the Knights (8:00 p.m. show)

FRIDAY, APRIL 23, 1965: Civic Center, Baltimore, MD, with Sam the Sham and the Pharaohs, the British Walkers, and the Uptowns (8:00 p.m. show)

Performing "Do You Wanna Dance" in Clearwater, Florida, on April 12, 1965. Ian Rusten Collection

didn't feel like I was being pressed to make something in an unnatural way. And all of a sudden I couldn't believe how much greater making music was when I did have the time and the naturalness to do it. It was so beautiful." *The Beach Boys Today* album (released in March) demonstrated that Brian's music was maturing at a phenomenal rate. The first half of the record showcased some of the group's best upbeat material, including "Dance, Dance, Dance" and "When I Grow Up (to Be a Man)," while the second half consisted of introspective ballads with incredible depth in arrangement and production. "Please Let Me

THE BEACH BOYS IN CONCERT

(Left to right) Carl, Mike, Glen, Dennis, and Al backstage in Washington, DC, on April 24, 1965. Photo: Jim Satcher

Wonder," "She Knows Me Too Well," and "Kiss Me Baby" were a departure from the breezy teen themes of previous albums and a move towards deeper reflection. Particularly arresting was "In the Back of My Mind," featuring lush orchestration and a melancholy lyric sung by Dennis that hinted at the direction Brian would turn to on *Pet Sounds* the following year.

Brian was also capable of creating extremely commercial material that also showcased his progress as an arranger/producer. The group scored

Ian Rusten Collection

SATURDAY, APRIL 24, 1965: Washington Coliseum, Washington, DC, with the Jumping Jacks, the British Walkers, Danny and the Elegants, and Jimmy Jones (8:00 p.m. show)
Over 7,000 fans attended the Beach Boys' first show in the nation's capital. Ronnie Oberman of the *Washington Star* reported, "Brian Wilson will not participate in tours in the immediate future. Two other singers, who will alternate, have been found to replace Brian on tours. They are Glen Campbell, who is frequently seen on *Shindig*, and Bruce Johnston, formerly of the Rip Chords. Campbell appeared on stage with the Beach Boys in Baltimore and Washington and Bruce was around too. 'I've known these guys for three or four years,' 20-year-old Bruce says. 'It's groovy on the road with them. They never hassle. It's a gas and I just dig them.'"

SUNDAY, APRIL 25, 1965: Carney Hall, Kansas State College, Pittsburg, KS (Canceled)
The Beach Boys' management never approved this show. The college negotiated the booking with an agent named David Ren, who claimed to represent the group, but in fact had no relationship with them. Ron Gates reported in the *Collegio* newspaper that it was a common problem of "local agents offering colleges acts which they are unauthorized to represent. These 'paper agents' receive a down payment—oft times substantial—and either contact the school one day before the scheduled concert to announce the act has become 'unavailable' and suggesting an act they can produce, or they don't return the down payment." The agent eventually returned the money after threats of court action. The Beach Boys never played at Kansas State College.

FRIDAY, MAY 7, 1965: Legion Field, Birmingham, AL, with the Rolling Stones, the Righteous Brothers, Marty Robbins, Sonny James, Cannibal and the Headhunters, Skeeter Davis, Archie Campbell, and Del Reeves (7:00 p.m. show)
The group, with Glen Campbell on bass, played to one of the largest audiences of their career to that date, with over 15,000 people in attendance. Emmett Weaver of the *Birmingham Post* noted, "The audience fell into two definite categories: 1) the screaming hand-waving teens and younger set who were quite obviously dyed in the wool champions of this noisy form of 'music' and 2) parents with their stolid, patient faces who had been dragged to this teenage shindig under the stars . . . The Birmingham police kept the youngsters from the Rolling Stones and the Beach Boys whenever they made an entrance or exit. Also it took a special wire fence across the width of the field to separate spectators from performers."

This was the second and last time the Beach Boys shared a bill with the Rolling Stones. Mike Love later recalled that "they were the act that directly preceded us . . . they came on and they did their best to bury us but it didn't work too well because I happen to know the state motto of Alabama. And I came out and said 'Hey this has been real nice . . . real fun, but it's about time we stood up for Alabama.' The state motto is 'Stand Up for Alabama.' They stood up, yelled, screamed, cheered, and forgot about the Rolling Stones." The Beach Boys and the Stones spent little time socializing backstage, since the Stones drove straight to the gig and left immediately after for Florida. They did, however, share a dressing room and, according to roadie Ron Swallow, "Dennis almost got into a fight with Mick Jagger because Dennis was offended by his poor hygiene!"

WEDNESDAY, MAY 12, 1965: Alan B. Shepard Civic Center ("The Dome"), Virginia Beach, VA, with the Sir Douglas Quintet and the Swinging Machine (Two shows at 7:00 and 9:00 p.m.)
The Beach Boys returned for a second set of shows in the Tidewater area, sponsored by WGH radio. A press release stated, "This will be one of the first return concerts ever done by our group and this is the only night we can come back as we will be on the East Coast to do *The Ed Sullivan Show* and will fly down from New York for WGH and all our Tidewater fans."

THURSDAY, MAY 13, 1965: Springfield Auditorium, Springfield, MA, with the Long Island Sounds (7:30 p.m. show)
Three thousand fans were treated to a twenty-five-song performance, which included "Surfin'

1965

USA," "Surfer Girl," "Little Old Lady from Pasadena," "Monster Mash," "Do You Wanna Dance" (sung by Dennis), and "Papa-Oom-Mow-Mow." According to the *Springfield Union*, "The Beach Boys concert literally left the huge audience breathless. The boys chewed them up, swallowed them, and spit them out and they came up yelling for more. Getting most of the loud screams was Dennis, who received an ovation with every shake of his long, blonde hair. At one point in the program, a group of girls ran up to the stage and presented their idol with a large sheet on which was printed 'Denny the Sexy One.'"

Glen Campbell was still playing bass for the group and he told a reporter, who inquired about the Beach Boys leader's whereabouts, that Brian was home suffering from fatigue because "Brian writes and arranges all our songs and in addition, he manages recording sessions, acts as a public relations man, and works fifteen or sixteen hours a day. Add to this public appearances and one show stands, and it's no wonder he became sick."

FRIDAY, MAY 14, 1965: Boston Arena, Boston, MA (8:00 p.m. show)
This show was almost canceled as a result of the Boston police department's decision to ban all rock 'n' roll concerts in the city, to prevent the violence associated with such events. The group was eventually allowed to perform because the police deemed that the Beach Boys "have a history of non-violence."

SATURDAY, MAY 15, 1965: New Haven Arena, New Haven, CT (8:00 p.m. show)
This was probably Glen Campbell's last appearance with the Beach Boys. The group headed to New York following this concert for what was supposed to be their second appearance on *The Ed Sullivan Show*. They were scheduled to perform their current single "Help Me Rhonda" and a version of "Graduation Day." According to Ron Swallow, the group, including Brian, took part in rehearsals at the CBS studio. As they waited to go on, they were unexpectedly told that their appearance would have to be rescheduled because the show was running long. They did not appear on the show again until 1968.

WEDNESDAY, MAY 19, 1965: Canton Memorial Auditorium, Canton, OH, with Sam the Sham and the Pharaohs, the Motions, and Glen Campbell (7:30 p.m. show)
The Beach Boys performed on this night before 4,718 people. The show grossed $13,312 and the group received $8,500. Bruce Johnston joined for the rest of the tour while Glen Campbell served as an opening act. Ron Swallow was given the opportunity to perform as Glen's drummer during his set.

THURSDAY, MAY 20, 1965: Sports Arena, Toledo, OH, with Sam the Sham and the Pharaohs, the Vandaliers, and Glen Campbell (8:15 p.m. show)
Five thousand fans attended the Beach Boys' first appearance in Toledo.

FRIDAY, MAY 21, 1965: Hara's Sports Arena, Dayton, OH, with Sam the Sham and the Pharaohs, and Glen Campbell (8:30 p.m. show)

SATURDAY, MAY 22, 1965: Victory Field, Indianapolis, IN, with Sam the Sham and the Pharaohs and Glen Campbell

SUNDAY, MAY 23, 1965: Cobo Arena, Detroit, MI, with Sam the Sham and the Pharaohs and Glen Campbell (7:30 p.m. show)
Following this show, the Beach Boys returned home to work on their upcoming *Summer Days (And Summer Nights!)* album.

FRIDAY, MAY 28, 1965: Centennial Coliseum, Reno, NV, with Glen Campbell and Dick and Dee Dee
The near-constant touring began to wear on more members of the group. Al commented to Earl Leaf, "The most grueling part of traveling is the one-nighters. We reach a new town a little late and leave a little early. This leaves us really no time to find out what a city or our fans are like. We have

their second number one single in May with "Help Me Rhonda" and followed that with the equally brilliant "California Girls," which hit number three on the *Billboard* charts. Both songs were instant classics and became staples of future Beach Boys concerts. The two singles appeared on the group's summer 1965 LP *Summer Days (and Summer Nights!)*. The LP also contained the rich ballad "Let Him Run Wild," featuring a fabulous vocal from Brian, the Beatles-inspired "Girl Don't Tell Me" (sung by Carl), the bubbly pop of "You're So Good to Me," and the Spector remake "Then I Kissed Her." Notably the latter three tracks featured the Beach Boys as musicians at a time when Brian was expanding his studio scope to include more session pros on his tracks.

Brian's ambition grew.

Ian Rusten Collection

Rather than rush the group's next album, Brian hit on the idea of recording a "live" Beach Boys album in the studio to buy more time. *Beach Boys' Party* was recorded at five sessions in September 1965

"It was just incredible to be onstage with them, then run for the limos to make our escape from the screaming fans. It was so much fun and so exciting. It was just like the Beatlemania I had seen in the film *A Hard Day's Night*, except it was Beach Boys mania."

to satisfy the label's demands for Christmas product. It featured the group singing loose covers of other artists, including the Beatles and Bob Dylan. The band held a special session with invited guests

to sacrifice sightseeing in order to get the rest we need. After a concert, we are always tensed up and can't get to sleep for hours afterwards, though we usually have to get up and go to the airport early in the morning." Carl stated, "It can get quite lonely on a tour away from home. After a show, there's often nothing to do but grab a bite to eat, then return to our hotel room and play cards or have a bull session. I love to meet new people but it isn't always as easy as you think. Most girls who come to meet us and get our autographs at the hotel travel in packs. We don't get to know them as individuals or to date just one out of the group."

SATURDAY, MAY 29, 1965: Lagoon, Farmington, UT, with Glen Campbell and Dick and Dee Dee (Two shows at 7:00 and 10:00 p.m.)

SUNDAY, MAY 30, 1965: Denver Auditorium Arena, Denver, CO, with the Moonrakers, Glen Campbell, and Dick and Dee Dee (8:00 p.m. show)

MONDAY, MAY 31, 1965: Municipal Auditorium, Oklahoma City, OK, with the Swinging Conner Family, Glen Campbell, and Dick and Dee Dee (7:30 p.m. show)
According to John Acord III of the *Daily Oklahoman*, "Signs were held up in the audience with the name of their favorite Beach Boy. Every time one of the favorites took a solo spot, there was a run to the stage with cameras clicking and flash attachments popping . . . The Beach Boys are a good group of entertainers . . . They sang several of their big record hits, such as 'Surfer Girl,' 'Shut Down,' 'Help Me Rhonda,' 'Johnny B. Goode,' 'Do You Want to Dance,' and a frantic version of 'Little Old Lady from Pasadena.'"

FRIDAY, JULY 2, 1965: Community Concourse Arena, San Diego, CA, with Sonny and Cher, Ian Whitcomb, and Sam the Sham and the Pharaohs (8:30 p.m. show)
Having decided to play the Hollywood Bowl show the next day, Brian Wilson also played this warmup show in place of Bruce Johnston. Steve Vivona of the *Evening Tribune* commented, "The five Southern California dynamos were the kingpins to the 3,000 strong, there's no doubt. They twanged out tunes like 'Louie, Louie' and 'California Girls' to the accompaniment of hysteria."

SATURDAY, JULY 3, 1965: Hollywood Bowl, Los Angeles, CA, with the Righteous Brothers, Sam the Sham and the Pharaohs, Donna Loren, Ian Whitcomb, Dino, Desi and Billy, Sonny and Cher, the Byrds, the Liverpool Five, the Sir Douglas Quintet, and the Kinks (8:15 p.m. show)
The group's first hometown show in almost a year was a huge event, billed as "The Summer Spectacular" and attended by 15,000 people. Brian Wilson joined the group for what turned out to be his last full concert until August 1967. Mike Fessier Jr. of the fledgling *LA* magazine captured the scene that night as the group waited to go on. "They've been at this game three years but they're still nervous. 'You guys know your lyrics? Hey remember when we used to paste them on the back of something?' Even now lead vocalist Mike Love has written in ink on the palm of his hand the order of songs they'll sing. Brian Wilson, group leader and composer of most of their songs, is taut as a guitar string. His fingers tremble violently. Little Alan Jardine says something and Brian barks, 'Shut up.' The time has arrived and Irving Granz pushes them out towards the stage to meet the 15,000 people." Despite the high pressure of following such popular acts as the Byrds and the Kinks, the *Los Angeles Times* critic Charles Champlin and his teenage daughters agreed: "the Beach Boys seemed by all odds the most polished performers of the evening."

Watching from backstage, teenager Billy Hinsche of opening act Dino, Desi, and Billy recalled, "It was a thrill to see the Beach Boys about to take the stage, dressed in their trademark striped shirts and white pants, with Brian towering over everyone with his bass strapped on his shoulder. They sounded great live, a tight unit of instrumentation and harmonies—real professionals." Hinsche (born June 29, 1951, in Manila, the Philippines) was so impressed by the Beach Boys' sound that he sought out Carl Wilson during rehearsals. The two hit it off, and Billy was soon introduced to the rest of the band. Billy recalled that the Beach Boys "acted then as they acted throughout their lives and career, each individual portraying their own personalities. Dino, Desi, and I were just young teenagers, so we didn't really pose a threat to them on any level so it was easy to talk with them."

1965

SUNDAY, JULY 4, 1965: Cow Palace, San Francisco, CA, with the Kinks, Sonny and Cher, the Ronettes, Donna Loren, Ian Whitcomb, Sam the Sham and the Pharaohs, Drusalee and the Dead, the Emeralds with Linda Dawn, the Westwinds, the Decibels, and the Coachmen (4:00 p.m. show)
This concert turned out to be a big disappointment for promoters. Only 3,500 fans attended. According to the KEWB newsletter, "The show took place on a Sunday afternoon. But not any Sunday afternoon—this was a national holiday. Further, the show went on at four in the afternoon. The promoter, perhaps, should have known better. Traditionally, the Fourth of July is a day for the family. And a hot, muggy mid-July afternoon is no time to ask people to trek to a show." There was also backstage drama at this concert. The mercurial Kinks refused to play because the promoter couldn't pay them up front. They waved to the audience and then left the building.

TUESDAY, JULY 6, 1965: Canobie Lake Park, Salem, NH
The group flew to New Hampshire to begin their big summer tour. Dick Duryea, Roy Hatfield, and Ron Swallow accompanied them.

WEDNESDAY, JULY 7, 1965: Hampton Beach Casino, Hampton Beach, NH

THURSDAY, JULY 8, 1965: Municipal Auditorium, Bangor, ME, with the Mar-Vels (8:00 p.m. show)

FRIDAY, JULY 9, 1965: Portland Exposition Building, Portland, ME, with the Mar-Vels and the Headlighters (8:00 p.m. show)
The Beach Boys played to an audience of 6,500 people.

SATURDAY, JULY 10, 1965: Convention Hall, Asbury Park, NJ (Two shows at 7:30 and 9:30 p.m.)

SUNDAY, JULY 11, 1965: Berkshire Music Barn, Lenox, MA (8:30 p.m. show)

MONDAY, JULY 12, 1965: Dorton Arena, Raleigh, NC, with the Embers, the Unknown IV, and the Inmates (8:00 p.m. show)
A huge crowd at the Raleigh-Durham airport welcomed the Beach Boys. After giving a radio interview, they traveled to their hotel and then the concert arena. J. G. Ligon of the *Raleigh News* stated, "Their performance was spiced with a little comedy by lead vocalist Mike Love, who emceed the show. Love 'jerked' and sang to the near-hysterical girls who were hanging from the railing just to touch him. The blue jean–clad group sang their odes to surfing, hot rods, and California girls. Their hour-long stand left the crowd cheering and singing the tunes after them."

TUESDAY, JULY 13, 1965: Greensboro Coliseum, Greensboro, NC, with the Roemans, the Unknown IV, and the Inmates (8:00 p.m. show)

WEDNESDAY, JULY 14, 1965: Charlotte Coliseum, with the Roemans and the Galaxies (8:30 p.m. show)
Prior to the concert, two teenage fans interviewed Carl and Al for WIST radio. Discussing the new *Summer Days (And Summer Nights!)* album, Carl stated that the "new album has something of a new sound, mostly instrumental, a little bit more 'intellectual,' a little bit older." That night, 6,746 fans attended the concert.

THURSDAY, JULY 15, 1965: Columbia Township Auditorium, Columbia, SC

FRIDAY, JULY 16, 1965: Memorial Auditorium, Chattanooga, TN, with the Vondels, Don Argo, Kris Jenson, Ronnie Bird, and Billy Osborn and the Tracers (8:00 p.m. show)

SATURDAY, JULY 17, 1965: Memorial Auditorium, Greenville, SC (8:00 p.m. show)

SUNDAY, JULY 18, 1965: City Auditorium, Atlanta, GA, with Billy Joe Royal and the Roemans (3:00 p.m. show)

to create the atmospehere of eavesdropping at a party at the Beach Boys' home. Meanwhile, Brian worked hard on composing music for what would become his magnum opus *Pet Sounds*.

Despite the casual aspect of *Beach Boys' Party*, everything Brian touched seemed to turn to gold. When "Barbara Ann," a fun sing-along on the LP with guest Dean Torrence, was released as a single, it shocked Brian by rising all the way to number two on the *Billboard* singles charts. Brian commented in *Teenset*, "It didn't represent any production talent, just a live sound. We didn't spend as much time polishing it, because we didn't know it would be forced out as a single. But don't get me wrong, I couldn't be happier that it went number one (in L.A.)."

The Beach Boys ended the year on top of the charts and were growing more popular all over the world. Brian was setting his sights even higher. Ninteen sixty-six would see the band reach the pinnacle of its popularity and Brian reach the apex of his creativity.

THE BEACH BOYS IN CONCERT

Opener Billy Joe Royal was riding the charts with his single "Down in the Boondocks."

MONDAY, JULY 19, 1965: Municipal Auditorium, Nashville, TN, with the Searchers, the Zombies, and Ray Lynn (8:15 p.m. show)

WEDNESDAY, JULY 21, 1965: Civic Center Arena, Tulsa, OK, with the Rondells, Gene Simmons, and the Uniques (8:30 p.m. show)

THURSDAY, JULY 22, 1965: Municipal Auditorium, Austin, TX, with the Rondells, the Uniques, and the Five Americans (8:00 p.m. show)
The Beach Boys' first Austin concert drew 4,500 fans. John Bustin of the *Austin American Statesman* commented dismissively that "their few stabs at any kind of showmanship or humor are of a most elemental sort—possibly in keeping with the level of their fans—and about their biggest non-musical device was to have Mike Love, a thinning-haired, 23-year-old front man unbutton his shirt (this got a great reaction) and do a monster takeoff."

FRIDAY, JULY 23, 1965: Memorial Auditorium, Dallas, TX, with the Rondells, the Uniques, and the Five Americans (8:00 p.m. show)
Dressed in blue and white striped shirts and white slacks, the group performed to a capacity crowd.

SATURDAY, JULY 24, 1965: Jacksonville Coliseum, Jacksonville, FL, with Lesley Gore, Del Shannon, the Shangri-Las, the Zombies, Del Reeves, the Searchers, Sam the Sham and the Pharaohs, and the Premieres (Two shows at 5:00 and 9:00 p.m.)

FRIDAY, JULY 30, 1965: Santa Clara County Fairgrounds, San Jose, CA, with Sonny and Cher, the We Five, and the Preps (8:30 p.m. show)

SATURDAY, JULY 31, 1965: Civic Auditorium, Bakersfield, CA, with Dino, Desi, and Billy and Barbara Lewis (8:30 p.m. show)
Dino, Desi, and Billy were invited to open for the Beach Boys at this show and also the next night in Fresno. Billy Hinsche recalled, "It was amazing to be asked on that tour. . . . I spent my time on the road with Carl mostly, hanging out in his room in Bakersfield and Fresno."

SUNDAY, AUGUST 1, 1965: Memorial Auditorium, Fresno, CA, with the Preps, Dino, Desi and Billy, and Barbara Lewis (8:00 p.m. show)
The set list for this show included "Little Deuce Coupe," "Shut Down," "Little Honda," "Surfin' USA," "Surfer Girl," "Papa-Oom-Mow-Mow," "Little Old Lady from Pasadena," "Girl Don't Tell Me," "Hawaii," "California Girls," "Do You Wanna Dance," "I Get Around," and "Wendy." Reviewer Spencer Mastick of the *Fresno Bee* singled out "the dancing and other antics of lead singer Michael Love and the thumping good performance of drummer Dennis Wilson." He reported, "Wadded-up notes started bouncing off the performers, mostly off Love, and a glitter now and then indicated some of the girls were pulling off their rings and tossing them too. Through the tunes 'I Get Around' and 'Little Wendy,' the policemen near the stage did a great job of keeping the girls in their seats and keeping down the barrage."

FRIDAY, AUGUST 6, AND SATURDAY, AUGUST 7, 1965: Waikiki Shell, Honolulu, HI, with Dino, Desi, and Billy and Barbara Lewis (8:00 p.m. shows)
The Beach Boys flew to Honolulu on August 4 and were greeted at the airport by hundreds of teenage fans. After signing autographs and talking to the press, the group settled in at the Hilton Hawaiian Village Hotel. During their ten-day visit, they played two concerts at the Waikiki Shell. Billy Hinsche recalled that "Dino, Desi, and I joined the Beach Boys onstage for the encore of 'Johnny B. Goode' and it was just incredible to be onstage with them, then run for the limos to make our escape from the screaming fans. It was so much fun and so exciting. It was just like the Beatlemania I had seen in the film *A Hard Day's Night*, except it was Beach Boys mania."

The Beach Boys with new member Bruce Johnston (top left) pose at Honolulu Airport on August 4, 1965. Jon Stebbins Collection

The trip was important for young Hinsche, who developed a close, lifelong friendship with Carl. Billy recalled, "Carl taught me how to play Chuck Berry guitar riffs in his suite at the Hilton Hawaiian Village Hotel that he shared with Mike Love. Desi and I went surfing with Bruce at Honolulu's Waikiki Beach—the one and only time I ever surfed. And [I went] mud sliding with Carl, Ron Swallow, and a few others in the rain forest. I returned to the hotel a muddy mess. It wasn't exactly my idea of fun, though Carl got a big kick out of it." Elvis Presley was also in Honolulu that week, filming scenes for his film *Paradise Hawaiian Style*, but there is no evidence that the Beach Boys met him while there.

FRIDAY, AUGUST 20, AND SATURDAY, AUGUST 21, 1965: Memorial Auditorium, Sacramento, CA, with Barbara Lewis, the Preps, and Group "B" (8:30 p.m. shows)
After their Hawaiian trip, the group returned to Sacramento for two concerts. According to Sean O'Callaghan of KXOA, "the Beach Boys certainly put on a show. For nearly an hour, both nights, they filled the auditorium with so many Beach Boys hits it's almost impossible to list them. Although some may have been disappointed at the absence of Brian Wilson, the show certainly did not suffer with the addition of Bruce Johnston."

The day after these shows, Mike and Carl flew to Portland, Oregon. Steve Brown of radio station KISN arranged for them to meet the Beatles backstage at the Portland Memorial Coliseum prior to the Beatles' August 22 concert. Brown recalled that despite their wealth and success, the musicians talked about "the same things that teenagers who didn't have $5 in their pockets talked about . . . girls, cars, and houses."

TUESDAY, AUGUST 24, 1965: Sioux Falls Arena, Sioux Falls, SD (8:00 p.m. show)
Over 6,000 South Dakota fans attended the Beach Boys appearance in Sioux Falls. According to the *Argus-Leader*, "The crowd went into hysterics as each singer took his turn at quivering his knees or hips. There was unadulterated ecstasy over a song titled 'Little Old Lady from Pasadena.' Police got a small scare while the 'Boys' were singing 'The Monster Mash.' One of the group hopped off the stage and teenage girls in the lower northeast corner of the Arena immediately prepared to close in as they came to their feet screaming. The 'Boy,' meanwhile, skipped back on the stage with a swarming mass of bobbing heads left screeching in the bleachers."

WEDNESDAY, AUGUST 25, 1965: Rosenblatt Stadium, Omaha, NE (8:00 p.m. show)

THURSDAY, AUGUST 26, 1965: Kentucky State Fairgrounds Stadium, Louisville, KY, with the Shangri-Las, Sir Douglas Quintet, and the Keyes (8:30 p.m. show)

FRIDAY, AUGUST 27, 1965: Cincinnati Gardens, Cincinnati, OH, with the Sir Douglas Quintet, Johnny and the Hurricanes, and Dave Osborn's Action Unlimited (8:30 p.m. show)
The group's third appearance in Cincinnati drew over 4,000 fans. The set included "California Girls," "Little Honda," "I Get Around," "Help Me Rhonda," and "Surfer Girl." According to Robert Demarr of *The Enquirer*, "The biggest delight for the screaming teenagers was the drum solo by Dennis Wilson in 'Do You Wanna Dance.' The show ended with an uproar and more than a hundred outstretched hands when Wilson threw his drumsticks into the screaming crowd."

SATURDAY, AUGUST 28, AND SUNDAY, AUGUST 29, 1965: Arie Crown Theater, Chicago, IL, with Shadows of the Knight and Jonathan David and Albert (8:30 p.m. on Saturday and 7:00 p.m. on Sunday)

WEDNESDAY, SEPTEMBER 1, 1965: Civic Arena, Pittsburgh, PA, with Peter and Gordon, the Shirelles, Tom Jones, and Brian Hyland
According to *Variety*, this Dick Clark "Caravan of Stars Show" grossed $26,000.

THURSDAY, SEPTEMBER 2, 1965: Auditorium Theatre, Rochester, NY, with Dickey Lee, Sonny and Cher, Bobby Comstock and the Counts (Two shows at 6:30 and 9:00 p.m.)
Over 5,148 fans attended the two concerts in Rochester. The band played fifteen songs, including "Surfer Girl," "Little Deuce Coupe," "Help Me Rhonda," and "California Girls." The microphone went dead and

THE BEACH BOYS IN CONCERT

Onstage in Rochester, September 2, 1965. Dick Hollaert/Joe Russo (www.therascalsarchives.com)

The group poses with promoters backstage in Rochester, New York, September 2, 1965. Dick Hollaert/Joe Russo (www.therascalsarchives.com)

one of the amplifiers broke during the performance, leading Al Jardine, who celebrated his twenty-third birthday that day, to call it "the most everything went wrong show we've ever done." It mattered little to the teenage fans that screamed throughout.

FRIDAY, SEPTEMBER 3, 1965: Utica Memorial Auditorium, Utica, NY, with Dickey Lee and Bobby Comstock and the Counts (8:30 p.m. show) An audience of 2,300 teenagers attended. Barbara Jones of the *Utica Observer* noted, "'Help Me Rhonda,' 'I Get Around,' 'Surfin' USA,' 'Shut Down,' and 'Little Honda' delighted the well-behaved audience. Although noted for their vocal talents, the Beach Boys sound much better on wax than live. They lack spontaneous humor and concert chatter between numbers with their admirers. Mike Love, seemingly a favorite of the females for his attempt at humor and his frug and jerk dance steps, soloed on 'Monster Mash.' As he told his fans, 'This is where my friends say I show my true personality.' The number flopped as far as any audience reaction. Other Beach Boy members took the spotlight on 'Papa-Oom-Mow-Mow,' 'Little Old Lady from Pasadena,' and 'Little Deuce Coupe.' The most applause was saved for the artists' latest record, 'California Girls.'"

SATURDAY, SEPTEMBER 4, 1965: YM/YWCA Auditorium, Ottawa, ON, Canada, with Dickey Lee, J.B. and the Playboys, the Esquires, the Rhythmics, and Little Caesar and the Consuls About 2,500 fans attended this show, a disappointing turnout considering that the Beach Boys had attracted over 5,000 on their previous visit in February. Dennis Foley of the *Ottawa Citizen* briefly noted, "The Beach Boys came on strong and cool, without any jiggling to buttress their numerous numbers, which included most of their hit records. The show's windup got a little ugly when the hired guards clenched and waved their fists as the eager flocked front and center. It subsided quickly when the Beach Boys made a hasty exit just as a few in front were taking off their coats and watches. This was fortunate as there were some pretty big boys in that crowd."

SUNDAY, SEPTEMBER 5, 1965: Maple Leaf Gardens, Toronto, ON, Canada, with Sonny and Cher, J.B. and the Playboys, the Big Town Boys, and Little Caesar and the Consuls The Beach Boys set included "Surfin' USA," "Surfer Girl," "Wendy," "Then I Kissed Her," "Do You Wanna Dance," "California Girls," "Little Honda," and "Monster Mash." The *Toronto Star* reported that the 9,500 fans at the show raised such a din that the music could barely be heard.

FRIDAY, SEPTEMBER 10 AND SATURDAY, SEPTEMBER 11, 1965: Lagoon, Farmington, UT, with the Runaways (One show at 9:00 p.m. on Friday and two shows at 7:00 and 9:30 p.m. on Saturday) The Beach Boys flew to Salt Lake City on Thursday and were given the keys to the city by Commissioner Joe L. Christensen. The group had remained phenomenally popular in the area and played three shows in two days to satisfy demand. Amongst the crowd who greeted the group at the airport upon their return to California was Billy Hinsche's sister Annie, who was introduced to Carl and soon became his steady girlfriend.

FRIDAY, SEPTEMBER 17, 1965: Civic Center, Baltimore, MD, with the Uptowns

SATURDAY, SEPTEMBER 18, 1965: Convention Hall, Philadelphia, PA, (8:00 p.m. show) About 3,500 fans attended this show and, according to Ralph K. Bennett of the *Philadelphia Inquirer*, "there were signs painted on bed sheets hanging all over the hall. They said things like 'Cherry Hill Girls Welcome the Beach Boys' and 'We Wish You Could All Be Philadelphia Boys.'"

SUNDAY, SEPTEMBER 19, 1965: National Guard Armory, Washington, DC, with the El Corrals and Little Wimpy and the New Bedford Set (8:00 p.m. show) As part of a concert promotion, Bruce gave away a Honda motorcycle to a lucky fan during this show.

1965

FRIDAY, SEPTEMBER 24, 1965: Exhibition Forum, Vancouver, BC, Canada, with Charlie Rich, the Castaways, and the Chessmen (8:30 p.m. show)

SATURDAY, SEPTEMBER 25, 1965: Memorial Coliseum, Portland, OR, with the Tempests and the Viceroys (8:00 p.m. show)

Over 7,000 fans attended this show. During the six-week hiatus that followed this concert the group recorded a new single, "The Little Girl I Once Knew," and taped television appearances on *The Andy Williams Show* and the *Jack Benny Show*.

SUNDAY, NOVEMBER 14, 1965: Madison Square Garden, New York, NY, with Alan King, Frankie Laine, Johnny Carson, Bobby Vinton, Robert Vaughn, Anthony Newley, Mia Farrow, Carol Baker, the Supremes, Joan Crawford, Henry Fonda, Ed Sullivan, Peter Falk, Duke Ellington, Sammy Davis Jr., and others (8:00 p.m. show)

This concert was a star-studded USO benefit show. The Beach Boys made a brief appearance singing only a few songs. As revealed in a 1966 *Tiger Beat* interview, Carl proposed to his girlfriend Annie Hinsche over the phone following this show, after only two months of dating!

THURSDAY, NOVEMBER 18, 1965: Mayo Civic Center, Rochester, MN, with the Gentrys, the Strangeloves and the Castaways (7:30 p.m. show)

This was the first of four dates the Beach Boys played with the Gentrys, riding the charts with their hit "Keep On Dancing." Dick Duryea, Roy Hatfield, promoter Irving Granz, and Steve Korthof accompanied the group.

FRIDAY, NOVEMBER 19, 1965: Minneapolis Auditorium, Minneapolis, MN, with the Gentrys, the Strangeloves, and the Castaways (8:30 p.m. show)

SATURDAY, NOVEMBER 20, 1965: Municipal Auditorium, Kansas City, MO, with the Gentrys and the Strangeloves (8:30 p.m. show)

Jack Lloyd, then an employee of Irving Granz, was asked to fly to Kansas City to handle the production of this concert while Granz returned home for personal reasons. Lloyd would accompany the Beach Boys on a number of later tours, joining their American Productions Company in April 1968. According to Lloyd, Audree Wilson and Dennis' wife Carole had just flown in for a visit. Audree remained with the group for the rest of the tour.

SUNDAY, NOVEMBER 21, 1965: Kiel Opera House, St. Louis, MO, with the Gentrys and the Strangeloves (7:30 p.m. show)

TUESDAY, NOVEMBER 23, 1965: Curry Hicks Cage, University of Massachusetts, Amherst, MA, with the Prince Spaghetti Minstrels, the Boss Tweeds, and the Bold (8:30 p.m. show)

This show was a benefit for the JFK Fund, with profits used to build a library. It marked the group's first appearance before a college audience. The Beach Boys were well received and more university appearances were booked for 1966. The band was growing tired of the high school kids who grabbed their hair and screamed nonstop at shows. Carl was particularly impressed by the college show and told a reporter, "This audience can be wonderful—so quiet. If it's quiet at a regular date, that's disaster."

WEDNESDAY, NOVEMBER 24, 1965: Rhode Island Auditorium, Providence, RI, with Teddy and the Pandas and Cheryl-Ann and the Pilgrims (8:00 p.m. show)

According to Steve Gilkenson of the *Providence Journal*, the Beach Boys' female fans started screaming at the beginning of this show and never let up, making it virtually impossible to hear anything. "The impression we get is that just being in the same room with the Beach Boys was well worth the price and certainly something to scream about. Their program, for those who might be interested, included 'Little Honda,' 'Surfin' USA,' 'Then I Kissed Her,' and 'Surfer Girl.'"

FRIDAY, NOVEMBER 26, 1965: Boston Garden, Boston, MA (8:00 p.m. show)

THE BEACH BOYS IN CONCERT

The Beach Boys played to a capacity crowd in Boston. Following the show, reporter Linda McVeigh interviewed Dennis in the group's suite at the Sheraton Hotel. McVeigh was given exclusive access to the band because she had attended Hawthorne High with the Wilsons. Her article provides an interesting snapshot of the Beach Boys on the road in 1965. She noted that Dennis, dressed "like an expensively tailored cowboy," sat in the hotel living room with his mother Audree while "hangers-on" waited on him (refilling buckets of ice and taking care of room service) and "unidentified girls" sat nearby saying nothing. Fans had discovered what room the group was in and a security guard brought an admirer in every 15 minutes or so to obtain an autograph. Dennis, under the watchful eye of his mother, dutifully obliged until finally he grew fed up and gave the order to stop letting people up. In a reversal of their later image, McVeigh reported that during the interview Carl sat on a bed in the other room nursing a gin and tonic, while Dennis drank only 7-Up. He offered McVeigh a Coke with a sheepish apology and explained that he didn't drink because, "I can't afford to. With everything that's wrong with me, I'd be dead in a year."

SATURDAY, DECEMBER 4, 1965: Civic Auditorium, Albuquerque, NM, with Lindy and the Lavells, the Viscounts, and the Defiants (8:30 p.m. show)

WEDNESDAY, DECEMBER 29, 1965: Circle Star Theater, San Carlos, CA, with Jackie Lee, Mitch Ryder, and the T-Bones (8:30 p.m. show)
Dennis Wilson played drums at this show with a bandaged hand, but according to the *San Mateo Times,* he still stole the show. "They received the most enthusiasm when Dennis Wilson sang 'You've Got to Hide Your Love Away' and 'Do You Wanna Dance.' After their last song, the entire house marched down upon the Beach Boys."

THURSDAY, DECEMBER 30, 1965: Oakland Auditorium, Oakland, CA, with the Turtles, Mitch Ryder and the Detroit Wheels, Jackie Lee, and the T-Bones (8:00 p.m. show)
The Beach Boys drew 4,000 screaming teenage fans, who braved a torrential downpour to see them at the Oakland Auditorium. Bernie Hughes of the *Oakland Tribune* reported, "The Boys did 'Surfin' USA,' 'Little Honda,' 'California Girls,' 'Surfer Girl,' and their newest hit, 'Barbara Ann.' The screamers in the audience went wildest during Dennis Wilson's 'Hide Your Love Away,' in which he imitated Beatle John Lennon—and those who know about these things claim he does it perfectly . . . When Mike Love, the only bearded member, winked at the darkened crowd, the worshippers gave their all. They knew the Beach Boys by name and now and then a piercing voice from the balcony would yell out 'Dennyyyyy!' Denny would gaze up, keep on singing, and the screaming would begin anew."

FRIDAY, DECEMBER 31, 1965: UPS Field House, Tacoma, WA, with Gary Lewis and the Playboys, the Yardbirds, the Beau Brummels, the Vejtables, Alexys and the Mojo Men
Discussing this New Year's Eve show, Bruce Johnston told Richard Green of *Record Mirror* that "we had 10,000 people in the audience and at the end they all got up and rushed the stage. I thought it was all over. We got out of there fast. It was frightening." Bruce also recalled that the Yardbirds, with lead guitarist Jeff Beck, were one of the support acts at this show and at the subsequent show in Seattle. On one of the two nights, "Their amplifiers had blown up, so we lent them our equipment. Dennis plays drums so he doesn't understand equipment and Mike just sings, so he doesn't understand what's going on with amps either. Jeff Beck turns his guitar towards the amps to get feedback and Dennis and Mike were going to pull the plugs out. They thought the Yardbirds were harming the equipment. I had to stop them and explain what was happening. They were getting really mad."

CONCERTS NOT PLAYED
A poster exists advertising a Beach Boys show in Hartford, Connecticut, on June 25, 1965, but the group did not play there that day. Another version of this poster purports to advertise an Indianapolis show on the same day. Neither poster is legitimate.

Author Keith Badman's book listed a show in Montreal on September 6, but we could find nothing to substantiate this claim.

1966

I N EARLY 1966, Brian Wilson was suffused with ambition. He told Peter Jones of *Record Mirror*, "I know that in some circles we're not regarded as all that 'hip' or 'in.' This is maybe because we haven't just arrived from nowhere with something new with a new label. But I don't care too much what anyone says, so long as I know I'm staying ahead—right up to the limit of my present capabilities. I don't put out anything I don't respect. And I know for sure that the Beach Boys brought something new into rock 'n' roll." While the Beach Boys toured Japan, Brian was busy working on what many consider his masterpiece, *Pet Sounds*. The LP was the result of over five months of planning by Brian, who wrote and arranged most of its songs with collaborator Tony Asher. Brian chose to work with Asher, an advertising executive, over frequent collaborator Mike Love. Brian explained at the time, "I felt I needed a fresh approach." The move was symbolic of Brian's restless desire to leave behind the style the group was known for. Brian had been heavily influenced by the Beatles' fall 1965 release *Rubber Soul* and the unity of mood it conveyed. Rather than just a collection of songs, the Beatles LP made an artistic statement as a whole. Songs flowed from one to the next organically. Brian vowed to make an album on which each track had a synergistic relationship and the entire record came together as a concept.

Brian told a KRLA reporter that he was "experimenting . . . with combinations of instruments which aren't generally associated with the rock 'n' roll business." Brian used French horns, piccolos, trumpets, accordions, strings, and other jazz- and classical-associated textures on *Pet Sounds*. On "Wouldn't It Be Nice" alone, Brian used strings, kettle drums, accordions, and a banjo. Brian was determined to give each track a particular mood. He was particularly pleased with the instrumental track "Let's Go Away for Awhile." He told Pete Goodman of *Beat Instrumental*, "For me it's the most satisfying piece of music that has yet been released. I think the chordal changes are very special. I applied a certain secret set of dynamics through the arrangement. I believe honestly that the result is exactly what the song says."

Pet Sounds was a very personal statement by Brian. Although Tony Asher wrote many of the lyrics, they were the result of heartfelt conversations with Brian and reflected his deepest feelings and beliefs. The brilliant ballad "I Just Wasn't Made for These Times" seems, in retrospect, an eerie portrait of the problems Brian would face in dealing with his family and his obligations. The heartbreaking album closer "Caroline, No" projected a very real sense of regret. Bruce Johnston commented to *NME* reporter Nick Kent, "That song was directly about Brian himself and the death of a quality

CONCERTS PLAYED IN
1966

SATURDAY, JANUARY 1, 1966: Coliseum, Seattle, WA, with Gary Lewis and the Playboys, the Yardbirds, the Beau Brummels, the Vejtables, Alexys and the Mojo Men (8:00 p.m. show)

FRIDAY, JANUARY 7, 1966: Shibuya Koukaido, Tokyo, Japan
The Beach Boys left California on January 5 and arrived in Tokyo on January 6, 1966. The group held a press conference that night at which they thanked the Japanese fans for supporting them. Steve Korthof, Roy Hatfield, and Dick Duryea accompanied them. The set list for the band's opening concert consisted of "Fun, Fun, Fun," "Hawaii," "Surfin' USA," "Surfer Girl," "Little Honda," "Papa Ooo-Mow-Mow," "Monster Mash," "Instrumental," "Little Deuce Coupe," "Barbara Ann," "California Girls," "I Get Around," "Johnny B. Goode," and "Do You Wanna Dance." A special tour program was prepared, with song lyrics translated into Japanese. The program featured only photos of the band with Brian Wilson, with no photos of Bruce Johnston included in any of the publicity materials.

SATURDAY, JANUARY 8, 1966: Nagoya-shi Koukaido, Nagoya, Japan

SUNDAY, JANUARY 9, 1966: Osaka Sankei Hall, Osaka, Japan

MONDAY, JANUARY 10, 1966: Kyoto Kaikan Hall, Kyoto, Japan
Prior to this show, the group dressed in samurai garb for photographers. Some of the photos were later used on the back of the *Pet Sounds* album.

WEDNESDAY, JANUARY 12, 1966: Kobe Kokusai Kaikan, Kobe, Japan

THURSDAY, JANUARY 13, 1966: Osaka Sankei Hall, Osaka, Japan

FRIDAY, JANUARY 14, 1966: Fukuoka Kyuden Taikukan, Fukuoka, Japan

SATURDAY, JANUARY 15, 1966: Otemachi Sankei Hall, Tokyo, Japan

SUNDAY, JANUARY 16, 1966: Shinjuku Kousei Nenkin Hall, Tokyo, Japan

TUESDAY, JANUARY 18, 1966: Miyagi Kenmin Kaikan, Sendai, Japan

THURSDAY, JANUARY 20, 1966: Sumpu Kaikan, Shizuoka, Japan

FRIDAY, JANUARY 21, 1966: Yokohama Bunka Taikukan, Yokohama, Japan

SATURDAY, JANUARY 22, 1966: Shinjuku Kousei Nenkin Hall, Tokyo, Japan

SUNDAY, JANUARY 23, 1966: Ootaku Taikukan, Tokyo, Japan (day) and Shinjuku Kousei Nenkin Hall, Tokyo, Japan (Night)
Following these shows, Carl, Al, and Dennis headed to Hawaii. Bruce, Mike, and Dick Duryea spent time in Hong Kong. During their stay, they went to see a Searchers concert. Bruce told a reporter, "When we walked into the club the announcer recognized us and we had to stand up and take a bow." They held a press conference at the Mandarin Hotel on January 25. Mike and Bruce told a reporter from the *China Mail* that they loved Hong Kong and hoped to play there one day. Duryea noted that in less than a month they "had passed through three New Years and boy that was something. We had an American-style New Year in the United States, then a Japanese-style one in Tokyo. In Hong Kong, we had the tail end of the Chinese New Year and we liked it."

SATURDAY, JANUARY 29, 1966: HIC Arena, Honolulu, HI, with Jackie Lee, Lou Christie, the Mop Tops, the Undertakers, Frankie Samuels and the Kinfolk (8:30 p.m. show)
The Beach Boys gathered in Hawaii for a one-off concert. Following the show they flew to the states to begin intensive work on *Pet Sounds*, which Brian had been recording in their absence.

THURSDAY, FEBRUARY 17, 1966: Masonic Temple Auditorium, Davenport, IA, with the T Bones and the Sheep (8:00 p.m. show)
Jack Lloyd, working on behalf of promoter Irving Granz, accompanied the Beach Boys on this short tour. The group easily sold out the 2,700-seat Masonic Auditorium. Rita Mueller of the *Times-Democrat* reported, "The girls went wild when Alan Jardine sang 'Then I Kissed Her' and the girls were jumping to their feet when Dennis Wilson sang 'You've Got to Hide Your Love Away.' . . . The whole show was gaining momentum, the tempo was wild, and the crowd was with it as they went into 'California Girls,' 'Help Me Rhonda,' and finally what everyone was waiting for, number one on the pop charts, 'Barbara Ann.' It is a wild sight to watch over 2,000 people swaying, clapping, and cheering all at the same time." Police were on hand to ensure order after the final number "Do You Wanna Dance" finished and they seemed to have things under control until Dennis opened the curtain again and tossed a drumstick into the crowd. A small riot broke out as teenagers scrambled to capture the valuable souvenir.

FRIDAY, FEBRUARY 18, 1966: KRNT Theater, Des Moines, IA, with the T-Bones and the Sheep (8:30 p.m. show)

SUNDAY, FEBRUARY 20, 1966: Tulsa Assembly Center, Tulsa, OK, with the T-Bones and the Sheep (7:30 p.m. show)
Following this show, the band spent the night in Tulsa and then flew to Dallas on Monday morning to catch a connecting flight to Los Angeles.

FRIDAY, MARCH 4, 1966: State University of Oregon, Corvallis, OR
In the midst of finishing work on *Pet Sounds*, the Beach Boys flew to Oregon for a short college tour. In addition to Lynda Jardine, William Morris agent Pete Goldman, road manager Richard Duryea, and Roy Hatfield, the group were accompanied by *Los Angeles Times* reporter Art Seidenbaum, who was gathering material for a three-part profile of the band. He reported that the group flew from Los Angeles to Portland and then rented cars for the drive to Corvallis. This led to an amusing incident. Dennis started to get behind the wheel of one of the cars and was stopped by manager Dick Duryea, who insisted that the "speed demon" hand the wheel over to someone else.

SATURDAY, MARCH 5, 1966: McArthur Court, University of Oregon, Eugene, OR, with Noel Harrison, the Heirs, and the Critters (8:00 p.m. show)
Although held at the university, this general-admission show attracted many younger fans and a riot broke out. As the group headed backstage, they encountered a mob waiting in the corridor. Seidenbaum reported, "Little girls hurled themselves at police lines as if they were rabid dogs . . . Outside the dressing room kids began throwing stones at the windows . . . Inside more than 300 young people—most of them high school age—surged, thrashed, kicked, no longer human. The Beach Boys cringed and changed in the dressing room, staying clear of the windows. 'Now you know what it's like to be a sandwich,' yelled one. 'This is still mild,' mumbled another." Mike laughed it off, telling a university reporter, "This is the first college where we got mobbed . . . we love it . . . I'll bet the college kids were amazed though."

SUNDAY, MARCH 6, 1966: Southern Oregon State College, Ashland, OR (3:00 p.m. show)
The band spent most of their free time apart on this tour. Mike preferred to hang out with manager Duryea, while Al spent most of his time skiing with his wife Lynda. Dennis, described by Seidenbaum as "the farthest out and furthest in Beach Boy," spent time at the hotel playing gin rummy with the crew. Carl, though only 19, struck Seidenbaum as the most mature, and "the anchor on road trips around which the others can rally."

"I know that in some circles we're not regarded as all that 'hip' or 'in.' This is maybe because we haven't just arrived from nowhere with something new with a new label. But I don't care too much what anyone says, so long as I know I'm staying ahead—right up to the limit of my present capabilities. I don't put out anything I don't respect. And I know for sure that the Beach Boys brought something new into rock 'n' roll."

—Brian Wilson

Jon Stebbins Collection

within him that was so vital. His innocence . . . he knows it too." For many fans, however, the standout track was "God Only Knows," an absolutely breathtaking ballad with an otherworldly vocal by Carl Wilson, who was now revealing a vocal ability that other singers would envy.

Upon *Pet Sounds'* release, Brian declared proudly, "It's the first time that we've ever had an album that was completely produced throughout; what I mean is, every cut on it has been treated like a single." Sadly, Brian was crushed by the reaction his proudest accomplishment received at Capitol Records. As Carl later related to writer Geoffrey Himes, "Capitol didn't support *Pet Sounds*; I think they tried to talk Brian out of having it. Can you imagine that album not coming into being? It was a glorious album in our ears, but the record company gave it a real lukewarm reception. That really worried Brian; it really bothered Brian. He'd put his

THE BEACH BOYS IN CONCERT

FRIDAY, MARCH 11, 1966: Public Music Hall, Cleveland, OH, with Mickey and the Cleancuts, Noel Harrison, and the Lovin' Spoonful (8:30 p.m. show)
This was the first Beach Boys show in Cleveland since November 1964. Ironically, the town that later became the home of the Rock and Roll Hall of Fame had banned rock concerts after some violent incidents. *Cleveland Press* teen reporter Judy Prusnek noted that the group "played to a rather subdued capacity teenaged audience of madras, long hair, and flashbulbs." Prusnek managed to get a backstage interview with a visibly exhausted Dennis Wilson, who apologized for his sleepiness but told her frankly, "When you stand on your feet for 10 hours and holler, then hop a plane to the next show, you're beat. But we've grown dependent on those screams out there . . . that's why we keep going."

SATURDAY, MARCH 12, 1966: Memorial Hall, Muhlenberg College, Allentown, PA, with Noel Harrison and the Lovin' Spoonful (8:15 p.m. show)

SUNDAY, MARCH 13, 1966: Syria Mosque, Pittsburgh, PA, with Noel Harrison, the Lovin' Spoonful, Harold Betters Quartet, and the Fenways (7:30 p.m. show)

WEDNESDAY, MARCH 16, 1966: Memorial Auditorium, Canton, OH, with Noel Harrison and the Lovin' Spoonful (7:30 p.m. show)

THURSDAY, MARCH 17, 1966: Field House, University of Dayton, Dayton, OH, with Noel Harrison and the Lovin' Spoonful (8:00 p.m. show)

FRIDAY, MARCH 18, 1966: Fordham College, Bronx, NY, with Noel Harrison, the Lovin' Spoonful, and the Uncalled for Three (Two shows at 7:00 and 10:00 p.m.)
The group's first college concerts in New York were sellouts. The opening comedy act, the Uncalled for Three, were added to the bill by the William Morris Agency, but their racy performance upset the Fordham administration and they did not perform at the second show. They soon changed their name to the Pickle Brothers and were eventually signed to Brother Records, with Mike even producing a single for them. They appeared as a support act with the group at many shows.

SATURDAY, MARCH 19, 1966: 109th Armory, Wilkes-Barre, PA, with Noel Harrison and the Lovin' Spoonful
The King's College senior class sponsored this show, with the profits benefitting the Pope John XXIII Scholarship Fund. Despite a thunderstorm, the group played a well-received show. The *Wilkes-Barre Record* noted that "the five Californians, with one sporting a rust-colored beard and wearing a cap, sang and played many of their smash hits. Included were such numbers as 'Barbara Ann,' 'Help Me Rhonda,' 'Little Deuce Coupe,' 'I Get Around,' 'Papa-oom-mow-mow,' and a McCartney-Lennon favorite, sung by Dennis, 'You've Got to Hide Your Love Away.'" Dennis also grabbed attention when, with his back to the crowd, he threw one of his drumsticks over his shoulder into the seats, where it landed in a student's lap. During the concert, he flipped a tambourine behind his back into the crowd as well.

FRIDAY, APRIL 1, 1966: Memorial Auditorium, Dallas, TX, with the Lovin' Spoonful and Chad and Jeremy (8:30 p.m. show)
This was the first show of a nine-day southern tour. The entourage included Dick Duryea, Roy Hatfield, Steve Korthof, and Carl's new wife Annie.

SATURDAY, APRIL 2, 1966: Will Rogers Coliseum, Fort Worth, TX, with the Lovin' Spoonful, Chad and Jeremy, and the Elite
The U.K. duo Chad and Jeremy, who had hits with "Yesterday's Gone" and "A Summer Song," opened for the Beach Boys. Their musical director and guitarist was a young man named James William Guercio. He later recalled that his friendship with Dennis Wilson developed at this time. Guercio would become heavily involved in the management and production of the Beach Boys in the mid-1970s.

SUNDAY, APRIL 3, 1966: Music Hall, Houston, TX, with the Lovin' Spoonful and Chad and Jeremy (Two shows)

MONDAY, APRIL 4, 1966: Municipal Auditorium, San Antonio, TX, with Chad and Jeremy and the Lovin' Spoonful (7:30 p.m. show)

TUESDAY, APRIL 5, 1966: Palmer Municipal Auditorium, Austin, TX, with the Lovin' Spoonful and Chad and Jeremy (7:30 p.m. show)

WEDNESDAY, APRIL 6, 1966: Auditorium Amphitheatre, Memphis, TN, with the Lovin' Spoonful and Chad and Jeremy (8:00 p.m. show)
More than 6,300 fans attended this show.

THURSDAY, APRIL 7, 1966: Civic Auditorium, Jacksonville, FL, with Chad and Jeremy and the Lovin' Spoonful (Two shows at 7:00 and 9:30 p.m.)

FRIDAY, APRIL 8, 1966: Bayfront Center Arena, St. Petersburg, FL, with Chad and Jeremy and the Lovin' Spoonful (8:00 p.m. show)
Over 7,554 fans attended this show, which grossed about $20,000. The Beach Boys received forty percent of the gross, after taxes. Fred Wright of the *Evening Independent* noted, "They were the hit of the night, though their stage patter and off-color jokes brought laughs from only about one-third of the audience."

SATURDAY, APRIL 9, 1966: Convention Hall, Miami, FL, with the Lovin' Spoonful, the Bird-watchers, the Morlocks, and the Dedd (8:30 p.m. show)
Despite heavy rain, a full house turned out for this concert sponsored by WQAM radio. Student Sharon Trainor reported for the *Miami News* that "Mike Love was a riot. Dennis sang two songs. And Bruce Johnston, who has taken Brian Wilson's place, sang one song."

THURSDAY, APRIL 28, 1966: Duke University, Durham, NC (7:00 p.m. show)
The Beach Boys were a replacement for the Motown act the Supremes, who had backed out of the engagement at the last minute. This show was attended by 8,000 people.

FRIDAY, APRIL 29, 1966: Barton Hall, Cornell University, Ithaca, NY, with the Lost and the Uncalled for Three
The group's first appearance at Cornell was marred by the poor sound system. The microphones malfunctioned throughout the show. According to the *Daily Sun*, "It did give Mike a chance to be gross, knowing the audience couldn't hear or realize the change in lyrics to 'I Get Around.' . . . The song 'You've Got To Hide Your Love Away,' borrowed directly from the Beatles without any change in style, made Dennis Wilson standing upfront with his tambourine sound very much like P.J. Proby without the gyrations or the splitting pants."

SATURDAY, APRIL 30, 1966: Robert Hall, Boston College, Boston, MA, with the Lost and the Uncalled for Three (4:00 p.m. show) and Crane's Beach, Ipswich, MA, with Bob Newhart, Carolyn Hester, the Brandywine Singers, Noel Harrison, the Lost, the Original Sinners, the Reveliers, and the Uncalled for Three
The Beach Boys scheduled two concerts on the same day. The Crane's Beach show was part of the spring weekend festivities for the Massachusetts Institute of Technology. The group raced from their afternoon show at Boston College towards Crane's Beach, but their driver got lost. They arrived very late and were only onstage for twenty minutes before the show had to be halted due to curfew. The Beach Boys graciously agreed to play a makeup show for fans, which was hastily scheduled for May 6.

SUNDAY, MAY 1, 1966: Worcester Memorial Auditorium, Worcester, MA, with the Lost (3:00 p.m. show)
Only 1,200 fans attended this show, causing anguish for promoters, who blamed the poor turnout on scheduling. There was talk of cancelation and the show only went on, an hour late, following last-minute negotiations between Richard Duryea and the promoter. Jack Tubert of the *Worcester Telegram* captured the backstage scene: "Dennis the drummer sat in a rehearsal hall toying with the

heart and soul on the line."
Pet Sounds managed to reach a respectable number ten on the *Billboard* LP charts, and generated three hit singles, but it was considered a commercial disappointment. Nevertheless, Brian always remained proud of *Pet Sounds*. In a 1970 radio interview, he stated, "I think we brought a new bag to the Beach Boys with *Pet Sounds*. In fact we brought a new synthesis bag to the industry. I believe it brought a little more thought and care into the album process. It's by far our best album."

In the midst of recording *Pet Sounds*, Brian began composing a new tune called "Good Vibrations." Brian developed a new process of recording, which he'd also use on the next Beach Boys album. Rather than create a single instrumental backing track at one session, he would create short, seemingly unrelated, snatches of music and then piece them together like a puzzle. Brian recorded sections of the "Good Vibrations" track at multiple studios. He believed each studio had a unique sound that added something special to the record. Capitol Records questioned Brian over the mounting production costs. But Brian doubled down, bringing electro-theremin, tack piano, bass harmonica, and his favorite touch, a cello, into the single's mix. He later boasted to writer David Felton that "It was the first utilization of a cello in rock 'n' roll music to that extent—using it as an upfront instrument, as a rock instrument."

When the time came to add vocals, Brian showed the same determination to achieve perfection that he had displayed during the recording of *Pet Sounds'* instrumental tracks. Mike recalled that "on one passage of one little thing on "Good Vibrations," we did it over and over and over . . . and not only was it because to get the note, we wanted the notes right, but the timbre and quality of each note, and how the four parts would resonate together." According to Carl, "'Good Vibrations' had a lot of texture on it, because we did so many overdubs. We'd double or triple or quadruple the exact same part, so it would sound like 20 voices." No one could argue with the results. The record was released as a single on October 10, 1966, and became an international number one hit, the biggest success of the Beach Boys' career to date.

The group toured Europe, where they were scheduled to debut at the Paris Olympia on October 25, before heading to Germany, Austria, and Sweden. The real focus of the trip, however, was the U.K., where the Beach Boys' popularity was peaking. Bruce Johnston flew there in May to preview the *Pet Sounds* LP for the music world's movers and shakers, including Lennon and McCartney. In addition, publicist Derek Taylor made sure to keep the British music magazines full of stories about the Beach Boys. When the Beach Boys arrived in London, they encountered a scene resembling Beatlemania. Over a thousand fans, reporters, and press photographers were at the airport to greet them. On top of that, filmmaker Peter Whitehead filmed their arrival for the TV show *Top of*

keys of a piano. Carl sat with a girl and his electric guitar. Al Jardine, the married one, sat in a corner fiddling with his guitar, ignoring hellos. Love moped about, looking like Gauguin with ears, behind his full red beard. Brian was not present, although the youngsters who paid to get in did not know the 'Chairman of the Board' was not to appear."

MONDAY, MAY 2, 1966: Mayser Gym, Franklin and Marshall College, Lancaster, PA (8:00 p.m. show)
According to a student who attended this show, the Beach Boys had a clause in their contract requiring the school to have televisions available so they could take a break during the concert to catch their appearance on *The Andy Williams Show*, which aired on this night (it had been filmed the previous October).

WEDNESDAY, MAY 4, 1966: Catholic Youth Center, Scranton, PA (Canceled)
The Beach Boys traveled to Scranton for this concert, but never actually played. Instead, they remained ensconced at their hotel. Road manager Dick Duryea explained to *Variety* that the promoter had promised to supply twenty police officers, but that only five were at the venue when he went to check. "We simply could not let the boys go on stage without proper policing." The promoter was understandably furious and later sued the group and their management.

THURSDAY, MAY 5, 1966: Bushnell Memorial, Hartford, CT, with the Lost and the Barry Goldberg Blues Band (8:15 p.m. show)

FRIDAY, MAY 6, 1966: Rockwell Cage, Massachusetts Institute of Technology, Cambridge, MA (4:00 p.m. show), and Four Seasons Arena, Walpole, MA
The MIT concert was a makeup show for fans that had to leave early during the group's April 30 appearance at Crane's Beach. Following the afternoon concert, the Beach Boys headed to Walpole for another show that night.

SATURDAY, MAY 7, 1966: Providence College, Providence, RI, with the Lost and the Uncalled for Three (8:00 p.m. show)
The Beach Boys' performance at this college was marred by problems with the sound system. Rock 'n' roll concerts were a new world for academic institutions and required better PA systems and microphones than they were used to. Most of these shows were played in gyms and auditoriums with bad acoustics. College newspaper reviewers into the 1970s frequently mentioned sound system problems.

SUNDAY, MAY 8, 1966: Nassau Community College, Garden City, NY, with the Lost, the Uncalled for Three, and the Belvederes (2 p.m. show)
Almost 4,000 people attended this outdoor show. According to *The Vignette*, "The Beach Boys set up quickly and went right into their first song, 'Fun, Fun, Fun.' The audience was lively as they went through twenty songs. These included such Beach Boys hits as 'Help Me Rhonda' and 'Surfin';' songs made popular by other groups ('You've Got to Hide Your Love Away') and comedy ('What a Day for a Rainstorm'). The last song was a riff on the Lovin' Spoonful's song "Daydream."

WEDNESDAY, MAY 11, 1966: Ball State University, Muncie, IN, with the Caravans and the Sir Douglas Quintet (8:00 p.m. show)
The group performed in the round at the Men's Gym at Ball State. Bonnie Williams of the *Muncie Evening Press* reported, "Mike Love proved to be a capable, likable emcee, with a sense of humor . . . The performance was interspersed with laughter: Dennis complained of having a dry throat, so he was brought a soothing drink, and once, when they were unable to get the speakers to work, their 'sound man' came on stage to discover that the speakers were only unplugged."

THURSDAY, MAY 12, 1966: Lansing Civic Center, Lansing, MI, with Sam the Sham and the Pharaohs
Over 5,000 fans attended the group's first appearance in Lansing.

FRIDAY, MAY 13, 1966: Memorial Coliseum, Fort Wayne, IN

SATURDAY, MAY 14, 1966: Milwaukee Arena, Milwaukee, WI, with the Chieftones and the Sir Douglas Quintet (8:00 p.m. show)
The Beach Boys performed in gray and white striped shirts before an audience of 5,000 teenagers. Peggy Murrells of the *Milwaukee Journal* reported, "The Boys put their young audience in a receptive mood with several of their more recent hits—'Sloop John B,' 'Barbara Ann,' and 'California Girls.' Brian Wilson, the group's original bass guitarist, was not present . . . His replacement was Bruce Johnston, an impishly handsome redhead, whom Love presented to the audience about midway through the performance. They then proceeded to provoke a bit of pandemonium with a series of old favorites such as 'Fun, Fun, Fun,' 'Surfin' USA,' 'Little Old Lady from Pasadena,' and 'Papa-Oom-Mow-Mow.' 'I Get Around,' and 'Do You Wanna Dance' concluded the performance and got the biggest ovations."

SUNDAY, MAY 15, 1966: Memorial Stadium, Terre Haute, IN, with the Sir Douglas Quintet (7:00 p.m. show)

TUESDAY, JUNE 7, 1966: Greenville Memorial Coliseum, Greenville, SC, with Harry Deal and the Galaxies (8:00 p.m. show)

WEDNESDAY, JUNE 8, 1966: Civic Coliseum, Knoxville, with the Plesbians, the Krustations, the Echoes, and King Kent (8:00 p.m. show)

FRIDAY, JUNE 10, 1966: "Sound Blast 66," Yankee Stadium, Bronx, NY, with Stevie Wonder, Ray Charles, the McCoys, the Cowsills, Jerry Butler, the Guess Who, the Byrds, and the Marvelettes (7:30 p.m. show)
Although Yankee Stadium had a concert seating capacity of 75,000 people, only 9,000 attended this show due to heavy rain. Joe Cohen of *Variety* theorized that teens might also have been saving their money for the upcoming Beatles show at Shea Stadium.

SATURDAY, JUNE 11, 1966: New Haven Arena, CT (8:30 p.m. show)

FRIDAY, JUNE 24, 1966: "Summer Spectacular" at the Cow Palace, San Francisco, CA, with the Lovin' Spoonful, Chad and Jeremy, Percy Sledge, the Outsiders, the Leaves, the Sir Douglas Quintet, the Sunrays, Neil Diamond, the Byrds, and the Jefferson Airplane (8:00 p.m. show)
Irving Granz and his assistant Jack Lloyd produced this event, attended by 15,000 fans. Murry Wilson was in attendance to support his new protégés the Sunrays and begged Lloyd to give the band a prime spot on the bill. Lloyd informed him that he would have to go and ask the Beach Boys, who apparently consented. According to the *Oakland Tribune*, "The combination of screams and over-amplified guitars" made it impossible to hear much of the performers.

SATURDAY, JUNE 25, 1966: "Summer Spectacular," Hollywood Bowl, Los Angeles, CA, with Love, Percy Sledge, Captain Beefheart, the Outsiders, Neil Diamond, the Leaves, Chad and Jeremy, the Byrds, the Lovin' Spoonful, and the New Motown Sound.
Irving Granz produced this concert. He paid $9,000 to rent the venue and charged an average of $4.00 for each of the roughly 17,000 seats, grossing about $68,000 in ticket sales. Of this then princely sum, the Beach Boys only received $4,000, while a number of the other acts made less than $1000. Although Brian had played with the group at the Bowl the previous year, he did not come out of retirement for this appearance. However, he attended the show and was photographed backstage for *KRLA Beat*. It was probably just as well that he didn't play, since according to Charles Champlin of the *Los Angeles Times*, "the vocals were completely lost in a distorted blah of rhythm guitars and percussion."

FRIDAY, JULY 1, 1966: Convention Center, Las Vegas, NV, with the Association and the Sir Douglas Quintet (8:30 p.m. show)

SATURDAY, JULY 2, 1966: County Bowl, Santa Barbara, CA, with the Association and the Sir Douglas Quintet (8:30 p.m. show)

the Pops (Whitehead ultimately used the footage to make a documentary narrated by Marianne Faithful). The Beach Boys' 1966 U.K. visit was, quite simply, the event of the year.

> "I think we brought a new bag to the Beach Boys with *Pet Sounds*. In fact we brought a new synthesis bag to the industry. I believe it brought a little more thought and care into the album process. It's by far our best album."
>
> **—Brian Wilson**

The group found being thrust into the role of pop messiahs exciting, but also difficult to live up to. The publicity barrage created a huge audience eagerly awaiting their U.K. shows, and the growing "hype" created a potential backlash. Many critics seemed more eager to pounce on them for not being able to reproduce the sounds of their records than to enjoy their performance. Some took it a step further suggesting that the real talent of the group was at home in California and that the others were a hollow shell without him. Alan Walsh asked in *Melody Maker*: "Are the five touring Beach Boys merely puppets of sound genius Brian Wilson? The question is prompted by the vast blast of publicity, which has proclaimed Wilson as the architect of the Beach Boys' recorded sound. Are they just the instruments which BW uses to paint his pop pictures in sound?" Carl defended the group from such attacks, declaring "No, we are not just Brian's puppets . . . Brian plays the major creative role in the production of our music, but everyone in the group contributes something to the finished product. It's not like an orchestra translating the wishes of the conductor. We all have a part to play in the production of the records." He also sought to quash any unrealistic expectations for the stage show right away. He told writer David Griffiths: "Of course we can't reproduce the full effect of our records on stage. We just try to get the best sound we can, in the circumstances. People who come to hear us will hear an honest effort, that's all." The vast majority of U.K. reviewers praised the group and audiences enthusiastically received the shows. Although the Beach Boys had no way of knowing it, this tour was probably the absolute peak of their career. They returned to the U.S. eager to gush to Brian

SUNDAY, JULY 3, 1966: Memorial Auditorium, Fresno, CA, with the Association and the Sir Douglas Quintet (8:15 p.m. show)
The set list for this concert included "Fun, Fun, Fun," "Shutdown," "Surfin' USA," "California Girls," "Papa-Oom-Mow-Mow," and "Little Old Lady from Pasadena." According to Spencer Mastick of The *Fresno* , Dennis stole the show as far as the fans were concerned. "'Surfer Girl' was allowed to be heard with a dreamy beat and warm, quiet harmonies, until drummer Dennis Wilson began a solo. At this point, the screaming was about as loud as human ears can stand. Dennis again turned on the crowd again with 'Do You Wanna Dance.' 'Papa-Ooom-Mow-Mow' was thumping good rhythmically but seemed rather meaningless musically . . . The program included another Dennis solo in the glare of the blue spotlight and flashbulbs. The closing tune was 'Hide Your Love Away,' an old Beatles song."

MONDAY, JULY 4, 1966: Community Concourse Arena, San Diego, CA, with the Association and the Sir Douglas Quintet (8:00 p.m. show)
Steve Vivona of the *San Diego Evening Tribune* criticized the group for their conservative set list. *Pet Sounds* had been released months earlier, but they only played one song ("Sloop John B") from it. Vivona noted, "Instead it was a rehash of their 'golden goodies'—'Little Deuce Coupe,' 'Hawaii,' 'Barbara Ann,' and a half dozen others, all performed in a listless manner . . . "

SATURDAY, JULY 16, TO MONDAY, JULY 18, 1966: Arie Crown Theater, Chicago, IL, with the Chieftones and Yesterday's Children (One show on Saturday at 8:30 p.m., one show on Sunday, and one show on Monday at 7:30 p.m.)
Attesting to their great popularity, the group sold out all three of these shows.

THURSDAY, JULY 21, 1966: Memorial Auditorium, Buffalo, NY, with the Lovin' Spoonful, the Rogues, and Stan and the Ravens (8:00 p.m. show)
The Beach Boys played before 7,000 fans at the Memorial Auditorium.

FRIDAY, JULY 22, 1966: War Memorial Auditorium, Syracuse, NY, with Carmen and the Vikings and the Monterays (8:30 p.m. show)
About 4,500 fans attended this show. Peter Bell of the *Syracuse Herald Journal* reported, "Sparked by the constant mimicry of bearded and bereted Mike Love, the famous five were most impressive not for their songs, which sound as good on records, but for their stage professionalism and the heroic efforts of drummer Denny Wilson . . . With their seven guitars and Wilson in his own world . . . on the drums, the Beach Boys pounded an admiring audience with the staples ('Little Old Lady from Pasadena,' 'California Girls,' etc.) and left them swinging in their seats."

SATURDAY, JULY 23, 1966: Convention Hall, Asbury Park, NJ (Two shows at 7:30 and 9:45 p.m.)

SUNDAY, JULY 24, 1966: Iona College, New Rochelle, NY, with Chain Reaction (8:30 p.m.)
A local group called Chain Reaction opened this show. Their vocalist, Steven Tallarico, later became Steven Tyler of Aerosmith fame. They'd won a "battle of the bands" contest, allowing a local group the privilege of opening for the Beach Boys.

THURSDAY, JULY 28, 1966: Boys Club, Pittsfield, MA, with the Ruins (8:30 p.m. show)
The Beach Boys, dressed in red and white striped shirts and white jeans, took the stage at 9:50 p.m., forty-five minutes after the local opening act the Ruins finished their set. The delay was caused by technical difficulties with the equipment. Pat Francis of the *Berkshire Eagle* commented that despite the delays, the audience seemed to enjoy themselves, though some were disappointed at the shortness of the Beach Boys' set, which clocked in at a brisk forty-five minutes. Francis noted that the group played all their hits but that his own favorite song performed was "God Only Knows," which the group announced that they were playing for the first time ever onstage. "While the boys sang it, there wasn't one sound in the auditorium. In fact during most of the concert there wasn't much noise. Screams from the girls came mostly when Mike announced what song they would sing next . . . His

Performing in Pittsfield, Massachusetts, on July 28, 1966. Photo: Russ Bodnar

between-songs patter is enough to make you hope that the group members are all related, as the stories say, some of his jokes could only be buffeted between family."

FRIDAY, JULY 29, 1966: Virginia Beach High School Stadium, Virginia Beach, VA, with the Wild Kingdom and Bill Deal and the Rhondels
The 6,500 fans attending this concert experienced a 30-minute delay due to issues with the sound system, which the Beach Boys were renting for $1000 a day.

SATURDAY, JULY 30, 1966: Atlantic City Convention Hall, Atlantic City, NJ (9:00 p.m. show)
This was the final show of the tour and the group returned to California on Sunday.

TUESDAY, AUGUST 9, 1966: Auditorium Arena, Denver, CO, with the Benze Cyrque, the Moonrakers, King Louie and the Laymen, and the Astronauts
The air traffic controllers' strike in California led to problems with commercial airlines, so the Beach Boys chartered a DC-3 owned by racecar driver Carroll Shelby. Shelby had recently befriended Dennis, who owned one of his Shelby Cobra roadsters. The group enjoyed the experience so much that they seldom used anything but chartered airlines on future tours.

In Denver, the group performed before 6,000 fans. Thomas MacCluskey of the *Rocky Mountain News* reported, "The Beach Boys shone in their ballads, both musically and performance-wise. In nearly all their tunes, the harmonic progressions are interesting. Also, their sound is unique among the rock groups due to their use of four-part vocal harmony." However, he complained that the "spokesman, Mike Love, was quite unfunny."

WEDNESDAY, AUGUST 10, 1966: Civic Auditorium Arena, Omaha, NE
The group played a brief set of twelve songs for 6,856 people in Omaha.

THURSDAY, AUGUST 11, 1966: Memorial Auditorium, Fargo, ND, with the Uglies and the Little People (8:30 p.m. show)
The Beach Boys were greeted upon their arrival in Fargo by over 1,500 fans gathered at Hector airport. Later that night, they played for 4,500 fans. The set list consisted of "Do You Wanna Dance," "Help Me Rhonda," "Surfer Girl," "Surfin' USA," "God Only Knows," "Wouldn't It Be Nice," "Barbara

about the trip and to inform him about the Rolls Royce that they were having shipped to him.

Meanwhile, Brian was immersed in the next Beach Boys album, which he titled *Smile*. Brian was determined to make an even grander artistic statement and he wanted the lyrics to match the music. As Brian stated at the time in *KRLA Beat*, "Popular music . . . has to expand and has to gain more widespread respect as a result of someone making an art out of that kind of music." He was aware that many people in the industry still didn't take him seriously. Writer Jules Siegel related, "Among the hip people he was still on trial, and the question discussed earnestly among the recognized authorities on what is and what is not hip, was whether or not Brian Wilson was hip, semi-hip, or square." Brian understood what was at stake and was determined to show everyone in the industry that the Beach Boys were very definitely not square. The collaborator he chose was one of the more eclectic figures in the Los Angeles music scene, Van Dyke Parks. Parks was a southerner with an eccentric sensibility who had moved to Los Angeles to be a child actor. By the 1960s he was writing songs for other acts and doing session work. Brian met him one night at a party and was struck by his fantastic way with words. By late summer the two were meeting at Brian's house to compose songs at the piano he'd placed in a sandbox. The collaboration immediately produced a number of tunes, including "Wonderful," "Heroes and Villains," and

THE BEACH BOYS IN CONCERT

"Surf's Up." The songs that Brian and Van Dyke wrote were dramatic, poetic, and complex. Brian believed that this new music would transform the pop music world.

It was a period of incredible creativity for Brian.

"They announced that the show was being recorded for a live album and we should all cheer enthusiastically. When Brian came out at the end for a curtain call, it was absolutely surreal . . . A great, great memory."

He believed that this creativity was aided by experimentation with drugs. Beginning in 1965, he'd been regularly smoking marijuana and late that year his friend Loren Schwartz introduced him to LSD. Brian explained to writer Tom Nolan in the fall of 1966, "About a

Ann," "California Girls," "I Get Around," "Little Deuce Coupe," "Sloop John B," "You're So Good to Me," and "You've Got to Hide Your Love Away."

FRIDAY, AUGUST 12, 1966: Illinois State Fair, Springfield, IL, with Sam the Sham and the Pharaohs (8:00 p.m. show)
The group played to a huge audience of over 21,000 people. Unfortunately, the Fair hired just six policemen to handle security, and chaos reigned. Promoter Jack Lloyd recalled that Mike, Bruce, and Carl flew to Chicago after this show to meet up with the Beatles, who were starting their last American tour there. They rejoined the tour in Duluth the next day.

SATURDAY, AUGUST 13, 1966: Duluth Arena, Duluth, MN
This show, at the new Duluth Arena, was attended by 7,189 fans. Jack Lloyd noted that after this concert he took the Beach Boys to eat at a restaurant with live music and a dance floor. The musicians were just about to pack up their gear when Dennis, Bruce, and Carl asked if they could jam a bit. For the next hour or so, patrons at the eatery were treated to an impromptu show.

SUNDAY, AUGUST 14, 1966: Fort William Gardens, Thunder Bay, Ontario, Canada, with the Bonnvilles and Bobby Kris and the Imperials (8:00 p.m. show)
Although Thunder Bay promoters had tried to book the Beach Boys in 1965, this show marked the group's first and only appearance in the area until the 1980s. The 3,000 fans that attended were extremely enthusiastic. The Finnish-language *Canadan Uutiset* reported, "When the Beach Boys stepped onto the stage they received a tremendous ovation. The audience was excited and teenagers were screaming . . . when 'Help Me Rhonda' blasted, nobody would stay still. The young audience were stomping their feet and clapping their hands to the rhythm of the music . . . The Beach Boys' faces were gleaming and they looked like they enjoyed performing their songs that created such ecstasy."

Prior to the show, Bruce spoke to a fan named Liisa, who worked for a local paper catering to the Finnish community in Thunder Bay. One amusing exchange came when the reporter asked Bruce to respond to John Lennon's controversial comments that "the Beatles were bigger than Jesus." Bruce answered, "The Beatles said it that way. We say this . . . we are not as well known as even Moses."

MONDAY, AUGUST 15, 1966: Municipal Auditorium, Minot, ND, with Chad and Jeremy, the Sunrays, and the Embermen Five (8:00 p.m. show)

TUESDAY, AUGUST 16, 1966: Stampede Corral, Calgary, AB, Canada, with Chad and Jeremy and the Sunrays (8:15 p.m. show)
Carl's wife Annie traveled with the group on this tour. Carl explained to *Tiger Beat*, "Having a girl in our dressing room raises the whole level of the atmosphere. Backstage conversations are such a bore. But when Annie's there, it's always nicer."

WEDNESDAY, AUGUST 17, 1966: Memorial Arena, Victoria, BC, Canada, with Chad and Jeremy and the Sunrays
This show was attended by 4,044 fans. Bob Donahue of the *Victoria Daily Times* called the group "difficult to appreciate because their sounds were largely unintelligible and their voices weak."

THURSDAY, AUGUST 18, 1966: Queen Elizabeth Theatre, Vancouver, BC, Canada, with Chad and Jeremy and the Sunrays (Two Shows at 6:00 and 8:30 p.m.)
Jack Lloyd recalled that this Vancouver date was memorable for him because "the money from all the tour book sales was stolen from my briefcase, which I had placed in the manager's office for safe keeping."

FRIDAY, AUGUST 19, 1966: Spokane Coliseum, Spokane, WA, with Chad and Jeremy and the Sunrays (8:30 p.m. show)
About 5,000 fans attended this sold-out show.

88

SATURDAY, AUGUST 20, 1966: Memorial Coliseum, Portland, OR, with the Tempests, the Live Five, and the Tweedy Brothers
Dressed in red and white striped shirts, the Beach Boy played before 5,500 screaming fans.

FRIDAY, SEPTEMBER 9, AND SATURDAY, SEPTEMBER 10, 1966: Lagoon, Farmington, UT (One show at 9:00 p.m. on Friday and one show at 7:00 p.m. on Saturday)

THURSDAY, SEPTEMBER 29, 1966: Tully Gym, Florida State University, Tallahassee, FL (8:00 p.m. show)
The Beach Boys performed before an estimated 4,000 people. Prior to the show, the group gave an interview to Ronnie Stock of the *Tallahassee Democrat*. Asked about the strain of touring, Dennis replied, "It gets tiring, but this is the first time we've ever come to Tallahassee . . . and we're enjoying it." Responding to a comment from Bruce that teenagers needed a good education, Carl replied, "An education though . . . is not all received from books alone. We have learned a lot working with hundreds of people throughout the years. This kind of education, how to work with people, how to handle people—personal contact—has helped us learn a lot about people themselves." When asked about the future, Bruce optimistically referred to *Smile*, "We have another album coming . . . it should be ready in December."

FRIDAY, SEPTEMBER 30, 1966: Alabama State Coliseum, Montgomery, AL, with Peter and Gordon, Lou Christie, the Happenings, the Hollies, Ian Whitcomb, the Count Five, and the Rocking Gibraltars (8:00 p.m. show)

SATURDAY, OCTOBER 1, 1966: "WVOK Fall Shower of Stars," Municipal Auditorium, Birmingham, AL, with Peter and Gordon, Lou Christie, the Happenings, the Hollies, Ian Whitcomb, and the Count Five (Three shows at 2:00, 6:00, and 9:00 p.m.)
Gene Butts of the *Birmingham News* reported that despite the impressive roster of stars, "it was the Beach Boys whom everyone had come to hear, and they obliged in high style with their repertoire of past and present hits. With this group the sound, not the song, is what really counts with their fans. In a way it's a pity. Much of the words and music of their original compositions are very good. Their fame, however, rests on their 'Surfing sound.'"

Following these shows, the Beach Boys flew to L.A. to participate in vocal sessions for *Smile*. They also made a promo film for the soon-to-be released single "Good Vibrations." Brian directed the clip, which depicted group members sleeping in a fire station and hastily waking, getting dressed, sliding down a pole, and jumping in a fire truck. In addition, they were seen harmonizing with a shirtless Brian on the street. The band also taped a TV appearance on the syndicated show *Boss City*, hosted by DJ Sam Riddle, to premiere "Good Vibrations." It aired while the band was in Europe, but was taped at some point in mid-October. The Turtles also appeared on the show.

FRIDAY, OCTOBER 21, 1966: Jenison Field House, Michigan State University, Lansing, MI (8:00 p.m. show)
With "Good Vibrations" ready for release, the Beach Boys felt quite confident as they stopped in Michigan for the first of three warmup concerts before flying on to Europe for their second tour. There was, however, some controversy at this show. Some students picketed outside the venue because the group "undermined the cultural advancement of America." Mike made fun of the protesters the following night in Ann Arbor, declaring "Right! We don't even know how to spell that!"

SATURDAY, OCTOBER 22, 1966: Hill Auditorium, University of Michigan, Ann Arbor, MI, with the Standells (Two shows at 6:00 and 8:00 p.m.)
The Beach Boys chose these shows to debut "Good Vibrations." Brian flew to Michigan, with friend Michael Vosse, to record the shows for a possible live album. Photographs exist of him rehearsing the band. Mike Love was especially nervous because he was given the task of playing the electro-theremin necessary to recreate the sound of the single. The set list for the first show consisted of "Help Me Rhonda," "I Get Around," "Surfin Safari/Fun Fun Fun/Shut Down/Little Deuce Coupe/

year ago I had what I consider a very religious experience. I took LSD, a full dose of LSD, and later another time, I took a smaller dose. And I learned a lot of things, like patience, understanding. I can't teach you, or tell you, what I learned from taking it. But I consider it a very religious experience." Whether or not LSD was responsible for the increasingly complex compositions that Brian was creating, observers agreed that he was at the peak of his powers. The phrase "Brian is a genius" was becoming commonplace. Beach Boys publicist Derek Taylor introduced the slogan via the press. According to Taylor, "Brian told me that he thought he was better than most other people believed him to be . . . Then I thought, 'Well if that's so, why doesn't anyone outside think so?' Then I started putting it around, making almost a campaign out of it." The buzz caught the attention of the *Saturday Evening Post* editors, who commissioned Jules Siegel to write about Brian. CBS television chose to focus on Brian in an upcoming documentary called *Inside Pop*, which would be hosted by composer Leonard Bernstein. They all seemed to believe something special was happening in Southern California.

Some of Brian's friends were wary. When the Beach Boys returned to L.A. in late November, Brian played them the in-progress *Smile* tracks. Tension arose between Mike Love and Van Dyke Parks. Mike prided himself on writing lyrics that the group's young audience could relate to. He believed that many fans would have trouble understanding the abstract themes in Parks' lyrics. He interrogated Parks about the meaning of certain songs. Mike told Ken Sharp in 1992, "I thought his lyrics were alliterate prose, which is great if you appreciated his prose and his alliteration. He's brilliant. But as far as translating to mid-American commercial appeal, I don't think so." Sessions became progressively more fraught and Brian seemed to lose both his confidence and his ability to know when tracks were finished. Capitol expected delivery of the LP in January 1967, but it became clear Brian needed more time.

Despite the misgivings certain Beach Boys had regarding *Smile*, the group still had faith in Brian. He had never failed them and signs of his genius were all around. Not only did they have the number one single in the U.S. and the U.K. with "Good Vibrations," but that December the *New Musical Express* reader's poll voted the Beach Boys the number one group in the world, ahead of the Beatles. A stunned Al Jardine had to sit down when he heard the news, while Bruce Johnston wandered around in a daze mumbling, "Wow! I just can't believe we're that popular." It seemed as though things could only get better in 1967, but in truth the Beach Boys had reached their peak and a decline was imminent.

Surfin' USA" (medley), "Surfer Girl," "Papa-Oom-Mow-Mow," "You're So Good to Me," "You've Got to Hide Your Love Away" (sung by Dennis), "California Girls," "Sloop John B," "Wouldn't It Be Nice," "God Only Knows," "Good Vibrations," "Graduation Day," and "Barbara Ann." The second show was basically the same, but with one surprise twist. According to local fan Bill Freedman, "They announced that the show was being recorded for a live album and we should all cheer enthusiastically. When Brian came out at the end for a curtain call, it was absolutely surreal . . . A great, great memory." Brian was dragged onstage and strapped on a bass for the encore of "Johnny B. Goode."

Following the concert, Brian grabbed a plane back to L.A., where he arranged to have a group of friends, including Danny Hutton, Dean Torrence, and Van Dyke Parks, meet him at the airport to pose for a famous photograph. It is reproduced in the booklet that accompanies the 2011 release *The Smile Sessions*.

TUESDAY, OCTOBER 25, 1966: Paris Olympia, Paris, France, with Michel Polnareff, Casey Jones, and the Coco Briavel Quartet (8:00 p.m. show)
The group arrived in Paris on October 24 to begin their second visit to Europe. They spent Monday sightseeing, despite freezing weather, before performing a sold-out show the next day at the Olympia. Surprisingly, the group allowed Murry Wilson to accompany them. When the Beach Boys skipped a 6:30 p.m. rehearsal and photo op, it was Murry who entertained the assembled media. Many of the journalists were from the U.K., where "Good Vibrations" was a current smash and the Beach Boys' popularity was peaking.

Disc and Music Echo dispatched writer Wendy Varnals to Paris to get a peek at the group before their imminent U.K. arrival. She wrote, "I have no doubt that many bets were being made to see whether the Beach Boys can reproduce onstage their highly complicated but knockout new release, the product of many months in the recording studio in Los Angeles. I think they can—very successfully. It is their vocal strength that is The Beach Boys. Onstage they have no act. Mike Love does a little clowning around when he introduces the numbers, but on the whole it's just a case of standing up and singing—beautifully." Loekie de Bruin reviewed the Olympia concert in *Hitweek*: "during the complex, more recent hits, Brian's absence was more noticeable. Bruce can't replace that fantastic talent. 'God Only Knows' and 'Good Vibrations' were both very good, but still . . . it did not appear totally clearly, even though Mike Love used that electronic device, the theremin. But then again, one can always hear those songs on the turntable. For the rest the boys were fantastic." The next day the Beach Boys taped two French television appearances, before traveling to Germany.

THURSDAY, OCTOBER 27, 1966: Friedrich Ebert-Halle, Ludwigshafen, West Germany, with Peter and Gordon, Graham Bonney, Ambros Seelos, and the Lords
Although the group visited Germany in 1964 to make promotional appearances, this was their first concert in the country. Mike told Keith Altham, "Germany was fantastic. They really believe in security precautions out there. When we arrived at the airport there were about 300 police to meet us—we just walked into the lobby threw up our hands and surrendered! The people were real nice."

FRIDAY, OCTOBER 28, 1966: Ernst Merck Halle, Hamburg, West Germany, with Peter and Gordon, Graham Bonney, the Lords, and the Beat-Hoven (Two shows at 5:30 and 9:00 p.m.)
Hamburg fans stormed a train transporting the Beach Boys from Frankfurt and had to be dispersed by the police. As a result of the wildness of the teenagers, over 500 German police surrounded the stage during the concert. The group performed in matching checkered shirts. After years of playing to audiences composed mainly of screaming teenage girls, the predominantly male audiences they attracted at these German shows surprised the group.

SATURDAY, OCTOBER 29, 1966: Gruga-Halle, Essen, West Germany, with Peter and Gordon, Graham Bonney, the Lords, and Ambros Seelos
Over 9,000 enthusiastic fans attended this show. German security police were out in force and a number of fans that tried to rush the stage were ejected. According to the *Munsterischer*

Stadtanzeiger, "the high spirits were systematically dampened by the watchful security men. As soon as it became too lively in one corner, security led the colorfully dressed Beat-boys and Beat-girls out of the hall. Only a handful of fanatics managed to get to the stage and get an autograph."

Opening act Graham Bonney became friendly with the group and penned a short article about them for the German magazine *Bravo*. The Beach Boys informed him that while they were on tour, their wives were staying together at one house in L.A. for companionship. Bonney noted that Carl was so devoted to new wife Annie Hinsche that while in Germany he rang up expensive phone bills calling her. "In Essen he talked with his Annie for more than an hour. This happened every evening. During the day he belonged to the fans. In the evening he was only thinking of Annie." Bonney noted Dennis was completely the opposite of his brother and never spoke with his wife Carol. Dennis commented that it wasn't necessary because, "she knows me and I know her."

SUNDAY, OCTOBER 30, 1966: Halle Munsterland, Munster, West Germany, with Peter and Gordon, Graham Bonney, the Lords, and Ambros Seeelos (Two shows at 3:00 and 7:00 p.m.)
The Beach Boys played two capacity shows in Munster. Afterwards, the tour group boarded an overnight train through the picturesque snow-covered Alps to Austria. Peter Asher of Peter and Gordon remarked, "The Beach Boys were knocked out. They didn't go mad like tourists, but the scene was like one huge Christmas card and they just couldn't resist taking pictures."

MONDAY, OCTOBER 31, 1966: Stadthalle, Vienna, Austria, with Peter and Gordon, Graham Bonney, the Lords, and Ambros Seelos (Two shows)
The *Arbeiter Zeitung* reported that the afternoon show attracted just 3,000 fans, but the evening show was a sellout and police had to patrol the venue to prevent riots. Bruce Johnston commented on the loudness of the Vienna fans to writer Alan Freeman: "It seems crazy that when they come into the hall they make so much noise that they can't hear what they've paid to listen to."

TUESDAY, NOVEMBER 1, 1966: Circus Krone, Munich, Germany, with Peter and Gordon, Graham Bonney, the Lords, and Ambros Seelos

---

THURSDAY, NOVEMBER 3, 1966: Falkoner Centret, Torsdagm, Denmark, with the Red Squares, the Defenders, and the Scarlets (Two shows at 7:00 and 10:00 p.m.)
The group visited Denmark in 1964 to sightsee, but these were the first Beach Boys concerts there. The *Berlingske Tidende* noted that the audience "began humming along with the known songs; and the (security) guards themselves, standing in great numbers along the sides of the hall, were seen swinging along. The Beach Boys' repertoire was known numbers, which it felt good to hear from the creators themselves. It was an opportunity to once again note that the group really is musical and well sounding, which has made them the American answer to the Beatles."

FRIDAY, NOVEMBER 4, 1966: Koncerthuset, Stockholm, Sweden, with the Red Squares and the Swede Singers (Two shows at 7:00 and 9:30 p.m.)
This was the Beach Boys' second appearance at this venue, where they had played in 1964. The audience at the 7:00 p.m. show was reportedly disappointed by the band's inability to duplicate their recorded sound live, but the *Svenska Dagbladet* argued that the Beach Boys "made a much more powerful and playful impression than the records which often fascinate just by being so artificial and clean . . . With Brian Wilson a safe distance away one almost got the impression that the other Beach Boys decided to live a little and take a somewhat easier and fresher approach to it all."

SATURDAY, NOVEMBER 5, 1966: Konserthallen, Liseberg, Gothenberg, Sweden (Two shows at 6:00 and 9:00 p.m.)

SUNDAY, NOVEMBER 6, 1966: Finsbury Park Astoria, London, England, with Lulu, David and Jonathan, Sounds Incorporated, the Golden Brass, and Jerry Stevens (Two Shows at 6:00 and 8:30 p.m.)

Onstage at the Circus Krone in Munich on November 1, 1966.
Photo: Gene Oppermann

The Beach Boys were aware that the stakes were high for the first U.K. show of the tour. Bruce Johnston turned up at the Astoria gig wearing a heavy overcoat and scarf to prevent catching a cold. He told Keith Altham of *New Musical Express* that he was "worried about my throat. My voice is almost clapped out. I've done so much singing on this tour and I've got a sore throat. We're very conscious of the fact that people are expecting a lot from us and I couldn't bear to be the one who let them down." Adding to the pressure were many celebrities who attended, including Beatles manager Brian Epstein, TV host Cathy McGowan, and pop singer John Walker, who in earlier days had been Carl and David's guitar teacher.

The group's English trial by fire was a success with most fans and critics. *Record Mirror* stated "It's unlikely anyone who goes to see the Beach Boys will be disappointed with their stage sound . . . If there was any complex backing sound lost, it was more than made up for by excitement and a professional stage presence, especially by Mike Love. Surprisingly enough the group excelled on what one might think would be the hardest sounds to reproduce. 'Good Vibrations' was sensational, and so was Carl's atmospheric 'God Only Knows.'" Chris Welch declared in *Melody Maker*, "Any doubts about the Beach Boys' ability on stage were completely dispelled and all those who have said 'the Beach Boys are no good live, only on record' had better keep quiet from now on." Only Ray Coleman, of *Disc and Music Echo*, sounded a slightly sour note. "They just about made it. Carl Wilson's sweet voice braved 'God Only Knows,' and it sounded pretty authentic. 'Good Vibrations' was less successful. But then, nobody expected them to sound as good 'live' as on record. And this was where they fell down: . . . It isn't enough for five imageless Americans to stand up and sing. They made no attempt to project personality, unless it lay in their fresh California-sun outfits of blue and white striped shirts and pure white trousers . . . The question now is: Would it have been any different if Brian Wilson had been with them?"

TUESDAY, NOVEMBER 8, 1966: Granada Theatre, Tooting, London, England, with Lulu, David and Jonathan, Sounds Incorporated, the Golden Brass, and Jerry Stevens (Two shows at 7:00 and 9:10 p.m.)
The group did not play shows on Monday. Instead, Peter Whitehead filmed them, driving to EMI House in Manchester Square, in two Mini-Moke cars. There they posed with two attractive women for photographers, before holding a press conference inside. Following the conference, a cocktail party was held for specially invited guests, including Rolling Stones manager Andrew Loog Oldham. Dennis was particularly impressed by Oldham's Rolls Royce and spent much of the tour working to acquire one.

WEDNESDAY, NOVEMBER 9, 1966: Leicester DeMontfort Hall, Leicester, England, with Lulu, David and Jonathan, Sounds Incorporated, the Golden Brass, and Jerry Stevens (Two shows at 6:35 and 8:50 p.m.)
Al Jardine was quite impressed with the reception the group received and noted that he greatly preferred "the smaller auditoriums over here where everyone can see and hear and where we can communicate much more closely and with more reality than in America, where there may be, say, 20,000 [-seat] auditoriums or baseball fields."

THURSDAY, NOVEMBER 10, 1966: Odeon Theatre, Leeds, England, with Lulu, David and Jonathan, Sounds Incorporated, the Golden Brass, and Jerry Stevens (Two shows at 6:00 and 8:30 p.m.)

FRIDAY, NOVEMBER 11, 1966: Odeon Theatre, Manchester, England, with Lulu, David and Jonathan, Sounds Incorporated, the Golden Brass, and Jerry Stevens (Two shows at 6:15 and 8:45 p.m.)
Fan hysteria for the Beach Boys in England had reached an all-time high, forcing the group to carefully plan their entrance and exit from each venue to avoid being mobbed. Roger Easterby, who handled publicity for tour promoter Arthur Howes, recalled in a BBC interview that prior to this show, "The others had gone on ahead, but Mike was finishing a meal at the hotel and we had to think of a way of getting him into the theatre and in fact what we did . . . there was a news seller down the road . . . we borrowed his cloth cap . . . we put a muffler around Mike, put this cloth cap on him and we walked in with the crowd. We walked down the center aisle and we used the exit under the stage."

SATURDAY, NOVEMBER 12, 1966: Capitol Theatre, Cardiff, Wales, with Lulu, David and Jonathan, Sounds Incorporated, the Golden Brass, and Jerry Stevens (Two shows at 6:15 and 8:50 p.m.)
Before the first show, Carl accidently put his right hand through a plate glass window, cutting his arm. He visited a local hospital accompanied by Dennis to receive a few stitches. Driving through town, he noted to a reporter, "So this is Cardiff. Well at least I saw a bit of the city this time."

SUNDAY, NOVEMBER 13, 1966: Birmingham Theatre, Birmingham, England, with Lulu, David and Jonathan, Sounds Incorporated, the Golden Brass, and Jerry Stevens (Two shows at 5:40 and 8:00 p.m.)

MONDAY, NOVEMBER 14, 1966: Hammersmith Odeon, London, England, with Lulu, David and Jonathan, Sounds Incorporated, the Golden Brass, and Jerry Stevens (Two shows at 6:45 and 9:00 p.m.)
Prior to these shows, Peter Whitehead filmed Al and Dennis shopping on Portobello Road. Whitehead also filmed the group onstage at the Hammersmith Odeon.

THE BEACH BOYS IN CONCERT

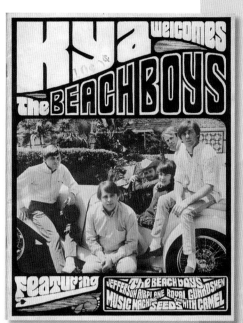

Program for the group's concert in San Francisco on December 28, 1966.
Collection of Chris Woods

WEDNESDAY, NOVEMBER 16, 1966: Rhode Island Auditorium, Providence, RI, with the Ascots and Chad and Jeremy (7:30 p.m. show)
The Beach Boys had little time to savor their success in the U.K. They flew back to the states to begin yet another tour, without even stopping at home to unpack.

THURSDAY, NOVEMBER 17, 1966: Bushnell Memorial, Hartford, CT, with Chad and Jeremy (7:30 p.m. show)
The Beach Boys' state of exhaustion was evident to a reporter from the *Hartford Courant* who tried to interview them backstage. Carl (joined on the tour by wife Annie) and Bruce hid out, while "Mike Love, Dennis Wilson, and Al Jardine did manage the interview, although they didn't answer the questions with much more than a word or two."

FRIDAY, NOVEMBER 18, 1966: Indianapolis Coliseum, Indianapolis, IN, with Chad and Jeremy
Over 12,000 rowdy teenagers attended this show, and problems quickly developed. The Beach Boys had barely begun their set when the house lights had to be switched on because members of the audience were smashing chairs in the box-seat sections. According to *Variety*, "Repeated threats to stop the show did no good. They only heightened the reaction of the kids. Before long, the stage was well crowded with members of the audience. Somebody was swinging a guitar wildly. Police, station personnel, and Coliseum workers sought to protect the performers . . . At long last, sponsors decided to terminate the show despite the number of Beach Boys' ditties left unsung and chair slats left un-slung."

SATURDAY, NOVEMBER 19, 1966: Farleigh Dickinson University, Teaneck, NJ, with Chad and Jeremy, and St. John's University, New York, NY, with Chad and Jeremy (8:30 p.m. show)
The afternoon concert at Farleigh Dickinson for homecoming weekend grossed $9,700. The St. John's show later that evening grossed $32,000.

SUNDAY, NOVEMBER 20, 1966: Maple Leaf Gardens, Toronto, ON, Canada, with the Last Words, the Ugly Ducklings, and Chad and Jeremy (7:30 p.m. show)
The crowd of 7,500 fans that attended this show was notably subdued. According to Joan Fox of the *Toronto Globe*, "The audience in the half-empty Maple Leaf Gardens was enthusiastic for all the Beach Boys' hits, but it was as though the teenyboppers in their white stockings and lank hair had come out to pay their respects to the group rather than to have an experience."

MONDAY, NOVEMBER 21, 1966: Kitchener Memorial Auditorium, Kitchener, ON, Canada, with Chad and Jeremy and the Thanes (8:00 p.m. show)

TUESDAY, NOVEMBER 22, 1966: South Hill Gym, Ithaca College, Ithaca, NY, with Chad and Jeremy (8:15 p.m. show)

WEDNESDAY, NOVEMBER 23, 1966: Baltimore Civic Center, Baltimore, MD, with Tommy Van and the Echoes, the Minus Four, and Chad and Jeremy (8:00 p.m. show)
This show drew an audience of 10,003 and grossed $38,800.

TUESDAY, DECEMBER 27, 1966: Seattle Coliseum, Seattle, WA, with the Royal Guardsmen, the Sopwith Camel, the Wailers, Don and the Goodtimes, the Emergency Exit, and the Standells (8:00 p.m. show)

WEDNESDAY, DECEMBER 28, 1966: Civic Auditorium, San Francisco, CA, with the Jefferson Airplane, the Seeds, Sopwith Camel, Music Machine, and the Royal Guardsmen (8:15 p.m. show)
The Beach Boys played a well-received show, though they were somewhat overshadowed by hometown favorites the Jefferson Airplane. One humorous moment occurred when Mike commented, "I know a lot of you are wondering where Brian Wilson is tonight. Unfortunately he's developed a condition where he had to stay home this evening . . . he's pregnant!"

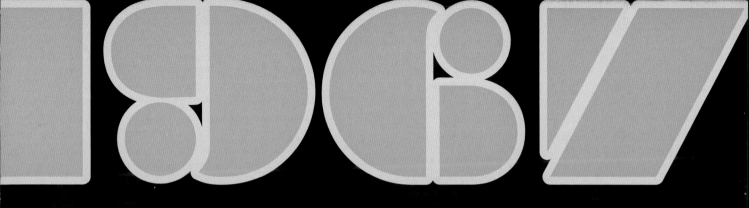

AS 1967 BEGAN, it became evident that *Smile* was incomplete and overdue. A wealth of awe-inspiring snippets and sections were on tape. Everyone believed that Brian would be able to pull it all together for a March release if he could focus and work in a disciplined way. Yet, with Capitol Records breathing down his neck, Brian chose to spend much of January tinkering endlessly with "Heroes and Villains," the single he saw as his brilliant followup to "Good Vibrations." As *New Musical Express* writer Tracy Thomas noted, Brian had become a "fanatical perfectionist. He will listen to a track over and over for twenty minutes before throwing it out. I've been at a three-hour recording session during which only one

CONCERTS PLAYED IN
1967

contract says that whatever we make has to be checked and finally worked out by Capitol. We signed this contract years ago . . . It's not possible anymore to go to Capitol with an idea of Brian's, then wait fourteen days because they have to talk about it . . . There's only one way out for us: our own record label. Well, Capitol did not want to do this." The group's manager Nick Grillo simultaneously conducted an audit that revealed the band had been shortchanged, and that Brian had not been paid properly for producing their records. The Beach Boys launched a lawsuit on February 24 demanding that the label pay them $225,000 in unpaid royalties. They believed that their suit had merit and even if a judge refused to grant them the money, they would "probably succeed in getting the court to rule that they are no longer obliged to record for Capitol, and thus may be their own best-selling stars for the new label." A side effect of the suit, however, was that the group held back on giving the label any new material. "Heroes and Villains" remained on the shelf.

The second big problem was one of great consequence to the completion of *Smile*. Brian's collaborator Van Dyke Parks suddenly departed the project in March. He was increasingly uncomfortable defending his lyrics and had relied on Brian to maintain the integrity of the album. However, Brian began to suffer his own doubts about some of Van Dyke's more abstract lyrics. Speaking to writer Tom Nolan in 1971 about the collapse of *Smile*, Brian said, "That was because . . . the lyrics, Van

FRIDAY, FEBRUARY 10, 1967: Convention Hall, Miami, FL, with Question Mark and the Mysterians, the Left Banke, the Electric Prunes, and Keith (8:30 p.m. show)
In the midst of recording sessions for *Smile*, the Beach Boys embarked on a ten-day tour. Dick Duryea, Steve Korthof, and Roy Hatfield accompanied them. The eclectic bill included Michigan band Question Mark and the Mysterians, then riding high on the success of their single "96 Tears," the Left Banke, who had success with "Walk Away Renee," the Electric Prunes, who had scored a hit single with "I Had Too Much to Dream (Last Night)," and Keith, of "98.6" fame.

SATURDAY, FEBRUARY 11, 1967: Bayfront Center Arena, St. Petersburg, FL, with Question Mark and the Mysterians, the Left Banke, the Electric Prunes, and Keith (8:15 p.m. show)
The Beach Boys performed for 7,700 fans at this show. Bob Blumberg of the *Evening Independent* noted, "Every song they sang was well known and heartily applauded. The most-liked group effort seemed to be the slow and sedate 'Surfer Girl.' The drummer, Dennis Wilson, left his drums to sing a beautiful and inspiring rendition of 'You've Got to Hide Your Love Away.' An interesting note of the evening was that the lesser groups all either had long hair or wild clothes, while the famous Beach Boys were a group of clean-cut young men, simply attired."

SUNDAY, FEBRUARY 12, 1967: Civic Auditorium, Jacksonville, FL, with Question Mark and the Mysterians, the Left Banke, the Electric Prunes, and Keith (Two shows at 6:00 and 8:30 p.m.)
James Lowe, of the Electric Prunes, usually watched the Beach Boys' set and recalled, "as with all bands, some nights the Beach Boys sounded a little disjointed, but when there were large venues they shined. I can still remember Carl singing 'In My Room' with a huge blue spotlight on him . . . it was amazing."

TUESDAY, FEBRUARY 14, 1967: Memorial Gym, Middle Tennessee State University, Murfreesboro, TN, with the Left Banke, the Electric Prunes, and Keith (8:00 p.m. show)

THURSDAY, FEBRUARY 16, 1967: Roberts Stadium, Evansville, IN, with the Left Banke, the Electric Prunes, and Keith (8:00 p.m. show)

FRIDAY, FEBRUARY 17, 1967: Bradley University, Peoria, IL, with the Left Banke, the Electric Prunes, and Keith (8:00 p.m. show)

SATURDAY, FEBRUARY 18, 1967: Memorial Hall, Dayton, OH, with the Electric Prunes, Keith, and the Left Banke (Two shows at 3:00 and 7:30 p.m.) and Veterans Memorial Auditorium, Columbus, OH, with the Electric Prunes, Keith, the Left Banke, the Rebounds, and the Grayps (Two shows at 6:00 and 8:45 p.m.)
In a truly insane setup, the Beach Boys played in Dayton at 3 p.m., rushed to Columbus for an evening show, returned to Dayton for a 7:30 show, and then went back to Columbus for their fourth concert of the day. Sterling Smith, then a keyboardist for the Columbus band the Grayps, recalled, "Steve Korthof rented Vox amps for the shows from a local music store and in the first show, Carl was getting some bad hum or crackling (either from the amp or a bad cord). Mike Love sarcastically told the crowd, 'These are the same amps the Beatles (sneer) use.'" Despite the technical problems, however, Smith was very impressed by the Beach Boys. "The five of them playing with no sidemen through the house PA sounded phenomenal . . . It was just simple, crisp. I wasn't a major Beach Boys fan, I was more of a Beatles, Rolling Stones, British Invasion guy, but I was really impressed. I was blown away by how good they were."

SUNDAY, FEBRUARY 19, 1967: Masonic Auditorium, Detroit, MI, with the Electric Prunes, Keith, and the Left Banke (7:30 p.m. show)

A capacity crowd attended this show. Lorraine Alterman of the *Detroit Free Press* commented, "The Beach Boys breezed through a collection of their hits like 'Surfer Girl,' 'Sloop John B,' and 'Good Vibrations' . . . The bearded Mike Love, wearing a white fur cap à la Dr. Zhivago, joked around with the audience between numbers in a casual way that made the crowd feel they were at a friendly get-together, not a concert. Unfortunately, the Beach Boys gave the impression on their songs that this was just another job to them. It was, but you still would like to think they were singing and playing their hearts out for you. They didn't project that added zing of excitement which distinguishes a great performance from a good one."

FRIDAY, MARCH 17, 1967: Western Illinois University, Macomb, IL, with the Standard Deviationists and the Contents Are
The set list at this concert included "Help Me Rhonda," "I Get Around," "Surfin' USA," "Wouldn't It Be Nice," "God Only Knows," "Good Vibrations," "Barbara Ann," and a cover of Gary U.S. Bond's 1961 hit "New Orleans."

SATURDAY, MARCH 18, 1967: Masonic Temple, Davenport, IA, with Keith, the Casinos, and the Harper's Bizarre (Two shows at 7:00 and 9:30 p.m.)

SUNDAY, MARCH 19, 1967: Municipal Auditorium, Kansas City, MO, with Keith, the Casinos, and the Harper's Bizarre (Two shows at 6:30 and 9:00 p.m.)
This show was attended by 2,576 people.

MONDAY, MARCH 20, 1967: Kiel Opera House, St. Louis, MO, with Keith, the Casinos and the Harper's Bizarre (8:00 p.m. show)

TUESDAY, MARCH 21, 1967: Tulsa Assembly Center, Tulsa, OK, with Keith, the Casinos, and the Harper's Bizarre (8:00 p.m. show)

WEDNESDAY, MARCH 22, 1967: Mid South Coliseum, Memphis, TN, with Keith, the Casinos, the Buckinghams, and the Wild Kingdom (8:00 p.m. show)
This show was attended by 6,000 enthusiastic fans. The *Commercial Appeal* praised the group as "masters of showmanship" but questioned their sarcastic in-between song patter. "When they called for requests, one of the Beach Boys said, 'What? Leave town?' Before introducing the song 'God Only Knows,' which several in the audience said they had never heard, the quintet warned, 'We're going to do a song that's kind of quiet, so you can all leave now . . . If anyone knows the words, just feel free to go ahead and shut up because we're going to do the song."

THURSDAY, MARCH 23, 1967: Municipal Auditorium, Austin, TX, with Keith, the Casinos, and the Buckinghams (8:00 p.m. show)
The Buckinghams, who had a huge hit with "Kind of a Drag," opened at these shows. Guitarist Carl Giammarese recalled, "I was in a locker room and Bruce Johnston was playing me their new song 'Heroes and Villains.' He was sure it was going to be a hit. The feeling I got from Bruce was they had huge expectations for 'Heroes and Villains.' Bruce was very engaging, very friendly. Always took the time to ask what you were doing. He was the most engaging of the group, in my opinion." Giammarese also noted, "I was really blown away by how great their vocal harmonies were live. The way they used to blend their voices was incredible. When we toured with them I would always listen to their sound checks. I never thought Dennis was that good a drummer, but vocally they were amazing."

FRIDAY, MARCH 24, 1967: Will Rogers Auditorium, Fort Worth, TX, with Keith, the Casinos, and the Buckinghams (7:00 p.m. show) and Dallas Memorial Auditorium, Dallas, TX, with Keith, the Casinos, and the Buckinghams (8:30 p.m. show)
After each group played in Fort Worth, they rushed to nearby Dallas to play there as well. The Dallas show was a complete sellout, attended by 10,500 fans.

Dyke Parks had written lyrics that were . . . it was all Van Dyke Parks and none of the Beach Boys. The lyrics were so poetic and symbolic they were abstract . . . " Parks was offered a chance to record for Warner Brothers Records and decided to abandon what had become an increasingly bizarre situation. The loss threw Brian into a depression. For over a month, Brian avoided the studio and did not work on anything related to *Smile*.

In April 1967 Brian and Van Dyke briefly reunited and Brian reentered the studio to begin work on "Vegetables." Brian's sporadic flirtations with physical fitness and nutrition inspired the humorous song, complete with sounds of carrots and celery being chomped. Brian threw himself into the recording of the song, focusing entirely on it for ten days. On April 10 Paul McCartney dropped in on the proceedings. Brian and Paul made a late night visit to the home of John and Michelle Philips (of the Mamas and Papas). There Brian directed them all in a jam with, "Brian on glasses of water filled to various levels, Paul on cello, Michelle on drums and John on bugle." The evening, however, had a greater significance for Brian. Paul played him some of the Beatles music slated for their new album, due for release in June. When Brian heard the dazzling songs he understood that his race with the Beatles was at an end. The Beach Boys were leaving for another tour on April 13 and would proceed directly to Europe after that. There was no way that *Smile* would be finished before *Sergeant Pepper's Lonely*

Hearts Club Band. On April 14, Brian held a last recording session for "Vegetables" and then again abandoned the studio.

Meanwhile, the Beach Boys had already left California for another series of concerts. When the tour reached New York, the band received a major shock. On April 26, prior to an evening show in Long Island, Carl was seized by FBI agents and charged with draft evasion, a serious charge with a potential five-year prison sentence. His arrest shocked friends and family. The group had always maintained an apolitical image, avoiding comments about Vietnam and other controversies. Carl, however, had developed strong anti-war beliefs. In court that June he stated, "I love my country very much, but I won't take part in the destruction of people." Carl posted bail and played the group's remaining U.S. concert dates before flying to L.A. to appear in court.

The Beach Boys were under a darkening cloud. The stress of *Smile* and Brian in shambles was now compounded by fears that Carl might be forced to spend time in jail. The group also had a very important European tour in front of them, so they had no choice but to fly to Dublin without Carl on the night of April 30. At a press conference in Ireland on May 1, Mike stated "For our part, we are hoping that the big, strong U.S. will find it in their hearts to let him come. We admit that this will affect our act. Carl sings a lot of our leads and has done so on a couple of records . . . " Luckily, that same day Carl received permission

THE BEACH BOYS IN CONCERT

SATURDAY, MARCH 25, 1967: Music Hall, Houston, TX, with the Casinos, the Buckinghams, and Neil Ford and the Fanatics (Two shows at 6:30 and 9:30 p.m.)

THURSDAY, APRIL 13, 1967: Animal Husbandry Building, Mississippi State University, Starkville, MS (8:00 p.m. show)
With *Smile* increasingly in doubt and a lawsuit against Capitol underway, the group somewhat dispiritedly hit the road. They were scheduled to play in the states until April 29 and then fly to London to begin a European tour. For the first time in the states, a mini orchestra, including cellist Igor Horoshevsky of the Robert Shaw Chorale, accompanied the group. Bruce Johnston told a reporter, "Our biggest problem on stage had been the actual reproduction of our records' sounds. We have solved this problem by bringing our entire band with us on this trip." Despite the lofty ambitions, the tour got off to a rough start when two of the group's guitars were stolen during this opening show. Steve Korthof began shouting and cursing and was arrested by local police. The group had to bail him out of jail that night.

FRIDAY, APRIL 14, 1967: Civic Center, Charleston, WV, with the Collegiates, Jim and Jean, the Casinos, and the Left Banke (8:00 p.m. show)

SATURDAY, APRIL 15, 1967: University of Virginia, Charlottesville, VA (7:00 p.m. show), and Washington Coliseum, Washington, DC, with the Casinos, Jim and Jean, the Minus IV, Weam Redcoats, and the Chartbusters (8:30 p.m. show)
The Beach Boys performed as part of Easter celebrations at the University. One student complained, "The lead singer was obnoxious and they appeared to put very little effort into their performance." The group then headed to Washington, DC, for a late-night performance there.

SUNDAY, APRIL 16, 1967: Cambria County War Memorial Arena, Johnstown, PA, with Tommy James and the Shondells, the Uncalled for Three, the Left Banke, and Jim and Jean (2:30 p.m. show) and Penn Theatre, Pittsburgh, PA, with Tommy James and the Shondells, the Uncalled for Three, the Left Banke, and Jim and Jean (Two shows at 5:00 and 7:30 p.m.)
The Johnstown show was attended by 2,700 fans. The group then performed two evening shows in Pittsburgh, both of which were sellouts.

MONDAY, APRIL 17, 1967: Metheny Fieldhouse, Geneva College, Beaver Falls, PA, with Jim and Jean and the Pickle Brothers
The group, dressed in striped shirts, played another sold-out gig. Dave Davison of the *Beaver County Times* wrote, "The group . . . seemed to appreciate the opportunity to have their music listened to and, despite several technical difficulties with their amplification system, gave a well balanced and entertaining show . . . The group sang a selection of their biggest hits, spaced with occasional ballads, and although screaming was kept at a low level, several young people could be heard singing along with the group. An indication of how entranced some of the kids were came when the group sang 'Graduation Day,' dedicated to all upcoming graduates. Many in the young audience, perhaps thinking of their own graduation, broke into tears as they sang along."

TUESDAY, APRIL 18, 1967: State Farm Arena, Harrisburg, PA, with the Pickle Brothers (7:30 p.m. show)

WEDNESDAY, APRIL 19, 1967: Defiance College, Defiance, OH, with Jim and Jean, the Casinos, and the Pickle Brothers (8:00 p.m. show)
The Tau Kappa Epsilon Fraternity sponsored this show, attended by 3,500 fans.

THURSDAY, APRIL 20, 1967: Alumni Coliseum, Eastern Kentucky University, Richmond, KY, with the Pickle Brothers (8:00 p.m. show)
The Beach Boys arrived at Eastern Kentucky University in the late afternoon and took part in a pick-up game of softball with local students prior to their well-attended evening concert. Bruce

commented to Craig Ammerman of the campus paper *The Progress* that he was too worn out from touring to take part in the game, but added, "This is one of the high points of our trip. For once, we are able to carry on normal communication with people . . . This is what we miss most: the chance to lead normal lives and enjoy the things other people are able to take part in."

FRIDAY, APRIL 21, 1967: V.P.I. Coliseum, Virginia Tech University, Blacksburg, VA (8:00 p.m. show)

SATURDAY, APRIL 22, 1967: Assembly Hall, University of Illinois, Champaign-Urbana, IL, with the Casinos, Jim and Jean, and the Pickle Brothers (8:00 p.m. show)
University of Illinois records show that Carl signed a contract on behalf of the group on January 5 stipulating that the group would receive a guarantee of $7,500 for the appearance against sixty percent of the gross. The contract also stated that the Beach Boys would supply opening acts to fill out the bill at no cost to the University and that they would appear onstage for no less than 50 minutes. The University agreed to supply no less than 20 police or private security officers, two stage hands, a sound system, four microphones, colored stage lights, and a riser for Dennis's drums.

The *Daily Illini* reviewer reported that "The Beach Boys roared into town Saturday and when they left no one could doubt that they were the kings of good, clean all-American rock 'n' roll music . . . While it is difficult to perform some of their more recent hits without the added electrical gimmicks of a recording studio, the fine job they did on such songs as 'Good Vibrations,' 'Wouldn't It Be Nice,' and 'God Only Knows' practically brought the crowd to their feet. 'Good Vibrations' was the one the audience seemed to enjoy the most."

SUNDAY, APRIL 23, 1967: Canton Memorial Auditorium, Canton, OH, with the Buckinghams, Jim and Jean, and Terry Knight and the Pack (7:30 p.m. show)
Terry Knight and the Pack, a Flint, Michigan band that had a regional hit with "Mister, You're a Better Man Than I," opened for the Beach Boys at this show and in Akron the next night. Members of the group later formed the 1970s band Grand Funk Railroad.

MONDAY, APRIL 24, 1967: Akron Civic Theatre, Akron, OH, with the Buckinghams, Jim and Jean, and Terry Knight and the Pack (7:30 p.m. show)

TUESDAY, APRIL 25, 1967: Westchester County Center, White Plains, NY, with Jim and Jean, the Buckinghams, the Chain Reaction, the Teardrops, and Satan's Helpers (8:00 p.m. show)
This was the second time that a Beach Boys show was opened by Chain Reaction, a local White Plains group that featured a young Steven Tyler of future Aerosmith fame.

WEDNESDAY, APRIL 26, 1967: Long Island Arena, Commack, NY, with Jim and Jean, and the Buckinghams (8:15 p.m. show)
Prior to this show, Carl was arrested in New York City by FBI agents and charged with draft evasion. He posted bail and was released in time for the show. His arrest threw a cloud over the group's future and threatened to disrupt an upcoming European tour. The Selective Service Board informed Carl they were opposed to letting him leave the country with the group.

Onstage in Kentucky, April 20, 1967. With permission of Eastern Kentucky University Special Collections and Archives

Performing at Eastern Kentucky University on April 20, 1967. With permission of Eastern Kentucky University Special Collections and Archives

to leave the country to fulfill the Beach Boys' concert obligations.

Adding to the group's mounting problems, the British musician's union refused to allow them to use the four extra musicians they had brought from America in an effort to recreate the sound of their records. The group was furious. They had specifically hired extra

THE BEACH BOYS IN CONCERT

musicians to avoid criticisms of their live act that the British press had emphasized during their previous U.K. visit. Mike told reporter Keith Altham, "That really burned me up . . . All we were trying to do was give the British public the best possible value for money . . . When it means the public must suffer I can't see the sense of it." Yet another negative issue popped up when the group arrived in Europe to find that EMI had released the 1965 track "Then I Kissed Her" as a single without their approval. The song sounded horribly dated in the wake of Pet Sounds and the much-celebrated "Good Vibrations." One reviewer commented, "To release 'Then I Kissed Her' as the Beach Boys' 'new' single is to go backwards and can do the Beach Boys nothing but harm." Expressing the group's feelings, Bruce exclaimed, "It's really ridiculous. The record is in no way representative of the kind of things we are doing now . . . this is not the music that won us the *NME* award as the World's Top Vocal Group."

The Beach Boys' frustrations only increased when they flew to London on May 4 for two concerts at the Hammersmith Odeon. The press pounced on the group for failing to live up to their increasingly complex records onstage. The U.K. music papers were clearly expecting much more than a rehash of the 1966 tour. Even as they picked up their *New Musical Express* Poll Winner's award for World's Best Vocal Group on May 7, the Beach Boys found themselves in the unenviable position of apologizing for failing to live up to the hype. *Disc and Music Echo*'s Jonathan

THURSDAY, APRIL 27, 1967: Community War Memorial, Rochester, NY, with Tommy James and the Shondells, Jim and Jean, and the Buckinghams (7:30 p.m. show)
Fans were concerned that Carl would not be present, but despite the stress he was under, he performed with the group. *The Rochester Democrat and Chronicle* reported, "Seven thousand youngsters or more, wired with flash bulbs and equipped with screams, welcomed the Beach Boys back to Rochester last night. The rock 'n' roll group, including Carl Dean Wilson, whose travels are currently limited by the FBI on account of draft board troubles, caused a phenomenon like one long, continuous flash of lightning as thousands of cameras 'shot' the celebrities."

FRIDAY, APRIL 28, 1967: Back Bay Theatre, Boston, MA, with Tommy James and the Shondells, Jim and Jean, and the Buckinghams (Two shows at 7:00 and 9:30 p.m.)
While the rest of the group continued on to Boston after their Rochester show, Carl was forced to return to New York for a hearing in U.S district court. He was informed that he would have to appear before a judge in Los Angeles to receive permission to go to Europe. He agreed to show up in court in L.A. on Monday. After the hearing, Carl hurried to Boston to appear with the group.

SATURDAY, APRIL 29, 1967: Symphony Hall, Newark, NJ, with Jim and Jean, the Buckinghams, and the Doughboys (2:00 p.m. show), and Memorial Field House, Union College, Schenectady, NY, with Jim and Jean, the Casinos, David Frye, and the Buckinghams (8:00 p.m. show)
The Beach Boys concluded their American tour with a matinee show in New Jersey followed by an evening appearance at Union College. The tour had been a stressful affair for the entire band, but it especially affected Dennis. The strain of watching his younger brother arrested by the FBI and facing the possibility of jail time proved too much for him. Guitarist Carl Giammarese of the Buckinghams recalled that in Newark, the local opening act the Doughboys "asked permission to use Dennis's drums for their performance. They did a Who kind of act and the drummer knocked over Dennis's drums during their set." The Doughboys were stunned when Dennis raced onstage, while the band was finishing their set, and attacked band member Myke Scavone. Doughboys' guitarist Richard Heyman recalled in his book *Boom Harangue*, "Dennis was throwing punches and wrestling down our front man to the floor. The curtains hadn't even closed yet. The members of the audience had that look of astonished horror and bewilderment for that moment before the curtains came together." Once the curtain went down, the fight got even worse, with Dennis and Scavone trading punches until their respective camps pulled them apart. Dennis later apologized for his behavior. Giammarese, who had gotten to know Dennis a little bit on tour, was not that surprised by the drummer's outburst and commented "Dennis could be a really nice guy sometimes, but he had a split personality."

TUESDAY, MAY 2, 1967: Dublin Adelphi, Dublin, Ireland, with Derek, Billy and the Freshmen, the Vampires, the Strangers, and Joe Cahill (Two shows at 6:45 and 9:00 p.m.)
The Beach Boys flew to Ireland without Carl Wilson, while he returned to Los Angeles to appear before U.S. District Court Judge A. Andrew Hauk. He pleaded innocent to the charge and was ordered to appear in court on June 20. The judge then granted him permission to go to Europe in return for a $25,000 bond. Carl chartered a private plane, at a cost of $5,000, to fly to Dublin in time for the concert. The group nervously paced backstage, hoping that he would arrive in time for the 6:30 show, but instead they were forced to play without him.

They opened with "Help Me Rhonda," "I Get Around," "Do You Wanna Dance," and "Surfer Girl." The crowd quickly made their displeasure known by chanting, "We want Carl." Rather than change the act, the group soldiered on with the usual set, which led to a problem when it came time to perform "God Only Knows." It was left to Bruce to sing the lead and apparently it did not go well. Ray Coleman of *Disc and Music Echo* reported, "This was a brave, misguided failure. Bruce forgot the words. To say it was an embarrassing moment would be minimizing an electrifyingly disastrous moment . . . It should not have happened . . . it was utterly unbelievable that any member of a group reckoned by some to be the world's number two could not know the words of any part of their repertoire before going on stage. Especially as they'd had time to plan things if Carl failed to arrive in time." Boos rained down on the group and seventy members of the audience demanded their money back. B. P Fallon of *Melody Maker* commented, "It was to, to be as polite and charitable as possible, a disaster. The audience wanted Carl, but not as much as the four men who were struggling to make do without him. They seemed at a complete loss, like some amateur group struck with stage fright at the local talent contest."

The Beach Boys recognized how badly things had gone and were reluctant to return the stage for their second show. Soon they received word Carl had landed in Dublin and was being speedily driven to the Adelphi. Much to their relief, he arrived midway through the set and raced onstage, still dressed in the clothes he wore on the plane. Fallon remarked, "From then on it was the same act, if rougher, that audiences heard on the last tour. We had 'God Only Knows,' 'Sloop John B'—the number booed in the disastrous first house—'Good Vibrations,' and 'Graduation Day.'"

Ian Rusten Collection

WEDNESDAY, MAY 3, 1967: ABC Theatre, Belfast, Ireland, with Derek, Billy and the Freshmen, the Vampires, the Strangers, and Joe Cahill (Two Shows at 6:45 and 9:00 p.m.)

THURSDAY, MAY 4, 1967: Hammersmith Odeon, London, England, with Helen Shapiro, Simon Dupree and the Big Sound, the Marionettes, Alan Field, and Terry Reid with Peter Jay's Jaywalkers (Two shows at 6:45 and 9:00 p.m.)
After two dates in Ireland, the group flew to London, where an increasingly skeptical British press awaited them. If the media had given the group a relatively easy time in 1966, they seemed intent on taking the opposite tack on this tour. *Melody Maker* writer Nick Jones wrote a scathing review of their opening shows at the Hammersmith Odeon. "One expects a group as experienced as the Beach Boys . . . to have far more presence on stage. As the curtain slides up, the impact should strike you dumb. But one just hears the disjointed, empty, nervous instrumental sound." Although Jones was undoubtedly aware that the group was prevented by the U.K. musicians' union from using extra musicians at the show, he singled out their inability to replicate their recorded sound as the biggest sin. "Maybe it is the polished perfection and the wealth of sound and orchestration that one is used to on their records that makes the live Beach Boys seem so comparably amateurish—floundering weakly as though their umbilical cord to Brian Wilson had been severed." The group was stung by the negative reviews and lashed out at their critics. Mike told Bill Harry in the *Record Mirror*, "If I said we could reproduce that record sound on stage I'd be nuts. We get the occasional comments from people who say we don't sound like the records. But it's a dumb comment to make because naturally we're not like the records. It's the people who usually don't pay to come in and see the show who criticize."

FRIDAY, MAY 5, 1967: Finsbury Park, Astoria, London, England, with Helen Shapiro, Simon Dupree and the Big Sound, the Marionettes, Alan Field, and Terry Reid with Peter Jay's Jaywalkers (Two shows at 6:40 and 9:10 p.m.)

SATURDAY, MAY 6, 1967: Odeon Theatre, Birmingham, England, with Helen Shapiro, Simon Dupree and the Big Sound, the Marionettes, Alan Field, and Terry Reid with Peter Jay's Jaywalkers (Two shows at 6:30 and 9:00 p.m.)

SUNDAY, MAY 7, 1967: *NME* Poll Winner's Concert, Empire Pool, Wembley, London, England, with Jeff Beck, Cream, the Dubliners, Simon Dee, Dusty Springfield, Georgie Fame, Paul Jones, Lulu, the Move, Cliff Richard, the Small Faces, the Spencer Davis Group, the Alan Price Set, Cat Stevens, the Tremeloes, the Troggs, Steve Winwood, and Geno Washington and the Ram Jam Band (2:00 p.m. show)
The Beach Boys appeared at the *New Musical Express* Poll Winner's show to pick up their award as "World's Top Vocal Group" and perform a short set. As a result of the "Then I Kissed Her" debacle and the negative comments about their recent concerts, the group's morale was low and they expressed some anxiety about accepting the award. Bruce Johnson told Keith Altham, "Frankly I

King piled on, "Wax wizard Brian Wilson may still be, but it has to be said, in this country, the Beach Boys are finished. This tour and this record ("Then I Kissed Her") were the decline . . . Very sad." It was a demoralizing experience for the group, who had come to England expecting to be treated as triumphant heroes.

While the group was in Europe, momentous events were unfolding in America. On May 6, publicist Derek Taylor broke the news in *Disc and Music Echo* that *Smile* had been "SCRAPPED. Not destroyed, but scrapped. For what Wilson seals in a can and destroys is scrapped. As an average fan of the Beach Boys, I think it is bitterly disappointing." Dennis told reporters, "We got a little frightened. We've got a lot of songs recorded, but we got nervous about whether they were good enough. We've got afraid to put anything out, unless it comes up to a certain standard." The demoralized group soldiered on with their European tour, while Brian stayed mum. Speaking years later, he suggested that he needed at least another year to work on *Smile*, but he knew that this was impossible. Time had run out.

The decision to abandon *Smile* haunted the group for the next forty years. Nearly every interviewer felt obliged to ask about it. It became the most famous unreleased album of all time and a millstone of regret around the Beach Boys' necks. Reviewers compared albums the group released in succeeding years to the LP they chose not to release. The Beach Boys themselves fed the myth of *Smile* by dribbling out bits and pieces on their albums released over the next five years. Often the *Smile* songs dominated and overshadowed the rest of the material the group was trying to promote.

For Brian, the abandonment of *Smile* was a life-altering occurrence. After all the hype, and talk of his genius, he had failed to deliver his masterpiece. In 2004 Brian suggested that the collapse of *Smile* caused him to have another nervous breakdown. Friends certainly believed that the failure to complete *Smile* virtually destroyed Brian. David Anderle told Paul Williams, "I think Brian is probably saying to himself . . . 'I should have gone ahead the way I was going to go ahead and abandoned the Beach Boys.' He's gotta be thinking of that sometimes."

Derek Taylor released a statement that the Beach Boys wouldn't tour during the summer of 1967 because they felt "that they haven't been turning out enough in the studio, so they're going to start concentrating on recording." But the group had already made one important commitment. In the heady days of *Smile*, Brian had

was little embarrassed to be receiving a world's top vocal group award from the *NME* . . . I mean to all of us there is only one number one and that's the Beatles. I told Ringo about this and he said that was nonsense and wished us the best of luck in your poll again next year. I thought that was really nice." Later that night, members of the group attended Jimi Hendrix's concert at the Saville Theatre, along with Ringo Starr and Brian Jones.

MONDAY, MAY 8, 1967: Odeon Theatre, Manchester, England, with Helen Shapiro, Simon Dupree and the Big Sound, the Marionettes, Alan Field, and Terry Reid with Peter Jay's Jaywalkers (Two shows at 6:15 and 8:45 p.m.)
While in Manchester, Carl granted an interview to *Melody Maker* about his draft case. He told the paper, "I am an objector on the grounds of conscience. I have to make them believe me; otherwise the alternative is jail—and in America it is usually for a term of three years. But I have feelings about these things and I feel absolutely certain that the worst will not happen. I only hope I'm right!"

TUESDAY, MAY 9, 1967: Odeon Theatre, Glasgow, Scotland, with Helen Shapiro, Simon Dupree and the Big Sound, the Marionettes, Alan Field, and Terry Reid with Peter Jay's Jaywalkers (Two shows at 6:40 and 9:00 p.m.)

WEDNESDAY, MAY 10, 1967: A.B.C. Theatre, Edinburgh, Scotland, with Helen Shapiro, Simon Dupree and the Big Sound, the Marionettes, Alan Field, and Terry Reid with Peter Jay's Jaywalkers (Two shows at 6:30 and 8:50 p.m.)

FRIDAY, MAY 12, 1967: Grona Lund, Stockholm, Sweden (8:00 p.m. show)
With their controversial British tour completed, the group flew to Sweden to play in Stockholm for the third time in their career.

SATURDAY, MAY 13, 1967: Messuhalli, Helsinki, Finland, with Jormas and Topmost (8:00 p.m. show)
The group made their first appearance in Finland, playing with two well- known Finnish bands. Following their performance, they flew to Holland for a scheduled concert. Unfortunately, bad luck continued to mar the group's European tour. The Beach Boys were unable to obtain work permits necessary to perform and the show was canceled. Instead they held a press conference at the Amsterdam Hilton on Sunday. *Hit Week* reporter Peter Schroder questioned the group's insistence on wearing outdated clothing onstage. Bruce replied, "Oh those clothes, we simply perform in clothes we find comfortable." Schroder asked why they didn't take a greater interest in how their records were packaged and Carl testily answered, "Are you from EMI or something?" When Schroder expressed enthusiasm for the proposed *Smile* album jacket that had been advertised in *Hit Week*, Carl softened and declared, "You might have a point. We used to not think about it too much, and left it to others. From now on we'll make sure that it's in good hands."

While at the Hilton, the group also taped a television interview for the VARA TV show *Fanclub* with Judith Bosch. During the interview, Carl revealed that problems with work permits had led to the cancelation of not only the show in Amsterdam but also a proposed concert in Paris.

WEDNESDAY, MAY 17, 1967: Sport-Halle, Cologne, West Germany, with the Beat Stones, the Barking Dog, the Twangy Gang, the Small Faces, the Smoke, and David Garrick (7:00 p.m. show)
Over 3,000 German fans attended this show. The *Kolner Stadt-Anzeiger* reviewer noted that there was a long delay before the Beach Boys came out "because of photographers crowding the stage and fans occupying the incline of the cycling track. The compere tried in vain to get the crowd to return to their seats but it was only when security men marched up and threatened to kick them out that the fans drew back." *The Berlin Telegraf* reported, "The American band managed to make the hall into an inferno from the very beginning. Girls in multicolored miniskirts were screaming 'Darling!' and emitting jungle-like sounds. Male fans on the other hand stripped for the Beach Boys, undressing piece by piece, leaving only swim trunks. The especially wild crowds were held back by security men when they tried to get onstage."

FRIDAY, MAY 19, 1967: Berliner Sport Palast, Berlin, West Germany, with the Small Faces, the Smoke, and David Garrick

This was the final show of the ill-fated tour. Prior to the concert, the group held a press conference at the rooftop bar of the Hilton Hotel. *The Berlin Telegraf* reported that "drummer Dennis Wilson was out of sorts but the other four Beach Boys entertained the press and radio people in an unusual manner. 'Please get together for a picture,' Bruce Johnston called to the cameramen and took a flash picture for his souvenir album. Alan Jardine rummaged through an *Electrola* press kit and burst into laughter every time he found a funny picture of himself or his partners. Stubbornly sluggish Mike Love scratched his red beard and gave a play-by-play account to an AFN reporter. At the end of the bar Carl Wilson gave an interview for TV reporter Helmut Lohmeyer and his *Zwischenstation* program."

Although this was their first concert in the city, the group had planned to appear in Berlin in 1966. The authorities at that time had denied the permit because they were afraid that fans would riot and damage the Sport Palast. Referring to this trip, Bruce told *NME* reporter Norrie Drummond "We played in Germany with the Small Faces and we had a really great time but Berlin really frightened me. I went into East Berlin and that's a pretty grim place, but strangely enough away from the main streets there's a real warmth."

Following the tour, Bruce flew to Ibiza for a vacation and then stopped off in London in early June. He told Norrie Drummond of *NME* that even after two years in the band he still felt somewhat isolated. "The others never telephone me. But then I suppose we have very little in common. They're all married and have their own circle of friends and I have mine. They do ask me around to dinner occasionally but I seldom manage to make it."

SATURDAY, JUNE 17, 1967: Monterey Pop Festival, Monterey, CA (Beach Boys set canceled)

FRIDAY, AUGUST 25, AND SATURDAY, AUGUST 26, 1967: Honolulu International Center Arena, Honolulu, HI, with Paul Revere and the Raiders; the Pickle Brothers (Friday only); Dino, Desi, and Billy (Saturday only); Bobbie Gentry; and Val Richards Five (One show each night at 8:30 p.m.)

The Beach Boys single "Heroes and Villains" stalled at number twelve on the *Billboard* charts and the band had serious doubts about the commercial appeal of their upcoming *Smiley Smile* LP. A decision was made to record a live album and rush it out that fall in hopes of reversing the group's fading fortunes. The band flew to Hawaii to perform two concerts, which would be recorded for the proposed release. Brian agreed to play his first full concerts with the group since 1965. Bruce told the *New Music Express*, "This is definitely a one-shot appearance by Brian. I was invited to take part in the Hawaii concert, but I shall not do so. However, I'll be playing with the group throughout its U.S. tour next month." While rehearsing with the group on Thursday, Brian explained to reporter Wayne Harada that he was appearing with the band because, "We wanted to do another live album where the mood's good. And it's great here. We're calling it *Lei'd in Hawaii*." Despite his upbeat mood, Brian admitted that he "had a particular insecurity about traveling, so I stopped doing the live shows with the group. Now that I'm back again, it's a bit frightening." Brian seemed both proud and resentful of the group. He told Harada, "I think rock 'n' roll—the pop scene—is happening. It's great. But I think basically, the Beach Boys are squares. We're not happening—but we've been so lucky in the past. It doesn't hurt now. We get enjoyment in our recordings. I write most of the songs and I've taken some drugs, which have opened my mind to a wider range of musical creativity. I write anywhere, usually at home. I don't write about drugs and those things, though. As I said, we're not a hip group. We're pretty square."

Certainly, the band looked pretty square when they emerged onstage in their matching blue and white striped shirts, which one reviewer disparagingly noted, "might have been borrowed from basketball referees." Brian took an active part in the proceedings, singing lead on a number of songs, including an interesting version of "Heroes and Villains." He alternated between his bulky Baldwin organ, which he insisted on lugging to Hawaii, and bass guitar. With Bruce absent, this meant that Carl had to play bass when Brian was on the organ. The Beach Boys debuted both of their summer 1967 singles, "Heroes and Villains" and the instantly forgotten "Gettin' Hungry." The set list for the first show was: "The Letter," "Hawaii," "You're So Good to Me," "Surfer Girl,"

promised that they would appear at a large California music festival being planned by John Phillips and Lou Adler. The Monterey Pop Festival quickly developed into the music event of the year, with nearly every important band of the time on the bill. The Beach Boys were scheduled to headline the night of June 17 following performances by the Byrds, the Jefferson Airplane, and Otis Redding. But in early June, the group suddenly announced that they would not appear. They stated that they were canceling because of Carl's draft issues and because "the pressure from their record company for a new single and album had become overwhelming." Festival organizer John Phillips later alleged to writer David Leaf that the real reason they didn't appear was because "Brian was afraid the hippies from San Francisco would think the Beach Boys were square and boo them." Whatever the reason, the decision proved a costly one. Monterey marked the symbolic birth of the counterculture and signaled a major shift in the American music scene. By not being there, the Beach Boys were quickly defined as part of the past. As Carl noted years later, "Monterey was a turning point in rock 'n' roll. Overnight the whole scene changed and we felt as if we'd been passed by."

On June 20, Carl appeared in court to answer his draft evasion charges. At the hearing, his attorney J. B. Tietz argued that Carl had been denied due process, because the draft board had denied his request to be classified as a conscientious objector without granting him a hearing. Judge Andrew Hauk interviewed Carl and asked him if he was willing to serve his country in a capacity other than fighting, such as working in a VA hospital. Carl stated "Most definitely, I just want to do something good." As a result, he was released with the understanding that he would serve in some other way. Carl's lawyers and the court would sort out the details in the future. The Beach Boys also settled their issues with Capitol, since it was in neither party's interest to continue the lawsuit. It was mutually agreed that the Beach Boys would record for their own Brother Records label in the United States, while Capitol would press and distribute the records. As Mike related to Derek Taylor, "Now they realize that after all it is not a bad deal for them at all, because Bruce, Dennis, and Brian are going to produce records separately for Brother Records . . . and the records will be released by the Capitol industries . . . Everything is settled perfectly."

With legal matters resolved, the Beach Boys began recording sessions at Brian's newly thrown-together home studio. Jim Lockert, the band's engineer, explained to Byron Preiss, "we found a room adjacent to the large music room and built a control room in there and installed a remote console and speakers . . . We physically changed the music room into a recording studio." Brian remained excited about the potential of "Heroes and Villains" as the next Beach Boys single. That July he insisted on personally bringing the disc to KHJ-AM to premiere it. The DJ on duty, however, told Brian that he was not allowed to play a song that

"Surfin'," "Getting' Hungry," "California Girls," "Wouldn't It Be Nice," "Heroes and Villains," "God Only Knows," "Good Vibrations," and "Barbara Ann." The second show consisted of "Hawthorne Boulevard," "Hawaii," "You're So Good to Me," "Help Me Rhonda," "California Girls," "Wouldn't It Be Nice," "Gettin' Hungry," "Surfer Girl," "Surfin'," "Sloop John B," "The Letter," "God Only Knows," "Good Vibrations," "Heroes and Villains," and "Barbara Ann."

Dino, Desi, and Billy opened for the Beach Boys on Saturday night and Billy Hinsche recalled that at the rehearsals, the Beach Boys discussed "what the set list should be. Carl loved the Box Tops hit 'The Letter' and this might have been the debut of them doing it. I believe Brian suggested that they should start the show by all shouting a variation of a popular song titled 'Let's Take a Trip down Whittier Boulevard' and change it to 'Hawthorne Boulevard,' and then launch into 'The Letter.' It seemed a mildly amusing albeit unconventional beginning, but turned out to be a little too 'inside' for the audience that night. They didn't 'get it' . . . also the fact that Brian was playing his white Baldwin organ, Carl on bass, Al on guitar, and Dennis playing bongos, with his back turned sideways to the audience when the effects of the LSD he took finally got a hold of him, didn't help. It was like the *Smiley Smile* version of a concert . . . unorthodox, unexpected, and unusual. The show was very unlike any other Beach Boys show I had ever witnessed and I felt badly for them . . . the audience was nonplussed."

The Beach Boys professionally recorded both Hawaii shows. However, when they listened to the tapes they were underwhelmed. The performance was somewhat odd, possibly due to hallucinogenic substances the Wilson brothers ingested before taking the stage. Recognizing the Hawaii tapes were unreleasable, the group assembled, with Bruce back in the fold, at Wally Heider's studio in September to basically rerecord the concert in the studio. That didn't work either. Soon the whole idea was scrapped. Capitol did release a live version of "Heroes and Villains" from one of the shows as a bonus track on the *Beach Boys Concert/Live in London* CD release. A portion of one of the concerts was also filmed, at Dennis' instigation, on 16mm Kodachrome stock, without sound. Some of this footage, with audio from another concert dubbed onto it, can be seen in the *American Band* documentary. The group is seen performing "God Only Knows," with Brian on organ. In addition, Dennis or an assistant shot home movie footage of the band riding around on motorcycles, swimming, rehearsing (probably on August 24), and listening backstage to the recently recorded audio. There is also footage of sound engineer Steve Desper watching the show on a closed-circuit TV monitor.

Desper probably began touring regularly with the group at this time. A Florida native, he had moved to California in the mid-'60s and found employment at Universal Sound Studios working on TV shows such as *The Man from U.N.C.L.E.* and *Star Trek*. While there, he became friendly with a relative of Mike Love's wife. Desper recalled, "He informed me that Mike Love wanted to build a sound system that he would own and rent to the Beach Boys . . . I designed a portable sound system for them and got together with an audio company and specified the system and the time allotted to build it and they built the console and the cases. So we went out on the road with that. Initially [the relative] was the mixer and I was the roadie. I helped set it up, tear it down, and took care of it. He mixed for a couple of weeks and then one weekend he got sick and they asked if I would cover for him. So I did. Carl liked my mix so much that he asked if I would do it again, so I wound up finishing the tour as mixer."

Desper recalled that being on the road with the group could be a stressful experience for a sound mixer. "I remember the first show I did with them, it was a big venue with fifteen or twenty thousand people there and I plugged in the speakers and they didn't work, nothing worked. It turned out the speaker cables were connected backwards. So it was a mad frantic thing. They had 20,000 kids stomping and screaming and were madly taking connections apart and re-soldering the connections. We were late about an hour but we finally got it up and running and the system worked quite well from then on." The Beach Boys were all enthusiastic about the better sound at their gigs. Dennis noted to a reporter in 1968 that, "Five years ago when we first started touring, audiences would scream all through a performance. Today they listen to the music then scream. Other groups have noticed the same change and suddenly found themselves handicapped by inadequate sound systems. We decided to do something about the problem and I fully suspect other groups will soon follow suit."

FRIDAY, OCTOBER 6, 1967: Indianapolis State Fairgrounds Coliseum, Indianapolis, IN, with the Box Tops, the Idle Few, and the Chosen Few (7:00 p.m. show) and Freedom Hall, Louisville, KY, with Soul INC., the Alphabetical Order, and the Box Tops (8:45 p.m. show)

In the midst of recording *Wild Honey*, the group flew to the Midwest for a short tour with Alex Chilton and the Box Tops. The Beach Boys appeared in their usual stage outfits of striped shirts, with Bruce now sporting a moustache. The shows featured the debut of bassist Ron Brown as a Beach Boys sideman. His presence freed up Bruce to play keyboards, resulting in a fuller band sound.

The Indianapolis show was a return to the days of 1964, as the audience spent most of the show screaming their heads off. Wendell Fowler of the *Indianapolis News* commented, "The Beach Boys . . . seemed to accept the enthusiasm of the screaming youngsters with an air of humility when they appeared. Despite all the screams, the veteran, striped-shirt group sings to the best of their ability despite what people say about the lack of enthusiasm in groups today. The last song of the show was the world premiere of 'Wild Honey,' which will be released in two weeks." Following the evening show, the group appeared in Louisville later that night.

SATURDAY, OCTOBER 7, 1967: Music Hall, Cleveland, OH, with the Box Tops, King Kirby and the U.S. Male, and the Ohio Express (Two Shows at 7:00 and 9:30 p.m.)

In between the two Cleveland shows, the group answered questions from 30 local high school reporters backstage. Questions ranged from why Al's hair looked blonder than usual (the sun lightened it), to the group's feelings about LSD (they opposed it). Asked his opinion of hippies, Mike replied, "You've asked the wrong person, I don't agree with their principles." *Smiley Smile* sweatshirts were given to reporters after the conference.

SUNDAY, OCTOBER 8, 1967: Civic Opera House, Chicago, IL, with the Box Tops (Two shows at 5:00 and 8:00 p.m.)

FRIDAY, NOVEMBER 17, 1967: Masonic Auditorium, Detroit, MI, with Buffalo Springfield, the Strawberry Alarm Clock, the Soul Survivors, and the Pickle Brothers (8:30 p.m. show)

This was the opening date of a ten-day trip billed as the "Fifth Annual Thanksgiving Tour." It was the group's first tour in their new stage outfits, matching white suits. While arguably an improvement over the archaic striped shirts, the outfits were hardly hip in comparison to the flamboyant stage clothes worn by most rock groups of the time. Ron Brown played bass on this tour and was joined by a second sideman, Daryl Dragon, who was hired to play keyboards.

Later to achieve fame as the "Captain" of the mega-hit act Captain and Tennile, Dragon came from a musical family with similarities to the Wilsons. Like Brian, Dennis, and Carl Wilson, Daryl and his two brothers Doug and Dennis all became professional musicians. While they would all tour with the Beach Boys at various times, Daryl was the first of the Dragon brothers to perform with the group. He was introduced to them through Bruce Johnston, whom he had known for many years. Daryl recalled, "I discovered Bruce at a nightclub in Venice, California and I thought he was a really talented guy. This is long before the Beach Boys. I think he was about 16. All the girls were melting over him and his great piano playing. He was the king. I was a boogie guy and he was a romantic guy. So then Bruce, Doug, and I used to work together in clubs and I also worked with Bruce alone. We used to do occasional gigs." When the Beach Boys decided to add a keyboard player to the touring band, Bruce thought first of Doug Dragon, who passed on the offer and recommended Daryl. According to Daryl, "The Beach Boys auditioned me. My elder brother Doug knew that he couldn't cut those charts. They're very sophisticated chords. They're not rhythm and blues you know, they're classic songs. The songs from Pet Sounds and those kinds of things are very difficult to figure out. So I think they gave me a tape to learn the stuff and I auditioned at a studio for Carl Wilson. I wasn't sure I was going to get the gig but he hired me. But he told me, 'You have to really beat the piano to death when you play Beach Boys stuff!' So I learned to do that."

Brian rehearses for his first concert appearance in two years. Hawaii, August 1967.
Jon Stebbins Collection

wasn't on his playlist. A huge argument ensued, until the manager of the station finally gave permission to play the song on the air. However, the damage was done. In a 1971 interview with Tom Nolan, Terry Melcher, an eyewitness to the event, recalled, "Brian almost fainted. It was all over. He'd been holding the record, waiting for the right time. He had astrologers figuring out the correct moment. It really killed him." Nothing seemed to come easy anymore. The single only made it to number twelve on the *Billboard* charts.

As a followup to "Good Vibrations," it was considered a failure. For Brian, "Heroes and Villains" marked the end of his previously unquestioned leadership role in the Beach Boys. He continued to be involved in the group but no longer seemed willing or able to take command of their direction. As Mike Love put it, Brian took "a benign, passive interest, instead of a dominating interest. At that time something had happened to his whole ego drive . . . Brian had lost interest in being aggressive and he went in the other direction—still creative, and different, but it wasn't competitive."

When the group's new LP *Smiley Smile* was released that September, the production was credited to the Beach Boys. It made sense, since the extremely minimal presentation bore little comparison to any previous Brian Wilson production. A man once so concerned about perfection now seemed content to allow a record release that lacked almost any technical finesse. Mistakes were intentionally left in, and due to the limitations of the home studio, the record had an unusual, stripped-down sound. As Brian explained in a radio interview, they used no echo on it, "because we didn't have an echo chamber in the studio and we just liked the sound without echo." Songs slated for *Smile* were rerecorded with vastly simplified arrangements. The LP was dominated by the coldish sound of Brian's Baldwin organ, which he used on many of the tracks. Instead of using session musicians, the Beach Boys played most of the simple instrumental parts themselves.

Daryl Dragon ended up working with the group until the end of 1972 and regarded it as his "education" in the industry. Unfortunately, he joined just as the Beach Boys' popularity was in decline, and he left before they re-emerged as a stadium filler. "I always said that when I joined them their demise started happening. They were really happening, really moving and as soon as they hired me there was less interest, less money, less everything! Of course I took it personally. It was my fault." Soon after he joined the group, Daryl earned a nickname that would stick with him for the rest of his career. "Mike Love was sort of the spokesman of the group and I told him as a joke . . . I got a Captain's hat one day at an old army surplus store . . . so I told him 'Call me Captain Keyboards when you give me a solo on 'Help Me Rhonda' . . . so (during the show) he said 'And now here's Captain Keyboards!' And I started jumping around like Jerry Lee Lewis and that started it."

The legendary Buffalo Springfield opened for the group at all of the shows on the November '67 tour. They had a hit record at the time, the Stephen Stills classic "For What It's Worth." The Springfield was composed of guitarists Stills, Neil Young, and Ritchie Furay; drummer Dewey Martin; and bassist Bruce Palmer. In 1968, Bruce Johnston told Ann Moses of *New Musical Express*, "The Buffalo is the only group I've seen all the Beach Boys really dig since the Beatles." Mike Love told Springfield biographer John Einarson that the Buffalo Springfield "was incredible. We used to go onstage and sit behind the speakers and listen to them." The Beach Boys particularly loved the Stephen Stills song "Rock and Roll Woman" and by 1969 it was part of their act. Members of the two groups maintained friendships off the road as well. In the biography *Shakey*, Neil Young explained that he became quite close with Dennis and the two hung around together. Neil clearly remembered the day in 1968 when Dennis introduced him to his friend Charles Manson.

The Beach Boys began recording many of their concerts on two-track tape (one track for the band and one ambient audience track). Most likely they were taped so that the band could use them to study their performances. The set list for the concert in Detroit consisted of "Barbara Ann," "Darlin'," "Country Air," "I Get Around," "How She Boogalooed It," "Wouldn't It Be Nice," "God Only Knows," "California Girls," "Wild Honey," "Graduation Day," "Good Vibrations," and "Johnny B. Goode."

SATURDAY, NOVEMBER 18, 1967: Lemoyne College, Syracuse, NY, with Buffalo Springfield, the Strawberry Alarm Clock, the Soul Survivors, and the Pickle Brothers (2:00 p.m. show) and Memorial Auditorium, Buffalo, NY, with Buffalo Springfield, the Strawberry Alarm Clock, the Soul Survivors, the Pickle Brothers, and Caesar and His Romans (8:30 p.m. show)

On the second day of the tour, the group played a doubleheader in upstate New York. The afternoon show in Syracuse was frustrating for the group since they were forced to play it without their new keyboardist. Daryl Dragon recalled, "I didn't know how touring worked. I'd never done a major tour like that. The road manager said we were going to meet in the lobby and I thought they were going to call me in my room. So when I got down to the lobby no one had called me and they had all left. So I missed the gig. It was very embarrassing." The evening show in Buffalo was attended by 6,000 enthusiastic fans.

SUNDAY, NOVEMBER 19, 1967: Mosque, Richmond, VA (Matinee), and Constitution Hall, Washington, DC, with the Strawberry Alarm Clock, the Soul Survivors, the Pickle Brothers, and Buffalo Springfield (Two shows at 7:00 and 9:30 p.m.)

The Beach Boys gave three performances on this day, one of which (the 9:30 p.m. show) they taped. Christine Moorhead of the *Annapolis Capitol* noted, "Strangely enough throughout the concert there wasn't any of the usual screaming—only hand clapping, unlike many other rock 'n' roll concerts. Mike Love . . . was the main spokesman for the popular group. His jokes interspersed between songs added humor and zest to the program and thrilled the audience. The program included such songs as 'Surfer Girl,' 'I Get Around,' 'God Only Knows,' 'California Girls,' 'Barbara Ann,' and 'Wouldn't It Be Nice.'"

MONDAY, NOVEMBER 20, 1967: Bushnell Memorial, Hartford, CT, with Buffalo Springfield, the Strawberry Alarm Clock, the Soul Survivors, and the Pickle Brothers (7:00 p.m. show) and Fairfield University, Fairfield, CT, with Buffalo Springfield, the Strawberry Alarm Clock, the Soul Survivors, and the Pickle Brothers (8:30 p.m. show)

1967

Waiting for the curtains to open. Al and Carl (with road manager Steve Korthof) in Buffalo, New York, November 18, 1967. Dick Hollaert/Joe Russo (www.therascalsarchives.com)

The group played concerts in two different cities on the same night. Following the Fairfield show, Patrick Long of *The Stag* interviewed Carl. Asked about the significance of *Smiley Smile*, he replied, "How were we to follow up Pet Sounds? Use an 800-piece orchestra to back us up? *Smiley Smile* is a collection of sounds without any deep meaning. It is a very personal album and because of this there is a lot about it that the average listener doesn't understand."

TUESDAY, NOVEMBER 21, 1967: Westchester County Center, White Plains, NY, with Buffalo Springfield, the Soul Survivors, the Strawberry Alarm Clock, and the Pickle Brothers (8:00 p.m. show)
This show was sponsored by Iona College.

WEDNESDAY, NOVEMBER 22, 1967: Penn Theatre, Pittsburgh, PA, with Buffalo Springfield, the Strawberry Alarm Clock, the Soul Survivors, and the Pickle Brothers (Two shows at 7:00 and 9:30 p.m.)
Once again, the Beach Boys taped one of their two shows. The 9:30 p.m. set list consisted of "Help Me Rhonda," "Darlin'," "I Get Around," "Surfer Girl," "Wouldn't It Be Nice," "God Only Knows," "California Girls," "Wild Honey," "Good Vibrations," "Graduation Day," "Sloop John B.," and "Johnny B. Goode."

THURSDAY, NOVEMBER 23, 1967: Back Bay Theatre, Boston, MA, with Buffalo Springfield, the Strawberry Alarm Clock, the Soul Survivors, and the Pickle Brothers (8:00 p.m. show)

FRIDAY, NOVEMBER 24, 1967: Rhode Island Auditorium, Providence, RI, with Buffalo Springfield, the Strawberry Alarm Clock, the Soul Survivors, and the Pickle Brothers (7:30 p.m. show) and Back Bay Theatre, Boston, MA, with Buffalo Springfield, the Strawberry Alarm Clock, the Soul Survivors, and the Pickle Brothers (9:00 p.m. show)

SATURDAY, NOVEMBER 25, 1967: West Point Military Academy, Highland Hills, NY, with Buffalo Springfield, the Strawberry Alarm Clock, the Soul Survivors, and the Pickle Brothers and St. John's University, Jamaica, NY, with Buffalo Springfield, the Strawberry Alarm Clock, the Soul Survivors, and the Pickle Brothers (8:30 p.m. show)

Perhaps the decision was an attempt to repair the harmony within the group that had been shattered by *Smile*. Or perhaps, after *Smile*, Brian just no longer cared enough. The LP had a very stoned and slightly creepy vibe. Group members later admitted to taking drugs while recording it.

No one in the Beach Boys seemed under any illusions that it was a masterpiece. Carl seemed almost apologetic about the record, telling a reporter that September that the group had "decided not to have a complicated album this time. We did *Smiley Smile* in a couple of weeks, to get something out. It's not nearly as ambitious an album as *Pet Sounds* was." Dennis dismissed the album to the *New Musical Express* writer Keith Altham as "just something we were going through at that time, connected with drugs, love, and everything." Still, it came as a shock when *Smiley Smile* peaked at number forty-one on the *Billboard* charts, by far the worst showing of any Beach Boys LP to date. Critically, the album was an even bigger disaster. After all of the hype about Brian and *Smile*, the album that was eventually released seemed an admission of defeat. Jann Wenner of the new San Francisco–based music paper *Rolling Stone* declared that Brian's "promotion men started to tell him and his audience that he was a 'genius' and on a par with Lennon and McCartney. That's cool cause were all just folks, but no one is John Lennon except John Lennon and no one is Paul McCartney except Paul McCartney and the Beach Boys (let alone Chad and Jeremy) are not the Beatles . . . The Beach Boys are just one prominent example of a group that has gotten hung up in trying to catch the Beatles. It is a pointless pursuit."

The group shook off the bad vibes and hastily headed back into the studio to record a followup LP. Brian showed no inclination toward a big production, so the group went for simplicity again. The result, *Wild Honey*, was a homespun Beach Boys R&B record. Like *Smiley Smile*, the LP had a low-tech vibe, but the group sounded brighter, more focused, and less stoned. While not a huge seller, it made it to a decent number twenty-four on the *Billboard* charts, helped immensely by the great single "Darlin.'" Brian and Mike composed the upbeat rocker while Carl gave the track its deliciously soulful lead vocal. The LP also contained the dynamic title track, the bucolic "Country Air," Brian's amusing "I'd Love Just Once To See You," and the sunshine pop ditty "Aren't You Glad." In retrospect, the Beach Boys seemed proud of the LP. Carl told writer Geoffrey Himes in 1983, "Wild Honey was underrated. It didn't have the polish and pizzazz, but it brought out all our R&B influences that had always been there but people had overlooked."

The release of *Wild Honey* in December sounded a modestly positive last note in a year of bad news. There were obvious dents in the Beach Boys' aura of invincibility and serious reasons for concern. Their leader was no longer engaged in the struggle to keep them at the top and the group had major doubts that they could maintain that position without his help. The year 1968 would put them all to the test.

The concert at the military academy was attended by "the largest audience ever to see a show at West Point," according to the West Point yearbook. The appearance at St. John's later that night was also a sellout.

SUNDAY, NOVEMBER 26, 1967: Seton Hall University, South Orange, NJ, with Buffalo Springfield, the Strawberry Alarm Clock, the Soul Survivors, and the Pickle Brothers (2:00 p.m. show) and Civic Center, Baltimore, MD, with Buffalo Springfield, the Strawberry Alarm Clock, the Soul Survivors, the Pickle Brothers, and Bob Brady and the Concords (8:00 p.m. show)

FRIDAY, DECEMBER 15, 1967: UNICEF Gala, Paris, France, with Marlon Brando, Lena Horne, Victor Borge, Johnny Halliday, Ravi Shankar, Elizabeth Taylor, and Richard Burton

The Beach Boys arrived in Paris on Wednesday, December 13 to prepare for their appearance at this high-profile event on behalf of the United Nations Children's Fund. Highlights were aired on BBC1 television on December 27. It was also filmed by *Eurovision* and aired in its entirety on Christmas Eve in France. The eclectic gathering of talent included Marlon Brando performing Polynesian dances, Ravi Shankar playing Indian ragas on the sitar, and Richard Burton singing a song from *Camelot*, while wife Liz Taylor held up a sign with his name on it. The Beach Boys performed "Barbara Ann," "God Only Knows," "Good Vibrations," and "O Come All Ye Faithful" in white suits. Ron Brown (bass) and Daryl Dragon (keyboards) accompanied them onstage.

In a 1973 interview, Mike mentioned that this was one of the few times he got nervous at a gig because "it was a big important show; you know everyone in the audience was in tuxes and everything in this really posh theater there. There was a big huge orchestra behind us. In the front there were three guys that we knew pretty well; they were pretty famous at the time . . . that was the Maharishi and John Lennon and George Harrison." Following the show, John and George introduced the Beach Boys to the Indian holy man, who gave them a mantra and explained transcendental meditation. Ironically, Mike, who would become the most devout TM devotee in the group, traveled to London after the show and missed the Maharishi meeting. An excited Dennis called Mike and convinced him to return to Paris. By the time the group flew to London on December 17, they had all become enthusiastic disciples of TM. At a reception in their honor at the Hilton Hotel, Mike stated, "Maharishi's ideas are so simple and so right that I cannot begin to explain how impressed I was." While Carl gushed "He's the purest, most honest human being I've ever met . . . I've only been into this meditation practice for two days but I'm completely convinced that it is a good and constructive thing." Al, who would also become a lifelong TM devotee, was equally won over. He told a reporter, "The Maharishi is really sincere. He's no con man. At least, this is what I feel." The group was so taken with Maharishi that in January they talked Brian into flying to New York to meet him and receive his mantra.

The main purpose of the group's year-end visit to England was to discuss yet another tour of the U.K. with promoter Arthur Howes. The band originally planned to return in the spring of 1968, but ultimately the tour did not happen until November. While in England, the group made no TV appearances, but did consent to an interview for Alan Freeman's BBC Radio program *Pop Inn* on December 18. Although the rest of the group flew home soon afterwards, Mike and Bruce remained in the U.K. long enough to attend the Beatles' party at the Royal Lancaster Hotel on December 21 to celebrate the upcoming premiere of their *Magical Mystery Tour* television special, which aired on December 26. All the guests turned up in wild costumes, including John Lennon, who wore his black leather stage outfit from the early Cavern Club days.

CONCERTS NOT PLAYED

The most notable concert not played in 1967 was the Monterey Pop Festival. The Beach Boys were included in concert advertising and the festival program, which only seemed to magnify their embarrassing last-minute cancellation.

The Beach Boys were originally scheduled to play at Painters Mill Theater in Maryland on October 29, but the show was canceled.

1968

THE YEAR 1968 began on a hopeful note. The Beach Boys enthusiastically embraced the concept of Transcendental Meditation while in Paris. Upon their return to L.A. they gushed to Brian about the peaceful feelings that it inspired in them. Brian was excited. He told an interviewer that January, "I had already been initiated a year before and for some ridiculous reason I hadn't followed through with it . . . And now all of a sudden we're all meditating together and it just seems to be right on time . . . We've been meditating and doing this Maharishi thing and it's just been beautiful." For the time being, interest in meditation united the group and also inspired their next LP, to be titled *Friends*.

Friends set the pattern that the next five Beach Boys albums would follow. Rather than a Brian Wilson production, it was a democratic project, with everyone contributing songs and production ideas. It's hard to say whether this change came about because Brian could not focus enough to lead (or no longer cared enough to lead), or because the rest of the group was no longer willing to defer to him. As a result, *Friends* is a peaceful and uplifting album, but it lacks the dynamism of the Beach Boys' more commercial material. The brilliant "Busy Doin' Nothing" is a definite highlight and showed Brian's composing and arranging skills were intact. Dennis surprisingly provided two of the album's most interesting songs. His lovely "Little Bird" and deeply spiritual "Be Still" suggested that the Beach Boys had more than one

CONCERTS PLAYED IN 1968

impressive songwriter named Wilson. Predictably the LP was a commercial bomb. The Beach Boys' confidence was already shaken by the relative failures of *Smiley Smile* and *Wild Honey*. The public's reaction to *Friends*, which peaked at a horrifying number 126 on the *Billboard* charts, emphasized the reality of a very difficult time for the group. Though the Beach Boys continued to release high-quality albums, sales figures suggested that the public did not care in the slightest. It was telling that their lone commercial success of the year came with a nostalgic summer single titled "Do It Again." The simple and rocking Brian Wilson/Mike Love song was a throwback to the old Beach Boys sound. It hit the top twenty in the U.S. and a surprising number one in Britain, but the temporary relief of a U.K. hit was short-lived.

Although their problems were many, the Beach Boys were still a fairly popular concert attraction. Plans were underway for a major spring tour of southern cities, which the group was mostly handling through their own American Productions. Jack Lloyd went to work for the group at this time. Lloyd recalled the Beach Boys had high hopes for the tour, which was set to begin on April 5 in Tennessee. They flew to Nashville on April 4, 1968, but, as business manager Nick Grillo related to *Amusement Business*, "Exactly as we boarded the plane for Nashville we got the news that Dr. King had been shot; when we landed in Nashville the announcement was made that he was dead."

As a result of Dr. Martin Luther King's tragic assassination, the opening

THURSDAY, FEBRUARY 1, 1968: Everett Community College, Everett, WA, with Buffalo Springfield
The first tour of the year was a quick and profitable swing through the Pacific Northwest. The group grossed $60,000 on the four-day tour, including $8,050 at this opening show. It was a sellout, with tickets priced between $2.00 and $5.00.

FRIDAY, FEBRUARY 2, 1968: Seattle Center Arena, Seattle, WA, with Buffalo Springfield and Springfield Rifle (8:00 p.m. show)
The group hit Seattle in the midst of a major snowstorm, but Ed Baker of the *Seattle Times* reported that they "entertained an audience of 5,500 screaming, whistling, flash-bulb-popping teeny boppers (and a few older fans) at the Arena last night . . . The Beach Boys gave generously. The numbers were short and plentiful. Screams of recognition greeted each opening bar. With the Arena's amplification system revved up to about 10,000 decibels, the lyrics were unintelligible to the uninitiated but the Beach Boys' faithful following seemed to get every message loud and clear."

SATURDAY, FEBRUARY 3, 1968: Agrodome, Vancouver, BC, Canada, with Buffalo Springfield (8:00 p.m. show)
This was another sellout, for which the Beach Boys netted $10,000.

SUNDAY, FEBRUARY 4, 1968: Memorial Coliseum, Portland, OR, with Buffalo Springfield (2:00 p.m. show) and St. Martin's College, Lacey, WA, with Buffalo Springfield and the Smiling Castle
The Beach Boys netted $18,918 for the Portland matinee and another $8,000 for the Lacey concert that night. St. Martin's College was the sort of venue the group came to prefer. Carl told writer Gene Hurley there was "no screaming like we used to get a couple of years ago. Sometimes they dance and just groove. No riots or anything like there used to be. I think kids are growing up . . . Well, not only kids, but everybody. I'm glad about that. Before about all you'd have to do is strum the guitar and the audience would supply the sound with all that yelling. But no more, now they listen."

FRIDAY, APRIL 5, 1968: Municipal Auditorium, Nashville, TN, with Buffalo Springfield and the Strawberry Alarm Clock (Canceled)
The Beach Boys embarked on an ambitious tour with Buffalo Springfield and the Strawberry Alarm Clock on April 4, but it quickly ran into trouble in the wake of Martin Luther King's assassination. All three groups spent a dreary day at a Holiday Inn, while management scrambled to do damage control.

Steve Desper, Dick Duryea, Jack Lloyd, Steve Korthof, and Jon Parks accompanied the group on this tour. Keyboardist Daryl Dragon, however, was ill and was replaced by his older brother Doug. Doug Dragon recalled, "Daryl taught me all the parts so I could go out with them . . . I didn't play with the group that long, but I had some great memories. Crazy ones, perverted ones, you know the typical rock band thing . . . it wasn't all mom and apple pie. On the other side, I got to learn some really great tunes, like 'Good Vibrations.' My favorite was 'God Only Knows.' I loved the piano part on that." Doug's younger brother, percussionist Dennis Dragon, also was on the tour. He remained with the Beach Boys, off and on, through 1972. Later to achieve fame with his band the Surf Punks, Dennis got his start as a jazz drummer with Blue Note Records. Daryl Dragon recalled, "Dennis played extra percussion and when Dennis Wilson went a little crazy he'd play drums too. Dennis Wilson would run off the stage sometimes and throw the sticks at Dennis and say 'Take it!'"

SATURDAY, APRIL 6, 1968: Minges Coliseum, East Carolina College, Greenville, NC, with Buffalo Springfield and the Strawberry Alarm Clock (1:00 p.m. show)
The afternoon show at East Carolina College took place as scheduled, but an evening show in Raleigh was postponed until April 23.

1968

Taping a TV appearance, **March 1968.** Ian Rusten Collection

SUNDAY, APRIL 7, 1968: Clemson University, Clemson, SC, with Buffalo Springfield and the Strawberry Alarm Clock (2:30 p.m. show) and Columbia Township Auditorium, Columbia, SC (Canceled)

The Beach Boys were scheduled to appear in Greensboro, but the concert was postponed until April 23. They played an afternoon show at Clemson, as part of the Junior-Senior weekend festivities. A concert scheduled for that night in Columbia was canceled.

MONDAY, APRIL 8, 1968: County Hall, Charleston, SC, with Buffalo Springfield and the Strawberry Alarm Clock (7:00 p.m. show)

TUESDAY, APRIL 9, 1968: Florida Southern College, Lakeland, FL, with Buffalo Springfield and the Strawberry Alarm Clock (4:30 p.m. show) and Sports Stadium, Orlando, FL, with Buffalo Springfield and the Strawberry Alarm Clock (7:00 p.m. show) and Memorial Stadium, Daytona Beach, FL, with Buffalo Springfield and the Strawberry Alarm Clock (8:00 p.m. show)

After a bumpy start, the tour picked up steam with three concerts in Florida. Steve Desper recalled, "On that tour we were doing two or three shows a day and we had two sound systems and two sound crews and we would leapfrog each other. So a lot of the time I would be with the Beach Boys and I would just come in and mix and my crew would set it up (at the next venue) and I would be in contact with them over the telephone." Dennis Dragon recalled the tour with mixed feelings. "It was *insane*, with sometimes three performances booked in three different places in a day! Too much! I watched Neil Young's health decline with multiple bouts of epilepsy due to the stress. It was not a good tour."

WEDNESDAY, APRIL 10, 1968: University of Florida, Gainesville, FL, with Buffalo Springfield and the Strawberry Alarm Clock (7:00 p.m. show)

The Beach Boys' contract with the University of Florida stated that the three acts would receive seventy percent of the gate, which ended up being $6,500. As a result, after expenses the Inter Fraternity Council who sponsored the show only made $1,500. There were 5,200 attendees, of which only 3,500 were actually from the University. The Council blamed the low attendance on the race riots and the decision to have the show on a weekday. The group generously donated $1000 from their own pockets to help offset the short fall.

THURSDAY, APRIL 11, 1968: City Auditorium, Macon, GA, with Buffalo Springfield and the

show of the tour was abruptly canceled. From there, the tour experienced an ongoing series of problems. Due to fear of riots by African-Americans, curfews were instituted in a number of southern cities. Concerts in North Carolina and Memphis had to be rescheduled to later in the month. *Amusement Business* stated that shows in Nashville, Tennessee (April 5); Columbia, South Carolina (April 7); Atlanta, Georgia (April 11); Macon, Georgia (April 11); Little Rock, Arkansas (April 16); and Jonesboro, Arkansas (April 17) were canceled. Racial unrest kept audiences away in droves and many of the concerts that managed to go on suffered from low attendance. The tour proved to be a financial drain on the group, who were fronting the money for the dates themselves. Nick Grillo estimated it cost them at least $350,000 in revenue.

The group's financial problems were compounded by an even bigger fiasco, which directly followed the miserable southern tour. In May 1968 the Beach Boys decided to tour in tandem with their Indian guru Maharishi Mahesh Yogi. Though all the Beach Boys had become devoted followers, it was Mike Love who was so fascinated by Transcendental Meditation that he flew to Rishikesh, India in February to participate in a meditation retreat with Maharishi, the Beatles, Donovan, and Mia Farrow. While in India, Mike suggested that a tour with Maharishi would help spread his message to more young people. Mike explained to a reporter, "because the Beach Boys are the top American group, he agreed to tour with us. He wants to get his message across to American youth . . . that man was not born to suffer. Anyhow his meditation will do a lot of good by getting kids away from LSD, pot, booze, and speed because you really don't need it if you understand what the Maharishi is saying." The group planned for thirty-five concerts, which would include a Beach Boys performance and a Maharishi lecture.

The tour proved to be ill-fated from the very start. Maharishi failed to arrive for an important press conference in New York on May 2. He had flown from India to Istanbul but missed his connecting flight because he was meditating. He arrived in New York at 4 p.m. on May 3 and had to be rushed to the first show, which was only sparsely attended. It soon became apparent that, as one promoter remarked, "The Guru couldn't draw flies." Newspaper advertisements that pictured Maharishi rather than the Beach Boys didn't help. Teenagers that might have attended a music concert didn't want to go hear a lecture. Interest was so low that a show at the Singer Bowl in NY sold just 800 tickets. By May 5, Maharishi had decided to abandon the whole idea and the rest of the tour was canceled. As some tickets for these canceled concerts had already been sold, the Beach Boys were forced to issue refunds. In a BBC Radio interview, Dick Duryea called the tour "the biggest fiasco of anything I've been involved with. The Maharishi was a nice man but nobody wanted to listen to him. They came to

Strawberry Alarm Clock (7:00 p.m. show canceled) and Municipal Auditorium, Atlanta, GA, with Buffalo Springfield and the Strawberry Alarm Clock (8:00 p.m. show canceled)
The Macon show was postponed due to rioting and rescheduled for later in the month. Ultimately it was canceled, though the group returned to honor the date in October. The Atlanta appearance also was canceled.

FRIDAY, APRIL 12, 1968: Jacksonville Coliseum, Jacksonville, FL, with Buffalo Springfield and the Strawberry Alarm Clock (8:00 p.m. show)
Part of the proceeds from this concert benefitted the Heart Fund, an organization that donated surgical tools needed for open-heart surgery to hospitals. During the day, the group watched a film showing an open-heart surgery and gave the fund a $1000 donation.

Doug Dragon recalled some crazy moments on this tour. "My brother Dennis threw cherry bombs down the hallway in one of the international hotels and Steve Stills flipped out. I said to Dennis, 'We better get out of here!' So we went back to our room and boarded it up in case there was any retaliation."

SATURDAY, APRIL 13, 1968: Robart's Sports Arena, Sarasota, FL, with Buffalo Springfield and Bobby Goldsboro (7:00 p.m. show) and Curtis Hixon Hall, Tampa, FL, with Buffalo Springfield, the Frogs, and Bobby Goldsboro (8:30 p.m. show)
The first "big name rock concert" in Sarasota drew 5,000 fans. Judy Copeland of the *Sarasota Journal* gushed, "The Beach Boys in person are even more fabulous than the Beach Boys on records. They held the whole audience spellbound from the first notes of 'Darlin'' through older numbers such as 'California Girls' and 'Rhonda' to their latest hit, 'Friends.' The old standard, 'Graduation Day' was beautifully sung but 'Good Vibrations' and 'God Only Knows' seemed to be the fans' favorite numbers . . . Members of the audience who expected a T-shirt and jeans uniform were surprised to see the Beach Boys in white double-breasted suits. The only thing reminiscent of the surfer image was Dennis Wilson in his sandals."

The Tampa show was attended by 5,000 fans, and started late due to sound system issues. Steve Desper told a reporter, "something happened to the power source for the system and we are running the whole thing on two car batteries." The Beach Boys did not go onstage until 10:45 p.m. To make up for the late start, they played for an extra forty-five minutes. Kay Donahue of the *Evening Independent* called it a "mind blowing night . . . As the Beach Boys did one after another of their top ten hits—from the recent 'Darlin'' to the earlier sounds of 'Surfer Girl'—the audience swayed and clapped to the beat." According to Donahue, one unnamed Beach Boy (undoubtedly Dennis) sat onstage by himself playing songs on the piano long after the crowd left the venue.

SUNDAY, APRIL 14, 1968: Convention Hall, Miami, FL, with the Strawberry Alarm Clock, Buffalo Springfield, Bobby Goldsboro, and the Echoes (8:00 p.m. show)

MONDAY, APRIL 15, 1968: Municipal Auditorium, San Antonio, TX, with the Strawberry Alarm Clock and Buffalo Springfield (7:00 p.m. show) and Municipal Auditorium, Austin, TX, with the Lavender Hill Express, the Strawberry Alarm Clock, and Buffalo Springfield (8:30 p.m. show)

TUESDAY, APRIL 16, 1968: Robinson Auditorium, Little Rock, AR, with the Strawberry Alarm Clock and Buffalo Springfield (7:30 p.m. show canceled)

WEDNESDAY, APRIL 17, 1968: Arkansas State University, Jonesboro, AR, with the Strawberry Alarm Clock and Buffalo Springfield (Canceled)
A Memphis show was rescheduled for April 24. The Jonesboro show was canceled.

THURSDAY, APRIL 18, 1968: John M. Parker Agricultural Center, Louisiana State University, Baton Rouge, LA, with the Strawberry Alarm Clock and Buffalo Springfield (7:00 p.m. show) and Loyola University, New Orleans, LA, with the Strawberry Alarm Clock and Buffalo Springfield (8:45 p.m. show)
The tour headed to Louisiana for two concerts. Eldridge Roark reviewed the LSU show for the *Daily*

1968

Reveille. He dismissed the group as unhip bubblegum pop and declared, "If it were not for the mass of teeny boppers in the place, the show would have been a complete flop. The Beach Boys, arriving in their super-cool white suits and sneakers, sang in the style that most of the upperclassmen on campus twisted to at their high school prom. Songs like 'Help Me Rhonda' and 'Surfer Girl' were quite popular five years ago, but drew snide comments and yawns from the older element of the crowd. Of course, the 12-year-olds completely blew their minds."

David Cutforth of the *Baton Rouge Advocate* had a different take. He commented, "The Beach Boys kicked off an impressive forty-five minutes with 'Help Me Rhonda' and it was immediately apparent a treat was in store. The help their orchestra gave was welcome in the first selections. The brass in 'Darlin'' was out of sight. Perhaps one of the most complex compositions performed by touring rock groups is 'Good Vibrations.' The Beach Boys had all the goods needed to duplicate studio sound on the live stage and they proceeded to do so . . . The audience was still applauding as they ran out on their way to New Orleans for their next show."

FRIDAY, APRIL 19, 1968: Birmingham City Auditorium, Birmingham, AL, with the Strawberry Alarm Clock, Buffalo Springfield, and Randy's World (8:30 p.m. show)
Gene Butts of the *Birmingham News* noted that the group "declared that meditation gave them increased energy and they unleashed it all. Their ability to score in different musical styles was apparent from the first minute. They played a medley of their original surfing songs and other successes, including 'Sloop John B,' and 'Good Vibrations.' Dennis the barefoot drummer leaped down from the bandstand to join the group in their newest release 'Friends.'"

SATURDAY, APRIL 20, 1968: Will Rogers Coliseum, Fort Worth, TX, with the Strawberry Alarm Clock, Buffalo Springfield, and Bobby Goldsboro (7:00 p.m. show) and Market Hall, Dallas, TX, with the Strawberry Alarm Clock, Buffalo Springfield, Bobby Goldsboro, and the Soul Society (8:30 p.m. show)
The group played in both Fort Worth and Dallas despite the two cities' close proximity. According to Cheryl Russell of the *Dallas Morning News*, "The Beach Boys achieved a clear, choir-like harmony with their treatment of 'Graduation Day' while their pulsating 'Good Vibrations' literally shook the bandstand. The Beach Boys tide of hits engulfed the young listeners, as they revived memories of 'Barbara Ann,' 'I Get Around,' 'California Girl,' and 'I Want to Go Home (Sloop John B).'"

SUNDAY, APRIL 21, 1968: Moody Civic Center, Galveston, TX, with the Strawberry Alarm Clock and Buffalo Springfield (2:30 p.m. show) and McDonald Gym, Lamar Technical College, Beaumont, TX, with the Strawberry Alarm Clock and Buffalo Springfield (4:30 p.m. show) and Sam Houston Coliseum, Houston, TX, with the Strawberry Alarm Clock and Buffalo Springfield

MONDAY, APRIL 22, 1968: Municipal Coliseum, Lubbock, TX, with the Strawberry Alarm Clock and Buffalo Springfield

TUESDAY, APRIL 23, 1968: Greensboro Coliseum, Greensboro, NC, with the Strawberry Alarm Clock and Buffalo Springfield (7:00 p.m. show) and Dorton Arena, Raleigh, NC, with the Strawberry Alarm Clock and Buffalo Springfield (8:30 p.m. show)
The group played two shows originally scheduled for April 6 and 7.

WEDNESDAY, APRIL 24, 1968: Mid-South Coliseum, Memphis, TN, with the Strawberry Alarm Clock and Buffalo Springfield
This show, originally scheduled for April 17, drew 5,400. The group played "Help Me Rhonda," "I Get Around," "Friends," "Surfer Girl," "Sloop John B," "Wouldn't It Be Nice," "Darlin'," "God Only Knows," "Good Vibrations," "Surfin' Safari," "Fun, Fun, Fun," "Shut Down," "Little Deuce Coupe," "Surfin' USA," "Papa-Oom-Mow-Mow," "Graduation Day," and "Barbara Ann." Dorothy Beith of the *Commercial Appeal* reported the audience was so enthusiastic that, "after the West Coast group played through a program of old and new favorites like 'Let's Be Friends,' 'Help Me Rhonda,' and 'Surfer Girl,' the crowd kept them on stage more than fifteen minutes playing encores."

"Mike Love was the guy that put that whole thing together. I thought it was kind of a stretch but I didn't say anything. I mean you have a highly evolved dude like Maharishi Mahesh Yogi and you're going to try and work in 'Help Me Rhonda' into that? Is that going to work? And it just didn't work."

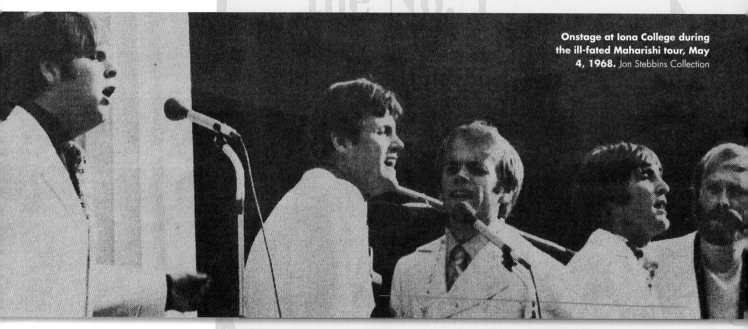

Onstage at Iona College during the ill-fated Maharishi tour, May 4, 1968. Jon Stebbins Collection

hear the Beach Boys and when he went on stage and started talking, they all left . . . they must have lost a quarter of a million dollars on that tour."

Tours for July and August were hastily booked as an attempt to recoup the huge losses of two consecutive money-draining tours. The shows were relatively successful, but the Beach Boys were still performing what was basically the same show that they had in 1966. By 1968 standards, their concerts were quite short and minimal. Groups like Cream and the Jimi Hendrix Experience routinely played for one and a half or even two hours, while the Beach Boys were gone after 40 minutes. The college-age audiences that bands relied on to buy tickets expected more from a live performance than the Beach Boys were offering.

Rock fans began to reject the Beach Boys and their wholesome image. They looked very square compared to the groups coming out of San Francisco and London. As Bruce Johnston put it in

FRIDAY, MAY 3, 1968: Washington Coliseum, with Maharishi Mahesh Yogi (6:30 p.m. show) and Civic Center, Baltimore, MD, with Maharishi Mahesh Yogi (8:45 p.m. show)

After a week's respite, the Beach Boys embarked on the ill-fated tour with Maharishi Mahesh Yogi. They made a live appearance on the *Tonight Show* while in New York on May 2. That same day a taped appearance on *The Les Crane Show* also aired. The group intended to give the best concerts possible and hired a full contingent of backup musicians. Doug Dragon again filled in for brother Daryl on piano. Dennis Dragon played extra percussion. The Beach Boys also had a four-piece horn section lined up, but at the last minute, they dropped out. Doug Dragon recalled, "I was in New York and Nick Grillo called me. I didn't know Nick that well, but he told me that he was in a jam. He said, 'my four musicians just stood me up in New York. You've got twenty-four hours to get me four musicians.' So I had to figure that out in New York, a place that I didn't even know about . . . I called my cousin who lived there and in twenty-four hours I got the names of four guys. I don't remember all the names, but Joel Peskin was one (on saxophone) and Glenn Lewis was on trumpet and Ernie Small on trombone . . . So, I called back Nick and said 'OK, I got the musicians but what about the money?' He said, 'Don't worry about the money.' I said, 'These guys aren't going to get on your chartered plane from New York unless they are getting paid in cash.' So he passed the buck to Jack Lloyd. The plane was literally revving up ready to go, and I still didn't have the money. So I went up to Jack Lloyd and said 'Jack, this is no bullshit, these guys are not getting on the plane.' So at the last minute Jack pulled out the $2,500 and they boarded the plane."

Unfortunately, despite all the hard work, the tour quickly fizzled. Only 1,500 fans showed up at the 8,000-seat Washington Coliseum. According to Charley Impaglia of *The Hoya*, "whole sections were abandoned and those who actually paid the $5.50 top [price] felt cheated since you could sit where you liked in the one-third-full auditorium." He noted that audiences missed a great performance as "the five-some strove for absolute fealty to the recording studio sound and succeeded brilliantly. Even the most rabid detractor would have been forced to concede that their renditions of 'Darlin',' 'Sloop John B,' and 'God Only Knows' were letter-perfect." In Baltimore, 2,888 people turned out for the evening show at a venue capable of comfortably seating 11,500. Hecklers interrupted Maharishi's lecture repeatedly. The Beach Boys were not amused and Bruce later disparagingly recalled, "The kids in Baltimore were really vulgar."

SATURDAY, MAY 4, 1968: Singer Bowl, Flushing, NY, with Maharishi Mahesh Yogi (2:00 p.m. show canceled) and Iona College, New Rochelle, NY, with Maharishi Mahesh Yogi (4:30 p.m. show) and Spectrum, Philadelphia, PA, with Maharishi Mahesh Yogi

May 4 was a discouraging day for the group. To begin with, the early show at the Singer Bowl was canceled at the last minute. According to *Go* magazine, "a threat of rain was given as the reason, but more likely was the fact that few tickets had been sold." June Harris reported in *New Musical Express*, "The Beach Boys arrived some time before the concert and set up their equipment ready to go on stage when the news reached them that Maharishi was still in his New York hotel suite, unwilling to appear before a reported crowd of less than 1,000 people."

The concert at Iona College went on as planned but only brought out about 1,800 students. The sparse audience enjoyed the group's set, which included a rare performance of the *Friends* track "Transcendental Meditation." Maharishi's lecture, however, was less well received. *Go* magazine noted that "as the Maharishi attempted to explain his philosophy of transcendental meditation to the crowd, hecklers demanding the return of the Beach Boys interrupted him. Other hecklers denounced him as seeking money. Finally Mike Love . . . was forced to come onstage and quiet the crowd. Mike said: 'I would personally appreciate it that, if you don't want to listen, you would leave. There are a lot of young people here but you will get older and want to remember the Maharishi.'"

About 6,000 people attended the evening show at the 17,162-seat Spectrum, but half of them walked out after the Beach Boys' set, rather than stay for the Maharishi's lecture. Mike Love told the *Philadelphia Inquirer* that this did not surprise Maharishi. "He knows it's going to happen . . . they aren't quite ready for meditation." The Philadelphia show, which had the largest audience of the tour, grossed barely enough for promoters to break even.

SUNDAY, MAY 5, 1968: Bushnell Memorial, Hartford, CT, with Maharishi Mahesh Yogi (7:00 p.m. show) and Rhode Island Auditorium, Providence, RI, with Maharishi Mahesh Yogi (8:30 p.m. show canceled)
In Hartford, 3,000 fans attended the show. *The Hartford Times* noted, "Backed by their own band and augmented by seventeen microphones, the Beach Boys poured out a concert of their most famous hits in the first half of the program. They were enthusiastically received by an audience of mostly high school students." Doug Dragon recalled, "That was the only place where we had a good response to that package. Mike Love was the guy that put that whole thing together. I thought it was kind of a stretch but I didn't say anything. I mean you have a highly evolved dude like Maharishi Mahesh Yogi and you're going to try and work in 'Help Me Rhonda' into that? Is that going to work? And it just didn't work." Maharishi agreed. After the Hartford gig he informed the group he was leaving the tour due to a film commitment. The second show of the night in Rhode Island, where an audience of 3,500 was already lining up, was abruptly canceled. The treasurer of the auditorium begged Dick Duryea to bring the Beach Boys anyways, but Duryea told him that it was a package show and they weren't prepared to play without Maharishi. The group returned to California.

Scheduled concerts were canceled for the Boston Garden (May 6); Brandeis University (May 7); New Haven Arena (May 7); Quinnipiac College (May 7); Memorial Auditorium, Buffalo (May 8); Ohio State University (May 9); Syracuse University (May 10); Lemoyne College (May 10); Richfield Coliseum, Cleveland (May 11); Chicago University (May 12); Capitol Theatre, Madison (May 13); St. Paul's Arena (May 14); Veteran's Memorial, Des Moines (May 15); Municipal Auditorium, Kansas City (May 15); and Kiel Auditorium, St. Louis (May 16). Maharishi initially agreed to return for shows at the Denver Arena (May 17), Oakland Stadium (May 18), the Hollywood Bowl (May 19), Las Vegas (May 19), Stanford University (May 20), Sacramento (May 21), and San Diego (May 21), but these ultimately did not take place.

SATURDAY, JUNE 15, 1968: Lagoon, Farmington, UT, (Two shows at 7:00 and 9:30 p.m.)
A month after the Maharishi fiasco, the Beach Boys headed to Salt Lake City, Utah where they could always rely on attracting a sizable audience. There the group took part in a photo shoot for *Fabulous 208* magazine. Accompanied by writer Cyril Maitland, they took a jeep ride to locations Al Jardine had previously visited and thought would look good in photos. They posed at an old amusement park and pier, as well as on the shores of the Great Salt Lake. Mike Love had adopted an 1890s look, complete with handlebar mustache, while Dennis sported a full beard. Always a risk-taker, Dennis "asked a local inhabitant if there was any quicksand about and was shown where it was and told that it only dragged you to the thighs . . . this obviously didn't put him off and he decided to try the feel of the quicksand." It's possible that they also filmed the promo film for "Friends" on this trip.

a 1970 radio interview, "the public thinks of us as surfing Doris Days." It didn't help that Capitol Records continued to promote them as the "number one surfing group in America" and used outdated photographs of them. While this was not a problem in the heartland, the Beach Boys were *persona non grata* in places like New York. In October

> "When he got up to the mic, Dennis had this silly grin on his face and looked like he was either really high, totally bombed on alcohol, or both . . ."

when they performed at Bill Graham's Fillmore East, they were given a chilly reception. The influential *Village Voice* attacked Graham for booking a "bubble gum" group. Bill Reed of *Rock* magazine described the Fillmore concert as a near-disaster. "They came onstage decked out in matching ice cream—colored suits and since, generally, Fillmore habitués like their groups grungy, raw, and *au courant*, the Good Humor hallucination on the stage couldn't help but bring out the sadistic side of the audience. By the end of their set, the aging 'Beach Boys' were like panicky circus ponies . . . too much goosing and horsing around betrayed the fact that they really were ashamed of being simply the Beach Boys."

"Brian's a very sensitive, artistic, musical genius who is paranoid of being in any environment other than in his home and family. He's a very domestic kind of person."

Morale was low when the group departed in late November for yet another European tour. However, this time it proved to be just what the group needed. Dick Duryea, told writer Keith Altham that though "coming to Britain is not really a very good commercial proposition for them . . . they genuinely love England." The Beach Boys were eager to avoid

TUESDAY, JULY 2, 1968: RKO Orpheum Theatre, Davenport, IA, with Gary Puckett and the Union Gap and the Human Beinz (Two shows at 6:30 and 9:00 p.m.)
This sixteen-date tour billed the group with the Union Gap and the Human Beinz. The Beach Boys brought ten extra musicians with them, including a full brass section led by saxophonist Ernie Small. Percussionist Mike Kowalski and bassist Ed Carter, who would both have long relationships with the group, also were on this tour. They were hired as a result of Kowalski's friendship with Bruce Johnston. Based on Bruce's recommendation, they auditioned for Carl Wilson at the Moulin Rouge club in Hollywood. Kowalski played extra percussion and took over drums when Dennis Wilson came up front to sing. Carter handled bass duties, freeing up Bruce to play keyboards. Carter would go on to work countless tours as bassist or guitarist with the Beach Boys over the next thirty years.

The group taped some shows on this tour. However, they used only two tracks (one board and one ambient audience mic) and the sound is somewhat subpar. It's likely that the shows were recorded only for the band's personal archives, rather than for any live album. Steve Desper, who accompanied them as sound mixer, recalled that it was not unusual for the band to record gigs in this period, though few survive. "We made a recording every night of the show, listened to it and critiqued it and then usually erased it and made another recording the next night on top of it. We just used the same tape over and over again."

WEDNESDAY, JULY 3, 1968: Sioux Falls Arena, Sioux Falls, SD, with Gary Puckett and the Union Gap and the Human Beinz

THURSDAY, JULY 4, 1968: Majestic Hills, Lake Geneva, WI, with Gary Puckett and the Union Gap and the Human Beinz

FRIDAY, JULY 5, 1968: Auditorium Theatre, Chicago, IL, with Gary Puckett and the Union Gap and the Human Beinz (8:30 p.m. show)
Robb Baker of *The Tribune* criticized the group for sticking to the "oldies" rather than performing songs from post-Pet Sounds albums. "It's not that their Top Forty songs are really bad: In fact, for what they attempt, they're rather good. The distinctive beat, the quick tempo changes, the harmonizing in the upper registry are all effective, but they're a bit like circus dogs who keep wagging their tails (and making their feeble jokes) long after the crowd has tired of their single trick."

The Human Beinz, noted for their hit single "Nobody But Me," opened for the group. Lead vocalist/guitarist Ting Markulin recalled that he and drummer Mike Tatman were asked to find a missing Dennis on Friday afternoon as the Beach Boys suspected that he had gotten lost in downtown Chicago when he didn't show for the pre-concert soundcheck. They drove around Chicago in their motor home until they finally located him. "He wasn't that hard to spot because he always wore a white suit with no shirt and he was always barefoot. He recognized us as we were shouting his name and got in the motor home. He thanked us for finding him and taking him back to the hall. He invited us to meet at his room after the concert for a little party. Dennis loved pink champagne in frosted glasses and when we showed up that night, he had cases of pink champagne and a cooler full of frosted glasses. Well I guess you can imagine how trashed we got. The worst part was that we had to leave and drive all night, while the Beach Boys had their own plane to fly to the next city in the morning. But we didn't care because Dennis was a cool guy and a lot of fun."

SATURDAY, JULY 6, 1968: Anderson High School Gym, Anderson, IN, with Gary Puckett and the Union Gap and the Human Beinz (8:00 p.m. show)

SUNDAY, JULY 7, 1968: Duluth Arena, Duluth, MN, with Gary Puckett and the Union Gap and the Human Beinz (7:30 p.m. show)

MONDAY, JULY 8, 1968: Memorial Auditorium, Fargo, ND, with Gary Puckett and the Union Gap and the Human Beinz (Two shows at 7:00 and 9:30 p.m.)
The group recorded these shows.

TUESDAY, JULY 9, 1968: St. Paul Auditorium Theatre, St. Paul, MN, with Gary Puckett and the Union Gap and the Human Beinz (Two shows at 7:00 and 9:30 p.m.)

WEDNESDAY, JULY 10, 1968: Waterloo, IA, with Gary Puckett and the Union Gap and the Human Beinz
This was a fill-in date booked by Irving Granz. The accommodations were less than glamorous considering the group's dressing room was in a horse stable. The band recorded the show.

THURSDAY, JULY 11, 1968: Ice Arena, Des Moines, IA, with Gary Puckett and the Union Gap and the Human Beinz

FRIDAY, JULY 12, 1968: Memorial Hall, Salina, KS, with Gary Puckett and the Union Gap and the Human Beinz (Two shows at 7:00 and 9:30 p.m.)

SATURDAY, JULY 13, 1968: Pershing Auditorium, Lincoln, NE, with Gary Puckett and the Union Gap and the Human Beinz (8:30 p.m. show)
The band taped this show. The set list consisted of "Darlin'," "Help Me Rhonda," "California Girls," "Sloop John B," "Surfer Girl," "Friends," "Little Bird," "Wouldn't It Be Nice," a medley of "Fun Fun Fun/Shut Down/Little Deuce Coupe/Surfin' USA," "Do It Again," "Wake the World," "God Only Knows," "Their Hearts Were Full of Spring" (the Beach Boys introduced the number as the song they had performed on the *Tonight Show*), "Good Vibrations," "Barbara Ann," and "Johnny B. Goode."

SUNDAY, JULY 14, 1968: Memorial Hall, Kansas City, KS, with Gary Puckett and the Union Gap and the Human Beinz

MONDAY, JULY 15, 1968: Civic Auditorium, Albuquerque, NM, with Gary Puckett and the Union Gap and the Human Beinz (8:30 p.m. show)
This show was attended by 3,000 fans. Prior to their performance, the Beach Boys gave an interview to Brian Tafoya of *The Albuquerque Journal*. The group was asked how its music compared to the records they made three years previous. They replied, "We dip back into our old songs but we try to write new songs—it's what's happening for us." Bruce told the reporter, "The audiences of today are listening first then screaming—not like a few years ago. They used to scream during the whole concert, but now they are listening." The group also stated that they expected Brian's unreleased gem "Can't Wait Too Long" to be their next single, but this did not happen.

TUESDAY, JULY 16, 1968: Exhibition Building, Arizona State Fairgrounds, Phoenix, AZ, with Gary Puckett and the Union Gap and the Human Beinz (8:30 p.m. show)
The group recorded this concert.

WEDNESDAY, JULY 17, 1968: Convention Hall, San Diego, CA, with Gary Puckett and the Union Gap, and the Human Beinz (8:00 p.m. show)
This was the last concert of the tour. The set list consisted of: "Darlin'," "Shut Down/Surfin' USA/ Little Deuce Coupe/Surfin' Safari/409" (medley), "Friends," "Surfer Girl," "Do It Again," "Wake the World," "Little Bird," "Help Me Rhonda," "Fun, Fun, Fun," "Wouldn't It Be Nice," "Sloop John B," "God Only Knows," "Their Hearts Were Full of Spring," "California Girls," "Barbara Ann," "Good Vibrations," and "Johnny B Goode."
According to longtime fan Rob Shepherd, "Mike Love seemed far less upbeat than he had been the previous time I had seen the group in concert a year and a half earlier . . . Carl seemed really exuberant and happy and his positive attitude and obvious joy in singing and playing the music really enhanced the group's onstage presence . . . At some point Mike announced that Brian Wilson was in the audience and Brian, sitting in the center of around the third or fourth row, stood up and waved, turning in all directions. I was disappointed that he didn't come up on stage for at least a few songs . . . During the concert, Dennis had a guy standing next to him, watching him on the drum kit . . . I couldn't figure out why he was there until Dennis came up to the front of the stage to sing

the major criticism of their previous UK tours, that they could not reproduce their records onstage. To remedy this, Steve Desper and the $250,000 sound system he had designed for the group, as well as a talented horn section, accompanied them. *Disc and Music Echo* commented, "they came to Britain, saw, were seen and heard, and they definitely conquered the nation's pop fans with one of the most exciting tours for many years." The group played to capacity houses and cemented a bond with audiences in Europe that would enable them to survive their declining popularity in the states.

THE BEACH BOYS IN CONCERT

'Little Bird' . . . He seemed quite wobbly, and the guy who was standing next to him was holding onto Dennis' arm. When he got up to the mic, Dennis had this silly grin on his face and looked like he was either really high, totally bombed on alcohol, or both . . . In any event, Dennis did a great job singing 'Little Bird,' as well as drumming . . . The Beach Boys had a number of backing musicians, including four or five guys on horns who were sitting behind those little bandstand boxes, and when it came time for them to play they would stand up. Back then you would often see such an arrangement in older adult bands such as the musicians on the *Lawrence Welk* [TV] *Show*, but it seemed totally uncool to me for a rock band, like something an old geezer like Murry would have suggested."

FRIDAY, AUGUST 2, 1968: Ottawa Civic Centre, Ottawa, ON, Canada, with the Box Tops, the Pickle Brothers, and 3's A Crowd (8:30 p.m. show)
The group embarked on a three-week tour with the Box Tops and the Pickle Brothers. Jack Lloyd accompanied them on the Canadian dates, while Dick Duryea handled gigs in the states. Ed Carter played bass, Dennis Dragon played extra percussion, and Doug Dragon played piano/keyboards. The group rented a customized four-engine Viscount airplane from John Mecom, owner of the New Orleans Saints, to travel to shows. They flew to major cities and then switched to a car, bus, or charter plane to get to that night's gig. Carl told an Ottawa reporter, "The Viscount is really our main base of operations, and we are always happy to see that big bird waiting for us with its comfortable seats and room to move around."

SATURDAY, AUGUST 3, 1968: Paul Sauve Centre, Montreal, QB, Canada, with the Box Tops, the Pickle Brothers, and the Munks (8:30 p.m. show)
Wilder Penfield III of the *Montreal Star* noted that the group came across as "well-adjusted, affluent good-time kids. Their hair is still short; their dress (aristocratic, knife-creased suits of electric white) more couth than ever . . . The new songs are something quite different . . . the era of 'Do You Wanna Dance' has been succeeded by the age of 'When a Man Needs a Woman' . . . Saturday's performance, though, had the advantage of both; the old was generously mixed in with the new, and a medley of 'Surfin' Safari,' 'Shut Down,' 'Little Deuce Coupe,' and 'Surfin' USA' was enough of a memory bath to work the audience into a revivalist frenzy."

SUNDAY, AUGUST 4, 1968: Lord Beaverbrook Rink, Saint John, NB, Canada, with the Box Tops, the Pickle Brothers, and F.J. and the Soul-Fingers (8:30 p.m. show)
Almost 6,000 fans attended this show. Teenagers lined up around the block to catch a glimpse of the group. Many also turned up to see the Box Tops, who were quite popular in Canada.

MONDAY, AUGUST 5, 1968: Halifax Forum, Halifax, NS, Canada, with the Box Tops and the Pickle Brothers (8:00 p.m. show)
Jack Lloyd recalled that the tour ran into trouble when the Canadian government demanded that the Beach Boys pay taxes on the money they made in the country. Since money was tight, the group relied on what they made each night to pay their expenses. Luckily, Lloyd persuaded the government to not take the money from the band.

Doug Dragon recalled, "One of the funniest things I remember (on that tour), leave it to Dennis Wilson to do this! He had some young gal up there in Canada . . . maybe seventeen or eighteen, and he stashed her in the upper cabin stowaway thing to get her over the border. When we got back to the States, Jack Lloyd just saw red! He said, 'Get that blonde back to Canada, man!'"

TUESDAY, AUGUST 6, 1968: Bangor Auditorium, Bangor, ME, with the Box Tops, the Barracudas, and the Pickle Brothers (8:00 p.m.)

WEDNESDAY, AUGUST 7, 1968: Hampton Beach Casino, Hampton Beach, NH, with the Box Tops, the Pickle Brothers, the Spectras, and the Vogues
Dick Ray, of the local band the Spectras, recalled that they were invited by the Beach Boys "back to their hotel for a few cold ones after the show. They stayed at Lamie's Tavern in downtown Hampton,

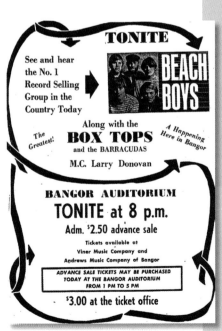

TONITE

See and hear the No. 1 Record Selling Group in the Country Today

BEACH BOYS

The Greatest!

Along with the
BOX TOPS
and the BARRACUDAS

A Happening Here in Bangor

M.C. Larry Donovan

BANGOR AUDITORIUM
TONITE at 8 p.m.
Adm. $2.50 advance sale

Tickets available at
Viner Music Company and
Andrews Music Company of Bangor

ADVANCE SALE TICKETS MAY BE PURCHASED
TODAY AT THE BANGOR AUDITORIUM
FROM 1 PM TO 5 PM

$3.00 at the ticket office

Ian Rusten Collection

Performing at the Pittsfield Boy's Club, August 8, 1968. Photo: Russ Bodnar

which is about three miles inland from the beach. They said they didn't like the beach atmosphere and didn't want to stay at the beach, which I thought was unusual, given their name." Ray related that trumpeter Bob Lassonde ended up hanging out with Dennis that night. "Dennis wanted to rent a bike and pedal around Hampton Beach. Dennis put on dark glasses and a hat so he wouldn't be recognized, and they rented a tandem bike. Dennis was still pretty drunk, so Bob had to do the lion's share of the pedaling. Eventually, some girls recognized Dennis. They started screaming and running after the bike. Bob had to pedal like crazy to get out of there because Dennis wasn't much help. They did manage to elude them."

THURSDAY, AUGUST 8, 1968: Boy's Club, Pittsfield, MA, with the Box Tops and the Pickle Brothers (8:00 p.m. show)

FRIDAY, AUGUST 9, TO SUNDAY, AUGUST 11, 1968: Steel Pier, Atlantic City, NJ, with the Box Tops and the New Christy Minstrels
Doug Dragon recalled, "We did three gigs on the Steel Pier. It was great . . . A very responsive audience. I had a ball! Those summer tours were always fun." *Amusement Business* listed shows in Reading, Pennsylvania (August 13), Harrisburg, Pennsylvania (August 14), Wheeling, West Virginia (August 15), and Charleston, West Virginia (August 16), but none of them took place. Instead, the group took a five-day break for promotion, including TV appearances on *The Mike Douglas Show* (where they performed "Do It Again," "Wake the World," and "Darlin'") and *The Dick Cavett Show*.

SATURDAY, AUGUST 17, 1968: Convention Hall, Asbury Park, NJ, with the Box Tops and the Pickle Brothers (Two shows at 7:30 and 9:45 p.m.)

Backstage in Pittsfield, Massachusetts, on August 8, 1968. Photo: Russ Bodnar

THE BEACH BOYS IN CONCERT

SUNDAY, AUGUST 18, 1968: Dane County Memorial Coliseum, Madison, WI, with the Box Tops and the Pickle Brothers (7:30 p.m. show)
This was a makeup date for fans that bought tickets for the canceled May 13 show with Maharishi. Only a paltry 1500 people attended. John Gruber of the *Wisconsin State Journal* reported that the group played in a perfunctory manner without their "usual dash." He suggested that they stuck to their older surf songs too much and only seemed to come alive when they played some of their newer numbers, which predictably got less crowd response. "For a listener, the most notable exceptions were 'Good Vibrations,' 'Wake the World,' and 'God Only Knows,' songs whose gentle lyrics and winding melodies reflect the 'new' Beach Boys."

MONDAY, AUGUST 19, 1968: Winnipeg Auditorium, Winnipeg, Manitoba, Canada, with the Box Tops, the Surprise Package, and the Pickle Brothers

TUESDAY, AUGUST 20, 1968: Exhibition Stadium, Regina, SK, Canada, with the Box Tops, the Surprise Package, and the Pickle Brothers (8:30 p.m. show)
The show was attended by 5,000 fans, filling all but the rear section of the stadium.

WEDNESDAY, AUGUST 21, 1968: Edmonton Gardens, Edmonton, Alberta, Canada, with the Box Tops, the Surprise Package, and the Pickle Brothers (8:30 p.m. show)
Lydia Dotto of the *Edmonton Journal* reported that the Beach Boys' "competence and professionalism on stage were beyond question. An especially good sound system (their own, I believe) enabled them to overcome the very considerable acoustics problem at the Edmonton Gardens, which is no small feat . . . In all, a completely enjoyable show."

THURSDAY, AUGUST 22, 1968: Stampede Corral, Calgary, Alberta, Canada, with the Box Tops, the Surprise Package, and the Pickle Brothers (8:00 p.m. show)

FRIDAY, AUGUST 23, 1968: Spokane Coliseum, Spokane, WA, with the Box Tops, the Surprise Package, and the Pickle Brothers (8:30 p.m. show)
Only 4,000 fans turned out for this concert. Jack Swanson of the *Spokesman Review* declared that the "five aging millionaires . . . drew mixed reactions from the half-full Coliseum of young fans . . . They treated their clapping audience to several old favorites, a bit of teen-level smut, and some new tunes from their latest hit record . . . Hecklers interrupted the quiet songs with shouts of 'speak up' and 'where's your razor?'"

SATURDAY, AUGUST 24, 1968: Boise High School Auditorium, Boise, ID, with the Box Tops and the Pickle Brothers (Two shows at 7:00 and 9:30 p.m.)

SATURDAY, SEPTEMBER 7, 1968: Lagoon, Farmington, UT, with the Box Tops (Two shows at 7:00 and 9:30 p.m.)

FRIDAY, SEPTEMBER 20, AND SATURDAY, SEPTEMBER 21, 1968: Hall of Music, Purdue University, Lafayette, IN, with Odetta and Rich Little (Two shows each night at 7:00 and 9:30 p.m.)

FRIDAY, SEPTEMBER 27, AND SATURDAY, SEPTEMBER 28, 1968: Melodyland Theatre, Anaheim, CA, with Grassroots and Sweetwater (One show on Friday at 8:30 p.m. and two shows on Saturday at 7:00 and 10:00 p.m.)
While he did not join them onstage, Brian attended at least one of these concerts and took part in a pre-show event. He and the other Beach Boys each stood at a different entrance to the circular venue and signed autographs. One Hawthorne High alumni that came through Brian's door struck up a conversation with him about their alma mater and was invited to sit in the family section. Brian spent the entire concert peppering him with questions about the Hawthorne High football team.

David Mark Dashev of the *Los Angeles Times* reviewed the opening show. He noted, "In spite of the starchy arrangements, their voices never sounded better. At times their harmonies were quite

intricate and there were moments of genuine excitement, as in their rendition of 'God Only Knows.' For the most part, however, the performance seemed programmed, with the group wearing the tedium of singing the same songs too many times." Alex Del Zoppo, keyboardist of opening act Sweetwater, was greatly impressed by the Beach Boys. He recalled that the "gig was the first that we had seen where a band took their own PA system along, used small amps, mic'd and pumped the instrumental sound through said sound system after being perfectly balanced through their mixing board, along with the exquisite vocal mix. Of course, with the vocals being so very important to the group, it was almost necessary for them to do it that way . . . We were just so completely blown away with the vocal mix and indeed, the overall mix (as it sounded exactly like the records, but with even more power, and therefore, excitement)."

Performing "Their Hearts Were Full of Spring" at the Fillmore East, October 11, 1968. Photo: Russ Bodnar

FRIDAY, OCTOBER 11, 1968: Fillmore East, New York, NY, with Creedence Clearwater Revival (Two shows at 8:00 and 11:30 p.m.)

The Beach Boys spent a full week in New York during October 1968. In addition to performing two concerts, they appeared on *The Ed Sullivan Show* on October 13, singing live versions of "Do It Again" and "Good Vibrations" over prerecorded backing tracks. The group also spent three days in a recording studio working on their upcoming *20/20* LP.

The Fillmore booking was controversial from the start. The Beach Boys and the Turtles were scheduled to appear on the same weekend at the venue owned by Bill Graham. It led to howls of protest by the intelligentsia, who viewed both bands as bubblegum music and not hip enough to play the Fillmore. The *Village Voice*, the leading underground paper in the city, argued Graham was selling out to gain mass appeal and declared it "the weekend the Fillmore tried out as a whore." Robert Shelton of the *New York Times* noted that 1,900 fans were in attendance for the first show.

Russ Bodnar was one of those fans and he recalled, "The highlight was mid-show when Dennis Wilson stepped away from the drums to the spotlight and sang 'Little Bird' with the tasty horns and a banjo part (played by Al) . . . one of my all-time favorite live music experiences!" Other critics, however, were less kind. Robert Shelton contended that the Beach Boys failed to measure up to their recordings and were overshadowed by opening act Creedence Clearwater Revival. The *Village Voice* argued that the group had nothing new to say and disparagingly noted that they received applause "as every old tune was trotted out . . . Nostalgia alone can't support even 'California Girls' and 'Wouldn't It Be Nice.' It's no news that going home again is a bad trip." The group was stung by the negative reviews. Bruce Johnston contended that the reviewers were biased against them. He told the *Hartford Courant*, "there was criticism from reviewers, but they were all 'heavy' reviewers. I think they were bugged because we sold out . . . they were hoping we'd bomb. I think they thought we were too flashy. We're not trying to be 'in' with any group . . . with the hippies or the teens. We just do what we like and try to do it the best we can."

Although the group would work with promoter Bill Graham in the future, their relationship got off to a rocky start on this night. According to Chip Rachlin, who worked for Graham, the group challenged the Fillmore's box office sales figures and demanded a stub count, which meant that the Fillmore staff had to spend hours after the show re-counting each ticket stub by hand while a Beach

Marquee at Fillmore East, October 1968. Jon Stebbins Collection

THE BEACH BOYS IN CONCERT

Performing "Good Vibrations" on *The Ed Sullivan Show*, October 13, 1968. Joe Russo Collection

Rocking at Bill Graham's Fillmore East in New York, October 11, 1968. Photo: Russ Bodnar

Boys representative watched. Graham angrily swore he'd never book them again, which proved to be an empty threat.

FRIDAY, OCTOBER 18, 1968: Civic Coliseum, Knoxville, TN, with the 1910 Fruitgum Company and the Pickle Brothers (8:00 p.m. show) The Pickle Brothers and the 1910 Fruitgum Company supported the group on this tour. The backup band consisted of Ed Carter, Dennis Dragon, and either Daryl or Doug Dragon. It's conceivable that all three Dragons were present. Dennis Dragon insists they played one tour together, though neither Daryl nor Doug recall. Jack Lloyd acted as road manager with Steve Desper, Jon Parks, and Steve Korthof also along.

SATURDAY, OCTOBER 19, 1968: Greenville Memorial Auditorium, Greenville, SC, with the 1910 Fruitgum Company and the Pickle Brothers (8:30 p.m. show)

SUNDAY, OCTOBER 20, 1968: Greensboro Coliseum, Greensboro, NC, with the 1910 Fruitgum Company and the Pickle Brothers (8:00 p.m. show)

TUESDAY, OCTOBER 22, 1968: Freedom Hall, Louisville, KY, with the 1910 Fruitgum Company, the Pickle Brothers, and Tom Dooley and the Lovelights (7:30 p.m. show)

THURSDAY, OCTOBER 24, 1968: Dobyns-Bennett High School Gym, Kingsport, TN, with the 1910 Fruitgum Company and the Pickle Brothers (8:00 p.m. show)
This concert attracted 2,100 people.

FRIDAY, OCTOBER 25, 1968: Virginia Polytechnic Institute, Blacksburg, VA, with the 1910 Fruitgum Company and the Pickle Brothers (7:00 p.m. show) and Salem-Roanoke Civic Center, Salem, VA, with the 1910 Fruitgum Company and the Pickle Brothers (8:30 p.m. show)

SATURDAY, OCTOBER 26, 1968: Civic Center, Charleston, WV, with the 1910 Fruitgum Company and the Pickle Brothers (8:30 p.m. show)

SUNDAY, OCTOBER 27, 1968: Municipal Auditorium, Columbus, GA, with the 1910 Fruitgum Company, Johnny Barfield, and the Antique Zoo (2:00 p.m. show) and Macon Coliseum, Macon, GA, with the 1910 Fruitgum Company, the Pickle Brothers, and ten unnamed bands from Georgia (3:00 p.m. show)
The Beach Boys played an early afternoon show in Columbus before heading to Macon for the

last concert of the tour. The Macon show was a makeup for the April 11 concert canceled in the wake of Dr. King's death. Unfortunately, the Beach Boys, who were supposed to go onstage around 4:30 p.m., did not get to the venue until 7:00 p.m. The late arrival angered many young fans and their parents. Promoter Junior Watts complained to the *Macon News* that the group ripped him off. He claimed that he specifically paid them an extra $500 so that they could fly to Macon and make the gig on time, but the group pocketed the money, driving there in a bus instead. Watts claimed that he lost $2,000 on the show because he had to issue refunds to many people. The group claimed that flying wouldn't have gotten them there any sooner and refused to give the promoter back his money.

SATURDAY, NOVEMBER 23, 1968: Children's Hospital, Columbus, OH (Afternoon show) and Veterans Memorial Auditorium, Columbus, OH, with the Gears, the Grass Roots, and the Pickle Brothers (8:00 p.m. show)
After a hectic month spent trying to complete their *20/20* album, the group flew to Columbus to begin a short tour before heading to Europe. Ed Carter, Mike Kowalski, and Daryl Dragon accompanied them. The Beach Boys played an afternoon benefit at Children's Hospital, prior to that night's concert. A number of charity shows were performed during this period to help Carl's draft case. While the judge had requested that he report for duty at a military hospital, Carl preferred to play benefit shows instead. Unfortunately, it did not please the court and he would find himself back before a judge in 1969.

SUNDAY, NOVEMBER 24, 1968: Canton Memorial Auditorium, Canton, OH, with the Grassroots, the Chylds, and the Pickle Brothers (3:00 p.m. show)
The Beach Boys performed in Canton for the fourth year in a row. Sue Scott of the *Dover Times Reporter* noted, "The crowd came . . . alive with their opening number, 'Darlin',' and the audience enthusiasm continued to build through 'California Girls' and 'Sloop John B.' Carl sang the popular 'Surfer Girl' and Al . . . was featured in 'Wouldn't It Be Nice.' A medley of their best-known numbers followed. 'Do It Again' gave the audience an opportunity for hand clapping and then Mike went 'wild' on his electric organ during a new dimension in sound, 'Good Vibrations.' The concert concluded with a longtime Beach Boy favorite, 'Barbara Ann.'"

MONDAY, NOVEMBER 25, 1968: Bushnell Memorial, Hartford, CT, with the Grassroots, Damn Yankees, and the Pickle Brothers (7:30 p.m. show)
Reviewer Barry Gilbert of the *Hartford Courant* reported the Beach Boys "were better than they've been on records or TV for a long time. Backed by a band from New York City, their singing, which has been their base for years, once again broke through, although they couldn't quite make the high notes of their older hits." The group informed Gilbert backstage that they enjoyed the concert, which included three songs from their upcoming *20/20* album: "Do It Again," "Bluebirds Over the Mountain," and "All I Want to Do." Dennis remarked, however, that "where I sit I can't see too much of the audience so I don't have the chance to form any opinion. There are two speakers aimed back at me so I can hear how things sound and adjust the band accordingly."

TUESDAY, NOVEMBER 26, 1968: Stanley Theatre, Jersey City, NJ, with the Grassroots and the Pickle Brothers (8:00 p.m. show)
The set list for this show consisted of "Darlin'," "Sloop John B," "California Girls," "Wouldn't It Be Nice," "I Get Around," "Do It Again," "Wake the World," "Bluebirds Over the Mountain," "God Only Knows," "Their Hearts Were Full of Spring," "Good Vibrations," "Barbara Ann," and "All I Want to Do."

WEDNESDAY, NOVEMBER 27, 1968: Boston Music Hall, Boston, MA, with the Grassroots, the Pickle Brothers, and the Beacon St. Union (Two shows at 7:00 and 9:30 p.m.)

SUNDAY, DECEMBER 1, 1968: London Palladium, London, England, with Barry Ryan, Bruce Channel, Vanity Fare, Eclection, and Sharon Tandy with Fleur De Lys (Two shows)
The Beach Boys flew to the U.K. on Thursday, November 28, to begin a three-week tour of Europe. Engineer Steve Desper and his $250,000 sound system accompanied them. To further bolster their

WKAZ RADIO AND THE LASHINSKY BROS. PRESENT

IN PERSON

WITH THEIR SHOW

MANY TOP ACTS!

THE BEACH BOYS

SATURDAY OCT. 26 • CIVIC CENTER
ONE PERFORMANCE ONLY AT 8:30 P.M.
PRICES $4.00 $3.00 $2.00 ALL SEATS RESERVED
TICKETS AT CIVIC CENTER - GALPERINS TURNER'S - GORBY'S - SEARS

Courtesy of PosterCentral.Com

sound they also hired a large horn section for the tour. Ed Carter (bass), Mike Kowalski (percussion), and Daryl Dragon (keyboards) completed the touring group.

Upon arrival in London the group immediately held a series of press interviews with U.K. music publications. Asked about their hectic schedule, Mike told Bob Dawbarn of *Melody Maker*, "We've certainly been doing a lot of touring in the States and we are planning to cut it down, but we will keep up the international side. Traveling doesn't bother me . . . we all enjoy it pretty much. And we really like coming to Britain . . . who wouldn't?" The group spent Saturday, November 30, rehearsing at BBC studios, where they taped an appearance for the Christmas edition of *Top of the Pops*. Later that night, Bruce, Al, and Mike visited Bee Gees singer Barry Gibb's house where they "sang songs and strummed guitars until 4 a.m."

This U.K. trip was very well documented. In addition to extensive coverage by magazines, cinematographer Vic Kettle and crew filmed much of it for a proposed documentary that the group financed. Kettle captured the group's arrival at Heathrow airport and their meeting with the press. A BBC TV crew also spent Friday, November 29, and Saturday, November 30, filming the group for a *Colour Me Pop* episode that aired on BBC2 on December 14.

For their English dates, the Beach Boys toured with a traditional U.K. package show, featuring five support acts. As headliners, they closed the concerts with a set of eleven songs. The tour kicked off with two sold-out shows at the London Palladium. Keith Altham of *New Musical Express* wrote, "the Beach Boys . . . proved once again that they have that little magic which distinguishes the great from the good in pop music . . . Mike Love smiled through his beard and said 'Hi to all those in the cheap seats' while Carl was beautifully benign and Dennis dashing on the drums. Al Jardine was chirpy and Bruce looked more like a Beach Boy than anyone else. Their sounds were sun and surf and full of California fun." Lon Goddard of *Record Mirror* stated, "The Beach Boys put on what may be termed the best stage presentation yet. Applause was universal as a prelude to every number, and the set included exceptional reproductions of such memorable greats as 'Sloop John B,' 'God Only Knows,' 'California Girls,' 'Darlin',' 'Barbara Ann,' and a very fine version of 'Good Vibrations.'"

EMI recorded the Palladium shows for a possible album. However, the British Musician's Union and the American Federation of Musicians failed to reach an agreement, preventing the tapes from being used. The dispute was eventually settled in time for the Astoria shows on December 8 to be recorded. Vic Kettle filmed Bruce Johnston taking a walk through London prior to the concerts and pretending to conduct a symphony in Hyde Park.

MONDAY, DECEMBER 2, 1968: Colston Hall, Bristol, England, with Barry Ryan, Bruce Channel, Vanity Fare, Eclection, and Sharon Tandy with Fleur De Lys (Two shows)

WEDNESDAY, DECEMBER 4, 1968: City Hall, Sheffield, England, with Barry Ryan, Bruce Channel, Vanity Fare, Eclection, and Sharon Tandy with Fleur De Lys (Two shows at 6:30 and 8:50 p.m.)
Dennis celebrated his twenty-fourth birthday in Sheffield. Bob Farmer for *Disc and Music Echo* interviewed him and his fellow Beach Boys backstage at Sheffield City Hall. Asked to comment on the continual absence of Brian, Mike stated, "He gets too uptight and that doesn't help when you're touring. Brian's a very sensitive, artistic, musical genius who is paranoid of being in any environment other than in his home and family. He's a very domestic kind of person." When asked if they had considered cutting back on touring, as the Beatles had, Mike replied, "The thing is, unlike the Beatles, we feel that if we're in the pop business, we should do the touring because that's all part of it. It helps keep you current."

THURSDAY, DECEMBER 5, 1968: Odeon, Manchester, England, with Barry Ryan, Bruce Channel, Vanity Fare, Eclection, and Sharon Tandy with Fleur De Lys (Two shows)
Prior to these shows, the group made a promotional appearance at New Century Hall where the BBC interviewed them for *Radio 1 Club*.

FRIDAY, DECEMBER 6, 1968: Odeon, Birmingham, England, with Barry Ryan, Bruce Channel, Vanity Fare, Eclection, and Sharon Tandy with Fleur De Lys (Two shows)

SATURDAY, DECEMBER 7, 1968: Capitol Theatre, Cardiff, Wales, with Barry Ryan, Bruce Channel, Vanity Fare, Eclection, and Sharon Tandy with Fleur De Lys (Two shows)

SUNDAY, DECEMBER 8, 1968: Finsbury Park Astoria, London, England, with Barry Ryan, Bruce Channel, Vanity Fare, Eclection, and Sharon Tandy with Fleur De Lys (Two shows)

EMI recorded these shows and performances were edited together and released in the U.K. for the 1970 release *Live in London*. American fans had to wait until 1976 for the release in the states, under the title *Beach Boys '69*. While the LP has many fans, the Beach Boys were initially against its release. Sound mixer Steve Desper alleged that neither he nor the group was informed that the concerts were being recorded. Desper recalled, "EMI ran some cables and taped some mic feeds . . . We were only there for one night but EMI lived there and they knew the tricks of the trade, so they captured the vocals and the overall sound and came out with an album. They had every right to do it. I just wish they had said something about it. They treated me as if I was just the house mixer. They had their agenda and as long as it didn't interfere with my agenda, which was to deliver sound to the theatre, they figured it was all right. But we didn't find out about it until the album was released and we all figured out what happened." Regardless, the performances on *Live In London* beautifully display the live Beach Boys of late 1968 in a highly positive light.

TUESDAY, DECEMBER 10, 1968: Odeon, Glasgow, Scotland, with Barry Ryan, Bruce Channel, Vanity Fare, Eclection, and Sharon Tandy with Fleur De Lys (Two shows)

The Beach Boys spent part of Monday filming a segment for *Top of the Pops* that was ultimately scrapped. They were on the River Thames, boarding a barge piloted by an old man and sailing around. Vic Kettle's color footage of the shoot was seen in the 1985 documentary *The Beach Boys: An American Band*. Kettle also accompanied them to Scotland and shot footage of Al and Bruce visiting a castle.

FRIDAY, DECEMBER 13, 1968: Kongresshalle, Dusseldorf, West Germany, with the Black Cats (8:00 p.m. show)

The Beach Boys flew to Munich on December 12 to tape appearances on the ZDF TV shows *Star Parade* and *Musik Fur Junge Leute* (aka *4, 3, 2, 1 Hot and Sweet*). Vic Kettle shot behind the scenes footage at the tapings. On Friday the group performed the first of two German concerts. Martin Blok of the *Rheinische Post* was unimpressed by the group's live sound: "In the Kongresshalle the amps were too loud. The five stars from the West Coast, aided by an eight-man orchestra, followed suit. They weren't avant-garde pop-authors but rather darlings spoiled by the audience, getting the applause anyhow. They played and sang many of their best creations in a clichéd manner, showing their vocal and instrumental abilities from time to time, but mainly affecting the audience with their aggressive rhythm . . . As long as the instruments on stage were warm the audience was on fire, but as soon as they left the stage, the applause faded away. Of course they didn't come back for an encore and there wasn't any magic left."

SATURDAY, DECEMBER 14, 1968: Concertgebouw, Amsterdam, Netherlands, with Geebos

The Beach Boys spent the day at the Theater De Brakke Grond recording a mini concert for the NCRV TV show *Twien*. They mimed to "Do It Again," "Friends," "California Girls," "Darlin'," "Wouldn't It Be Nice," "Sloop John B," "Good Vibrations," "God Only Knows," and "Barbara Ann" before a live audience.

The nighttime appearance at the Concertgebouw marked the group's first Dutch concert. A reporter from *Muziek Express*, who heard of their reputation as a weak live act, commented, "Fortunately the Beach Boys realized that a live performance is not just playing a few hits, but must also be worth seeing. They apparently have worked on their appearance and also the instrumentation has been upgraded to a higher level. The result: the first concert of the Beach Boys has become one of the finest pop happenings of the year 1968!"

SUNDAY, DECEMBER 15, 1968: Palais des Beaux Arts, Brussels, Belgium

The concert in Brussels was televised on Belgian TV.

The Fillmore booking was controversial from the start. The Beach Boys and the Turtles were scheduled to appear on the same weekend at the venue owned by Bill Graham. It led to howls of protest by the intelligentsia, who viewed both bands as bubblegum music and not hip enough to play the Fillmore.

MONDAY, DECEMBER 16, 1968: Stadthalle, Bremen, West Germany, with the Black Cats (8:00 p.m. show)

The Beach Boys spent the afternoon at the Osterholz television studios recording the first of two appearances on *Beat Club*. They mimed to three songs, which were broadcast separately. "Bluebirds over the Mountain" aired on December 31, 1968; "Do It Again" was shown on January 25, 1969; and "California Girls" aired on March 29, 1969. Although the shows aired in black and white, Vic Kettle filmed color footage of the taping. He also shot film of Carl walking outside of his hotel, looking at birds. Footage of the group at an ice skating rink was probably also shot on this day.

The concert that night was well received by 3000 fans, many of who lit sparklers that brightened the venue. Margot Walther of *Bremer Nachricten* reported, "Dressed in blinding white . . . the sunny boys from California supremely dominated the show. Pop music fully developed for a concert. Vocalists with heavenly self-confidence . . . they succeeded in seducing their fans from far away within little more than 30 minutes . . . They conjured up 'Bluebirds Over the Mountains,' came with the sensational 'Pet Sounds,' and passionately interpreted 'Wake the World.'"

The Weser Kurier reported, "'Do It Again' made the female audience scream in a frenzied way, which in turn animated the choirboys on the stage. Dennis, the drummer of the California skylarks, beat so vehemently on his drums that the calfskin tore apart." The *Norddeutsche Volkszeitung* added that he "furiously threw the pedals of his [snare] drums across the stage [into the audience] and eventually jumped over boxes and bins to complain to the engineer about the instrument's lack of quality. The microphone apparently also wasn't a match for Mike Love's needs and requirements, so that it had to be hastily replaced. It didn't break the mood." Many fans were disappointed by the shortness of the concert. The group was onstage for little more than a half hour and played no encore. According to Walther, "Only two fans were completely happy. They had confiscated drummer Dennis's drum sticks that had flown with a high curve into the audience."

Following the Bremen concert, the Beach Boys traveled to Frankfurt on Tuesday, December 17 and caught an afternoon flight to Milan to appear on Italian television. RAI TV news was at the airport to film their arrival. The group taped appearances for the show *Settavocci (Seven Voices)* that aired on December 22, 1968, and January 22, 1969. They also attended a cocktail party held in their honor by EMI Italy.

The group was back in London to tape another piece for *Top of the Pops* on December 18. While there, Al and Carl visited Blaises nightclub to see a South African band called the Flame, who'd opened a weeklong engagement on December 15. Steve Desper recalled, "It was Alan who first saw them and he tried to convince Carl to go back and check them out. Eventually he convinced Carl to go back the next night to this bar where they were playing and then Carl took the reins from that point on. He saw the talent and wanted to get them out of Europe and South Africa and over to the states to sign them up." Carl spent much of 1969 working to get them visas so they could come to California, where he planned to produce them for Brother Records.

OTHER 1968 CONCERTS

According to a Buffalo Springfield box set, concerts were played in Statesboro, Georgia, and Montgomery, Alabama, but these dates have not been confirmed.

CONCERTS NOT PLAYED

A February 11 concert in Las Vegas listed by author Keith Badman was actually a Buffalo Springfield concert. The Beach Boys did not appear.

Amusement Business stated in its June 29, 1968, issue that the group would play dates in Alaska and Canada in July, but they did not take place.

Concerts scheduled for Reading, Wilkes-Barre, and Harrisburg, Pennsylvania and Wheeling and Charleston, West Virginia in August also were canceled.

Amusement Business listed Vancouver shows for August 23 and 24, but the group played in Spokane and Boise on those dates.

1969

T HE HIGHLY SUCCESSFUL December 1968 visit to Europe reminded the group that they were still popular around the world. However, a continuing downward spiral in their U.S. standing had the Beach Boys in a near panic. The latest single release, "Bluebirds over the Mountain," produced by Bruce, was a commercial failure. It peaked at number sixty-one on the *Billboard* charts, the lowest ranking for a Beach Boys single to date. The truth was that the Beach Boys were unsure what direction to go in. They sought to emulate Brian's style in his absence but they also knew that they needed to create new sounds. Life without Brian was both a difficult and liberating journey for the other Beach Boys. 1969 would reflect that dichotomy in many ways.

When the Beach Boys flew to Vancouver on January 16, 1969, University of British Columbia student Mike Quigley asked if they were concerned about their decline in popularity. Bruce replied, "Well, a lot of our concerts do okay, and I know we still get royalty checks . . . We're just doing our thing and why should everyone dig us? Everybody can dig the Beatles, but why should everyone dig us? You know the Beach Boys image is kinda like a group Doris Day, you know what I mean? A lot of people stopped digging the Beach Boys, you know, and in their minds that image is probably still that Doris Day image and I think a lot of kids are going away from all that 'clean' thing because that's where their parents are at."

CONCERTS PLAYED IN
1969

Meanwhile, capacity crowds at their Pacific Northwest concerts showed that the band remained a viable concert draw in many regions. The Beach Boys were optimistic that their new album would stop their commercial slide.

"We were used as a reference point as to what was lame about the time. It was nonsense, but people still associated us with cars and surfboards. When the hits stopped coming, we all felt a lot of pressure. It was back to the real world after the fairy tale."

—Carl Wilson

A final studio album under their original Capitol Records recording contract was released on February 10, 1969. It was titled *20/20* because it was the band's twentieth album on the label. The group, minus Brian,

THURSDAY, JANUARY 16, 1969: Memorial Arena, Victoria, BC, Canada, with Joe Hicks, Tommy James and the Shondells and the Tunnel (8:00 p.m. show)
For this short tour, an eight-piece orchestra, conducted by pianist John D'Andrea, accompanied the group. It consisted of saxophonist Roger Neumann, trumpeters Mike Price and Daryl Eaton, saxophonist Earle Dumler, bassist Bob Boyack, guitarist Jeff Kaplan, and drummer Joe Lasky.

Despite heavy snow, over 4,000 fans attended the show in Victoria. Russell Freethy of the *Victoria Daily Times* praised the Beach Boys and wrote, "Dressed all in white, they flipped through their hits with an incredible precision and ease that delighted the crowd. The polish and professionalism of their stage appearance and their performance is welcome in this era of unconscious stage-struck statues."

FRIDAY, JANUARY 17, 1969: Seattle Center Arena, with Joe Hicks and Tommy James and the Shondells (8:00 p.m. show)
A capacity audience turned out for this appearance. Susan Schwartz of the *Seattle Times*, noted, "The Beach Boys really sing—they don't shout or scream . . . Their beat and their harmony are precise. Their music is melodic. They don't go in for feedback or fancy instrumental solos. Whatever it is they've got, 'Help Me Rhonda,' and 'I Get Around,' and 'Barbara Ann,' not to mention 'Good Vibrations' are still catchy songs . . . Nine years from now, maybe the Beach Boys will be working on their 40th record album as they're on their 20th now."

SATURDAY, JANUARY 18, 1969: Agrodome, Vancouver, BC, Canada, with Winters Green, Joe Hicks, and Tommy James and the Shondells (8:00 p.m. show)
Over 6,000 fans attended this show. Bob Smith of the *Vancouver Sun* picked the Beach Boys' a capella performance of "Their Hearts Were Full of Spring" as the highlight, declaring, "It was top-flight harmonizing reminiscent of Mel Torme's Meltones or the Hi-Lo's, for example."

SUNDAY, JANUARY 19, 1969: Gymnasium, Eastern Montana College, Billings, MT (8:15 p.m. show)
The group made their first known appearance in Montana, before returning home to promote their new single "I Can Hear Music."

FRIDAY, FEBRUARY 7, 1969: Municipal Auditorium, San Antonio, TX, with Rene and Rene, the Bob Seger System, and Joe Hicks (8:00 p.m. show)
This was the first date of a six-day Texas tour with opening act Bob Seger, then on the charts with "Ramblin' Gamblin' Man." Soul singer and Brother Records' protégé Joe Hicks performed as well.

SATURDAY, FEBRUARY 8, 1969: Music Hall, Houston, TX, with Rene and Rene, the Bob Seger System, and Joe Hicks (Two shows at 7:00 and 9:30 p.m.)

SUNDAY, FEBRUARY 9, 1969: State Fair Music Hall, Dallas, TX, with Rene and Rene, the Bob Seger System, and Joe Hicks (3:00 p.m. show) and Will Rogers Auditorium, Fort Worth, TX, with Rene and Rene, the Bob Seger System, and Joe Hicks (7:30 p.m. show)

MONDAY, FEBRUARY 10, 1969: Memorial Coliseum, Corpus Christi, TX, with Rene and Rene, the Bob Seger System, and Joe Hicks (7:30 p.m. show)
About 2,500 fans attended this concert. Carl announced from the stage that Dennis had flown home due to illness and would not appear. Either Dennis Dragon or Mike Kowalski filled in. Dean Thorpe of the Corpus Christi *Caller Times* noted, "Even lacking one member, the group turned in a performance the audience thoroughly enjoyed."

Thorpe interviewed the Beach Boys backstage. Al Jardine informed him that the group employed a staff of eighteen people to manage their activities. While stressing that they were in a strong financial state, Al admitted, "hits don't come as easily as they did only a few years ago, when members of the group were in their teens and could relate to their audience on an equal-age basis." Carl noted that "California Girls" was still a very popular number in their stage act and that they played it on the NBC TV show *Kraft Music Hall*, which aired on February 19. They also mimed to "I Can Hear Music" on the same program.

TUESDAY, FEBRUARY 11, 1969: Municipal Auditorium, Austin, TX, with Rene and Rene, the Bob Seger System, and Joe Hicks (7:30 p.m. show)

WEDNESDAY, FEBRUARY 12, 1969: Heart O' Texas Coliseum, Waco, TX, with Rene and Rene, the Bob Seger System, and Joe Hicks (7:30 p.m. show)

This was the last night of the tour and the group returned to California to continue work on their new album. Dennis held a session for his *Sunflower* rocker "Got to Know the Woman" on February 13.

THURSDAY, APRIL 3, 1969: Alan B. Shepherd Civic Center ("The Dome"), Virginia Beach, VA, with the Classics IV (Two shows at 7:30 and 9:30 p.m.)

This tour was supposed to begin in March, but Carl would not go on the road until his wife Annie gave birth to their first child Jonah Wilson. Carl and Annie's first son was born on March 22. The group flew to Philadelphia prior to the concert to tape an appearance on the *Mike Douglas Show*, which aired on April 9, 1969. They sang "I Can Hear Music" and "Never Learn Not to Love" over taped backing tracks. During "Never Learn Not to Love" Dennis, dressed in an orange silk shirt, took center stage to sing. Few knew at the time that the song was actually composed by Dennis' friend and future convicted murderer Charles Manson.

FRIDAY, APRIL 4, 1969: All Children's Hospital, St. Petersburg, FL (Afternoon), and Curtis Hixon Hall, Tampa, FL, with the Classics IV, Tommy Roe, and Joe Hicks (8:30 p.m. show)

Prior to this concert, the Beach Boys played a free show for patients at All Children's Hospital. It was one of a number of benefits to aid Carl's draft case. Brian explained to Bernard Barry of *Disc and Music Echo*, "It's a kind of unofficial way of the group paying off our debt to the American government for allowing Carl to become a conscientious objector. A few concerts here and there is the alternative to him emptying some bed pans in some hospital to substitute for military service."

About 7,000 fans turned out at Curtis Hixon Hall. The newspaper reviews of the concert illustrate the growing divide among rock fans over the Beach Boys' "clean" image. Though he admitted that "the harmonics were interesting . . . and each slow number was a gem," Dave Hawpe of the *St. Petersburg Times* disparagingly referred to the group as "an appallingly decent rock act" and proclaimed that despite the fact that they let their hair grow, "one still gets the impression they would rather be back in the garage working on the Little Deuce Coupe." Kay Donahue of the *St. Petersburg Evening Independent* countered that the group, "just keep getting better. Harmony is the Beach Boys' biggest selling point. 'Good Vibrations,' the symbol of their harmonic perfection, sounded better than ever last night. The blended surf sound of 'California Girls,' 'Rhonda,' and 'Do It Again' was marvelous. Songs from the early days and from *20/20* . . . filled their all too short hour on stage."

SATURDAY, APRIL 5, 1969: Miami Beach Convention Hall, Miami, FL, with the Classics IV, Tommy Roe, and Joe Hicks (8:30 p.m. show)

A portion of the proceeds from this show benefitted the Heart Fund Charity.

MONDAY, APRIL 7, 1969: Peabody Auditorium, Daytona Beach, FL, with the Crazy Elephant, Shadows of Knight, and Joe Hicks (8:30 p.m. show)

TUESDAY, APRIL 8, 1969: Orlando Municipal Auditorium, Orlando, FL, with the New Colony Six, Tommy Roe, and Joe Hicks (8:00 p.m. show)

was pictured on the cover in modern garb, while Brian was cryptically shown inside the gatefold hiding behind an eye chart. The first single released from the album, a beautiful arrangement of the Spector/Ronettes classic "I Can Hear Music," was a modest hit in many U.S. radio markets, eventually peaking at number twenty-four on the *Billboard* charts. Produced and sung by Carl, with Dennis on drums, the single had zero participation from brother Brian. The only new composition credited to Brian on the *20/20* album, "I Went to Sleep," was actually from the *Friends* period. Brian did produce a version of the old Leadbelly song "Cotton Fields" featuring Al, but he had little to do with the rest of the LP. Baby brother Carl, who was emerging as the group's studio leader, oversaw the record. The Beach Boys were learning to cope without Brian but were simultaneously raiding the vaults for his scrapped 1966 *Smile* tracks. They also included a Beach Boys–sung version of the gorgeous "Time to Get Alone," a song Brian had written in 1967 for the band Redwood. Carl took charge of the lead vocal, although Brian's voice was in evidence on backgrounds. Despite its grab-bag quality, the album was another high-quality release. The group made a number of TV appearances to promote it, but *20/20* was a commercial dud, peaking at number sixty-eight on the *Billboard* LP charts.

Ellen Willis of the *New Yorker* succinctly summed up the group's growing problems when she noted that the Beach Boys "have never really been accepted as serious, by the heads or even by themselves . . . Even though they had a hit record not long ago, it is hard to keep from thinking

Onstage in the Netherlands on June 1, 1969. Courtesy of Klaas Jelle

of them as relics." The group recognized their predicament but had no idea to remedy it. Carl explained to Geoffrey Himes, "We were used as a reference point as to what was lame about the time. It was nonsense, but people still associated us with cars and surfboards. When the hits stopped coming, we all felt a lot of pressure. It was back to the real world after the fairy tale." Brian sporadically tried to lend a hand. He wrote and produced a single for the group with his father (credited as Reggie Dunbar) titled "Breakaway." But, despite appearances on the *Mike*

WEDNESDAY, APRIL 9, 1969: St. Vincent's Hospital, Jacksonville, FL (Morning), and Hope Haven Children's Hospital, Jacksonville, FL (2:30 p.m. show), and Duval Medical Center, Jacksonville, FL (4:00 p.m. show), and Civic Auditorium, Jacksonville, FL, with the New Colony Six, Tommy Roe, and Joe Hicks (Two shows at 6:00 and 8:30 p.m.)
April 9, 1969 was a very busy day for the Beach Boys. The group had become interested in Jacksonville charity the Heart Fund during their previous visit to the city in 1968, and they agreed that a portion of their profits on this night would be given to it. Due to their curiosity, the Heart Fund arranged for the group to watch an operation. The boys arrived in Jacksonville at 8:30 a.m. and traveled to St. Vincent's Hospital, where they witnessed open-heart surgery. Afterwards, the Beach Boys performed for the children's ward in the hospital. They then traveled to Hope Haven Children's Hospital, where they gave another performance at 2:30 p.m. Following that show, they traveled to Duval Medical Center and played yet another free show for patients at 4 p.m., before heading to the Civic Auditorium for their evening concerts. At 6 p.m. the group played a benefit for the disadvantaged children of the city, and then performed a second show at 8:30 p.m.

THURSDAY, APRIL 10, 1969: Municipal Auditorium, Atlanta, GA, with Tommy Roe, the New Colony Six, and Joe Hicks (8:00 p.m. show)
This concert was advertised as "the show you've waited for." It was a reference to the fact that the group had canceled their last appearance in the city as a result of rioting in the wake of Dr. Martin Luther King's assassination. A portion of the profits from the show benefitted the Georgia Heart Association.

FRIDAY, APRIL 11, 1969: Fieldhouse, Sikeston, MO, with the Yellow Payges, the Serfs, the New Colony Six, and Joe Hicks (8:00 p.m. show)

1969

The Beach Boys were originally scheduled to perform in Memphis, but the show was canceled and they instead played in Sikeston, a town midway between Memphis and St. Louis. The local Jaycees sponsored the show, which was played on an elevated stage resting on three trailer-truck beds. According to the *Daily Standard*, "The Beach Boys' concert was a rousing success as teenyboppers of every size and description packed the Field House to the gills . . . 'I Can Hear Music' and 'Barbara Ann' brought immediate applause as did a few other numbers the Beach Boys presented."

SATURDAY, APRIL 12, 1969: Municipal Auditorium, Nashville, TN, with Tommy Roe, Joe Hicks, the Serfs, and the Yellow Payges (8:00 p.m. show)

SUNDAY, APRIL 13, 1969: "Decency Rally," Fairgrounds Pavilion, Tulsa, OK, with the Spurlows (1:00 p.m. show) and McAlester State Prison, Oklahoma City, OK (Evening show), and Children's Memorial Hospital, Oklahoma City, OK (Evening show)
The Beach Boys started the day by appearing at a "Decency Rally" in Tulsa. It was hardly likely to aid their counterculture credentials. The Governor of Oklahoma and nine conservative high schools sponsored the event "to show that not all teenagers support the protest movements popular with some youths today." About 5,000 showed up for the concert, which began with performances by selected high school students. Most of the crowd was only interested in seeing the Beach Boys and lurked outside hoping to get a glimpse of their arrival. When the band took the stage, the youthful audience clapped along and rushed the stage at the end to get photos. There was a near-riot by the kids when it was announced that the group's performance was coming to its end. The Beach Boys quieted them down by performing an a cappella version of "Their Hearts Were Full of Spring." According to the *Tulsa World*, "an estimated 1,000 youngsters left their seats after the Beach Boys finished their part of the show and clogged the path of the executive limousines which were to take . . . the Beach Boys to McAlester."

Following the show, the group accompanied Lt. Governor George Nigh to McAlester State Prison, where they performed for convicts in the prison yard. Bruce later joked with writer Richard Green that "Nobody left during the show. It was a captive audience! We did forty-five minutes, then it started raining. The concert was in the open air and we were the first big group they'd had for 15 years." Dennis told Bernard Barry of *Disc and Music Echo* that the prison show "was a bit of a drag" because many of the inmates didn't like the group and were unresponsive to the performance. Despite mixed feelings about the concert, the Beach Boys performed at a number of prisons between 1969 and 1973.

FRIDAY, APRIL 18, 1969: Hawthorne High School Prom, Beverly Hilton Hotel, Beverly Hills, CA, with Joe Hicks
The Beach Boys accepted an unusual request to play at the prom of the Wilsons' alma mater. It was more of a favor, as the school could hardly pay the large sums the group usually demanded. They apparently received just $900 for the concert. Nevertheless, they were enthusiastic about putting on a good show for the kids and added Joe Hicks to the bill for no extra cost. Despite requests, Brian did not join them.

It was a memorable night for many Hawthorne students who had heard stories of the famous Beach Boys attending their school but had never seen them in the flesh. According to Jack Lloyd, who traveled with Dick Duryea to the date, "We were all decked out in tuxedos for the evening. The Beach Boys played a full dance set; Joe Hicks sang, and the kids loved the show and dance. Duryea and I tried to go from backstage to the floor to talk to some of the kids but the chaperones wouldn't let us, so no one got to mingle."

APRIL?, 1969: Louisberg, NJ
In a June interview in *Melody Maker* Carl mentioned that they had recently played at a prison in this town. Author Keith Badman referred to the gig as taking place in North Carolina, but Carl said it was in New Jersey. No further information is known.

FRIDAY, MAY 2, 1969: University of Oklahoma, Norman, OK (8:00 p.m. show)

Douglas Show and elsewhere to promote it, the record charted at a disappointing number sixty-three on the *Billboard* charts.

"Breakaway" was the group's last single for Capitol Records until 1989. In 1969 Capitol executives expressed some interest in re-signing the Beach Boys, but the band had grown disenchanted with the label and its reluctance to embrace their changing music. As Carl related to *Rock* magazine in 1970, "They were against Pet Sounds and all the albums that came after. They wanted us to stick with surfing and hot rod records, you know. But we said, well you know, we don't want to do that. We're doing other music now. But they really weren't going for it. And so they had all these hundreds of people in their organization pushing another thing. People were bound to get the wrong impression about the group." In April 1969, the band made the decision to formally terminate their relationship with Capitol, and simultaneously pursue a lawsuit against them, demanding back payments that they claimed they were owed. Capitol responded by deleting their back catalogue, thus cutting off the group's record royalties and much of their income stream.

The action came at a bad time, as the Beach Boys needed money to cover their huge overhead. They were in the midst of upgrading their studio to sixteen tracks and were determined to get their stillborn Brother Records label off the ground. Carl was hard at work making plans to obtain visas for the South African group the Flame, whom he intended to sign to Brother Records. To raise cash, another European tour was quickly arranged. Before it even began, however, the group

Dennis rehearsing in Norman, Oklahoma, May 2, 1969. Jack Lloyd

The Beach Boys took time out from recording to play a few Midwest shows. Carl's brother-in-law Billy Hinsche joined them. Engineer Steve Desper and road manager Jack Lloyd, who left American Productions shortly afterwards, also accompanied the group.

This first concert proved memorable because Mike Love missed it. He traveled to India in late April to personally deliver a check to Maharishi from the Beach Boys. He told Richard Green of the *New Music Express* that "I got snowed up in Kashmir . . . for five days I was stuck in the snow and I missed my first ever Beach Boys concert. Who replaced me? I am irreplaceable, didn't you know?" Jack Lloyd recalled that the band "split the songs among the other guys. Billy Hinsche sang some but had trouble remembering the lyrics. Bruce and Carl sang some, and the audience didn't seem to care. They sounded just fine."

SATURDAY, MAY 3, 1969: Eppley Care Center, Omaha, NE (Afternoon), and City Auditorium Music Hall, Omaha, NE, with the Spiral Staircase (Two shows at 6:30 and 9:30 p.m.)

Mike Love flew into Omaha in time to take part in an hour-long benefit concert for 250 children from the Omaha Home for Boys, Girl's Town, Immanuel Hospital, the Nebraska Psychiatric Institute, and Ula-Halee Home for Girls at the Eppley Care Center. Due to the intimate size of the venue, the show was relaxed and low-key. The group wore their street clothes rather than their customary white suits. Mike opted for a "royal blue Edwardian bell-bottom outfit" at the benefit. Following the show, the Beach Boys were made admirals in the Nebraska Navy in a small ceremony.

The shows at the Music Hall in Omaha that night drew 4,385 people. According to Steve Jordon of the *Omaha World Herald*, "Recent talk about the group's new versatility was borne out when they sang creditable versions of the Buffalo Springfield's 'Rock and Roll Woman' and an older tune called 'Riot in Cell Block Number Nine.' But their magic begins when they perform, live, older hits like 'Help Me Rhonda,' 'Good Vibrations,' and 'I Get Around.' Their newest hit 'I Can Hear Music' has the same magic their fans never get tired of."

SUNDAY, MAY 4, 1969: Shriner's Hospital for Crippled Children, St. Louis, MO (3:00 p.m. show), and Kiel Opera House, St. Louis, MO, with the Crazy Elephant, the Spiral Staircase, and Joe Hicks (7:30 p.m. show)

Once again the Beach Boys played an afternoon benefit for the Crippled Children's charity. John Brod Peters of the *Globe Democrat* reviewed the evening show at the Opera House. He noted, "The group performed many of its well known selections for the appreciative audience although nothing comparatively new seemed to emerge. It seems to depend heavily on the protective acoustics of a recording studio, and doesn't come across as strongly in person. The necessary reinforcement of a band does nothing to help."

FRIDAY, MAY 30, 1969: Brighton Dome, Brighton, England, with Paul Revere and the Raiders and Joe Hicks (Two shows at 6:15 and 8:45 p.m.)

The Beach Boys arrived in London early on Thursday, May 29, accompanied by Dick Duryea, Steve Desper, bassist Ed Carter, and pianist Daryl Dragon to begin their European tour. They also brought John D'Andrea with them and he took charge of the eight-piece horn section hired in the U.K. The opening acts were Joe Hicks and Paul Revere and the Raiders. Bruce later expressed regret that the Beach Boys had not toured with a more respected U.K. band, like Fairport Convention. He told the BBC "We shouldn't have toured with the Raiders because it was a bubblegum kind of band, but we didn't have any direction. Unfortunately when you don't have a manager, you don't have good perspective . . . so, we were making our own decisions and a lot of them were really dumb." Bruce's comment about the Raiders mimicked the exact narrow-minded misperception that had befallen

became mired in controversy. On May 27, 1969, Brian held an impromptu press conference where he announced that the group was in deep financial trouble and were considering filing for bankruptcy. He told *Disc*, "We spent a heck of a lot of corporation money on Brother Records, our own company, and in boosting other recording artists who just didn't make it, and didn't have a single hit. When our records started to bomb out we looked around desperately for something to save ourselves. We had one hit, 'I Can Hear Music,' but one isn't enough to pay for our tremendous overheads . . . We all know that if we don't watch it and do something drastic inside

the Beach Boys. The Raiders' equally large body of work was high-quality and varied, with only a small fraction of it being anything close to bubblegum.

Upon their arrival in England, the group spent the day rehearsing and giving interviews. Filmmaker Vic Kettle accompanied them for the tour because the group was preparing a film to be shown on BBC TV. Kettle captured a great deal of footage in Brighton, including film of the group fooling around on bumper cars and relaxing in a park. He also filmed portions of the opening shows at the Brighton Dome, including an energetic performance of Buffalo Springfield's "Rock and Roll Woman." Richard Green of *New Musical Express* was also there and wrote, "Opening with 'I Can Hear Music,' they included 'Wouldn't It Be Nice,' 'California Girls,' 'Darlin','' 'I Get Around,' 'Cotton Fields,' 'Do It Again,' 'Breakaway,' 'Barbara Ann,' 'God Only Knows,' a medley of their slow numbers, and 'Their Hearts Were Full of Spring,' which they sang without instrumental backing and went down a storm . . . The Beach Boys delighted everyone and gave us as good a concert as I've seen for many a year."

SATURDAY, MAY 31, 1969: Hammersmith Odeon, London, England, with Paul Revere and the Raiders and Joe Hicks (Two shows at 6:45 and 9:15 p.m.)
The British music press was out in force for two sold-out concerts at the Hammersmith Odeon. Dressed in their all-white suits, the group kicked off the show with high-energy renditions of "I Can Hear Music," "Wouldn't It Be Nice," and "Darlin'." They then slowed things down with a medley of "The Warmth of the Sun" (just the musical intro with no vocals)/"Don't Worry Baby"/"Please Let Me Wonder"/ "Surfer Girl"/ "In My Room" that was practically drowned out by screaming girls in the audience. Mike silenced them by screaming "*Shaddap!*" into his microphone, and they regained control with "I Get Around," followed by "Cotton Fields" from *20/20*.

After performances of "Sloop John B" and "Do It Again," they played their new U.K. single "Breakaway," as well as "Rock and Roll Woman" and "Barbara Ann." Carl then performed "God Only Knows" and the full group sang "Their Hearts Were Full of Spring" a cappella. Bruce got his chance to shine with a solo piano rendition of "The Nearest Faraway Place." The full band returned for closing number "Good Vibrations" and headed offstage, but returned for an encore of "Johnny B. Goode."

David Hughes of *Disc and Music Echo* reported, "If the Beach Boys are really in Britain to make some quick money and get themselves in the black again . . . they're certainly making sure they earn it! At the sedate Hammersmith Odeon on Saturday the world's most popular active group turned an uncommonly apathetic first house audience into rousing cheers with fifty non-stop minutes taking in no less than eighteen hit songs." Royston Eldridge of *Melody Maker* commented, "The Beach Boys proved that they can produce onstage both intricate and simple songs without losing any of the control that most groups can only attain in the studio." He especially singled out their performance of "Rock and Roll Woman" for praise. "Carl Wilson, playing acoustic guitar, had a controlled yet powerful voice and the group's harmonies are tremendous."

SUNDAY, JUNE 1, 1969: De Doelen, Rotterdam, Netherlands, with Paul Revere and the Raiders and Joe Hicks (3:00 p.m. show) and Concertgebouw, Amsterdam, Netherlands, with Paul Revere and the Raiders and Joe Hicks (8:15 p.m. show)
The group flew to the Netherlands to play two concerts and tape a special TV show with Paul Revere and the Raiders. The TV show, *De Raiders and De Beach Boys*, was probably taped on June 2. Each group performed a mini concert for the cameras. The Beach Boys mimed to "Good Vibrations," "Breakaway," "I Can Hear Music," and "Cotton Fields." Instead of wearing stage clothes, Bruce wore a black leather jacket, Mike wore a dark suit, Carl wore a blazer and T-shirt, Dennis wore a striped shirt, and Al sported a tan coat and pants. The footage aired in July.

TUESDAY, JUNE 3, 1969: Brussels, Belgium, with Paul Revere and the Raiders and Joe Hicks
The group returned to Brussels for a show, partially filmed for the TV show *Vibrato*. On June 4 they were in Bremen, Germany, to tape appearances on the TV show *Beat Club*. They mimed to "Surfin' USA" and "Breakaway." The "Breakaway" clip aired on June 7, 1969, while the "Surfin' USA" clip was broadcast on August 2, 1969. The footage is easily distinguishable from their 1968 appearances

a few months we won't have a penny in the bank."

Brian's bombshell threatened to overshadow the tour and the Beach Boys' management exercised damage control. Dick Duryea told the U.K. press that Brian was "making a mountain out of a molehill and things are not nearly as bad as he says." Nick Grillo also downplayed the group's problems, telling reporter Bernard Barry that, "the Beach Boys' assets, if sold, would add up to around five million dollars . . . bankruptcy is unlikely. We could always sell off assets to pay bills, but we don't want to do so." He also explained that Brian "gets nervous when the bills start coming in. The business end of this operation was always too much for him to handle. But we are putting things in order and paying off our debts."

Despite the statements, the British press grilled the Beach Boys when they arrived in London on May 29. Carl told Richard Green of *New Musical Express*, "That was Brian being paranoiac, I think. He's said some things like that before. He was probably referring to a period about two and a half years ago when we had a cash shortage." Mike, accompanied on tour by his 22-year-old brother Steve, also weighed in. When reporter Alan Walsh asked if the group was broke, he replied, "Beach Boys broke? Well all I can say is that it's a relative word and there are relative truths in it. I know Brian said that but I believe it was an elaboration of the situation, which obtained last year. We were booked for a 30-day tour of the southern states of America when a certain gentleman named Martin Luther King was murdered and the tour was canceled."

Although Brian's statements

had created an unwanted controversy, the European tour was still a success. The Beach Boys remained phenomenally popular there. The same *20/20* album that had bombed commercially in the states hit a lofty number three on the U.K. album chart, while the single "I Can Hear Music" made the top ten. The group played to packed houses wherever they went, including concerts behind the Iron Curtain in Czechoslovakia. They arrived

"After he left, I said, 'Denny who is that? And he said, 'Fred, it's a guy named Charlie Manson and you don't want to know anything about him.'"

only months after the Soviet occupation had sent 750,000 troops into the country to crush fermenting anti-Communist reforms. In this climate of repression, the Beach Boys represented a breath of freedom. Large crowds swarmed around the concert venues to greet them. As Bruce recalled, "They wanted to know all about America, the latest records and rock 'n' roll." The European tour, especially the Czechoslovakian shows, bolstered their confidence and the Beach

because of Mike's long beard and "Maharishi" robes. Footage of the group eating in a restaurant and discussing the upcoming visit to Czechoslovakia that appeared in the 1985 *American Band* film was probably shot on this night.

FRIDAY, JUNE 6, 1969: Birmingham Odeon, Birmingham, England, with Paul Revere and the Raiders and Joe Hicks (Two shows at 6:30 and 9:00 p.m.)
The group returned to England on June 5. They were stopped at customs and spent several hours at the airport while officers searched their luggage and looked closely at all of the vitamins in the group's possession. Valerie Mabb of *Record Mirror* attended the Birmingham show and reported, "The boys opened their set with 'In My Room' and after making light-hearted quips about their financial status they continued with 'I Get Around,' 'Sloop John B,' and 'Do It Again,' which displayed incredibly well-balanced and perfectly reproduced harmonies. One of the highlights of the group's act was their current release 'Breakaway' which must renew every fan's faith in the Beach Boys' musical talent."

SATURDAY, JUNE 7, 1969: Liverpool Empire, Liverpool, England, with Paul Revere and the Raiders and Joe Hicks (Two shows at 6:10 and 8:40 p.m.)

SUNDAY, JUNE 8, 1969: King Edward's Nursing Home, Leeds, UK (Afternoon), and Free Trade Hall, Manchester, England, with Paul Revere and the Raiders and Joe Hicks (Two shows at 6:00 and 8:30 p.m.)
In the afternoon, the band visited the children's ward at King Edward's Nursing Home with BBC DJ Jimmy Savile and performed a free concert for 150 delighted nurses and patients. The concert was filmed for *Top of the Pops*. Jimmy Savile recalled on BBC Radio that Bruce had phoned from California to set up the show prior to the tour. "I said, 'What have you brought with you?' and they said 'Nothing. We have three acoustic guitars and a set of drumsticks . . .' With three acoustic, with the drummer sitting on a chair, playing on the top of a packing case . . . and with one microphone between . . . them . . . they gave us a session the like of which I could never even remember . . . They sang so good that they knocked themselves out. They sang for an hour and a quarter. They sang every song they knew, including 'Good Vibrations' because the nurses kept shouting [for it]. Nobody was sitting down, everyone was standing up . . . It was too fantastic for words."

MONDAY, JUNE 9, 1969: Glasgow Odeon, Glasgow, Scotland, with Paul Revere and the Raiders and Joe Hicks (Two shows at 6:15 and 8:45 p.m.)
Following these concerts, the group spent a few days relaxing. Mike spent his time at a TM center in Brighton. Carl and Dennis were spotted at London's Revolution Club drinking champagne. Carl undoubtedly spent time with the Flame, for whom he was working to get visas to come to the states.

On June 12, Dick Duryea, the group's road manager since 1965, collapsed due to complications from a blood clot and had to be rushed home. Duryea had already announced his decision to quit after the tour was over, and this marked the end of his relationship with the group.

FRIDAY, JUNE 13, 1969: Jahrhunderthalle-Hööchst, Frankfurt, Germany, with Paul Revere and the Raiders and Joe Hicks (Two shows at 7:00 and 9:45 p.m.)
Rumors that the Beach Boys were bankrupt almost ground the tour to a halt. Fearing that they might not get paid, the charter air company and the English musicians they were utilizing demanded that they receive cash up front. As a result, the group was unable to leave for Germany until money was raised to pay everyone. They arrived in Frankfurt after midnight. On Friday morning they were interviewed for German TV and Bruce recorded an interview with Tony Prince of Radio Luxembourg.

Ulrich Olshausen for the *Frankfurter Allgemaine Zeitung* briefly reviewed the concerts that night and noted, "What the Beach Boys bring together with intricate and interesting written parts . . . not only in the recording studio, but also on the concert stage in the roar of their own guitars is impressive and can't be replicated by others. Their lyrics are trivial . . . their music is clinically polished . . . But the sooner one tolerates pop music of the totally leisure-entertainment variety, the sooner one appreciates the musical and unsentimental way the Beach Boys deliver it."

1969

SATURDAY, JUNE 14, 1969: Deutschland Halle, West Berlin, Germany, with Paul Revere and the Raiders and Joe Hicks

While in Berlin, the group met with Deutsche Grammophon about a recording contract, but the deal was never finalized.

MONDAY, JUNE 16, 1969: Olympia Theatre, Paris, France, with Paul Revere and the Raiders and Joe Hicks (9:00 p.m. show)

A concert scheduled for June 15 in Munich was canceled, so the group flew to Paris on Sunday night. On Monday afternoon they taped a television appearance on the *Midi Premiere* show. Their show at the Olympia that night was filmed for *Musicorama*. It was their first show in Paris since 1966, as concerts scheduled in 1967 and 1968 were both canceled. It was also the last concert that they played with Paul Revere and the Raiders, who returned to the U.S. due to TV commitments. The Olympia set list consisted of "Darlin'," "Wouldn't It Be Nice," "California Girls" (introduced by Mike as "one of my favorite songs because I sing it"), "I Can Hear Music," a medley of "Warmth of the Sun" (only the introduction, no vocals)/"Don't Worry Baby" (with dual lead by Al and Bruce)/"Please Let Me Wonder" (with Bruce on lead vocals)/"Surfer Girl," and "In My Room," "I Get Around," "Sloop John B," "Do It Again" (with Bruce on tambourine and organ), "Breakaway," "The Nearest Faraway Place" (piano instrumental by Bruce), "Cotton Fields," "Barbara Ann" (introduced by Mike as "dedicated to everyone interested in improving Franco-American relations;" the group then proceeded to sing the chorus as "Pom-Pom-Pom-Pom Pompidou"), "God Only Knows," "Their Hearts Were Full of Spring," "Good Vibrations," and "Johnny B. Goode."

TUESDAY, JUNE 17, 1969: Lucerna Music Hall, Prague, Czechoslovakia, with Saze, Atlantis, and Blue Effect (Two shows)

The Beach Boys' legendary visit to the Eastern Bloc began with two shows in Prague, which was just recovering from a Soviet crackdown due to their anti-Communist reform efforts. The Beach Boys were one of the first big groups to visit Prague, and the Czech people filled the streets to get a glimpse of the American icons. Over 6,000 fans that were unable to get tickets to the sold-out concerts stood outside the venue to try to hear the group. The large crowds forced the police to bring reinforcements to maintain order and cope with traffic jams.

That night the group gave memorable performances in the intimate Lucerna Hall and received rapturous ovations. The reviewer from the Czech language *Rude Pravo* noted, "The Beach Boys themselves confirmed that they are one of those groups that possess a different sound on their studio recordings compared to when they appear on the stage. Whilst on record they excel vocally . . . on stage it is difficult to recognize the presence of the main lead voices under the domineering instrumental accompaniment, although, if we overlook the musical shortcomings then they created an incredible atmosphere . . . The whole evening was spiced up by the distinctive performance of singer Mike Love. I dare not say whether or not the Beach Boys failed to live up to expectations. Quite clearly though they demonstrated that no matter how good a recording it can never capture the atmosphere of their live performance, and no matter how brilliant the atmosphere of a live performance, it does not capture the musical standard which we are accustomed to on their records."

According to Daryl Dragon, "the most interesting thing about Prague was that they didn't have air conditioning in that country. And when I was sitting there playing the piano, the water and dew from all of the people and the sweat and everything made the piano like a big grease pit. I couldn't even play the piano. It was all wet, all the keys. It was like somebody hosed it down. So that was really a weird sensation. I was thinking, 'How many germs am I breathing right now?' But the fans really appreciated the band. They really appreciated Americans."

WEDNESDAY, JUNE 18, 1969: Bratislava Lyre IV International Festival of Popular Song, Bratislava, Czechoslovakia (11:30 p.m. show)

The group played one show at this four-day music festival and song competition. Preceding them were many Czech and Slovak acts taking part in the actual competition. Czech TV filmed the show. In addition, Vic Kettle shot footage of the group at the Carlton Hotel.

Boys returned home with greater purpose to rebuild their career.

Around this time Fred Vail rejoined the Beach Boys organization. The group had not forgotten that Vail had been helpful to them in their early days and they sought his assistance at this troubled time. Vail recalled that while he was in Denver setting up a show for Teenage Fairs International (which had employed him since 1966), "I got a call from Carl asking me if I would fly to L.A. because he wanted to talk to me about coming back and being in charge of all their concerts and their promotion and their marketing. They had their business manager Nick Grillo, but I was going to be in charge of all their marketing and production and touring. So I flew out and met them on a weekend and decided I would leave Teenage Fair." Vail arrived to find the Beach Boys' finances in chaos. He recalled, "They had major bills and that was one of my jobs. To deal with American Airlines, Diner's Club, American Express, Sheraton Hotels, etc. We had huge bills with those people and I had to fend off collection calls . . . So I was booking the group, I was fending off collection calls, doing some of the press releases, and I was trying to help some of the guys individually. . . . I was doing a ton of things."

When Vail joined the Beach Boys they were hard at work on their first post-Capitol LP. The sessions for what ultimately became the *Sunflower* album would stretch into the spring of 1970. The group recognized that they needed to hit a home run this time and were not willing to rush it. They were still seeking a willing record label in the States and were playing smaller venues and attracting fewer fans. The group's Thanksgiving tour that year was a dismal affair, with a show in South Dakota attracting an embarrassing 300 people. The group's problems were compounded by the distractions posed by Carl's ongoing legal struggle over his draft status.

The L.A. district attorney announced in early August that they intended to indict Carl for his failure to report to a military hospital for alternative service, as per his 1967 agreement. His arraignment was scheduled for August 18, 1969. Nick Grillo told *Rolling Stone* that Carl had in fact reported to the Los Angeles County Hospital as mandated and had been ordered to serve as an institutional helper. Carl would have been assigned to whatever task the hospital deemed fit. Jobs included clerking in an office, cleaning up after the patients, and working in the kitchen. Carl argued that his talents might be better served teaching handicapped children to play the guitar, and wrote a ten-page proposal that he submitted. According to Grillo, the hospital was enthusiastic but the Selective Service Board ignored the request. The Beach Boys attempted to placate the Draft Board by playing numerous benefit shows in 1969, but to no avail. Carl pleaded guilty and an initial trial date of November 4 was set. The case would drag on into 1970 and make touring difficult.

Dennis' name was also dragged into a court case, though of a very different sort. That December he was questioned about his relationship with the notorious Manson Family. Dennis had met Charles Manson and his

THURSDAY, JUNE 19, 1969: Winter Stadium, Brno, Czechoslovakia, with Blue Effect, Progress Organization, and Synkopy 61
This was the group's last concert behind the iron curtain. Bruce Johnston recalled a few weeks later on *The Mike Douglas Show* that the communist government "wouldn't allow us to take all of the income home. We had to spend half of the income we made there. So in the remaining two or three hours we had in the country after we did all of our work, we had to run around and try to get rid of the money. Dennis bought about two suitcases."

FRIDAY, JUNE 20, AND SATURDAY, JUNE 21, 1969: Keimolan Juhannus Juhla, Vantaa, Finland, with Joe Hicks, Spede and Simo Show (Friday at 6:00 p.m. and Saturday at 2:00 p.m.)
The group played two shows at this venue outside Helsinki. It was actually a rink used for auto racing and they were on the bill with an act that performed car stunts!

SATURDAY, JUNE 21, 1969: Antwerp Pop Festival, Antwerp, Belgium

SUNDAY, JUNE 22, 1969: Finsbury Park Astoria, London, England, with Rainbow People and Marmalade (Two shows at 6:00 and 8:30 p.m.)
The Beach Boys' popularity in the U.K. led to the addition of these shows to satisfy demand. Since Paul Revere and the Raiders had flown home, Marmalade and Rainbow People were added to the bill. Mike Ledgerwood of *Disc and Music Echo* reported, "the Beach Boys certainly left us with some good vibrations. A full-blooded, power packed bumper programme which included most of their big hits and Carl Wilson's clever, if at times a tiny bit flat, rendering of 'God Only Knows' . . . Musically they might not exactly reproduce their famous studio sounds, but they have a damned good try and the result is not disappointing." Ledgerwood singled Bruce out for special praise for his solo piano performance of "The Nearest Faraway Place," which "went down a storm."

Following the shows, the group spent a few days in London. On June 23 Carl and Mike visited an editing studio on Oxford St. to have a look at footage shot by Vic Kettle of the tour. Dennis, Carl, and Al most likely returned to the U.S. on June 24. Mike and Bruce remained in Europe a bit longer, appearing on *Top of the Pops* on June 25 to introduce the footage shot at Leeds. Bruce also worked on a single for Graham Bonney. Mike spent time at the Brighton Meditation Center and returned to the states on June 29.

SATURDAY, JULY 19, 1969: Long Island Arena, Commack, NY, with the Box Tops and the Buchanan Brothers
This was the first tour organized following the 1969 hiring of Fred Vail. Ed Carter (bass), Daryl Dragon (keyboards), and Dennis Dragon (percussion) were the backup musicians on these dates. The group also utilized a three-piece horn section. The Wilsons' cousin Steve Korthof acted as stage manager. Stephen Desper, who was also on the tour as live mixer, recalled, "Korthof was like a bulldog. He was always worried about something and always pushing everybody. He had high blood pressure. He got the job done but he was like a Tasmanian devil. He was quite a character. I really enjoyed his company."

While on the East Coast the group taped two television appearances in Philadelphia. They sang "Breakaway" on the syndicated *Hy Lit Show*. Lit was an influential radio personality, who had emceed the group's first Philly show. The group also appeared on *The Mike Douglas Show*. Dressed in their white stage outfits, the group sang live vocals for "Breakaway" and Dennis' composition "Celebrate the News."

SUNDAY, JULY 20, 1969: Troy Armory, Troy, NY, with the Box Tops and the Buchanan Brothers
A fan that attended this show recalled, "It was the night that we landed on the moon and the show got interrupted in the middle of the slow song medley when the local DJ brought a black and white TV onto the stage and played the landing. The Beach Boys had to leave the stage and Al was pissed off and made an audible comment to that effect."

MONDAY, JULY 21, 1969: Wentworth Curling Club, Hamilton, ON, Canada, with the Box Tops and the Buchanan Brothers

The Beach Boys were one of the first rock acts to play in Hamilton. Mayor Vic Copps came to greet them and presented them with special hats to commemorate their visit. In addition, Capitol Records Canada threw a press party for the group. Carl gushed about being a new father: "Man, it's just the greatest thing." Dennis took the opportunity to proclaim, "No one should be unhappy. It's all in the mind. You haven't got to let things get to you." Asked about Vietnam, Dennis said, "That's abstract. I won't believe it till I see it . . . I'd like to go there and have a look around and see what it's all about, but not to fight. I'm a conscientious objector." Dennis also stated his continued support for the Maharishi's teachings. "He's got the answer you know. Meditation, that's the answer to all your problems . . . It's got nothing to do with money. In business I'm a multimillionaire, but I don't have a place of my own in L.A. I live with my friends and sleep wherever I put my head down. I've got peace and happiness man."

The Hamilton police were unprepared for the large crowds that turned out to see the Beach Boys. Cars were parked in no-parking zones near the venue and police threatened to ticket and tow the vehicles. Bruce Johnston had to personally call the police station to beg them not to. *The Spectator* reviewer Jerry Rogers praised the Box Tops, led by their dynamic singer Alex Chilton. About the Beach Boys, he stated, "While their total sound has become a bit familiar they still have a few surprises. Last night's set—forty-five minutes of top forty tunes like 'Sloop John B,' 'Good Vibrations,' 'I Get Around,' and 'Help Me Rhonda'—was a quick, almost effortless way for them to earn $8,500 that delighted the audience."

TUESDAY, JULY 22, 1969: Manhattan College Summer Music Festival, Gaelic Park, New York, NY, with the Box Tops and Brooklyn Bridge (8:30 p.m. show)
This concert was sponsored by Manhattan College and WOR-FM radio. It was opened by the Box Tops and Brooklyn Bridge, a new group that had a hit with Jimmy Webb's "The Worst That Could Happen." It was probably the next day that the Beach Boys taped their first appearance on *The David Frost Show*. Their appearance aired on August 8.

THURSDAY, JULY 24, TO SATURDAY, JULY 26, 1969: Steel Pier, Atlantic City, NJ, with the Buchanan Brothers and the Box Tops
Fred Vail recalled a very embarrassing incident involving this engagement and a misprint poster. "Back in those days, when you signed a union contract, the leader would sign it. So (it read), 'Carl Wilson and four musicians known as the Beach Boys.' The union would have the leader sign it and the promoter sign it and the agent sign it. So my guess is that the Steel Pier gave the contract to some secretary who was probably new on the job and told her to order posters like you always do for this act. So I can just imagine the Beach Boys getting to the Steel Pier for the gig and Michael getting out of the car and just dying when he saw the poster! Because in huge letters it said 'Carl Wilson' and in smaller letters 'and the Beach Boys.' Love must have been having a hemorrhage when he saw that!"

SUNDAY, JULY 27, 1969: Oakdale Musical Theatre, Wallingford, CT, with the Buchanan Brothers and the Box Tops (8:00 p.m. show)

MONDAY, JULY 28, 1969: Merriweather Post Pavilion, Columbia, MD, with the Buchanan Brothers, the Box Tops, the Fugitive Six, and Bill Myers and the Younger Americans (8:00 p.m. show)
This was a benefit concert for the March of Dimes. The set list stuck mainly to the hits with the exception of Bruce's performance of "The Nearest Faraway Place" and an a cappella "Their Hearts Were Full of Spring."

TUESDAY, JULY 29, AND WEDNESDAY, JULY 30, 1969: Hampton Beach Casino, Hampton Beach, NH, with the Buchanan Brothers, the Box Tops, and the Spectras

THURSDAY, JULY 31, 1969: Irwin's Winnipesaukee Gardens, Weir's Beach, Laconia, NH, with the Buchanan Brothers, the Box Tops, and the Spectras

"family" in the spring of 1968 in between Beach Boys tours. He'd picked up two young female hitchhikers who led him towards a nightmare that haunted him until his death. Dennis told David Griffiths of *Record Mirror* that he had told the girls about Maharishi "and they told me they too had a guru, a guy named Charlie who'd recently come out of jail after twelve years. His mother was a hooker, his father was a gangster, he'd drifted into crime, but when I met him I found he had great musical ideas." Charles Manson impressed Dennis enough that he arranged for him do some recording at Brian's home. Steve Desper recalled to writer Steven Gaines, "Dennis was really taken in by Manson. He went on for days about how much he loved Manson and how he wanted to help him out, saying that he really had talent, and that he was terribly misunderstood." Dennis also got Manson an audition with producer Terry Melcher and invited him to tour with the Beach Boys on their February trip to Texas. Fortunately, Manson's parole officer refused to allow him to leave California and his gig opening for the Beach Boys ended before it started.

Dennis was deeply intrigued by Manson's harem of confused young runaways, who viewed Charlie as a father figure and were willing to do anything for him. Seventeen scantily clad young women who were more than willing to engage in any sexual fantasies that Dennis could dream up held his interest, and by the summer of 1968 Manson and his family were living with him at his expansive ranch-style

THE BEACH BOYS IN CONCERT

Al Jardine backstage at the Delaware State Fair on August 2, 1969. Photo: Jack Lloyd

home on Sunset Boulevard. Dennis immersed himself in the communal lifestyle and free-love atmosphere. He told writer Lon Goddard in 1969, "We'd make love and discuss things while contributing to one purpose—to help others. The girls would go out on the streets and beg money from those that looked like they could afford it, then bring it home . . . we would make clothes for those who needed them or give the money to charity."

FRIDAY, AUGUST 1, 1969: Schaefer Music Festival, Wollman Rink, Central Park, NY, with Lonnie Mack (Two shows at 8:00 and 10:30 p.m.)
Neil Young was scheduled to co-headline, but he canceled and Lonnie Mack opened instead. The set list consisted of "Do It Again," "Darlin'," "Wouldn't It Be Nice," "Sloop John B," "California Girls," a medley of "Warmth of the Sun" (instrumental)/"Don't Worry Baby"/ "Please Let Me Wonder"/"Surfer Girl"/"In My Room," "I Can Hear Music," "Breakaway," "Cotton Fields," 'Riot in Cell Block Number Nine," "God Only Knows," "Their Hearts Were Full of Spring," "Good Vibrations," and an encore of "Rock and Roll Woman."

SATURDAY, AUGUST 2, 1969: Delaware State Fair, Harrington, DE (Two shows at 7:30 and 9:00 p.m.)
Despite bad weather, the group attracted over 23,000 fans to the fair. Former road manager Jack Lloyd took photos of the group onstage. According to Lloyd, after they returned to L.A. he took some of the Beach Boys to Las Vegas to see Elvis Presley perform. Brian and his wife Marilyn were among the attendees.

FRIDAY, SEPTEMBER 5, AND SATURDAY, SEPTEMBER 6, 1969: Lagoon, Farmington, UT, with Paul Revere and the Raiders (One show at 9:00 p.m. each night)
The Beach Boys' touring schedule was temporarily derailed by Carl's draft case. It was not until early September that they were able to play a few dates.

SUNDAY, SEPTEMBER 7, 1969: Bronco Football Stadium, Boise, ID, with Paul Revere and the Raiders, the Filmore West, Rick McClellan, and the Crystal Ship of Ontario (7:00 p.m. show)
About 6,500 fans attended this show. Paul Revere and the Raiders, who were from Boise and were making their first appearance in their hometown since attaining stardom, overshadowed the Beach Boys. The *Idaho Statesman* noted that, "with unique vigor, sophisticated corn, and sufficient electronic amplification to be heard by anyone within blocks of the Bronco Stadium, both groups won a storm of whistles and applause from their fans, after playing over an hour each to satisfy the crowd."

WEDNESDAY, NOVEMBER 26, 1969: Aragon Ballroom, Chicago, IL (Two shows at 7:30 and 10:30)
The group began their seventh Thanksgiving tour. Daryl Dragon (piano), Ed Carter (bass), Dennis Dragon (percussion), Fred Vail, Stephen Desper, and road manager Jon Parks accompanied them. The Beach Boys taped a television appearance on *The Dennis Wholey Show* in Cincinnati prior to this concert. They performed Dennis' as-yet-unreleased "Slip On Through" before a live audience.

THURSDAY, NOVEMBER 27, 1969: Corn Palace, Mitchell, SD (3:00 p.m. show), Sioux Falls Arena, Sioux Falls, SD, with the Apostles (7:00 p.m. show) and Sioux City Auditorium, Sioux City, IA, with the Pilgrims (11:00 p.m. show)
Poor record sales were beginning to affect bookings. Fred Vail recalled, "We were back to what we had been doing in 1963. We were playing in secondary markets where the kids seldom saw entertainment." The group would remember this Thanksgiving Day as a bottoming-out moment in their career. Bruce has often recounted his bleak memory of playing for 300 people in Mitchell at the Corn Palace. Daryl Dragon recalled, "Half a house showed up. That was so pathetic. I think I said, 'You guys should just hang it up.'" Fred Vail commented more charitably, "It wasn't an absolute disaster but I love to kid people and say, 'There were more people on stage than in the audience.' We had Thanksgiving dinner in styrofoam to-go boxes. It was definitely one of the low points."

The infamous Corn Palace concert was an afternoon affair and one of three concerts played that day. After eating their modest Thanksgiving meal, the group traveled to Sioux Falls for a 7 p.m. show and then moved on to nearby Sioux City, Iowa for a late-night concert there.

1969

SATURDAY, NOVEMBER 29, 1969: Edmonton, Alberta, Canada

In Edmonton, Fred Vail witnessed a very disturbing incident involving Dennis. "Denny got a panicky call from (his ex-wife) Carole that (their son) Scotty was missing. And Dennis was really upset

Carl performing in Delaware on August 2, 1969. Photo: Jack Lloyd

There was a darker side to all of this free love. Manson and his followers were soon helping themselves to all of Dennis' possessions, including furniture, stereo equipment, and cars. Eventually, all the leeching disillusioned Dennis. Instead of kicking out the family, he allowed the lease to expire on his house and he moved into his friend Gregg Jakobson's garage. The Family then moved to the Spahn Ranch in the desert, but continued to occasionally come around to beg Dennis for more cash. Fred Vail recalled being at Dennis's once when Charles Manson came to visit. "I met him once. The guy was a creep. He was a real asshole. Not only was he evil, but also he was a manipulator and a deadbeat. I remember Dennis was living in a rental apartment. And I was over there on a Saturday and Denny got a phone call. And he said, 'Oh crap! This guy is coming over.' I didn't even know who it was. So he came over in a jeep and came in and kind of grunted 'Hi Denny. I need some of your stuff.' And he

Bruce onstage in Delaware on August 2, 1969. Photo: Jack Lloyd

goes into the closet and takes an armful of clothes off the rack and he goes out to the jeep and throws it in the back and takes off. No conversation. After he left, I said, 'Denny who is that? And he said, 'Fred, it's a guy named Charlie Manson and you don't want to know anything about him.'"

Dennis belatedly realized that he'd connected with something evil. His fears were amply confirmed when in the summer of 1969 the Tate-La Bianca murders horrified the world and Manson and his family were charged with the brutal carnage. When stories of Dennis' involvement with Manson surfaced in the press, it threatened to tarnish the Beach Boys' clean image. Ultimately, it demonstrated just how far their star had fallen in the states when the story came and went with little fanfare. Dennis, however, continued to be harassed by reporters about the episode for the rest of his life. He seldom answered, but friends knew the stress and shame of his Manson association took a toll on him and forever changed his happy-go-lucky demeanor.

Nineteen sixty-nine was definitely a dark year for the group, but they believed in themselves and were continuing to produce good music. Dennis, Mike, Carl, Bruce, and Al were all busy writing songs and even Brian was becoming more involved again. Towards the end of the year, the Beach Boys secured a new recording contract with Warner Brothers/Reprise Records. While they knew it would be a steep climb back to the top, the Beach Boys were optimistic as the turbulent 1960s came to an end.

because we were like 2500 miles away and Carole's just really upset because Scotty's not there. He's gone and she can't find him. She'd already gone around the neighborhood and they lived in Benedict Canyon Drive, which was pretty isolated. So something could have happened and nobody would know about it. So anyways we did the show and Denny is in a panic. He was saying, 'I want to leave.' And I was saying, 'You won't get a flight because it's Saturday.' So he said, 'Charter me a plane.' And I had to break the news to Denny that we couldn't afford to charter him a plane. So I just said, 'Let's just give it a little more time. They're probably doing everything they can down there. I think by that time the Sheriff's department had been called and all that stuff. We got back (to the hotel) and I was trying to get him on a red-eye to Minneapolis-St. Paul so that he could then catch a flight back to L.A. But as it turned out Carole had called and said 'Don't worry, we found him.' It was just an innocent mistake, he was just at a friend's. The mother thought Carole knew he was at the friend's, so they didn't call to say he was at the friend's. It was just a big mess. So we didn't have to get Denny on a plane. But I am absolutely certain to this day that when Carole called and said Scotty was missing, the first thing Dennis thought was that Charles Manson had taken him."

SUNDAY, NOVEMBER 30, 1969: Winnipeg Auditorium, Winnipeg, Manitoba, Canada, with the Fifth and Eddy Laham (7:30 p.m. show)
The group returned to Winnipeg for what turned out to be the last night of a dismal tour. The *Winnipeg Free Press* noted, "the Beach Boys came remarkably close to duplicating the marvelous sound they achieve on their recordings . . . "

MONDAY, DECEMBER 1, 1969: University of Duluth, Duluth, MN (Canceled)

TUESDAY, DECEMBER 2, 1969: University of North Dakota, Grand Forks, ND (Canceled)
The Beach Boys were scheduled to play shows in Duluth and Grand Forks but they canceled. Fred Vail told a reporter from the *Dakota Student* that "Mike Love has been ordered to appear in court for divorce proceedings and he can't get out of it. We've gotten continuances before so Mike could make their engagements, but we couldn't get another one." The group promised both schools they would play makeup shows, but this did not happen. Fred Vail reveals that Mike's divorce proceedings may not have been the real reason for the cancelations. "I think they may have been canceled by the promoters because there wasn't enough advance sales. And you never want to admit that your shows are being canceled for lack of fans."

The group headed back to L.A., where a hellish media storm was brewing. Vail recalled, "When we got back on Monday to Los Angeles the story broke about Charles Manson and all hell broke loose. The D.A. called us up and they told me to field all the questions to the district attorney because there is going to be a lot of press. They said, 'You guys are the Beach Boys. You have millions of fans and there is going to be a lot of stuff in the papers about Denny's connection to Manson. You may get threats. Lock the door.' That was the beginning of that whole thing."

OTHER 1969 CONCERTS
The Beach Boys may have played shows on November 28. Author Keith Badman wrote that they played at Minot State University, but the school had no record of this.

CONCERTS NOT PLAYED
Author Keith Badman wrote that the Beach Boys played in Budapest in June 1969, but the only Iron Curtain country they visited was Czechoslovakia.

According to *Variety*, the group was to appear in Buffalo on August 3. But a check of the local papers disclosed no mention of it. It's possible it was canceled due to Carl's ongoing draft case.

The Beach Boys were scheduled to play a seven-date Canadian tour in October, including a stop at the Saskatoon Arena on October 18, but the tour was canceled.

1970

T HE BEACH BOYS spent the first few months of 1970 working on their first Brother/Reprise album, tentatively titled Add Some Music to Your Day. Mo Ostin, the president of Warner/Reprise, agreed to sign the Beach Boys on the promise that Brian would be an active contributor. The group was at such a low point popularity-wise that despite all of their past success, many Warner executives referred to the contract with the Beach Boys as "Mo's Folly." Despite the common perception that the group's best days were behind them, the Beach Boys themselves were convinced they were still getting better. That February they submitted a finished LP to the label. Since recent Beach Boys album releases had sunk like a stone, Reprise decided to test the market by throwing out a trial balloon before releasing a full album. A single, "Add Some Music To Your Day," was released on February 23, 1970. It proved to be a major failure. Fred Vail spent much of 1970 working to get the Beach Boys' new music played on the radio and recalled, "The 'Add Some Music' single was a huge disaster. It should have been a top ten record. It was perfect lyrics of the time. It's just that the Beach Boys weren't cool. Jay Cook of WFIL in Philadelphia said, 'Fred I can't play the record.' I asked him why and he said, 'Because the Beach Boys

CONCERTS PLAYED IN
1970

aren't hip anymore." That kind of sums up the whole period." When the single stalled at number sixty-four on the *Billboard* charts, the label rejected the proposed LP and ordered the group to work on it some more.

It was a stressful time for the group, especially Carl. He was busy with the Beach Boys' new album and also producing the first album by his protégés the Flame. However, most of Carl's time was taken up by legal problems stemming from his failure to report for alternate service. On January 29, 1970, Carl was given three year's probation and fined $4,000 by U.S. District Court Judge Harry Pregerson. The judge ordered Carl to spend two of his three probation years working as an institutional helper for the County Department of Hospitals. Carl was reluctant to use his time and talents this way, so his legal battles continued until the fall of 1971. Due to these issues and the fact that all of the Beach Boys other than Bruce had young children, the Beach Boys toured very little in the U.S. in 1970.

The band was also having a hard time obtaining bookings. Fred Vail recalled, "The Beach Boys were not making big money. I had trouble putting together the Pacific Northwest tour (in February–March 1970). . . . I had promoters who had made hundreds of thousands of dollars off the Beach Boys who wouldn't return my calls. Or they would offer me ridiculous guarantees or no guarantees. They were still a legendary act at that point, and they still had a big fan base, but there were so many other people involved in the music scene then. We were up against a lot of heavyweight acts of that era."

THURSDAY, FEBRUARY 26, 1970: Kennedy Pavilion, Gonzaga University, Spokane, WA, with Paul Revere and the Raiders

This was the opening date of a four-day tour of the Pacific Northwest, with Brian making his first appearances onstage since August 1967. The shows were played without Mike, who had become quite ill as a result of fasting too strenuously, and was hospitalized. Fred Vail, who booked the tour and traveled with the group, recalled, "Michael basically had a meltdown. So Brian played it. It was always exciting to see Brian onstage." The *Gonzaga Bulletin* reported, "The second half of the program was presented by the Beach Boys who also blew the collective mind of the audience. They played many of their older and more familiar hits to a large conglomeration of old fans and new converts."

FRIDAY, FEBRUARY 27, 1970: Queen Elizabeth Theatre, Vancouver, BC, Canada, with Paul Revere and the Raiders (Two shows at 7:00 and 9:30 p.m.)

SATURDAY, FEBRUARY 28, 1970: Seattle Opera House, Seattle, WA, with Paul Revere and the Raiders (Two shows at 7:30 and 9:30 p.m.)

A low-quality audiotape of one of these two Seattle shows exists. Brian and Carl opened the show with a dual lead on "Do It Again," Carl took the lead on "Darlin'," Brian and Al sang "Surfer Girl," Carl sang the lead on "Sloop John B," Al took his usual lead on "Help Me Rhonda," Carl sang "I Can Hear Music," Al sang the lead on "Wouldn't It Be Nice" with Brian singing the bridge, all the Beach Boys sang "Add Some Music to Your Day" with Brian singing Mike's parts and his own from the record, Al sang "Cotton Fields," Carl sang "God Only Knows," Brian took the lead on "Barbara Ann," Bruce played a solo piano version of "Nearest Faraway Place," and Carl sang the lead on "Good Vibrations" with accompaniment by Brian.

The performance captured on tape is quite good, but reporter Jeanine Gressel of the *Seattle Times* was unimpressed. She argued that the Beach Boys' problems were "entirely due to their performance. For a group that has traded on their harmonic blend, they certainly didn't live up to past achievements in that area. The harmony was sloppy and often out of tune . . . True Mike Love, a regular member of the group, was absent. Love was replaced by Brian Wilson, who hadn't been with them in performance for five years. But excuses are not allowed to professionals. Besides, the trouble didn't seem to lie in Brian Wilson's work at all, but was rather an overall sloppiness that seemed to infect the entire group."

SUNDAY, MARCH 1, 1970: Portland Civic Auditorium, Portland, OR, with Paul Revere and the Raiders (Two shows at 6:00 and 8:30 p.m.)

This was the last day of the tour. Though he enjoyed the experience, Brian did not play with the group again until November, when he joined them onstage at the Whisky a Go Go.

SATURDAY, APRIL 18, 1970: Town Hall, Auckland, NZ, with Dave Allenby (Two shows at 6:00 and 8:15 p.m.)

The Beach Boys traveled to New Zealand for the second time in their career. Due to commitments, Fred Vail stayed home, but Daryl Dragon and Ed Carter traveled with the group, along with Jon Parks, who acted as stage manager, having replaced Steve Korthof. Steve Desper also accompanied them, though his sound system remained in California. He told a reporter from *The Australian* that if they had brought the system, it would have cost them $180,000 to ship and reassemble it.

The Beach Boys arrived in Auckland on April 17 to begin a four-city tour of New Zealand with opening act Dave Allenby, a British comedian. The band was delayed at the airport because Carl was missing a smallpox vaccination form and had to receive a shot from an airport physician before he could be admitted into the country.

Bruce and Al share a microphone at Gonzaga University on February 26, 1970. Courtesy of Gonzaga University Libraries

MONDAY, APRIL 20, 1970: Town Hall, Wellington, NZ, with Dave Allenby (Two shows at 6:00 and 8:15 p.m.)

The Beach Boys played to two full houses. *The Wellington Evening Post* reported, "Confetti and streamers fell on the group as Al Jardine, rhythm guitar, led the vocal into 'Help Me Rhonda' followed by Carl Wilson in 'God Only Knows.' Even without studio recording techniques, they produced enough effect with their smash hit 'Good Vibrations' to set the Town Hall rocking when fans saw the group reproduce their unique harmonizing . . . Mike Love . . . despite a somewhat marked difference in appearance from the early days of the group, sang 'California Girls' in true Beach Boys style . . . Even though the surfing sound in pop music which the Beach Boys pioneered may have become faded, the groups' earlier hits received great response from a hard to stir Wellington audience."

TUESDAY, APRIL 21, 1970: Majestic Theatre, Christchurch, NZ, with Dave Allenby and Tap Heperi and the Chaptah (Two shows at 6:00 and 8:15 p.m.)

The *Christchurch Press* reported, "The Beach Boys concert last evening at the Majestic Theatre was a knockout . . . Their playing was superb. The number 'Good Vibrations,' the group's biggest selling single, was probably the highlight of the performance. The presentation of this was flawless and showed how far the boys have come since their first surfing music . . . "

While it may have been hard to set up, ultimately the short tour of the Pacific Northwest was quite memorable. Mike Love became ill and was unable to tour. Much to everyone's surprise, Brian agreed to fill in for him. Brian sang and played piano at the shows, and showed that his high falsetto voice was still intact. In a radio interview that July, Brian enthusiastically recalled, "I was scared for a few minutes in the first show . . . it had been a while since I was in front of so many people. But after it started to cook I really got with it. It was the best three days of my life, I guess." Brian was so enthused by the experience that he considered going on the group's tour of Australia and New Zealand in April. He went so far as to fill out a visa application before abandoning the idea.

The Australian–New Zealand tour was a much more low-key affair than their 1964 visit. Indeed, it culminated with a residency at a small dinner theater in the Chevron-Hilton Hotel in Sydney. Fred Vail recalled, "We really needed the money. I talked them into doing it. We had an offer from the Sydney [Chevron] Hilton to do a two-week gig and I had to really fight with them to get them to do it. They said, 'We don't want to be a lounge act. We don't want to be a Vegas act. We don't want to be an oldies act.' And I said, 'You're not. You're still big stars in Australia. You have always been big there. This is a premiere room and they're paying us great money.' They were taking care of the per-diem and the rooms. I said, 'You guys will make money if you do that gig.' And they finally agreed to do it."

When the Beach Boys

THE BEACH BOYS IN CONCERT

Dennis keeps the beat in Spokane, February 26, 1970.
Courtesy of Gonzaga University Libraries

WEDNESDAY, APRIL 22, 1970: Town Hall, Dunedin, NZ (Canceled)
The group was scheduled to play two shows in Dunedin, but the *Otago Daily Times* announced the group had canceled the engagement, possibly due to poor ticket sales.

THURSDAY, APRIL 23, 1970: Festival Hall, Melbourne, VIC, Australia, with Dave Allenby
The Beach Boys flew to Australia on Wednesday night, landing in Melbourne around midnight. Despite their exhaustion from the flight, the entire group, except Bruce, stayed up until 4 a.m. talking with reporter Jean Gollan. Asked about Brian's absence, Carl replied, "Well, he did join us for a weekend in the states recently . . . and he said that he might join us in Europe, but you can never tell with Brian . . . He just doesn't like to travel . . . he didn't like anything about touring, and he didn't like being away from his home environment, which consists of a piano and fridge and peanut butter and wild honey and a couple of masseurs and a constant temperature above seventy-five degrees." Asked about recent musical changes, Dennis said, "The music we do now is just for fun." Carl added, "In a way we had to catch up with Brian. We've been developing rapidly as a group and as individuals in the last year. I guess we've gone into another whole cycle. We're much stronger, independently stronger. I'm a much better singer now than I used to be. But we aren't looking for any direction, just to have fun and be as good as we can."

FRIDAY, APRIL 24, 1970: Perry Lakes Stadium, Perth, WA, Australia, with Dave Allenby (8:00 p.m. show)
The group flew to Perth on Friday. About 3,500 fans attended the concert that night at the outdoor Perry Lakes Stadium.

SATURDAY, APRIL 25, 1970: Apollo Stadium, Adelaide, SA, Australia, with Dave Allenby and the Incase (8:00 p.m. show)
The group's rented sound system was lost in transit and this concert was delayed while the crew struggled to set up a hastily compiled substitute. Over 4,000 fans waited patiently. Harold Tidemann of the *Adelaide Advertiser* wrote, "despite sound distortion, microphone feedback, and cramped conditions, there was no denying the group's talent when they got going. Much of their appeal lay in their easy manner, the way-out gear they wore, and their sense of style and ensemble. Their greatest hits came towards the end, with 'Barbara Ann,' 'Good Vibrations,' and 'Johnny B. Goode.' Teenagers went wild and screamed for more, but the boys said goodbye after about an hour on stage."

SUNDAY, APRIL 26, 1970: Canberra Theatre, Canberra, ACT, Australia, with Dave Allenby (Two shows at 5:00 and 8:00 p.m.)
Daryl Dragon recalled this tour with fondness. "It was lot of fun in Australia. I liked it because I got to hang out with Dennis Wilson a lot."

MONDAY, APRIL 27, 1970: Sydney Stadium, Sydney, NSW, Australia, with Dave Allenby and Catch 22 (8:00 p.m. show)
The lack of a sophisticated sound system caused problems at larger venues. Michael Symons of *The Sydney Herald* reported that the group's delicate harmonies "were not exactly heard to advantage at the Stadium . . . All the same, Brian's brothers Carl and Dennis, with Al Jardine, Mike Love, Bruce Johnston, and two extra unnamed musicians ran through a series of two-minute hits without inflicting too much pain on the large crowd . . . Dressed impeccably in white, the group looked even more precious than they have sounded since leaving their original surf phase. Mike Love puffs a magnificent red beard, Carl Wilson hides his plumpness in a military jacket, and his contrastingly lean, broad-shouldered brother really belted the hide out of the drums."

TUESDAY, APRIL 28, 1970: Capitol Hall, Wollongong, NSW, Australia, with Dave Allenby, Tamam Shud, Fantasy, and the Turkish Green Electric Band (Two shows at 7:30 and 10:30 p.m.)
Surprisingly, the group allowed Murry Wilson to join them for part of this tour. However, despite his backstage request that they all wear the exact same white outfits, the Beach Boys chose to abandon their stage uniformity in favor of more casual attire. Carl wore a dark military jacket rather than his white coat, while Mike sported a blue and white Cossack hat. The group received $3600 Australian for the shows after playing to about 4,000 people.

WEDNESDAY, APRIL 29, 1970: Century Theatre, Newcastle, NSW, Australia, with Dave Allenby (Two shows at 7:30 and 9:30 p.m.)

THURSDAY, APRIL 30, 1970: Festival Hall, Brisbane, QLD, Australia, with Dave Allenby (8:00 p.m. show)
This concert was attended by 3,853 fans. Peter Brady of the *Brisbane Courier Mail* declared, "Looking nothing like the Ivy League surfers of their last Australian tour in the early '60s, the Beach Boys showed they had lost no support from Brisbane fans. The crowd clapped and cheered during the onstage antics which culminated with a 'Happy Birthday' singalong for the group's manager, and group poses for anyone who wanted to take their picture. An unaccompanied version of 'They Had Spring in Their Hearts' and a driving version of 'Johnny B. Goode' also proved they had not lost any of the harmony and versatility which made them famous."

SATURDAY, MAY 2, 1970: Beachcomber Tiki Village Motel, Surfer's Paradise, QLD, Australia, with Dave Allenby (8:00 p.m. show)
This concert was filmed as part of an odd BBC TV special, which the group agreed to take part in for Channel Seven. The show was described at the time as a "send-up many of the age-old myths about Australian life" and a bicentennial celebration of Captain Cook's landing at Botany Bay. It would be a comedic film with the Beach Boys in the role of members of Cook's crew. In addition to the concert, further filming took place in Sydney the following week. However, the show never aired, with the exception of a small excerpt that shows the group riding in a car dressed in pirate costumes being chased by Captain Cook (played by Dave Allenby), while a live version of "I Get Around" plays. The group allegedly hated the finished product and prevented its release.

BIG EXCLUSIVE!

NEW 2UW PRESENTS THE BEACH BOYS IN CONCERT SYDNEY STADIUM Monday 27th April, 8pm TICKETS AVAILABLE AT MITCHELLS BOOKING AGENCY AND SYDNEY STADIUM

Ian Rusten Collection

returned to the states in May, they headed back into the studio to complete their first LP for Warner Brothers. At the request of the label, the group replaced five tracks from the originally proposed LP with stronger songs, and the group also convinced Brian to let them finish an unreleased track that had germinated in the late *Smile* through *Wild Honey* period titled "Cool, Cool Water." With these changes made, the album, retitled *Sunflower*, was accepted by the label and released on August 31, 1970. The Beach Boys were extremely proud of it. In retrospect, several of the Beach Boys referred to *Sunflower* as their favorite LP. Carl told *Rock* magazine, "*Sunflower*, I'd say, is the truest group effort we've ever had. Each of us was deeply involved in the creation of almost all the cuts." Brian was more involved than he had been in years. He contributed the gorgeous "This Whole World," an instant harmony classic featuring an incredible group vocal arrangement. Bruce contributed the dreamy "Deirdre" and the wistful "Tears in the Morning," Carl composed the gently affirming "Our Sweet Love," and Mike sang one of his best vocals on a shimmering co-composition with Brian called "All I Wanna Do." Perhaps the biggest star of *Sunflower* was Dennis, who contributed the slinky soul-pop opener "Slip On Through," the Jerry Lee Lewis-esque "Got to Know the Woman," his truly sublime ballad "Forever," and a blazing rocker that he co-wrote with Carl and Al titled "It's About Time."

The LP received rave reviews from critics, but audiences in America had long ago rejected the Beach Boys and they ignored the release. It flamed out at a dismal number 151 on the *Billboard* charts, the worst chart performance of any Beach Boys LP. Fred Vail recalled, "It was the best of times and it was the worst of times. It was great because the guys were working as a group on *Sunflower*, which was really the first group album per se. You know Denny had three singles on it, Bruce had a couple of singles on it, and

MONDAY, MAY 4 TO WEDNESDAY, MAY 13, 1970: Silver Spade Room, Chevron-Hilton Hotel, Sydney, NSW, Australia, with Lorrae Desmond (Two shows each night)
This residency at the Chevron Hilton Hotel marked the Beach Boys' debut as cabaret performers, playing two shows a night. They were originally scheduled to perform for five nights, but the residency was extended to nine days due to demand. The unusual booking initially bemused the group. The venue itself seemed representative of their decline in popularity. Unlike the giant concert halls they had played in their mid-1960s heyday, the Silver Spade only held about 250 people. The group also found themselves playing to different audiences than they were used to, mostly middle-aged couples that sat at candlelit tables surrounding the stage. Carl later recalled, "That was so bizarre, so different. We've never done another concert where the curtain opens and there are candles out there." Nevertheless, the group enjoyed the experience. Bruce told journalist Roy Carr, "The Chevron is a very exclusive place. But every night without fail, the people all joined in and danced all over the floor. It proved to be really great fun for all of us."

Murry Wilson was also at the Chevron engagement, where he gave a bombastic interview to *The Australian*. He told the paper "I have to give them a pep talk occasionally. Yesterday I let them have it for forty minutes. I don't stand any guff—none of that big star stuff washes with me. I let them know they have to work for a living just like everybody else . . . that's where my boys are so good. They're still normal . . . they haven't let all this star stuff go to their heads. Plenty of people in show business are mixed up with drugs and girls, but I've warned them well off all that. Some people might say I meddle in the boys' careers. But I only butt in when they ask me. I was their original manager, but I gave up after two years when the ulcers came on and my nerves were giving me hell."

Dennis gave an interview to Matt White of the *Sydney Daily Mirror*. Dennis told him that the group had finally begun to get out of the financial hole they were in. He blamed their troubles on "our big-headedness. We thought we were so great that nothing could go wrong. Then in 1967 we launched a tour of America with the Maharishi Mahesh Yogi, but nobody came and we lost half a million dollars on rented halls and air tickets. Even when we sold most of the things we had, we were still $200,000 in debt, and there were times when creditors threatened to close our office doors." Dennis also told White about his personal life, including his plans to marry his girlfriend Barbara Charren that August. He admitted "If I'd known I would be spending $1200 in telephone calls to her in two and a half weeks I would have brought her with me. Being apart from her is terrible and I can hardly wait to meet her in Hawaii when we leave Sydney next week." Following the Silver Spade residency, the group remained in Sydney one extra day to tape a TV appearance and then flew to Hawaii on May 15.

SUNDAY, JUNE 14, 1970: Milwaukee Pop Fest, County Stadium, Milwaukee, WI, with the Supremes, Tommy Roe, John Phillips, the Jaggerz, Ides of March, Frijid Park, Frankie Avalon, Andy Kim, Edison Lighthouse, the Ventures, the Lettermen, Jack Blanchard, and Misty Morgan (1:30 p.m. show)
The Beach Boys arrived in Milwaukee for their only concert appearance in the summer of 1970. It was sponsored by radio station WOKY. All the performers appeared for a minimum fee, so that profits could be donated to the Children's Outing Association and the Milwaukee County Mental Health Center. The all-day show, attended by 22,000 fans, featured many "bubblegum" acts, like Andy Kim and Tommy Roe. As a result, the concert attracted more twelve-year-old girls than the Beach Boys had performed for in a while. The kids reacted enthusiastically to the group, who went onstage after 5:00 p.m. Hundreds of fans left their seats and poured onto the field during "Good Vibrations," forcing the band to leave the stage for ten minutes while order was restored. During the chaos Mike Love lost a very important item, his Cossack hat. When the band returned to the stage he announced, "Would whoever took my hat please bring it back." The newspapers reported that Mike "performed the nearly impossible task of singing 'Good Vibrations' with an exposed bald spot." A photo from this concert graced the cover of the 1971 Capitol Records compilation album *Fun, Fun, Fun/Dance, Dance, Dance*.

JULY 1970: Big Gus Club, Santa Monica Blvd, Hollywood, CA
The Beach Boys made no other concert appearances in the summer; however, members of the

group turned up at a now-defunct club in West Hollywood that July. Billy Hinsche recalled that the event "was basically a showcase for the Flame. They opened their set with the Beatles' 'I've Got a Feeling' and then played their own material like 'See the Light.'"

After the Flame's performance, Carl, Brian (looking quite healthy in a paisley shirt), and Bruce took part in an impromptu jam session. Billy Hinsche, Marilyn Wilson and her sister Diane Rovell, Desi Arnaz Jr., and a young Ricci Martin also joined in. Earl Leaf captured the jam with his camera, but what songs were played remains a mystery, as no known tape or documentation survives.

SATURDAY, SEPTEMBER 12, 1970: Lagoon, Farmington, UT (9:00 p.m. show)
This was the group's final appearance at this legendary venue.

SATURDAY, OCTOBER 3, 1970: "Celebration: A Day of Music," Big Sur Folk Festival, Monterey Fairgrounds, Monterey, CA, with Kris Kristofferson, Joan Baez, Mimi Farina, John Phillips, John Hartford, Country Joe McDonald, Mark Spoelestra, Linda Ronstadt, and Merry Clayton (Two shows)
These were the first performances given by the Beach Boys as part of Jack Rieley's "comeback" strategy. They played both in the afternoon and again in the evening. Dennis was missing due to his acting commitment for the film *Two Lane Blacktop*. Mike Kowalski replaced him on drums.

Performing in Milwaukee on June 14, 1970. Jon Stebbins Collection

Al contributed. It was a great album, but it just didn't catch the attention of the media at the time because the Boys were so overshadowed by all the love generation and all the acts that were happening at the Fillmore . . . All these groups were happening that were all counterculture and the Beach Boys were very establishment. But the creativity was still there." Vail blamed much of

Sunflower's commercial failure on the label. "The Boys were not properly promoted and marketed by Warner Brothers. . . . It was just another album that they had. You know, they had James Taylor on the label and they had Van Morrison. It was a hot little label at the time. But I don't think they really ever gave Sunflower or 'Add Some Music' 110 percent and the Boys didn't have the money to buy independent promotion people. That was basically my job. I was doing promotion, running the label, working with Warner Brothers, going out on the road, going to radio conferences, going to radio stations, etc. I was on the road seven months in 1970, which is a long time. But I couldn't do it all."

It was was no longer enough for the group to record and release great music. They also needed to convince people to buy it. Jack Rieley, a charismatic radio DJ and journalist claimed that he could help them. He met the Beach Boys when Brian granted an increasingly rare radio interview to promote Sunflower. Brian, Bruce, and Mike appeared on Rieley's Radio Pacifica show on July 29, 1970. During the interview Brian commented, "The first half of our career the surf thing was projected so much. It was so clean—the sound was so clean, we looked clean, and about 1966 I think people started rejecting the image. We got a little funkier about that time, but they didn't know it . . . I'm proud of the group and the name, but I think the clean American thing has hurt us. And we're really not getting any kind of real airplay today." After the interview, Rieley seized the chance and offered his services to the

Daryl Dragon was also present on keyboards. The set list included a smattering of oldies but concentrated more on album cuts from recent records. The complete set list included "Wouldn't It Be Nice," "Sloop John B," "Country Air," "California Girls," "Aren't You Glad," "Darlin'," "Tears in the Morning," "Wake the World," "Vegetables," "God Only Knows," "Cotton Fields," "Their Hearts Were Full of Spring," "Riot in Cellblock Number Nine," and "Good Vibrations." The show was recorded and a performance of "Wouldn't It Be Nice" was included on the concert album Celebration. The tapes are owned by Lou Adler and, as of this writing, there is no agreement to allow the full set to be officially released.

The Big Sur performance was very well received. Robert Hilburn gushed in the Los Angeles Times: "It was easily the best moment of the recent Big Sur Folk Festival in Monterey. The Beach Boys, a group that seemed irrevocably drowned in its own surfing image only a few months ago, were on stage playing some of the songs (both old and new) that have made them one of the handful of best and most important groups in the history of rock music." A few days after the festival, Carl and Brian granted an interview to Bill Reed of Rock magazine. Asked about the shows, Carl said, "It went fine. I only wish we'd had a little more time. There were a lot of acts, so even with two sets we didn't get a chance to play as much as we'd have liked to. I liked playing there, though." He also commented that the band had altered their entire concept of concert performing. "We're not so much trying to redo the records now, although we still travel with that big sound system. We're loosening up in our interpretations. It seems like a much more realistic thing to be doing."

WEDNESDAY, NOVEMBER 4, TO SATURDAY, NOVEMBER 7, 1970: Whisky A Go Go, Los Angeles, CA, with the Flame (Two forty-five-minute sets each night)
The Beach Boys engagement at the Whisky drew huge audiences, with lines of fans backed up around the block hoping to get in. Despite the small size of the club, the full band, including Daryl Dragon (keyboards), Ed Carter (bass), Mike Kowalski (percussion), and a five-piece horn section were utilized. There was one more surprise for fans. When the curtains opened on the first night, Brian Wilson was also there. The booking marked the first time all six Beach Boys were onstage at the same time for a full concert. Daryl Dragon recalled, "those shows were memorable because Brian played with us. But it's always a problem when you don't work with one musician and out of the blue start to work with them, because you have to learn their style and start to meld with them. Even though Brian wrote the music and it's all his stuff, I wasn't familiar with his style (of playing) so it was kind of like flying blind, waiting to see what he was going to do. He wasn't that familiar with the band either. But the people were so blown away. It didn't make a difference anyways."

Judy Sims of Disc and Music Echo commented that "the Beach Boys didn't play so long, but they covered a wide range of old and new songs. There were fifteen people on that stage . . . plus the, much heralded, appearance of Brian Wilson, who hadn't performed in years. Brian looked slimmer and more handsome than the last time I saw him. He sat down at the electric piano near the Moog and didn't really seem to do a heck of a lot. Carl still carries the group, with Mike and Al close by. Carl's voice and guitar are the mainstays, and he handles that role with enthusiasm, something which seemed to be lacking in the others." Elliot Tiegel of Billboard praised the Beach Boys for retaining their "characteristics: softly subtle backing voices working harmonically behind soloists, hard rhythmic patterns, strong melodies . . . The boys pulled 'California Girls,' 'Cotton Fields,' 'Sloop John B,' 'Good Vibrations,' and 'I Get Around' from their flashback files. The 'nowness' of the band was strengthened with 'Cool, Cool Water' from their new LP. 'Riot in Cellblock Number Nine' was a marvelous excursion into good funky soul patterns and some gutsy singing."

Brian seemed to enjoy himself on opening night, singing and alternating between piano and Moog. He told a reporter from Melody Maker afterwards, "It was good to get up there again. When I first got on stage I felt a little self-conscious. A lot of eyes were on me. So I thought, 'OK, I'm gonna have some fun.'" Unfortunately, he did not make it through the whole engagement. He returned on November 5, but left midway through the show. Mike commented, "It was during our second set that Brian started complaining about the pain in his right ear. He had to leave the stage and was taken by car straight to a specialist. He was in considerable pain." With the exception of two brief cameos at local shows in 1971 and 1973, Brian would not play another concert until 1976.

Unfortunately, no tape of the first two nights with Brian has surfaced (though Bruce has hinted that he might have a soundboard recording). A tape of the November 6 show without Brian makes the rounds. The set list consisted of "Darlin'," "Aren't You Glad," "Wouldn't It Be Nice," "Wake the World," "Cotton Fields," "Country Air," "Sloop John B," "Riot In Cell Block Number Nine," "God Only Knows," "Good Vibrations," "It's About Time," "I Get Around," and an encore of "Johnny B. Goode." "Cool, Cool Water" and "California Girls" are not on the tape, but based on the *Billboard* review, it's clear that they were performed during at least one of the Whisky shows as well.

TUESDAY, NOVEMBER 10, 1970: Civic Auditorium, Bakersfield, CA
This was a benefit concert on behalf of Bakersfield and Foothill High Schools. The schools had won the KAFY radio school spirit contest.

THURSDAY, NOVEMBER 19, 1970: New Theatre, Oxford, England, with the Flame (Two shows)
The Beach Boys flew into London on Monday, November 16 to begin their sixth European tour. Brian told reporters he might accompany the group, but in the end the reclusive Beach Boy stayed home. Bruce told Lon Goddard of *Record Mirror*, "We never believe him when he says he'll show up until he does, because he often changes his mind. Nice things happen when he does play with us, but people don't ooh and aah and applaud loudly. It's just nice." While Brian opted out, the group brought over a large contingent of people including Steve Desper, Jack Rieley, Daryl Dragon, Ed Carter, and Mike Kowalski. They also hired five British horn players. The Flame was the opening act at most of the shows.

Upon arrival in London, the group headed to the Inn on the Park Hotel to rest before holding an afternoon press conference on the "Sloop John B," a floating discotheque on the Thames. The group's new look attracted the press' attention. Carl now had a full beard, which he'd grown prior to the Big Sur show and would from this point maintain as his normal look. Bruce briefly sported a moustache, but it was gone by the time the tour hit Birmingham. The group spent their first three days in London doing promotion, including an appearance on *Top of the Pops* on November 18 to mime their new single "Tears in the Morning."

FRIDAY, NOVEMBER 20, 1970: Hammersmith Odeon, London, England, with the Flame and Colin Scott (Two shows)
The set list for these shows consisted of: "Cotton Fields," "Darlin'," "Wouldn't It Be Nice," "Country Air," "I Can Hear Music," "Vegetables," "Sloop John B," "Riot in Cell Block Number Nine," "Tears in the Morning," "God Only Knows," "Forever," "Good Vibrations," "I Get Around," and "It's About Time." Bruce was late coming onstage and apologized to the audience. He recalled in 1989 during the "campfire" sequences of the *Endless Summer* TV show that he'd been at a bar with Keith Moon and raced back to the theatre where he quickly gargled with mouthwash before heading onstage. However, he soon realized to his horror that it was actually shampoo!

Lon Goddard of *Record Mirror* enthusiastically reported, "When Mike Love pranced on stage in a tight-fitting, pale blue farmer suit with matching cowboy hat, it was apparent this was the top billed act. Numbers like 'Darlin'' and "I Can Hear Music' confirmed this . . . Beautifully performed versions of marvelous material proved yet again the Beach Boys are one of the foremost recording and touring groups in the world." Andy Gray of *New Musical Express* gushed, "The Beach Boys have lost none of their fire when it comes to stoking up some rock 'n' roll flames . . . They really attack their numbers and inject a happy sound into it . . . I liked Bruce's 'Tears in the Morning,' the new single, and Dennis deserting his drum kit for a solo singing spot on 'Forever' . . . Great act as always."

However, Ray Coleman of *Melody Maker* was more critical, commenting, "The Beach Boys' panache was missing . . . There wasn't any spark . . . If their future shows are not going to reach the standard of previous years, we will all be better off staying at home playing Pet Sounds. There is nothing sadder than a diminishing magic." Gavin Petrie in *Disc and Music Echo* reserved his criticisms for Dennis, noting that when he sang "Forever," "his lack of frontline stardom showed in the way he constantly pulled up his trousers, scratched himself, and generally looked like a five-year-old reciting for the first time at a Sunday school concert." Dennis told Keith Altham a few days later, "I read that a few of the critics thought I was nervous when I performed out front during the

group. He laid out an action plan to change the Beach Boys' image. He argued persuasively that they needed to ditch their matching stage uniforms and devote more time to developing their live act. The ultimate goal of Rieley's plan involved changing the public's perception of the group, especially the perceptions of the politically active college audiences that had rejected them. As he told the BBC in 1974, "One of the things, and we did it in a series of advertisements, was to just say it right out . . . It's safe now to listen to the Beach Boys. And I remember it was a headline in one of the first ads we ran . . . it was sort of silly, but people were afraid to say they were into the Beach Boys."

Not everyone was a Rieley fan. His arrival led to the departure of Fred Vail. Vail recalled, "I came back from a tour one time and I walked into my office and Jack is sitting at my desk. I said, 'What are you doing here?' He said, 'Oh, they said I could use your office for a little while.' I was really ticked and then I found out he'd been talking to Bruce and talking to Mike and running a number on them . . . I finally left because of the whole thing with Jack Rieley and my lack of respect for Nick Grillo. I didn't think he was treating the boys well. I think he was looking out for Nick number one. The surviving boys know to this day that I was loyal to them. For me, it was always about my friendship and love for the boys and my respect for their music. If I had done it for the money, I would have stayed at Teenage Fair because I made a lot more money there and I would have a lot less frustration, but then I wouldn't have been around for *Sunflower*."

Program for the Beach Boys' residency in Sheffield, November to December 1970.
Ian Rusten Collection

Vail felt the group had recorded a masterpiece and that audiences would eventually come back to them. He opposed the drastic changes and embrace of the counterculture image that Rieley envisioned. Vail recalled, "We had a meeting one time at the Ivar offices. The Beach Boys were in a panic. I was telling them that it was getting hard to book them. And they were panicking. The record wasn't going up the charts like they thought it would. And I was saying the old political line that presidents always use, 'Stay the course.' I was basically saying, 'This is a blip on the radar screen. Your loyal fans are out there and they will support you.' But unfortunately they did not want to stay the course, they wanted to take a left turn." Although some members would later turn against Rieley, there was initially a united belief in

stage act with 'Forever' but that wasn't really so. I just felt humbled in front of so many people . . . I'd feel humble in front of an audience of two."

SATURDAY, NOVEMBER 21, 1970; Palace Theatre, Manchester, England, with the Flame (Two shows at 6:15 and 8:30 p.m.)

SUNDAY, NOVEMBER 22, 1970: Coventry Theatre, Coventry, England, with the Flame (Two shows at 6:00 and 8:30 p.m.)

MONDAY, NOVEMBER 23, 1970: Gaumont Theatre, Southampton, England, with the Flame (Two shows)

TUESDAY, NOVEMBER 24, 1970: Capitol Theatre, Cardiff, Wales, with the Flame (Two shows)

WEDNESDAY, NOVEMBER 25, 1970: Odeon, Birmingham, England, with the Flame (Two shows)
While in Birmingham, Dennis gave an interview to Keith Altham for *Record Mirror*. Asked about his solo single "Sound of Free/Lady," which was released in the U.K. on December 4, Dennis said, "This is really what having your own record company is all about. Brother gives us the freedom to do individual things. I cut my record exactly three days before leaving for England . . . Frankly I prefer the B-side, 'Lady,' which was a love song that I wrote for my wife, but everyone at EMI seemed convinced that 'Sounds of Free' was more commercial. I intend to follow it up by next April with a solo album called *Poops* or maybe *Hubba Bubba*." The "Sound of Free" single was credited to Dennis Wilson and Rumbo. Daryl Dragon recalled, "That was the (toy) elephant I had when I was three years old. I had three of them; one was Rumbo, one was Dumbo, and one was Chumbo. I did the string arrangements for him on that. I didn't want credit as Daryl Dragon. I wanted Dennis to get the credit for writing it. There were people around him who said they wrote songs. They'd write one line and take a credit for writing it."

THURSDAY, NOVEMBER 26, 1970: Green's Playhouse, Glasgow, Scotland, with the Flame (Two shows)

FRIDAY, NOVEMBER 27, TO SUNDAY, NOVEMBER 29, 1970: Fiesta Club, Stockton-on-Tees, England, with the Flame
The group played residencies at the Fiesta cabaret clubs in Stockton on Tees and Sheffield on this tour. Al explained to Richard Green, "We accepted an offer to do a cabaret week in Sydney and we had such a far-out time we decided to try and get one in England. We're looking forward to it, but there's only one show a night and that's going to leave a lot of idle time. One thing we've never had is time."

MONDAY, NOVEMBER 30, TO SUNDAY, DECEMBER 6, 1970: Fiesta Club, Sheffield, England, with Jimmy Marshall, Keeley Ford, and the Flame
The band played one week at the Sheffield Club. A reporter from *Beat Instrumental* noted that Al announced onstage, "Man, this is the greatest club we have ever played!" Dennis was also taken with it. He gushed that, "This place is an exception to most of the places we get asked to appear in. Even in Las Vegas we don't get dressing rooms like these." Dennis also commented on his larger vocal role. In addition to "Forever" and "Lady," he also performed "Barbara" (a great composition that never found a place on a Beach Boys album until a demo version was belatedly released on the 1998 *Endless Harmony* CD). Dennis remarked, "Put it this way, I sang more tonight than I have ever done on a Beach Boys show before. If you didn't quite understand the words on the second song, don't worry about it . . . I forgot them, and made some new ones up as I went along." However, he was quick to quash rumors that he was angling for a solo career by releasing his own single. "We do have a great deal of free time . . . so we can do our own thing."

~~~~~

1970

TUESDAY, DECEMBER 8, 1970: Gaumont Palace, Paris, France
This was a special benefit in support of the relatives of 142 dancers who died in a recent fire. It was filmed in color and the group's riveting performances of "Country Air," "Wouldn't It Be Nice," "Riot in Cellblock Number Nine," "Cotton Fields," "Their Hearts Were Full of Spring," and "It's About Time" aired on the TF2 program *Pop2* in April 1971. The Beach Boys, minus Bruce, were also interviewed prior to the show while lying on a large bed together. Amongst other subjects, they discussed their recent concert at Big Sur and their outdated image as a surfing group.

WEDNESDAY, DECEMBER 9, 1970: Palais D'Hiver, Lyons, France, with the Flame

FRIDAY, DECEMBER 11, 1970: Finsbury Park Astoria, London, England, with the Flame (Two shows)
Mike Ledgerwood of *Disc and Music Echo* praised the Beach Boys performance at the Astoria but sensed dissension, noting that Mike, Dennis, and Bruce seemed to be "competing against each other for the solo spotlight . . . Dennis for instance did solo numbers in the second show yet appeared sadly devoid of either enthusiasm or presence out front. But he struggled defiantly through three songs when one would have been enough. Later seemingly not to be outdone, bouncy Bruce interrupted the group during 'Tears in the Morning' to take his solo entirely alone, except for his own piano accompaniment. I must admit it went down a storm . . . but if you'd seen the expressions and heard the mutterings of the others of the group as they were ordered off, it looked decidedly as though Bruce could find himself in the 'doghouse.'"

Neil Roberts of *Melody Maker* declared the group would have been better if "they had scrapped some of the weaker material, like the cod rock 'n' roll number, and one or two other less typical songs, and performed more of the standards that have made them." Roberts' review was illustrative of a problem that would confront the group throughout the next few years. At the same time they were trying to get away from their archaic surfer image, many fans just wanted oldies. Bruce commented to Georgina Mells, "What brings me down more than anything is when people review our shows and only want to know about the old songs, the old surfing type things we used to do. Now we play half old stuff and half the kind of music that's on our new LP *Sunflower*, and even the old things are new-old, nothing before '66."

SATURDAY, DECEMBER 12, 1970: Winter Gardens, Bournemouth, England, with the Flame (Two shows)
Beach Boys fanatic Keith Moon joined the group onstage for a closing jam on this night.

SUNDAY, DECEMBER 13, 1970: Empire, Liverpool, England, with the Flame (Two shows)
This was the last scheduled date of the UK tour. Bruce told Georgina Mells the tour was "great, really lovely . . . I think we all feel really happy when we're in England. The audiences are very good here and it seems like a good place to be. I love it and it's more than possible that next year we may settle here, find a place in London, or the country nearby and build a studio for recording using Britain as a base for Europe."

Following these shows, the group concentrated on promotion. They taped an appearance for Radio Luxembourg on December 14 and Bruce Johnston was in Amsterdam on December 15 to perform a solo version of "Tears in the Morning" on the Dutch TV show Top Pop. He sang a live vocal over the pre-recorded track. The group also appeared on Belgian TV on the December 16 before heading back to the U.K. for a special charity show.

THURSDAY, DECEMBER 17, 1970: "Save Rave," Christmas Concert, Royal Albert Hall, London, England, with the Flame, Magna Carta, and the Flirtations (7:30 p.m. show)
This was a benefit concert on behalf of the Invalid Children's Aid Association. When asked why they performed so many charity events, Al replied, "Man, we made it, we got money. We're all healthy (well sort of), so it just seems right that we should do something for others, it makes me feel good. The bad thing is that once you say you like charities, hundreds of letters come pouring in, asking us to play for free, or to give bread." For the "Save-Rave" event, Bruce convinced

his vision to help the Beach Boys regain the limelight.

The seventh annual Big Sur Festival gave the group their first chance to connect with audiences that had rejected them. The group was somewhat apprehensive about playing to the hippies at Monterey. Carl Wilson commented to Robert Hilburn, "I didn't know if the audience would give us a chance. I thought they would, but you can never be sure." Another reason for their hesitation was the fact that the concert took place while Dennis was unavailable. He'd been cast in the feature film *Two Lane Blacktop* for Universal Pictures and had filming commitments that clashed with the festival date. The group also failed to convince Brian to join them, giving them even more trepidation. Despite their fears, the Beach Boys turned up at Big Sur and scored a knockout. *Los Angeles Times* critic Robert Hilburn called the appearance "a triumph," while *Rolling Stone* publisher Jann Wenner, who had dismissed the group in an influential editorial in 1967, raved "the Beach Boys, quite objectively, were excellent . . . They were the best act there that day. Monterey Pop really did happen again because they were the one act, the one part of Monterey Pop that had yet to occur."

The group continued their comeback by returning to the Sunset Strip for the first time since 1962 to play a four-night stand at the popular Whisky a Go Go. Mike Love saw the engagement as part of a new beginning for the group. He told Robert Hilburn, "I look at us as a whole new group starting up again. We do things now that we never did before. Much of the audience will be hearing some of the things for the first time. We're just as much a part of the times now as we were in 1963. There's more creativity, more maturity." With Dennis present, and Brian joining the group for the first two shows, the band received rave reviews. The Whisky shows proved to influential Los Angelenos, who had written them off as squares, that the Beach Boys were a relevant musical force deserving of reappraisal.

Another European tour was the next hurdle to clear. Carl told Eliot Tiegel of *Record Mirror*, "We'll be playing in places which have beautiful facilities. We're playing some cities in which we haven't appeared before. We're all really looking forward to the trip because we'll be playing for friends and be able to do some traveling and get around." The tour began on November 16 and, although most critics raved about the group, the Beach Boys were not altogether happy. The tour was a financial success, but that wasn't enough. Jack Rieley later told the BBC that the group "were terribly, terribly dissatisfied with it . . . That tour was for us, from an artistic standpoint, a disastrous tour and I think it was with that, that I was able to sell the group completely on the idea of being themselves." By this he meant that members of the group felt straitjacketed onstage by the need to perform only the hits written by Brian. The music they had been writing and recording without him seldom found a place in the show. The forty-five-minute sets the Beach Boys performed at most U.K. shows didn't give them the chance to stretch out and show their full spectrum. Within months this would all change.

promoter Arthur Howes to supply a small string section for "God Only Knows." Bruce was excited about the show, which was attended by the Queen's sister. He later told a reporter that "the best part of the whole trip was when we did the Royal Albert Hall concert and I got introduced to Princess Margaret. It's the first time I've ever met a real Princess and she was a really nice lady and very polite to me."

FRIDAY, DECEMBER 18, 1970: Concertgebouw, Amsterdam, Netherlands, with the Flame (12:30 a.m. show)
With the U.K. tour over the group prepared to leave England to play the remaining continental dates. They had shows scheduled in the Netherlands and Belgium and had made tentative plans to play in Yugoslavia (December 23 and 24), Germany (Christmas Day), Scandinavia (December 26-27 and 29-31) Rome (December 28) and Montreux, France (January 2). None of these concerts took place. One reason for the cancelations was that Carl suffered an attack of appendicitis and was playing the tour in tremendous pain. Bruce gave an interview on Friday morning to Georgina Mells for *Fabulous 208* and told her that Carl's health was "not too bad really, although he has been in pain for quite awhile, but I know how it is with an appendix because I had pains from mine for a long time before I finally had it out. I think when you're under stress it makes it worse. Anyway, unless we miss our date in Amsterdam tonight because of the fog and have to play it later, we should be going home in a few days and he can rest and get well at home in the States."

The Amsterdam show performed that night has since taken on legendary status. It didn't start until 4:00 a.m. because the Beach Boys were delayed in London by fog, but the promoter refused to cancel. As Jack Rieley later explained to Rob Bartlett of *Beat Instrumental*, "By six o'clock that evening we had virtually given up, but the promoter had hired a jet from Gatwick for us, so we drove down there, boarded the plane, and made Brussels by 10 p.m. There were twelve limousines waiting for us when we arrived and after the drive to Amsterdam the Beach Boys finally went on stage at 5:30 in the morning . . . to a completely packed house, not an empty seat in the place. It was incredible and we decided there and then that there was something 'strange' about the place!"

SATURDAY, DECEMBER 19, 1970: De Doelen, Rotterdam, Netherlands, with the Flame (12:15 p.m. show)
Radio Caroline taped this show and a portion of it was aired. At the beginning of the broadcast, Bruce announced "Very nice to be here. Tonight we're not late . . . last night . . . eh . . . we brought some English fog with us and that made us very late, but anyway here we are," and the band launched into show opener "Cotton Fields." The group then performed "Country Air," "Aren't You Glad," "Vegetables," and "Tears in the Morning" before the broadcast ended.

SUNDAY, DECEMBER 20, 1970: Congresgebouw, The Hague, Netherlands, with the Flame (8:30 p.m. show)
The Beach Boys sold out the Congresgebouw.

MONDAY, DECEMBER 21, 1970: Palais Des Beaux Arts, Brussels, Belgium, with the Flame (8:30 p.m. show)
This was the last show of the tour. Mike remained in Europe until January 25, 1971, spending his time at the meditation retreat in Brighton. Bruce spent most of January in New Zealand.

CONCERTS NOT PLAYED
Although author Keith Badman posited in his book that the group postponed a number of shows on the late February Pacific Northwest tour and played them in March, advertisements, reviews and photographs of the Gonzaga and Seattle shows prove he was incorrect.

A number of European dates that the Beach Boys were tentatively scheduled to play in late December 1970 and early January 1971 did not take place.

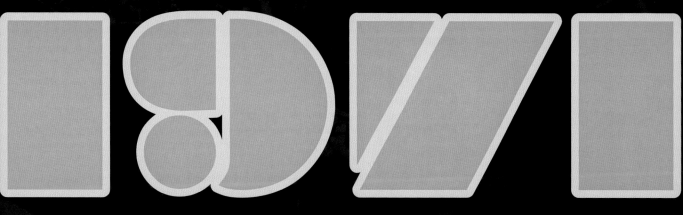

AS 1971 BEGAN, the Beach Boys faced numerous challenges. Their record sales had plummeted to an all-time low. They still attracted large audiences in the heartland, but college-aged music fans on both coasts had forgotten them. In many circles they were regarded as a passé oldies act. Bands like the Grateful Dead; Crosby, Stills, Nash and Young; the Rolling Stones; and Led Zeppelin were far more popular and influential with young people. The Beach Boys recognized that they would have to tour more heavily than they had in recent years if they wanted to get the word out that their band was no longer about little deuce coupes and striped shirts. Nineteen seventy-one would see them crisscross the country while playing dozens of concerts at major colleges and universities.

Jack Rieley convinced the group that they needed to follow up the good reviews they received at the Big Sur Folk Festival and the Whisky A Go Go by completely revamping their stage act. As Bruce explained at the time, "we're building our stage show from about forty-five minutes to ninety and leaving a lot more room for solo spots." The Beach Boys abandoned the "greatest hits" sets for good and instead focused on presenting more recent material and deeper album cuts. The hits were reserved for the end of the show, which was now divided into two separate segments. The group would play one set, take an intermission, and return for a second set. Daryl Dragon

CONCERTS PLAYED IN
1971

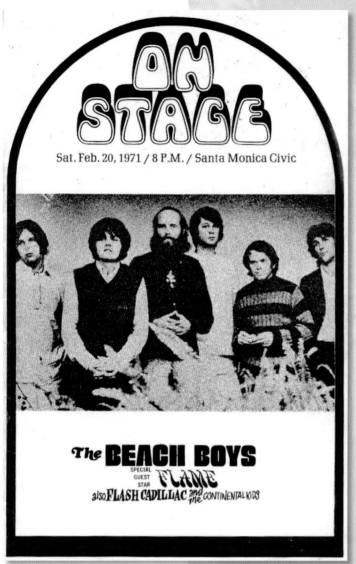

Sat. Feb. 20, 1971 / 8 P.M. / Santa Monica Civic

The **BEACH BOYS**
SPECIAL GUEST STAR *FLAME*
also **FLASH CADILLAC** and the CONTINENTAL KIDS

Collection of Chris Woods

FEBRUARY 20, 1971: Civic Auditorium, Santa Monica, CA, with the Flame and Flash Cadillac (8:00 p.m. show)
For the Beach Boys' first concert of 1971, Daryl Dragon, Ed Carter, two percussionists, and a five-piece horn section accompanied them. They played for ninety minutes, giving the group more opportunity to showcase their newer music, while also satisfying the crowd's insatiable demand for oldies. The expanded set list included "Heroes and Villains," "Help Me Rhonda," "Country Air," "Wouldn't It Be Nice," "Cool, Cool Water," "God Only Knows," "Vegetables," "Good Vibrations," "Surfer Girl," "I Get Around," "Riot in Cell Block Number Nine," Merle Haggard's "Okie from Muskogee," "Caroline No," "Tears in the Morning," "Their Hearts Were Full of Spring," two songs by Dennis ("Forever" and "Barbara"), and a cover of Elton John's "Your Song" (sung by Bruce).

According to Todd Everett of the *Los Angeles Free Press*, "To nobody's great surprise (although slightly offensive to the group's artistic instincts) most of the applause came for the old numbers . . . The group's ensemble vocalizing was generally more interesting than their solos. In this respect, Brian's presence was sorely missed; his high, pure voice is one of Southern California's natural wonders . . . Bruce Johnston's two numbers, the original 'Tears in the Morning' and Elton John's 'Your Song,' were quite nicely done. Dennis Wilson, with two numbers of his own, also did well."

Robert Hilburn of the *Los Angeles Times* remarked, "The focus in the Beach Boys' music is always crisp. The songs move forward with economy and direction. There is no flashy, self defeating, self indulgence in the music." Hilburn, however, was aware that the group was trying to change their image and commented, "They should stick to business between songs rather than slow down the pacing by unnecessary chatter. And there's no reason they should waste their time allowing Bruce Johnston to sing Elton John's 'Your Song.' The group has too much at stake now not to make every moment on stage count." The reviewers also noted that Brian attended the show and stood backstage watching the performance. Mike repeatedly tried to cajole him onto the stage, even getting the audience to chant his name, but Brian stayed put.

WEDNESDAY, FEBRUARY 24, 1971: Carnegie Hall, New York, NY (8:00 p.m. show)
The Beach Boys continued their "comeback" by performing several highly publicized east coast shows. Ed Carter (bass), Daryl Dragon (piano), and Dennis Dragon (extra percussion) accompanied them, along with a five-piece horn section. The set list for the Carnegie Hall concert consisted of "Heroes and Villains," "Help Me Rhonda" (with Carl on lead), "Aren't You Glad," "Cotton Fields," "Okie from Muskogee," "Country Air," "Wouldn't It Be Nice," "Vegetables," "Cool Cool Water," "Lady" (sung by Dennis), "Forever" (sung by Dennis), "Darlin'," "Caroline No," "Riot in Cell Block Number Nine," "Tears in the Morning" (sung by Bruce), "Your Song" (sung by Bruce), "You Still Believe in Me," "Their Hearts Were Full of Spring," "Sloop John B," "In My Room," "God Only Knows," "Good Vibrations," "California Girls," "Surfer Girl," "It's About Time," "I Get Around," and "Johnny B. Goode."

Reporters from numerous influential newspapers and magazines covered the Carnegie Hall show. Fred Kirby of *Billboard* reported, "The Beach Boys combined old and new material for a complete show, far more developed than in their New York appearances of several years ago. Mike

recalled, "They started doing that because they got cold. Cool bands played long shows. Jack was telling them, 'The Stones play two hours so you need to also.'"

For their first concert of 1971, they returned to the Santa Monica Civic Auditorium, a venue they had last appeared at in 1964. The concert attracted favorable critical notice, but in essence it was little more than a rehearsal for bigger things ahead. The real Beach Boys

Love, Bruce Johnston, Carl Wilson, and Alan Jardine singly and in perfect harmony were in good vocal form, while Dennis Wilson, a steady drummer, came out front for a couple of good vocal leads, including 'Forever.' The enthusiastic audience drew out several encores, including such big oldies as 'California Girls,' 'Surfer Girl,' and 'I Get Around.'" *Variety* stated, "Though Brian Wilson's presence was missed, the Beach Boys went over big with a mixed repertoire of songs that chronicled their long existence in the rock field. Dividing the show into two segments, the group appeared somewhat tight at first, but soon got it together for a show that highlighted their precise four-part vocal harmonies. 'California Girls' and 'Good Vibrations' stood out with the former showing that the Beach Boys have always been into melodic rock." *Rock* magazine declared "It makes no sense at all to tell you what went on, song by song, nor to describe to you how the hall was one sea of dipping bodies, nor try to recreate for you the glow on the faces onstage and in the audience . . . Well maybe I should try for some . . . Dennis Wilson announcing the birth of his son a few days before and dedicating a new song to his wife . . . the look of total astonishment on Carl's face as his strap broke and his guitar slid magically on his knees, where he finally reacted and grabbed it, to cheers of thousands. Oh hell, it's no use. You're never going to feel it, the joy, the warmth, the recreation of what six people shared for so long with people."

Afterwards, the band returned to the Chelsea Hotel, where a writer from *Crawdaddy* magazine interviewed them. Carl commented, "I enjoyed the concert very much tonight, especially the second half. The first half was all right. I was having fun. I always dig it but the second half was really nice." Bruce remarked, "Carnegie Hall knocked us out. Performing is such a beautiful thing. It's just as beautiful as making a record. You may be recreating songs you've recorded but it goes way past that. I would rather make records recording live than going into a studio because I think I'm a better performer creatively when I'm juiced up and really performing." While in New York they were also interviewed in their hotel by blues singer Barry Goldberg. A film of this interview is in the possession of Brother Records. A clip from this film showing the Beach Boys performing an impromptu version of "Their Hearts Were Full of Spring" while seated in a bathtub was used in the 2012 DVD *The Beach Boys: Doin' It Again.*

THURSDAY, FEBRUARY 25, 1971: Agora Auditorium, Columbus, OH
This was the first of numerous concerts that the group played for promoter Jim Koplik's Peace Island East. He recalled, "I was a big Beach Boys fan and they were not that popular at the time. So I just booked the show at the Agora, which was directly across the street from OSU (Ohio State University). A lot of northeast kids go to Ohio State and the Beach Boys were always popular in the northeast. I recall that it was a beautiful day in late February. It was like seventy degrees outside and I filled the place up. And (as a result) I got very friendly with the group, because they were shocked at how well they did."

SUNDAY, FEBRUARY 28, 1971: Symphony Hall, Boston, MA, with Seals and Croft (7:00 p.m. show)
The Beach Boys failed to impress Charles Martin of the *Boston Globe*. While he granted "the strong harmony, once it got off the ground, was still there," he complained that "the quintet . . . competed against a much too loud orchestral backup, a weak PA system, and a sell-out crowd which just wanted the oldies." Charles Giuliano of the *Boston Herald* was more enthusiastic. He declared "the Beach Boys, minus leader Brian Wilson, produced a masterful concert of more than two hours . . . and a smashing success on every level . . . For me the best moment was when Bruce Johnston offered a solo of 'Tears in the Morning,' from *Sunflower* . . . He followed it with a fine rendering of Elton John's 'My Song.' I could have enjoyed an entire evening of Bruce Johnston and his piano." While Giuliano

comeback began with their now-legendary Carnegie Hall concert on February 24. It was a return to New York City, where the Beach Boys were now a mostly forgotten relic. The show was set up by two enterprising young men named Michael Klenfner and Chip Rachlin.

Courtesy of Chip Rachlin

Ian Rusten Collection

loved the show, he noted that the crowd was resistant to the group's inclination to play newer material. Whenever a song ended, there were screams from all over the hall for "Good Vibrations" and "I Get Around." The Beach Boys were determined not to give in to nostalgia and refused to play these songs until the end of the show. Bruce yelled to the crowd at one point "This isn't a rock 'n' roll revival, so cool it." Mike fended off the requests with plenty of sarcasm as well. Carl told reporter Lisa Robinson, "If the people in the audience yell for a particular song, we'll do it. But we don't do any of the really early stuff unless somebody wants us to do it."

Former Beach Boy David Marks was attending music school in Boston at this time and recalled that he "hadn't seen those guys in a year or two and I was curious to see what they were like. So I bought a ticket to the show and when I went to hear them it made me feel kind of sad. Brian wasn't there, and they had all these horns and stuff. I don't know what I was expecting . . . it just seemed so different, so I split. But before I made it through the lobby I heard someone yell, 'Hey Dave!' . . . and I turned around and it was Dennis. With the show still in progress, somehow he found me. I asked him, 'What are you doing offstage while the band is still playing?' and he told me he was 'looking for chicks.'" Dennis convinced Dave to come say hello to the others, and he ended up joining them onstage, playing guitar on "Surfer Girl" during the encore. On March 1, when the Beach Boys returned to New York to tape a TV appearance on *The David Frost Show*, David was invited to attend, though he did not appear on camera. The group performed "Wouldn't It Be Nice" and "Cool, Cool Water."

FRIDAY, MARCH 12, 1971: Valley Music Theatre, Los Angeles, CA, with Pacific Gas and Electric and Red Wilder Blue (8:30 p.m. show)
The commercial failure of *Sunflower* and lack of radio airplay for their newer music caused the Beach Boys to reappraise the importance of live concerts. Al told *Creem*, "Our concerts seem to be doing our promotion for us. We get good reviews. Maybe that more natural kind of public relations is the way it's going to happen. We're not going to break up, so it's eventually going to happen again."

FRIDAY, APRIL 2, 1971: Porterville College, Porterville, CA, with the Flame

MONDAY, APRIL 12, AND TUESDAY, APRIL 13, 1971: Whisky a Go Go, Los Angeles, CA, with If and Uriah Heap
The Beach Boys returned for two more nights at the Whisky a Go Go. Although Brian did not join them, David Marks sat in with the group. He recalled, "When I was hanging around with the guys in Boston, Mike Love had convinced me to come back to California and rejoin the band. So I thought about it . . . and when I finally got there I was hanging out at Brian's place and Carl was there. Carl wanted me to play the bass and I said 'No, I'm not going to join the band and be the bass player.' But I sat in with them at the Whisky."

THURSDAY, APRIL 22, 1971: John F. Kennedy Stadium, Manchester, NH
This was the first date of the Beach Boys "comeback" tour of the Northeast. In addition to their horn section (which included trumpeter Terry Jones and saxophonist Sal Marquez), other musicians on this tour included Jeff Kaplan (bass), Daryl Dragon (piano), and his brother Dennis Dragon (extra percussion). A tape of this Manchester show exists. The set list consisted of "Heroes and Villains," "Do It Again," "Help Me Rhonda," "Aren't You Glad," "Cotton Fields," "Okie from Muskogee," "Vegetables," "Cool Cool Water," "Lady," "Forever," "Riot in Cell Block Number Nine," "Caroline

Klenfner was employed as a security guard at the Fillmore East, while Rachlin worked as a booking agent with Bill Graham's Millard Agency, which operated out of offices above the Fillmore on Second Avenue. The two men shared a common passion for the Beach Boys and approached Graham about booking them. Graham, still smarting from his very negative 1968 experience with the group, told Klenfner and Rachlin that there was no way he'd ever let the Beach Boys play at the Fillmore again. However, he gave them permission to try to find

No," "Tears in the Morning," "Your Song," "You Still Believe In Me," "Wouldn't It Be Nice," "God Only Knows," "Their Hearts Were Full of Spring," "Good Vibrations," "California Girls," "Surfer Girl," "I Get Around," "Sloop John B," "Barbara Ann," and "It's About Time."

Many concerts on this tour suffered from low attendance. At this particular show, when Chip Rachlin and Michael Klenfner went backstage to reach a financial settlement with the promoter, they were told that there were no remaining unsold tickets. Based on this information, Rachlin requested a check for $2,700 and the promoter went to get it. While he was gone, however, Rachlin noticed that Klenfner, who had the build of a football linebacker, was obstructing the view of a metal filing cabinet and that there was a box on top of it that looked like the type used to store tickets. "I said to Michael, 'Get the box . . . Get the fucking box!' We were the only two in the room and he shoved it in his bag. There were a thousand (unsold) tickets in it that they had overlooked." Rachlin had no hesitation about keeping his mouth shut. "There was no way on the first date that I was going to tell the Beach Boys that [even though] from the stage it looked like a full house, that they were a thousand tickets short of a sellout."

FRIDAY, APRIL 23, 1971: David Gym, Bucknell University, Lewisburg, PA (8:30 p.m. show)
According to Chip Rachlin, of 3000 available tickets for this concert only 1100 were sold. Despite the low turnout, the group gave it their all. But Dean Landew of *The Bucknellian* wasn't buying the Beach Boys' attempt to change their image. His review was typical of criticism the group encountered over the next three years. Landew commented, "So their hair got longer and they swapped their Good Humor suits for other clothes . . . and they do dope and meditation and they probably have got groupies too, but didn't you hear the same old band of last decade? . . . Some of their old stuff is done over so it's slower and sort of funkier, like 'Help Me Rhonda,' but wasn't it great to hear 'I Get Around' again like it really used to be? . . . They don't have to change. They shouldn't."

SATURDAY, APRIL 24, 1971: Wallace Wade Stadium, Duke University, Durham, NC, with the New Riders of the Purple Sage, the Grateful Dead, the Paul Butterfield Blues Band, and Mountain (3:00 p.m. show)
This outdoor concert began at 3 p.m. and lasted until 1 in the morning. Steve Emerson of *The Chronicle* was impressed by the Grateful Dead and Mountain and argued, "The Beach Boys were clearly outclassed in such company . . . After an hour or so of apologizing for the heavy changes the band had gone through, meaningless guru statements by Mike Love, a lot of wasted time, and some mediocre to poor recent songs backed up by a useless horn section, they realized that if anything was to be accomplished, they would have to play their old songs and forget about the irrelevance Love wanted to attribute to them. 'Surfer Girl,' 'Good Vibrations,' 'Sloop John B,' and 'I Get Around' brought the house down and capitalized on a common level of experience felt by all in the stadium. Jerry Garcia was clapping along, rocking and yelling 'Little Deuce Coupe' backstage."

TUESDAY, APRIL 27, 1971: Fillmore East, New York, NY, with the Grateful Dead and the New Riders of the Purple Sage (8:00 p.m. show)
As part of their effort to gain counterculture credentials, the group made a legendary guest appearance at a Grateful Dead concert. They played "Searchin'" and "Riot in Cell Block Number Nine" in tandem with the Dead, and then on their own they performed versions of "I Get Around" and "Good Vibrations" before the Dead rejoined them for "Okie from Muskogee" and "Johnny B. Goode." The Fillmore audience, if at first confused, was very appreciative of the group's performance. This appearance was an important step towards gaining acceptance from a demographic that had rejected the Beach Boys years earlier.

WEDNESDAY, APRIL 28, 1971: Lowell Auditorium, Lowell, MA, with Mist (8:00 p.m. show)
The group performed for 2,500 fans at this concert sponsored by Merrimack College. They were paid $2,000 and promised ninety percent of the gate.

THURSDAY, APRIL 29, 1971: Loew's State Theatre, Providence, RI, with Swallow (8:00 p.m. show)

another venue if they wished. Carnegie Hall was secured for two concerts and Rachlin then called American Productions in Los Angeles to arrange a contract with the Beach Boys. The group agreed to play the shows for a flat fee of $9,000, which included travel expenses. Unfortunately, tickets for the second show failed to sell and only one performance took place.

The group flew into New York on February 23, 1971,

> "Everything you've read was true. They were that fucking good! The vocals were perfect . . . it was amazing."

and taped a live interview for influential radio station WNEW. DJ Pete Fornatale was a huge Beach Boys fan and heavily promoted the show. He also emceed the concert. Chip Rachlin informed him that the group did not want to be referred to as an oldies act and that he shouldn't mention surfing or their old image. However, Fornatale had no intention of abiding by these dictates. Instead, he walked onstage on February

THE BEACH BOYS IN CONCERT

24 carrying a surfboard and announced, "Growing up wouldn't have been half as much fun without these guys. Ladies and gentlemen, the Beach Boys!" Rachlin, who refers to the show as "the moment that changed my life," recalled, "The lights came down and the opening song was 'Heroes and Villains' . . . and they brought the horn section out and it sounded so much like the album . . . Everything you've read was true. They were that fucking good! The vocals were perfect . . . it was amazing. I don't know what we expected. I'd been so busy working on the show and trying to con our way and get stories in the newspapers. I hadn't thought about what it would sound like and why we were doing a show in the first place."

The Carnegie Hall show turned out to be a triumphant reminder to the music world that the Beach Boys were still here. They followed it up with concerts in Columbus and Boston before returning to California for recording sessions. Before they headed west they made one important decision: they signed with the Millard Agency. Chip Rachlin had been so impressed by their performance at Carnegie Hall that he decided he would love to become the Beach Boys' booking agent. He flew out to Boston for the group's February 28 show and met with them backstage. The Beach Boys allowed Rachlin "on their bus, which was just a bus, no luxury coach, it was like a Trailways or Greyhound." Over drinks, he learned more about the intra-group dynamics, of which he was only dimly aware beforehand.

FRIDAY, APRIL 30, 1971: Painter's Mill Music Fair, Baltimore, MD (8:00 p.m. show)
Promoter Lawrence Steinbach slashed ticket prices in half and got the Beach Boys to take a fifty percent cut in their fee, but a disappointing turnout of less than 1,000 people attended. The concert began with "Heroes and Villains," and included performances of "Good Vibrations," "Cotton Fields," "Vegetables," "Riot in Cellblock Number Nine," "Wouldn't It Be Nice," "Okie from Muskogee," "I Get Around," and "Little Deuce Coupe." *Washington Post* reporter Tom Zito declared the concert "an almost perfect evening of harmony and rhythm."

SATURDAY, MAY 1, 1971: May Day Peace Demonstration, Potomac Park, Washington, DC, with the Tayles, Charlie Mingus, Linda Ronstadt, and Phil Ochs
Thousands of young people descended on Washington for a week of anti-war protests and planned to spend the weekend camping out in Potomac Park. Jack Rieley convinced the group to perform a free Saturday concert at this politically charged event. More artists were scheduled to play the following day, but the D.C. police kicked the demonstrators out of the park on Sunday morning. This event was filmed and a portion of it can be seen in the 1985 *American Band* documentary.

SUNDAY, MAY 2, 1971: Trinity College, Hartford, CT (Canceled), and Paris Cinema, Worcester, MA (Three shows at 4:00, 7:00, and 9:30 p.m.)
The Beach Boys were initially booked to appear at Trinity College on this date but high overhead forced the cancelation of the show.

TUESDAY, MAY 4, 1971: the Dome, C.W. Post College, Brookville, NY (8:00 p.m. show)
Eric Lesselbaum of the *C.W. Post Pioneer* raved that after hearing the Beach Boys, "it is obvious that they are perhaps the tightest and most masterful harmonizers in rock 'n' roll . . . The show was separated into two sets. The first included most of their rock stuff with an outstanding version of Merle Haggard's 'Okie from Muskogee.' The other feature of the first set was a 1953 tune [Riot in Cell-Block Number Nine], originally done by the Rockets, that let the brass section loose and exhibited the old-style Beach Boy vocals. The second set opened with an acoustic tune sung by Carl Wilson that proved his fine solo ability as well as making it obvious that big brother Brian Wilson is a great songwriter. Bruce Johnston followed with two solos at the piano, the second of which was the best version of Elton John's 'Your Song' that I've ever heard. Following this came the rest of the band and all the oldies but goodies, from 'Help Me Rhonda' to 'Good Vibrations.'"

THURSDAY, MAY 6, 1971: State University of New York, New Paltz, NY, with Happy and Artie Traum (7:30 p.m. show)

FRIDAY, MAY 7, 1971: Philadelphia Spectrum, Philadelphia, PA, with Taj Mahal and Boz Scaggs (8:00 p.m. show)
During the day the group taped an appearance on *The David Frost Show* that was particularly enjoyable for fans of Dennis Wilson. They performed a full band version of Dennis' "Forever," and acoustic versions of the *Smile* relic "Vegetables" and Dennis' solo single "Lady." Continuing to keep the focus on Dennis, Frost also interviewed him about his upcoming film release *Two Lane Blacktop*. Unfortunately, the footage is lost, though an audiotape survives.

The turnout for the concert that night was small, but those that attended were enthusiastic. Mark Russell of the *Lehigh University Brown and White* gushed that the Beach Boys "were able to play any song they ever recorded perfectly—that includes 'Sloop John B,' 'Good Vibrations,' 'Help Me Rhonda' . . . I could have listened to them for another two hours."

SATURDAY, MAY 8, 1971: University of Bridgeport, Bridgeport, CT

SUNDAY, MAY 9, 1971: State University of New York, Plattsburgh, NY (8:00 p.m.)
John Gregory of the *Cardinal Points* reported, "Musically, the Beach Boys are ingeniously, primitively sophisticated, backed by a strong five-man horn section and Dennis' pounding drums . . . The Beach Boys are a sophisticated good vibrations group, with an amazing endurance record. As their advertising says, 'the Beach Boys are better than ever.'"

TUESDAY, MAY 11, 1971: Manley Field House, Syracuse University, Syracuse, NY, with Peter Yarrow (8:30 p.m. show)
This show was a benefit concert to aid the Berrigan Brothers Defense Fund. Anti-war activist Phillip

Performing at Bucknell University on April 23, 1971.
Reproduced from the Special Collections/University Archives photograph collection, Bertrand Library, Bucknell University

Performing on *The David Frost Show* in New York, May 1971. Jon Stebbins Collection

Berrigan and his brother, Catholic priest Daniel Berrigan, were Syracuse University alumni who were charged by the government, along with six other individuals, with plotting to kidnap presidential aide Henry Kissinger and blow up government heating tunnels in Washington, DC. The Beach Boys' appearance at this event showed their support for the anti-war movement, though whether they truly had strong convictions or were simply trying to gain counterculture credentials is debatable.

Dennis had to return to California to record voiceovers for *Two Lane Blacktop*, which was due to be released in July. Dennis Dragon filled in on drums. A tape of this show makes the rounds. The set list consisted of "Heroes and Villains," "Do It Again," "Darlin'," "Aren't You Glad," "Cotton

Fields," "Vegetables," "Okie from Muskogee," "Cool, Cool Water," "Help Me Rhonda," "Student Demonstration Time," "Caroline, No," "You Still Believe In Me," "Sloop John B," "Your Song," "Wouldn't It Be Nice," "God Only Knows," "Good Vibrations," "California Girls," "Surfer Girl," "I Get Around," and "It's About Time." The group was in great form, though the audience occasionally showed impatience when newer material was played and Mike had to lecture them a few times.

THURSDAY, JUNE 24, 1971: Celebration of Life Festival, Pointe Coupee, LA, with Pink Floyd, Miles Davis, B.B. King, the Amboy Dukes, Boz Scaggs, Canned Heat, Chuck Berry, Country Joe McDonald, the Flying Burrito Brothers, Ike and Tina Turner, It's a Beautiful Day, John Lee Hooker, Melanie, Ravi Shankar, Richie Havens, Sly and the Family Stone, Taj Mahal, the Chambers Brothers, Ballinjack, Kate Taylor, Eric Burdon and War, Buddy Miles, Delaney and Bonnie, and the Dixieland Jazz Band

The Beach Boys played on the fourth day of a weeklong rock festival (June 21–28). They had been busy working on *Surf's Up* and also had to deal with the unexpected injury of Dennis. On June 11, in a drunken accident at home, he put his right hand through a pane of glass, severing crucial nerves in his hand and wrist. Doctors told Dennis that he'd probably be unable able to play the drums again. Mike Kowalski took over drums, with Dennis Dragon adding extra percussion.

Other musicians that played on this tour included Daryl Dragon (piano), Luther Coffee (bass), Sal Marquez and Mike Price (trumpets), Joel Peskin and Roger Neumann (Sax), Glen Ferris (trombone), and Carli Munoz (extra percussion). Munoz was an accomplished keyboardist and would soon become a longterm member of the backing band following Daryl Dragon's departure in late 1972.

SATURDAY, JUNE 26, 1971: Beggars Banquet Festival, Borough of York Stadium, Toronto, ON, Canada, with Blood Rock, Steppenwolf, Bread, Chilliwack, Alice Cooper, and Lighthouse (12:00 p.m. show)

According to the *Toronto Globe*, this all-day concert event was marred by a "thoroughly inept electronics system, which prompted John Kay, leader of Steppenwolf, to suggest a 'public lynching of the owner of the PA system after the show.'"

SUNDAY, JUNE 27, 1971: Fillmore East, New York, NY, with Country Joe McDonald, Albert King, the J. Geils Band, the Allman Brothers, Edgar Winter's White Trash, and Mountain (9:00 p.m. to 4:15 a.m.)

Bill Graham decided to close his legendary venue and this was the final concert held there. Fans who bought tickets were only expecting Albert King, the J. Geils Band and the Allman Brothers, but Graham surprised them by turning the night into a giant seven-hour celebration of rock with numerous surprise guests, including the Beach Boys.

They group played one forty-five-minute set, in between performances by Mountain and Country Joe McDonald. It consisted of "Heroes and Villains," "Do It Again," "Cotton Fields," "Help Me Rhonda," "Wouldn't It Be Nice," "Your Song," "Student Demonstration Time," "Good Vibrations," "California Girls," "I Get Around," and "It's About Time." *Billboard* called it "a remarkable set" which delighted the "nostalgic audience."

WEDNESDAY, JUNE 30, 1971: Theatre Maisonneuve, Place Des Arts, Montreal, QB, Canada (Two shows at 7:00 and 10:00 p.m.)

The Beach Boys arrived in Montreal on Monday and spent two days relaxing. Dennis rejoined them, with his arm in a cast. He would not play the drums regularly again until late 1974 and instead wandered the stage, singing harmonies and occasionally playing piano. Boredom set in fairly quickly, as Dennis needed the drums as an outlet for his manic energy and he seemed lost without them. His close friend Ed Roach confided, "That was when he started to have problems because he wanted to be center stage with Mike, and he didn't have that emcee thing that Mike had . . . So that's when Dennis started to get . . . well, he would get absolutely blotto before going on stage because he thought he'd be funnier like that and he didn't feel as self-conscious, but it wound up making him look more self-conscious. . . . Once the accident with his hand happened, he was drinking like I'd never seen before."

As Rachlin recalled, there was some confusion regarding whom he had to sell the idea to. "I spent time with Mike, and Mike told me he was the leader of the band, and I spoke to Dennis, who said 'Make sure you always come to me.'" After awhile, however, he realized that it was Carl he really needed to convince. "Carl and I started to connect just because he was the businessman and not the crazy (although everyone was kind of crazy)." Rachlin urged Carl and the others to allow him to be their main booking agent. "I explained to them that I wasn't a promoter by trade and that we had a small agency. I was really hammering home the Bill Graham connection, the Fillmore. I explained that we should put them in colleges, just to break the mold. Do what we did at Carnegie Hall." Rachlin returned to New York, still unsure if the group was sold on the idea, but "early the following week, I got a telegram from Rene Pappas of American Productions giving me ninety days to represent the band. So . . . whatever I was going to do, I had ninety days to do it."

Rachlin quickly booked the group into a series of East Coast venues, mostly college gymnasiums. To save money, the group traveled on a chartered Trailways bus. The Beach Boys were usually promised a $1000 guarantee and a percentage of the profits after the promoter recouped their expenses. However, they were no longer the solid draw that they had been in the 1960s. A number of promoters had trouble selling tickets on this tour,

> "I remember I was playing vibes and he said, 'OK, Daryl, play vibes' and I said, 'What do you want me to play?' and he said, 'Just think of something.' I didn't want that. I wanted the Beach Boys feedback. Brian was there and I wanted him to tell me more. But at those sessions, Brian was just hanging out."
>
> **—Ricky Fataar**

THURSDAY, JULY 1, 1971: Kingsbridge Armory, Bronx, NY, with Alice Cooper, Ike and Tina Turner, Chuck Berry, Wilson Pickett, Kate Taylor, Voices of East Harlem, Hooker 'N' Heat, 30 Days Out, Illusion, Powerhouse, and J.F. Murphy
The group played on day three of a week-long International Youth Expo.

FRIDAY, JULY 2, AND SATURDAY, JULY 3, 1971: Schaeffer Music Festival, Wolman Skating Rink, Central Park, New York, New York, with Ike and Tina Turner, Boz Scaggs, Kate Taylor, and Carly Simon (One show at 8:00 p.m. each night)
These two concerts were filmed for the ABC TV special *Good Vibrations From Central Park*. The film crew insisted on capturing two shows to ensure they had good footage. Director John Moffitt had the musicians wear the same outfits both days to create the illusion that they had only filmed one show. The Beach Boys performances "Heroes and Villains," "Okie from Muskogee," "Forever," and "It's About Time" appeared in the program, along with footage of the other artists.

The Beach Boys spent most of July completing the *Surf's Up* album. Carl was also busy preparing for another court appearance in his draft case. On September 14, U.S. District Court Judge Harry Pregerson freed him from his four-year legal nightmare by granting him the right to perform the alternative service that he had requested. Carl agreed to play a number of shows at hospitals, orphanages, and prisons over the next two years. He also promised to spend time with inmates teaching them about music. In addition, Carl agreed to promote voter registration at upcoming concerts.

WEDNESDAY, SEPTEMBER 22, 1971: Ramada Inn, Portsmouth, RI
With Carl's draft-related legal problems finally over, the group embarked on a ten-day tour. As part of the terms of Carl's settlement, they displayed a 20x8-foot banner with the slogan "We Win" above the stage, encouraging people to register to vote at booths set up in the halls. The group featured over fifteen musicians onstage for these concerts. Not only did the Beach Boys bring along a five-piece horn section with them (composed of Joel Peskin, Roger Newman, Sal Marquez, Glenn Ferris, and Mike Price), but they also recruited Ricky Fataar, of the recently disbanded Flame, as a percussionist/drummer, along with Daryl Dragon (keyboards), Ed Carter (bass), Mike Kowalski (drums), and Bobby Torres (extra percussion). Carl's brother-in-law Billy Hinsche also joined this tour, mostly to sing harmony. Billy remembered the tour fondly as "a very special time for me, as I had moved to the next level in my musical experience and career. I had gone from being in Dino, Desi, and Billy to being in the Beach Boys and it felt good. I was very proud and honored to be included in their band."

The Beach Boys opening show at a Ramada Inn was sponsored by Roger Williams College. The *Newport Daily News* noted, "They opened some people's eyes, as does their new album *Surf's Up* . . . The group has grown so much since the surf days. The new songs sometimes utilize four keyboards at once in a concert . . . Overall, the group puts on a great show, and parts of their album are brilliant." The Beach Boys were not impressed by the venue. Al told a reporter from *The Quill* that his ear was ringing from all the noise because "the room was acoustically ill-suited for us. All that sound in such a small room is just not good. There should be a law providing minimal acoustical standards for any place where concerts are to be held."

THURSDAY, SEPTEMBER 23, 1971: Music Hall, Boston, MA, with Boz Scaggs (8:00 p.m. show)
A disappointing crowd of less than 2,500 people turned out for this concert. Critics agreed that fans that stayed home missed a great show. Charles Giuliano of the *Boston Herald* reported, "The music leaned toward new works which saw Bruce Johnston and Carl and Dennis Wilson singing solos that proved to be the most moving segments of the exquisite evening . . . The artistry of the Beach Boys blossomed in the second set with the masterpiece 'Surf's Up' providing an emotional pivot for the program. Bruce Johnston scored with his 'Disney Girls' and Carl was superb with 'Caroline.' California conquered Boston as the set climaxed with a rocking encore of 'Johnny B. Goode.'" Michael Nicholson of *The Globe* expressed slightly less enthusiasm but noted that "Carl Wilson was surprisingly good on guitar, and Mike Love's talks kept things loose. The new stuff like 'Surf's Up' and 'Student Demonstration Time,' and the old stuff like 'Heroes and Villains' and 'Do It Again' worked out fine. Dennis Wilson, absent on drums because of a hand injury, contributed the

great, great song 'It's About Time,' and sang to his own piano accompaniment (in darkness because of his embarrassment of playing alone) a beautiful song to his wife, Barbara."

FRIDAY, SEPTEMBER 24, 1971: Carnegie Hall, New York, NY (Two shows at 7:30 and 11:00 p.m.)
Seven months after their triumphant show at Carnegie Hall, the Beach Boys returned. Prior to the shows, they held an afternoon press conference. Nancy Lewis reported in *New Musical Express*, "The conference was held for the purpose of dispelling all fresh rumors that the group was falling apart. And also to announce the good news that Carl Wilson has emerged triumphant from his five years of legal wrangling with the draft board." The break-up rumors were caused by reports that Dennis had clashed with Carl and pulled his songs from the *Surf's Up* album. The appearance of both brothers at the conference put an end to any breakup gossip.

As was now their custom, the band played two sets with a short intermission in between. The first set consisted of "Good Vibrations," "Take a Load off Your Feet," "Don't Go Near the Water," "Wouldn't It Be Nice," "Darlin'," "Student Demonstration Time," "Cool Cool Water," "Long Promised Road," "God Only Knows," "Sloop John B," and "It's About Time." The second set began with Mike reading a poem about TM, followed by performances of "Feel Flows," "Disney Girls," "Looking at Tomorrow," and "Caroline, No." Dennis then performed a solo piano version of "Barbara," before the group concluded with "Surf's Up" and "Heroes and Villains." They had to be pleased by fan reaction at these shows. They were called back onstage numerous times for encores, during which they played the oldies "Do It Again," "Little Deuce Coupe," "I Get Around," "Johnny B. Goode," and "Help Me Rhonda." Fred Kirby noted in *Variety*, that the band pulled out "Surfin' USA," which they had not played in years, for their fifth encore. "Carl Wilson took vocal lead as he had for most of the show, aided by some of the finest vocal blending around. The encore followed an updated version of 'Help Me Rhonda,' which the Beach Boys had done during a late-set jam with the Grateful Dead at Fillmore East last spring."

SATURDAY, SEPTEMBER 25, 1971: Fieldhouse, Villanova University, Villanova, PA
This show drew 4,000 people. Frequent calls for older songs were met with promises that "This is a long show and we'll get to that." The audience accepted the message stoically but the group were frustrated by the crowd's unwillingness to embrace their new music with the same fervor as the oldies. Nevertheless, Jack Correia of *The Villanovan* reported, "As had been promised . . . after an excellent hour of *Surf's Up* recordings that included 'Disney Girls (1957),' 'Student Demonstration Time,' and 'Surf's Up,' the Beach Boys came back and rocked the building with surf music. 'I Get Around' and 'Little Deuce Coupe' brought the audience to a state of pandemonium. Then ceaseless chanting and pounding brought them back again for sing-a-long 'Surfer Girl,' a new arrangement of 'Help Me Rhonda,' and 'Surfin' USA.'"

SUNDAY, SEPTEMBER 26, 1971: State University of New York, Stony Brook, NY, with Boz Scaggs

TUESDAY, SEPTEMBER 28, 1971: Keaney Gymnasium, Rhode Island University, Kingston, RI (8:30 p.m.)

WEDNESDAY, SEPTEMBER 29, 1971: Taft Auditorium, Cincinnati, OH (8:00 p.m. show)
Mike O'Connor of the *Journal News* called the resurgent Beach Boys "the hottest act in the business" but took them to task for pretending that it was their new music that was attracting the fans. "They're playing games with themselves and their fans . . . Carl and his cohorts literally demolished an audience playing three encores and performing for a total of two and one half hours. But it wasn't anything from their newer albums that crazed the throng. You guessed it, 'Little Deuce Coupe' and 'I Get Around' blew the place down . . . Why did the Beach Boys have to force their current styles on us, when we came to hear 'Surfer Girl'?"

THURSDAY, SEPTEMBER 30, 1971: Warner Theater, Erie, PA (8:00 p.m.)
This concert was sponsored by the student union of Behrend College. Carol Hughes of the *Behrend Collegian* declared, "The old songs 'Do It Again,' 'I Get Around' are the same as they always were, full of action and fun. They contrast sharply with the new Beach Boys sounds and together made a show that pleased everyone at Warner. The concert made it very obvious that the Beach Boys could

which took place in April 1971. Nevertheless, the tour was important. The group demonstrated that they were determined to rebuild their fan base and would do whatever it took to restore their standing in the rock world. The often-fractious Beach Boys became a focused team motivated by a common goal.

The group played any and all jobs that they were offered and checked their egos at the door, despite sometimes-spotty venues and less than glamorous accommodations. One infamous appearance was at the Paris Cinema in Worcester, Massachusetts. The group were promised a $5,000 guarantee for these shows, the highest pay they received on the low-grossing tour. However, they received quite a surprise when they arrived at the venue. According to Chip Rachlin, "Carl called me at my mother's house and said 'Are you familiar with this theater?' I said, 'Yeah, it's about 900 seats.' Carl said, 'They run pornographic films and strip shows.' I said 'Yeah.' He said 'I just thought you'd want to know.' He was very polite, but said 'Please don't do this again.'"

The tour was designed to encourage counterculture audiences to reassess their perceptions of the Beach Boys. The group made appearances at the May Day peace celebration in Washington, DC, and at a benefit for anti-war activists the Berrigan Brothers in Syracuse, N.Y. They also made a legendary guest appearance at a Grateful Dead concert at the Fillmore East. The group was apprehensive about what sort of response they'd get from the Deadheads.

But Chip Rachlin recalled, "When they came out and everyone realized that this was not a joke and they weren't just on a bad trip, it started in the back of the hall. This one clap, became two, became a hundred, became literally a wave and it was a stunning aural sensation, which just sort of reverberated through the hall." Rachlin watched the show from the mixing booth and was joined briefly by Bob Dylan, who was friends with the Dead and had come to see them perform. Dylan turned to Rachlin during the Beach Boys' performance and exclaimed, "They're fucking good, man!"

While the tour was not a financial success, the good will it generated led to more bookings and soon the Beach Boys had become a fixture on the college concert circuit. Chip Rachlin recalled, "The renaissance hadn't really started. Sunday nights at the colleges they only made the $1000. But by booking them with artists like Boz Scaggs and Taj Mahal, we were at least putting them in something a little more *Rolling Stone*–worthy." The band was happy enough with Rachlin's efforts on their behalf to agree to a long-term contract and he continued to represent them until January 1978.

Rachlin worked hard to land important bookings that would show off the Beach Boys to audiences that were ignorant of how good they were live. It proved to be an uphill climb for much of 1971. At times the Beach Boys and their management were their own worst enemies. When Rachlin and Klenfner managed to get the group on the bill for the closing concert

teach harmonically orientated groups such as Crosby, Stills, and Young and the Jefferson Airplane quite a few tricks."

FRIDAY, OCTOBER 1, 1971: Clowes Hall, Butler University, Indianapolis, IN
The *Indianapolis Star* declared "There were a lot of 'Good Vibrations' at Clowes Hall last night . . . We expected to hear a lot of the group's contemporary sound . . . Not only did they oblige us with 'Don't Go Near the Water' (an anti-pollution offering) and 'It's About Time,' but also an old favorite thrown in, every other song. And did the audience dig on it? You bet your sweet dune buggy!"

SATURDAY, OCTOBER 2, 1971: Athletic and Convocation Center, Notre Dame University, South Bend, IN (8:30 p.m. show)
This first of many Beach Boys concerts at Notre Dame drew 8,000 people. To stave off the catcalls and screams for "Surfin' USA," Carl announced at the start of the show, "We're going to be here for a long time, so relax. We'll get to everything." From then on the concert proceeded smoothly. Nevertheless, Mike George of the *Notre Dame Observer* argued that the audience, while respectful, was waiting for oldies. "Mike Love set the mood for the celebration during the first encore saying, 'You know the words, sing along. You're part of this.' And so we sang along: to 'California Girls,' to 'I Get Around,' to 'Fun, Fun, Fun,' and especially to 'Surfer Girl' . . . We enjoyed being kids again. We enjoyed it so much that we brought the Beach Boys back from the dressing room three times to help us." Following this show, the band spent the night at Randall's Inn.

SATURDAY, OCTOBER 23, 1971: "People's Concert," Municipal Stadium, Phoenix, AZ, with Taj Mahal, Woodlord Haven, Joe Benthencourt, and Miguel (12:00 p.m. show)
This was a benefit show sponsored by radio station KRIZ and the Mayor's Youth Advisory Board, with the proceeds going to CODAC (the Council on Drug Abuse Control). The Beach Boys played for a minimal fee and closed the six-hour outdoor concert. Over 15,000 people showed up, despite overcast skies. Voter registration booths were set up at the venue and the group made personal pitches from the stage encouraging people to register. The group offered one dollar refunds to any fan who presented their voter registration card at the gate. Carl told the *Arizona Republic*, "The idea is to get everyone involved. If people don't like things the way they are, then voting is the only way to make things that are unfair fair and bad things good."

Adding to their gradually improving fortunes, the Beach Boys were featured on the cover of *Rolling Stone* magazine this week as part of a two-issue feature chronicling the group's history and comeback.

FRIDAY, NOVEMBER 5, 1971: Gymnasium, Fairfield University, Fairfield, CT (8:00 p.m. show)
To promote *Surf's Up*, the Beach Boys embarked on a seventeen-day East Coast tour. In addition to the musicians who'd played with them on their recent shows, Jeff Kaplan joined the band on electric piano, replacing Billy Hinsche.

The group was paid $7,000 to perform during homecoming festivities at Fairfield University. All 2,350 tickets sold, and Al remarked that the crowd was one of the most enthusiastic he ever performed for. Dennis took a prominent role, performing the rarely heard "Celebrate the News" and a great new song that he finished that afternoon during rehearsals, "I've Got A Friend" (which never appeared on a Beach Boys album). Dennis also briefly took over drumming duties, for the first time since May, on "God Only Knows" and "Sloop John B." which only irritated his slowly healing hand.

Chuck Frissora of the *Fairfield Free Press and Review* reported, "The Beach Boys harmonized, blended, and rocked on home some of the best vibrations this place will ever hear." He was particularly impressed by Carl's contributions, noting that "Carl, apparently a bit edgy and nervous at first, dominated, arranged, and guided the group through their entire repertoire . . . It was Carl's version of 'Caroline No' that provoked genuine sensitivity in a tremendous rendition of a most beautiful song."

SATURDAY, NOVEMBER 6, 1971: University Hall, University of Virginia, Charlottesville, VA, with the Byrds (8:00 p.m. show)

This double bill featured the two most popular L.A. bands of the mid-60s and expectations were high among the 10,000 plus fans that turned out. The Byrds played a strong set, sprinkling their new songs amidst their hits. There was then an intermission while the stage was reset for the Beach Boys. Unfortunately, the celebratory mood was quickly broken. The audience refused to be patient and repeatedly interrupted the group with requests for oldies. Audiences unwilling to give their new music a chance undoubtedly frustrated the group and things reached a boiling point at this show. Fifteen minutes into the concert, a fan yelled out, "Play Barbara Ann," just as the group was about to perform a new song. A frustrated Mike lost his temper and proceeded to lecture the audience on their behavior. Tension in the hall only grew, though opinion was divided on who was to blame.

Bob Ramsey of the *Cavalier Daily* blamed the Beach Boys for refusing to give the audience what it wanted. He ripped the group for introducing songs with "long awkward pauses" and odd comments like "My wife left me two weeks ago," and took Mike to task for launching into a long rap about meditation. When the group finally played the oldies at the end of the show, Ramsey was still unsatisfied. The encores were "the final insult. The Beach Boys left the stage . . . and forced us to beg them to come back and do each of their three (or was it four) big hits. I found myself . . . screaming approval at a bunch of people at whom I was very pissed off. Ten thousand screaming dentists were forced to extract each encore from five men who knew exactly what the audience wanted and had for three hours angrily refused to give."

University student Michael Cascio offered a very different viewpoint, placing the blame on the crowd. He argued that rock concerts were no longer an opportunity to simply listen to music, but instead had become social events in which the audience insisted on having equal billing. "'We want oldies' they shrieked; hardly embarrassed when the group made it very plain again that they did not need to be told what to play. The loud mouthing kept up, and the audience was not satisfied until the Beach Boys did 'oldies' in a deserved (if only for sheer stamina) encore."

SUNDAY, NOVEMBER 7, 1971: McDonough Arena, Georgetown University, Washington, DC (8:00 p.m. show)

The set list consisted of "Good Vibrations," "Don't Go Near the Water," "Darlin'," "Wouldn't It Be Nice," "Disney Girls," "Long Promised Road," "Student Demonstration Time," "God Only Knows," "Take a Load off Your Feet," "Sloop John B," "It's About Time," and "Surfin' USA," followed by an intermission. Then the band returned and played "Cool, Cool Water," "Lookin' at Tomorrow," "Barbara," "I've Got a Friend," "Okie from Muskogee," "Surf's Up," "Heroes and Villains," "Do It Again," "California Girls," "I Get Around," "Help Me Rhonda," and "Fun, Fun, Fun."

A fan that attended the concert recalled, "The show looked sold out. I was surprised. They opened with 'Good Vibrations' and played for two hours with an intermission. Mike was cracking his usual lousy jokes ('Take a load off your feet by elevating your consciousness!'). Dennis had a solo spot ('My Friend' and 'Barbara'). Bruce Johnston asked people to register to vote (a registration booth was out front). Dennis played drums during the encore of hits. Carl had a cowboy-tyle jumpsuit on and Mike also had a jumpsuit. Someone in the crowd kept yelling out 'Don't Back Down!' (Jack Rieley had admonished the crowd at the beginning not to request songs until the encore.) Mike introduced 'Cool, Cool Water' by saying, 'Imagine you are in Brian Wilson's recording studio.' Mike played a theremin-like device during the songs that needed it and used it as a siren during 'Student Demonstration Time.' It was a riveting show." The *Washington Star* noted that the sons of legendary bluegrass banjo player Earl Scruggs, Randy and Gary, came out to sing "Okie from Muskogee" with the band.

TUESDAY, NOVEMBER 9, AND WEDNESDAY, NOVEMBER 10, 1971: The Dome, C.W. Post College, Brookville, NY

Fans that attended the second of two shows at C.W. Post witnessed quite a different performance from those who attended the first night. Dennis's hand injury clearly frustrated him, as he could go no longer play drums for more than a song or two. In addition, he had shown some mercurial behavior in recent months, such as pulling all his compositions from the *Surf's Up* album. Earl Leaf alleged, in his regular column in *Teen Magazine*, that a major cause of Dennis's "emotional dive" was that his wife Barbara temporarily left him and threatened divorce. Whatever the reasons, Dennis' demons flared up at the Wednesday concert.

of the Fillmore East in June 1971, Rachlin recalled, "Jack Rieley nearly got them thrown off by insisting that they close the show, even though you had J. Geils there and you had the Allman Brothers there. The Beach Boys were lucky to be on the show and we had to work very hard to convince Bill (Graham) to put them on the show, and then for Jack to take the idiotic position that they had to close the show. Klenfner showed his disgust with Jack in the lobby of the Fillmore, with the glittering lights and all the beautifully lit Fillmore posters. Klenfner threw Jack into a glass case and said he would kill him if he didn't change his mind . . . He told him 'If we go to Bill with this request he'll throw you out of the theater, so don't hurt the band by being such a jerk!' We won that one."

In July the Beach Boys were filmed for the ABC TV special *Good Vibrations: Live From Central Park*. The show aired in August 1971 to good reviews and helped to alert America that the group was still around and worthy of reevaluation. Relentless touring began to pay off and when the group returned to Carnegie Hall in September for two shows, they sold out both and grossed $30,000. Clearly the band's stock was rising. Only seven months before, they had been unable to sell out one show at the same venue despite a great deal of promotion.

Renewed interest in the group gave a boost to their fall 1971 album *Surf's Up*. While not a million-seller, it sold respectably, hitting number twenty-nine on the *Billboard* charts in the U.S., and an even stronger number fifteen in the

U.K. It also garnered excellent reviews from the increasingly important rock press. Daryl Dragon, however, who took part in some of the sessions, missed Brian's presence. "I felt there was limitation in the production, not the recording, but in the production values compared to when Brian Wilson was in charge. When Brian was recording at Capitol or at Western, he would go over and tell Hal Blaine to play this and the trombone player to play that. He never did that (during this period) like he did then. And I think that was part of the magic. I remember I was playing vibes and he said, 'OK, Daryl, play vibes' and I said, 'What do you want me to play?' and he said, 'Just think of something.' I didn't want that. I wanted the Beach Boys feedback. Brian was there and I wanted him to tell me more. But at those sessions, Brian was just hanging out."

Despite Brian's minimal involvement in the album as a whole, he still managed to steal the show thanks to the inclusion of two of his most stunning tracks. His 1966 *Smile* jewel "Surf's Up" was beautifully completed by the group for the album, and another mesmerizing Brian composition called "'Til I Die" was included as well. The two Brian masterpieces were miles above anything else on the album. Although Carl contributed two strong collaborations with Jack Rieley, "Feel Flows" and "Long Promised Road," and Bruce supplied one of his best songs, "Disney Girls (1957)," there was something else missing. Dennis had a major disagreement with Carl over the sequencing of the

W. Sachs Gore of the *C.W. Post Pioneer* reported that Dennis "appeared to be slightly disorientated and wandered around the stage muttering things like 'a girl who I love . . . a baby nine months long, divorced, married, now let me try that again.' The high point of the night came when he wandered onstage and announced that the Beach Boys were donating the proceeds of the concert to poverty, whereupon Bruce Johnston replied, 'Our own.'" The reviewer noted that, in contrast, the night before, "Dennis, if I may call him that, was 'into' the music, but the only difficulty encountered was a faulty electric piano, whereupon he arose, and sat himself down with no more than a 'hell' or something to that effect. And Carl Wilson stood on the side of the stage smiling, not as though the world was ending (as he seemed to think on Wednesday night as he rushed to the limousine after the end of the second encore). It was unfortunate." As a result of this incident, Dennis flew home to get himself together. He was not present for the remaining November shows. Since he was no longer relied upon to play the drums, his absence was not difficult to fill. But his sudden departure from the tour led to rumors in various magazines that he was leaving the group.

THURSDAY, NOVEMBER 11, 1971: Memorial Field House, Indiana University of Pennsylvania, Indiana, PA (8:30 p.m. show)
The group showed up an hour late but a crowd of 2,700 greeted them warmly. Greg Harris of the *Indiana Penn* noted that "The harmony could not, of course, have been as clean as on their records but, all things considered, the effect came across well . . . Songs like 'Student Demonstration Time,' 'Surfin' USA,' and 'Okie from Muskogee' received standing ovations even though they were in the middle of the program. The Boys were called out to do two encores . . . in which they did a total of five numbers . . . smiles were beaming from every direction, which seems to indicate the concert was somewhat of a success."

FRIDAY, NOVEMBER 12, 1971: Central Theater, Passaic, NJ (Two shows at 8:00 and 11:30 p.m.)

SATURDAY, NOVEMBER 13, 1971: Dillon Gym, Princeton University, Princeton, NJ (Two shows at 8:00 and 11:00 p.m.)
The Beach Boys' first Princeton University concert was a sellout and an 11:00 p.m. show was added. While the group's harmony was unified and tight, members' individualism was on display: Carl wore a blue Nudie cowboy shirt decorated with butterflies, Mike opted for bib overalls and an old Stetson hat, and Al wore an old bush hat and ascot. Asked about Dennis' absence, Mike replied, "Dennis went home. He wasn't feeling well. He'd cut his hand and he was just getting back into playing the drums and then he OD'd or something . . . He didn't OD. I take that back. He wasn't feeling well and rather than take planes and all that, he decided to go get well." Another fan then called out 'Where's Brian?' and Mike replied, 'Brian's at home . . . Brian's in the music."

Alan Edwards of the *Trenton Times* was impressed by the set, which included "a breathtakingly lovely 'Surf's Up,' medium oldies like 'Darlin'' and 'Sloop John B,' and one or two surprises like 'Okie from Muskogee,' which they proudly mentioned they'd jammed on with the Grateful Dead at the Fillmore. But the encore was what it was really all about. 'California Girls,' that state's unofficial anthem, and then the most orgiastic version of 'I Get Around' imaginable, everybody on his feet, dancing, and singing and grinning in pure ecstasy. The group returned for a second encore, playing a new arrangement of 'Help Me Rhonda' and then the ultimate '60s song, the one all the shouted requests had been for, 'Fun, Fun, Fun.'"

SUNDAY, NOVEMBER 14, 1971: State University of New York, Fredonia, NY

TUESDAY, NOVEMBER 16, 1971: Syria Mosque, Pittsburgh, PA (8:00 p.m. show)

WEDNESDAY, NOVEMBER 17, 1971: Arie Crown Theatre, Chicago, IL (8:00 p.m. show)

THURSDAY, NOVEMBER 18, 1971: Arena Annex, St. Louis, MO (7:30 p.m. show)
About 3,000 fans attended this show at the small arena annex.

FRIDAY, NOVEMBER 19, 1971: Masonic Auditorium, Detroit, MI (8:30 p.m. show)
Although they performed to a half-empty auditorium, John Weisman of the *Detroit Free Press* declared that the Beach Boys put on "an exquisite concert." He noted that "'Don't Go Near the Water' and 'Student Demonstration Time,' based on 'Cellblock Number Nine' with new lyrics by Love, were marvelous . . . Then came Bruce Johnston's 'Disney Girls (1957)' . . . the dreamy, fragile poetry of this song is simply incredible. Bruce sang in a solo spotlight. The only other lights onstage were the red 'on' bulbs from the amps. It gave a fantasy-like setting to this 1957 sense-memory exercise. There were old favorites too. 'Good Vibrations,' 'Sloop John B,' 'Surfin' USA,' and many more, all greeted with enthusiastic applause."

SATURDAY, NOVEMBER 20, 1971: Music Hall, Cleveland, OH (8:30 p.m.)
The group received a rapturous reception from Cleveland fans that demanded three encores. Mike told the audience "This is ridiculous. But we love every minute of it." Jane Scott of the *Plains Dealer* commented, "The Beach Boys have left the beach and they're no longer boys . . . Their songs have progressed and deepened and their later lyrics are poetic and intricately woven. Their old 'Riot in Cell Block Number Nine' had new words to it, 'Student Demonstration Time,' and other references to May 4, 1970 at Kent State."

SUNDAY, NOVEMBER 21, 1971: Guthrie Theater, Minneapolis, MN (Two shows at 8:00 and 11:00 p.m.)
The Beach Boys played two enthusiastically received shows. Michael Anthony of *The Star* reported, "With sound problems abounding—excessive feedback and too much bass, the lyrics were not always clear so that the best numbers were uptempo . . . But there were still some lovely moments: Bruce Johnston's vocals on 'Disney Girls,' 'Caroline No' sung by Carl Wilson, as well as the group's contrapuntal 'Good Vibrations.'"

MONDAY, NOVEMBER 22, 1971: Milwaukee Performing Arts Center, Milwaukee, WI (Two shows at 7:00 and 10:00 p.m.)
Neither of the two Milwaukee shows was a sellout. The first concert attracted 2,000 fans and the second only 1,300. However, the group soldiered on. According to Dean Jensen of the *Milwaukee Sentinel*, the Beach Boys made a "mockery of pronouncements about the fleeting fame of rock artists . . . [and] showed here Monday night that, after ten years, they're still making big waves with audiences." Jensen declared that "the most brilliant solo performances were turned in by Bruce Johnston with his nostalgic glance back at his youth, 'Disney Girls,' and Carl Wilson with 'Surf's Up,' a poetically and melodically lavish song written by his brother, Brian, and Van Dyke Parks."

FRIDAY, DECEMBER 3, 1971: Long Beach Arena, Long Beach, CA, with Elvin Bishop and Seatrain (8:00 p.m. show)
The Beach Boys returned to Long Beach to celebrate their tenth anniversary. The turnout was smaller than promoters had hoped for, but the 8,000 fans that attended witnessed a special show. The group, including Dennis, took the stage at 11 p.m. and opened with "Good Vibrations," "Don't Go Near the Water" and "Darlin'." The rest of the set consisted of "Wouldn't It Be Nice," "Long Promised Road," "Student Demonstration Time," "Disney Girls," "Take a Load Off Your Feet," "Sloop John B," "Surfin' USA," "It's About Time," "Cool, Cool Water," "A Day in the Life of a Tree," "Lookin' At Tomorrow," "Caroline No," "I've Got a Friend," "Okie from Muskogee," "God Only Knows," "TM Poem," "Surf's Up," "Do It Again," and "Fun, Fun, Fun."

Jeff Sherwood of *Staff Magazine* reported, "For nearly 100 minutes, the group served up a tasty offering of songs from their past and present which never failed to be anything below what one might expect to hear from one of the greatest rock 'n' roll bands ever to be reckoned with." A tape of this show reveals that Carl gave one of his most beautiful performances of 'Caroline, No' while Dennis' 'I've Got a Friend' was equally mesmerizing. The highlight of the concert was the surprise appearance of Brian, who emerged from the audience to perform "A Day in the Life of a Tree" with Jack Rieley. It's possible Brian might have been convinced to perform a few more numbers but unfortunately, Long Beach police forced the show to end at 12:30 a.m. due to city curfew laws.

album and pulled his tracks off the record. Based on the quality of Dennis' unreleased recordings from this time, this omission left the *Surf's Up* LP significantly short of the masterpiece it could have been.

Meanwhile, many fans that bought tickets for Beach Boys concerts still expected to hear the old hits. The band had to deal with constant resistance to their decision to play mostly newer music. The group understood their fans' thirst for nostalgia, but refused to be diverted from their goals. Asked about the response they got when they played older numbers, Mike said, "The beautiful aspects of nostalgia and the truths that we were expounding in the '60s, two, three, and four like 'Fun, Fun, Fun' and 'Don't Worry Baby,' 'Good Vibrations,' and things like that. Those are very enjoyable to people in that they are related to good memories and good times. We're still saying 'Have a good time,' but now the issues are just a little broader, you know." Asked by a reporter from the *Behrend Collegian* for his reaction to the fans' preference for oldies over newer material, Carl replied, "I don't know how to give an accurate answer at this time, because our new record is essentially a new record as of now. I think in several months to a year it can be gauged more accurately. I think as those songs become more familiar to the people and they get to recognize those songs, I think that then we'll know more about these new songs."

By the end of 1971, the Beach Boys appeared to be heading in the right direction again. For their tenth anniversary they returned to Long Beach, California for a celebratory concert that even got Brian out of the house. It was his first appearance onstage since the Whisky shows in November 1970. Overall, it felt like an upswing was in progress. Beach Boys fans had good reason to be encouraged that the ensuing years would see the band thrive.

SATURDAY, DECEMBER 4, 1971: Sports Arena, San Diego, CA, with Elvin Bishop and Seatrain (8:00 p.m. show)
The Beach Boys' first San Diego concert since 1968 only attracted 2,000 people. Those that attended heckled the group when they performed anything other than oldies. Performances of "Don't Go Near the Water" and "Surf's Up" received a tepid response, while "Surfin' USA" and "Darlin'" were greeted enthusiastically. At one point, the band got the audience to join in singing happy birthday to Dennis, who turned twenty-seven that day. He performed "I've Got a Friend" on piano for the crowd. Frank Green of the *San Diego Union* trashed the group's attempts at relevance and declared their music passé. He commented, "The Beach Boys should begin to realize that their era is over and that they have been unable to make the transition from the music of the '60s to that of the '70s. The group is far too old to be singing such juvenile ditties as 'Surfer Girl,' 'Wouldn't It Be Nice,' and 'Sloop John B."

SUNDAY, DECEMBER 5, 1971: HIC Arena, Honolulu, HI, with Elvin Bishop (8:00 p.m. show)

FRIDAY, DECEMBER 10, AND SATURDAY, DECEMBER 11, 1971: Winterland, San Francisco, CA, with Stoneground and Mason Profitt (One show each night at 8:00 p.m.)
The Beach Boys reunited with promoter Bill Graham for two nights at Winterland. Kathy Mackay of *Earth Magazine* captured the backstage scene. Fred Vail, Steve Love, and Jack Rieley were all milling about, as wine flowed freely. Mackay cornered Dennis, who was accompanied by an amply endowed young lady named Monica, and asked whether Brian was the group's leader. Dennis replied, "We don't really have a leader. We're equal you know—brothers. Yes, we've stuck together because we're a family." Dennis also discussed why none of his compositions were on the last album: "I didn't write any of the songs on the *Surf's Up* album. I really wasn't into it that much. I'm a little tired of rock 'n' roll. I like blacks . . . I'm working on a symphony now, I just got it together a couple of days ago."

Dennis Hunt of the *San Francisco Chronicle* was disappointed that the band "insisted on doing material from their latest album, *Surf's Up*, which consists mostly of thoughtful, sluggish songs characterized by pretentiously intricate arrangements." Phillip Elwood of *The Examiner*, however, argued they didn't play *enough* new material. He commented, "The Beach Boys are at the point of confronting themselves. Do they move ahead, perhaps losing some of their loyal old followers, or do they try to straddle the years and satisfy some of the people all of the time, mixing old and new? I'd vote for progress, leaving the past to accumulate dust in the microgrooves. The Beach Boys are much too together to want to waste their energetic inventiveness on musical nostalgia."

OTHER 1971 CONCERTS

It's probable that the group played a few prison shows during the fall as part of Carl's draft settlement. In an interview with the *Honolulu Advertiser* in February 1983, Bruce recalled appearing with the Beach Boys at Terminal Island Prison near Los Angeles.

CONCERTS NOT PLAYED

According to *Amusement Business*, the Beach Boys were booked to play a Pacific Northwest tour from December 15 to 19. The dates were Vancouver (December 15), Salem (December 16), Seattle (December 17), Portland (December 18), and Spokane (December 19). However, there is no evidence that the shows took place.
The group was signed to appear at the Vega Baja Fair in Puerto Rico, to be held around Thanksgiving. However, it was postponed until 1972 and ultimately, the group did not play.

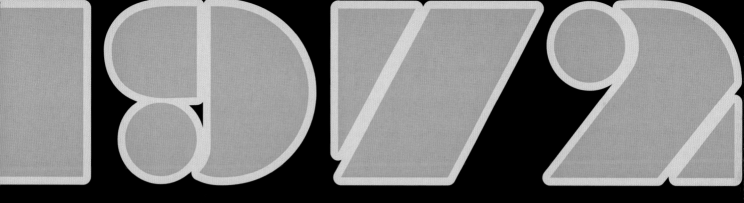

NINETEEN SEVENTY-TWO was a year of hard work for the Beach Boys. They recorded two albums and toured relentlessly, including two trips to Europe. The group continued their effort to get the message out that they were no longer the clean-cut, striped-shirted "surfers" that people recalled. Their November 1972 shows were advertised in newspapers with the slogan, "The Beach Boys: They've changed even more than you." There was a continued focus on presenting newer material in their sets, with oldies relegated to the encores. At times this led to hostile reactions from some fans. But changing an image so firmly cemented in the minds of the general public called for an uncompromising approach.

The group had been scattered apart since December, with Bruce spending time in Mexico, and Mike and Al in Spain, where they had been studying TM. On February 25 the Beach Boys played at the Grand Gala du Disques, the major annual pop music event in the Netherlands. Aside from performing, the group was scouting locations for a possible long-term stay. They were bored with their usual recording routine. The group hoped that moving to an exotic location away from the distractions and hangers-on in L.A. might awaken more creativity in them, and especially in Brian. At a press conference, Bruce stated that the group wanted "to find somewhere in France, get the Stones' mobile recording truck, and do an album. That way, with all of us together, we'd get more done in six weeks than we do in three months at home."

The press conference took place on February 28 in London at the Royal Gardens Hotel with Bruce, Carl, Dennis, and Jack Rieley present. The main purpose of the conference was to announce the upcoming

> "Jack Rieley had this idea for me and Blonds to join the group and I just thought it was so ridiculous. It just didn't seem possible because it seemed like such a tight-knit family thing."
>
> —Ricky Fataar

European tour. Carl told Martin Hayman of *Sounds* that he didn't "remember having so much fun on stage before," and that their May 1972 U.K. tour would be far superior to their last visit in 1970. "It used to be a variety show, with lots of other groups, and a compere. In the future it will be nothing like that. Any resemblance will be strictly coincidental now."

CONCERTS PLAYED IN 1972

FRIDAY, FEBRUARY 25, 1972: Grand Gala Du Disques, RAI-Congres Hall, Amsterdam, Netherlands, with Brass United, Gene Pitney, Roy Black, Middle of the Road, Peret, Helen Reddy, Charles Aznavour, the New Seekers, Gilbert O'Sullivan, Rod McKuen, the Bee Gees, Johnny Cash, and John Woodhouse (8:30 p.m. show)

The Beach Boys' first concert of the year was a huge show, headlined by Johnny Cash. It was televised on AVRO TV as well as being broadcast on radio. The group performed "Heroes and Villains," "Sloop John B," "Surf's Up," and "Student Demonstration Time."

THURSDAY, MARCH 16, 1972: State University of New York, Oneonta, NY

To prepare for their first tour of the year, the group commandeered the auditorium of North High School in Binghamton, New York on March 15 to rehearse. The rehearsal was especially necessary because of new additions to the band. Blondie Chaplin was now prominently featured on guitar and Ricky Fataar took over as full-time drummer. Daryl Dragon remained on keyboards, while Jeff Kaplan took over bass duties. The five-piece horn section the band had been utilizing since the previous year also accompanied them. Also present at the rehearsal was manager Jack Rieley and a young female pianist/singer from California named Toni Shearer, who was friendly with Daryl Dragon.

In an online post, Shearer recalled that her employment with the Beach Boys came about because Billy Hinsche, who had been playing acoustic piano with the group, had to return to film school and "Daryl thought that Carl Wilson, who acted as the band's music director, might be open to hiring me to fill that spot while Billy was away . . . Daryl was able to convince Carl that I could do the job, and he agreed to bring me along on their next tour." Daryl remembered, "I taught her the right way of banging the piano. A good test was that song "Darlin'," because you really had to bang the piano hard on that one. Carl looked her over and he said 'OK,' so she did the tour. She was really invaluable because sometimes one of the guys, Ricky Fataar or Blondie, would lose their voice or something and Toni would fill in, in a heartbeat. She's such a talented person. That's the only time they did that. After all, it was the Beach Boys and she was a Beach Girl. It was kind of weird that they did that."

The opening concert of the tour took place at SUNY Oneonta. The group played for 2,500 fans. The *Oneonta Star* review reiterated the usual tiresome theme: "At Thursday night's concert the crowd was moved by the oldies . . . The stomping and clapping of an audience is not unusual for a concert but the lack of it during the part of the Beach Boys show covering their last few musical years is. The truth of it is the Beach Boys are a group of the 1960s. Surf boards and hot rods are their medium and their concerts prove it."

FRIDAY, MARCH 17, 1972: Philadelphia Spectrum, Philadelphia, PA, with It's a Beautiful Day (8:00 p.m. show)

The group drew 8,000 fans to the 10,000-seat Spectrum. David Marziale of the *Bucks County Courier Times* reported that the Beach Boys "combined some of their later hits—'Wouldn't It Be Nice,' 'Good Vibrations' etc.—with some of the older ones like 'I Get Around' and the direct take from Berry, 'Surfin' USA' . . . The new songs they played, 'Surf's Up' and 'Student Demonstration Time,' combine modern themes with basic Beach Boy music. They have not resorted to copying the new groups but are blending new ideas into their music. They are changing but in their own way."

SATURDAY, MARCH 18, 1972: Montclair State College, Montclair, NJ (Two shows at 8:00 and 10:00 p.m.)

SUNDAY, MARCH 19, 1972: Lusk Field House, Cortland College, Syracuse, NY (8:00 p.m. show)

MONDAY, MARCH 20, TO WEDNESDAY, MARCH 22, 1972: Carnegie Hall, New York, NY (One show each night at 8:00 p.m.)

The group sold out three nights at Carnegie Hall, grossing $50,100. The set list on March 22 was "Wouldn't It Be Nice," "Long Promised Road," "Sloop John B," "Take a Load off Your Feet," "Cool, Cool Water," "Disney Girls," "Do It Again," "Heroes and Villains," "Wild Honey" (with Blondie on lead), and "Surfin' USA." The second set included "Surf's Up," "Let the Wind Blow," "My Friend" (sung by Dennis), "Darlin'," "Wonderful/Don't Worry Bill," "God Only Knows," "Help Me Rhonda," "Student Demonstration Time" and "Good Vibrations." For the encore they played "California Girls," "Surfer Girl," "I Get Around," and "Fun, Fun, Fun." Sam Sutherland of *Billboard* noted, "Both 'Surf's Up' and 'Wonderful' were stunning, revealing that they really could bring the shimmering clarity of tone and structure into the concert hall."

In Holland preparing for their appearance on the Grand Gala du Disque, February 25, 1972. Courtesy of Klaas Jelle

Ian Rusten Collection

The Beach Boys also revealed that they were adding two new official members to the group: Blondie Chaplin and Ricky Fataar from the now defunct Flame. Ricky had been involved with the Beach Boys as a backup musician since 1971, and both of them were recording with the group, so it was a smooth transition.

It was, however, a controversial move. The addition of two racially mixed South Africans to the lineup instantly altered their all-American image, which was probably the main reason Jack Rieley suggested it. Both Ricky and Blondie were initially baffled at the idea that they could be Beach Boys. Ricky told the BBC that "Jack Rieley had this idea for me and Blonds to join the group and I just thought it was so ridiculous. It just didn't seem possible because it seemed like such a tight-knit family thing." Daryl Dragon also felt it was an odd fit. "I never understood why they added those guys . . . because they weren't Beach Boys. Carl had

THURSDAY, MARCH 23, 1972: Kleinhan's Music Hall, Buffalo, NY (8:00 p.m. show)
While audiences often sat on their hands until the oldies were performed, there was evidence that the Beach Boys' new music was slowly being embraced. Jack Rieley told the BBC in 1974 that he took great personal satisfaction at concerts when "'Long Promised Road' got the biggest ovation of the show, and that's from *Surf's Up*. So I think it was accepted by people. We didn't want to have people turn off to what the Beach Boys were but only to be aware that there was still stuff going on and it was also very exciting music and still is." Rieley may have been referring to this concert. Reviewer Dale Anderson reported that "Long Promised Road" received great applause and dubbed it "the anthem of the latter-day Beach Boys fan." He also noted that the group "didn't dip back to their surfer days too early or too often. Mike Love stroked something akin to a theremin to produce sirens for 'College Demonstration Time' and Bruce Johnston soloed on his 'Disney Girls (1957)' with nostalgia piano, a little harmony, and such charm that the half verses he forgot seemed to fit anyway . . . Once they got the puny PA system turned up, it was just right for 'Heroes and Villains,' with Al Jardine leading the voices through a conclusion of awesome beauty and complexity."

FRIDAY, MARCH 24, 1972: Roberts Center, Boston College, Boston, MA (8:00 p.m. show)

SATURDAY, MARCH 25, 1972: Alumni Hall, St. John's University, Jamaica, NY (8:00 p.m. show)
The Beach Boys played before a sold-out crowd at St. John's. The set list included "Wouldn't It Be Nice," "Long Promised Road," "Sloop John B," "Take a Load off Your Feet," "Cool, Cool Water," "Disney Girls," "Do It Again," "Heroes and Villains," "Wild Honey" (sung by Blondie), "Surfin' USA," "Surf's Up," "Let the Wind Blow," "Darlin'," "Wonderful/Don't Worry Bill," "God Only Knows," "Help Me Rhonda," "Student Demonstration Time," "Good Vibrations," "California Girls," "Surfer Girl," "I Get Around," and "Fun, Fun, Fun." Mary Caslin of *The Torch* reported, "'Darlin'' definitely brought screams and 'Good Vibrations' created an uproar . . . And they really deserved it, for they truly made an effort of performing one of their best concerts . . . They played together excellently and the backup group with piano, sax, trumpets, and guitarists added even more to the vibrating sounds of their concert."

A good quality tape of this show exists. The highlight of the show was probably a truly rocking five-minute-plus version of "Wild Honey" with a great vocal by Blondie. During the medley of "Wonderful/Don't Worry Bill," the group stopped playing because a fight broke out in the audience. Carl threatened to walk off stage if the people involved didn't cool it. He yelled, "You want to get it straightened out! People are fighting and it's fucking stupid!" Mike chimed in, "If anyone wants to fight, they can go to Madison Square Garden and get paid for it."

SUNDAY, MARCH 26, 1972: Muhlenberg College, Allentown, PA

MONDAY, MARCH 27, 1972: Mayser Center, Franklin and Marshall College, Lancaster, PA (8:00 p.m. show)
This show was marred by a bomb threat after the opening number, which caused a long delay. As a result, the group played a truncated show without an intermission. Nevertheless, Dave Fenster of the *College Reporter* declared the concert "a triumphant return, evidenced by the tumultuous vibrations of Mayser Gym's bleachers and floors . . . the voices blended relatively well, and after some early mixing problems, truly complemented the accompanying instrumentalists."

TUESDAY, MARCH 28, 1972: Maryland State Prison, Baltimore, MD (Afternoon), and Cole Fieldhouse, University of Maryland, College Park, MD (8:00 p.m. show)
The Beach Boys played a free afternoon show at Maryland State Prison prior to their evening concert at the university. The contracts for the latter engagement reveal that the university signed an agreement with the Millard Agency to obtain the group's services on January 11, 1972. The university agreed that the group would be sole headliners, that there would be a short intermission during the show, that they would not sell any merchandise without permission, and that it had a responsibility to advertise the show starting no later than three weeks prior to the concert. The group requested two dressing rooms with a security officer to watch them, a drum riser, two

sound technicians, two roadies, twenty-five amps of power, a standby sound system with four microphones in case their system had a problem, a dolly to move equipment, a grand piano at 440 pitch, a Hammond B-3 organ with one Leslie speaker, two spotlights with different colored gels, and at least two police officers to protect the group. The university agreed to pay the Beach Boys $8,500 before the show and to promise them sixty percent of any profits at the gate over $17,000.

Fan George Heon recalled that although it was not a sell-out there was "almost a full arena. It was a good crowd. It was one of the last shows with Bruce. He sang 'Disney Girls' and his voice broke during the line 'all my life, I've spent the night with dreams of you.' It was very emotional. The encore was one of the most rocking ever. I never dance at shows and I was dancing. Bruce was on bass. Dennis announced the motel they were staying at (Carl was not happy about that) and we went over after the show and Al and Bruce were in the bar. My sister (fifteen at the time) and her friends all got into Dennis' room and he was charming; nothing happened though, at least while she was there."

THURSDAY, MARCH 30, 1972: Alexander Memorial Coliseum, Georgia Tech, Atlanta, GA (8:00 p.m. show)

FRIDAY, MARCH 31, 1972: Memorial Coliseum, Auburn University, Auburn, AL (7:30 p.m. show)

SATURDAY, APRIL 1, 1972: Convention Hall, Miami, FL (8:00 p.m. show)
This was the second show the group played for promoter Jim Koplik's Peace Island East. Koplik had booked their February 1971 Columbus appearance and the group was so impressed by the attendance at that show that they offered him "a present." He recalled, "They said I could book the Beach Boys anywhere I want. And being a kid from the northeast, I always went to Miami Beach. So I booked them at the Convention Center over Easter weekend, which is when all the northeast kids go down to Florida. We sold 7,000 tickets. It was just great. But I always made money with them. They were amazing."

According to Fran Peterman of the *Miami Hurricane*, the crowd at this show was so enthusiastic that they sang along with every song, all but drowning out the band. "With each new selection, the crowd grew more excited and people stood atop their chairs to boogie along with the group. The tremendous applause almost brought the Convention Hall's ceilings down upon the crowd, and the Beach Boys returned for a brief encore."

SUNDAY, APRIL 2, 1972: Fort Homer Hesterly Armory, Tampa, FL (8:00 p.m. show)
The Beach Boys played to a less-than-capacity crowd at the Armory. This marked the last full concert Bruce played with them until 1978. Perry Fulkerson of the *Evening Independent* was disappointed by changes that had taken place in the group since he last saw them in 1966. He felt that in the process, they had lost what made them unique. "Now they are like all of the other rock groups, not only in appearance but in sound. They've added a few new members to their group, none of which I felt really fits in. Their new lead guitarist (Blondie Chaplin) was very loud and hard rockish. Their bass player (Jeff Kaplan) was freaky and their drummer (Ricky Fataar) was too basic. The total volume was extremely loud, out of character, distorting, and nearly covering the rumble of the surf."

FRIDAY, APRIL 14, 1972: Hilton Coliseum, Iowa State University, Ames, IA, with It's a Beautiful Day and the Ides of March (7:30 p.m. show)
In the midst of trying to complete the *Carl and the Passions: So Tough* LP, the group headed to the Midwest for two concerts. They arrived in Des Moines on Friday afternoon, bleary-eyed from a long recording session the night before, and then piled into rental cars for the trip to Ames. Their first show after Bruce's departure was a volatile affair. An audience of 12,000 waited restlessly through two opening acts and numerous delays because of a faulty sound system. By the time the group emerged, the audience was in a hostile mood. Despite requests for oldies, the Beach Boys stuck to their usual set and trouble erupted.

According to Gordon Meyer of the *Ames Daily Tribune*, over 5,000 people walked out during

this thing where he wanted to spread out and try different types of music. He wanted people to appreciate that the Beach Boys was no longer just Brian Wilson music. I think it was faulty logic . . . they were good musicians but I didn't hear anything that unique." Dennis and Carl, however, were enthusiastic about the decision. Dennis told Richard Williams of *Melody Maker*, "We've been playing with the same people for ten years. That's not necessarily a bad thing, but I don't remember ever having this much fun, just listening to the band." Following the conference, the group headed back to the States to continue work on their next LP, to be titled *Carl and the Passions: So Tough*.

Due to the relative success of the *Surf's Up* LP, expectations were high for the next album. Unfortunately, the record that emerged in the spring of 1972 puzzled many people. *Carl and the Passions: So Tough* was not the follow-up smash the group needed and they had no one to blame but themselves. They recorded it hastily between tours, and it showed. After "Feel Flows" and "Long Promised Road," fans were hoping that Carl would carry the Wilson baton, but his contributions to the album simply didn't match up. Dennis, who'd sat out the *Surf's Up* album, contributed a few nice moments, including the epic ballad "Cuddle Up," but the album felt disjointed and slight, a feeling compounded by its short running time. Warner/Reprise showed their lack of faith in the finished product by oddly attaching a reissue of *Pet Sounds* to it . . . to theoretically boost sales.

Nineteen seventy-two also saw the departure of one of the group's principals. The March–April tour of the states was their last with Bruce Johnston until 1978. He had become disenchanted with Jack Rieley and the artistic direction the group was moving towards. Exactly what caused Bruce to leave, and whether he resigned or was fired, remains a murky subject. It is interesting to note that as early as 1969, Carl and Dennis offered Bruce's position in the band to Billy Hinsche, an offer that Billy declined. Bruce told the BBC in early 1974, "the last tour I was on, I kind of felt strange because the group had gotten kind of clubby again. You had two guys, Mike and Al, who were deeply involved in meditation, you had Carl and Ricky that were kind of tight, you had Blondie who was kind of alone and Dennis (who) wasn't quite sure of his role because he had an accident with his hand and he couldn't play drums for a long time and he was trying to get used to the role of finally singing. And so the group kind of felt a little uncomfortable with each other and we just kind of decided that it would be better to not play together and feel comfortable."

The Beach Boys had their own take on Bruce's departure. Brian told *Record World* in June 1973 that Bruce "got into a horrible fight with Jack Rieley. Some dispute and they got into a horrible fight and the next day he was gone." Mike opined to Val Mabbs of *Record Mirror* that Bruce "left because he wasn't too happy about things. It was decided that because of a couple of feelings harbored by different members of the group and the way things went

the performance. Meyer placed the blame on the group. He contended that they tried to play beyond their "capabilities" and that their new songs "came off distorted, jumbled, and in many cases, they were just noise." He dubbed their performance "disappointing" and blasted them as prima donnas who "seemed more concerned about what they were doing than with what the audiences wanted them to do. They acted as if they had made it and didn't have to worry about playing for other people anymore. Even if they didn't feel that way, they certainly played that way."

James Healey of the *Des Moines Register* also believed that the Beach Boys "weren't quite together and the electronic problems magnified their imprecision." However, he placed some of the blame on the audience. Even if the group had been perfect, "nostalgia was rampant and the folks wanted to hear old Beach Boys music, period." According to Healey, things got so heated that "a verbal skirmish erupted between bandsmen and fans over just who was going to dictate the program. Band member Dennis Wilson at one point denounced the audience for its impatience and for shouting during songs. Some in the audience later hurled ugly names at the group." Dennis later apologized for his remarks and dedicated a song to them. Some audience members also recognized that they had gone overboard and approached the Beach Boys at the end of the show to apologize. Despite the problems, Healey noted in a separate review for the *Iowa State Daily* that "the group jelled for the proverbial rousing finale. 'Good Vibrations,' errors and all, sent a shiver through the crowd, which by then had diminished by a few thousand. Those that remained just had to be hardcore fans, so the final trio of tunes—'Little Deuce Coupe,' 'I Get Around,' and 'Fun, Fun, Fun'—summoned from the rockers something approaching delight. Too bad the night couldn't have started there and worked up."

SATURDAY, APRIL 15, 1972: Brewer Fieldhouse, University of Missouri, Columbia, MO (8:00 p.m. show)
Unlike the problematic concert the previous night, this show before a small but appreciative audience of 3,800 was stress-free. Barbara Schuetz of the *Columbia Missourian* applauded their performance: "The Boys were together musically; instruments never drowning out the vocals and the mix was balanced and harmonically well done. From 'Good Vibrations' on, everyone was standing, rocking with the music, packed solid to the stage . . . The group could not get away without an encore, 'Fun, Fun, Fun,' which appropriately summed up the evening."

Following this concert, the group returned to L.A. for last-minute work on their new album. With a week of shows scheduled in the Midwest and then a trip to Europe, the album had to be completed and hastily mixed before they again left for the road.

FRIDAY, APRIL 21, 1972: Memorial Coliseum, University of Kentucky, Lexington, KY (8:00 p.m. show)
Prior to this show, the group gave an interview for the *Kentucky Kernel* newspaper. Discussing their newer material, Carl commented, "Our songs don't pretend to be other than what they say." Dennis added, "When I was sixteen, I was thinking about driving a fast car and going surfing. Now we sing about other things. We sing about what we're into." Ricky, who was sitting nearby, chimed in cryptically, "Being a Beach Boy is nice, except for Dennis Wilson."

SATURDAY, APRIL 22, 1972: Rec Hall, Penn State University, University Park, PA (8:00 p.m. show)
The group's appearance at Penn State marked yet another clash with their audience over what songs should be played. Things got so heated that a pointed exchange took place between members of the audience and the band. An unnamed Beach Boy asked whether many groups came to Penn State to play and when the audience said yes, the group member asked whether they ever came back a second time. An audience member replied, "Not unless we ask them to!" A Beach Boy retorted, "You know, we occasionally give refunds." The audience member shouted back, "Good, please tell us where the lines are forming!"

Two students who attended weighed in with their view of who was to blame. John Mort took the Beach Boys' side. In a letter to *The Daily Collegian*, he denounced the audience as "one of the worst and tasteless and least sophisticated I have ever witnessed at a concert anywhere." He accused them of wanting only "to hear nothing but a juvenile exhibition of surfing songs and a revival of hot-rod mania." John Vitkow, however, blamed the group for the bad feeling in the hall. He attacked their "endless pauses between songs, the mumbled tones of the groups' spokesman, as well as the lack of any definitive sign of professionalism as reflected by the performers." He also criticized the decision to stick with new music rather than playing hits, a decision he believed showed the "indifference of the group to the needs of an entertainment-starved audience."

SUNDAY, APRIL 23, 1972: Ferris State College, Big Rapids, MI (8:00 p.m. show)
This was a nostalgic show for Al, who briefly attended school here in 1961.

MONDAY, APRIL 24, 1972: Finch Fieldhouse, Central Michigan University, Mount Pleasant, MI (9:00 p.m. show)

TUESDAY, APRIL 25, 1972: Brown County Veterans Memorial Arena, Greenbay, WI (8:00 p.m. show)
This concert, sponsored by St. Norbert College, was again considered a disappointment because of the band's unwillingness to cater to nostalgia. Mike Bielmeier of the *St. Norbert Times* commented, "I'm not saying that the Beach Boys didn't perform well, for they did. What I am saying, quite simply, is that they didn't play what the audience wanted them to play. The night started off well with the band resurrecting 'Wouldn't It Be Nice.' The crowd seemed quite pleased with this. But from then on throughout the first set it was all down hill with the exceptions of 'Sloop John B' and 'Surfin' USA.' The second set was much of the same frustration with only sporadic bursts of nostalgia coming from the mammoth speaker system." Bielmeier noted that when the group finally let loose with oldies during the encore, a large part of the audience had left the arena.

THURSDAY, APRIL 27, 1972: Agora, Columbus, OH (Two shows at 7:00 and 10:00 p.m.)

FRIDAY, APRIL 28, 1972: John Carroll University, University Heights, OH (8:30 p.m. show)
The group performed at the kickoff of Spring Weekend. Tim Russert, future anchor of NBC TV's *Meet the Press*, was student union president at the time and was instrumental in arranging this appearance.

SATURDAY, APRIL 29, 1972: Elliot Hall of Music, Purdue University, Lafayette, IN (Two shows at 7:00 and 9:30 p.m.)
These appear to have been the last shows of the short tour.

SUNDAY, MAY 7, 1972: Saarlandhalle, Saarbruecken, Germany
The Beach Boys headed back to Europe for the second time in 1972. Musicians that accompanied them included Daryl Dragon (keyboards), Dennis Dragon (percussion), Billy Hinsche (guitar/piano), and Ed Carter (bass).

MONDAY, MAY 8, 1972: Jahrhunderthalle, Frankfurt, Germany (8:00 p.m. show)

TUESDAY, MAY 9, 1972: Deutsches Museum, Munich, Germany
The set list for this show consisted of "Sloop John B," "Long Promised Road," "Wouldn't It Be Nice," "God Only Knows," "Here She Comes," "Wonderful/Don't Worry Bill," "Do It Again," "Heroes and Villains," "Wild Honey," "Surfin' USA," "Cool, Cool Water," "Let the Wind Blow," "I've Got a Friend," "Surf's Up," "Darlin'," "You Need a Mess of Help to Stand Alone," "Student Demonstration Time," "Good Vibrations," "Help Me Rhonda," "I Get Around," "Fun, Fun, Fun," "Johnny B. Goode," and "Fun, Fun, Fun." While not played at this concert, "Caroline, No" and "Cotton Fields" were also performed on the tour.

WEDNESDAY, MAY 10, 1972: Villa Louvigny, Luxembourg (10:00 p.m. show)
The group performed a live concert for Radio Luxembourg. Tony Tyler of *New Musical Express* reported, "There have been some heavy changes in the Beach Boys since their last visit to

with Bruce developing a solo career it made it more or less an uncompromising situation." Dennis told Martin Lewis of *New Musical Express*, "musically we didn't . . . appreciate each other, so one day we both said 'OK, that's it.' He's a good guy but he was writing stuff for a solo artist . . . we're a band." Chip Rachlin noted, "Bruce didn't really have a buddy in

> "I didn't think it was a good financial move on the Beach Boys' part to move an entire studio over to Holland to record there. I thought it was a crazy, stupid idea and I said 'I'm not going to go . . ."
>
> —Stephen Desper

the group and he was sort of the odd man out. He didn't get along with Jack Rieley and he could be a little meddlesome." Bruce was gone before the group returned to the road on April 14.

Another issue in the band's dynamic was Dennis's undefined role. Since injuring his hand the previous summer, he often seemed lost onstage. He strolled around, sometimes

THE BEACH BOYS IN CONCERT

Europe . . . Dennis Wilson's move from drums to front-line vocals has strengthened the Beach Boys' already tight vocal textures. Dennis also played a solo-piano-accompanied piece of his own composition—unrecorded as yet—called 'A Friend of Mine' which was really moving and received some of the warmest applause of the night." Tyler also noted that Carl had "developed in confidence enormously and now resembles brother Brian in more ways than one, being totally responsible for the cueing and (I suspect) most of the arrangements . . . There's no doubt who's the kingpin, musically speaking."

THURSDAY, MAY 11, 1972: Martinihal, Groningen, Netherlands (8:15 p.m. show)
About 2,000 fans attended this concert. The *Nieuwsblad van het Noorden* reported, "What's remarkable about the Beach Boys is that their already years old songs still appeal to audiences. With regard to their musical approach and lyrics . . . there's no progression to be found. We could hear that yesterday evening (in their performance of) their new single, 'You Need a Mess of Help,' and in one song from the yet to be released album called 'Here She Comes' (written and sung by drummer Ricky Fataar). Nothing new under the sun and fortunately for the Beach Boys that's not so bad. What these Boys do is perfect and one can be satisfied with that."

FRIDAY, MAY 12, 1972: Forest-National, Brussels, Belgium (Canceled)

SATURDAY, MAY 13, 1972: Sportspaleis Ahoy, Rotterdam, Netherlands (8:15 p.m. show)
Thom Olink of the *Leidsche Dagblad* reported, "The Beach Boys, with drummer Ricky Fataar and singer-guitarist Blondie Chaplin sing old and new [songs], a bit of everything. Dennis, the oldest, and most unsettled Wilson . . . therefore has nothing to do. During the concert in the Ahoy-hal in Rotterdam he was woefully intoxicated searching for his spot on the stage. He played one solo (on the piano) 'My Friend' . . . Blondie clearly is an inspiration, an advocate of the harder line in the music . . . A sublime bass and solo guitarist, hard and to the point voice-wise. The fusion 'Wonderbill'—Wonderful (from *Smiley Smile*) and a Fataar-Chaplin composition—worked on all fronts. Carl sang beautifully, all evening by the way. Wilson-cousin Mike Love is stable and in good voice . . . For the Ahoy-happening . . . there were more people on stage than showed up. A horn section was announced. They couldn't be heard, but they could very well have been there, because the stage was filled with 'Flame'-leftovers, and piano, drums, congas, and timpani-playing roadies and publicity people. It seems they want to go in all kinds of directions . . . What will this lead to?"

Dennis and Blondie Chaplin onstage in Rotterdam, May 13, 1972. Photo: Gabriel Witteveen

1972

TUESDAY, MAY 16, 1972: City Hall, Newcastle, England (Two shows at 6:30 and 9:30 p.m.)

The group flew to London on Monday and headed to the BBC TV studios to tape an appearance on *The Old Grey Whistle Test*. They sang live vocals over a backing track for "You Need a Mess of Help to Stand Alone." They also held a press conference for U.K. music publications. The U.K. concerts began the next day in Newcastle. Billy Hinsche recalled that like most of their recent tours of the States, it was a no-frills affair. "It was a bus tour. The halls were sometimes small, almost like community centers. One had a huge pipe organ behind the stage and Daryl played it on 'Good Vibrations.' It was an awesome sound."

THURSDAY, MAY 18, 1972: Kinetic Circus, Birmingham, England (8:00 p.m.)

New Musical Express reporter Martin Lewis, who'd been skeptical of the group's ability to deliver live, reported that in Birmingham the group "proved their strength beyond a doubt. With steaming zest they zipped through such goodies as 'Heroes and Villains,' 'God Only Knows,' and 'Do It Again.' The sound was rich, fat and satisfying, with Carl, Al, and Blondie laying down thick, gutty guitar sounds over back up musicians, Dragon Brothers. Their vocal blends were delivered in all their fullness, falsettos, et al." Mark Plummer of *Melody Maker* declared the concert "one of the best gigs I have been along to see for a long time . . . You forget how many great songs they have written. . . . They have to be one of the most exciting live bands seen in a long time, and the audience was right there behind them."

FRIDAY, MAY 19, 1972: Belle Vue, Manchester, England (8:00 p.m.)

Melody Maker reported that "numbers old and new were played, the new single, 'You Need a Mess of Help to Stand Alone' coming over far stronger and much more exciting live . . . 'Surf's Up' showed the ends they have gone to get the best sounds possible on stage . . . The vocal parts on 'Surf's Up' are quite amazing. The harmonies are note-perfect, and only once did Carl slip as he sang that strange little hymn part ending with 'domini.'"

After the show, Mike told a reporter that he enjoyed "doing the old songs plenty, but I also like doing the new ones. I don't think there are enough new songs in the show. We're recording a double album in Holland this summer, so I think then we'll get a lot of new material rehearsed and ready for the stage."

SATURDAY, MAY 20, 1972: Liverpool Empire, Liverpool, England (Two shows at 6:15 and 8:35 p.m.)

SUNDAY, MAY 21, 1972: Leicester DeMontfort Hall, Leicester, England (8:00 p.m. show)

MONDAY, MAY 22, 1972: Top Rank Suite, Reading, England (Two shows at 7:30 and 10:00 p.m.)

According to *Record Mirror*, the group put on a flat show and "appeared to be indifferent to the somewhat strangely assorted Top Rank audience." Mike later admitted that he wasn't enjoying the U.K. tour that much "basically because we're playing awful bars here, like that Top Rank Reading with people talking and drinking."

TUESDAY, MAY 23, 1972: Top Rank Suite, Bristol, England

WEDNESDAY, MAY 24, 1972: Dome, Brighton, England (Two shows at 6:30 and 9:00 p.m.)

Daryl Dragon recalled that on this tour, "they kept having me pose with them for pictures and they literally asked me to be a Beach Boy. But I told them I would rather not because I don't sing and I don't think I have enough of the Beach Boys harmony thing in my gut to pull it off . . . But they liked the way I was capturing a lot of their album cuts instrumentally so they could reproduce them on stage. So they actually took a lot of promotional pictures of me in the band in Holland. I told them please put me in the back so you can edit me out when I decide not to become a Beach Boy."

U.K. tour ad, 1972. Ian Rusten Collection

playing piano, sometimes singing, sometimes not. He often appeared onstage drunk, occasionally delivering inappropriate remarks. There were times he'd just leave the stage mid-show and disappear. On the band's May European tour, a reviewer from *Phonograph* magazine noted that Dennis "looked barely interested in what was going down. He spent most of the time wandering vaguely around the stage, hands thrust deep into his jean pockets. When it came time for him to help with the harmonizing, he inched up to the mike (but not too close) and opened and closed his mouth at the appropriate moments. I couldn't tell if he was actually singing or not." Nevertheless, Dennis remained the "sex symbol," and reviewers often noted that he received the most applause. And when he did perform it could be mesmerizing. Future star Elvis Costello attended one of the 1972 U.K. shows and recalled Dennis' performance of "Cuddle Up" as the highlight of the concert.

When the Beach Boys' 1972 European tour was over,

THE BEACH BOYS IN CONCERT

they did not return to the U.S. At Jack Rieley's suggestion, it was decided the group would record their next album in Holland. The controversial move resulted in the departure of longtime engineer Stephen Desper, who was replaced by Steve Moffitt. Desper recalled, "Mike had met Steve Moffitt somewhere or other through his interest in Transcendental Meditation. He was getting more and more into that and he was getting rid of people in the Beach Boys organization that didn't meet his criteria, which was that you had to meditate. I didn't think it was a good financial move on the Beach Boys' part to move an entire studio over to Holland to record there. I thought it was a crazy, stupid idea and I said 'I'm not going to go . . . You're just going to go over there and get stoned and get sidetracked with the ways of Amsterdam and it will be more problems than it is worth. But Jack Rieley was instrumental in getting them to go to Holland and make an album there. Simultaneously, Mike was getting more friendly with Steve Moffitt, who had done some speaker research, and he talked Michael into using his control-room monitor speakers, which I didn't like at all. I resented being told what monitors to use in the studio and I made that apparent to them. Mike Love was becoming more and more insistent that everyone in the organization meditate, and I told him flat out that I wasn't going to meditate. I was very happy in the religion that I had and I wasn't going to change. So Steve Moffitt replaced me basically because of my religious beliefs."

SATURDAY, MAY 27, 1972: Royal Festival Hall, London, England (Two shows at 6:15 and 9:00 p.m.)

Micheal Oldfield of *Melody Maker* knew it was going to be a great show when the band walked onstage and launched into "Heroes and Villains," playing every note perfectly. He gushed, "Those records that sound so complicated they can only be repeated in a recording studio can be and are done live . . . there's no West Coast surfer tininess about them now: they're a ten-piece band that can call on three keyboards, three percussion, and four guitarists when they want to rock." *Phonograph Magazine* was also impressed by the changes to the band, noting that Blondie and Ricky "don't make radical changes in the sound but their presence is felt. When Blondie Chaplin switches over from bass to lead you'll notice a few licks that didn't used to be there before, but would have been fine if they were . . . for me the highlight of the show was the much-deserved encore. I'd been waiting all night to hear 'I Get Around' and 'Fun, Fun, Fun' and the Boys wisely saved them for the end. It was one of those great encores with everyone leaping around *joie de vivre* style."

SUNDAY, MAY 28, 1972: Great Western Express Spring Bank Holiday Festival, Bardney, England, with Sly and the Family Stone, Lindisfarne, Slade, Spencer Davis, Monty Python, the Average White Band, Brewers Droop, Focus, and the Natural Acoustic Band

The Beach Boys closed day three of this four-day festival. Artists that played on the other three days included Rory Gallagher, Joe Cocker, Don McLean, Humble Pie, the Faces, Ry Cooder, Genesis, Billy Joel, and Sha Na Na. Despite the impressive talent arrayed, many in the press declared the Beach Boys the best of the lot. *Melody Maker* gushed that they "were so good that at least one of your correspondents lost his voice from singing along and shouting requests . . . The vocals and turbulent guitar of Blondie Chaplin were a revelation, and the vocal harmonies were so pure and faultless that they made the field feel like some acoustically perfect concert hall." Ray Telford of *Sounds* commented, "The most obvious change in the Beach Boys of late has been in their building up of an incredibly powerful rhythm section. Certainly in the past, one of the Beach Boys' biggest hang-ups in performing live has been in achieving a faithful reproduction of their recorded sound but now that the band has a more solid foundation this no longer seems to be an obstacle."

SATURDAY, JUNE 3, 1972: Crystal Palace Concert Bowl Third Garden Party, Crystal Palace Bowl, London, England, with David Blue, Joe Cocker, Melanie, Richie Havens and Sha Na Na, hosted by Keith Moon (12:00 to 9:00 p.m.)

This was a special "happening" hosted by Keith Moon, with each act playing for an hour. NBC TV filmed the concert and a one-hour special aired in the U.S. on June 28 as *Good Vibrations from London*. It featured the group performing "Do It Again," a fantastic "Wild Honey" sung by Blondie, and "Help Me Rhonda," with Elton John on piano.

For the benefit of the TV crews, all the acts performed a full rehearsal on June 2, a beautiful sunny day. However, on June 3 it rained almost the entire day, making the taping difficult and diluting the sound. The group was not happy and announced that they considered it "the worst set of conditions for playing in ten years of live appearances." Tony Stewart of *New Musical Express* argued that the Beach Boys still put on a great show. He noted that although they played mostly oldies "with the new rhythm section, the tunes were put over with more funk and good old unsophisticated balls."

Although *New Musical Express* announced that the group had plans to play additional U.K. shows in July and film a special for BBC TV's *In Concert* series, in the end none of this took place. The Crystal Palace Bowl concert was their last European appearance until 1975. The Beach Boys may not have been pleased with the show, but Dennis Dragon recalled it fondly. "I think the greatest experience I had with those dudes was playing the concert outside of London in the rain. Keith Moon showed up in a small boat (totally drunk) and he proceeded to jam with me on a couple of tunes. We broke a bunch of percussion instruments, and it was worth it!"

WEDNESDAY, AUGUST 16, 1972: Mississippi River Festival, Edwardsville, IL (8:30 p.m. show)

After completing an all-night recording session for *Holland*, the Beach Boys flew to the States on

Tuesday. There were changes to the backing band. The horn section was now gone and instead musician Charles Lloyd filled in on saxophone and flute. Ed Carter sat out this tour and Billy Hinsche subbed for him on bass. Toni Shearer rejoined on piano, while Daryl Dragon remained on keyboards and synthesizers. Mike Kowalski played extra percussion. The set list included many cuts from recent albums, including two rarely performed ballads by Dennis, "Only With You" and "Cuddle Up." One new addition to the show was a cover of the Rolling Stones standard "Jumpin' Jack Flash," which became the closing number for the next several years. Mike Love explained to a reporter in November that the song was added "just for shock value . . . people don't leave saying, 'Wow, the Beach Boys,' they leave thinking it was a great concert. I've wanted to put it in the show for a long time, because it's a good show piece."

THURSDAY, AUGUST 17, 1972: Auditorium Theatre, Chicago, IL (8:00 p.m. show)
David Witz of the *Chicago Daily News* reported, "In the first half, the Boys ran through new things ('Only With You,' a lovely Dennis ballad), a Flame song, 'Mama, Won't You Hold On?' and favorites such as 'Wild Honey,' 'Sloop John B,' and 'Do It Again,' closing with a high spirited 'Surfin' USA.' After intermission and a voter registration bid, the second half started with a spacey intro to 'Cool Water,' washed into 'Surf's Up' and 'Cotton Fields,' and ended with a smashing 'Good Vibrations' . . . Coming back for the first of two encores, Dennis yelled out, 'Whaddya wanna hear?' Roar. Everyone in the hall screamed out titles of Beach Boys songs . . . 'Help Me Rhonda' had a wild solo from Captain Keyboard who, with deadpan face, jumped all over the piano like a rocking Jerry Lee Lewis. Segue right into 'I Get Around' and off to screams. Back on stage, all the lights on, and closing with a dynamite 'Fun, Fun, Fun.'"

FRIDAY, AUGUST 18, 1972: Dillon Stadium, Hartford, CT, with the Kinks, the Phlorescent Leech, and Eddie and the Doors (7:00 p.m. show)
The Beach Boys and the Kinks were both represented by the Millard Agency and were booked for a few joint concerts. This show featured a particularly "nostalgic" lineup with the Doors (who had chosen to carry on without Jim Morrison) and Flo and Eddie of the Turtles rounding out the bill. The concert was marred by heavy rain, which led to a long delay before the Beach Boys came onstage. Nevertheless, Ron Georgeff of the *Hartford Times* declared the concert a success and singled out "Blondie Chaplin for his lead guitar and Daryl Dragon for his keyboard playing, especially his handling of the Moog synthesizer which added many happy moments."

SATURDAY, AUGUST 19, 1972: New Jersey State Fairgrounds, Hamilton Township, NJ, with the Kinks and Looking Glass (7:30 p.m.)
The show was supposed to take place at Roosevelt Stadium but the venue was changed. The group spent the night in Allentown, where they played the next day.

SUNDAY, AUGUST 20, 1972: Allentown Fairgrounds, Allentown, PA, with the Kinks and Orleans (7:00 p.m. show)
According to Ed Roach, Dennis had a "knockdown drag-out fight" with Ray Davies of the Kinks after this show. "They fought over this groupie and [the road crew] took Dennis away all bloody. They really fought it out and I didn't see Dennis again till we got to New York . . . and I knocked on his door and the woman, that he had the fight with Ray Davies over, answered the door of his hotel room!"

MONDAY, AUGUST 21, 1972: Nassau Coliseum, Uniondale, NY, with the Kinks (8:00 p.m.)
This show was a sellout that grossed $96,000.

WEDNESDAY, AUGUST 23, AND THURSDAY, AUGUST 24, 1972: Boston Common, Boston, MA, with the Boston Philharmonia Orchestra (One 6:00 p.m. show each night)
Large crowds turned out for these outdoor shows (there were over 14,000 on the first night). The presence of thirty-eight musicians from the Boston Philharmonic Orchestra there to accompany the group made these shows especially memorable. Daryl Dragon wrote out arrangements for the

While the band was playing gigs in May, Moffitt completed a makeshift studio in Holland. Houses were rented for Mike and Al in Haarlem, while Carl rented one in Hilversum. Dennis did not like the climate in Holland and had management look for

"Mike Love was becoming more and more insistent that everyone in the organization meditate, and I told him flat out that I wasn't going to meditate. I was very happy in the religion that I had and I wasn't going to change."

a place for him on Tenerife in the Canary Islands. Brian eventually made the trip as well, renting a house in Laren.

Al explained to Tony Tyler of *New Musical Express* that the group decided to record in the Netherlands because "Number one: we're here. Number two: our equipment is here.

Nineteen seventy-two ad with the Jack Rieley–inspired slogan, "They've Changed Even More Than You." Ian Rusten Collection

Rickie Fataar on steel guitar at Clemson University, November 4, 1972. Special Collections, Clemson University Libraries

orchestra. The Wednesday set consisted of "Marcella," "Wouldn't It Be Nice," "Long Promised Road," "Here She Comes," "Heroes and Villains," "Only With You," "Wild Honey," "Surfin' USA," "Student Demonstration Time," "God Only Knows," "Let the Wind Blow," "Cuddle Up," "Wonderful/Don't Worry Bill," "Surf's Up," "Do It Again," "Sloop John B," "Good Vibrations," "I Get Around," "Fun, Fun, Fun," and "Jumping Jack Flash."

FRIDAY, AUGUST 25, 1972: Hampton Roads Coliseum, Hampton, VA, with Brownsville Station (8:00 p.m. show)
Reviewer Steve Abramson of the *William and Mary Flat Hat* was impressed by the group's "vocal pyrotechnics" and bemoaned the fact that there seemed to be very few new fans at the show. He was pleasantly surprised that the group played "'Wonderful' because it represents an experimental period in their career that was unpopular five years ago. But the complex vocal workouts in this, 'Heroes and Villains,' and 'Surf's Up' . . . and 'Good Vibrations' proved to me that the Beach Boys are the masters of vocal arrangements."

SUNDAY, AUGUST 27, 1972: Eastside Speedway, Waynesboro, VA
After a rare day off, the group played in Waynesboro, where they spent the night. The next day the five Beach Boys and Jack Rieley headed to Wilmington, Delaware for business meetings while the rest of the musicians headed to Baltimore.

WEDNESDAY, AUGUST 30, 1972: Merriweather Post Pavilion, Columbia, MD (7:30 p.m. show)
A restless audience turned up at this show. There was constant talking while the Beach Boys played their recent music and the crowd only settled down when they turned to oldies. Richard Harrington of the *Evening Star* noted that the show "started with their latest single 'Marcella' and ended with a foot stomping dancing in the aisles rendition of the Rolling Stones' song 'Jumping Jack Flash' . . . Changing with the times, as always, the Beach Boys let their band take the spotlight occasionally and it becomes very obvious that by doing so, they avoid tiring of doing the same songs. Instrumentally the band is as hard as any, occasionally using four guitars at once."

Fan George Heon recalled, "Dennis was strange during this show. The Captain and Tenille were playing with them and Dennis kept trying to push Daryl Dragon out of his seat. He pulled the seat out from under him and then pushed the electric piano over, laughing the whole time, but the Captain was a good sport. Mike got mad at the bouncers at one point for stopping people from dancing . . . and the crowd roared its approval."

FRIDAY, SEPTEMBER 1, 1972: Wildwood Convention Hall, Wildwood, NJ (8:00 p.m. show)
The group flew to Philadelphia on August 31 and drove to Wildwood, where they spent the next two nights.

SUNDAY, SEPTEMBER 3, 1972: Convention Hall, Ocean City, MD (Two shows at 7:00 and 10:00 p.m.)
George Heon, who attended one of the two concerts, recalled, "It was a good show—I remember Carl singing "Surf's Up" . . . There was a parking garage overlooking the water below the venue. After the show we met Mike, Al, and Dennis sitting around the garage, just talking to anyone . . . very friendly. Al answered my questions about the *Smile* album, saying it was coming out soon. Dennis talked to my sister but left after a few minutes. Mike was friendly and answered all my teenage fanboy questions and gave me his attention."

MONDAY, SEPTEMBER 4, 1972: Pine Knob Music Theater, Clarkston, MI (7:30 p.m. show)
This was the first of many appearances at this venue outside Detroit.

WEDNESDAY, NOVEMBER 1, 1972: Carolina Coliseum, Columbia, SC (8:00 p.m. show)
The group began a three-week East Coast tour. Dennis' wife Barbara accompanied him for part of it. Also present were Ed Carter on bass, guitar, and congas; Daryl Dragon on organ, vibes, and synthesizer; Toni Shearer on piano and vocals; and Mike Kowalski on extra percussion.

1972

THURSDAY, NOVEMBER 2, 1972: Varsity Gym, Appalachian State University, Boone, NC (8:00 p.m. show)
The Beach Boys were extremely well received by the Appalachian student body. According to Dave Wright of *The Appalachian*, "Mixing old standards with exciting new material, they held the crowd for the entire two hours . . . a time that seemed all too brief . . . The addition of several stage musicians gave the group an added depth and versatility, especially in the areas of vocal harmony and guitar work . . . But for the most part, the evening belonged to two brothers, their cousin, and a good friend from Hawthorne, California, who gave those of us in the audience a concert that stirred the memory and touched the soul."

FRIDAY, NOVEMBER 3, 1972: Diddle Arena, Western Kentucky University, Bowling Green, KY (8:30 p.m. show)
Over 7,000 fans attended this show and were on their feet for the opening number "Sloop John B." The band followed with a series of recent numbers and lost the crowd. According to Scott Johnston of the *College Heights Herald*, "throughout the first set . . . many people were chattering away, throwing Frisbees, and otherwise entertaining themselves . . . Those in the audience who wanted to hear and enjoy this new dimension of the group really could not; there was simply too much noise coming from the inconsiderate crowd." The second set was more politely received, but Dennis still had to lecture the audience that "the concert experience would be heightened for both the group and the crowd if the non-essential communication was curtailed. In other words . . . shut up!"

Carl sings at East Carolina College, November 5, 1972.
Courtesy of Joyner Library, East Carolina University

SATURDAY, NOVEMBER 4, 1972: Littlejohn Coliseum, Clemson University, Clemson, SC (8:00 p.m. show)
The group played to a sizable crowd, but failed to sell out the Coliseum. Their newer material received a tepid crowd reaction, prompting Mike to lecture the audience that the band was not willing to only perform oldies, "because we're great today. And I'm saying this with all the humility I can muster. Plus we would be bored. We'd rather set up some films and a jukebox and just sit there and watch ourselves."

SUNDAY, NOVEMBER 5, 1972: East Carolina College, Greenville, NC (Afternoon show)
Peter Greenspan of *The Fountainhead* noted that the "performance featured many recent songs such as 'Long Promised Road' and 'Marcella' plus several unreleased cuts from their next album, like 'Leaving This Town' and 'Only With You.' The encore consisted of two oldies from their successful past and then a brilliant take off on Mick Jagger's Rolling Stones hit 'Jumping Jack Flash.'"

MONDAY, NOVEMBER 6, 1972: Coliseum, University of Georgia, Athens, GA (8:00 p.m. show)
This show attracted a near-capacity audience. However, the majority came to hear oldies and sat on their hands until the band played them. Charles Orck of the *Red and Black* expressed the majority view when he noted, "with every new song they played, I as well hundreds around me groaned in disappointment." However, student Steven Ernst declared that "the audience ripped off the Beach Boys . . . The audience was just disgustingly like outdated parents who refuse to acknowledge that people change, that kids don't stay the same, that people outgrow certain things and move into new ones, who refuse to listen even when their attention is specially requested and who insist that everyone should grow up in their image."

WEDNESDAY, NOVEMBER 8, 1972: Minneapolis Armory, Minneapolis, MN (8:00 p.m. show)
Rich DeYoung of *The Carletonian* argued that a lukewarm audience response led the band to

Number three: our personnel are all here. So why rush back to the States to do an album, which has always been the case? Let's just stay here and settle down—the weather's beautiful." The group settled in and spent the next several months recording an album they simply titled *Holland*. Recording in the Netherlands was not without difficulties. Steve Desper recalled, "Steve Moffitt had an in with the brand new console company called Olive. They were one of the first companies to come up with an automated console, but it was very, very troublesome. And the Beach Boys took delivery of one of

Dennis, Carl, and Mike performing in Atlanta, November 6, 1972. Photo: Ray Taylor

deliver a "flat" show. "'Heroes and Villains' came across like barbershop duet. Al Jardine couldn't hold his falsetto for 'Don't Worry Baby' (heart-breaker!) . . . I did like 'Long Promised Road' and 'Student Demonstration Time' but the set as a whole was disappointing . . . Fortunately, the second set was much better . . . With the encore of 'Surfin' USA,' 'Fun, Fun, Fun' and (no this is not a misprint) 'Jumping Jack Flash' they clobbered the house for the first time all night."

THURSDAY, NOVEMBER 9, 1972: Dane County Memorial Coliseum, Madison, WI, with Poco (8:00 p.m. show)
Over 5,000 fans attended this concert. Michael Bauman of *The Wisconsin State Journal* criticized the Beach Boys for being out of tune for half the show and frequently "going through the motions" and argued opener Poco put on a better show. However, he admitted that the crowd did not agree with him and they gave the Beach Boys a standing ovation.

FRIDAY, NOVEMBER 10, 1972: Xavier University, Cincinnati, OH (8:30 p.m. show)

SATURDAY, NOVEMBER 11, 1972: Ford Auditorium, Detroit, MI (7:30 p.m. show)

MONDAY, NOVEMBER 13, 1972: Niagara University, Lewiston, NY (8:00 p.m. show)

TUESDAY, NOVEMBER 14, 1972: Palace Theater, Albany, NY (9:00 p.m. show)
A large crowd turned up for this show despite an early blizzard. Bob Altman of the *Albany Student Press* reported, "The audience was on their feet for most of the second set as the Beach Boys and band ran through mind blowing renditions of 'Surfin' USA,' 'Daddy Took Her T-Bird Away,' and 'Help Me Rhonda.' This all turned out to be mere foreplay as the Palace reached a climax with Mike Love doing 'Jumpin' Jack Flash.' It takes quite a band to pull off that song and the Beach Boys did it right. 'California Girls' and 'Barbara Ann' were saved for a rousing encore."

WEDNESDAY, NOVEMBER 15, 1972: Fordham University, Bronx, NY (8:30 p.m. show)
This show attracted about 5,000 fans. Carl was not happy with the venue, criticizing the stage as 'restrictive and stocky.' The poor acoustics may have affected their performance. Gerry Meagher of the *Fordham Ram* noted, "It was just as well that everybody was singing along for the Beach Boys have performed much better. I doubt if they've been worse." Meagher declared the highlight of the show to be the moment when Mike Love, "in the midst of a superb version of Jagger's 'Jack Flash,' ripped off his work shirt to reveal a tank top with a frappe (the country version of a malted) embossed on it. One girl appeared on the verge of orgasm as he flipped a red rose to her."

THURSDAY, NOVEMBER 16, 1972: War Memorial Auditorium, Syracuse, NY (8:00 p.m. show)
Daryl Dragon recalled, "Sometimes there were problems with Dennis Wilson because of his drinking. At one show he called out, 'Carl Wilson's hotel room is #4800. See you tonight!' . . . that's the kind of stuff that would happen sometimes."

FRIDAY, NOVEMBER 17, 1972: Barton Hall, Cornell University, Ithaca, NY (8:30 p.m. show)
This concert was attended by 8,000 fans. Lawrence Bassoff, of the *Cornell Daily Sun*, gushed that the group "performed at their tightest, nay most casual, peak, mixing older, newer, and

Mike with Toni Shearer at the University of Georgia, November 6, 1972. Photo: Ray Taylor

yet to be released material deftly. The trademark rock choir harmony; credible stomping-rock instrumentation, notably on 'Student Demonstration Time;' their standard 'surprise' showstopper-closer 'Jumpin' Jack Flash;' and Mike Love's golly-gee commentary (right down to his white socks) made for a near flawless two hours of real American rock 'n' roll music."

SATURDAY, NOVEMBER 18, 1972: Music Hall, Boston, MA (Two shows at 7:30 and 10:30 p.m.)

SUNDAY, NOVEMBER 19, 1972: Capitol Theatre, Passaic, NJ (Two shows at 7:30 and 11:00 p.m.)
The group decided their follow-up to *Holland* would be a live album and began recording their shows. Both performances on this night were taped and some tracks appeared on the 1973 *Beach Boys in Concert* album. The songs used were "Wouldn't It Be Nice," "Let the Wind Blow," "Marcella," "Don't Worry Baby," and "Good Vibrations."

TUESDAY, NOVEMBER 21, 1972: New Haven Coliseum, New Haven, CT (8:00 p.m. show)
The Beach Boys were the first rock act to play at the newly built coliseum, which replaced the New Haven Arena. Around 7,000 people turned out. Unfortunately, the group was delayed in arriving and did not take the stage till 10 p.m. They needed to depart the venue by 11:40, so much to the crowd's disappointment, they departed with many oldies left unplayed.

WEDNESDAY, NOVEMBER 22, 1972: DAR Constitution Hall, Washington, DC (Two shows at 8:30 and 11:30 p.m.)
Paul J. Dallman of the *Evening Star* attended the first of two concerts at Constitution Hall and was impressed by the group's effective mix of old and new music. He dubbed the show "a ten-year

the first consoles Olive made in Holland and had nothing but trouble with it." Much of June was wasted trying to get the makeshift studio up and running, but the group remained enthusiastic about the experience. Carl told a reporter from *MuziekKrant OOR*, "It's very peaceful here and the sphere is relaxed. I'm glad that it's exactly as I imagined it would be when I made the plan to go and live here for a while. I convinced the others that it would be good for all of us to catch our breath in the Netherlands and to get some new impulses . . . the truth is that we want to quietly work on a new album, and we think we need about three months for it in a calm environment."

The group's enthusiasm was soon tempered by their record label's lukewarm response to the material. When Warner/Reprise executives first heard the proposed album that August, the label expressed dismay over Brian's diminished role. The move to the Netherlands had not resulted in a return to form for Brian, who concentrated on a bizarre fairy tale he titled "Mt. Vernon and Fairway." When Carl questioned the pseudo-suite's appropriateness for the album, Brian lost interest and absented himself from further recording sessions. The label rejected the proposed LP, insisting that the band drop a song by Blondie and Ricky called "We Got Love" that didn't sound "Beach Boys" enough and replace it with something more commercial, preferably written by Brian. In an oft-told story, Van Dyke Parks, now an executive at Warner Brothers, was asked to cajole Brian into writing a tune to save the album. The two worked on a song that Brian had partially written years earlier. The Beach Boys quickly recorded it that November. The legendary track, "Sail on Sailor," turned out to be another Brian Wilson classic and its addition to the LP satisfied the label execs. *Holland*, released in January 1973, would be the last LP of new material that the Beach Boys would produce for four years.

retrospective rock concert. It's done well, with good sound mixing, decent lighting, and talent and taste. They are able to approximate their studio sound on stage, quite an accomplishment in itself . . . They'll probably be filling halls 10 years from now. See you there."

While the band did fill the hall for the first show, the second concert was a big disappointment, only attracting 400 people. George Heon, who attended both shows, declared it a better performance and recalled, "They played a set just as long as the first show and really put a lot into it. I remember 'We Got Love' and Dennis' 'The River Song' got played. Mike talked about the new *Holland* album."

THURSDAY, NOVEMBER 23, 1972: Carnegie Hall, New York, NY (Two shows at 8:00 and 11:30 p.m.) The Beach Boys grossed $34,000 for these Thanksgiving shows. Both were recorded for possible inclusion on the proposed live LP, but the performances were not used. Two songs, however, appeared on the *Endless Harmony* CD in 1998. Fred Kirby of *Variety* attended the early show and noted, "There was plenty of fun during the evening, including the comments of Love, clad in an orange and gold mandarin outfit, and such oldies as 'Sloop John B,' 'Darlin', ' 'Wouldn't It Be Nice,' 'I Get Around,' and 'Help Me Rhonda' . . . The combination of old and new is keeping the Beach Boys on top. The clogged aisles and standing response of the young audience bear this out." The 11:30 show, however, was a tense affair. According to Henry Edwards of the *New York Times*, a number of people actually charged the stage, demanding that the band stop playing new music and switch to oldies. Mike Love, dressed in a "salmon colored meditation outfit and a crocheted beanie," stopped the show and "gave the crowd a firm talking to. Using some choice language along the way, he finally remarked 'Don't be a bunch of punks!'"

OTHER 1972 CONCERTS

In the spring of 1972, Carl played a number of shows at hospitals and prisons to fulfill his legal settlement. He enlisted friends to play with him at these unpublicized events. Musicians that took part included Blondie Chaplin, Ricky Fataar, and Alex Del Zoppo, of the band Sweetwater. Del Zoppo met Carl through Ricky Fataar, who briefly drummed for Sweetwater after the breakup of the Flame in 1971.

Del Zoppo recalled that one day in late 1971 or early 1972, "Ricky called me up to do a studio gig the next morning at Brian's studio (on Bellagio Road). When I showed up, Ricky, Blondie, Carl, Billy Hinsche, and (pedal steel guitarist) Red Rhodes were assembled in the studio to work on a couple of tracks that Ricky and Blondie had written. I played that funky upright piano that Brian had done so many cool-sounding experiments with—making up piano riffs as I learned the songs. In fact, all of the rest of us were still learning it, fitting in what we could . . . a very spontaneous way to record. Having one's own studio at that time was a fairly unique luxury, allowing that sort of evolving creative process to take place. Brian would occasionally stand in the doorway and silently nod approval. Those songs were 'Here She Comes' and 'Hold on Dear Brother,' which came out on *Carl and the Passions: So Tough*. Both were quite different from the usual [Beach Boys] fare, but both were beautiful musical and lyrical statements. Red played that incredible pedal steel guitar on 'Brother'—still one of the most amazing pieces of work I've ever heard from any steel player . . . It's an extremely soulful song, still one of my personal favorites to this day."

Del Zoppo continued, "We would go along with Carl to help him fulfill his 'conscious objector' status requirements. Keep in mind that this was in the days of everyone being eligible for the draft. . . . Carl would play jails and odd places like that. Really odd—singing 'Help Me Rhonda' to hundreds of scary-looking reprobates!"

CONCERTS NOT PLAYED

Despite author Keith Badman's listing of shows in Sweden, there is no evidence they played there in 1972.

NINETEEN SEVENTY-THREE was an important transitional period for the Beach Boys. A renewed focus in recent years had made them a disciplined and powerful stage act. With excellent new material and a growing reputation as a killer live act, their bookings began to improve. While the year was not without struggles, by the end of 1973 they would find themselves in a much stronger position.

CONCERTS PLAYED IN
1973

thirty-six on the *Billboard* charts, and is considered one of the most listenable Beach Boys LPs from beginning to end.

The recording trail went cold after this. Sadly, the group would not reenter the studio until late 1974, and no new studio album would appear until mid-1976. There were numerous reasons for this, but the most troubling of them was Brian's continued drift away from reality. While he still showed interest in making music, he devoted more of his energies in 1973 to sleeping and taking drugs. In the recent past, the Beach Boys had been able to cajole Brian into occasionally joining their sessions because their recording studio was in his home. But during the *Holland* period, the equipment was removed from Brian's house. Brian told Richard Williams, "Marilyn wanted some more room. She was tired of having musicians coming in and out of the house . . . but it was a great studio. We got a nice sound here." If, in the words of

FRIDAY, MARCH 16, 1973: **University of California, Riverside, CA (8:00 p.m. show)**
The Beach Boys' first concerts in 1973 were benefits on behalf of the Love Foundation, a non-profit entity formed by Mike and his brother Steve. Mike told a reporter from the *UC Santa Barbara Nexus* that he launched the foundation because "I wanted to do something other than amass a large personal fortune. My objective was to use my individuality in any area where I could be of use in improving the quality of life." The Love Foundation initiated a prison reform program and the group played a number of shows to aid it.

One of Mike's motivations to aid prisoners was his knowledge of the case of "Humble" Harv Miller, a famous KHJ DJ who'd been convicted of killing his wife. Miller wanted to start a prison radio station and give prisoners training in broadcasting skills. In addition, the foundation aimed to help prisoners cope with incarceration by teaching them meditation techniques. Carl told Lisa Robinson of *Disc* that after visiting a number of prisons, he solidly supported "trying to get meditation in prisons. It would really be helpful to them. Because all the prisons I've been to are really tense, and the feeling inside is just so frustrating. It draws all of your energy out to go to a prison."

The Beach Boys' backup band suffered a major loss during this time. After almost six years of service, keyboardist Daryl Dragon left and took Toni Shearer with him. The pair would soon achieve massive chart and television success as the Captain and Tennile. The parting between Dragon and the group was not altogether amicable. Daryl recalled, "They couldn't believe I wanted to quit. I told them I was going to go work in nightclubs with Toni and they couldn't believe it. They were making much better money by then but I had complete faith that Toni was good enough to be a recording star." Billy Hinsche replaced Shearer, while Carli Munoz (who'd played percussion for the Beach Boys in 1971) rejoined on keyboards. Munoz remained with the band until 1979. The current lineup also included Ed Carter on bass.

SATURDAY, MARCH 17, 1973: **Robertson Gym, University of California, Santa Barbara, CA**
The proceeds from this show were split between the Love Foundation and the Santa Barbara Society for Public Education and Reform. At the request of Mike, ex-road manager Jack Lloyd organized this show as well as one in Irvine the next day. It was his first encounter with the group in almost four years. He recalled that Dennis was offered a jug of wine as he was heading to the front of the stage to take a vocal solo. Lloyd grabbed the jug from Dennis, infuriating him. As soon as the song was over, Dennis rushed backstage to confront him. Lloyd recalled, "I could see that he was upset, so I handed the wine to someone, walked towards him and wrapped my arms around him, pinning his own arms at his sides, so he couldn't do anything . . . 'Now Dennis,' I said, 'Do you remember you once promised me you would never do anything like that on one of my shows?' It stopped him long enough to think about it and he said, 'OK, Jack, I won't.'"

THE BEACH BOYS
"WE'RE NOT COMING DOWN UNLESS THE SURF'S UP!"

ASUCI Concert and Dance Committee will present The Beach Boys in a benefit concert for prison reform Sunday, March 18 at 7:30 p.m. in Crawford Hall. Tickets, $3 for students and $4 for non-students, are on sale now at Ticketron.

CARL WILSON

BLONDIE CHAPLIN

BRIAN WILSON

RICKY FATAAR

MIKE LOVE

DENNIS WILSON

ALAN YARDINE

Ad for the group's appearance at UC Irvine on March 18, 1973. Ian Rusten Collection

SUNDAY, MARCH 18, 1973: **Crawford Hall, University of California, Irvine, CA (7:30 p.m. show)**
The third benefit for the Love Foundation took place at this campus in Orange County. John Timpane of the *New University* gushed, "The Beach Boys gave the best concert. Without so much as a shove, they moseyed on stage, and gave a crowd, that was determined to be reserved, a big jolt. They forced them out of their seats, they compelled them to clap and shout and carry each other around and watch the searchlights and even the band on occasion and most of all they had us looking around and saying, 'Aren't we great?'" British writer Nick Kent noted in *New Musical Express* that Murry Wilson watched the second half of the show with the promoter, while Marilyn Wilson danced in the aisles. Brian was nowhere to be seen. This show was broadcast live on student radio station KUCI. In addition, Mike was interviewed on the station after the show.

1973

SATURDAY, MARCH 24, 1973: California Men's Colony, San Luis Obispo (Afternoon) and Men's Gym, California Polytechnic University, San Luis Obispo (8:00 p.m. show)

The group played an afternoon show at the local prison, before performing a benefit appearance that night. The Cal Poly gym was filled with 4,100 people, who turned up at and greeted the band with "thunderous applause." According to a reporter from the *Poly Post*, "Mike got the crowd going early in the show when he taunted them by yelling 'Santa Barbara was dancing' in reference to the show a week earlier. "From then on, through the three songs until intermission and through the rest of the evening, the bleachers rocked as people poured down the crowded aisles to the gym floor or boogied right where they were. Old favorites from earlier records such as 'Surfin' USA' and 'I Get Around' alternated with 'Good Vibrations,' 'Funky Pretty,' 'Sail on Sailor,' and many more."

THURSDAY, MARCH 29, 1973: UD Arena, University of Dayton, Dayton, OH (8:00 p.m. show)

The group embarked on a major tour to promote their new LP *Holland*. Musicians accompanying them included Ed Carter (bass), Carli Munoz (piano), Billy Hinsche (keyboards), Joe Pollard (extra percussion), and Richard Didymiss Washington (congas).

The first concert of the tour was somewhat of a downer. The Beach Boys were eager to present their new sounds but the Ohio audience greeted the recent material with impatience. According to Mike Clarke of the *UD Flyer News*, "Only 'Funky Pretty' succeeded in garnering a favorable reaction, due to Chaplin's soulful vocal and brilliant solo, whipping his head and swaying his body like a hypnotized snake in time to the churning strains of his guitar. The show stopper was a not to be believed rendition of the Stones' 'Jumpin' Jack Flash.' Mike Love, pompously strutting about the stage, eclipsed the performance with a perfect imitation of Mick Jagger's concert choreography. It's a shame that the evening was marred by the selfish attitudes of the audience."

FRIDAY, MARCH 30, 1973: Arie Crown Theatre, Chicago, IL (8:00 show)

As on the previous night, the group was tumultuously applauded for oldies, while new material received a tepid response. A fan in attendance recalled: "The guys (quite understandably) wanted to play mainly their more recent stuff from *Holland*, *Carl and the Passions*, and *Surf's Up*, but the audience was very resistant right from the outset and almost outright hostile toward the group while they played some of their newer stuff. And so they stopped playing for a couple of minutes while they had a meeting on stage, and then proceeded to rip through a veritable jukebox of their old hits. And while they were doing this Carl looked angry, Al looked detached, Mike looked bored, and Dennis kind of wandered around the stage. But the younger musicians (including Blondie, Ricky, and Billy) played the songs with gusto, and really seemed to be enjoying themselves. They saved the show."

SATURDAY, MARCH 31, 1973: Athletic and Convocation Center, Notre Dame University, South Bend, IN (8:00 p.m. show)

The set list consisted of "Sloop John B," "Darlin'," "Do It Again," "Sail on Sailor," "Heroes and Villains," "Funky Pretty," "Caroline No," "Don't Worry Baby," "Surfin' USA," "Marcella," "California," "Leaving This Town," "Help Me Rhonda," "Let the Wind Blow," "Wouldn't It Be Nice," "Wild Honey," "Good Vibrations," "I Get Around," "Fun, Fun, Fun," and "Jumping Jack Flash."

According to Pat Small of the *Notre Dame Observer*, "The triumphant return of the Beach Boys was everything and more as the Boys thrilled an enthusiastic audience at the ACC." Small was particularly impressed by performance of "Caroline No," "which was simply exquisite featuring Carl Wilson on vocal and some nice flute by Rickie Fataar." He also singled out 'California,' with Ricky Fataar on pedal steel guitar and Al Jardine on banjo, 'Help Me Rhonda,' with Dennis "on raunchy vocal" and Billy Hinsche on piano, and "a soulful 'Heroes and Villains,' with Al Jardine laughing through the last verse" for special praise. Small later made it backstage and interviewed Jack Rieley, who informed him that "Brian Wilson is singing less now because he considers himself more of a producer and because he wants the group to sound more exact live." Whether this was true or simply an attempt to cover up Brian's increasing indifference is a matter of conjecture.

SUNDAY, APRIL 1, 1973: Assembly Hall, University of Illinois, Champaign-Urbana, IL (8:00 p.m. show)

Steve Desper, the studio had been installed in Brian's home to "bring the mountain to Mohammed," then conversely the removal of it led to a greater distance between Brian and the group.

The death of Murry Wilson that June also haunted

> "At one point Murry complained to Brian (in the wrong ear!) that the Beach Boys weren't playing the songs in the right order. Still Murry was surprisingly jovial and seemed to enjoy the concert."

Brian and his brothers. Neither Brian nor Dennis could handle attending their father's funeral. Brian nervously told reporters from *Record World* that his father's death made him "feel a lot more ambitious . . . I'm gonna try a little harder now . . . It's making a man outta me. Makes me want to produce a little more." In

Onstage at Notre Dame University, March 31, 1973 (left to right: Ed Carter, Billy Hinsche, Richard Didymiss Washington, Blondie Chaplin, Al Jardine, Joe Pollard, Carl Wilson, and Mike Love). Photo: Notre Dame Archives

Flyer for a 1973 show in Atlanta with misspelled opener Bruce Springsteen.
Courtesy of Ray Taylor

The crowd at the Assembly Hall didn't respond well to the group's new material during the show's first half, but became very enthusiastic when, according to Bob Hykan of the *Daily Illini*, the Beach Boys played "one of the many old hits which the crowd had been begging for . . . 'Help Me Rhonda.' They followed that with one more mellow number, 'Let the Wind Blow,' and some more terrific 1960s songs—'Wouldn't It Be Nice,' 'Good Vibrations,' 'I Get Around,' and 'Fun, Fun, Fun.' Both the crowd and the group then reached new heights of frenzy as the Boys played the Rolling Stones' 'Jumping Jack Flash' with a bare-chested Mike Love prancing around ala Mick Jagger."

Mike told a reporter that he enjoyed the show, though he felt the first half lacked energy. He commented that the addition of Ricky and Blondie added, "quite a unique chemistry to the group. We play kind of a little harder rock than we did before when we played a good kind of rock 'n' roll. Now it can get a little more outrageous, which is good. We expanded to do stuff like 'Jumping Jack Flash.'"

TUESDAY, APRIL 3, 1973: Stokes Physical Education Building, Saint Francis College, Loretto, PA (8:30 p.m. show)

WEDNESDAY, APRIL 4, 1973: Alumni Hall, St. John's University, Jamaica, NY, with the Charles Lloyd Band (7:00 p.m. show) and The Dome, C.W. Post College, Brookville, NY, with the Charles Lloyd Band (11:00 p.m. show)

The St. John's Alumni Hall "was too hot and stuffy," according to Al, but the group still put on an energetic show. Gerard Lewandowski of *St. John's Torch* reported, "The Beach Boys are excellent entertainers and know a lot about crowd psychology. While the Beach Boys still play their old songs, they usually add something new. 'Do It Again' has the kind of beginning that lends itself to improvising on the guitar, and Carl Wilson is no slob when it comes to playing. Listen to what he did on 'Surf's Up.'" Lewandowski singled out Blondie Chaplin for special praise, declaring, "His absence would certainly be missed, especially on such songs as 'Sail on Sailor' and 'Leaving This Town' . . . He can play anything lying around on the stage, as do most of the Beach Boys. 'Wild Honey' is 'his' song in concerts."

The St. John's show ran late and the C.W. Post concert didn't begin until one a.m. Despite being tired, the group performed for over two hours, before a sellout crowd of 3,000. It was almost three a.m. when the show ended, but the band returned to the stage for encores of "California Girls" and "Barbara Ann." Frank Aimetti of the *C.W. Post Pioneer* commented, "The Beach Boys showed remarkable vocal ability throughout, especially on the intricate harmonies of 'Heroes and Villains.' Carl Wilson did a beautiful job soloing on 'Caroline No,' a pretty ballad from the *Pet Sounds* album, which he played on acoustic guitar . . . I really can't say enough about the show . . . the vocals were perfect, song selection excellent, and their rapport with the audience was, as usual, great . . . I was also happy that the Beach Boys now fully integrate their show with both old and new materials. They seem satisfied that they are being accepted for what they do now as well as their oldie hits."

THURSDAY, APRIL 5, 1973: State Farm Arena, Harrisburg, PA, with Argent (8:00 p.m. show)
The Doobie Brothers were originally advertised as appearing, but were replaced by Argent.

FRIDAY, APRIL 6, 1973: Philadelphia Spectrum, Philadelphia, PA, with Spooky Tooth and Argent (8:00 p.m. show)
Over 20,000 fans attended this show. John Fisher, of the *Bucks County Courier Times*, expressed surprise that the crowd, the vast majority of whom were teenagers, stayed for the Beach Boys' set. He noted, "Many of the kids in the audience were too young to appreciate the Beach Boys when they were in their prime but the same youth rock and rolled furiously when the group began to play."

SATURDAY, APRIL 7, 1973: Norfolk Scope, Norfolk, VA, with Bruce Springsteen and the E Street Band (8:00 p.m. show)
This concert featured a young Bruce Springsteen and the E Street Band, then promoting their first album, *Greetings From Asbury Park*. Springsteen opened for the Beach Boys twice on this tour, giving him access to a larger audience. Chip Rachlin recalled that, "back then it was not so complicated to put an opening act on. If you got a call from Walter Yetnikoff asking for a little help on Billy Joel or Bruce, you knew that would come back to you at some point. And the Beach Boys, particularly Carl, were very good about that sort of stuff. Mike didn't pay that much attention to it."

Steve Abramson of the *Flat Hat* noted that in comparison to a performance he'd witnessed in 1972 at Hampton Coliseum, the group focused more on oldies, though they were just as impressive as before. He commented, "Carl has matured the most since the 'Surfin' Safari' days . . . Vocally he seems to have followed in Brian's footsteps, phasing beautifully with a clear, bright falsetto that would make your ears smile if they could . . . Jardine, like Carl, has a likable voice which is highlighted on a vivid, satisfying rendition of 'Heroes and Villains.' Chaplin was in especially good voice and his hard-edged R&B-trained style was put to good use on the soul-oriented 'Wild Honey.'"

SUNDAY, APRIL 8, 1973: French Fieldhouse, Ohio State University, Columbus, OH, with the Muledeer and Moondogg Medicine Show and the Doobie Brothers (8:00 p.m. show)
Over 7,000 people attended this show. Cynthia Robins of the *Columbus Dispatch* noted that the audience had trouble sitting through the slower numbers and "Mike Love literally had to cajole people to allow Carl Wilson to solo on 'Caroline No,' a quiet, bittersweet memoir, more David Gates than Brian Wilson." Nevertheless, despite sound problems, caused by the late arrival of the equipment truck, the group won over the crowd. Robins complimented, "the dynamism of an already excellent group too interested in growth to rust on their golden discs for long." J.N. Agnew of the *Ohio State Lantern* concurred "that there's not much to find fault with from a group that's been on the road for over eleven years . . . Bad notes here and there, missed cues, equipment failure, flaws in their performance, yes. But rather like the flaws in a fine piece of leather—only adding to the quality. Personally more material from the *Holland* album would have suited me. But it's a toss-up. 'Help Me Rhonda,' 'Wouldn't It Be Nice,' and all the other oldies sure sounded good again."

TUESDAY, APRIL 10, 1973: Carmichael Auditorium, University of North Carolina, Chapel Hill, NC

WEDNESDAY, APRIL 11, 1973: Omni, Atlanta, GA, with Mother's Finest and Bruce Springsteen (8:00 p.m. show)
This was a benefit concert to raise money for muscular dystrophy.

THURSDAY, APRIL 12, 1973: Florida Gym, University of Florida, Gainesville, FL (8:00 p.m. show)

truth, the passing of Murry had the exact opposite effect on Brian. He lost all interest in recording and retreated to his room, where he slid downward into depression and addiction. The Beach Boys were resigned to soldiering on without him.

For the others, most of 1973 was spent on the road. It was decided that a live concert LP displaying the band's much-improved chops would be a natural to promote while touring. At first Carl compiled a single album, using recordings from their November 1972 Carnegie Hall and Passaic, New Jersey concerts for a proposed release in early 1973. But Warner/Reprise was once again less than thrilled with the submitted album, probably due to Carl's choice of including only a few oldies in the set. Brian agreed with the label. In June 1973 he told Robert Nash and Mike Sigman of *Record World* that when the band played him the live tapes from the November '72 shows he told them not to release it because "I just didn't think it was that good." The group went back to the drawing board and recorded a selection of summer '73 shows for what would become the *Beach Boys in Concert* LP. This time, instead of proposing a single album, Carl compiled a double LP, thus satisfying the record label's desire for oldies while still allowing space for more recent material.

By the time the record was released, a dramatic shift in the band's management had occurred. Although Jack Rieley accompanied the group on the road in April 1973, he was spending more time in Holland than in the U.S.

Many people in the Beach Boys organization were not fans of Rieley and his absence provided an opportunity to plot against him. Chip Rachlin recalled, "Jack allegedly claimed to have got a Pulitzer while working for AP or UPI in Puerto Rico . . .

"The skill is not to try to live the past down, but to try to overshadow it. What we want people to know is that we're still alive now, and we're still working and progressing."

and the people at the Grillo office never bought into that. As it turned out, there was no Puerto Rican bureau and there was nothing in the Pulitzer history that suggested Jack was awarded the prize. Private detectives got involved in checking this out and it became a whole scene." By the fall, enough doubt had been

E. A. Gorman of the *Independent Florida Alligator* reported that when an equipment failure temporarily disabled the amplifiers, "the crowd continued their life beating claps and lyrics to 'Jumping Jack Flash,' the second encore song. This continued non-stop for fifteen minutes" even after the power was restored. Al Jardine called the student participation "incredible."

FRIDAY, APRIL 13, 1973: Memorial Coliseum, University of Alabama, Tuscaloosa, AL, with Focus (8:00 p.m. show)

SATURDAY, APRIL 14, 1973: Pirates World Arena, Dania, FL (8:00 p.m. show)

THURSDAY, APRIL 19, 1973: Winterland, San Francisco, CA, with Jesse Colin Young and Barbara Mauritz (8:00 p.m. show)
Proving that two years of hard work was showing results, the group's second appearance at this venue was attended by a near-capacity crowd. Joel Selvin of the *San Francisco Chronicle* reported, "During the 100 minute performance they concentrated on material recorded since *Pet Sounds*, though they opened with 'Help Me Rhonda' and threw in 'Surfin' USA,' politely dropping the 'round Frisco bay' line. They also dusted off 'I Get Around' and 'Fun, Fun, Fun' for the encore."

FRIDAY, APRIL 20, 1973: Hollywood Palladium, Los Angeles, CA, with Mason Profitt and Jesse Colin Young (8:00 p.m. show)
This sold-out concert was originally scheduled for March 16 but was postponed until this date. The hometown appearance brought out the entire Wilson clan. Fan Rob Shepherd recalled, "Audree Wilson arrived early, sat in the balcony, and chatted with several fans, including me. Murry Wilson arrived just before the concert, as did Brian, with one of the Rovell sisters (I believe Diane). Several rock stars came to pay tribute to Brian, including Dewey Bunnell of America and Danny Hutton (of Three Dog Night) . . . At one point Murry complained to Brian (in the wrong ear!) that the Beach Boys weren't playing the songs in the right order. Still Murry was surprisingly jovial and seemed to enjoy the concert." Chip Rachlin recalled, "Murry Wilson was there and it was the only time I ever saw him. I met Brian for the first time at the Palladium show. Brian was dressed, despite the eighty- or ninety-degree heat, in a cashmere, navy blue overcoat."

Brian's friend Danny Hutton coaxed him onstage for the encore. But Carl told *LA Times* reporter Paul Bernstein, "They were just messing around. I think what he was really doing was checking the audience out. He wanted to come out and see what all the fuss was about." The brief cameo was Brian's last appearance onstage until July 1976. Bruce Johnston was also on hand and came out for the encore. The show was recorded for possible use on the *Beach Boys in Concert* album and the tapes still exist in the Beach Boys vault. In addition, a photographer was on hand and took numerous pictures, some of which were eventually used for the LP's cover and inner gatefold.

Steve Rosen of *Sounds* declared, "The impact that the band had on the audience Friday night was as great as this concert-goer has ever seen. The screaming and shouting between numbers, the nonstop foot tapping and dancing, near hysterical greetings for each song, all combined to place this performance (easily) in the top five of the year." Dennis Hunt of the *Los Angeles Times* raved that it was "a thrilling, roof rattling concert . . . Their formula is unbeatable—heavy beat, silly lyrics, and good harmony . . . Among the hits they played were 'I Get Around,' 'Fun, Fun, Fun,' 'Surfin' USA,' 'Help Me Rhonda,' and 'California Girls.'"

SATURDAY, APRIL 21, 1973: Music Hall, Houston, TX, with the Doobie Brothers (8:00 p.m. show)
A day after their hometown show, the group traveled to Texas for two concerts with the Doobie Brothers.

SUNDAY, APRIL 22, 1973: Bronco Bowl, Dallas, TX, with the Doobie Brothers

WEDNESDAY, APRIL 25, 1973: Celebrity Theater, Phoenix, AZ (7:30 p.m. show)
The Beach Boys attracted a capacity crowd for their first Phoenix appearance in a year and a half.

THURSDAY, APRIL 26, 1973: Fieldhouse, Regis College, Denver, CO, with Steeleye Span (8:00 p.m. show)

This concert was another sellout. David Youngstrom of the *Denver Post* declared that the old songs such as "I Get Around" were "as much fun now as they were eight years ago. The group has also produced some of the richest, most fulfilling music in rock. 'Sail on Sailor,' 'Heroes and Villains,' and of course 'Good Vibrations' were all in the show, proving that the Beach Boys know, perhaps better than anyone else in rock, how to make good music."

FRIDAY, APRIL 27, 1973: Kiel Opera House, St. Louis, MO

SATURDAY, APRIL 28, 1973: Allen Field House, University of Kansas, Lawrence, KS (8:30 p.m. show)

Tim Bradley of the *University Daily Kansan* dubbed the show a success due to "the unbridled brilliance of the band in its many good moments . . . Newcomer Blondie Chaplin more than proved his worth with his fine vocal and tasty guitar work and Carl Wilson's rendering of 'Caroline No' was genuinely touching and unashamedly vulnerable. Mike Love's stage antics far belied his Gandhi-garbed appearance on numbers like 'Fun, Fun, Fun' and 'California Girls' and a tumultuous (but sincere) ovation followed the second set. The audience left assured that the Beach Boys are well into their second heyday."

SUNDAY, APRIL 29, 1973: City Auditorium Music Hall, Omaha, NE (7:00 p.m. show)

This concert attracted a small but eager crowd of 2,610. However, a long delay due to technical problems led to tension. Shouts of "Just sing!" sprung up around the hall while the Beach Boys took time tuning up their instruments, and the heckling continued throughout the show. According to James Bresette of the *Omaha World Herald*, "Dennis Wilson and Love responded in kind and adopted sloppy, couldn't care less stage demeanor that didn't help matters. But as the hits, garbled though they were, kept coming, much of the crowd was won over, until the whole house stood and clapped for 'Good Vibrations,' which closed the regular program. The audience called the group back after that for another round of hits, including 'California Girls' and 'Fun, Fun, Fun.'"

SUNDAY, MAY 6, 1973: Farleigh Dickinson University, Teaneck, NJ

The group flew to New York to play two weeks of East Coast dates.

MONDAY, MAY 7, 1973: Colden Auditorium, Queens College, Queens, NY (Two shows at 7:00 and 10:00 p.m.)

These two concerts were both sellouts. At each concert, the Beach Boys performed for an hour and forty-five minutes with a fifteen-minute intermission. David Rosenbloom of *Newsbeat* commented that "Funky Pretty" and many of the other songs the group performed "sounded much fuller than on their respective albums . . . 'Sail on Sailor' and 'Sloop John B' kept the concert at its already blazing pace. The group kept the crowd active by playing 'Wouldn't It Be Nice' and then 'Wild Honey' which contained great guitar by Blondie Chaplin. Dennis Wilson then told the crowd that they better sing along with this one because 'this is what it is all about.' That was his plea to the audience to have 'Good Vibrations' which closed the second set . . . the concert ended with an energetic version of 'Jumping Jack Flash.'"

WEDNESDAY, MAY 9, 1973: Gym, Genesee Community College, Batavia, NY (8:30 p.m. show)

The Beach Boys flew to Rochester on May 8 and spent the night in Batavia. About 1,000 students turned out for the show at the local community college. The group arrived forty-five minutes late, but the *Sur Esprit* declared the show "phenomenal . . . During the first set, both audience and the Beach Boys were a bit laid back, but the second set hit like an explosion. Within minutes, the crowd was on its feet to dance, to sing, to laugh, to clap . . . I've never been a Beach Boys fanatic myself, but after seeing them—I'm almost converted. They did some cuts off *Holland* (their latest album), which went over well, as did assorted oldies and middle-agers. But the very highest point of the evening was their encore 'Jumping Jack Flash'—pure dynamite."

sown about Rieley's past that even the Wilsons, who had been his main champions, began to question Rieley's credibility. With Rieley no longer living in the States, it seemed appropriate to terminate his position. Mike's brother, Steve Love, who was already employed by the group as an assistant to Nick Grillo, began to consolidate power and rose to a stronger position within the group's management structure.

As soon as Love took control of the band, Blondie Chaplin was gone. His last show took place at Madison Square Garden in December. According to photographer and Beach Boys confidant Ed Roach, "When they were on their way to New York they got word that Blondie's father had died and Blondie was inconsolable, and after the show he told them he had to go back to South Africa. Steve Love told him, 'Fuck you. You have to come back to Los Angeles.' Now this was after the whole band had stopped working for a while after (Murry) had died. So they had a big fight and Blondie left." In a March 1974 interview with *Sounds*, Mike remained coy about the reasons Blondie had left, but noted "he'd been unhappy for some time" before his departure. Carl commented in 1974 that Blondie was "into a different type of music. Even though he helped compose a lot of the music on the *Holland* album, his style was much different than the rest of the group." Unfortunately for Blondie, he left just as the group was catching a huge popularity wave that would take them back to the absolute top of the music industry.

THE BEACH BOYS IN CONCERT

FRIDAY, MAY 11, 1973: Farrell Hall Gym, State University Agricultural and Technical College at Delhi, Delhi, NY (8:00 p.m.)
The group spent the night of May 10 in Binghamton, drove to Delhi on May 11 for this show, and then returned to Binghamton for a second night.

SATURDAY, MAY 12, 1973: Gym, SUNY Binghamton, Binghamton, NY (Two shows at 8:00 and 10:30 p.m.)
The Beach Boys were scheduled to play one free afternoon concert outdoors. However, bad weather conspired to force the promoters to move indoors to the gym and postpone the show until 8:00 p.m. As the gym only held 3,300 people, promoters announced that only students from the campus could have tickets. This created a very tense situation, since people from as far away as Pittsburgh were coming and would have to be turned away. Luckily, road manager Jon Parks informed the school that they were willing to play two shows that night. The group graciously performed both gigs for the original agreed-upon price of $12,500.

SUNDAY, MAY 13, 1973: Wadsworth Field House, Colby College, Waterville, ME (Two shows at 7:00 and 9:30 p.m.)
The group flew to Boston and then drove to Waterville, where they gave an exciting performance for a small college audience. L. Phil Gagne III of the *Lewiston Evening Journal* declared, "The response to the second set was a constant standing ovation. Of course the urge to dance and jump into the music was augmented when the Beach Boys performed their out now hit 'Sail on Sailor.'"

MONDAY, MAY 14, 1973: Massachusetts State College, Framingham, MA

THURSDAY, MAY 17, 1973: Fort Meade, Laurel, MD
The group spent a few days in Boston before flying to Baltimore on May 16. They drove to Laurel, where they spent the night. The concert took place on the U.S. Army base.

FRIDAY, MAY 18, 1973: Dillon Gym, Princeton University, Princeton, NJ (Two shows at 8:00 and 11:00 p.m.)
The group planned to play only one show, but a second was added due to high demand.

SATURDAY, MAY 19, 1973: Roberts Center, Boston College, Boston, MA (Two shows at 7:00 and 10:30 p.m.)

SUNDAY, MAY 20, 1973: Convocation Center, Ohio University, Athens, OH, with Argent (8:00 p.m. show)
This was the last show of a string of March–May dates, and it attracted over 7,000 fans. Robert P. Tkacz and Tom Barker of the *Ohio University Post* noted, "Music from the Beach Boys' *Holland* album pleased the crowd but it was the music from the '60s that released them from the present and propelled them back to the summer sun of the '60s . . . Starting with 'Surfin' USA,' dedicated by Dennis to those who had attempted 'the art of surfing, all my brothers,' each oldie doubled and redoubled the force of that wave they began riding in 1962."

Interviewed afterwards, Dennis remarked that he wasn't surprised by the strong response the '60s music received, because "today there's nothing to relate to," but he admitted that for him and Carl the excitement of performing the oldies was gone: "It's just music."

SUNDAY, AUGUST 12, 1973: Nippert Stadium, University of Cincinnati, Cincinnati, OH, with Linda Ronstadt (7:30 p.m. show)
The June 4, 1973, death of Murry Wilson was quite traumatic for the Wilsons and the band took a long hiatus. When they returned to the road, Ed Carter (bass), Billy Hinsche (guitar/keyboards), Robert Kenyatta (percussion, saxophone and flute), Carli Munoz (piano), and Mike Kowalski (extra percussion) accompanied them. In addition, the Wilsons invited their mother Audree on tour. She was introduced from the stage at a number of shows. Also traveling with them was

Rick Nelson, who had replaced Jon Parks as tour manager. Nelson had served as West Coast regional coordinator for the Student's International Meditation Society. He was introduced to Mike and Al in 1972 and as Nelson recalled, "We became friends. Mike later asked me if I would like to come to work for the Beach Boys." Nelson started out as a touring sound engineer in the summer of 1972, assisting Steve Moffitt at the gigs. He recalled, "Steve Love recognized that I was educated and responsible, and was instrumental in having me become the tour manager and tour accountant. I instituted several revolutionary, at the time, procedures for auditing the box office at each performance, ensuring that the band was properly compensated."

The group also brought engineer Steve Moffitt with them to record a number of shows for the eventual *Beach Boys in Concert* album, including this Cincinnati concert. Rick Flynn of the *Journal News* commented, "The PA system wasn't completely adjusted and feedback glared out at times . . . However, the Beach Boys still reigned as the kings of surf music—a style that no other group has been able to duplicate since its origin . . . Mike Love's vocals on 'Surfin' USA' and . . . 'Sunny California' were great, while Carl Wilson continued to reach his usual spectrum of high notes in as clear a voice as humanly possible . . . Dennis, who began as 'Denny on the drums' back in 1962, was up front as vocalist and MC on this tour . . . "

Al and Carl performing at Newark State College on December 13, 1973. Photo used with permission of Matt Caruso, Kean University

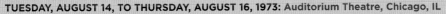

TUESDAY, AUGUST 14, TO THURSDAY, AUGUST 16, 1973: Auditorium Theatre, Chicago, IL
The Beach Boys recorded the opening show and an AFM contract was filled out for the performances of "Sloop John B," "The Trader," "Sail on Sailor," and "Help Me Rhonda." Ultimately nothing from this night appeared on the *Beach Boys in Concert* album.

FRIDAY, AUGUST 17, 1973: Tiger Stadium, Massillon, OH (Canceled)
This concert was canceled for reasons unknown.

SATURDAY, AUGUST 18, 1973: Mosque, Richmond, VA, with Jonathan Edwards (8:00 p.m. show)
The versions of "Heroes and Villains" and "Caroline No" performed at this show were included on the *Beach Boys in Concert* LP.

SUNDAY, AUGUST 19, 1973: Nassau Coliseum, Uniondale, NY, with Jonathan Edwards (8:00 p.m. show)
The set list consisted of "Sail on Sailor," "Long Promised Road," "Sloop John B," "The Trader," "Leaving This Town," "California Girls," "Marcella," "Funky Pretty," "You Still Believe In Me," "Caroline No," "We Got Love," "California Saga," "River Song" (this Dennis song, which appeared on his 1977 solo album *Pacific Ocean Blue*, was performed at a number of shows on the tour), "Wild Honey," "Surfer Girl," "Help Me Rhonda," "Wouldn't It Be Nice," "Surfin' USA," "Good Vibrations," "I Get Around," "Fun, Fun, Fun," and "Jumping Jack Flash." This night's performances of "Sloop John B," "Leaving This Town," "Help Me Rhonda," "We Got Love," and "California Girls" were included on the *Beach Boys in Concert* LP.

MONDAY, AUGUST 20, 1973: Schaefer Stadium, Foxboro, MA, with Loggins and Messina and Jonathan Edwards (8:00 p.m. show)
Over 35,000 people attended this concert at an open-air venue near Boston. Although several songs from this concert were recorded for possible inclusion on the *Beach Boys in Concert* LP, none of them were included on the released album. It may have been due to the muted audience reaction. The group underwhelmed the crowd, which had already sat through performances by Jonathan Edwards and Loggins and Messina. Stephen Williams of the *Boston Globe* commented, "The group

sounded raw and at times competitive, and the programmed selections they are playing during this tour are obviously the songs they want to play, and not always what their audience wants to hear. There was only an occasional concession to the oldies 'Surfer Girl,' 'Sloop John B,' 'California Girls.' The group did a number of their softly pretty ballads but it was evident that a crowd like Monday's wanted loudness before intimacy."

THURSDAY, AUGUST 23, 1973: Danbury Prison, Danbury, CT
As far can be determined, this was the last prison concert the Beach Boys played in the 1970s.

FRIDAY, AUGUST 24, 1973: Dillon Stadium, Hartford, CT, with Jonathan Edwards and Poco
Approximately 14,000 people attended this show, which was recorded. The group came onstage at 9:30 p.m. and played until after midnight. Recorded evidence suggests that both band and audience were in a celebratory mood. In what was a usual routine on this tour, Mike Love introduced Audree Wilson, who was seated at the side of the stage, with this tribute: "She's the person responsible for the Beach Boys. She's my aunt." Henry McNulty of the *Hartford Courant* singled out two new songs performed this night for special praise: "'River Song,' by Dennis Wilson, and 'We Got Love,' by Ricky Fataar, are both full, rich numbers making full use of the group's multipart harmonies."

SATURDAY, AUGUST 25, 1973: Roosevelt Stadium, Jersey City, NJ, with Poco and Stanky Brown (7:30 p.m.)

SUNDAY, AUGUST 26, 1973: Hampton Coliseum, Hampton, VA, with Jonathan Edwards
The band played before a small crowd of 3,700. According to Teresa Taylor of the *Times Herald*, fans greeted more recent material with "polite patience . . . rushing forward to the stage only when a golden oldie was mixed in. But the rock 'n' roll they came to hear was played during the encore and the dancing mob brought them back for a second time. They were still the Beach Boys of ten years ago, as if music hadn't undergone any changes in the past decade."

MONDAY, AUGUST 27, 1973: SPAC, Saratoga, NY (8:00 p.m. show)
The group performed to over 13,000 people who mostly were there to hear the oldies. According to Bill Dantini of *The Amsterdam Recorder*, "It wasn't until they performed 'Sloop John B' . . . that the crowd became genuinely excited. In a sense, this was the story of the evening. The new songs were received half-heartedly throughout the concert, while the 'oldies' frequently brought the crowd to its feet. Songs like 'California Girls,' 'Surfer Girl,' 'Wouldn't It Be Nice,' and 'Surfin' USA' all ended in standing ovations."

THURSDAY, AUGUST 30, 1973: Merriweather Post Pavilion, Columbia, MD (7:00 p.m. show)

FRIDAY, AUGUST 31, 1973: Syria Mosque, Pittsburgh, PA (8:00 p.m. show)
The performances of "You Still Believe in Me," "Funky Pretty," and "Surfin' USA" from this show were included on the *Beach Boys in Concert* album. According to Pete Bishop of *The Pittsburgh Press*, the recording marred the show since it contributed to long delays between songs. Despite the technical problems, however, the second half got the crowd on their feet and by the time they played "Surfer Girl" there were "big cheers that didn't stop through 'We Got Love' . . . fast, boogying 'Darlin'' (it should have been recorded this way), and 'Help Me Rhonda,' 'Wouldn't It Be Nice,' and a 'Surfin' USA' like you wouldn't have believed. The Beach Boys trotted off to a howling standing ovation and returned for an encore of 'I Get Around' played harder and 'Good Vibrations,' their most sophisticated hit . . . 'Barbara Ann' and 'Fun, Fun, Fun' played as never before . . . and as a nightcap—if you can believe it—the Beach Boys doing that nasty classic, 'Jumping Jack Flash' while the whole place was jumping right along with them."

SATURDAY, SEPTEMBER 1, 1973: Century Theatre, Buffalo, NY (Two shows at 7:00 and 10:00 p.m.)
The group included a performance of "Darlin'" from one of these shows on the *Beach Boys in*

"At midnight, a voluptuous young lady flung herself onto Carl Wilson with a pure, uninhibited desire to make love to him, but at that time everybody was flinging themselves on everybody else."

Concert LP. According to Joe Wilhelm of the *Courier Express*, a receptive audience cheered the oldies but "responded almost as equally to a hard driving rock delivery of 'We Got Love,' which they perform for the first time on this tour; to several funky offerings; and to some movingly romantic folk blues interpretations . . . If you went there expecting a night of repetitious surfing harmony . . . you would have been disappointed. Instead you would have found a talented outfit, up to date, but never out of tune."

SUNDAY, SEPTEMBER 2, 1973: Massey Hall, Toronto, ON, Canada, with Myles and Lenny (8:00 p.m. show)
This concert got off to a less-than-promising start when scheduled opener Michael Tarry stormed out of the building after an argument. Violinist Lenny Solomon offered his services and called his partner Myles Cohen, who raced to the theater to save the day. Of course, the audience was really there to see the Beach Boys. According to Bruce Kirkland of the *Toronto Star*, the group gave an "electrifying concert" that "climaxed . . . with two encores, the second one a rendering of their old 'Fun Fun Fun,' which exploded into a frenzied version of the Rolling Stones' 'Jumping Jack Flash.'"

MONDAY, SEPTEMBER 3, 1973: Pine Knob Music Theater, Clarkston, MI (7:30 p.m. show)
Recordings of "Sail on Sailor," "Trader," and "Surfer Girl" taped at this show were included on the *Beach Boys in Concert* LP.

FRIDAY, NOVEMBER 2, 1973: Paramount Northwest Theater, Seattle, WA, with Billy Joel
A young Billy Joel opened this show with his three-piece band. He'd impressed Chip Rachlin, who agreed to represent him and pushed the Beach Boys to allow Joel to open for them. Joel received a strong audience response. In a DVD tribute to Carl Wilson, Saxophonist Richie Cannata, who was then in Joel's band, recalled that Carl Wilson took an interest in the group and was often in the wings to watch them "religiously . . . he kind of always showed up. He was the only one (from the Beach Boys) that really showed up."

SATURDAY, NOVEMBER 3, 1973: Paramount Northwest Theater, Portland, OR, with Billy Joel (8:00 p.m. show)
A capacity crowd of 3,000 attended this show. John Wendeborn of *The Oregonian* reported, "The theater virtually rocked from the rafters when the group began one of those tunes . . . They do play contemporary rock and managed to get a lot of their recent works out, showing not only a reversal of that pretty, harmonic, choral sound but also a tendency to get involved in some tasteful and sparklingly arranged tunes . . . There is a lot of talent in the band and they proved it with exciting sounds."

SUNDAY, NOVEMBER 4, 1973: War Memorial Gym, University of British Columbia, Vancouver, BC, with Billy Joel (8:00 p.m. show)
Lance Ware of *The Ubyssey* reported that the Beach Boys worked the crowd up to such a fever pitch that when they left the stage after "Good Vibrations," one had to "imagine the Beatles walking offstage, waving goodbye a few years ago. Listen to 6,000 stamping, cheering, happy people lighting matches and asking for more! More! More!" After a break, the group returned to the stage for high-energy performances of "I Get Around, "Barbara Ann," and "Fun, Fun, Fun" and then left the stage to a massive standing ovation that continued until they reemerged to play one more tune. According to Ware, "This was an encore to remember. 'Jumping Jack Flash' with Mike dressed in purple belted silk jacket and bells, big sun on his chest, and a wide brimmed hat, dancing, a perfect Mick Jagger, miming him and jumping while three guitars, three keyboard men, and three drummers played one of the finest rock 'n' roll songs I've ever seen."

WEDNESDAY, NOVEMBER 7, 1973: Myrum Memorial Fieldhouse, Gustavus Adolphus College, St. Peter, MN (8:00 p.m. show)
The group flew to Minneapolis and then drove to St. Peter to play this small college. Tim Colburn and J. L. Fleer of *The Gustavian Weekly* complained that excellent performances of "The Trader," "Leaving This Town," and "Long Promised Road" received only a tepid response, while the encore

THE BEACH BOYS IN CONCERT

performances of "Barbara Ann," "I Get Around," "Fun, Fun, Fun," and "Jumping Jack Flash" were applauded with orgasmic enthusiasm. "The indiscriminate pandemonium which resulted from these selections gave these reviewers the distinct impression that the Beach Boys could have collectively taken a shit on stage and still have bowed to a thunderous standing ovation."

THURSDAY, NOVEMBER 8, 1973: Quincy College, Quincy, IL (8:00 p.m. show)
The Gyrfalcon Yearbook noted that the "largest concert of the year was by the Beach Boys, who earned the well-deserved respect of the audience throughout their harmonies."

FRIDAY, NOVEMBER 9, 1973: William L. White Auditorium, Emporia, KS (8:00 p.m. show)
Kansas State Teachers College sponsored this concert.

SATURDAY, NOVEMBER 10, 1973: Pershing Auditorium, Lincoln, NE (7:30 p.m. show)

SUNDAY, NOVEMBER 11, 1973: Music Hall, Oklahoma City, OK (8:00 p.m. show)
Following this show, the group visited Jim Guercio's Caribou Ranch in Colorado. While there, Dennis, Carl, and Al contributed backing vocals to Chicago's future hit single "Wishing You Were Here."

WEDNESDAY, NOVEMBER 14, 1973: Denver Coliseum, Denver, CO, with the Steve Miller Band and Eric Anderson (8:00 p.m. show)
Ed Roach filmed part of this show to create a TV commercial for the *Beach Boys in Concert* LP.

THURSDAY, NOVEMBER 15, 1973: Celebrity Theater, Phoenix, AZ (Two shows at 7:30 and 11:00 p.m.)
The Beach Boys easily sold out the tiny 2,700-seat venue. Reviewer Hardy Price of the *Arizona Republic* commented that it "was not a great wave of nostalgia that generated all the excitement in Celebrity Theater, but the genuine spontaneous reaction to one of the better performing rock 'n' roll bands around. There's no question in anyone's mind that the Beach Boys have a lock on harmony and now that the group includes eleven (remember when they were only five) talented musicians, the end result is a tightly packed hour and a half of good time rock 'n' roll."

FRIDAY, NOVEMBER 16, 1973: Convention Center, Anaheim, CA, with Three Man Army
Ed Roach filmed a portion of this show.

SATURDAY, NOVEMBER 17, AND SUNDAY, NOVEMBER 18, 1973: Winterland, San Francisco, CA, with Commander Cody and His Lost Planet Airmen and Three Man Army
Ed Roach again filmed a portion of one of the concerts. Adam Block of *New Musical Express* bluntly wrote that the Beach Boys' performance "stank . . . Blondie Chaplin, normally a fine player, was barely functional . . . Dennis Wilson's main function was to look pretty, and lean at odd moments, plugging one ear, closed-eyed, into the microphone as he rubbed his crotch up and down the pole and produced ill matched harmonies. Even Carl Wilson and Al Jardine were having trouble filling their vocals." A fan who attended recalled that he personally witnessed Carl and Al wrestling with "a crying and screaming" Blondie to get him to go onstage. This drama undoubtedly contributed to his exit from the group in December.

Interviewed the next day, Carl blamed the bad performance on colds band members had all caught. He candidly admitted, "Our voices were really shot. Blondie was a bit wasted, I noticed. It was one of the few times I've ever really felt trapped by the older numbers. I'm beginning to get tired of them."

TUESDAY, NOVEMBER 20, 1973, North Gym, California State University at Chico, Chico, CA, with Three Man Army
About 3,000 fans attended this concert. *The CSUC Wildcat* gushed, "the Beach Boys created a charged atmosphere filled with cheering and rock-n-rolling from stage front to bleacher tops . . . everyone dug it . . . One of the best gigs to come to town in a long time."

"The group sounded raw and at times competitive, and the programmed selections they are playing during this tour are obviously the songs they want to play, and not always what their audience wants to hear."

WEDNESDAY, NOVEMBER 21, 1973: Memorial Auditorium, Sacramento, CA, with Three Man Army (7:30 p.m. show)

After an eight-year absence, the group returned to Sacramento. John Hurst of the *Sacramento Bee* reported, "While balloons floated, lights flashed and the bobbing crowd on the main floor stood for a better look, the BBs ripped through a total of songs—mostly familiar hits from early bubblegum to latter day powerhouse. Twice they left the carpeted stage but returned for encores after two minutes each time of uninterrupted cheering from the multitude. They then finished with a romping 'Jumping Jack Flash' that included a visual climax of dancing lights—from mirrored spheres spinning high overhead and from a backdrop of colored lights on the stage."

FRIDAY, NOVEMBER 30, 1973: Assembly Center, Louisiana State University, Baton Rouge, LA, with Billy Joel (8:00 p.m. show)

The Beach Boys embarked on another tour encompassing the South, Midwest, and East Coast. Musicians accompanying them included Billy Hinsche, Ed Tuduri on extra percussion, Carli Munoz, Richard Didymiss Washington on congas, and Putter Smith (famous for his acting role as "Mr. Kidd" in the 1971 James Bond film *Diamonds Are Forever*) on bass. Billy Joel opened and proved a hard act to follow. Jim Whittum of the *Baton Rouge Advocate* argued that he stole the spotlight from the group who "seemed to warm the half-filled Assembly Center only when they launched into their 1960s songs . . . The lack of acceptance of any current songs of the group was at least partially the fault of the band itself, for they wandered aimlessly about the stage at times and only infrequently were able to manage a cohesiveness of music and lyric."

SATURDAY, DECEMBER 1, 1973: Auditorium North Hall, Memphis, TN, with Billy Joel (8:00 p.m. show)

SUNDAY, DECEMBER 2, 1973: Memorial Gym, Vanderbilt University, Nashville, TN, with Billy Joel (8:00 p.m. show)

Over 6,000 rowdy fans attended this concert. According to the *Nashville Tennessean*, there were frequent shouts of "Play the oldies!" After the show, Mike was philosophical about the crowd reaction. He admitted that it was true "that the old stuff is liked more here than in some parts of the country" but argued that "the skill is not to try to live the past down, but to try to overshadow it. What we want people to know is that we're still alive now, and we're still working and progressing."

MONDAY, DECEMBER 3, 1973: Kiel Auditorium, St. Louis, MO, with Billy Joel (7:30 p.m. show)

WEDNESDAY, DECEMBER 5, 1973: Dane County Coliseum, Madison, WI, with New Riders of the Purple Sage (8:00 p.m. show)

About 4,000 fans attended this show. Michael Vena of the *Wisconsin State Journal* was unimpressed by the Beach Boys' "bored, almost lackadaisical" performance and wrote that their new songs sounded like their old songs, "which is what everyone wanted to hear." Robert LaBrasca of the Capital Times was also disappointed, but not for the same reason. He argued that the group's performance "was more nostalgic and less experimental than last years. They did 'California Girls,' 'Fun, Fun, Fun,' 'Good Vibrations,' 'Help Me Rhonda,' and 'Surfin' USA,' which Dennis Wilson introduced, saying, 'Well, it paid the rent.' There were a few newer things, but with far less instrumental interplay than they used last year."

THURSDAY, DECEMBER 6, 1973: Lantz Gym, Eastern Illinois University, Charleston, IL (8:00 p.m. show)

This show was completely sold out and promoters had to create a special SRO section to squeeze more people in. *The Eastern News* reported that "at times more than half of the crowd was on their feet dancing, clapping, and dancing in the aisles . . . Old standards like 'Sloop John B' and 'California Girls' were played in a perfection of sound and balance that one only hears on a disc." Jennifer Clark of the *Warbler* noted, "Singers Love and Carl Wilson, both dressed in flashy outfits . . . made a particularly big hit with the audience when they asked the ushers in red T-shirts . . .

THE BEACH BOYS IN CONCERT

Mike and Blondie onstage, December 13, 1973. Photo used with permission of Matt Caruso, Kean University

to stop trying to restrict audience members from getting close to the stage area . . . The conga players added newer dimensions to the sound, so that every number was not in keeping with the same musical patterns. Also, Richard Fataar, who played flute in several of the numbers and did an exceptionally fine excerpt on the organ in one portion of the concert, added to the contrast that the Beach Boys had in all of the numbers that they played."

FRIDAY, DECEMBER 7, 1973: Public Hall, Cleveland, OH, with Linda Ronstadt and the Electric Light Orchestra (7:30 p.m. show)
Prior to this concert, the Beach Boys and Linda Ronstadt made a promo appearance at radio station WMMS.

SATURDAY, DECEMBER 8, 1973: Music Hall, Boston, MA

SUNDAY, DECEMBER 9, 1973: Keaney Gym, University of Rhode Island, Kingston, RI

MONDAY, DECEMBER 10, 1973: UNH Field House, University of New Hampshire, Durham, NH (8:00 p.m. show)

TUESDAY, DECEMBER 11, 1973: the Dome, C.W. Post College, Brookville, NY, with Henry Gross (8:00 p.m. show)
The group's fourth appearance at C.W. Post was a sellout. W. Sachs Gore of the *Post Pioneer* noted that their repertoire had not altered much from their previous appearance in April but gave this performance the edge because "the sound was fuller. With two drummers, also an extra percussionist, three guitars, piano, synthesizer, and bass going on at the same time it is bound to sound full."

Despite attempts by the band's PR people to keep them away, two student reporters managed to grab comments from the group after the show. Dennis, dressed in a grey suit and bowtie, was asked what influenced his increasing use of orchestration on his songs. He responded, "Wagner." When the reporters inquired what he listened to, he replied, "I like Marvin Gaye and Otis Redding, but I'm really not into the blues." The interview might have continued longer, but when they asked Dennis for the real story of how he hurt his hand, he replied curtly, "I cut it in two. Merry Christmas," and then abruptly walked away. The reporters correctly surmised that his inability to drum had affected him more than he let on. They also managed to talk to Carl, who told them, erroneously as it turned out, the band was "planning to release *Smile* in a more or less original form, within the coming year." To the inevitable question of how Brian was, Carl answered, "Brian is Brian, you know? He's working on a lot of new ideas. Aside from that he's still recovering from the effects of the car accident he was involved in last summer."

WEDNESDAY, DECEMBER 12, 1973: DAR Constitution Hall, Washington DC (8:30 p.m. show)
The Beach Boys performed before a capacity crowd of 3,700. Richard Harrington of the *Washington Star* praised the group for playing "all its music with an infectious enthusiasm that is matched by a solid professional delivery. There was certainly no energy crisis on the part of either the band or the audience . . . With a brace of lead singers . . . and with thoughtful arrangements, there was no way this group was going to deliver a bad show." However, while Harrington saw a band on top of its game, Tom Zito, of the *Washington Post*, saw a band in crisis. He noted that, in the midst of all

the revelry, "a tell-tale sign lingered, Dennis Wilson . . . stayed stage left most of the night, dressed in a dark three-piece suit and tie, singing halfheartedly into a microphone, looking bored, bored, bored . . . The music may have sounded fresh and novel to a new audience whose older brothers and sisters grew up on the Beach Boys, but twelve years on the stage with the same act has to become a drag. And it's starting to show."

Carl sings "Long Promised Road" at Newark State College on December 13, 1973. Photo used with permission of Matt Caruso, Kean University

THURSDAY, DECEMBER 13, 1973: Newark State College, Union, NJ, with Henry Gross (Two shows at 7:00 and 10:00 p.m.)

FRIDAY, DECEMBER 14, 1973: Spectrum, Philadelphia, PA, with Jo Jo Gunne (8:00 p.m. show)
Over 16,000 fans attended this concert, which featured a few unusual songs. Dennis, decked out in a full three-piece suit and tie, sang an impromptu "Forever" (rarely in the set after 1972) with a ten piece children's maraca group. The group also pulled out "Little St. Nick" for their first encore.

SATURDAY, DECEMBER 15, 1973: Springfield Municipal Auditorium, Springfield, MA (Two shows at 7:00 and 11:00 p.m.)
Over 4,000 fans attended each of these concerts.

SUNDAY, DECEMBER 16, 1973: Walsh Auditorium, Seton Hall University, South Orange, NJ
The '74 Seton Hall yearbook gushed, "The group rocked the auditorium, exhibiting the majestic stage presence that is theirs alone. Carl Wilson, at the piano, sang several of their most popular ballads, including 'Let the Wind Blow' and 'Caroline, No.' Michael Love led the 'oldies but moldies' such as 'Surfin' USA' and 'Fun, Fun, Fun,' while Alan Jardine and Dennis Wilson provided the vocals on such favorites as 'Surfer Girl.' Several selections from their newest album, the *Beach Boys in Concert*, were included. The crowd enjoyed 'Sail on Sailor' and 'Heroes and Villains.' Blondie Chaplin was featured on 'Leaving This Town.' The group answered the clamor for an encore with a rendition of their seasonal hit, 'Little Saint Nick.'"

THE BEACH BOYS IN CONCERT

Mike Love in New Jersey, December 13, 1973. Photo used with permission of Matt Caruso, Kean University

TUESDAY, DECEMBER 18, 1973: Brooklyn College, Brooklyn, NY

WEDNESDAY, DECEMBER 19, 1973: Madison Square Garden, New York, NY, with Linda Ronstadt (8:00 p.m. show)

The Beach Boys' first appearance at the rebuilt Madison Garden brought out a large and boisterous crowd. The party atmosphere all but drowned out opening act Linda Ronstadt. Fred Kirby of *Variety* reported, "The Beach Boys roused the throng with newer material, but especially with such oldies as 'Wouldn't It Be Nice,' 'Darlin', 'Surfer Girl,' 'Help Me Rhonda,' 'Surfin' USA' and 'Sloop John B' . . . The vocal blends were exceptional, a key for the old rock 'n' roll clicks as well as the newer stuff."

Adding to the nostalgia was the surprise appearance of Bruce Johnston, who came out for 'Good Vibrations' and remained for the encores. However, backstage the mood was less then celebratory. This was the night that a backstage confrontation between Steve Love and Blondie Chaplin led to the Blondie's permanent departure after almost two years as a Beach Boy. In his absence, Billy Hinsche took over lead vocals on "Sail on Sailor."

SATURDAY, DECEMBER 29, 1973: Swing Auditorium, San Bernardino, CA

A capacity crowd filled the Swing Auditorium for the group's first show at the venue since 1963. Despite the sudden absence of Blondie Chaplin, Steve Cooper of the *Sun-Telegram* called the concert "near flawless" and singled out Carl for special praise, noting that he "was superb throughout the night and deserved the appreciative response for his solo on 'Caroline No.' Bathed in a light blue spotlight, he tamed a rocking audience with his fragile love song."

SUNDAY, DECEMBER 30, 1973: Sports Arena, San Diego, CA, with Joe Walsh and Barnstorm (7:30 p.m.)

A crowd of over 12,700 attended this show. The group did not take the stage until 11:30 p.m. because the plane carrying their equipment was late arriving from L.A. Carol Olten of the *San Diego Union* noted when they finally appeared, "the Beach Boys in concert Sunday performed exactly the tunes everyone came to hear— 'California Girls,' 'Surf's Up,' 'Good Vibrations,' etc . . . Their performance lasted until almost one a.m. with practically every song bringing rounds upon rounds of applause."

MONDAY, DECEMBER 31, 1973: Long Beach Arena, Long Beach, CA, with Joe Walsh and Barnstorm (8:00 p.m. show)

The Beach Boys returned to Long Beach for a festive New Year's Eve show. Ed Roach was on hand to film part of it for posterity. The last show of the year was a moment to take a deep breath and reflect on the long journey the group had already taken. Mike commented, "We played Long Beach twelve years ago and got paid $60, and I thought, 'Wow that's a lot of money and I don't even have to work.' Today we've increased our income over 1000 percent per concert." The group took the stage at 11:00 p.m. and played for two and a half hours, with Joe Walsh joining them on guitar for part of the show. They opened with 'Wouldn't It Be Nice,' bringing the crowd to its feet and, according to Terri Ray of the *East L.A. College Campus News*, "this is the way everybody stayed for the rest of the evening." The band was in a celebratory mood, with Mike decked out in a pink satin suit and Dennis armed for the night with a champagne bottle in his hand. There was even an unexpected stage invasion when "at midnight, a voluptuous young lady flung herself onto Carl Wilson with a pure, uninhibited desire to make love to him, but at that time everybody was flinging themselves on everybody else."

CONCERTS NOT PLAYED

Billboard magazine stated the Beach Boys were playing in Knoxville on December 2, but the show took place in Nashville.

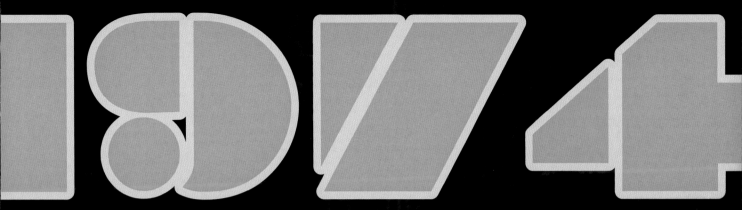

1974

A S 1974 BEGAN, the Beach Boys' popularity was on the rise. The depressing reality of Vietnam and Watergate led to a nationwide longing for the simpler times of the 1950s and early 1960s. This romantic vision of nostalgia was perfectly encapsulated in the 1973 film *American Graffiti*, which featured Beach Boys music prominently in its soundtrack. The group's early sound represented an America that lived in a joyful celebration of fun and was void of the cynicism and negativity that permeated current times. The *Beach Boys in Concert* album, released in November 1973, was boosted by a building revival of interest in the California icons. The LP reached number twenty-six on the *Billboard* charts and gave the Beach Boys their first RIAA Gold Record Award in many years.

It was at this critical time that James William Guercio entered the picture. Guercio started out as a musician, playing with the early Mothers of Invention and serving as Chad and Jeremy's guitarist and musical director. He parlayed that into a producer's role for Columbia Records. He first had hits with the Buckinghams, and then moved on to massive commercial success with the horn-rock trend of Chicago and Blood, Sweat, and Tears. A genuine fan of the Beach Boys music, Guercio offered his services as an occasional bass player in their touring band, and also in an advisory and managerial capacity. Chip Rachlin stated, "I helped get Jimmy in. Because

Poster for a show at Utah
State University in 1974.
Courtesy of Utah State University

I thought the records he
produced with Chicago were
great . . . I thought it would
be a very good association
[for the Beach Boys], so I used
whatever influence I had (to
get him in)."

For the Beach Boys,
1974 was another year spent
continuously on tour. Guercio
accompanied the band and
played an important role in
mediating tensions that had
been simmering within the
group. By the mid-1970s, Carl
and Dennis could usually be
counted on to vote exactly
the opposite of Mike and Al
on any band decisions. There
were frequent flare-ups, as the
partiers (Dennis and Carl)
had little in common with the
TMers (Mike and Al). Once
Guercio arrived on the scene,
he managed to gain the respect
of both factions and promoted
peace. Road manager Rick
Nelson recalled that Guercio
made "the show totally work.

CONCERTS PLAYED IN
1974

THURSDAY, FEBRUARY 14, 1974: Fieldhouse, Montana State University, Bozeman, MT (8:00
p.m. show)

After a short hiatus, during which time Mike took a five-week TM course in Belgium, the Beach
Boys returned to the road for a weeklong swing through the western states. Ed Carter, Ed Tuduri
(second drummer) and Carli Munoz were probably with them.

Their opening show in Bozeman was plagued by sound problems, for which the band
apologized after the intermission. Unfortunately, the problems persisted, marring what would
otherwise have been a great show. According to Pat Dawson of *The Exponent*, "'the sound
system was spitting out tinny highs on the drums, pronounced stumbling lows on the bass, and
feeble vocal mixing." Despite these issues, the group were called back for an encore, "a time
when they called for requests. 'Barbara Ann' did the trick. A Chuck Berry 'Johnny B. Goode'-style
intro led into the final number for the night 'Fun, Fun, Fun.' Love and Dennis Wilson showed their
appreciation by slapping palms which were extended over the edge of the stage."

FRIDAY, FEBRUARY 15, 1974: The Spectrum, Utah State University, Logan, UT, with Jim Stafford
(8:00 p.m. show)

The reviewer for the *Student Life* newspaper noted, "Although the audience seemed to appreciate
the group's more recent arrangements, it wasn't until the group went into such musical milestones
as 'Good Vibrations,' 'California Girls,' and 'God Only Knows' that the crowd hit the ceiling, rewarding
the group's efforts with four standing ovations." For reasons known only to him, Dennis Wilson
appeared at this show and other concerts on this tour dressed in a full tuxedo.

SATURDAY, FEBRUARY 16, 1974: Adams Field House, University of Montana, Missoula, MT, with
Jim Stafford (8:00 p.m. show)

The group appeared as part of the three-day Fasching Festival, attracting 5,000 fans.

SUNDAY, FEBRUARY 17, 1974: Air Force Academy, Colorado Springs, CO, with Jim Stafford

MONDAY, FEBRUARY 18, 1974: City Auditorium, Colorado Springs, CO, with Jim Stafford (Two
shows at 7:00 and 9:30 p.m.)

The 9:30 show was added after the 7:00 p.m. appearance sold out.

TUESDAY, FEBRUARY 19, 1974: Moby Gym, Colorado State University, Fort Collins, CO (8:00 p.m.
show)

Over 7,000 fans attended this tour-ending concert.

FRIDAY, MARCH 15, 1974: Salem Armory Auditorium, Salem, OR, with Jim Stafford (8:00 p.m.
show)

The Beach Boys hit the road for a short Pacific Northwest tour. In addition to Carli Munoz and Billy
Hinsche, James Guercio joined them on bass. Also in the lineup was a new face: drummer Bobby
Figueroa. He was a native Californian and a longtime Beach Boys fan. Figueroa had first seen them
play at the Azusa Teen Club in 1962. By 1974 he was a professional musician playing with an eight-
piece soul band at a club in Pasadena when he received a call from Carli Munoz. Figueroa recalled,
"I had given Carli a job when he first came out to the West Coast from Puerto Rico via New York. He
was a fantastic musician and we played together for about a year. Then we lost track of each
other for a while. He called me up in 1974 and said he was playing with the Beach Boys and they
were looking for a percussionist. He said, 'You want to give it a shot?' And I said, "Yeah, that sounds
pretty cool!' He gave me the address of Brother Records in Santa Monica. So I went down there
and I was the first guy in the studio and there were several other guys that were going to audition

as well for the same position. . . . I started playing and one by one Al and then Mike and the others individually walked into the studio and asked me to play different feels on the drums. So I obliged everybody and then they said 'Thank you very much.'"

Figueroa thought he stood little chance of getting the gig. "I was leaving the audition and pushing my stuff out the door and the other guys were getting ready to do their auditions and then I heard Dennis scream from down the hall, 'Hey, where are you going?' So I said, 'Well you have to audition the other guys too right?' And he said, 'No come over here.' So we went in the back to the office where he was set up and he said, "We want you to go on the road with us.' And I said, 'When?' And Dennis said, 'Tomorrow. We'll have them send a car for you and we'll see you in Washington.' It literally happened that fast. So I had to go back to the nightclub that night and tell the guys I was playing with, 'I'm leaving tomorrow and I won't be back.' Which was a shock to them. But I had a really good feeling about it. At that particular point in their career, the Beach Boys were doing the colleges and the 2500-seaters and weren't playing the really large venues, but I had a hunch [they would be big again] because I was familiar with them and was a fan. And of course within a year of my joining them they were again playing in the larger venues, like Wembley Stadium, as a result of the release of *Endless Summer*. It was a really good time to join. And because of Dennis and Carl trusting me to do certain things and the rest of the guys following suit, I loved being there."

SATURDAY, MARCH 16, 1974: Olson Auditorium, Pacific Lutheran University, Tacoma, WA, with Jim Stafford (Two shows at 6:00 and 9:45 p.m.)
Bobby Figueroa recalled, "I was little nervous and apprehensive at those first couple of shows. I didn't have any rehearsal and here I was within two days on stage with them and doing it. But that was probably the one and only time I felt like that because after that it was really great. And I went bowling with Dennis and Carli and some of the guys after the show and it was a really fun scene. And I thought, 'Wow, what a strange thing to be doing.' I went through the whole rookie, hazing thing. It was a new thing for me. I'd been playing small clubs for money for eight years and never really got to do the things I did with the Beach Boys . . . But Dennis was a great tutor in my drumming technique and calming me down into not doing so much and playing more feel than anything else. And Carl was kind of my vocal coach. And I felt like I was welcomed."

SUNDAY, MARCH 17, 1974: Pacific Coliseum, Vancouver, BC, Canada, with Jim Stafford and Chilliwack (8:00 p.m. show)
The set list for this show consisted of "Wouldn't It Be Nice," "The Trader," "Long Promised Road," "California Girls," "Funky Pretty," "California," "Marcella," "Surfer Girl," "Darlin'," "Little Deuce Coupe," "Caroline No," "God Only Knows," "We Got Love," "Sloop John B," "Help Me Rhonda," "Surfin' USA," "I Get Around," "Fun, Fun, Fun," and "Good Vibrations."

Don Stanley of the *Vancouver Sun* noted that "Funky Pretty" and "California" were greeted by "polite applause followed by a puzzled silence, which shaded from respectful to surly," while oldies like "Sloop John B" had the audience on their feet and dancing. Stanley singled out Mike for appreciation, noting that "between cheerleading and Ed Sullivan impressions ('really big shew') he made no fewer than three costume changes: a pink suit with a solar explosion on the chest, purple velvet with a purple wool cap, and a quick switch into Dennis Wilson's lumberman's basic. With his blonde hair and bushy blonde beard, he looked like a spaced out, lanky walrus." Stanley, however, seems to have missed the real reason why Mike switched briefly into Dennis' duds. According to *Rolling Stone*, while Carl was singing "Caroline No," Mike and Dennis ran across the stage stark naked and then switched into each other's clothes. The streaking cousins caused Carl to crack up in the middle of his performance.

MONDAY, MARCH 18, 1974: Victoria Memorial Arena, Victoria, BC, Canada, with Jim Stafford and Chilliwack (8:00 p.m. show)

TUESDAY, APRIL 9, 1974: Coliseum, University of Mississippi, Oxford, MS, with Jim Stafford (8:30 p.m. show)
The group flew to Memphis on April 8 and drove to Oxford, where they spent the night.

Jim was more than the bass player on the tours. He'd get them to sit down and do critiques after the shows, which they'd never done."

Guercio convinced the Beach Boys to revamp their live show and add more oldies. Carl and Dennis had fought to keep the show relevant, but it was an uphill battle with fans. Dennis rather glumly told a reporter from Utah State's *Student Life* in February that the "audiences don't seem to give the new material much of a chance. I personally enjoy our old material, but if the audiences gave us a chance I think they would begin to enjoy our more recent releases." Everyone in the band was

Carl (with new drummer Bobby Figueroa), March 16, 1974. Pacific Lutheran University Archives

THE BEACH BOYS IN CONCERT

weary of constantly struggling with crowds who only wanted hits. The practice of playing mainly newer songs in the first set and saving the majority of oldies for the end of the

> "They did a little less than an hour because CSNY wouldn't let them do more than that. It was all greatest hits. And it was unbelievable. I had never seen them received like this by a crowd and I remember saying to myself 'Hah! Let Crosby, Stills, Nash, and Young follow this!'"

show simply wasn't working. Under Guercio, the Beach Boys revamped their stage show to include more of their classic hit songs sprinkled evenly throughout the set. While they still played songs from *Holland*

Accompanying them were Jim Guercio, Billy Hinsche, Bobby Figueroa, Carli Munoz, and Don Lewis, who was hired to play synthesizer.

About 3,000 fans turned out for the tour opener at Ole Miss. Benjamin Smith of the *Daily Mississippian* noted, "The band alternated between songs such as 'I Get Around,' 'Little Surfer Girl,' 'Good Vibrations,' and 'Little Deuce Coupe,' with recent material from their *Holland* album . . . The audience never seemed to lose attention to what was happening on stage. Unlike many artists today, who play lengthy songs which sooner or later are apt to become monotonous, the Beach Boys allowed each number just enough time to catch on before going into something else."

WEDNESDAY, APRIL 10, 1974: Municipal Auditorium, New Orleans, LA, with Jim Stafford and the James Gang (8:30 p.m. show)
The Beach Boys attracted a large crowd eager to hear the hits. Bill Shearman of the *Times Picayune* noted, "'Surfin' USA,' 'Little Deuce Coupe,' and their classic 'California Girls' brought the whole place to its collective feet and for an encore the band didn't play anything past 1966 . . . One gets the impression from watching the band that it stills enjoys performing, a feeling you distinctly didn't get from the Rolling Stones in non-action a summer ago in Mobile."

Billy Hinsche's porta-pak camera filmed portions of this show, including performances of "The Trader" and "Marcella." (Ed Roach actually filmed the concert sequences, since Billy was busy performing.) Billy also captured a visit backstage by Van Dyke Parks. In addition, Hinsche filmed an earlier conversation at the hotel between Dennis, Carl, and Rick Nelson about the tour itinerary. The footage appeared in Hinsche's 1974 documentary *1974: On the Road with the Beach Boys*.

THURSDAY, APRIL 11, 1974: Municipal Auditorium, Atlanta, GA (7:30 p.m. show), and Fieldhouse, Auburn College, Auburn, AL, with Jim Stafford and the James Gang (9:30 p.m. show)
Despite playing an earlier show in Atlanta, the group performed until 2 a.m. for the Auburn audience. According to David Nordness of the *Auburn Plainsman*, "The group was visibly beat. (But) It was like the half-awake giddiness you get after two all-nighters in a row, with more polish and enthusiasm than most groups ever thought of having . . . They gave it everything they had and then some more . . . Everyone who was there felt the good vibrations of the truly great American band."

FRIDAY, APRIL 12, 1974: Curtis Hixon Hall, Tampa, FL, with Jim Stafford and the James Gang (8:00 p.m. show)
This show was almost derailed when the James Gang failed to show up, forcing promoters to offer refunds to those who wanted them. However, there were just as many fans that had wanted to purchase tickets and quickly snatched up the available seats to make the concert a success.

SATURDAY, APRIL 13, 1974: Sportatorium, Hollywood, FL, with Jim Stafford and the James Gang (8:30 p.m. show)
The group played a sold out concert for 13,000 fans at this barn-like venue near Miami. Once again the James Gang was billed but did not appear. Reviews were mixed. R. J. Dewhurst of the *Miami Herald* noted, "Despite the typically atrocious conditions at the Sportatorium, the overall impact of the show was rewarding and refreshing because the Beach Boys view the past with a clear affection and humor unhampered by clowning sentimentality." However, Dave Goldstein of the *Miami Hurricane* panned the performance as the worst he had ever seen. He argued that the group were sloppy and performed their new material in a shoddy fashion. "Lead guitarist Carl Wilson obviously has the strongest voice and at times carries the group as they haplessly forget lines and meander off stage. The group, in particular Mike Love, was condescending to the audience, sometimes to the point of lewdness. Brother Dennis turned his back to the crowd and mumbled the whereabouts of the band's sleeping accommodations—obviously for 'interested' fans."

SUNDAY, APRIL 14, 1974: Sports Stadium, Orlando, FL, with Jim Stafford
A tape exists of this concert. The set list consisted of "Wouldn't It Be Nice," "Darlin'," "Little Deuce Coupe," "The Trader," "Long Promised Road," "Surfer Girl," "Funky Pretty," "California," "Marcella," "God Only Knows," "We Got Love," "Don't Talk," "Heroes and Villains," "Surf's Up," "Don't Worry

1974

Baby," "Sloop John B," "Help Me Rhonda," "Surfin' USA," "Good Vibrations," "California Girls," "Barbara Ann," "I Get Around," and "Fun, Fun, Fun."

MONDAY, APRIL 15, 1974: State College, Edinboro, PA (8:00 p.m. show)

TUESDAY, APRIL 16, 1974: Long Center, University of Scranton, Scranton, PA (8:00 p.m. show)

WEDNESDAY, APRIL 17, 1974: Civic Arena, Pittsburgh, PA, with Steely Dan (8:00 p.m. show)

THURSDAY, APRIL 18, 1974: Coliseum, West Virginia University, Morgantown, WV, with Wet Willy (8:00 p.m. show)

Mike Hasch of the *Uniontown Morning Herald* reported, "They opened the evening with several old favorites which got most of the crowd in the right mood. Then came several of the newer songs, which I had rarely if ever heard. To be perfectly honest, the group handled themselves quite well on stage and the performance was excellent . . . For the next hour and a half, the Wilsons, Love, and company kept a fast paced and smooth running combination of the old and new . . . I left the Coliseum with the realization that it was one of the best concerts I'd seen in a while."

FRIDAY, APRIL 19, 1974: Marietta College, Marietta, OH (6:00 p.m. show), and St. John's Arena, Ohio State University, Columbus, OH, with the Talbot Brothers and Steely Dan (8:30 p.m. show)

The group performed back-to-back shows. The Columbus show was their third straight sold-out concert in three consecutive years at OSU. The fans eagerly applauded the oldies, though Anne Warner of *The Lantern* noted it was unfortunate that "the group's popularity cannot be extended with their current innovations. Fans are steadfast to songs such as 'California Girls' and they make it quite difficult for the group to break the ice to a new image. In this case, the Beach Boys might do better to elaborate on their old style."

SATURDAY, APRIL 20, 1974: Calvin College, Grand Rapids, MI (5:00 p.m. show), and Athletic and Convocation Center, Notre Dame University, South Bend, IN, with Stanky Brown (7:30 p.m. show)

Despite playing an earlier show in Grand Rapids, the Beach Boys showed no signs of fatigue at Notre Dame, performing a twenty-two-song set and two encores. Although there were problems with the sound system, which made Carl's vocals on "Long Promised Road" all but inaudible, Jerry Lutkus of *The Observer* reported that "while they're onstage, the group has the uncanny talent of making you feel that they're having a great time entertaining you . . . The key to it is Mike Love, whose stage personality is nothing short of amazing. He clowns, he dances and jokes while moving from one end of the stage to the other . . . Carl Wilson's voice showed the wear and tear of constant performing and Dennis Wilson gave a little more evidence to the fact that his voice has been going for years, but despite all that, when their voices worked together, there is no better vocal work in the business."

SUNDAY, APRIL 21, 1974: Morrow Field House, Slippery Rock State College, Slippery Rock, PA (2:00 p.m. show), and Beeghley Gym, Youngstown State University, Youngstown, PA, with Henry Gross (8:00 p.m. show)

About 3,000 fans attended this afternoon concert at Slippery Rock. Although they were only contracted to play a minimum of one hour, the group performed for more than two. They were paid $10,000 for the appearance.

Over 6,000 fans attended the evening show at Youngstown. Dennis McEaneny of *The Jambar* noted that when the group broke into "'Sloop John B' the crowd rose to its feet and remained standing for the remainder of the scheduled performance: 'Help Me Rhonda,' 'Surfin' USA,' and 'Good Vibrations.' They left the stage after 'Good Vibrations' but the screaming, clapping, stomping, cheering, clamoring crowd . . . brought them back for two more encores. Extended, all-stops-out versions of 'California Girls,' 'Barbara Ann,' 'I Get Around,' and 'Fun, Fun, Fun' closed out the show."

SATURDAY, MAY 11, 1974: Millett Hall, Miami University, Oxford, OH (7:30 p.m. show)

The Beach Boys began a string of Midwest dates. The musical personnel remained the same as the

Al performing at Pacific Lutheran University on March 16, 1974. Pacific Lutheran University Archives

and *Surf's Up*, nostalgia began to play the dominant role in their concerts.

At Guercio's suggestion, the band also sought to broaden their audience by accepting the position of opening act for supergroup Crosby, Stills, Nash, and Young. Bill Graham was promoting their massive 1974 concert tour. Graham had once scorned the Beach Boys, but had since become a supporter. Chip

THE BEACH BOYS IN CONCERT

Rachlin approached his old boss. Rachlin recalled, "Bill Graham went to the mat for the Beach Boys and convinced Crosby, Stills, and Nash. The CSNY camp was pretty much hipper than thou and [didn't

> "Dennis was late. We couldn't find him and we were set to go on. Bill Graham said, 'OK, Beach Boys, it's time to go on.' But we couldn't find Dennis. So then at the last minute he came cruising in as if nothing had happened. It drove Bill Graham bananas."

want them] . . . but Bill was an advocate for it." As a result, the group opened for CSNY at eight highly publicized concerts over the summer. The tour put them back in front of huge stadium crowds that had not been exposed to their exciting

April tour, except with Ed Carter in place of Jim Guercio on bass. Once again, Billy Hinsche had his porta-pak movie camera with him. The Miami University show attracted over 8,000 fans. John Fisher of the *Miami Student* declared the group "good but not great" and argued that while they did "demonstrate some impressive harmonies and vocals," the "clean tight sound they used to have just wasn't there. The awful sound system could very well have been responsible for the whole thing, but voices do change over the years."

SUNDAY, MAY 12, 1974: Sports Arena, Toledo, OH (7:30 p.m. show)
Prior to this night's concert, Billy Hinsche filmed "The Match," a highly charged backgammon game between Dennis and Carli Munoz with Ricky Fataar supplying color commentary and Billy and Bobby Figueroa acting as "coaches."

MONDAY, MAY 13, 1974: Physical Education Center, Wooster College, Wooster, OH, with the Apple Butter Band (8:00 p.m. show)
A paltry 966 students attended this show. The promoter blamed the low attendance on the change of date for the show. The concert had originally been scheduled for May 12.

TUESDAY, MAY 14, 1974: Western Illinois University, Macomb, IL

WEDNESDAY, MAY 15, 1974: Municipal Auditorium, Kansas City, MO, with Henry Gross (8:00 p.m.)
A show was scheduled at Kent State but it was canceled and the group played in Kansas City instead. Nancy Ball of the *Kansas City Times* noted that it took time for the crowd to build up enthusiasm. She blamed the "sheer number of men on the stage" for the tepid response in the first half, noting that it led "to a good deal of confusion as to just who was playing what, and the horrendous back echoes of the arena played havoc with the delicately balanced vocal and instrumental harmonies."

THURSDAY, MAY 16, 1974: Southern Illinois University Arena, Carbondale, IL, with Henry Gross (8:00 p.m. show)
Jimmy Dean of the *Southern Illinoisan* called this concert "unbelievably fantastic . . . Two encores to such greats as 'Barbara Ann' and 'Good Vibrations' and others had people standing in aisles and chairs for the final forty-five minutes. The first part of the two-hour concert had the Beach Boys playing some of their more recent tunes that didn't quite hit it off as well with the good-sized crowd. But once the nostalgia started, the Arena was filled with clapping hand and singing right along."

FRIDAY, MAY 17, 1974: Louisville Downs, Louisville, KY, with Earl Scruggs Revue (8:30 p.m. show)

SATURDAY, MAY 18, 1974: Jenison Fieldhouse, Michigan State University, Lansing, MI (8:00 p.m. show)
Dan Riddle of the *Michigan Daily* reported that the group "wowed the Jenison crowd with everything from 'Wouldn't It Be Nice' to 'Barbara Ann' and worked in several more introspective songs from recent albums . . . But the most fun of all was 'I Get Around' at the end of the regular set. As Mike Love and Dennis Wilson danced side by side a woman in a green sweater leaped on the stage to join them. But it only lasted for a few seconds. Love motioned to the guards who pulled the woman from the stage while the Beach Boys sang, 'You leave your best girl home on a Saturday night.'"

SUNDAY, MAY 19, 1974: "Joliet Jam," Joliet Memorial Football Stadium, Joliet, IL, with Bachman Turner Overdrive, the New Colony Six, Henry Gross, Fresh Start, and Fast Eddie (1:00 p.m. show)
Billy Hinsche filmed this concert, as well as a photo session that took place prior to it. The group was scheduled to play a gig on Monday in Indianapolis, but it was canceled and they flew home after the Joliet concert.

SATURDAY, JUNE 8, 1974: Oakland Coliseum, Oakland, CA, with the Grateful Dead, Commander Cody and his Lost Planet Airmen, and the New Riders of the Purple Sage (9:00 a.m. to 7:00 p.m. show)
The group arrived late for this event, forcing them to cut short their set. The *San Francisco Chronicle*

noted, "Promoter Bill Graham barely concealed his ire." Bobby Figueroa recalled, "Dennis was late. We couldn't find him and we were set to go on. Bill Graham said, 'OK, Beach Boys, it's time to go on.' But we couldn't find Dennis. So then at the last minute he came cruising in as if nothing had happened. It drove Bill Graham bananas. We finally did the show but Bill was just beside himself. Later I appeared with him in the movie *Bugsy* and we were talking about it. He said, 'That Dennis drove me crazy!' The funny thing was that the next time we played for him we each were given these wardrobe cases, and on each case there was a clock, like you'd find on a wall of an office building. When we were making the movie I said, 'So did you give us those clocks because of Dennis?' And he said, 'Yep!'"

The group went on just prior to the Grateful Dead, playing before a crowd estimated at over 30,000. In addition to the hits, they did songs from *Holland* including "Funky Pretty," "The Trader," and part of "California Saga." Pete Cowan of the *Oakland Tribune* reported, "Love and Carl Wilson did most of the lead vocals, with Al Jardine and Dennis Wilson helping out on backup. No longer the group's drummer, Dennis played keyboards at times. For an encore they did 'California Girls' and 'Fun, Fun, Fun' which seemed to be their motto from the start."

Al and Dennis at the "Day on the Green" concert in Oakland, California, June 8, 1974. Photo: Ed Roach ©1974, 2012

THURSDAY, JUNE 13, 1974: Civic Center, Providence, RI, with Kiki Dee (8:00 p.m. show)
Musicians that played on this ten-day tour included Carli Munoz, Billy Hinsche, and Bobby Figueroa.

FRIDAY, JUNE 14, 1974: Nassau Coliseum, Uniondale, NY, with Kiki Dee (8:00 p.m. show)
This show was broadcast on radio. The set list consisted of "Wouldn't It Be Nice," "Sail on Sailor," "Funky Pretty," "Marcella," "California," "We Got Love," "Little Deuce Coupe," "Trader," "All This Is That," "Feel Flows," "Surfer Girl," "God Only Knows," "Heroes and Villains," "Don't Worry Baby," "Sloop John B," "Help Me Rhonda," "I Get Around," "Good Vibrations," "California Girls," "Barbara Ann," "Surfin' USA," and "Fun, Fun, Fun." Both Paul Simon and Elton John made surprise guest appearances during the Beach Boys set. Elton came out during "Barbara Ann" and remained onstage until the end of the show. Paul Simon came out for the closing number, "Fun, Fun, Fun."

SATURDAY, JUNE 15, 1974: Yale Bowl, Yale University, New Haven, CT, with Kiki Dee (8:00 p.m. show)
Over 7,000 fans attended this concert.

SUNDAY, JUNE 16, 1974: Saratoga Performing Arts Center, Saratoga, NY, with Kiki Dee (7:00 p.m. show)
The Beach Boys performed before 15,000 people on a rainy, humid night. Nancy Curran of the *Schenectady Gazette* noted that they had "learned" from their 1973 appearance in Saratoga, where fans demonstrated distaste for the new material and made clear their desire for "oldies." Although they opened with a few numbers from *Holland*, "they finally returned to the days of yesteryear with a barrage of their hits that kept the crowds in their thrall."

TUESDAY, JUNE 18, AND WEDNESDAY, JUNE 19, 1974: Cape Coliseum, South Yarmouth, MA, with Kiki Dee
The group was one of the first acts to play at this 7,200-seat venue on Cape Cod.

live show. As Rachlin said, "These were the moves that you did to make them not simply an oldies act but to make them relevant."

The strategy worked. Even if reviewers sometimes overlooked them, the fans were blown away. "They did a little less than an hour because CSNY wouldn't let them do more than that. It was all greatest hits. And it was unbelievable. I had never seen them received like this by a crowd and I remember saying to myself 'Hah! Let Crosby, Stills, Nash, and Young follow this!'" Even if the crowd wasn't

~~~~~~~

THE BEACH BOYS IN CONCERT

really there to see them, the Beach Boys got their message across.

The tour coincided with Capitol's decision to release a double album of classic Beach Boys hits titled *Endless Summer*. The album was released in July 1974 and to the surprise of the entire music industry, it rose all the way to number one on the *Billboard* charts. The

> "We determine what we play by the response it gets from the public, and with the success of things like *Endless Summer*, that material seems to be what's most in demand."
>
> —Mike Love

group's initial complaints about packaging and song selection were silenced by the exciting *Billboard* statistics reflecting the LP's massive sales across the U.S. The success of *Endless Summer* provided clear evidence that the Beach Boys' audience wanted oldies. As Mike said, "We determine what we play by the response it gets from the public, and with the success of things like *Endless Summer*, that material seems to be

FRIDAY, JUNE 21, 1974: Civic Centre, Ottawa, ON, Canada (8:00 p.m. show)
This show was attended by almost 14,000 people. Bill Provick of the *Ottawa Citizen* was almost deafened by the applause that washed over the Civic Centre when the group took the stage. He commented, "Unfortunately, the sound was sometimes atrocious especially in the early parts of the show. The lead vocals and accompanying harmony—a trademark— were embarrassingly bad at times with Dennis Wilson's rendition of 'Help Me Rhonda' still the worst example . . . The crowd . . . demanded nostalgia, got it, and left extremely happy. The Beach Boys remained trapped within their early charisma."

SATURDAY, JUNE 22, 1974: Broome County Veterans Memorial Arena, Binghamton, NY (8:00 p.m. show)

SUNDAY, JUNE 23, 1974: "World Series of Rock," Cleveland Stadium, Cleveland, OH, with Joe Walsh and Barnstorm, REO Speedwagon, and Lynyrd Skynyrd (2:00 p.m. show)
This tour-ending show, produced by radio station WMMS and Belkin Productions, was attended by approximately 40,000 people.

TUESDAY, JULY 9, 1974: Seattle Coliseum, Seattle, WA, with Crosby, Stills, Nash, and Young and Jesse Colin Young (8:00 p.m. show)
More than 15,500 fans attended the opening date of the much-hyped CSNY reunion tour. Bobby Figueroa recalled, "That was a fun tour for me because I was getting to see up close these icons . . . And what a great show it was to have both these great bands playing together. The crowds were really warming to us. You'd hear people saying, 'Oh wow I love 'Don't Worry Baby.' So I think people were starting to wake back up to the Beach Boys at that time."

FRIDAY, JULY 19, 1974: Royals Stadium, Kansas City, MO, with Crosby, Stills, Nash, and Young and Jesse Colin Young (6:30 p.m. show)
The group opened for CSNY but many people left the stadium exclaiming that the Beach Boys stole the show. The *Kansas City Times* noted, "The crowd's biggest reaction was saved for the Beach Boys, stars of the middle 1960s. The group was called back for an encore after performing for an hour and a half. Standing ovations followed each of the group's three encore numbers, including golden oldies 'Surfer Girl' and 'Good Vibrations.'" Bobby Figueroa agreed with reviewers that CSNY made a tactical mistake in letting the Beach Boys open for them. "I mean, how do you follow an hour and a half of nothing but hit songs? The crowd would go wild every time we started a new number."

SUNDAY, JULY 21, 1974: County Stadium, Milwaukee, WI, with Crosby, Stills, Nash, and Young and Jesse Colin Young (12:00 p.m. show)
A massive crowd of 52,000 turned out for this concert, simulcast on WQFM. Once again, despite preceding CSNY, the group made a strong impression. Damien Jacques of the *Milwaukee Journal* reported "After doing several sections from their fairly recent *Holland* album, they moved into a string of their old hits that brought the memories surging back. It was like a recitation of the number one hits of the last decade. 'Little Deuce Coupe,' 'Don't Worry Baby,' 'Surfer Girl,' 'I Get Around,' 'Surfin' USA,' and 'Good Vibrations' were played one after another. By the time the group got to 'Barbara Ann' the audience was dancing, clapping in unison and singing along . . . "

THURSDAY, JULY 25, 1974: Mile High Stadium, Denver, CO, with Crosby, Stills, Nash, and Young and Jesse Colin Young (8:30 p.m. show)

SATURDAY, JULY 27, 1974: "Oklahoma Jam," All Sports Stadium, Oklahoma City, OK, with Leon Russell and the Gap Band, Elvin Bishop, Trapeze, Babe Ruth, and Isis (2:00 p.m. show)
Over 13,000 fans turned out for this all-day event organized by Leon Russell.

SUNDAY, JULY 28, 1974: Jeppesen Stadium, Houston, TX, with Crosby, Stills, Nash, and Young and Jesse Colin Young (4:00 p.m. show)
With over 50,000 in attendance, the CSNY show at Jeppesen was more of an event than a concert.

The Beach Boys proved a tough act to follow. Bob Claypool of the *Houston Post* reported, "The Beach Boys came on full of zippy surf harmonies that came across tight and bright in the still blistering sunlight. The Boys ran through a big chunk of past triumphs—most of which came from the pre-psychedelic sun and surf era. It seemed to be what the crowd wanted most—'Little Deuce Coupe,' 'Little Surfer Girl,' 'I Get Around' and others—occasionally balanced by newer things, such as the Love-Jardine Transcendental Meditation tribute, 'All This Is That.'"

The Beach Boys performing at the Oklahoma Jam on July 27, 1974. Ed Roach © 1974, 2013

WEDNESDAY, JULY 31, 1974: Texas Stadium, Irving, TX, with Crosby, Stills, Nash, and Young and Jesse Colin Young (6:00 p.m. show)
Over 32,000 fans attended this show. Susan Barton of the *Dallas Times Herald* reported that the Beach Boys "had almost everybody up and dancing 1974 dances to their lighthearted, bouncy tunes depicting sunshine, convertibles and California girls. It has been a long time, in fact, since a group has caused such a rocking reaction to its music."

FRIDAY, AUGUST 23, 1974: Roosevelt Stadium, Jersey City, NJ, with the Eagles (8:00 p.m. show)
The group launched a ten-day tour with Carli Munoz on piano; Billy Hinsche on keyboards; Jim Guercio on bass; and Ross Salamone, formerly of the band Madura, and Robert Kenyata on extra percussion. While oldies definitely outnumbered post-1970 songs, the band still played "Sail on Sailor" (with Billy Hinsche on lead), "Long Promised Road," "California," "Marcella," "All This Is That," and "Feel Flows." Ricky Fataar, soon to depart the group, sang his usual lead on "We Got Love" as well.

SATURDAY, AUGUST 24, 1974: Capital Centre, Largo, MD, with the Marshall Tucker Band (8:00 p.m. show)
An estimated 20,000 fans attended this concert, demonstrating the renewed interest in the group as a result of the success of the current *Endless Summer* LP.

SUNDAY, AUGUST 25, 1974: Norfolk Scope, Norfolk, VA, with the Marshall Tucker Band and the Eagles (8:00 p.m. show)

MONDAY, AUGUST 26, 1974: Roanoke Civic Center, Roanoke, VA, with the Marshall Tucker Band (8:30 p.m. show)
By this time, drummer Bobby Figueroa had begun singing vocal parts in addition to playing percussion. He recalled, "We were backstage getting ready to go on one night and I just started singing something that they did and Carl came over and said, 'Do that again!' And then Al walked by and said 'Hey, you've got a voice!' And the next thing I knew Carl was telling Steve Moffitt 'Get him a mic.' And he gave me one vocal part to sing. I think it was in 'Feel Flows' . . . Eventually later on I sang 'Sail on Sailor' on my own and one night on a very rare occasion Carl couldn't hit the notes on 'Darlin'' and asked me to sing it."

WEDNESDAY, AUGUST 28, 1974: CNE Grandstand, Toronto, ON, Canada, with Bachman Turner Overdrive
Over 22,000 fans attended this concert. Lawrence O'Toole of the *Toronto Globe* argued that the clear harmony on their records was lost by the need to play to a stadium of rowdy fans. He commented, "The Beach Boys . . . have also juiced up their instruments to jump well over the

what's most in demand." While Dennis and Carl privately fretted about becoming a singing jukebox of ancient hits, the band publicly embraced their old songs. A number one album gave the group a whole new audience that was eager to hear them live.

By August 1974, the Beach Boys were regularly selling out much larger venues than they had in some time. For example, over 22,000 fans turned out for their show in Toronto. As Dennis explained to *Melody Maker*, "There was a time when it was uncool to be into the Beach Boys. Somehow the Beach Boys didn't fit at one period, but now . . . well, I guess were just fitting again. It's not uncool to like the Beach Boys anymore." Road manager Rick Nelson reasoned in an interview with the *New Times* that the group was having a renewed popularity because "the show is totally happy. I've never seen a down show. Night after night it's up, up, up. The music is a positive creative force . . . and people are ready for that these days. People need it or enjoy

"There was a time when it was uncool to be into the Beach Boys. Somehow the Beach Boys didn't fit at one period, but now . . . well, I guess were just fitting again. It's not uncool to like the Beach Boys anymore."

—Dennis Wilson

it or are looking for it." Mike credited the group's "hard work and determination" for the change in fortunes. He told *Melody Maker* that "over the last few years we've reached maybe a half-million people who weren't aware of the Beach Boys as a thirteen-year entity. Our concerts have got better and better and I think the new

lyrics (and some of their later lyrics are good stuff) . . . The heavier beat destroys that lovely, almost diaphanous quality songs like 'I Get Around' and 'Do It Again' once had. There was a basic innocence at the core which drew you back into hazy, summer days."

THURSDAY, AUGUST 29, 1974: Ohio State Fair, Columbus, OH (Two shows at 4:30 and 8:30 p.m.)
The group's equipment truck broke down and they were forced to use the fair's existing sound system. Despite pouring rain and sound problems, Cynthia Robins of the *Columbus Dispatch* reported that the crowd of roughly 23,000 "pulled a mini-Woodstock (and) grooved on very, very good vibrations and enjoyed a newer, tighter, cooking group of musicians." Robins argued the band was better than they'd been when they last played Columbus in April and gave credit to the addition of drummer Ross Salamone, who played in tandem with Ricky Fataar. The set list for the second show consisted of "Wouldn't It Be Nice," "California," "Marcella," "We Got Love," "Do It Again," "I Can Hear Music," "Little Deuce Coupe," "Long Promised Road," "Sail on Sailor," "The Trader," "Feel Flows," "All This Is That," "Sloop John B," "Surfer Girl," "Heroes and Villains," "Help Me Rhonda," "I Get Around," "Fun, Fun, Fun," "Good Vibrations," "California Girls," "Barbara Ann," and "Surfin' USA."

SATURDAY, AUGUST 31, 1974: Pocono International Raceway, Long Pond, PA, with the Allman Brothers and Edgar Winter, the Marshall Tucker Band, and Duke Williams and the Extremes (12 noon to 9 p.m. show) and Pine Knob Music Theatre, Clarkston, MI (7:30 p.m. show)
Following an afternoon show in Pennsylvania, the group flew to Michigan to appear at Pine Knob. This concert was added after two other scheduled dates at the venue sold out.

SUNDAY, SEPTEMBER 1, 1974: Assembly Hall, Indiana University, Bloomington, Indiana, with Kansas and the Eagles (1:00 p.m. show)
This concert was scheduled to take place at the outdoor Tenth Street Stadium, but monsoon conditions forced it indoors. The last-minute switch led to technical problems at the concert, but the crowd of roughly 12,000 was well-behaved. Peter Kaufman of the *Indiana Daily Student* noted that the new songs interspersed throughout the first half of the concert "received a polite but token reception," but when the group played older numbers "the crowd was ecstatic: from 'Sloop John B' through 'Surfer Girl,' 'Help Me Rhonda,' 'I Get Around,' 'Fun, Fun, Fun,' and 'Good Vibrations' the crowd loved it all. Then the encores 'California Girls,' 'Barbara Ann,' and "Surfin' USA' and the Beach Boys' seventy-five-minute set was over. And if the vocals occasionally wandered and the harmony was a little ragged here and there, nobody seemed to mind. It was too exhilarating to mind."

MONDAY, SEPTEMBER 2, AND TUESDAY, SEPTEMBER 3, 1974: Pine Knob Music Theatre, Clarkston, MI (One show each night at 7:30 p.m.)
The Tuesday show took place on Al's birthday and the joyous crowd of 10,300 sang to him when he came onstage. John Weisman of the *Detroit Free Press* reported, "While some of the group's subtleties were lost Tuesday night because of their leviathan sound system, the Beach Boys, backed by a group that included James William Guercio on bass, showed the audience exactly the kind of good time it had expected all along. They are still at the top of their form—something not many other pop groups can claim after having been on the concert and recording trail for more than a decade."

SUNDAY, SEPTEMBER 8, 1974: Roosevelt Raceway, Westbury, NY, with Crosby, Stills, Nash, and Young; Joni Mitchell; Tom Scott and the LA Express; and Jesse Colin Young (1:00 p.m. show)
The group opened for CSNY one last time at this eleven-hour event, attended by close to 80,000 people. The Raceway was owned by Madison Square Garden, which organized the show with Bill Graham. The Beach Boys took the stage at 2 p.m. and quickly won over the crowd. They played "Wouldn't It Be Nice," "Sloop John B," "Little Deuce Coupe," "Surfing USA," "Good Vibrations," "Barbara Ann," and "Fun, Fun, Fun." According to the *Stony Brook Statesman*, "The sound of the Beach Boys brought back memories of surfing and hot rods, scenes typical of the early '60s and the crowd responded wildly."

It is probable that this was Ricky Fataar's last concert. He made the decision to move on and was offered a job with Joe Walsh. Although it has been previously suggested in print that his last show was in December, keyboardist Ron Altbach confirmed that Ricky was already gone when he joined the Beach Boys' backing band in November. Bobby Figueroa commented, "He was a fantastic drummer . . . Watching him play really helped me a lot. He was a great guy and his drumming style was really cool . . . "

SUNDAY, OCTOBER 12, 1974: El Paso Civic Center, El Paso, TX (8:00 p.m. show)
This was one of a few concerts the band performed in October. They were spending much of the month recording at Jim Guercio's Caribou Ranch in Nederland, Colorado.

SATURDAY, OCTOBER 25, 1974: Pershing Municipal Auditorium, Lincoln, NE
This was another one-off show, in the midst of a two-month hiatus.

TUESDAY, NOVEMBER 12, 1974: Niagara Falls International Convention Center, Niagara Falls, NY, with the Raspberries
About 10,300 fans attended the opening date of the fall tour. The group added a number of older songs that they hadn't performed in years to the set, including "I Can Hear Music," "Warmth of the Sun," "In My Room," "Catch a Wave," and "I'm Waiting For the Day" (sung by Billy Hinsche).

The concert was notable for a number of reasons. Firstly, it marked Dennis' return to the drum kit after a three-year absence. Secondly, it marked the return of Bobby Figueroa, who would become a group mainstay, to handle extra percussion. Thirdly, Ron Altbach was added to the group, joining Billy Hinsche and Carli Munoz on piano and keyboards.

Altbach was a TM devotee and had been recruited by Mike, whom he'd met the previous year. He visited the band when they were in Toronto in late August and was not exactly made welcome. He recalled, "I saw Carl in the lobby. I walked up to him and said hi and that Mike had invited me to come over because I was going to join the band, and Carl said basically 'Go fuck yourself' and walked away." Carl considered himself the de facto bandleader and felt that hiring musicians was his job, not Mike's. He viewed Altbach with distrust as part of the "meditating" contingent. After that frosty reception, Altbach decided the gig was not going to happen. He was eventually invited to go to Switzerland to teach TM. "So I packed up . . . and went to Switzerland. But literally within hours of arriving there, I got a call from Rick Nelson who asked why I wasn't at Caribou Ranch rehearsing for the tour that was starting in less than a week. So after about an hour of soul searching, I got a flight back to the U.S. and went to Caribou, where the rehearsals were finished. Carl was there and grudgingly took me through the set and told me what to play on what songs."

Altbach's first show did not go well. He recalled, "I had been with my own band King Harvest through college, through a few years in Paris, through having a big hit ("Dancing in the Moonlight") and touring, and we always wore whatever, jeans, etc. But when I showed up on stage in a tee shirt, Carl was fuming. And after the show he attacked me verbally, saying I had rushed the little theremin part I played on 'Good Vibrations' and that I had played out of tune on another that required accuracy in some other place. Al was standing with me and in fact reminded me a couple of months ago of what I said to Carl, which was, 'I have forgotten more about music than you have learned, Carl, but it's your band, so if you want to fire me, this would be a good time to do it.' Unfortunately that set the tone. I was clearly marked as being in the meditator contingent and while I know Carl was a gentle and sweet man and a beautiful singer, we just never hit it off."

WEDNESDAY, NOVEMBER 13, 1974: Heiges Field House, Shippensburg State College, Shippensburg, PA, with the Raspberries (8:00 p.m. show)

THURSDAY, NOVEMBER 14, AND FRIDAY, NOVEMBER 15, 1974: Spectrum, Philadelphia, PA, with Billy Cobham (Thursday only) and Roger McGuinn (Friday only)
The group was only scheduled to play Thursday, but a Friday show was added due to demand. Matt Damsker of the *Evening Bulletin* reported that the group was "all in good form and voice, deftly triggering a super-charged, joyous, sing-along-clap-along audience with a shower of surf anthems."

Carl in his Nudie suit at Pacific Lutheran University, March 16, 1974. Pacific Lutheran University Archives

audiences and record buyers from twelve to twenty are now becoming aware."

Many reviewers were struck by the young age of the fans that turned out for the Beach Boys' concerts. Jack Reiley's strategy of constantly touring and performing for college audiences had created a second generation of fans, most of whom were too young to recall when "Little Deuce Coupe" was a new song. Quite a number of reviewers were dumbfounded that young people would embrace surf music, but as Scott MacRae of the *Vancouver Sun* noted, the Beach Boys gave people a chance to forget the problems

THE BEACH BOYS IN CONCERT

of today and "reflect that it might be fun to be an adolescent, if the biggest concern was that Daddy would take the T-Bird away."

Some reviewers criticized the band for bowing to the crowd's desire for nostalgia rather than challenging their expectations. Such criticisms

"They were so splintered . . . Dennis and Carl Wilson were on one path and Mike Love was on another. The only place they saw each other was occasionally at a board room or else on the road."

became louder as the '70s progressed and the band gave the audience more oldies at the expense of new material. This was the problem the Beach Boys faced. They were in the position of damned if you do and damned if you don't. If they catered to the fans that wanted progressive music, as they had in 1971–1973, then

SATURDAY, NOVEMBER 16, 1974: Jadwin Gym, Princeton University, Princeton, NJ, with Roger McGuinn (8:00 p.m. show)
The group's third appearance at Princeton attracted 8,000 people. The *Daily Princetonian* reported that the "vibrations" caused by the crowd's exuberant dancing loosened the beams in the gym and caused damage. As a result they banned further concerts there.

SUNDAY, NOVEMBER 17, 1974: Civic Center, Springfield, MA, with Roger McGuinn (8:00 p.m. show)
A capacity crowd of 10,000 people attended this concert, standing or sitting "wherever there was an inch of space in the auditorium," and thirty-six Springfield police were required to get them under control. Fans were thrilled to see Dennis back pounding out the beat and he seemed happy to play a more central role onstage then he had in recent years. Rick Nelson argued, "The greatest thing that ever happened for Dennis was to get back with playing drums. His whole attitude changed; he really felt vital to the group again."

MONDAY, NOVEMBER 18, 1974: Syracuse War Memorial, Syracuse, NY, with Roger McGuinn (8:00 p.m. show)
Over 9,000 fans attended this show. Andrew Reschke of the *Syracuse Herald Journal* reported, "The harmony which has been a trademark of the Beach Boys for many years has never sounded better. The distinctive blend of voices on which many of the younger members of the audience have been weaned since they were toddlers, is as pure and delicate as ever. . . . There was a polished quality to their performance, one that has been perfected in their dozen or so years in rock music, and they know what their fans want."

TUESDAY, NOVEMBER 19, 1974: Pucillo Gym, Millersville State College, Millersville, PA (8:00 p.m. show)
The Beach Boys charged the Millersville concert committee $15,000 to appear. The fee included a $4000 charge for miscellaneous expenses, such as wages for work crews and advertising.

WEDNESDAY, NOVEMBER 20, 1974: Patrick Gym, University of Vermont, Burlington, VT
The Raspberries were originally scheduled to open and the Beach Boys planned on only playing one sixty-minute set, but the University paid an extra $500 to get them to play two sets with no opening act. The group was promised $15,000 plus sixty percent of any gate over $22,000. The University made $26,000 from the show. Thus, the group ended up netting $17,400.

Carlo Wolff of the *Burlington Free Press* noted that the 5,000 fans "cheered the Beach Boys every time they swung into one of their hits, golden oldies like 'Little Deuce Coupe,' 'Surfin' USA,' 'Help Me Rhonda.' And their more complex songs like 'Heroes and Villains,' 'Good Vibrations,' and 'Waiting for the Day' came across with a power not usually associated with the group . . . Even though the Beach Boys didn't play any new material, it all sounded fresh . . . It felt like the group has finally caught up with its past and is ready to come out with new material after a pause of nearly two and a half years."

THURSDAY, NOVEMBER 21, 1974: Madison Square Garden, New York, NY, with Roger McGuinn
Despite heavy promotion, this appearance was not a sellout. Nevertheless, Fred Kirby of *Variety* reported, "Spirits were high onstage and offstage at Madison Square Garden Thursday as the happy surf-rock of the Beach Boys permeated the arena. The Coast combo spiced their full set and encores with many tunes they've never before done live plus some, such as 'In My Room,' their first encore, which they haven't done locally for about ten years."

FRIDAY, NOVEMBER 22, 1974: Baltimore Civic Center, Baltimore, MD, with the Raspberries (8:00 p.m. show)

SATURDAY, NOVEMBER 23, 1974: Boston Garden, Boston, MA, with John Sebastian (Two shows at 6:00 and 9:00 p.m.)
The Beach Boys sold out the Boston Garden, necessitating a 6:00 p.m. show being added. The

set list for the first show consisted of "I Can Hear Music," "Marcella," "Little Deuce Coupe," "Do It Again," "The Warmth of the Sun," "Sail on Sailor," "Surfer Girl," "Heroes and Villains," "Darlin'," "God Only Knows," "Don't Worry Baby," "Sloop John B," "Wouldn't It Be Nice," "I Get Around," "Good Vibrations," and encores of "In My Room," "Help Me Rhonda," and "California Girls."

Following this concert, the band returned to California to tape Dick Clark's *New Year's Rockin' Eve* TV special. It was filmed before a live audience at MGM Studios on November 26 and also featured Chicago, Herbie Hancock, Olivia Newton John, and the Doobie Brothers. The Beach Boys performed "Good Vibrations," "Darlin'," and "Surfer Girl." Mike, Al, and Carl also sang background vocals during Chicago's performance of "Wishin' You Were Here." Jim Guercio played bass with both bands during the show. Dennis was absent from the taping. He allegedly balked over the group's decision to appear in matching double-breasted blazers, white slacks, and polka dot scarves.

THURSDAY, DECEMBER 5, 1974: Denver Coliseum, Denver, CO, with Honk (8:00 p.m. show)
The group began a string of sixteen western dates. Bobby Figueroa, Ron Altbach, Billy Hinsche, Carli Munoz, and Jim Guercio accompanied them. A number of newer songs, such as "Trader," were dropped from the set in favor of more oldies. The *Denver Post* reported, "The coliseum was packed to the ceiling, even behind the stage. The young crowd was animated nearly to the point of hysteria."

FRIDAY, DECEMBER 6, 1974: University of Utah, Salt Lake City, UT, with Honk (8:00 p.m. show)
This show marked the first appearance by the group in Salt Lake City since 1970. According to Vandra Webb of the *Salt Lake Tribune*, the audience reacted as if they had never been away. "They didn't stop clapping, swaying, stomping, and screaming all night long as the Beach Boys presented old time favorites time after time. There was 'In My Room' and 'Surfin' Safari' and both brought renewed cheers from the audience . . . It's the kind of music that makes you happy and takes you back to that time when the biggest problem was finding a big wave."

SATURDAY, DECEMBER 7, 1974: Boise State University, Boise, ID (8:00 p.m. show)

MONDAY, DECEMBER 9, 1974: Coliseum, Spokane, WA

TUESDAY, DECEMBER 10, 1974: Seattle Center Coliseum, Seattle, WA (8:00 p.m. show)
Erik Lacitis of the *Seattle Times* noted that the crowd was mainly composed of teenagers. However, he pointed out, "The high schoolers who went to the Seattle Coliseum last night weren't on a nostalgia trip. They went because they are now discovering the Beach Boys for themselves. Last night as the Beach Boys sang tunes with titles such as 'Surfin' USA,' 'Barbara Ann,' 'Good Vibrations,' and 'Help Me Rhonda,' youths streamed down from their seats into the main arena to dance."

WEDNESDAY, DECEMBER 11, 1974: Pacific Coliseum, Vancouver, BC, Canada
Demand was so great in Vancouver that a second concert was added on Saturday.

FRIDAY, DECEMBER 13, 1974: Memorial Coliseum, Portland, OR, with Honk (8:00 p.m. show)
About 10,000 fans attended this show. John Wendeborn of *The Oregonian* reported, "It's a whole new generation that wants the Beach Boys—and it's got them. The noise surrounding all the oldies—'I Get Around' and the finale 'She had Fun, Fun, Fun 'til her daddy took her T-bird away,' among a dozen or more others—bordered on pandemonium. The only bad part was the sound; It didn't fill the Coliseum acoustically, only noisily."

SATURDAY, DECEMBER 14, 1974: Pacific Coliseum, Vancouver, BC, Canada (8:00 p.m. show)
As proof of their resurgence, Mike proudly proclaimed to *Melody Maker* reporter Harvey Kubernik that 17,500 fans attended this show and 5,000 more had to be turned away.

WEDNESDAY, DECEMBER 18, 1974: Selland Arena, Fresno, CA, with Little Feat (8:00 p.m. show)

THURSDAY, DECEMBER 19, 1974: Civic Auditorium, Bakersfield, CA, with Little Feat (8:00 p.m. show)

they were criticized for being selfish and disinterested in the majority of the audience's wishes. Conversely, if they gave in to audiences' constant demand for more oldies, then they were accused of selling out. No act in rock history shouldered this burden more intensely than the Beach Boys.

Meanwhile Brian seemed lost and showed little interest in being a Beach Boy. With the exception of a radio interview with Jim Pewter for KRTH in L.A., he kept a very low profile for the entire year, spending most of his time in bed. Guercio did manage to get Brian to accompany the group to his Caribou Ranch and recording studio in the fall of 1974 for proposed sessions, but nothing of any real value came out of it. Brian seemed temporarily bereft of creativity and his only released work of 1974 was a quirky Christmas record called "Child of Winter" that didn't see release until December 23, several weeks too late for any holiday relevance.

With little recording going on, band members pursued their own interests off the road. Most of Mike's free time was taken up by meditation. Al shared his passion for TM and it brought the two closer together during this period. However, TM alienated them from the Wilsons, whose devotion to meditation had lagged. Mike believed that it gave him the strength to resist the temptations of the road and grew increasingly impatient with the self-indulgent lifestyles of his cousins. Due to his disgust and sadness over seeing Brian's drug-related deterioration,

Manager, producer, and bass player James Guercio performs with the Beach Boys, March 16, 1974. Pacific Lutheran University Archives

Mike had become intolerant of recreational drug use and drinking. The Wilsons, on the other hand, were irritated by Mike's judgmental attitude and rigid sobriety. As Chip Rachlin commented, "They were so splintered . . . Dennis and Carl Wilson were on one path and Mike Love was on another. The only place they saw each other was occasionally at a board room or else on the road."

The band had risen from the ashes of a failing career and were becoming one of the mid-seventies' biggest concert draws. 1975 would see the Beach Boys hitting new heights of success, but tensions within the group would soon threaten everything they had worked so hard for.

The group received a hero's welcome in Bakersfield, with the audience drowning out the opening number with applause. The group kept them in the palm of their hands the rest of the night. John Ford of *The Californian* reported, "As the Beach Boys finished their last number and wished everyone a Merry Christmas, the crowd began to roar for them to do an encore. Hundreds of matches lit up the room like little stars while people pounded and chanted for more. As the group returned, the bandsmen showed their appreciation by building an already tremendous concert to a staggering climax. People sang, swayed and screamed at a group that has sold over seventy million records."

FRIDAY, DECEMBER 20, 1974: Civic Auditorium, San Francisco, CA (8:00 p.m. show)

SATURDAY, DECEMBER 21, 1974: Exhibit Hall, Earl Warren Community Center, Sacramento, CA, with Honk (Two shows at 1:00 and 8:00 p.m.)
The 8:00 p.m. show sold out only seven hours after tickets went on sale, causing a 1:00 p.m. show to be added. John V. Hurst of the *Sacramento Bee* noted "there was far less of their current music than of their California gold of the '60s . . . The fans were on their feet for most of the set, and they called the group back twice for encores."

SUNDAY, DECEMBER 22, 1974: Earl Warren Convention Center, Santa Barbara, CA

FRIDAY, DECEMBER 27, 1974: Inglewood Forum, Los Angeles, CA, with Honk
At their first hometown show in over a year, the band put on an exhilarating if ragged show, with Jim Guercio on bass. Harvey Kubernik of *Melody Maker* noted, "The harmonies are still excellent and as the years go by, the music is getting tighter and better. All of the eras of the group's existence were touched upon in the two-hour set . . . The concert ended with 'Good Vibrations,' possibly one of rock's finest songs. The crowd wouldn't leave. Then came the opening notes of 'California Girls,' with 'In My Room,' and a song of desperation, 'Help Me Rhonda,' then 'Barbara Ann,' and to close 'Fun, Fun, Fun.'"

SATURDAY, DECEMBER 28, 1974: Swing Auditorium, San Bernardino, CA, with Honk

SUNDAY, DECEMBER 29, 1974: Long Beach Arena, Long Beach, CA, with Honk (8:00 p.m. show)
The Beach Boys celebrated their thirteenth year as a live act with a ninety-minute concert in the city where they'd made their first major appearance in 1961. The *Long Beach Press Telegram* reported, "They worked an energetic crowd into near frenzy, played for an hour and a half and walked off stage two encores later without scratching their creative brains for new material . . . Comparing this concert to one given in the Arena last New Year's Eve, the Beach Boys would have to earn A-plus for their latest effort . . ."

CONCERTS NOT PLAYED
A concert at Kent State University scheduled for May 15 was canceled. A concert at the LA Coliseum scheduled for July 6 was canceled. A concert scheduled for August 3 at the Ontario Motor Speedway in California, that would have also featured CSNY, Joe Walsh, and Jesse Colin Young, was canceled.
The group was advertised in June as appearing in Chicago on September 6 and 7, but did not play.

I F 1974 WAS the year the Beach Boys regained mass popularity, then 1975 was the year they re-cemented their position as rock superstars. They played major arenas and stadiums in a highly publicized tour with the band Chicago (dubbed "The Beachago Tour") and took part in a massive concert in London with Elton John. In both cases, the consensus was that the Beach Boys stole the show. They won critical plaudits as the best live band in America, and were chosen as *Rolling Stone* magazine's "Band of the Year."

of money they'd seen CSNY grossing the year before. Chip Rachlin was thrilled because he knew "that tour couldn't miss if you tried. I mean combined, the Beach Boys and Chicago had forty top-ten records."

It was agreed that the Beach Boys would play first, followed by Chicago, and finally the two groups would come together for the last hour. For Chip Rachlin the highlight was when Dennis came out each night to sing

"That tour couldn't miss if you tried. I mean combined, the Beach Boys and Chicago had forty top-ten records."

"You Are So Beautiful." He recalled that at rehearsals, "The group discussed singing a few numbers with Chicago at the end of the show and then saying 'Thank you. Good night.' Dennis said, 'No, I want me and [Chicago keyboardist] Bobby Lamm to get up and sing 'You Are So Beautiful' together,' which was a big hit for Joe Cocker." Dennis, and others, claimed that he'd co-written the song with its credited author Billy Preston. Rachlin recalls initially disliking the idea of

CONCERTS PLAYED IN
1975

SATURDAY, JANUARY 4, 1975: HIC Arena, Honolulu, HI (8:00 p.m. show)
The Beach Boys opened the year with a concert in Hawaii, after which they began a twelve-week hiatus. Mike, who remained in Hawaii with his fiancée, told Penny Anderson of the *Cedar Rapids Gazette*, "Touring around the world . . . is really exhausting. The pace and pressure of the grind, plus the lack of a stable lifestyle, gets so bad that people can actually flip out from it all."

FRIDAY, MARCH 21, 1975: Community Center Arena, Tucson, AZ (8:00 p.m. show)
To prepare for their first shows in over two months, the group scheduled two days of rehearsals (March 19 and 20) at Caribou Ranch prior to flying to Arizona. The flight was not uneventful. Ron Altbach recalled, "Dennis and I flew to Tucson on a charter flight and . . . he insisted on smoking, and he was arrested when we got to Tucson. It was just Dennis being Dennis."

Larry Fleischman of *The Tucson Daily Citizen* declared the show that night "the greatest performance this town has ever seen." He went on to gush, "there were moments last night when absolutely everything was perfect. Like on 'Fun, Fun, Fun' when the entire crowd did the high harmony line so loudly that the entire place reverberated. Or on 'Little Deuce Coupe,' the first surprise of the evening, when the entire joy of that song made the audience stand as one."

SATURDAY, MARCH 22, 1975: Tempe Stadium, Tempe, AZ

SUNDAY, MARCH 23, 1975: UC Santa Barbara, Santa Barbara, CA, with Jesse Colin Young and Honk
Over 27,000 fans attended this concert on the UC campus. Though it wasn't evident to fans, Ron Altbach recalled that there was a lot of tension between Mike and Dennis. "When we played Santa Barbara, Dennis rode his motorcycle up to the gig drunk and showed up late. Mike just didn't get it at all. What was the fun of ruining the Beach Boys? From Mike's point of view, Dennis was just so unpredictable. Mike didn't get the whole rock star thing. He was much more professional and disciplined about the whole thing."

FRIDAY, MARCH 28, 1975: Memorial Stadium, Daytona Beach, FL (8:00 p.m. show)
The Beach Boys began a short southern tour, accompanied by Jim Guercio, Bobby Figueroa, Ron Altbach, Carli Munoz, and Billy Hinsche. While the set leaned heavily on oldies, there were a few surprises, including a cover of the Stones' "Brown Sugar."

SATURDAY, MARCH 29, 1975: Civic Center, Lakeland, FL (8:00 p.m. show)

SUNDAY, MARCH 30, 1975: Hollywood Sportatorium, Hollywood, FL, with Honk (8:00 p.m. show)

TUESDAY, APRIL 1, 1975: Freedom Hall, Louisville, KY, with Billy Joel (7:30 p.m. show)

WEDNESDAY, APRIL 2, 1975: Civic Coliseum, Knoxville, TN, with Billy Joel (8:00 p.m. show)

THURSDAY, APRIL 3, 1975: Omni Coliseum, Atlanta, GA (8:00 p.m. show)

FRIDAY, APRIL 4, 1975: Civic Center, Charleston, WV, with Billy Joel (8:00 p.m. show)
Over 7,000 fans turned to see the Beach Boys and Billy Joel. The group proved so popular with the crowd that they were called back for two encores and even that wasn't enough. Mike finally told the crowd, "OK, we'll stay 'til we sing them all."

SATURDAY, APRIL 5, 1975: Greensboro Coliseum, Greensboro, NC, with Billy Joel (8:00 p.m. show)

1975

SUNDAY, APRIL 6, 1975: Charlotte Coliseum, Charlotte, NC, with Billy Joel (8:00 p.m. show)
According to Marjorie David of *The Charlotte Observer*, "There was wave after wave of Beach Boys standards, from the opening with 'Sloop John B' to 'Help Me Rhonda,' 'Sail on Sailor,' and 'Surfer Girl.' And the crowd which had milled and fretted for part of the opening act—pianist composer Billy Joel, who was onstage for an hour, was on its feet and dancing for the Beach Boys."

MONDAY, APRIL 7, 1975: William and Mary College, Williamsburg, VA, with Honk
A capacity crowd turned out for this tour-ending concert. Wayne Studer of *The Flat Hat* noted, "On the slower selections like 'Surfer Girl' or 'Don't Worry Baby,' Love, Jardine, and the Wilsons once again demonstrated what *Rolling Stone*'s Arthur Schmidt meant a few years ago when he called the Beach Boys 'rock's only choir.' Their voices, similar to begin with, blend in such a way that their incredibly tight harmonies lend to many of their songs an almost spiritual air."

THURSDAY, MAY 1, 1975: Municipal Auditorium, Austin, TX
This was a special warm-up concert to gear up for the Chicago tour. Tickets were only given out to fans attending the University of Texas. Jim Guercio (bass), Bobby Figueroa (second drummer/percussion), and Ron Altbach, Carli Munoz, and Billy Hinsche (keyboards/pianos) accompanied the group on the tour.

FRIDAY, MAY 2, 1975: Jeppesen Stadium, Houston, TX, with Chicago and Flo and Eddie and the Turtles (7:00 p.m. show)
The opening concert of the twenty-one-date "Beachago" tour went on for five hours with long delays between acts. While two delays were simply opening-show technical problems, the need to reset the stage between the Beach Boys and Chicago sets led to the inclusion of a thirty-five-minute intermission at future "Beachago" shows. A female tightrope walker and a man specializing in flagpole stunts traveled with the tour and performed during intermission.

SATURDAY, MAY 3, 1975: Cotton Bowl, Dallas, TX, with Chicago and Flo and Eddie and the Turtles (7:00 p.m. show)
Kim Martin of the *Dallas Times Herald* declared that the "Beach Boys rarely achieved exceptional moments, did well to maintain, and far too many times failed at that." Martin blamed the poor performance on "technical problems, especially with sound mixing," which caused the harmonies to be drowned out by the instruments. She noted, "By their third tune, 'In My Room,' the musicians, most notably Mike Love and Carl Wilson, were looking at each other with distinct signals of uneasiness in their movements. The high vocals, meanwhile, trailed off inaudibly for the audience." However, Martin conceded that the crowd had a good time and stayed on their feet cheering for the whole last part of the show. •

SUNDAY, MAY 4, 1975: Myriad Arena, Oklahoma City, OK, with Flo and Eddie and the Turtles (8:00 p.m. show)
The Beach Boys headlined this concert, attended by close to 10,000 fans. Edwin Maloy of *The Oklahoman* reported, "'Little Deuce Coupe,' 'Wouldn't It Be Nice,' 'In My Room,' 'Do It Again,' and 'Help Me Rhonda' might be anthems for a happier, quieter, more peaceful time, but the mood is still catching. Sing-alongs on 'Rhonda' and 'Vibrations' were easy to join because everyone was having such a good time—except possibly the police security and ushers who were more than busy with enthusiastic fans."

SATURDAY, MAY 17, 1975: Arrowhead Stadium, Kansas City, MO, with Chicago (3:00 p.m. show)
The Beach Boys arrived in Kansas City on Friday and held a sound check that night to ensure they wouldn't experience the technical issues that marred the opening shows of the tour. Jess Ritter of the *Kansas City Times* noted, "The sound was for the most part favorable, the Beach Boys pumping a big bass sound from the walls of amps on the massive stage."

The band was certainly pumped up at these shows. Bobby Figueroa recalled, "The Beachago tour was wonderful. I was a big fan of Chicago and played a lot of their music in the nightclubs.

Dennis performing it. "I said, 'You're out of your mind! Why would you do that? First of all there may be no one left in the hall. Why would you do that?' And Dennis just said 'Watch.' Anyways, the opening show went great and the Beach Boys were great and the audience wanted more. So the house lights went down and Dennis came out and introduced Robert Lamm and I'm thinking to myself 'Dennis is currently dating Robert Lamm's former wife, this is already pretty nuts.' And then it [the performance of that song] literally brought the house down. It just was a spectacular moment and he was right. It was unbelievable." The song proved such a crowd pleaser that Dennis sang it at virtually every concert he appeared at for the next five years.

The tour was a huge success selling out six shows at Chicago Stadium, four concerts at New York's Madison Garden, and many other stadiums and arenas across the U.S. For the Beach Boys, it was a major triumph. In 1971 they'd struggled to sell out tiny Carnegie Hall, and now four years later they were able to sell out four nights at Madison Square Garden. Jim Guercio was singled out for managing the Beach Boys back to prominence, but in a TV interview he declared, "The Beach Boys did everything. The Beach Boys had the hopes and dreams and the talent and the music. They've always had it. The only ability I tend to have is that I can help people achieve what it is they want to achieve . . . my talent is making everybody ten feet tall."

217

THE BEACH BOYS IN CONCERT

The elation over the tour's success added to the festive vibe of the concerts, which many people, including Chip Rachlin and Rick Nelson, view as the highlight of the Beach Boys' performing career. The group played with an intensity and commitment to the material that they'd seldom display so fully again. Mike, usually dressed in a flashy gold lamé jacket and turban, hit his stride as a frontman. Always comfortable in front of large crowds, he seemed exuberant on the tour. He told *Cleveland Scene* reporters Mark Kmeztko and Cliff Michalski, "The two groups are very complementary to each other; both do vocal harmonies. Chicago has good percussion and horns. We add to each other. Some of our stuff together has been really outrageous—ten or twelve people singing at one time. Blowing people right out of the stadium."

So to stand at a microphone with Peter Cetera and trade parts with him was really great. Because here was one of my heroes, and I know Carl admired his voice quite a bit too, and that's saying something. And Bobby Lamm, Terry Kath, and the rest of those guys were fantastic musicians. So playing together with them and hearing that music live was really great. But what stuck out in my mind was the encore, where we came out together as one huge band and sang each other's songs. I think it set a mark for doing shows like that. I don't think anyone had done anything quite like that before. You had hits coming out your ears! By the time you left that theatre, you were just overwhelmed."

SUNDAY, MAY 18, 1975: St. Louis Arena, St. Louis, MO, with Chicago (7:00 p.m. show)
More than 16,000 fans attended this concert. Dick Richmond of the *Post Dispatch* declared it a big success because "the two bands complement each other. The Beach Boys basically concentrate on vocals and tight harmony. Chicago, which has a number of hits such as 'Saturday in the Park' and 'Harry Truman' that are vocals, are mostly inclined toward brass-dominated instrumentals . . . so the end result was that of a band supporting vocalists, the number of which ranged from one to twelve depending on the song."

For the encores, the two bands played "We Can Make It Happen," "Harry Truman" (accompanied by fireworks), "California Girls," "Fun, Fun, Fun," and a highly charged version of "Feelin' Stronger Every Day." However, the audience refused to leave and stomped and chanted "we want more" until the bands returned to the stage. Dave Schmitt of *Concert News* reported that "Mike Love led the total entourage back out for the final encore. The unexpected treat 'Jumping Jack Flash' with Love drove the fans crazy. Strutting his stuff, he dragged the mike across the stage, ripped off his shirt and amply pleased the crowd while both groups played right up 'til the house lights went on."

FRIDAY, MAY 23, 1975: "Together Concert," Anaheim Stadium, Anaheim, CA, with Chicago and Honk (6:00 p.m. show)
Over 50,000 fans piled into Anaheim Stadium to see this show, which promoters dubbed the "Together Concert." While admitting that the double bill attracted fans of both bands, Michael Jensen of the *Pasadena Star News* had no doubts that "the Beach Boys showed up Chicago that night." The audience response to the Beach Boys was so strong that stadium officials had to rush to the second and third stadium levels to request that thousands of fans stop dancing and jumping for fear that the whole stadium structure might collapse.

Amongst those present for this concert were Brian and his family. While still in his reclusive phase, he was convinced to check out the show. Photographers took numerous pictures of him backstage, looking overweight and scruffy. Carl later recalled that Brian was taken aback by the fact that so many young people, most of whom hadn't even been born when the group started, knew every word to their songs.

Carl, Al, Billy Hinsche, and Dennis harmonize at Anaheim Stadium, May 23, 1975. Photo: Ed Roach ©1975, 2012

SATURDAY, MAY 24, 1975: "A Day on the Green," Oakland Coliseum, Oakland, CA, with Chicago, Bob Seger, Richard Torrance, and Eureka (1:00 p.m. show) Over 55,000 fans attended this concert, and a festive atmosphere permeated the Coliseum. Kathie Staska of *The Hayward Daily Review* declared, "The Beach Boys have been stealing concerts away from headliners for many years now and Saturday afternoon was no different . . . The Beach Boys did a different musical set than they did last year and worked harder on their older material like 'Surfer Girl,' 'Little Deuce Coupe,' 'Wouldn't It Be Nice,' 'Good Vibrations,' 'Sloop John B,' and 'I Get Around.'"

1975

SATURDAY, MAY 31, 1975: "World Series of Rock," Municipal Auditorium, Cleveland, OH, with Chicago (1:30 p.m. show)

The Beach Boys flew into Cleveland on Friday and Carl was whisked off to radio station WMMS, one of the sponsors of this mega-show, where he acted as guest DJ. In the music memoir *The Buzzard: Inside the Glory Days of WMMS and Cleveland Rock Radio*, music director John Gorman fondly recalled that the appearance "was one of those once in a lifetime magic moments." Carl allegedly had too good a time with the radio crew, as did Dennis, who ended up getting drunk with the DJs at a nearby bar. The next morning Gorman was told that Mike was furious at him because Dennis could barely hold up his head and Carl was so out of it that he had uncharacteristically "told Love to take his TM and shove it."

Despite this backstage drama, the 35,000 fans that attended on Saturday afternoon didn't notice a thing. Jane Scott of the *Plains Dealer* praised the concert as "three and a half hours of just plain great vibrations," and declared that "the happy harmonies and get down boogie beat of the Beach Boys and the soaring jazz-rock sounds of Chicago were a fine blend . . . "

SUNDAY, JUNE 1, TO THURSDAY, JUNE 5, AND SATURDAY, JUNE 7, 1975: Chicago Stadium, Chicago, IL, with Chicago

The Beachago tour sold out five nights at Chicago Stadium and a sixth night was added. The shows were the high point of the tour. Chris Charlesworth of *Melody Maker* reported that it was obvious to all that, despite the fact that Chicago was nominal headliner, it was the Beach Boys who were the audience favorite. He added that when the two bands joined forces at the end of the show "the concert truly came alight." *Variety* opined that the Beach Boys' performance suffered from atrocious sound and threw some of the blame on "their needlessly intricate nine pieces which turned some songs like 'Heroes and Villains' and 'Good Vibrations' into extended shouting matches," but concluded, "their onstage presence is so strong that the handful of satisfying renditions of songs like 'Surfer Girl' and 'In My Room' seemed enough."

The *Chicago Tribune* accused Dennis of being inebriated when he went onstage, while *Variety* declared that he "gave the show a black eye with his senseless ramblings." Such behavior was still something of a rarity in 1975, but was also an ominous sign of troubles to follow in the ensuing years.

THURSDAY, JUNE 12, TO SUNDAY, JUNE 15, 1975: Madison Square Garden, New York, NY, with Chicago

The Beachago tour had no problem selling out four nights at Madison Square Garden. Portions of one show were filmed for a TV special called *Fun, Fun, Fun*, hosted by Tom Curtis. The Beach Boys and Chicago were seen performing "Feelin' Stronger Every Day" and "Fun, Fun, Fun" with Jim Guercio on bass in a New York Rangers jersey.

Bobby Figueroa recalled the Garden shows fondly. "We rocked Madison Square Garden! We put cracks in the walls. People were jumping around and getting into the music. When New Yorkers like you, they really like you!"

SATURDAY, JUNE 21, 1975: Wembley Stadium, Wembley, England, with Elton John, Joe Walsh, the Eagles, Rufus featuring Chaka Khan, and Stackridge (11:30 a.m. show)

The group took a break from the Beachago tour and flew to England for one massive U.K. show attended by 72,000 people. Although Elton John was the headliner, reviewers were adamant that it was the Beach Boys, making their first U.K. appearance since 1972, who were the real stars of the day. *New Musical Express* declared, "In soccer terms, it was Elton John 1, Beach Boys 3. Where the Beach Boys, with their close harmony, good-time sounds, and gospel of nothing more profound than the joys of teenage love, immediately connected with the audience, Elton John seemed obsessed with piano-dominated, moody music and was for most of the time on a cloud of his own." Chris Welch reported in *Melody Maker*, "It was the Beach Boys who stole the show . . . They went through the mother lode of their repertoire from 'Help Me Rhonda' and 'Little Deuce Coupe' through to 'Sail on Sailor' and 'Surf's Up.' The audience was on their feet for the entire set."

Bobby Figueroa recalled, "That show was when I realized how powerful the Beach Boys were

"When we played Santa Barbara, Dennis rode his motorcycle up to the gig drunk and showed up late. Mike just didn't get it at all. What was the fun of ruining the Beach Boys? From Mike's point of view, Dennis was just so unpredictable. Mike didn't get the whole rock star thing. He was much more professional and disciplined about the whole thing."

However, a few perceptive reviewers noted that potential problems remained. Max Bell of *New Musical Express*, noted a dichotomy within the group: "Fun lovin', life and soul of the party, Mike Love continues to project the most aggressive cheerleader mug. Carl, evidently, would prefer a bit more solemnity. After all

> Carl later recalled that Brian was taken aback by the fact that so many young people, most of whom hadn't even been born when the group started, knew every word to their songs.

'Surf's Up,' 'Trader,' 'Sail on Sailor,' and 'California' are the Boys now, but they have to be shoved into the middle of the set because not enough people pay them attention." While the entire band agreed on the set changes that Guercio had suggested, there was a clash brewing within the band over whether this was a temporary or a long-term career path.

Nevertheless, the Beach

internationally. It also showed how good we were. Here we are with the Eagles, Elton John in his prime, and Rufus (with Chaka Kahn), which I really liked, and I get up with the Beach Boys and just hear this thunderous recognition from the audience after every song . . . It was amazing that there were so many great bands at that time making their mark. And we could go up against any one of them and just blow them away."

TUESDAY, JUNE 24, TO SATURDAY, JUNE 28, 1975: Capitol Centre, Landover, MD, with Chicago
Over 100,000 people turned out for the five-night stint at the Capitol Centre. Even President Ford's children were in attendance and Susan Ford invited the Beach Boys to the White House for a special all-access tour.

The set remained the same for all the shows, with the exception of June 27. Chicago bassist Robert Lamm broke his leg that day while playing basketball and had to miss the concert, so the Beach Boys were asked to expand their set. The audience that attended that night was treated to extra songs, including, "Surf's Up," "Marcella," "I Can Hear Music," and "You're So Good to Me."

Tom Basham of the *Baltimore Sun* noted that when the Beach Boys joined Chicago onstage at the end of the show, "the energy level in the Capitol Centre climbed higher and higher through 'Saturday in the Park,' 'California Girls,' 'Fun, Fun, Fun,' and 'Feelin' Stronger Every Day.' Guitarist (Terry) Kath and Carl Wilson were sizzling, riding over the wave of sound generated by the screaming fans and the smoking bands. Spirits soared up to the roof and exploded into a two minute standing ovation on the last notes of 'Stronger' at 12:18. At 12:20 the bands were back and finished the show with a power version of 'Jumping Jack Flash . . . '"

Portions of one of these shows was filmed for the *Fun, Fun, Fun* TV special, including rousing performances of "I Get Around," "Catch a Wave," and "Good Vibrations." Mike Love and Jim Guercio were also interviewed backstage by Tom Curtis. In addition, TV cameras captured producer Phil Ramone recording the concert for a possible live album.

Ramone, stationed in the Washington Bullets' locker room, taped four of the shows (June 25–28). Alan Boyd, custodian of the Beach Boys archives, stated that in his opinion, these are some of the best live performances by the group that he's heard. Unfortunately, the album was never released due to the legal difficulties that occur when opposing record companies are involved. After many years where their whereabouts were unknown, the tapes of the group's performances are now safely ensconced in their vaults. Boyd noted that they "are missing the Beach Boys' tracks for the encores. When both bands took the stage, they ended up running a pair of 2" machines in sync: the main 24-track deck, and an additional sixteen track to record the Beach Boys' vocals and instruments. The Chicago portions of the encores were sent to Warners (along with the tapes of the main shows) as part of an ongoing legal settlement a few years back, but the Beach Boys' 16-track encore reels somehow didn't make the trip . . . We're not completely sure as to their exact whereabouts, but we think they exist."

SUNDAY, JUNE 29, 1975: Schaefer Stadium, Foxboro, MA, with Chicago (8:00 p.m. show)
This outdoor Beachago concert attracted over 62,000, making it, at the time, the biggest crowd to attend a concert in New England. By contrast, only 35,000 had attended the Beach Boys' 1973 appearance at the same venue. The show netted $620,000.

TUESDAY, JULY 1, 1975: Spectrum, Philadelphia, PA, with Michael Murphy (8:00 p.m. show)
The Beach Boys took a break from the Chicago tour to headline a few shows of their own. This concert drew 19,500 fans. Matt Damsker of the *Evening Bulletin* reported that the "concert hit a soaring pace, on its collective feet from the first notes, as the Beach Boys delivered strongly and euphoniously—the simple favorites, 'Surfer Girl,' 'Little Deuce Coupe,' 'Sloop John B,' 'California Girls' balanced against the later, more sophisticated ones, 'Sail on Sailor,' 'Heroes and Villains,' 'Good Vibrations.'"

THURSDAY, JULY 3, 1975: Marcus Amphitheater, Milwaukee, WI (Two shows at 3:00 and 7:30 p.m.)
The Beach Boys were paid $50,000 to appear at Summer Fest. The concert was marred by bad

weather, which caused technical problems and led to stops and starts. Nevertheless, the *Milwaukee Sentinel* commented that the group "demonstrated again that they are clearly masters at what they do . . . a crowd of about 30,000 stood, clapped and stomped as the band breezed through familiar yet still exciting renditions of 'I Get Around,' 'Surfer Girl,' and 'California Girls.'"

SUNDAY, JULY 6, 1975: Hughes Stadium, Colorado State University, Fort Collins, CO, with Chicago
About 37,000 fans attended the closing show of the Beachago tour and, according to the *Rocky Mountain Collegian*, were treated to "almost four hours of familiar hits from the past, some present day rock professionalism, and a good excuse to sit all day in the very warm sun." The biggest surprise of the show was the guest appearance by Elton John, who was recording at Caribou Ranch and was invited to the concert by Jim Guercio. Elton joined the Beach Boys for "Barbara Ann" and the big finale.

FRIDAY, JULY 25, 1975: Coliseum, Edmonton, AB, Canada, with Tim Moore (Two shows at 5:00 and 9:00 p.m.)
An estimated 24,000 fans attended these shows, which were part of "Klondike Days," a ten-day festival with numerous big name entertainers including Johnny Cash and Dionne Warwick. Audience response to the Beach Boys was extremely enthusiastic. Joe Sornberger of *The Edmonton Journal* reported, "Fans did more than applaud. They tuned in to the good vibrations flowing from the stage. They danced, sang along, stomped, hooted, cheered and in every way enjoyed the best show yet in the Coliseum. It was just a great evening of musical fun."

SATURDAY, JULY 26, 1975: McMahon Stadium, Calgary, AB, Canada, with Tim Moore (8:00 p.m. show)

SUNDAY, JULY 27, TO TUESDAY, JULY 29, 1975: Montana State Fair, Great Falls, MT (One show each night at 8:00 p.m.)

SUNDAY, AUGUST 10, 1975: Balboa Stadium, San Diego, CA, with Jesse Colin Young and Pure Prairie League (1:00 p.m. show)
Over 20,000 attended this show, a far cry from the measly 2,000 that had shown up when the band performed in San Diego in 1971. Donald Harrison of the *San Diego Union* noted that the crowd "responded enthusiastically to the downright insistent beats of such past favorites as 'Help Me Rhonda,' 'Surfer Girl,' 'Little Deuce Coupe,' 'California Girls,' 'I Get Around,' and 'Good Vibrations.' After hearing a fifteen-song set on such favorite Beach Boy topics as surfing, cars, and girls, the fans applauded and brought back the rock group for 'Barbara Ann,' 'Surfin' USA,' and 'Fun, Fun, Fun.'"

MONDAY, AUGUST 18, 1975: Iowa State Fair, Des Moines, IA (8:00 p.m. show)
The Beach Boys began a sixteen-date tour accompanied by Ed Carter, Carli Munoz, Billy Hinsche, Bobby Figueroa, and Ron Altbach.

TUESDAY, AUGUST 19, AND WEDNESDAY, AUGUST 20, 1975: Pine Knob Music Theatre, Clarkston, MI

THURSDAY, AUGUST 21, 1975: Dayton Hara Arena, Dayton, OH, with Ambrosia (8:00 p.m. show)

FRIDAY, AUGUST 22, 1975: Wings Stadium, Kalamazoo, MI

SATURDAY, AUGUST 23, 1975: Civic Arena, Pittsburgh, PA (8:00 p.m. show)
The Beach Boys were scheduled to play one concert in Pittsburgh on August 29, but demand was so great that this show was added. Tickets sold out in four hours, making it the fasting-selling show in Pittsburgh history. The audience was incredibly enthusiastic, though as usual more for the oldies than anything new, and Pete Bishop of the *Pittsburgh Press* noted that "aside from the slower

Boys were on top of the world again. Their August–September tour grossed over two million dollars and drew huge crowds. Spirits within the group were high. When Jane Scott of *The Cleveland Plains Dealer* asked if he could imagine the band breaking up, Carl replied, "I don't know. All I know for sure is that you never know. But right now we're having too much fun. And as long as people like us we'll be out there." The group had finally reclaimed their place as one of America's top bands and with Brian showing signs of emerging from his long hibernation, there was every indication that 1976 might make them even bigger.

Bobby Figueroa recalled, "That show was when I realized how powerful the Beach Boys were internationally. It also showed how good we were. Here we are with the Eagles, Elton John in his prime, and Rufus (with Chaka Kahn), which I really liked, and I get up with the Beach Boys and just hear this thunderous recognition from the audience after every song . . . It was amazing that there were so many great bands at that time making their mark.

numbers ('In My Room,' 'Surfer Girl,' and Dennis Wilson's rendition of 'You Are So Beautiful') and a couple less familiar ones from the *Holland* album, every song—every song—was an everybody up, clap along, sing along, cheer along, do-the-bump along."

SUNDAY, AUGUST 24, 1975: Allentown Fairgrounds, Allentown, PA, with the Captain and Tennille

MONDAY, AUGUST 25, 1975: Veterans Memorial Coliseum, New Haven, CT, with the Captain and Tennille (8:00 p.m. show)

TUESDAY, AUGUST 26, 1975: Civic Center, Hartford, CT (8:00 p.m. show)

WEDNESDAY, AUGUST 27, 1975: SPAC, Saratoga, NY, with Ambrosia (7:00 p.m. show)
This concert at SPAC had a turnout of 26,892. Scott L. Powers of the *Troy Times-Record* reported, "The Beach Boys gave a dynamite show, rendering true to the record imitations of all their old hits . . . The execution in most places was perfect, and in the case of songs like 'California Girls,' a little update work made the song stand up, even to today's musical tastes. For the most part, Brian Wilson's songs have stood the test of time. Not many writers can say the same."

THURSDAY, AUGUST 28, 1975: Nassau Coliseum, Uniondale, NY, with Gary Wright (8:00 p.m. show)
Demand for tickets was so great that a second show was added for September 1. The set consisted of "Sloop John B," "Do It Again," "In My Room," "Help Me Rhonda," "The Trader," "Sail on Sailor" (sung by Billy Hinsche), "California," "Heroes and Villains," "Little Deuce Coupe," "Catch a Wave," "Surfer Girl" (sung by Dennis), "Darlin'," "California Girls," "Wouldn't It Be Nice," "I Get Around," "Good Vibrations," "You Are So Beautiful," "Barbara Ann," "Surfin' USA," and "Fun, Fun, Fun."

The crowd was in the mood to let loose but many were intimidated by over-zealous security, who shined flashlights in fans' eyes when they stood up to dance. Tony Kornheiser of *Newsday* reported, "Beach Boys' drummer Dennis Wilson finally had enough and grabbing a mike, he shouted at the crowd, 'Hey, what is this? Stand up . . . I said stand up' . . . The guards were beaten. And the people never sat down until the concert was over."

FRIDAY, AUGUST 29, 1975: Civic Arena, Pittsburgh, PA, with Ambrosia (8:00 p.m. show)

SATURDAY, AUGUST 30, 1975: CNE Grandstand, Toronto, ON, Canada, with the Stampeders (Two shows at 7:00 and 11:30 p.m.)
Over 44,000 fans turned out for these sold-out shows emceed by Wolfman Jack. Robert Martin of the *Globe* noted, "All the audience wanted was hot sand and smoking tires. Whenever they got off that well-worn track, to play, for example, a couple of numbers from *Holland* . . . the crowd was polite but uninterested. The reaction of the audience was obviously not unexpected. Carl Wilson, who sang the *Holland* songs, said 'Thank you for listening,' as though he had encountered some audiences that have howled him down with cries of old favorites . . . "

SUNDAY, AUGUST 31, 1975: Montreal Forum, Montreal, Quebec, Canada, with Ambrosia (8:00 p.m. show)

MONDAY, SEPTEMBER 1, 1975: Nassau Coliseum, Uniondale, NY, with Ambrosia (8:00 p.m. show)

TUESDAY, SEPTEMBER 2, 1975: Great American Music Fair, Syracuse, NY, with the Doobie Brothers, America, Jefferson Starship, New Riders of the Purple Sage, and Stanky Brown (12:00 p.m. show)
The Beach Boys ended their summer tour with an appearance at this twelve-hour event promoted by John Scher. Bad weather turned the fairgrounds into a giant puddle of mud and delays led to the group not taking the stage till 11:30 at night. The *Syracuse Post Standard* noted, "By that time, many concertgoers had given in to the increasing cold and wind and gone home. But for those who

remained, the Beach Boys played the best of the surfing music they've made so popular over the past several years, including 'Sloop John B' and 'Help Me Rhonda.'"

SATURDAY, OCTOBER 25, 1975: ACC, University of Notre Dame, South Bend, IN, with Ambrosia (8:00 p.m. show)

For their fall tour, Mississippi native Elmo Peeler replaced Ron Altbach on keyboards and Jim Guercio took Ed Carter's place on bass. Making their fourth appearance at Notre Dame, the group received a gleeful reception from the Irish audience. Patrick Small of the *Observer* noted that the Beach Boys sounded under-rehearsed and "ragged." But Small also admitted that "the harmony on the softer songs was at times magnificent, particularly 'In My Room' and the end of 'Heroes and Villains' with the exquisite 'ahs' backing Al Jardine's vocal."

SUNDAY, OCTOBER 26, 1975: Eastern Michigan University, Ypsilanti, MI, with Ambrosia (8:00 p.m. show)

About 6,000 fans attended this concert. Bill Turque of the *Michigan Daily* wrote that while the group ran through all their hits and kept the crowd happy, "there was the inescapable feeling that something was missing. The gleeful abandon of youth had given way to a plodding listlessness suggesting the onslaught of middle age . . . Road fatigue seemed to be corroding their shows. The airy vocal harmonies were just not quite as tight as they used to be, with newcomer Billy Hinsche . . . the chief offender, nearly sending 'California Girls' down the tubes with his off key singing."

MONDAY, OCTOBER 27, 1975: Market Square Arena, Indianapolis, IN, with Ambrosia (8:00 p.m. show)

The set included "Sloop John B," "Marcella," "Do It Again," "The Trader," "In My Room," "Heroes and Villains," "Surfer Girl," "Little Deuce Coupe," "Catch a Wave," "California Girls," "Wouldn't It Be Nice," "Help Me Rhonda," "I Get Around," "Good Vibrations," "Barbara Ann," and "Fun, Fun, Fun."

TUESDAY, OCTOBER 28, 1975: University of Illinois, Champaign, IL

THURSDAY, OCTOBER 30, 1975: University of Missouri, Columbia, MO, with Ambrosia (8:00 p.m. show)

The Beach Boys were paid $20,000 to perform by the S.A. Concert Committee. The group also requested an organic Chinese dinner (which was cooked backstage and delivered to their dressing room), a carpeted stage (which the committee was unwilling to obtain and which the group themselves ultimately provided), and alcoholic beverages (which were not provided due to university regulations). The stage setup (including carpet and potted plants, lights, and amps) was shipped to the University on Wednesday and crew manager Jason Raphalian oversaw the setup on Thursday.

FRIDAY, OCTOBER 31, 1975: Lloyd Noble Center, University of Oklahoma, Norman, OK, with Ambrosia (8:00 p.m. show)

SATURDAY, NOVEMBER 1, 1975: Allen Fieldhouse, University of Kansas, Lawrence, KS, with the Eddie Boy Band (8:30 p.m. show)

This show attracted a capacity crowd of 13,332 people. Tim Bradley of the *University Daily Kansan* wrote that "a standing, whooping, whistling ovation greeted the stars, and from there, the Beach Boys blitzed through a polished all-oldies set to an exhausted, sweat soaked encore that had the audience bouncing up and down like pistons." Marshall Fine, of the *Lawrence Journal World*, argued that the audience was too undiscriminating and that "the Beach Boys' harmonies, their mark of distinction, were sloppy, off key, and even embarrassing." He also admitted that "while mistakes were numerous, the nine member group acquitted itself stunningly on several tunes, including 'Catch a Wave,' 'Darlin', ' 'Wouldn't It Be Nice,' 'Barbara Ann,' and 'Fun, Fun, Fun.'"

SUNDAY, NOVEMBER 2, 1975: Civic Auditorium, Omaha, NE (7:30 p.m. show)

And we could go up against any one of them and just blow them away."

No. 0216

SUNSHINE PROMOTIONS, INC.
BEACH BOYS
DAYTON HARA ARENA & I
DAYTON, OHIO
THURSDAY EVENING A
AUGUST 21 1975
GENERAL ADMIS
ADVANCE $5
Prem. / So. Tkt. Co. Cin., O.

Ian Rusten Collection

THE BEACH BOYS IN CONCERT

MONDAY, NOVEMBER 3, 1975: Civic Center, St. Paul, MN, with Little Feat and the Eddie Boy Band (8:00 p.m. show)
This tour-ending show was attended by 15,800 fans. Michael Anthony of the *Minneapolis Tribune* commented, "They're so good that one is willing to forget that the band hasn't produced any new material in years . . . Onstage, the group doesn't achieve quite the vocal finesse, the Four Freshmen sound, it achieves in a studio (but no other group does either). Still, the blend was almost perfect in 'I Get Around' and the solo vocals, especially from the increasingly rotund Carl Wilson on 'Sloop John B' (the opener) and 'Good Vibrations' were excellent."

SATURDAY, NOVEMBER 15, 1975: McGaw Auditorium, Northwestern University, Evanston, IL, with Eric Carmen (Two shows at 4:00 and 9:30 p.m.)
These concerts were originally planned for October 24, but rescheduled. They were the first dates of a sixteen-day swing through the Midwest, East Coast, and South. Ed Carter (bass), Elmo Peeler (synthesizer), Bobby Figueroa (percussion), Carli Munoz (organ), and Billy Hinsche (piano) accompanied the group. The set included a few surprises, including "Take a Load off Your Feet" and Chicago's "Wishin' You Were Here."

SUNDAY, NOVEMBER 16, 1975: Olympia Stadium, Detroit, MI, with Eric Carmen (8:00 p.m. show)
Eric Carmen of the Raspberries, who had a solo hit with "All By Myself," opened this show. In an interview, Carl commented that he really liked Carmen and that "his playing actually shows up better on stage than it does on records even."

MONDAY, NOVEMBER 17, 1975: Barton Hall, Cornell University, Ithaca, NY (8:00 p.m. show)

TUESDAY, NOVEMBER 18, 1975: Civic Center, Providence, RI, with Eric Carmen (8:00 p.m. show)
The Beach Boys began just before 10 p.m. with "Sloop John B" and played for an hour to a capacity audience. Tony Lioce of the *Providence Journal* reported that the band wasn't "as tight or quite as polished as they were the last several times they played here" and threw most of the blame on Dennis' drumming, "which was rudimentary at best. And a few times, he lost the beat completely which didn't really do much as far as a tight and polished sound was concerned."

WEDNESDAY, NOVEMBER 19, 1975: Boston Garden, Boston, MA (Two shows at 6:30 and 9:30 p.m.)
The set at this show included "Sloop John B," "Do It Again," "Help Me Rhonda," "Be True To Your School," "In My Room," "Take a Load off Your Feet," "Sail on Sailor," "Surfer Girl," "I Get Around," "California Girls," "Wouldn't It Be Nice," "Surfin' USA," "Good Vibrations," "Wishin' You Were Here," "Little Deuce Coupe," "Barbara Ann," and "Fun, Fun, Fun."

THURSDAY, NOVEMBER 20, 1975: State Farm Arena, Harrisburg, PA (8:00 p.m. show)

FRIDAY, NOVEMBER 21, 1975: Convention Center, Niagara Falls, NY

SATURDAY, NOVEMBER 22, 1975: Convocation Center, Ohio University, Athens, OH, with Magic (8:30 p.m. show)

SUNDAY, NOVEMBER 23, 1975: Riverfront Coliseum, Cincinnati, OH, with Dave Mason and Eric Carmen (7:30 p.m. show)
Eric Carmen and Dave Mason preceded the group onstage but the majority of the 14,250 fans were there to see the Beach Boys. Cliff Radel of the *Cincinnati Enquirer* declared that "from the first notes of the opener 'Sloop John B' to the finale 'Fun, Fun, Fun' an hour and fifteen minutes later, the audience was on its feet, standing on chairs, screaming, and dancing in the aisles."

MONDAY, NOVEMBER 24, 1975: Richfield Coliseum, Cleveland, OH, with Dave Mason and Eric Carmen (8:00 p.m. show)

Mike the frontman, University of Kansas, November 1, 1975. Photo used with permission of Spencer Research Library University of Kansas

THE BEACH BOYS IN CONCERT

TUESDAY, NOVEMBER 25, 1975: Frankfort Sports Center, Frankfort, KY (7:30 p.m. show)

WEDNESDAY, NOVEMBER 26, 1975: Mid-South Coliseum, Memphis, TN, with Eric Carmen (8:00 p.m. show)
A crowd of 8,000 attended this concert. Jess Bunn of the *Press Scimitar* reported, "After opening their two hour set with 'Sloop John B,' the Beach Boys rock 'n' rolled on and on through past hits like 'Be True To Your School,' 'California Girls,' 'Good Vibrations,' and 'Little Surfer Girl' . . . The crowd let the band know its music is still appreciated in Memphis by calling for an encore with a standing ovation."

THURSDAY, NOVEMBER 27, 1975: Municipal Auditorium, Birmingham, AL, with Eric Carmen (7:30 p.m. show)

FRIDAY, NOVEMBER 28, 1975: Carolina Coliseum, University of South Carolina, Columbia, SC (8:00 p.m. show)

SATURDAY, NOVEMBER 29, 1975: Veterans Memorial Coliseum, Jacksonville, FL, with the Outlaws (8:00 p.m. show)

SUNDAY, NOVEMBER 30, 1975: Sports Stadium, Orlando, FL, with Eric Carmen (8:30 p.m. show)

SATURDAY, DECEMBER 13, AND SUNDAY, DECEMBER 14, 1975: Pacific Coliseum, Vancouver, BC, Canada, with Cecilio and Kapono (One show each night at 8:00 p.m.)
The Beach Boys began a West Coast swing with Hawaiian duo Cecilio and Kapono. The set was heavy on oldies, with only a few recent numbers included. However, they did give a nod to the Beachago tour, performing Chicago's "Wishing You Were Here," and concluded shows with "Jumpin' Jack Flash." Nick Collier of the *Vancouver Sun* declared, "The reaction of the audience to tunes that are only slightly younger than they are, was almost fanatic."

MONDAY, DECEMBER 15, AND TUESDAY, DECEMBER 16, 1975: Seattle Coliseum, Seattle, WA, with Cecilio and Kapono (One show each night at 8:00 p.m.)
The group filled the Seattle Center for two nights, playing for close to 30,000 people.

WEDNESDAY, DECEMBER 17, 1975: Memorial Coliseum, Portland, OR, with Cecilio and Kapono (8:00 p.m. show)
Over 11,000 fans attended the last show of 1975. *Oregonian* critic John Wendeborn noted that the band played "as if it were 1965 all over again. 'I Get Around' and 'Barbara Ann' elicited more noise from the audience than any crowd in recent memory . . . It was a highly entertaining concert, one which sent most of the crowd (if not all of it) home still singing and humming the songs many of the fans had sung along with inside the Arena moments before."

CONCERTS NOT PLAYED

A Beachago Fourth of July show in Coldwater, Michigan, sponsored by Wings Stadium Organization of Kalamazoo, was canceled at the last minute because Christian groups complained it would bring "gross immorality" to the town.

1976

A S 1976 BEGAN, the group was busy, recording their first album of new material since 1972 and planning a giant summer tour. It was a tall order, but the Beach Boys were determined to make 1976 their biggest year ever. Steve Love came up with the idea for a "Brian's Back" campaign. The plan was to thrust Brian back into the limelight. It was expected that his participation in the group would generate massive record sales and boost concert attendance.

Brian's participation in the Beach Boys had diminished considerably after 1970. It was difficult to determine whether it was drugs, mental health issues, or disinterest that kept Brian away from the studio in the early 70s. The death of Murry in June 1973 had been a definite turning point. Brian retreated to his room, only occasionally emerging to attend a recording session or a party. By 1975 stories of his odd behavior and addictions had become the talk of Hollywood. Brian's weight had ballooned to 250 pounds, and his family was concerned that he might not survive another year of this lifestyle. That fall, he was placed under the care of therapist Dr. Eugene Landy, who coaxed Brian out of his room, took away his drugs, and forced him to exercise. The Beach Boys helped cover the exorbitant fees that Dr. Landy charged, with the understanding that he'd get Brian back in the studio and working. By early 1976 Brian was recording music for the album known as *15 Big Ones*.

Brian's return to the role of producer wasn't without problems. Publicly, the group painted a rosy picture of the joy they felt at his return, but behind the scenes there was tension over the decision to give him control. As Dennis commented to Janet Maslin of *Newsweek*, "He was always the absolute producer,

CONCERTS PLAYED IN
1976

but little did he know that in his absence people grew up, people became as sensitive as the next guy. Why should I relinquish my rights as an artist?" In truth, Carl and Dennis had surpassed the long-dormant Brian in their familiarity with the recording process at their own Brother Studio. But everyone agreed that the magic words "produced by Brian Wilson" generated excitement and expectation.

Initially the band planned on creating a record of all-new material, but Brian had written few new songs and those were mostly melancholy ballads. This was hardly a commercial direction, and commercialism was what was sought. The decision was made to record a selection of oldie cover tunes like "Sea Cruise" and "Rock and Roll Music." There were a few new originals, including Mike's "TM Song" and Brian's "That Same Song," but the emphasis was definitely on retro-classics. Even one of the "new" numbers, "Back Home," was something Brian had written in 1963.

Carl and Dennis were unhappy with the decision to release an oldies album. Carl told a reporter from the *Winnipeg Free Press* the initial plan was to "warm up with old rock 'n' roll classics and then do an album of new things. So I was at first disappointed when it was just a combination." They also were unhappy with the lack of care that went into the record. Carl

FRIDAY, JULY 2, 1976: "Day on the Green No. 5," Oakland Coliseum, Oakland, CA, with America, the Elvin Bishop Band, and John Sebastian (3:00 p.m. show)
After a seven-month hiatus, the Beach Boys returned to the road for the *15 Big Ones* tour. Carli Munoz, Billy Hinsche (piano/guitar), Bobby Figueroa (drums/percussion), Ron Altbach (synths), and Ed Carter (bass) accompanied them. A five-piece horn section dubbed the Hornettes included Michael Andreas (alto and tenor sax and flute), Rod Novak (sax), Charlie McCarthy (sax), Lance Bueller (trumpet), and John Foss (trumpet). Ron Altbach recalled, "Those were my guys. I put that together for the Beach Boys. They wanted to have horns. I thought it was stupid. I mean it didn't really add anything. But they wanted it, so they did it." A dramatic new stage set included a neon lit sailboat that formed a magical backdrop for performances.

The audience of 50,000-plus witnessed the Beach Boys show begin with twelve California girls in bikinis carrying surfboards, who saluted the crowd as balloons fell from the sky. The group then launched into 'California Girls" to thunderous applause. They played all the hits plus songs from their recent album, including "A Casual Look," "It's OK," "Palisades Park," and "Rock and Roll Music." The emotional highlight of the Oakland show was undoubtedly when Brian wandered onto the stage and took his place behind a white grand piano. Bobby Figueroa recalled, "It was exciting but you could tell he was a little uncomfortable. But he was trying really hard to be there and we tried to support him. We were having fun, doing our show but Brian being there added a whole other dynamic. It was pretty neat seeing him get into the show."

SATURDAY, JULY 3, 1976: Anaheim Stadium, Anaheim, CA, with America, Santana and Gerard
This concert was billed as "Southern California's Only Bicentennial Rock Event." Over 54,000 people attended. NBC TV filmed the Beach Boys portion of the concert for their upcoming TV special. Dressed in white tie and tails and a gold sequined vest, Mike introduced the songs and paid tribute to Brian, seated behind his piano. Brian received a thunderous ovation, but remained mute, save for his lead on "Back Home."

Michael Jensen of the *Pasadena Star News* reported, "The music got the crowd off so much that the patrons on the club level were asked to stop dancing and jumping for fear of structural damage to the stadium. The high point of the show came when the group turned on the lights in the stadium and sang 'Good Vibrations' . . . One thing is for sure, the Beach Boys will remain a strong and vital band that's going to be around for a long, long time."

MONDAY, JULY 12, TO WEDNESDAY, JULY 14, 1976: Pine Knob Music Theatre, Clarkston, MI, with Billy Joel (One show at 7:30 p.m. on Monday and one show at 1:00 p.m. on Tuesday and Wednesday)

FRIDAY, JULY 16, AND SATURDAY, JULY 17, 1976: Chicago Stadium, Chicago, IL, with Billy Joel (One show each night at 8:00 p.m.)

SUNDAY, JULY 18, 1976: Mile High Stadium, Denver, CO, with Gerard, Fleetwood Mac, and Santana (12:00 p.m. show)
A record turnout of 62,000 attended this show, jamming the aisles. Promoters declared it the largest audience ever at a Colorado show.

WEDNESDAY, JULY 21, 1976: Coliseum, Edmonton, AB, Canada (Two shows at 5:00 p.m. and 9:00 p.m.)
Edmonton fans were so enthusiastic to see the group that both concerts sold out.

Ian Rusten Collection

1976

FRIDAY, JULY 23, 1976: Arrowhead Stadium, Kansas City, MO, with the Doobie Brothers, Jeff Beck, Firefall, and the Ozark Mountain Daredevils
Despite sweltering 120-degree heat, 33,000 turned out for this six-hour event.

SATURDAY, JULY 24, 1976: Wisconsin State Fair, Milwaukee, WI, with the Doobie Brothers, Firefall, and Gerard (12:00 p.m. show)

SUNDAY, JULY 25, 1976: Iowa State Fairgrounds, Des Moines, IA, with Jeff Beck and the Jan Hammer Group, the Doobie Brothers, and Gerard
While he believed Jeff Beck stole the show, Jim Healey of the *Des Moines Register* declared that the Beach Boys "sang and played better than in any previous Iowa show. You could even hear some bass guitar and now and then a real guitar lead from Carl Wilson or Al Jardine." Following this show, the group returned to California to attend Bruce's wedding on July 29 in Catalina. They performed a few numbers at the reception, but it wasn't an actual concert, just an impromptu jam.

FRIDAY, AUGUST 6, 1976: Metropolitan Stadium, Bloomington, MN, with Tower of Power, Boz Scaggs, Todd Rundgren's Utopia, and Gerard (7:00 p.m. show)
This show was planned as a Beachago reunion, hence the decision to use Metropolitan Stadium, rather than the smaller Parade Stadium as originally planned. However, Chicago canceled and, despite the last minute addition of Tower of Power and Boz Scaggs, attendance suffered.

SATURDAY, AUGUST 7, 1976: UNI Dome, University of Northern Iowa, Cedar Falls, IA (8:00 p.m. show)
This was one of three concerts advertised with Billy Joel. He dropped out and the Bellamy Brothers were added, but they had a car accident on the day of the show and the Beach Boys played two sets instead.

SUNDAY, AUGUST 8, 1976: Kiel Auditorium, St. Louis, MO
The group played for 11,500 people. R.A. Wilber of the *Globe-Democrat* expressed regret that the audience was so enthralled by oldies since it meant "musically more complex and lyrically better songs from such albums as *Holland* and *Surf's Up* were only rarely heard during Sunday night's show, but the crowd never missed them . . . The crowd came to hear some good old fashioned Beach Boys music. And the Beach Boys delivered."

MONDAY, AUGUST 9, 1976: Glen Oak Park Amphitheatre, Peoria, IL, with the Watermelon Rhythm Band (7:00 p.m. show)
Joan Richardson of the *Journal Star* reported "The fine hip shaking music took the audience through 'Little Deuce Coupe,' 'Surfin',' 'Help Me Rhonda,' 'Be True To Your School,' 'Sloop John B,' 'Wouldn't It Be Nice,' 'I Get Around,' and 'Good Vibrations' . . . Al Jardine, rhythm guitarist, sang the lead on 'A Casual Look,' a song Mike Love said was 'for the elderly people in the audience, meaning people in their twenties.' Carl Wilson had the lead on 'Palisades Park,' where he 'gives the girl a hug in the tunnel of love.'"

TUESDAY, AUGUST 10, 1976: UD Arena, University of Dayton, Dayton, OH, with Heart (8:00 p.m. show)

WEDNESDAY, AUGUST 11, AND THURSDAY, AUGUST 12, 1976: Spectrum, Philadelphia, PA, with Heart (One show each night at 8:00 p.m.)
The group played two nights at the Spectrum. Matt Damsker of the *Evening Bulletin* reported the crowd "was on its feet and deliriously engaged in the music from the opening bars of the opening number, 'California Girls' . . . The focal point, stage wise, remains Beach Boy Mike Love, whose flippantly casual presence—last night in elegant summer white—perfectly complements the less theatrical energies of his partners, drummer Dennis Wilson and guitarists Carl Wilson and Alan Jardine."

FRIDAY, AUGUST 13, 1976: Hampton Coliseum, Hampton, VA, with the Cate Brothers (8:00 p.m. show)

Poster advertising the 1976 "15 Big Ones" tour. Ian Rusten Collection

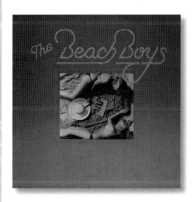

"15 Big Ones" tour program, 1976. Chris Woods Collection

recalled, "once we had finished a certain batch of songs, Brian said, 'That's it; put it out.' That's why the album sounds unfinished. Brian just wanted to do one cut and capture the moment rather than working on something." Meanwhile, Carl was laid up with a bad back and Dennis was spending his time recording a solo album. As a result, quality control on *15 Big Ones* suffered.

Despite the problems, an album was created and Brian had produced it. It turned out to be the Beach Boys' highest charting album of new material in over a decade, rising to number eight on the *Billboard* charts.

The album's single "Rock and Roll Music" did even better, hitting number five on *Billboard*. Steve Love organized a massive publicity campaign and reporters rushed to California to interview Brian. Lorne Michaels of NBC's *Saturday Night Live* agreed to produce a TV special about the Beach Boys, to air in August. Camera crews captured Brian's thirty-fourth birthday party (attended by Paul McCartney) and went inside Brother Studio to film Brian and the group performing "That Same Song." Probably the most memorable part of the show involved Dan Ackroyd and John Belushi posing as cops who barge into Brian's house, force him out of bed and drag him to the beach where he's instructed to "Go surfing." Brian only entered the water after receiving assurance from Dr. Landy that he wouldn't drown.

The "Brian's Back" campaign was predicated on getting him to participate as much as possible and he was cajoled into joining the group at their summer tour opener in Oakland. A nervous Brian, dressed in a white safari suit, came out during "God Only Knows" and sat at the piano, where he remained the rest of the night. It was his first appearance onstage since 1973. According to *Oakland Tribune* reviewer Peter Cowan, "at first, he seemed almost dazed, barely playing piano and singing in brief segments but as the crowd's enthusiasm warmed and he found his concert legs, Wilson gradually emerged from his shell. He even mugged for the people seated behind him, waving and smiling, and he took a lead vocal on a new song from the *15 Big Ones* LP, 'Back Home.'"

By the fall, Brian was well enough to travel. He played his

SATURDAY, AUGUST 14, 1976: Three Rivers Stadium, Pittsburgh, PA, with Gary Wright and Peter Frampton (2:00 p.m. show)
Over 48,000 people attended this show. Carl played in a red and white baseball jersey and briefly wore a Pittsburgh Pirates cap. The group also gained favor by tweaking the lyrics of "Back Home" to include a reference to Pennsylvania. The collegial atmosphere invited fan participation. One group of fans was invited onstage to present Mike with a cardboard surfboard, emblazoned with the words "Surfin' USA."

SUNDAY, AUGUST 15, 1976: St. John's Arena, Ohio State University, Columbus, OH (8:00 p.m. show)

THURSDAY, AUGUST 26, 1976: SPAC, Saratoga, NY (7:00 p.m. show)
After a ten-day break, the band regrouped for a performance at SPAC. Mike had been in England to lobby the BBC to air *The Beach Boys* TV show and flew on the Concorde to make it home in time.

FRIDAY, AUGUST 27, 1976: Civic Center, Providence, RI (8:00 p.m. show)
The Beach Boys were scheduled to play Buffalo, but that concert was postponed and they played Providence instead. Anthony Lioce of the *Providence Journal* noted, "A new horn section has been added and it plays sparingly and tastefully, adding subtle new colors to the bright old sound without overpowering it, as horns have a way of doing. Carl Wilson has developed into a master guitarist; energetic, clean lines flowed from his hollow-body electric all night long. And nobody but nobody can cavort like Mike Love."

SATURDAY, AUGUST 28, 1976: Roosevelt Stadium, Jersey City, NJ, with the Richie Furay Band (7:30 p.m. show)

SUNDAY, AUGUST 29, 1976: Civic Center, Hartford, CT, with the Cate Brothers

MONDAY, AUGUST 30, AND TUESDAY, AUGUST 31, 1976: Capitol Centre, Largo, MD, with the Artful Dodger (One show each night at 8:00 p.m.)
These appearances marked Brian's first shows outside California since 1970. He played both nights, seated behind a white piano, and played bass on "Back Home." Steve Parks of the *Baltimore Sun* noted Brian "still looks very tentative on stage—hiding behind the bass—perhaps because his shrink is never far off stage . . . To see him in person, one would never guess he wrote and performed the music that sold eighty million records." The next day he returned home and wasn't present for the rest of the tour.

WEDNESDAY, SEPTEMBER 1, 1976: Nassau Coliseum, Uniondale, NY (8:00 p.m. show)

THURSDAY, SEPTEMBER 2, 1976: Memorial Auditorium, Buffalo, NY, with the Cate Brothers and Jeff Beck with the Jan Hammer Group (7:30 p.m. show)
Among the 17,000 in attendance was Mo Ostin, president of Warner/Reprise. Dale Anderson of the *Buffalo News* praised the backing band, declaring that they "put a tidal wave of power behind the Beach Boys ocean of fabled surfing hits. 'Help Me Rhonda,' with three keyboards churning rhythm, threw all sheets to the wind halfway through the ninety-minute show. From there on it was nothing but old favorites right into their encore of Joe Cockers's 'You Are So Beautiful,' 'Barbara Ann,' 'Rock and Roll Music' and 'Fun, Fun, Fun.'"

FRIDAY, SEPTEMBER 3, AND SATURDAY, SEPTEMBER 4, 1976: CNE Grandstand, Toronto, ON, Canada, with the Garfield Band (One show on Friday at 8:30 p.m. and two on Saturday)
Over 65,000 people attended the Toronto shows.

SUNDAY, SEPTEMBER 5, 1976: Civic Centre, Ottawa, ON, Canada (8:00 p.m. show)

MONDAY, SEPTEMBER 6, 1976: Forum, Montreal, QB, Canada

This was the group's last appearance until late November. Ron Altbach recalled, "Mike got hepatitis when the Beach Boys were in Montreal. I saw him completely yellow and freaked out." Shows scheduled for BYU in Utah on September 16, Seattle on September 18, San Diego on September 24, Sacramento on September 25, and Santa Barbara on September 26 were canceled. The group planned to tour the Southwest in October, including dates in Arkansas and Texas, but these were canceled as well.

MONDAY, NOVEMBER 22, 1976: Riverfront Coliseum, Cincinnati, OH

The Beach Boys reconvened for concerts in Cincinnati, New York, and Boston. Flutist/saxophonist Charles Lloyd, who'd toured with the group in 1972, joined them again. He was a follower of TM and close friends with Mike. Lloyd told the *Seattle Times*, "Mike is my dearest friend. We were Dharmacly born on the same day, March 15. We were meant to get together. The Beach Boys are really good people and their music is a healthy, good vibe. It's a joy to work with them." Elmo Peeler also accompanied them, having taken Altbach's spot on piano and synths. More importantly, Brian was there too. He played most of the dates, mainly sitting behind the piano and playing bass a bit. The band perfromed "Airplane" and "Love Is a Woman," from the forthcoming *The Beach Boys Love You* album.

A disappointed Cliff Radel of the *Cincinnati Enquirer* reported, "The Beach Boys' legendary harmonies were out of tune and poorly balanced for the opener 'Wouldn't It Be Nice' and things did not get much better as the set progressed." However, Ken Williams of the *Journal News* declared the show exceptional, singling out Carl's performance of "God Only Knows" as the highlight. Williams noted, "The loudest ovation of the evening went to 'Suzy Cincinnati.' Even the real Suzy Cincinnati, an ex-cab driver now living in Covington, showed up for the excitement."

WEDNESDAY, NOVEMBER 24 TO FRIDAY, NOVEMBER 26, 1976: Madison Square Garden, New York, NY (One show at 8:00 p.m. each night)

The "Brian Is Back" campaign created such a buzz in New York City that the scheduled shows were SRO, necessitating the addition of a Wednesday concert. Close to 60,000 people saw the band over three days. Brian joined them the first two nights. Jim Fishel of *Billboard* noted, "Throughout the entire performance, many of the young concertgoers shouted his name in a worshipful manner and they were richly rewarded by Brian's vocal output."

SATURDAY, NOVEMBER 27, 1976: Boston Garden, Boston, MA (8:00 p.m. show)

Over 17,000 attended this show. If they were hoping to see Brian, they were out of luck. He was making a solo appearance on *Saturday Night Live* in New York. Dressed in a white suit, Brian performed "Back Home," "Love Is a Woman," and a very shaky version of "Good Vibrations." He also took part in a comedy sketch, dressed as a police officer.

WEDNESDAY, DECEMBER 15, 1976: Oakland Coliseum, Oakland, CA (8:00 p.m. show)

With the addition of Charles Lloyd and Brian, there were sixteen musicians onstage. Larry Kelp of The *Oakland Tribune* argued that the large band allowed "for little creativity or musical freedom by any player. They have to stick to a worked out format in order to keep the show together." While underwhelmed by the concert, Kelp was impressed by the return of Brian, dressed in a blue bathrobe with silver trim, his standard wardrobe for the tour. Steve Casey of the *San Diego Tribune* referred to it as "something that might have been a bargain item at Gorgeous George's estate sale."

Performing at the Nassau Coliseum, September 1, 1976.
Photo: Chuck Pulin.com

first concert outside California that August and was with the group on their Thanksgiving tour. Not everyone, however, believed Brian was "back." While fans loved seeing him, critics noted he appeared tentative before large crowds and spent most of his time hiding behind the piano, seldom joining in choruses of songs he wrote. Eudell Penski of the *Times-Herald Record* attended the November New York shows and argued, "those empty, worthless years—lying in bed, smoking marijuana—have taken their toll on the big man. The voice just wasn't there . . . After waiting so long to have Wilson perform with the group once again, it was a sheer letdown not to see him at his best." Chip Rachlin felt, "Forcing Brian out there then and parading him around like a trained monkey was detrimental. I didn't think that Brian being trotted around for the occasional date did him any good." Bobby Figueroa commented, "You know at times you could tell that he didn't want to be there. He didn't feel he should be there. He felt uncomfortable.

He was using every bit of energy he had to hold up his end and to come back and say 'OK, I'm gonna give it a shot.' At times he was into it and other times he just wasn't into it. But there were many nights where it was fine."

Brian's presence changed the group dynamic. Dr. Landy and his team of minders created problems within the Beach Boys entourage. Chip Rachlin recalled the period with distaste, noting, "The tension was so

"The music got the crowd off so much that the patrons on the club level were asked to stop dancing and jumping for fear of structural damage to the stadium."

great. Steve Love was managing the band. Dr. Landy had the Surf Nazis keeping an eye on Brian. It wasn't fun." However, reviewers continued to praise their performances. Bobby Figueroa commented, "In those days there were things going on backstage that were divisive but I think still that the integrity of the music won out over everything, because as soon as they got on the stage they were all friends again. We did some kick-ass shows in that period."

FRIDAY, DECEMBER 17, AND SATURDAY, DECEMBER 18, 1976: Seattle Coliseum, Seattle, WA (One show each night at 8:00 p.m.)
The Friday concert was SRO and the Saturday show almost sold out as well. Fans rapturously received the group but *Seattle Times* critic Patrick MacDonald was disturbed by Brian's return, noting that he looked "around from his piano bench frequently to get encouragement from somebody sitting behind him, presumably his psychoanalyst who is with him always . . . He acknowledged big signs that said 'Welcome Back' and waved back at people, but he had a blank, distant, unsmiling look on his face. At times it was eerie."

SUNDAY, DECEMBER 19, 1976: Coliseum, Spokane, WA (8:00 p.m. show)
Chuck Rehberg of the *Spokane Chronicle* reported that the group "wandered through a half dozen styles between their 'oldies,' seeking some chemistry with the audience, but finding little . . . Brian and brother Dennis Wilson did achieve a magical moment in their version of 'Surfer Girl,' and the audience responded warmly but such moments were all too infrequent."

TUESDAY, DECEMBER 21, 1976: Pacific Coliseum, Vancouver, BC, Canada (8:00 p.m. show)

THURSDAY, DECEMBER 23, 1976: Memorial Coliseum, Portland, OR (8:00 p.m. show)
This concert was a sellout, attracting 11,000 fans.

MONDAY, DECEMBER 27, 1976: Sports Arena, San Diego, CA (8:00 p.m. show)
Steve Casey of the *Evening Tribune* praised the band's performance, though he noted the sound was poor and that "their voices—when you could hear them—sounded strained, like the tour has taken its toll. In the softer numbers their voices seemed more at ease." He declared "Everyone's in Love with You" to be a highlight along with a rousing "Help Me Rhonda" that "was perfectly executed and caught the shouting, stomping, whistling crowd at the peak of an emotional high."

FRIDAY, DECEMBER 31, 1976: Forum, Los Angeles, CA
The Beach Boys commemorated their fifteenth anniversary with a hometown concert. Nearly 20,000 turned out for the show, which started late so they'd be onstage when New Year began. The group opened with "California Girls" and "Darlin'." David Leaf reported in *Pet Sounds* that he'd "never heard Carl sound hotter. His R&B gutsy lead vocal was a highlight of the evening." Brian, dressed in his blue bathrobe, sang "Sloop John B" and then the group performed "Little Deuce Coupe," "In My Room," (with Al on lead), "Sail on Sailor" (sung by Billy), "California," "God Only Knows" and "Airplane." Brian strapped on a bass for "Back Home" and then the group played "Catch a Wave," "Susie Cincinnati," and "Be True to Your School" to wrap up the first half. After a break, they launched into "It's OK" and "A Casual Look" from *15 Big Ones* and then played Brian's new song "Love is a Woman." A trio of meditative tunes followed: "Feel Flows," "Everyone's in Love with You" and "All This Is That." The group then performed "Surfer Girl" with Brian breaking out his falsetto, before picking up the pace with "Heroes and Villains," "Help Me Rhonda," "Wouldn't It Be Nice," and "I Get Around." Shortly before midnight they started 'Good Vibrations' but Carl stopped in the middle to countdown the last seconds of 1976. The group then played it again and closed with "Surfin' USA." For the encore, a large banner saying "The Beach Boys" descended behind them. Dennis sang "You Are So Beautiful" before the group returned for "Barbara Ann," "Rock and Roll Music," and "Fun, Fun, Fun."

CONCERTS NOT PLAYED

Keith Badman listed an appearance in Catalina on July 29 as an official concert. It was Bruce's wedding.

As discussed, the Beach Boys canceled shows scheduled for late September and early October due to Mike's illness.

A concert in Springfield, Massachusetts scheduled for November 29 was canceled as well.

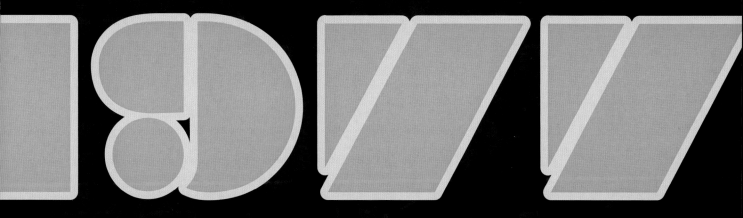

THE BEACH BOYS began 1977 with a successful East Coast tour. Brian was present for most dates and seemed to enjoy himself. He told the *Atlanta Journal* touring was "fun. I mean it's a remarkable experience . . . It's not normal by any means, but it is a lot more elaborate than the old days. We have a lot of good road management and we're taken care of with good accommodations." Some critics who observed Brian's behavior onstage questioned the genuineness of such statements and noted that minders watched him to make sure he didn't leave. But Brian appeared healthy and fans were excited to see him.

In general, it was a more productive period for Brian. By early 1977 he'd completed the album *The Beach Boys Love You*. With the group otherwise engaged, it was practically a solo album. He played most instruments on the record himself. The album divided critics and continues to divide fans. Many were turned off by the ragged harmonies, juvenile lyrics, and quirky tunes. However, others were thrilled by what looked like a real return to form after the disappointing *15 Big Ones*. Influential critic Lester Bangs called it "their best album ever" in *Circus*, though he admitted it was pretty weird. Songs such as "Solar System" and Brian's ode to his favorite talk show host, "Johnny Carson," were certainly bizarre but the musical arrangements showed traces of the old magic, especially "The Night Was So Young," featuring a pretty if slightly stoned lead from Carl and a high falsetto background vocal from Brian. Despite the encouraging elements, *The Beach*

Boys Love You proved to be a commercial failure. The band was leaving Warner/Reprise for CBS and the label did little to promote the inherently strange album.

The Beach Boys planned to reconvene in July for a U.K. tour. Carl flew to London at the end of June to announce that four open air concerts were booked; Cardiff Castle on July 23, Bellevue in Manchester on July 24, Wembley Stadium on July 30, and Dalymont Park Stadium in Dublin on August 1. The opening acts were to be Dr. Feelgood, Ricci Martin, and Dave Edmunds' Rockpile. The group also scheduled a July 26 show at Lorely Amphitheater in Germany. In addition, they committed to appear at the convention being held in London by CBS Records, their new record label. Just a week before the tour, the group abruptly canceled. The official reason was "inadequate time to make preparations," but behind the scenes, other explanations were proffered. Harvey Kubernik reported in *Melody Maker* that the group "had been overambitious in trying for the Wembley Stadium" and that they'd only sold 40,000 of the 60,000 tickets necessary to make the booking profitable. It was rumored that other shows had weak advance sales. Predictably, management denied this. However, such protestations rang hollow after Brian told *The Guardian* the tour was canceled because "the promotion didn't hold up—we had to cancel because tickets weren't selling."

While poor ticket sales played a part, it was also suggested that the cancelation had to do with changes in

CONCERTS PLAYED IN
1977

THURSDAY, JANUARY 6, 1977: Hollywood Sportatorium, Hollywood, FL (8:00 p.m. show)
The Beach Boys hit the road for a twelve-date winter tour. Accompanying them were Bobby Figueroa, Ed Carter, Charles Lloyd, Carli Munoz, Elmo Peeler, Billy Hinsche, and the Hornettes (Lance Bueller, John Foss, Michael Andreas, Rod Novak, and Charlie McCarthy Jr.), who were now dubbed Tornado because, according to Mike, "they blow up a storm." The promised presence of Brian created quite a buzz and demand for tickets was brisk.

Road manager Rick Nelson was leaving the Beach Boys' employ and Jerry Schilling was being groomed to succeed him. A close friend of Elvis Presley, Schilling had been road manager for Billy Joel in 1976. He would be associated with the group in a management capacity for the next ten years.

FRIDAY, JANUARY 7, 1977: Civic Center, Lakeland, FL (8:30 p.m. show)
A sellout crowd packed the Civic Center. For those who came to catch a glimpse of Brian, Bob Ross of the *St. Petersburg Times* declared the concert "was a moment of deep happiness. He looked great—played piano, sang, even danced around and smiled a bit."

SATURDAY, JANUARY 8, 1977: University of Florida, Gainesville, FL, with the Outlaws (2:00 p.m. show)

SUNDAY, JANUARY 9, 1977: Omni Coliseum, Atlanta, GA (8:00 p.m. show)
This show suffered from pacing problems. The group tried to play new material, rather than just oldies, but the audience proved resistant. They all but drowned out Mike while introducing his paean to Maharishi, "Everyone's In Love with You." The reviewer from the University of Georgia's *Red and Black* noted, "The crowd exhibited a pitiful lack of respect for the performers, greeting Mike Love's request for quiet with more noise." But Mark Parker, of the Georgia Tech *Technique*, blamed the group for playing so many unfamiliar songs and attacked Mike for yelling at the crowd: "something to the effect of 'Be thankful for what you're getting.'"

MONDAY, JANUARY 10, 1977: Von Braun Civic Center, Huntsville, AL (7:30 p.m. show)
Brian didn't appear at this show, having flown home for a few days. However, Lee Roop of the *Huntsville Times* argued that "four out of five can do just fine, and nobody in the audience wanted to be anywhere else . . . It was the best lit concert ever to play the Civic Center, the band and the audience had more fun, and the vibrations were so good even the Civic Center security guards were rapping their flashlights into their palms to keep time."

TUESDAY, JANUARY 11, 1977: Mid-South Coliseum, Memphis, TN (8:00 p.m. show)

WEDNESDAY, JANUARY 12, 1977: Market Square Arena, Indianapolis, IN (8:00 p.m. show)
A crowd of 15,000 turned up at the Arena. Zach Dunkin of the *Indianapolis News* declared it the best performance by the group he'd ever seen and noted that the "thirty songs ranged from those old surfing hits of the '60s to a pair of new numbers, 'Airplane' and 'Love is a Woman,' from the upcoming *The Beach Boys Love You* album to be released in February. In between there were songs for Beach Boys 'purists,' Carl Wilson's majestic 'Feel Flows' and 'This Is That.' His soaring vocals were unbelievably true to form for a live situation."

The set consisted of "California Girls," "Darlin'," "Sloop John B," "Little Deuce Coupe," "In My Room," "Sail on Sailor," "California Saga," "God Only Knows," "Airplane," "Back Home," "Catch a Wave," "Susie Cincinnati," and "Be True To Your School," followed by an intermission. After a break they played "It's OK," "A Casual Look," "Love Is a Woman," "Everyone's in Love with You," "Feel Flows," "All This Is That," "Surfer Girl," "Heroes and Villains," "Help Me Rhonda," "Wouldn't It Be

Nice," "I Get Around," "Good Vibrations," and "Surfin' USA," "You Are So Beautiful," "Barbara Ann," "Rock and Roll Music," and "Fun, Fun, Fun."

THURSDAY, JANUARY 13, 1977: Richfield Coliseum, Cleveland, OH (7:30 p.m. show)
A near-capacity crowd attended. Despite the absence of Brian and an hour delay, Jane Scott of the Cleveland Plains Dealer declared, "It was Good Vibrations from the opening 'California Girls' to the final encore 'Fun, Fun, Fun.'"

SATURDAY, JANUARY 15, 1977: Olympia Stadium, Detroit, MI (7:30 p.m. show)
The group headed to Detroit, where Brian rejoined the tour. John Laycock of the *Windsor Star* declared he'd never seen a happier audience and that the Beach Boys seemed just as enthusiastic to be there. He noted that Brian "bobbed Buddha-like at the baby grand piano, singing a little in a husky voice, waving like a victor and absorbing adulation—some of it from his brothers and cousins in the band, more of it from the totally blissed out audience."

SUNDAY, JANUARY 16, 1977: Maple Leaf Gardens, Toronto, ON, Canada (Two shows at 6:00 p.m. and 9:00 p.m.)

MONDAY, JANUARY 17, 1977: Forum, Montreal, QB, Canada (8:00 p.m. show)

TUESDAY, JANUARY 18, 1977: Spectrum, Philadelphia, PA
A crowd of over 19,000 attended. Many came to see Brian. John Fisher of the *Courier Times* commented, "His vocals added to the fullness of the Beach Boys' harmonies. For one number, he went back to playing the bass, which he originally played for the group. He pranced around showing a new energy and also a trimmed down waistline."

WEDNESDAY, JANUARY 19, 1977: Civic Arena, Pittsburgh, PA (7:45 p.m. show)

THURSDAY, JANUARY 20, AND FRIDAY, JANUARY 21, 1977: Capitol Centre, Largo, MD
Although Jimmy Carter's Inaugural Ball was taking place in DC, for many the biggest event in the area was the Beach Boys at the Capitol Centre. The first night alone was attended by 18,000 fans. The venue was one of the first to film performers so they could be seen on Jumbotron screens above the stage. A videotape of this feed exists. Dressed in a T-shirt and jeans, Brian was the center of attention. He sang with confidence, but there was self-parody in his delivery. He sang the words but seldom seemed invested in the performance. But fans that dreamed of seeing Brian onstage got their money's worth. He was an active participant, both vocally and instrumentally.

SATURDAY, JULY 30, 1977: CBS Convention, Grosvenor House Hotel, London, England, with Crawler and Teddy Pendergrass
Despite canceling their U.K. tour, the group appeared at the CBS Convention in London. U.K. fans expressed outrage that the band had snubbed its everyday fans while performing for record executives. Carl defended the decision, noting they'd signed papers in March committing them to appear. The purpose of the convention was to publicize major CBS acts and it was vital that their newest acquisition, the Beach Boys, be present. Despite scant rehearsal, the group closed the convention with a ninety-minute concert.

Most reviewers were pleased with the onstage effort. Alf Martin of *Record Mirror* noted that the band's harmonies were shaky but that by the time they performed "Help Me Rhonda," "it was a synch for the Beach Boys. The Grosvenor had never seen anything like it, people standing on chairs *and* tables. 'Wouldn't It Be Nice,' 'I Get Around,' 'Good Vibrations,' if you could spot a closed mouth in the place, its owner was either so drunk he couldn't hear or a waiter—and even one of those was standing on a chair, singing along."

Some, however, were more critical. Bruce Johnston, who attended separately, declined to join the group onstage for an encore because, as he related to *Melody Maker*, "The band sounded so shitty that I didn't want to be a part of it." Max Bell, of *New Musical Express*, admitted the

the group's management. With Mike out of the country in Switzerland, the Wilsons allowed Stephen Love's contract to lapse. The band again looked to James Guercio for management assistance. *Melody Maker* alleged that Guercio advised the group to back out of the U.K. tour since he "felt that certain contractual and other preparations had not been carried out as he wanted." However, by the time the tour was scheduled to begin, Henry Lazarus (an acquaintance of Carl's) had replaced Guercio. Some suggested that the tour fell apart because Lazarus failed to secure work visas for everyone in time.

Three weeks after the British debacle, the group embarked on a two-week trek through the states. The tour was highly successful and concluded with massive shows in New York and Rhode Island. While the concerts themselves were conducted without incident, behind the scenes the group was in turmoil. The individual Beach Boys were totally at odds with each other.

Until the early 1970s, the Beach Boys had been run as four-man corporation, which meant that when Mike disagreed with business decisions his cousins often outvoted him. Eventually Al was granted a voting share, but it made little difference as the three Wilson brothers usually formed a solid voting block and got their way. On the last day of the 1977 tour, the group held a divisive meeting to decide who'd now take control of the band. Mike was unhappy that managers and agents had fallen too far

A slimmed-down Brian backstage with fan Greg Shady, August 19, 1977. Photo courtesy of Greg Shady

into the Wilson camp and he insisted that his brother Stephen Love be re-signed as manager. Al also supported bringing Steve back, and Brian unexpectedly added his vote to the pro-Love contingent. Carl and Dennis were livid, and threatened to leave the group rather than accept Steve Love as manager. They left the meeting so dispirited that Dennis commented to *Rolling Stone* reporter John Swenson, "This could be the last Beach Boys concert tonight. I see the Beach Boys

crowd was enthusiastic but argued, "They're paid to like it. A real Beach Boys fan couldn't have dug it if he or she had been lost in a maze of acid. It was a nightmare of boredom." Harry Doherty of *Melody Maker* noted with concern that Brian, who'd slimmed down considerably, "looked totally zomboid and completely unaware of what was happening around him." Doherty was the only reviewer to notice tension between Mike and Brian. During "Fun, Fun, Fun," Mike rushed over towards Brian and "attempted to turn the grand piano over, but instead toppled Wilson's mike over. Wilson looked positively terrified at this and when the song ended, walked from behind the keyboard, keeping one eye on Love, waved and left the stage."

FRIDAY, AUGUST 19, 1977: Indiana State Fair, Indianapolis, IN, with Ricci Martin (8:00 p.m. show) The group started a two-week tour with Ricci Martin. The backing band consisted of Bobby Figueroa, Billy Hinsche, Charles Lloyd, Ron Altbach, Carli Munoz, Ed Carter, and Tornado. The biggest change was the new stage design, with Brian seated behind a keyboard built inside the shell of a 1957 Chevy convertible. However, it was missing from the opening show, because there wasn't enough room onstage.

Zach Dunkin of the *Indianapolis News* noted that the presence of Brian at this show made it special. "His vocals . . . on 'Sloop John B,' 'Airplane,' and 'Love is a Woman' were surprisingly better than what has been heard on the group's last two albums. He's looking much better too, with the smaller waistline. His short hair and beard were startling changes."

SATURDAY, AUGUST 20, 1977: Kentucky State Fairgrounds, Louisville, KY, with Ricci Martin (3:00 p.m. show)

SUNDAY, AUGUST 21, 1977: Mississippi River Festival, Edwardsville, IL, with Ricci Martin The Beach Boys arrived late, but the crowd of 9,200 was patient and cheered loudly throughout.

MONDAY, AUGUST 22, 1977: Iowa State Fair, Des Moines, IA, with Ricci Martin

WEDNESDAY, AUGUST 24, TO FRIDAY, AUGUST 26, 1977: Pine Knob Music Theater, Clarkston, MI, with Ricci Martin and Dennis Wilson (Five shows in three days) Dennis played short solo sets at these shows. He handled keyboards, while Bobby Figueroa manned drums, along with Carli Munoz, Ed Carter, Billy Hinsche, guitarist Ed Tuleja, and bassist Wayne Tweed. The decision to play was very last-minute. Bobby Figueroa recalled that they never rehearsed other than a sound check. "We did a half-hour set of mostly *Pacific Ocean Blue* songs. Most of us had played on that, so we were all familiar with it. We did it at Pine Knob and one or two other places but it didn't last very long."

SATURDAY, AUGUST 27, 1977: Castle Farms Music Theatre, Charlevoix, MI, with Ricci Martin (7:30 p.m. show)

SUNDAY, AUGUST 28, AND MONDAY, AUGUST 29, 1977: CNE Grandstand, Toronto, ON, Canada, with Ricci Martin

WEDNESDAY, AUGUST 31, 1977: SPAC, Saratoga, NY, with Ricci Martin (7:00 p.m. show)
Over 40,000 fans turned out at SPAC. Brian didn't say a single word, but took a few lead vocals. According to Donna Hartman of *The North Adams Transcript*, "His solo performance of 'In My Room,' a ballad he wrote, drew tremendous applause. But the old wailing falsetto was missing from what has become what some call his theme song." The concert featured a rare performance by Dennis of "You and I" from his solo album.

THURSDAY, SEPTEMBER 1, 1977: Central Park, New York, NY, with Ricci Martin (12:30 p.m. show)
The Beach Boys played a free concert for a crowd estimated to be between 75,000 and 150,000 people. WNEW and CBS Records sponsored the show, which cost $50,000 to set up. Chip Rachlin recalled, "The Central Park gig was one I fought really hard for. It was to celebrate the tenth anniversary of WNEW. My old partner from Carnegie Hall, Michael Klenfner, was on-air talent from midnight to six Saturdays and Sundays. The chance to headline Central Park for 100,000 people was huge. I said to the Beach Boys, 'You've got to do this. This is the most important market to this band. You are doing this show!' Then I had the task of finding $20,000 for expenses. If they were going to do a free show, they wanted the hotel and airfare covered. Mel Karmazin (VP of WNEW) looked at me like I had two heads. He said 'This is a free show!' But in the end I got the $20,000." For Rachlin, nearing the end of his time with the band, it was a sentimental moment. "I thought I'd put everything that's important to me on that stage. I gave a gift to the city of New York. That was the last hurrah . . . after that I said I can't do anymore . . . It became my entire life. At a certain point you have say, 'Look at what we fucking did!' and then you have to let go."

FRIDAY, SEPTEMBER 2, 1977: Narragansett Race Track, Pawtucket, RI, with Ricci Martin and Leo Sayer (6:00 p.m. show)
The tour culminated with this open-air concert that attracted 40,000 people. Chip Rachlin recalled that promoter Frank Russo wanted the group so badly he gave them the largest guarantee of their career, a promise of no less than $100,000 for two hours' work. To make up for the outlay, tickets sold for the unheard of price of ten dollars. Fans, many of whom arrived at noon to get a seat, were surprisingly sanguine about the prices and the endless delays, which resulted in the show starting two hours late. The concert, however, was a disappointment. Perhaps the group was tired after the exhilarating Central Park show or dispirited by a factious business meeting that'd just taken place in New York. Bob Kerr of the *Providence Journal* noted that the group "just went through the motions. They walked out in front of probably the largest rock audience ever assembled in Rhode Island and dogged it, giving the minimum for a maximum payday." Kerr singled out Brian's performance as particularly bad. Steve Morse of the *Boston Globe* commented, "Brian did sing a harsh lead on 'Sloop John B' and 'Back Home' but was shaky and vanished after four numbers, returning only for 'Help Me Rhonda.'" Morse was also disappointed that Dennis didn't perform a single song from his album.

Following this concert, the band flew to Newark to catch a connecting flight to L.A. The stopover proved to be a public relations nightmare. The group had a horrific argument on the tarmac in full view of a *Rolling Stone* reporter. All the Beach Boys' dirty laundry was thrown into public view. It took over a month to patch things up enough that they could play together again.

FRIDAY, OCTOBER 14, 1977: Allen Field House, University of Kansas, Lawrence, KS (8:30 p.m. show)
The Beach Boys flew to Kansas City for the first date of a hastily arranged three-day tour. The press speculated it might be the last chance for fans to see them. The group did not wholly refute the rumors. When quizzed by a local reporter, Dennis admitted the possibility of breaking up existed. However, when asked if it would be their last tour, he optimistically answered, "No, not if things work out." The lucky reporter was the only one to get a quote, as the band's management issued a gag order on interviews.

Even if they weren't talking, the group was under the microscope. Reviewers analyzed every movement onstage for clues to the state of the band. David Chartrand of the *Lawrence Journal World* claimed that one could "sense that the end is imminent as the band struggled through a

coming to a close and there's a lot of backstabbing and maliciousness going on." His words proved prophetic. Following the concert, the group had a very public fight at Newark Airport and came close to breaking up. Ron Altbach recalled that Dennis and Mike came to blows on the tarmac and had to be separated. John Swenson was there and spilled the entire incident to the public.

At the time, Dennis was seriously contemplating a solo career. That September his solo album *Pacific Ocean Blue* was released. While not a major commercial success, it generated strong critical buzz, with some hailing it as the best Beach Boys album of the '70s. Songs like "Thoughts of You," "Friday Night," "You and I," and "Farewell My Friend" showed Dennis had more to say than he'd been able to on recent Beach Boys' albums. He promoted the release at record store appearances during the August tour. He also performed solo sets during the group's residency at Pine Knob. With the band on the rocks, Dennis made plans for a solo tour, even rehearsing a backing band. Dates were booked for November at venues including Hofstra University (November 22), Avery Fisher Hall in New York (November 23), and the Academy of Music in Philadelphia (November 29). Dennis, however, lacked the confidence to push through his plan and canceled the tour. There were also claims of an ultimatum from the Love contingent that if Dennis toured solo he was out of the Beach Boys. Bobby Figueroa recalled, "The tour support wasn't there from the label for Dennis to go out on the road. They kind of pulled the plug on him a little as far as supporting him to go out and tour and play these songs. It was a great album but I think they were losing confidence in Dennis at that point. Dennis was wrestling with some problems of his own and that had a lot to do with it."

Dennis was back behind the drums for scattered dates with the Beach Boys that fall. The situation, however, remained tense. Dennis remarked to Dennis Hunt of the *Los Angeles Times*, "Everybody thinks the group is permanently back together just because we're doing these shows. That's pure bull. Nothing is finalized. We're doing these shows because it's been worked out that Steve Love won't be representing Carl and me in these gigs. This time they were willing to lean in our direction so we could do these dates." The Beach Boys, however, weren't comfortable being together. Writer Brad Elliot remarked that "if you looked closely, the group was disintegrating . . . It was obvious tempers were flaring over something."

The friction extended to the studio. Mike and Al decided to record at the Maharishi International University in Fairfield, Iowa. As Al related to Stan Soocher of *Circus*, "We had an invitation from the Maharishi himself to record at his facilities. We wanted to do something different, so we accepted. We renovated Building 154 of the university, put in a cafeteria, dorm rooms, [and] a studio in the basement, and did most of the arranging,

ninety-minute show here . . . Oh sure, the packed field house got what it wanted and came away thoroughly pleased . . . But there was so little effort." The *University Daily Kansas* commented that the band sounded all over the place and lacked tightness.

This was to be expected, since there'd been major shakeups in the backing band. Mike allegedly insisted that all non-meditators be fired. Billy Hinsche was gone after six years of service, Gary Griffin replaced Carli Munoz on keyboards, and Mike Kowalski took over for Bobby Figueroa on percussion. Ron Altbach recalled, "Mike (Love) believed that there's a certain kind of influence that happens when people are following a healthy lifestyle and doing TM and he wanted that around him." Bobby Figueroa commented, "I left because I wasn't given a choice. Things were going in a certain direction with the *MIU* album and meditation. I wasn't opposed to it but I didn't want to be forced into it either. . . . I don't like my philosophy being dictated to me. If they reached out to me in a better way I probably would've been more open to it but I was a little defiant about it. I was a hardass."

SATURDAY, OCTOBER 15, 1977: University of Iowa, Iowa City, IA
The band tried out new material at these shows, notably Al's "Lady Lynda" and Ron Altbach's "Country Pie."

SUNDAY, OCTOBER 16, 1977: Indiana State University, Terre Haute, IN (7:00 p.m. show)

FRIDAY, NOVEMBER 11, 1977: Freedom Hall Civic Center, Johnson City, TN (8:00 p.m. show)
As November began, the Beach Boys remained deeply divided. Mike, Al, and Brian settled in at MIU in Iowa to begin work on the *MIU* album, but Carl and Dennis pointedly stayed away. The band agreed to play a weekend of shows and they all dutifully appeared in Tennessee. But it proved impossible for them to hide their dissension.

Nancy Wingate of the *Kingsport Times* noted, "There was a static and tension among the group that could be felt by the fans. They didn't know what it was, but they didn't like it . . . From 'California Girls,' probably the most representative song from the early years, through 'Good Vibrations,' the largest selling hit they ever had, to cuts from their latest album, *The Beach Boys Love You*, they sang them all. But it didn't feel as if they loved anyone last Friday night. It felt as if they were having too many worries of their own."

SATURDAY, NOVEMBER 12, 1977: College of William and Mary, Williamsburg, VA (8:00 p.m. show)
While acknowledging that this concert suffered from off-key harmonies and the fact that the backing musicians hadn't had sufficient time together to develop a relationship, Ish Arango of the *Flat Hat* pronounced the group's appearance a success. He gave special praise to Dennis, whose "magnetic persona shone strongest when he sang Joe Cocker's 'You Are So Beautiful' and as he dropped to one knee (à la James Brown) at the end of 'Surfer Girl,' and to Brian, who briefly came alive while performing on bass before retreating behind his piano.

SUNDAY, NOVEMBER 13, 1977: Coliseum, Charlotte, NC (8:00 p.m. show)
Bob Drogin of the *Charlotte Observer* noted with concern that Brian "looked bored and kept staring glassy-eyed at the roof, or perhaps some point beyond. He only tried one verse of 'Sloop John B,' then went back to staring at the roof as his brother and lead guitarist Carl Wilson took over the lead."

FRIDAY, NOVEMBER 18, 1977: Hammons Center, SW Missouri State University, Springfield, MO (8:00 p.m. show)
Mike O'Brien of the *Springfield News and Leader* noted that "when the five members of what is perhaps America's most successful—certainly among the most important—rock music groups reached back to the early 1960s and dusted off their classic salutes to rolling waves and fast cars and California girls . . . well you could almost feel the sand between your toes."

SATURDAY, NOVEMBER 19, 1977: University of Illinois, Champaign, IL (8:00 p.m. show)

Performing at SW Missouri State University, November 18, 1977. Courtesy of *Ozarko* (student yearbook), Missouri State University

This show was marred by the audience's indifference to new material. Greg Allen of the *Daily Illini* noted that they booed when Mike introduced "Country Pie" and showed impatience when other recent numbers were played. Allen argued that, ironically, the old songs fans wanted to hear were the "material that was most lacking in execution. Most of the earlier material depends upon Brian Wilson's distinctive falsetto as an integral part of the Beach Boys' unique vocal blend. Sadly, he can't sing this way anymore, and his voice was acutely missed."

SUNDAY, NOVEMBER 20, 1977: UD Arena, University of Dayton, OH (7:30 p.m. show)
Following this concert, the group again went their separate ways. Mike, Al, and Brian returned to Iowa to record, while Carl and Dennis went home.

SUNDAY, DECEMBER 11, 1977: Pacific Coliseum, Vancouver, BC, Canada, with Foreman Young Band (8:00 p.m. show)
Having recorded almost two albums' worth of material in Iowa, the Beach Boys headed out on the road. The set list remained the same as in November, but the band dragged out "Papa-Oom-Mow-Mow" for the encore.

The opener in Vancouver was a disaster. The band remained fragile and there'd been no real rehearsal. Harmonies were flat, vocals were ragged, and the members of the band weren't on the same page. Dennis appeared inebriated and spent much of the show rambling inanities into the microphone. Vaughn Palmer of the *Vancouver Sun* declared it "one of the most disgracefully inept performances I have ever seen a major rock act mount."

MONDAY, DECEMBER 12, 1977: Memorial Coliseum, Portland, OR (8:00 p.m. show)

TUESDAY, DECEMBER 13, 1977: Seattle Coliseum, Seattle, WA (8:00 p.m. show)
This show was filmed for an unreleased documentary titled *Our Team*. Ron Altbach recalled, "It was done by Peter Marshall. I brought him out to California and set it up. I don't recall why it didn't come out. But there was so much negativity about that album within the Beach Boys. I think we financed that film, not the Beach Boys. It was done as a tax shelter." The rarely seen film has footage of the group performing "Fun, Fun, Fun" and "Surfin' USA," and of Dennis performing a moving

singing, and writing there." Mike told a reporter from the *Telegraph Herald* that the Institute would aid the creative process because "we all feel pressure; the music business is highly competitive, both while recording and after it's out. We have deadlines and delivery dates but here the tension doesn't build up." However, if he hoped the peaceful surroundings might ease strife within the group, Mike was soon proven wrong. Carl and Dennis had no desire to be cooped up on a meditation retreat and were mostly absent. Brian, under the watchful eye of his bodyguards, remained for the duration, but proved unwilling or unable to take charge and production chores fell to Al Jardine and Ron Altbach.

The resulting record, *MIU Album*, released in 1978, had some nice moments but was thin and unimaginative. Some felt that it sounded more like a Beach Boys album than their recent releases. The vocals were more polished and Brian was in somewhat better voice. He even broke out his falsetto for the fun opener, "She's Got Rhythm." However, the songs he sang on the record, especially "Match Point of Our Love," were banal in the extreme. The album was another commercial failure and did little to alter the critical perception that the Beach Boys were treading water as the 1970s waned.

Even as critics questioned their relevance, they were still a huge concert attraction. Reviewers often noted that the shows were sloppy and sluggish. The group couldn't summon the joy and energy they'd displayed in 1975.

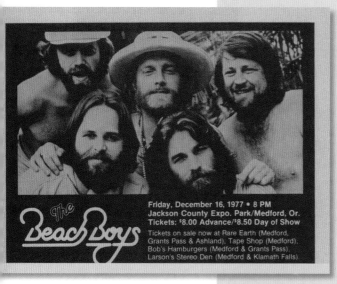

Poster for the Beach Boys' canceled concert in Medford, Oregon, on December 16, 1977. Ian Rusten Collection

Part of the problem was Carl's altered state. He'd gone through a painful divorce and had been sidelined by recurring and excruciating back pain that led him to self-medicate. Chip Rachlin recalled, "Carl was on a downward spiral . . . You get tired of fighting. Carl was not having much fun." And since Carl was the "quality control" of the group, his loss of focus couldn't help but affect performances.

The group ended a fractious year with a sold-out show at the Forum in L.A. Even at this celebration, tension was in evidence. Author David Leaf recalled in his book *The Beach Boys*, "Twice when songs were played that Mike or Al had written, Dennis stalked off stage, the second time taking Brian with him." The group should've taken a long break, but an Australian tour was already planned for February. 1978 would see the Beach Boys tour more than ever.

version of "You Are So Beautiful," which he dedicated to crippled children the group had met that day in a local hospital. In addition to visiting the children, the group went into Kaye Stevens' studio to record PSAs for Toys for Tots. While there, Dennis recorded a soulful lead vocal for Brian's new song "My Diane." *Our Team* features footage of a healthy-looking Dennis laying down this classic vocal. It also shows the group recording tracks at MIU, including "Pitter Patter," "Belles of Paris," and "Our Team."

WEDNESDAY, DECEMBER 14, 1977: Beasley Coliseum, Washington State University, Pullman, WA
The Beach Boys' appearance in Pullman was less than stellar. Once again the sound system was the culprit, frustrating fans and the group. Dennis grumbled throughout the show about his inability to hear other members. Bruce Spotleson of *The Lewiston Morning Tribune* noted, however, that Dennis seemed to have other issues: "He'd been slurring words all night, mumbling jumbles and generally singing off key whenever he was given the opportunity." His performance of "You Are So Beautiful" to begin the encore was apparently so incoherent that the band had to work hard to salvage the situation with their remaining three songs.

FRIDAY, DECEMBER 16, 1977: Jackson County Expo, Medford, OR (Canceled)

SATURDAY, DECEMBER 17, 1977: McArthur Court, University of Oregon, Eugene, OR (8:00 p.m. show)
The group played for 9,500 fans. It was apparently an incredible show culminating in spirited encores of "You Are So Beautiful," "Papa-Oom-Mow-Mow," "Barbara Ann," "Rock and Roll Music," and "Fun, Fun, Fun" that had the crowd on their feet. Fred Crafts of the *Eugene Register Guard*, however, was troubled by Brian's behavior. He noted that Brian looked "drawn and nervous" and that he "often screwed up his face in a nervous twitch." Crafts related that at one point during the concert, much to the surprise of band and audience, "Wilson mysteriously left the stage. Suddenly he wandered into the audience in front of the stage where, with a bemused grin, he waved at the band, signed autographs, left the arena, and went to his dressing room, then returned to the stage as if nothing had happened."

MONDAY, DECEMBER 26, 1977: Sports Arena, San Diego, CA (8:00 p.m. show)

TUESDAY, DECEMBER 27, 1977: Forum, Inglewood, CA (8:00 p.m. show)
The Beach Boys returned home to celebrate their sixteenth anniversary. It was a Love family reunion. Mike's sister Maureen guested on harp for "Catch a Wave" and "In My Room," and his sisters Stephanie and Margie sang backup vocals on one number. For once Loves outnumbered Wilsons, and Mike joked, "This kind of evens things up for all those years." Paul Grein of *Billboard* declared the concert "a triumph" but noted Brian seemed "lackadaisical and lost" and that "the only members who were really vital and dynamic were Dennis Wilson, the group's aggressive drummer, who also sang lead on 'Surfer Girl' and worked the keyboard banks, and Mike Love, lead singer on most of the songs and the group's crowd pleaser." A film of the show exists and shows the L.A. crowd giving Dennis a huge ovation during a soulfully rendered "You Are So Beautiful" encore.

WEDNESDAY, DECEMBER 28, 1977: Cow Palace, San Francisco, CA (7:30 p.m. show)
A fractious, difficult year came to an end with this concert. The set consisted of "California Girls," "Darlin'," "Sloop John B," "Little Deuce Coupe," "Love Is a Woman," "California Saga," "Airplane," "Back Home," "Surfer Girl," "Lady Lynda," "God Only Knows," "Honkin' Down the Highway," "Catch a Wave," "Be True to Your School," "It's OK," "In My Room," "Everyone's in Love with You," "All This Is That," "Country Pie," "Roller Skating Child," "Heroes and Villains," "Help Me Rhonda," "Wouldn't It Be Nice," "I Get Around," "Good Vibrations," "Surfin' USA," "You Are So Beautiful," "Papa-Oom-Mow-Mow," "Barbara Ann," "Rock and Roll Music," and "Fun, Fun, Fun."

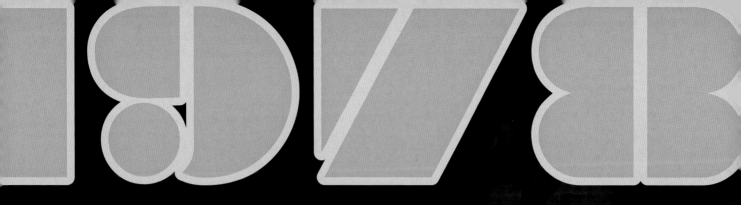

AS 1978 BEGAN, the Beach Boys were preparing for an Australia/New Zealand tour promoted by Paradine Productions (David Frost's company) and the AGC Corporation. The tour came at a tense time for the group, which remained divided between "the meditators" and "the partiers." Carl characterized the current situation as "a truce rather than an armistice." The tension made even the most trivial decisions difficult, since no one was in the mood to compromise.

The complications regarding hiring a replacement for Ron Altbach illustrates this. He'd announced he wouldn't accompany the band to Australia. Dennis immediately thought of a pianist named Sterling Smith, who'd performed on Dennis' solo recordings. Smith recalled, "Dennis hired me to do the tour but the meditating people had hired a piano player from New York, which was Wells Kelly. When we went to Las Vegas to do the rehearsals, Dennis and Carl were still at Caribou Ranch recording, so I flew to Vegas alone. I sat backstage but was pushed out of practices because at that point Al and Mike were planning to hold rehearsals with their meditating piano player . . . I was asked to return to L.A. the next day . . . So [Jerry Schilling] called Dennis and Carl and they said under no circumstance was I to leave. The next day when they got there, Dennis went around to everyone and said, 'If Sterling doesn't go, I won't go!'" Since the terms of the Beach Boys' Australian/New Zealand tour agreement specified that to receive their two and a half million dollars all five original Beach Boys had to be there, Dennis had the needed leverage and Smith joined the tour

CONCERTS PLAYED IN
1978

The 1978 Australian tour marked the absolute height of dysfunctional Beach Boys behavior. The tour was also the nadir of Carl's professional career. Australian TV filmed the band's second concert in Melbourne and his performance was painful to watch. Carl was substance-addled and his equilibrium screwed up, but it wasn't without reason. On the first night in New Zealand, Brian allegedly escaped his minders, Rocky Pamplin and Stan Love, and scored some drugs. As a result he exhibited wild behavior at the first show, twirling and marching about while playing bass. That night the group met with the tour's promoters at the Hilton. At the meeting, Carl commented sarcastically, "Nice going bodyguards. Good job watching Brian!" Bodyguard Rocky Pamplin allegedly responded by knocking Carl out and giving him a black eye. Even worse was the fact that Pamplin wasn't disciplined for his actions. Sterling Smith recalled that when he came into the Myer Music Bowl the next day to prepare for the televised show that night, he found Carl being worked on by makeup artists, and too afraid to go in the green room to get a sandwich because Rocky was there. It was a disturbing scene for the uninitiated. "[Carl's] on painkillers and he's screwed up, while this guy, who should have been fired and on a slow boat back to the States, is in the green room calmly eating a sandwich."

The tour became a misery for Carl and he bottomed out at a concert in Perth. He was in terrible shape, mumbling and stumbling about the stage. Newspapers across the country reported on his behavior. Over 300 angry fans demanded their money back. Promoters

THURSDAY, FEBRUARY 16, AND FRIDAY, FEBRUARY 17, 1978: Aladdin Hotel, Las Vegas, NV (One show each night at 8:30 p.m.)

With a tour of New Zealand and Australia imminent, the Beach Boys played a few warmup gigs. The backing musicians consisted of Wells Kelly, Ron Altbach (who joined them only to teach Kelly his parts), Sterling Smith, Carli Munoz (returning for the first time since September), Gary Griffin on keyboards and piano, Mike Kowalski on drums, Ed Carter on bass, and the Tornado horns. Sterling Smith recalled, "An hour before the first show there were just a few people in the auditorium and we started hearing these catcalls, 'Hey Brian . . . Brian! Hey Brian . . . ' So from backstage we came out to look and Brian's lying underneath the grand piano on his back looking straight up. He was overweight and had this Adidas warmup suit on . . . The bodyguards weren't around, so the stage manager got the road managers and they went and got him and said, 'Hey Brian, come on, let's go for a run!' And Brian said 'OK' and disappeared, but it was still like 'Wow! I mean he's really out of touch with reality.' And later (during the show), there he was . . . just sitting at the piano staring at it. His hands weren't even on the keys."

SATURDAY, FEBRUARY 18, 1978: Salt Palace, Salt Lake City, UT (8:00 p.m. show)

Brian didn't accompany the band to Salt Lake City and Will Grey of the *Deseret News* commented that his absence was noticeable in the high harmonies. "Nevertheless, the night was pure Beach Boys and we kept calling for more. . . . Songs such as 'Surfin' USA,' 'Help Me Rhonda,' 'Surfer Girl' and 'Little Deuce Coupe' were the biggest crowd pleasers . . . Dennis Wilson rendered a very moving version of the Billy Preston song 'Beautiful' which is the best way to describe the concert, beautiful."

SUNDAY, FEBRUARY 26, 1978: Western Springs Stadium, Auckland, NZ, with Stars (3:00 p.m. show)

The Beach Boys flew to Auckland to begin their third tour of New Zealand. Paradine Productions hired a familiar face to supervise the tour, Dick Duryea. Also present were Stephen Love and road manager Greg Berning, a meditator who'd been recruited by the Love camp. Engineer Tom Murphy recalled, "Greg was well behaved and treated the Wilsons well and was liked by everyone."

A crowd of over 30,000 turned out on Sunday. Robyn Langwell of the *New Zealand Herald* declared it "the best rock 'n' roll show seen in Auckland in years . . . the sound was bold and brassy with seventeen musicians cramming the stage. But the music emanated totally from the magic fingers and voices of the five Beach Boys. Their high, tight harmonies combined with a thumping powerful orchestra background to drive the crowd into a frenzy of dancing and screaming." Phil Gifford of the *Auckland Star* was troubled by the appearance of Brian. Gifford noted, "No matter how the others tried to encourage Brian to react (Love introduced him as 'The Big B' before a sad attempt by Brian—whose voice seems completely shot—to take a lead vocal), he sat stolidly at the piano, a stranger to his own music."

TUESDAY, FEBRUARY 28, 1978: Queen Elizabeth II Park, Christchurch, NZ, with Stars (8:00 p.m. show)

Following the Auckland show, the group flew to Christchurch and spent the night at Noah's Hotel, where they held a press conference the next morning. Asked how they felt about having Brian on the road with them, they replied, "We did not know how much we missed him until he came back on stage." Asked what their favorite Beach Boys album was, Dennis quickly replied *Pacific Ocean Blue!* Other members said, "The new ones coming out." Brian volunteered that *Smiley Smile* was his favorite, which prompted a surprised Carl to laugh and say, "I thought it was *Friends*."

The concert was attended by 20,000 fans and was filmed by New Zealand TV, and the group received an enthusiastic reception. However, Rob White of *The Christchurch Star* commented, "The

Beach Boys are getting old . . . They cannot hit the high notes, occasionally go flat and those wonderful Beach Boys harmonies are often rough."

FRIDAY, MARCH 3, TO SUNDAY, MARCH 5, 1978: Festival Hall, Brisbane, QLD, Australia, with Stars (One show on Friday and two on Saturday and Sunday)
The Beach Boys flew into Sydney on March 1. In Brisbane, the band performed five concerts in three days to capacity crowds. Brian was suffering from a cold and finished only two.

WEDNESDAY, MARCH 8, AND THURSDAY, MARCH 9, 1978: Myer Music Bowl, Melbourne, VIC, Australia, with Stars (One show each night at 8:00 p.m.)
The Beach Boys played two nights in Melbourne. Debbie Sharpe reviewed the opening night for the *Melbourne Herald* and noted that Brian and Dennis disappeared from the stage so often that "it was like 'Exodus' gone wrong." Nevertheless, Sharpe wrote that the audience had a great time. Fans were willing to overlook off-key harmonies and bad behavior that a lesser act might have been booed off stage for.

Performing at Sydney Sports Grounds on March 18, 1978.
Courtesy of Stephen J. McParland

The second Melbourne concert was filmed by Australian Channel 7 TV and aired in May as *Good Vibrations from the Myer Bowl*. Unfortunately, it wasn't the Beach Boys' finest hour. Carl looked and sounded stoned and was frequently off-key. His between-song patter was bizarre and Dennis had to keep him on track. At one point, Carl mentioned *Pacific Ocean Blue* was out and that he'd gone to the store and bought a copy. When Dennis told the audience his brother had gotten it for free, Carl exclaimed, "That's bullshit!" prompting Dennis to whisper to him that he was onstage. Dennis was in great form and looked healthier than he ever would again. Brian also looked well but seemed more like a side musician. He stayed in the background, playing bass while sitting on a riser.

SUNDAY, MARCH 12, 1978: Football Park, West Lakes, Adelaide, SA, Australia, with Stars (2:30 p.m. show)

Press conference at Sebel Town House in Sydney, Australia, March 17, 1978.
Courtesy of Stephen J. McParland

TUESDAY, MARCH 14, AND WEDNESDAY, MARCH 15, 1978: Perth Entertainment Centre, Perth, WA, Australia, with Stars (One show on Tuesday and two on Wednesday)
The Beach Boys' first Perth concert started twenty-five minutes late, allegedly because Carl needed to be put in a shower to sober up. Indeed, he was so out of it that he told reporters the next day he had no recollection of playing. Witnesses reported that he staggered about the stage, dropped his guitar a few times, and at one point, stumbled into the drum kit and fell over. He frequently missed high notes and failed to finish lines he was singing. Since he was the bandleader and responsible for counting off and ending songs, numbers rambled on interminably. Brian was so troubled by his brother's condition that the *Adelaide Advertiser* reported he "spent most of the evening sitting expressionless with his guitar near the back of the stage or off the stage." He did, however, rescue the group at the end. They were eager to get the show over with, but Carl kept singing choruses of "Good Vibrations." Brian moved things mercifully along by suddenly interrupting Carl and launching into the unreleased "hum-de-dum" section of the original track, which allowed the band to force the song to a conclusion.

The first Perth show was a major embarrassment. It affected the group in a major way,

were extremely alarmed and one of the organizers, Verity Byrne, confronted the band at their hotel and demanded an explanation. The band apologized and agreed to hold a press conference the next day. A contrite Carl told reporters that the combination of medications he was on and two beers that

The Wilsons share a microphone in Sydney, March 18, 1978. Courtesy of Stephen J. McParland

he drank had a major effect on him. He apologized to the band, noting that his behavior "made the rest of the group nervous and they did not perform as well as they could have done—I was frightening them."

Many in the Beach Boys' inner circle blamed Carl's troubles on Dennis' influence. Dennis was allegedly introduced to heroin a few months prior and his increased chemical dependencies, combined with his large alcohol intake, made him difficult to deal with. On a good night Dennis was great, but on a bad night he might do or say anything. As drummer Bobby Figueroa recalled, "He just started to become a different person. I didn't recognize him anymore."

Later in the year a Southwest tour was organized as a tie-in with the film *Almost Summer*, which featured a Mike Love offshoot act called Celebration on the soundtrack.

especially Carl. Critics noted the band was in much better shape for the shows the next day. *The Australian* reported, "The five plus their backup musos worked harder than any band seen at the Entertainment Centre, and not just for one concert, but two."

SATURDAY, MARCH 18, AND SUNDAY, MARCH 19, 1978: Sydney Sports Grounds, Sydney, NSW, Australia, with Stars (One show on Saturday night and one at 2:00 p.m. on Sunday)
The group concluded their tour with two massive outdoor shows in Sydney. Over 35,000 fans attended on Saturday, despite terrible weather. Lindsay Scott noted in the *Sydney Herald* that "probably only a rock concert would get people outdoors in such dreadful conditions. Probably only the fun of the Beach Boys' music could keep them happy, dancing and singing in the rain. The weather affected the sound quality, but what we could hear of the group sounded reasonably good, except for some of Brian Wilson's flat vocals."

MONDAY, MARCH 20, AND TUESDAY, MARCH 21, 1978: NBC Arena, Honolulu, HI, with Charles Lloyd (One show each night at 8:00 p.m.)
Brian's family attended these shows and his daughters, Carnie and Wendy, came onstage to help sing "Good Vibrations." Brian seemed happy, even manic, dancing around while playing bass. As John Christensen noted in the *Star Bulletin*, "Brian leaped and gyrated like a bear who'd been into the hard cider." Charles Lloyd opened this show. The group offered him a regular slot at Mike's insistence. On future tours, Carli Munoz, Ed Carter, Sterling Smith, Phil Shenale, and Mike Kowalski or Bobby Figueroa accompanied him. While the musicians had respect for Lloyd, there was grumbling behind the scenes because they allegedly received no compensation for backing him.

FRIDAY, APRIL 14, 1978: Summit, Houston, TX, with Charles Lloyd
This ten-day tour of the Southwest was a promotional tie-in with the film *Almost Summer*. Two actors from the movie, Lee Purcell and Tim Matheson, traveled to each date and screened a fifteen-minute clip from the movie prior to the concerts. Two songs that Mike had recorded with Celebration were in the set, "Almost Summer" and "Cruisin.'"

The Summit was equipped with Jumbótron screens and a video exists of this concert. The performances were rough due to a three-week break without rehearsal. Mike apologized for the ragged harmonies and noted that since the return from Hawaii "the whole thing had fallen apart."

SATURDAY, APRIL 15, 1978: Tarrant County Convention Center, Fort Worth, TX, with Charles Lloyd
Much of the focus at this show was on Brian. He didn't disappoint, dancing and racing around the stage manically. However, Pete Oppel of the *Dallas News* opined that in doing so, "he came across as rather bizarre. He never could settle into a lead vocal. He would pull away from the microphone at the most inopportune times and his singing never carried the forcefulness that his other stage antics portrayed."

SUNDAY, APRIL 16, 1978: Assembly Center, Tulsa, OK, with Charles Lloyd (8:00 p.m. show)

MONDAY, APRIL 17, 1978: Convention Center, Pine Bluff, AR, with Charles Lloyd (8:00 p.m. show)

TUESDAY, APRIL 18, 1978: Lloyd Noble Center, University of Oklahoma, Norman, OK, with Charles Lloyd

WEDNESDAY, APRIL 19, 1978: University of Texas, Austin, TX, with Charles Lloyd

THURSDAY, APRIL 20, 1978: Municipal Coliseum, Lubbock, TX, with Charles Lloyd (8:30 p.m. show)

FRIDAY, APRIL 21, 1978: New Mexico State University, Las Cruces, NM, with Charles Lloyd (8:00 p.m. show)

SATURDAY, APRIL 22, 1978: Arizona State University, Tempe, AZ, with Charles Lloyd

SUNDAY, APRIL 23, 1978: University of Arizona, Tucson, AZ, with Charles Lloyd (8:00 p.m. show)

Carl onstage in Sydney, March 18, 1978. Courtesy of Stephen J. McParland

According to Donna Hutchinson of the *Arizona Wildcat*, professionalism was completely absent in what was described as a "poor to fair show." Dennis was "too loaded to do his drumming [and] at one point stalked offstage until the rest of the band consented to play his favorite, 'Surfer Girl.' Brian Wilson on several occasions also had to leave the stage, apparently to see what the condition of his brother was."

Dennis continued to drink afterwards and picked up a sixteen-year-old girl, who accompanied him to his room at the Plaza International Hotel. The girl's mother got wind of it and called the police. Dennis was arrested on Monday morning and taken to Pima County Jail. He was charged with contributing to the delinquency of a minor. He flew home to California after agreeing to return to Superior Court on April 28. Luckily, the girl's parents chose not to pursue the case further and charges were dropped in May. However, the episode made the national news and pictures of Dennis being held by police were in newspapers across the country.

SATURDAY, MAY 13, 1978: Folsom Stadium, Boulder, CO, with Firefall, Bob Welch, and Journey
Over 35,000 fans attended this outdoor show. The group played a ninety-minute set that had fans forming conga lines around the stadium. According to *Boulder Camera* reporter John Leach, the band joined in the fun. "Mike Love, clad in an orange Hawaiian print shirt, pranced across the stage and joined the rest of the band in a series of chorus line kicks for 'Surfin' USA.'" This must have been difficult for Carl, since Leach noted "Wilson hobbled onto the stage on crutches with a 'broken foot' according to his brother, the often reclusive Brian, who was dressed in a yellow running suit."

SUNDAY, MAY 14, 1978: UNI Dome, University of Northern Iowa, Cedar Falls, IA, with Charles Lloyd (8:00 p.m. show)

SUNDAY, MAY 28, 1978: "Day on the Green," Oakland Coliseum, Oakland, CA, with Linda Ronstadt, Dolly Parton, Elvin Bishop, and Norton Buffalo (11 a.m. show)
This was a busy day for Mike, who made a morning appearance with Celebration in the San Fernando Valley before jetting north for the "Day on the Green." The event brought out 40,000 fans, many of which were nonplussed by the band's shoddy performance.

Joel Selvin of the *San Francisco Chronicle* titled his review "Have the Beach Boys Had It?" He declared the band's performance "not only listless and uninspired but fraught with the kind of technical incompetence—from both instrumentalists and vocalists—that even the rankest amateur bands have little trouble avoiding." He noted that Mike took most of the leads, while Carl hardly sang at all and that Brian, who was apparently suffering from laryngitis, gave a performance of "In My Room" that "was so off key and wretched that his brother Carl Wilson waved him away from the microphone and the group finished the song without a lead vocal."

The syndicated show *P.M. Magazine* filmed a portion of the set for a feature on the band. They were seen performing "Surfin' USA." Mike, Brian, and Carl were also interviewed backstage.

Celebration had come about in the fall of 1977 when director Marty Davidson contacted the Beach Boys about contributing to his film. Unfortunately, the soundtrack was on MCA and the group had an exclusive contract with CBS. While the Beach Boys couldn't participate, there was nothing stopping individuals from taking part. Mike got together with Brian, wrote three songs ("Almost Summer," "Crusin'," and "Sad, Sad Summer") and recorded them with a band consisting of Ron Altbach, Wells Kelly, Ed Carter, Mike Kowalski, Charles Lloyd, Gary Griffin, and Dave Robinson. In between Beach Boys shows, Mike and Celebration played free concerts to promote the film.

Mike enjoyed playing with Celebration because he didn't have to deal with his cousins. However, the Beach Boys continued to be Mike's bread and butter. In May they performed to huge audiences in Boulder and Oakland, while in June they became the first

THE BEACH BOYS IN CONCERT

Dennis onstage in Sydney, March 19, 1978. Courtesy of Stephen J. McParland

rock group to play at Giants Stadium. The band was also asked to participate in a massive free concert being organized by Bill Graham that would take place in Leningrad on July 4. The show would feature both Western and Soviet artists, and it was hoped that it would foster greater cultural exchange between the superpowers. The concert was to be documented by filmmaker Dmitri Gruenwald. Unfortunately, it never happened. By late June plans had run aground because officials from the Soviet Film Agency found historical inaccuracies in the script.

The highlight of 1978 was a tour with Jan and Dean in August. The singing duo's career had been derailed by Jan's horrific 1966 car accident that left him partially paralyzed. The recent TV movie *Deadman's Curve*, which depicted his slow recovery, had sparked new interest. Jan's condition remained shaky and he had trouble remembering the

FRIDAY, JUNE 16, 1978: Civic Center, Providence, RI, with Charles Lloyd (8:00 p.m. show)
The Beach Boys embarked on a ten-day East Coast tour. Backing musicians included the Tornado horns, Carli Munoz, Sterling Smith, Ed Carter, and Wells Kelly. Although Kelly had been acting as a keyboardist, he was originally a drummer and was enlisted to play percussion. John Philip ("Phil") Shenale was a new face in the band. He was a keyboard player who'd attended Brian and Al's alma mater El Camino College. He'd also studied TM and was recommended to Mike for Celebration. Instead, he ended up being employed by the Beach Boys. He recalled, "The funny thing was that I got the gig through Mike Love and everyone thought I was his guy because I was a meditator, but I grew to like Dennis much better. We confronted each other a few times on that first tour and got to be good friends. Dennis was a great guy. I think he was a real rock 'n' roll drummer and a great artist, as I later found when I worked with him at Criteria Studios. Dennis and Carli and Sterling and I hung around a lot together . . . I also liked Carl a lot. He was a truly spiritual man and he brought stability to the group."

Once again the concerts were tied in with *Almost Summer*. In the middle of each show, Mike played a solo set while the Wilsons took a break. It consisted of "Almost Summer," "Cruisin'," "Everyone's in Love with You," and "Country Pie." Sterling Smith recalled, "Dennis would leave because he didn't want any part of that, but to his credit he told us that whatever he thought of it, it was part of the Beach Boys show and we ought to be there."

SATURDAY, JUNE 17, 1978: Civic Center, Springfield, MA, with Charles Lloyd (8:00 p.m. show)
Illustrating the difficulties the Beach Boys were having with Dennis, promoter Jim Koplik recalled that he demanded Quaaludes prior to this show. When Koplik got them for him, "Carl told me what a mistake I made because he would eat them before the show. I felt terrible and I watched the whole concert terrified something would happen. When he came off the stage after the main show, I was standing right by the riser and his wife Karen Lamm said something to him and he said something back to her and she kicked him right in the balls! He went down like a ton of bricks and he didn't do the encore."

SUNDAY, JUNE 18, 1978: New Haven Coliseum, New Haven, CT, with Charles Lloyd

MONDAY, JUNE 19, 1978: Norfolk Scope, Norfolk, VA, with Charles Lloyd (8:00 p.m. show)

TUESDAY, JUNE 20, 1978: Spectrum, Philadelphia, PA, with Charles Lloyd (8:00 p.m. show)

WEDNESDAY, JUNE 21, 1978: Community War Memorial, Rochester, NY, with Charles Lloyd (8:00 p.m. show)
The band played for 10,000 fans at this show. Jack Garner of the *Democrat and Chronicle* commented, "Unlike many bands, that would blend several oldies into a kiss-off ten-minute medley, the Beach Boys did an incredible range of classic songs at full length. They also blended in just the right amount of new material, including two songs that are among the best California summer songs they've ever done ('Almost Summer' and 'Cruisin'')."

THURSDAY, JUNE 22, 1978: Forum, Montreal, QB, Canada, with Charles Lloyd (8:00 p.m. show)

FRIDAY, JUNE 23, 1978: Civic Centre, Lansdowne Park, Ottawa, ON, Canada, with Charles Lloyd

SATURDAY, JUNE 24, 1978: CNE Stadium, Toronto, ON, Canada, with Journey, Pablo Cruise, and the Steve Miller Band (12:00 p.m. show)

The group headlined this six-hour show. By the time they came onstage the crowd of 35,000 was spent and irritated, having been in the hot sun for five hours. They were in no mood for anything but hits. According to Stephen Godfrey of the *Globe and Mail*, when the group deviated from that formula to play "Lady Lynda," the crowd whistled disapproval. Godfrey didn't think it was the Beach Boys' finest hour, noting "they barely got by."

SUNDAY, JUNE 25, 1978: Giants Stadium, East Rutherford, NJ, with Pablo Cruise, Stanky Brown, and the Steve Miller Band
The Beach Boys played before a crowd of 61,128 at the first concert held at the newly constructed Giants Stadium. The set for this show, which aired on WNEW FM, consisted of "California Girls," "Sloop John B," "Do It Again," "Little Deuce Coupe," "In My Room," "God Only Knows," "Back Home," "Darlin'," "It's OK," "Peggy Sue," "Be True To Your School," "Catch a Wave," "Lady Lynda," "Almost Summer," "Cruisin'," "Everyone's in Love with You," "Country Pie," "Heroes and Villains," "Surfer Girl," "Help Me Rhonda," "Wouldn't It Be Nice," "I Get Around," "Rock and Roll Music," "Surfin' USA," "Good Vibrations," "Barbara Ann," and "Fun, Fun, Fun."

SATURDAY, JULY 15, 1978: Cal Expo Amphitheatre, Sacramento, CA
Brian was absent from this tour because he'd been admitted to Alvarado Hospital in San Diego. He wasn't the only musician missing. The horn section had been eliminated, with the exception of Charles Lloyd on saxophone. The group were looking to cut expenses and it came to their attention that one musician could replicate a five-piece horn section by skillful use of the Oberheim synthesizer, a new eight-voice keyboard. Thus, Phil Shenale alone supplied horn sounds. Though the horns were gone, Bobby Figueroa was back on percussion, after a ten-month absence.

SUNDAY, JULY 16, 1978: Memorial Stadium, Seattle, WA, with the Kinks, Randy Hansen, and Jr. Cadillac (3:00 p.m. show)
This six-hour rock fest was dubbed "Summer Sunday 78" and attracted 20,000 fans despite wet weather that turned the field into a soggy mess.

TUESDAY, JULY 18, 1978: Stampede Corral, Calgary, AB, Canada, with Zingo
The trip to Calgary was extremely memorable for Phil Shenale. He recalled, "Apparently Dennis took the furniture from two or three other rooms as a prank and stuffed it in Carl's hotel room while he was sleeping, so that Carl couldn't get out of the room . . . as a result we were late for the commercial flight and missed it. So they literally had to lease eight or ten four-seat planes to fly from Seattle to Calgary. It was the worst flight I've ever been on in my life. I mean, going over the Rockies in a four-seat prop plane . . . we were getting sick. And the plane we were on didn't have any extra oxygen. It was madness." Bobby Figueroa added, "The oxygen meter was faulty so we were all having trouble breathing, at least on our little plane. So we said to the pilot, 'Are you sure this is up? Because we're having trouble breathing.' And he said, 'Yeah, the oxygen gauge reads full.' Then he tapped it and it went all the way down to empty! So the meter said full but it was empty. That was scary. But we made it."

WEDNESDAY, JULY 19, 1978: "Klondike Days Festival," Edmonton Expo, Edmonton, AB, Canada (Two shows at 4:00 and 8:00 p.m.)
These shows were marred by Dennis' drunken behavior. He disappeared for large portions of both concerts and played dreadfully. He messed up the timing on "Sloop John B" and ruined "God Only Knows" by drumming over the vocal harmonies. According to Joe Sornberger of the *Edmonton Journal*, when Dennis returned to the stage after a twenty-minute break he "walked into a microphone; jumped up and walked across the top of a baby grand piano while dragging a mike stand with him at the same time; kicked over a speaker box near his drums; and frequently turned his back on the audience between songs."

THURSDAY, JULY 20, 1978: Agridome, Regina, SK, Canada, with Zingo (8:00 p.m. show)

"Carl had an acoustic guitar on the bus and they practiced 'The Little Old Lady from Pasadena' and two or three others and the harmony in its acoustic purity was phenomenal. They were doing the old songs and it was scary how good it was. I thought, 'Wow! If we went out and did this onstage it would be one of the best tours in the world!' But it all fell apart at the gig."

A wildly animated Brian steals the show in Hawaii, March 21, 1978. Photo: Ed Roach ©1978, 2012

words to his songs, but he was desperate to return to the stage. The Beach Boys were happy to lend a hand and invited him on tour. Dean Torrence accompanied him but was quick to remove pressure. He told the *St. Petersburg Press* that it wasn't a Jan and Dean tour. "We're just guests. We'll have the whole Beach Boys backup group behind us. It'll be fun, just traveling with the Beach Boys' tour and stepping on stage for three songs or so." For many fans it was heartwarming just to see Jan on a stage and the Beach Boys clearly got a buzz from having the duo along. The whole group remained onstage to help Jan and Dean perform "Surf City," "Deadman's Curve," and "Little Old Lady from Pasadena." There was a sense of fun at the concerts missing from recent tours.

FRIDAY, JULY 21, 1978: Civic Center, St. Paul, MN (8:00 p.m. show)
This Beach Boys' appearance before 13,000 was a huge success. However, the concert was almost derailed by Dennis. He wandered off stage early and returned later in a clearly drunken state. He then proceeded to ad-lib introductions for band members (introducing Carl as "the legendary Kenny Wilson") before actively requesting boos from the crowd. He exclaimed, "C'mon, let's hear some boos. Get vicious." The rest of the group did their best to ignore him, but he commandeered a spare keyboard and played off-key chords. Tim Carr of the *Minneapolis Tribune* reported, "Love was obviously upset, but brother Carl seemed to be taking it in stride and was laughing along with his brother's fraternity-style pranks. But the concert was in jeopardy of becoming a shambles. Then Dennis reclaimed the drums and began funneling his nervous energy into the music and kicked the band into a rousing final burst, propelling the songs along at a full-tilt pace."

SATURDAY, JULY 22, 1978: Chicago Stadium, Chicago, IL, with Charles Lloyd (8:00 p.m. show)

SUNDAY, JULY 23, 1978: Dane County Memorial Coliseum, Madison, WI, with Freeze (7:30 p.m. show)

THURSDAY, AUGUST 3, 1978: Carowinds Amusement Park, Charlotte, NC, with Charles Lloyd (Two shows)
Brian was again absent from this tour. The sailboat stage set that the group had played in front of in 1976, however, was back.

FRIDAY, AUGUST 4, AND SATURDAY, AUGUST 5, 1978: Merriweather Post Pavilion, Columbia, MD, with Charles Lloyd (One show at 8:00 p.m. on Friday and two on Saturday at 1:00 and 8:00 p.m.)

SUNDAY, AUGUST 6, 1978: SPAC, Saratoga, NY, with Charles Lloyd (7:00 p.m. show)

MONDAY, AUGUST 7, 1978: Boston Garden, Boston, MA, with Charles Lloyd (8:00 p.m. show)
The group took the stage after 10:00 p.m. and treated the audience to a twenty-five-song set. Bill Adler of the *Boston Herald* criticized their unprofessionalism, noting "the pacing was poor, the choice of tunes sometimes deliberately obscure, the playing and singing ragged." However, he admitted, "These failures aside, the opening chords of their classics never failed to trigger a familiar kind of kneejerk nostalgia and the mostly high school age audience enthusiastically clapped along."

WEDNESDAY, AUGUST 9, AND THURSDAY, AUGUST 10, 1978: Blossom Music Center, Cuyahoga Falls, OH, with Charles Lloyd (One show each night at 8:30 p.m.)

The Beach Boys made the first of many appearances at this venue thirty-three miles south of Cleveland. The Wednesday night crowd stood in drizzling rain for much of the night but most remained for the whole show. Mark Hruby of the *Cleveland Press* argued they stayed because "the Beach Boys means having a good time. They perform with style and cool. Their lyrics and melodies are among the most remembered of rock 'n' roll."

FRIDAY, AUGUST 11, TO SUNDAY, AUGUST 13, 1978: Pine Knob Music Theater, Clarkston, MI, with Charles Lloyd (One show on Friday and two each on Saturday and Sunday)

MONDAY, AUGUST 14, 1978: Illinois State Fair, Springfield, IL, with Charles Lloyd (Two shows at 7:00 and 9:00 p.m.)

FRIDAY, AUGUST 25, 1978: Buccaneer Stadium, Grand Haven, MI, with Jan and Dean and McGuinn, Clark, and Hillman (6:00 p.m. show) and Alpine Valley Music Theater, East Troy, WI, with Jan and Dean (8:00 p.m. show)

These were the first dates of the ten-day tour with Jan and Dean that took place while the Beach Boys were simultaneously recording in Miami. Brian was back and took an upfront role on bass. The rest of the musicians were Ed Carter on guitar, Charles Lloyd on sax, Sterling Smith on piano/keyboards, Phil Shenale on Oberheim synthesizer, Bobby Figueroa on drums, and Carli Munoz on keyboards.

As was often the case on the first show of a tour, the group was underrehearsed. Sterling Smith recalled that they didn't get around to practicing with Jan and Dean until the bus ride to the show. However, he noted, "Carl had an acoustic guitar on the bus and they practiced 'The Little Old Lady from Pasadena' and two or three others and the harmony in its acoustic purity was phenomenal. They were doing the old songs and it was scary how good it was. I thought, 'Wow! If we went out and did this onstage it would be one of the best tours in the world!' But it all fell apart at the gig." Jim McFarlin of the *Grand Rapids Press* declared the Beach Boys performance "like having sand kicked in your face . . . It was a melancholy sight to witness Brian Wilson . . . struggle through a lead vocal or turn away from the microphone in disgust, frustrated over his seeming inability to contribute fully. Mike Love, the gifted lead singer, now must muster all his resources to grasp the lilting tenor that once came so easily."

SATURDAY, AUGUST 26, 1978: Three Rivers Stadium, Pittsburgh, PA, with Jan and Dean, the Steve Miller Band, Axis, the Barkin Band, and Sweet Breeze (12:00 p.m. show)

This show, billed as the "Tri State Jam '78," was attended by 16,000 fans. Sandy Polarkoff of the *Beaver Times* noted, "The Beach Boys took the crowd through all the phases of their career from way back then to now . . . By the end, after an encore with Jan and Dean of 'Barbara Ann' and 'Fun, Fun, Fun,' the Beach Boys and Jan and Dean proved they still have the knack and talent to please their audience."

SUNDAY, AUGUST 27, 1978: Edgewater Raceway, Cincinnati, OH, with Jan and Dean, Blue Oyster Cult, the Cars, the Nitty Gritty Dirt Band, and Starcastle (12:00 p.m. show) and Charleston, WV (Canceled)

This was another all-day event, billed as the "Great Miami River Music Festival." The venue was, according to Sterling Smith, "the property next to a drag strip. Not your ordinary venue. It was like, 'Here is this outdoor venue and we're going to build a stage and invite everyone out to be hot and sweltering.'" The 7,000 fans that turned out were treated to a diverse bill, ranging from the new wave of the Cars to the hard rock of Blue Oyster Cult. Despite vast differences in styles, the members of Blue Oyster Cult professed to be Beach Boys fans and drummer Albert Bouchard was spotted singing along to "Surfer Girl." The concert concluded late, forcing cancellation of the show in West Virginia.

Brian went through a number of ups and downs in 1978. Early in the year he seemed on an upswing. But by the summer he'd sunk into a depression and he took time off to be treated at the Alvarado Medical Clinic. On his reemergence he seemed better, but when the group went to Miami's Criteria Studios to begin work on their

> "Mike told the audience that Brian was hungover from drinking too much the night before and couldn't hack it. 'C'mon everybody,' Mike announced, 'Let's boo Brian!'"

next album, it became evident Brian's participation would be limited. Maurice Gibb of the Bee Gees recalled Brian sitting outside the studio in a stupor for over an hour, not saying a word. In desperation, Bruce Johnston was called in to help.

Despite differences that caused Bruce to leave the Beach Boys in 1972, in the intervening years he had contributed to most of their albums. CBS Records was eager

Brian and Mike on the "Jan and Dean" tour, September 1978. Photo: Ed Roach ©1978, 2012

to have the Grammy-winning Bruce lend a hand to his old band. Bruce was summoned to Miami in August and took charge of what became the group's CBS debut, titled *LA (Light Album)*. Bruce somewhat diffused the tension present at the group's sessions for the past two years. Phil Shenale commented, "The thing I was wondering was, if Brian couldn't take charge, why didn't Carl take charge? But the reason was that the group had developed so many regions within the band. It was easier to have a guy from the external than for any of them to take charge." Bruce initially came just to aid them with the album, but after joining the group for some fall shows, he was back as a permanent member by early 1979.

FRIDAY, SEPTEMBER 1, 1978: Municipal Auditorium, Mobile, AL, with Jan and Dean
After a four-day hiatus, the tour resumed for some southern dates.

SATURDAY, SEPTEMBER 2, 1978: Omni, Atlanta, GA, with Jan and Dean and Le Roux (8:00 p.m. show)
Bruce Johnston appeared onstage with the group for the first time since 1973. He'd been working with them at Criteria and joined the band for the remaining tour dates. He told David Leaf that it was interesting being onstage, "because the only other time we'd ever officially played together, in terms of a set, all six of us, was the Whiskey (in 1970). The shows were good, a little sloppy, which is just a matter of rehearsing. A lot of times when you break for a few days it gets sloppy, but that's something every band goes through."

SUNDAY, SEPTEMBER 3, 1978: Lakeland Civic Center, Lakeland, FL, with Jan and Dean and Le Roux (8:30 p.m. show)
The Beach Boys took the stage after 10:00 p.m., but the crowd remained in a good mood throughout their set, which included a solo performance by Bruce of his composition "I Write the Songs." He told the audience it was the first time he'd performed the song, which had been a hit for Barry Manilow.

The only dark cloud affecting the concert was Dennis' behavior. According to the *Lakeland Ledger*, "The drummer disappeared halfway through the set, cutting the band's drum power in half, and reappeared to stagger around the stage, dance on the piano, and disassemble the microphones." Phil Shenale recalled that such behavior became increasingly common. "There were so many times where he'd jump on the piano and Sterling would be playing, and they'd put this fish net on the piano with big holes in it that his feet would fit into, and he would dance on the piano and he'd [frequently] almost crash thirty feet into the crowd."

MONDAY, SEPTEMBER 4, 1978: Civic Center, Savannah, GA, with Jan and Dean (6:00 p.m. show) and Coliseum, Jacksonville, FL, with Jan and Dean and Roundhouse (8:00 p.m. show)

FRIDAY, OCTOBER 27, 1978: Crisler Arena, University of Michigan, Ann Arbor, MI (8:00 p.m. show)
In addition to the five Beach Boys, the touring lineup for these dates consisted of Sterling Smith, Carli Munoz, Phil Shenale, Bobby Figueroa, and Ed Carter. The band pulled out the stage set used in late 1977 in which the piano was inside a '57 Chevy.

This opening show was plagued with technical problems. Brian received a shock from his bass guitar during "In My Room" and left the stage, never to return. According to a fan in attendance, "Mike told the audience that Brian was hungover from drinking too much the night before and couldn't hack it. 'C'mon everybody,' Mike announced, 'Let's boo Brian!' The crowd responded with a few half-hearted boos as Mike added his own 'Boo! Hiss!'"

SATURDAY, OCTOBER 28, 1978: Notre Dame University, South Bend, IN, and Arie Crown Theater, Chicago, IL (11:30 p.m. show)
Bruce was lecturing at Purdue and joined the group at Notre Dame. Afterwards, the group played a late-night concert in Chicago.

SUNDAY, OCTOBER 29, 1978: Milwaukee Arena, Milwaukee, WI (7:30 p.m. show)
A tiny crowd of less than 4,000 attended. Brian was absent.

T HE BEACH BOYS were putting the finishing touches on their upcoming *LA (Light Album)* as 1979 began. Dennis contributed the heartbreaking "Baby Blue," which had been intended for his unfinished *Bambu* project. Carl added the melancholy rocker "Angel Come Home," which featured one of Dennis' last lead vocals. Al weighed in with the ambitious "Lady Lynda," which became a huge hit in England. The new record featured little participation from Brian, other than an odd cover of "Shortnin' Bread," and the pretty "Good Timin'," a track leftover from the 1974 Caribou sessions. The album is chiefly remembered for the inclusion, at the behest of Bruce, of an eleven-minute disco-style remake of Brian's 1967 *Wild Honey* tune "Here Comes the Night." Bruce was excited by the idea of a Beach Boys disco single. He told a reporter from the *Phoenix*, "It's the best time to do it. Because it's out there, it's happening. I keep telling the guys it's like a costume to wear for one number if we were doing a show." The rest of the group seemed less sure. Carl commented, "We're not going disco . . . one of the cuts on the album is a disco cut. It was Bruce's idea to do it." Dennis was typically blunt, telling *Music World and Record Digest*,

CONCERTS PLAYED IN
1979

THURSDAY, MARCH 1, TO SUNDAY, MARCH 4, 1979: Radio City Music Hall, New York, NY

The Beach Boys played four nights at Radio City. The group mainly sang oldies, though cuts from *LA (Light Album)* were performed, including the disco "Here Comes the Night," which got a chilly reception at all four shows. Performing with the group were Ed Carter on bass, Bobby Figueroa on drums, Phil Shenale on Oberheim synthesizer, Sterling Smith on piano, Carli Munoz on organ, and newcomer Mike Meros on clavinette and synthesizer. Meros had played on "Here Comes the Night" and guested at these shows to teach the song to the band. He recalled in a 1984 interview with *The Baltimore Sun*, "I was blown away. Truth is, I wasn't that familiar with all their stuff. So I sat in my room and wrote down all the charts. We got out on stage, and it's Radio City, right? And I put the charts under my feet, and the crowd is cheering, and I'm looking down at my feet the whole night." Meros got the gig due to his association with Bruce, who was back permanently. Bobby Figueroa recalled, "I was happy to have Bruce there. He's a very talented guy. Also, he was very good at mediating between the guys and making suggestions and finding compromise. I noticed that he was kind of a peacekeeper at first."

Dressed in a jogging suit, Brian appeared on the first night, though after the opening number he headed backstage, occasionally peeking out from behind a curtain. Ken Emerson of the *New York Times* reported, "Finally he reappeared and picked inaudibly at the keys like a sulky child at his dinner while one or another of the group or its entourage sat beside him on the piano bench and cheered him on." Brian skipped the rest of the engagement. Dennis played all four nights, but was drunk on at least two and seemed bent on creating controversy, sporting a T-shirt that said, "Pity about Mike Love" at one show. Mike downplayed the problems with his cousin. He told *Record World*, "Dennis and I are the most obviously competitive in the group. Brian's passive, Carl is kind of a moderator, Al is very straight, while Dennis is the rebel and I am the eccentric. We get on each other's nerves sometimes . . . but it's not a big thing. We're both just very volatile."

Despite the intra-group issues, the band appeared well-rehearsed but somewhat uptight. Richard Forlenza of *NY Rocker*, who attended on Friday, noted, "The band seemed constricted, as if the slightest bit of spontaneity would send the whole structure tumbling. Only Dennis could be counted on for an occasional surprise, holding up the show so he could change his shoes, placing a Heineken bottle on the grand piano when the pianist began the Bach intro to 'Lady Lynda,' walking offstage for the performance of the discofied 'Here Comes the Night.' I sensed that Dennis is perhaps not all that happy with everything the band does, but his solid 4/4 drumming and spirited vocal on 'Angel Come Home' were the highlights of the show for me."

FRIDAY, APRIL 20, 1979: Market Square Arena, Indianapolis, IN, with Ian Matthews (8:00 p.m. show)

The group toured with Ian Matthews, a former member of Fairport Convention who had a hit with "Shake It." Musicians on the trip were Ed Carter, Carli Munoz, Phil Shenale, Charles Lloyd, Sterling Smith, and Bobby Figueroa. The tour was ostensibly to promote *LA (Light Album)* and the group played four songs from it. "Here Comes the Night" was dropped due to the bad reaction it received in New York.

In Indianapolis, 15,000 people turned out. Zach Dunkin of the *Indianapolis News* reported, "Last night's twenty-eight-song show opened the group's tour and like most tour openers it had its bugs . . . Three of the best done tunes were songs from the current *LA (Light Album)*—Love's 'Sumahama,' Jardine's 'Lady Lynda,' and Carl's 'Good Timin.' A rare misfire was 'Shortnin' Bread,' a song that was rehearsed heavily yesterday. It was supposed to be one of those sing-a-long jobs, but the crowd never quite got into it."

SATURDAY, APRIL 21, 1979: Riverfront Coliseum, Cincinnati, OH, with Ian Matthews (8:00 p.m. show)

The set consisted of "California Girls," "Sloop John B," "Darlin'," "Good Timin'," "Do It Again," "Little Deuce Coupe," "In My Room," "God Only Knows," "Shortnin' Bread," "Be True to Your School,"

"I hate it. I never did like it. Certain lines I like . . . certain disco songs I like . . . but that one is dead. It has the most boring drumming . . . thump . . . thump . . . thump."

"Dennis and I are the most obviously competitive in the group. Brian's passive, Carl is kind of a moderator, Al is very straight, while Dennis is the rebel and I am the eccentric. We get on each other's nerves sometimes . . . but it's not a big thing. We're both just very volatile."

—Mike Love

Despite mixed feelings, the group premiered the song at Radio City Music Hall in March. Things didn't go well. The crowd booed loudly when they played it, with red disco lights flashing above the all-white stage. Ken Emerson of the *New York Times* declared it

"Catch a Wave," "It's OK," "Lady Lynda," "Sumahama," "Surfer Girl," "Angel Come Home," "Heroes and Villains," "Help Me Rhonda," "Wouldn't It Be Nice," "Rock and Roll Music," "I Get Around," "Surfin' USA," "You Are So Beautiful," "Good Vibrations," "Barbara Ann," and "Fun, Fun, Fun."

SUNDAY, APRIL 22, 1979: University of Toledo, Toledo, OH, with Ian Matthews (7:00 p.m. show)
This concert attracted a crowd so bent on having a good time that they ignored feedback, bad sound mixing, missed cues on songs, and dysfunctional behavior. Jim Yavorcik of the *Toledo Blade* reported, "Dennis Wilson seemed disorientated as he pranced about the stage, forcing Brian and keyboard man Bruce Johnston away from their pianos at one point . . . He also had a few problems with his only lead vocal of the night, forgetting the words to 'Angel Come Home.' But Dennis returned to his drums for some inspired playing and finished the show quite strong."

MONDAY, APRIL 23, 1979: Southern Illinois University, Carbondale, IL, with Ian Matthews (8:00 p.m. show)

TUESDAY, APRIL 24, 1979: Middle Tennessee State University, Murfreesboro, TN, with Ian Matthews (8:00 p.m. show)
The April tour was enlivened by the presence of Fleetwood Mac's Christine McVie, who'd begun a romance with Dennis in the fall of 1978. Sterling Smith recalled, "It was fun for us but it ultimately kind of led to a little debauchery. Dennis . . . had stayed up all night in a partying mode and he missed the whole show (in Murfreesboro). I think that was the first time that had happened in the whole time I'd been there. And we thought, 'Wow, this isn't a good sign.'" While Dennis was absent, Roy Orbison came backstage to rehash old times with the group about their 1964 tour of Australia.

WEDNESDAY, APRIL 25, 1979: Civic Center, Roanoke, VA, with Ian Matthews

---

THURSDAY, APRIL 26, 1979: Carolina Coliseum, Columbia, SC, with Ian Matthews (8:00 p.m. show)

FRIDAY, APRIL 27, 1979: University of Tennessee, Knoxville, TN, with Ian Matthews (8:00 p.m. show)
A capacity crowd turned out at UT. Monica Langley of the *Daily Beacon* declared the group "nothing short of outstanding," but couldn't help noticing the dysfunctional behavior now commonplace at a Beach Boys show. Langley reported, "Dennis Wilson, the drummer, acted crazy as he jumped onto the piano, danced on his chair, laid down on the stage while kicking his feet in the air, and spilled his beer all across the stage. On the other hand, Brian Wilson, the oldest of the brothers, was so nonchalant that he contributed little to the concert's success. Wearing green sweatpants and a windbreaker, he played the piano and walked across the stage twice rather routinely with his arms in the air." While they were in Knoxville, a taped appearance by the group on *The Midnight Special* aired on NBC TV. They performed "Here Comes the Night," "Angel Come Home," "Good Vibrations," "Lady Lynda," and "Rock and Roll Music."

SATURDAY, APRIL 28, 1979: Rupp Arena, Lexington, KY, with Ian Matthews (8:00 p.m. show)
Christine McVie and Lindsey Buckingham of Fleetwood Mac joined the group for a few songs at this show.

SUNDAY, APRIL 29, 1979: Greensboro Coliseum, Greensboro, NC, with Ian Matthews (8:00 p.m. show)

MONDAY, APRIL 30, 1979: Capitol Centre, Largo, MD, with Ian Matthews (8:00 p.m. show)
For the last show of the tour, Christine McVie sang harmony on the encores of "Good Vibrations," "Barbara Ann," and "Fun, Fun, Fun."

FRIDAY, MAY 11, 1979: Broome County Veteran's Memorial, Binghamton, NY, with Ian Matthews
Perhaps hoping to drum up enthusiasm for the fading fortunes of their *LA (Light Album)*, the band played five songs from it on this tour. Even "Here Comes the Night" was back—and then gone again for good by May 15. The backing band was a stripped-down group consisting of Carli Munoz, Ed

an "out and out failure." Mike commented that detractors "were probably some hardcore Beach Boys fans who'd like us to play nothing but 'Barbara Ann' and 'Surfin' USA.'" His defense seemed half-hearted, considering he'd apologized to the audience before playing the song. It was soon evident that they'd made a misstep. Beach Boys fans weren't disco enthusiasts. The song was so badly received that it was almost immediately dropped from their set. Dennis was happy to see it go.

The "Here Comes the Night" single was initially hyped to the heavens by the group's new label CBS. But it tanked on the charts, as did the LP. The failure of *LA (Light Album)* had major repercussions for the Beach Boys. CBS had been subsidizing their tours, but as sound mixer Tom Murphy recalled, "When 'Here Comes the Night' and the album weren't selling well, that's when the record company stopped giving tour support and there were cutbacks. They started cutting members of the band and eventually they got down to cutting me." When Murphy flew to Indianapolis for the opening date of the April tour, Carl Wilson and Jerry Schilling asked him to take a walk with them. "I remember we were walking across the huge basketball arena in Indianapolis, Carl, Jerry, and me. Carl wasn't speaking. Jerry did all the speaking for him. Jerry said, 'Tom, we'd like you to help us. We have to do layoffs and cut expenses and we'd appreciate if you'd not go to Dennis about us laying you off so that the tour can continue and Dennis doesn't go nuts. So would you mind just leaving and not seeing Dennis first?' What was funny to me was that Carl wasn't talking, he was just standing there. So I said to

Carl, 'Is that your wish Carl?' Carl sort of nodded and Jerry said, "Yes that's Carl's wish too.' So I said, 'OK,' and Jerry and I flew back to L.A. together . . . I could have argued with them, but I was burned out by that point anyway."

Other cuts followed. Sterling Smith recalled that tour attendance was down and "at some point there was a business re-evaluation and they said, 'Hey, we have too many keyboard players,' which I could have told them when I joined! Bruce was friendly with Mike Meros and he said, 'Hey, my guy will work cheap,' and that appealed to the organization. So they looked at Carli Munoz and me, and Carli had greater seniority and was Dennis' buddy. They also wanted to fire Charles Lloyd, who was making $1000 a night and the consensus was that he wasn't bringing much to the party anymore. But Charles was Mike's buddy and he brought Mike great credibility because he's a world-class jazz guy and a meditator. So Mike liked all that. But Mike agreed he should be fired if a keyboard player was fired too. And that's where I became one of the pawns and was let go, along with Charles." By May, Charles Lloyd, Sterling Smith, and Phil Shenale were gone.

The cuts contributed to continuing tension within the group. At the center of the turmoil was Dennis. He'd been a heavy drinker and drug user for years and by 1979, as Tom Murphy recalled, "Drugs and alcohol were his life and music had become his secondary hobby." Many insiders felt that the problem was that he had few outlets for all his pent-up energy. He'd largely abandoned sessions for his second album *Bambu* when the Beach Boys were forced to

Carter, Bobby Figueroa, and Mike Meros. Bobby Figueroa had nothing but praise for Meros. "He was unsung in my mind. He was a great player, great guy, and a real fun dude."

SATURDAY, MAY 12, 1979: Civic Arena, Pittsburgh, PA, with Ian Matthews

SUNDAY, MAY 13, 1979: Community War Memorial, Rochester, NY, with Ian Matthews (8:00 p.m. show)

MONDAY, MAY 14, 1979: Nassau Coliseum, Uniondale, NY, with Ian Matthews (8:00 p.m. show)
Good quality tapes of this concert and the following night in Springfield survive. Dennis was in good form, as was the rest of the group.

TUESDAY, MAY 15, 1979: Civic Center, Springfield, MA (8:00 p.m. show)

WEDNESDAY, MAY 16, 1979: Memorial Auditorium, Buffalo, NY, with Ironhorse (8:00 p.m. show)
Randy Bachman's group Ironhorse opened on this tour. Carl hit it off with Bachman and ended up getting together with him to do some writing. Carl told a reporter, "We went to a ranch to write some songs. We had two days, and we cranked up five tunes." The songs appeared on the upcoming *Keepin' the Summer Alive* album.

THURSDAY, MAY 17, 1979: Community War Memorial Arena, Syracuse, NY, with Ironhorse (8:00 p.m. show)
Michael Kern of the *Syracuse Post Standard* noted, "Very little has changed as far as the group's live performances go. Mike Love is still a ringleader extraordinaire, Carl Wilson's vocals are still as sweet as ever, and brother Dennis Wilson remains the group's enfant terrible . . . Best of the new material was 'Angel Come Home,' in spite of Dennis Wilson's mumbled, raspy vocals (à la Joe Cocker)."

FRIDAY, MAY 18, 1979: Civic Center, Augusta, ME, with Ironhorse (8:00 p.m. show)

SATURDAY, MAY 19, 1979: Civic Center, Glens Falls, NY, with Ironhorse (8:00 p.m. show)

SUNDAY, MAY 20, 1979: Civic Center, Providence, RI, with Ironhorse (8:00 p.m.

MONDAY, MAY 21, 1979: Spectrum, Philadelphia, PA, with Ironhorse (8:00 p.m. show)

MONDAY, JUNE 4, TO SUNDAY, JUNE 10 1979: Universal Amphitheater, Los Angeles, CA, with Glenn Super (One show each night)
The group's weeklong engagement in their hometown started off on a note of triumph. June 4, 1979 was declared "Beach Boys Day" in L.A. and the group took part in a meet and greet for fans outside Peaches Records before heading to the Amphitheater. Daryl Dragon resumed his role of Captain Keyboards for the occasion.

Sylvie Simmons of *Sounds* attended the opener and declared it "an encyclopedic set of note perfect oldies, a smattering of new songs and the obligatory plug for the new album, explosive sound; we didn't even get that disco thing (though we did get Manilow solo from Bruce, 'I Write the Songs')." However, G. Brown of the *Denver Post* had a different take. He reported, "Musically things were a mess on opening night. Dennis Wilson can barely be termed a drummer, as he spent most of his time banging on the same two drums when he wasn't staggering around the stage in some chemically induced euphoria. Brian Wilson opened his mouth to sing 'Sloop John B' for the second number, then sat behind his piano for the duration of the set, chain smoking and clutching at his head in the best *Lost Weekend* tradition."

Both reviewers were alarmed by Dennis's drunkenness. Simmons commented that he fell over at one point, while Brown noted that Christine McVie refused to join him onstage despite repeated requests because "he was a little too buzzed to contend with." Dennis' behavior deteriorated as the week progressed, and on Friday, June 8 he went completely off the rails. At one point during the show, Mike seemed to be needling Dennis, bouncing on and off the drum riser, and glaring at him. A

1979

drunk and enraged Dennis reacted by attacking Mike in full view of the audience. As the audience gasped in horror Dennis kicked his drums off the riser and took off after Mike. He chased him down the side of the stage and began to beat on him. It was like watching a car wreck. Then a scrum of roadies, security personnel, and various band members separated the combatants and hustled them offstage. An unscheduled intermission was called. When the band returned to the stage, Mike made a speech downplaying the incident to the audience. Then Dennis appeared, grabbed a microphone, and began to repeat the words 'I love Mike Love.' Appearing to ignore this incantation, Mike kept himself as far away from Dennis as he could. The band finished the show, but the incident wasn't forgotten. Dennis was indefinitely suspended from the Beach Boys with the instructions to clean up his act or stay away. With the exception of a guest appearance at a show in Hawaii in August and a short tour in November, he'd be absent for an entire year.

Brian at the Universal Amphitheater, June 1979. Ed Roach © 1979, 2013.

TUESDAY, JUNE 19, AND WEDNESDAY, JUNE 20, 1979: Red Rocks Amphitheater, Morrison, CO, with Iron Horse (One show each night at 7:30 p.m.)

THURSDAY, JUNE 21, 1979: Aladdin Hotel, Las Vegas, NV

FRIDAY, JUNE 22, AND SATURDAY, JUNE 23, 1979: Greek Theater, UC Berkeley, San Francisco, CA, with Iron Horse (One show at 8:00 p.m. on Friday and 2:00 p.m. on Saturday)

SUNDAY, JULY 1, 1979: Midway Stadium, St. Paul, MN, with Atlanta Rhythm Section, Climax Blues Band, Jay Ferguson, and Iron Horse (2:00 p.m. show)
With Dennis gone, Bobby Figueroa took over on drums. Figueroa wasn't happy about the change. He recalled, "We'd sort of broken up the show to the point where neither of us would get tired but when he started playing less and less, I had to do more and more and it hurt me. I hurt my back at that time and eventually (in 1981) had to leave the band. I had tangled all the muscle." Drum technician Tony Leo tried to lessen the load for Figueroa, playing extra percussion, such as tympani on "Wouldn't It Be Nice."

MONDAY, JULY 2, 1979: Rosenblatt Stadium, Omaha, NE, with Jay Ferguson and the Atlanta Rhythm Section (4:00 p.m. show)

TUESDAY, JULY 3, 1979: Marcus Amphitheater, Milwaukee, WI (7:30 p.m. show)

WEDNESDAY, JULY 4, TO SATURDAY, JULY 7, 1979: Pine Knob Music Theater, Clarkston, MI, with Ironhorse
The group's Pine Knob shows sold out. Kim McAuliffe of the *Detroit Free Press* attended the opener and reported, "The show never really lagged, mainly because nearly every song was taken from the group's enormous history of hits. 'Help Me Rhonda,' 'Little Deuce Coupe,' and 'Be True to Your School' brought down the house, along with some beach balls and Frisbees."

Brian at the keyboards in Montreal, July 12, 1979. Ian Rusten Collection

SUNDAY, JULY 8, 1979: St. John's Hollow, Tiffin, OH (2:00 p.m. show)

MONDAY, JULY 9, AND TUESDAY, JULY 10, 1979: Blossom Music Center, Cuyahoga Falls, OH (One show per night at 8:00 p.m.)
A portion of one of these shows was filmed for a *PM Magazine* profile. Over 18,000 fans were expected opening night, but pouring rain kept many away. The crowd that remained was eager for oldies. "Roller Skating Child" was greeted with polite applause, but they grew restless when Bruce played "I Write the Songs." Mike pleaded with the crowd to be attentive and listen to the new music. But Anastasia Pantsios of the *Cleveland Plains Dealer* reported, "It didn't work, no matter how thick he laid it on. Songs like 'Sumahama' weren't what the people came to hear, and they weren't buying any. It took tunes like 'California Girls' and 'I Get Around' to command their attention."

WEDNESDAY, JULY 11, 1979: Rockland Community College, Suffern, NY

THE BEACH BOYS IN CONCERT

THURSDAY, JULY 12, 1979: Montreal Forum, Montreal, QB, Canada, with Long John Baldry (8:00 p.m. show)

FRIDAY, JULY 13, 1979: Monmouth Park, Oceanport, NJ

SATURDAY, JULY 14, 1979: "Sunfest 79," Yale Bowl, New Haven, CT, with the Cars, Eddie Money, the Henry Paul Band, and Flo and Eddie (12:00 p.m. show)
More than 35,000 turned out for this concert to benefit the Easter Seals charity. The temperature reached a sweltering ninety-five degrees and over 300 people had to receive medical treatment for heat exhaustion.

SATURDAY, AUGUST 4, AND SUNDAY, AUGUST 5, 1979: "Japan Jam," Enoshima Beach, Japan, with Heart, Firefall, TKO, and the Southern All Stars
The group returned to Japan for the first time since 1966. The backing band consisted of Mike Meros, Bobby Figueroa, Carli Munoz, Tony Leo, and Ed Carter. The group was in Japan by August 3, when they appeared on a bizarre TV show at which guests sat at a round table with cocktails. The host showed no interest in the Beach Boys and spent most of the time talking in Japanese to the people seated with him. After ten minutes, he finally turned to the group but only to ask what they knew about Japanese music! The band appeared on the show to promote "Japan Jam," two mammoth outdoor shows at a popular beach resort. Over 60,000 fans attended.

TUESDAY, AUGUST 7, 1979: Osaka, Japan, with Heart
Carl greatly enjoyed the Japan trip. He told Mike Powell of *Super Pop*, "It's funny really, when I first went to the U.K. I thought it was the most beautiful part of the world, and the same goes for France and Spain. But this month Japan just blew my mind. The climate's very tropical and humid and the plants are so green—at present, Japan's my favorite part of the entire globe."

WEDNESDAY, AUGUST 8, 1979: Momoyama Castle, Kyoto, Japan, with Heart
Unfortunately for fans that bought tickets to this event, foul weather prevented the group from taking the stage. Bobby Figueroa commented, "There was a storm brewing and after Heart performed, the whole place fell apart. The roof actually fell in. They had to cancel the rest of the show. We went all the way to Kyoto to play it, but we couldn't play. We stayed in Kyoto for a few days and it was a fun experience, other than the fact that we couldn't play."

SATURDAY, AUGUST 11, 1979: Aloha Stadium, Honolulu, HI, with Heart (2:00 p.m. show)
On their way back from Japan, the group stopped in Hawaii for one concert. Though officially suspended from the Beach Boys, Dennis was in Hawaii and was invited onstage. Bobby Figueroa recalled, "He knew that they were going to be there. You could see that he missed it and he was going to try to find a way to get back in and say 'Let's put that behind us.'" However, it was a one-night reunion, and he wasn't allowed to participate in the upcoming tour.

SATURDAY, AUGUST 18, 1979: "Chicago Jam," Comiskey Park, Chicago, IL, with Pure Prairie League, Sha Na Na, and Blondie (10:00 a.m. show)
This was one of two concerts held on the same weekend that were dubbed the "Chicago Jam." Promoter Sandy Feldman described it as a Midwest version of Woodstock. However, instead of the 70,000 expected on the first day, only about 8,000 showed up due to ominous clouds in the sky.

SUNDAY, AUGUST 19, 1979: Mississippi River Festival, Southern Illinois University, Edwardsville, IL

MONDAY, AUGUST 20, 1979: Iowa State Fair, Des Moines, IA (8:00 p.m. show)
Jim Healey of the *Des Moines Register* praised the band for streamlining their act. He commented, "By cutting back the group to a more manageable size, and by getting Johnston to sign on again, the Beach Boys have drawn tighter the yarn that binds them and their music. The result was a truly exciting set here Monday, one that re-established the group as a prime force in modern rock 'n' roll."

Carl onstage in Japan, August 5, 1979. Photo: photosets.net/ Brannon Tommey

sell their studio. Sterling Smith recalled, "When they sold Brother Studio, that was the real decline of Dennis. Because when Dennis came back [from the road], instead of harnessing his drug-confused but nevertheless very creative talent to some positive degree, Dennis had nowhere to go so he ended up just being the partying guy." He seemed to no longer care about how his behavior affected the group. During an interview with *NY Rocker* during the Radio City Hall engagement, Dennis exclaimed he'd just "quit

TUESDAY, AUGUST 21, 1979: Norfolk Scope, Norfolk, VA (8:00 p.m. show)

FRIDAY, AUGUST 31, 1979: Allentown Fair, Allentown, PA (7:30 p.m. show)

SATURDAY, SEPTEMBER 1, 1979: "Festival II," Aqueduct Raceway, NY, with Flo and Eddie (5:30 p.m. show) and Merriweather Post Pavilion, Columbia, MD, with Doucette (8:30 p.m. show)
The Beach Boys played the first of two dates at Aqueduct. Tom Zatorski of the *Stony Brook Statesman* noted, "The playing was flawless, their showmanship was excellent and the songs couldn't have been better . . . From the first song, 'Help Me Rhonda,' to the last chorus of 'Fun, Fun, Fun,' the audience was clapping and singing along—a response that the Beach Boys engender at almost every performance." Following the gig, the group flew to Maryland for an evening show.

SUNDAY, SEPTEMBER 2, 1979: Festival II, Aqueduct Raceway, NY, with Flo and Eddie (5:30 p.m. show) and Music Inn, Lenox, MA (Canceled)

MONDAY, SEPTEMBER 3, 1979: CNE Grandstand, Toronto, ON, Canada, with Long John Baldry

FRIDAY, SEPTEMBER 28, 1979: Mid-South Coliseum, Memphis, TN, with Target (8:30 p.m. show)
Bobby Figueroa, Ed Carter, and Mike Meros accompanied the group on these dates, but Carli Munoz was gone. Bobby Figueroa recalled, "That was a bummer because he was the reason I was there, him and Dennis Wilson. It wasn't totally his choice but he had other things he wanted to do anyways. But he was a great player. I loved his presence. I loved what he did on stage."

SATURDAY, SEPTEMBER 29, 1979: Zoo Amphitheater, Oklahoma City, OK, with the Lienke Brothers (3:00 p.m. show) and Kansas Coliseum, Wichita, KS, with Prism (8:00 p.m. show)

SUNDAY, SEPTEMBER 30, 1979: Blackham Coliseum, University of Southern Louisiana, Lafayette, LA (2:00 p.m. show), and Texas A&M, College Station, TX (Night)
For the second straight day, the group played two shows in separate states.

MONDAY, OCTOBER 1, 1979: Convention Center, Dallas, TX (8:00 p.m. show)

THURSDAY, OCTOBER 4, 1979: Convention Center, San Antonio, TX, with Prism

FRIDAY, OCTOBER 5, 1979: Summit, Houston, TX, with Prism

SATURDAY, OCTOBER 6, 1979: Hirsch Coliseum, Shreveport, LA (Canceled)
On October 3, 3,000 ticket holders were informed that the group was canceling due to "equipment difficulties" and a conflict with their recording schedule.

SUNDAY, OCTOBER 7, 1979: Reed Green Coliseum, University of Southern Mississippi, Hattiesburg, MS, with Prism (2:00 p.m. show) and Riverside Centroplex, Baton Rouge, LA (Canceled)
The Hattiesburg show was scheduled for 8:00 p.m. but was changed to 2:00 so the group could be in L.A. for a recording session on Monday. The change of plans necessitated the cancelation of a Baton Rouge show. Frank Rives of the *Student Printz* gushed, "The Beach Boys put on a superb performance. They started with 'California Girls' and worked up the audience steadily. Halfway through the show the audience was on its feet, clapping and singing along and there the audience stayed until after the encore."

THURSDAY, NOVEMBER 15, 1979: Arizona State University, Phoenix, AZ, with John Stewart (8:00 p.m. show)
While recording their upcoming *Keeping the Summer Alive* album, the group played a few dates. Surprisingly, Dennis, who'd been suspended since June, temporarily rejoined them. John Stewart, formerly of the Kingston Trio, had a hit record with "Gold," and opened the show as well as joined the Beach Boys for the encore of "Barbara Ann."

Brian in Japan, August 5, 1979. Photo: photosets.net/ Brannon Tommey

drugs." Then he asked the reporter if he had any pot and invited him back to his room, where a mirror and steel straw lay in plain sight. He began missing shows and was often not in a condition to play when he was there, though his magnetism was so great that audiences still welcomed him.

The Beach Boys were bewildered. They'd tried to control Dennis. Tom Murphy noted, "One of my unspoken jobs on the road was to try to keep Dennis from disrupting the shows." But no one could really contain Dennis. As Bobby Figueroa recalled, "He was unstable. He was wrestling with some serious demons." Things came to a head in June. A drunken Dennis physically attacked Mike onstage at the Universal Amphitheater, causing his suspension from the Beach Boys. He was out of the group for most of the next year.

While the group practiced tough love with Dennis, Brian remained a subject of concern. In early 1979 he was a patient at the Brotman Memorial Hospital, where he'd been committed in an effort to cure his depression, which had been compounded by the breakup of his marriage. After his release, he continued to tour but his involvement varied widely. Often his only participation would be to sing a line of "Sloop John B" or a hoarse verse of "Surfer Girl." He usually sat glumly at the piano, smoking cigarettes, and only occasionally playing. Some musicians argued it was better when he didn't play, since he sometimes wreaked havoc when he participated. Sterling Smith recalled, "When Brian would be playing the gig he'd sometimes go to the original key that the song was in. The record of 'Help Me Rhonda' was recorded in D flat, but everyone plays it in C because it's an easier key to play and probably easier for the world to sing. One night we're all in C and Brian is in D flat, which created a real cacophonous noise. Carl just said, you could hear it on the PA, 'Brian, it's in C,' in a real gentle voice." Brian's piano playing was so erratic that Tom Murphy was instructed to turn him down in the mix so audiences couldn't hear him.

The year 1979 ended much as it had begun, with a fractured band trying to pull together a new album. Questions about their dwindling relevance would have to wait until 1980 to be answered.

Performing at "Japan Jam," August 5, 1979. Photo: photosets.net/Brannon Tommey

Hardy Price of the *Arizona Republic* reported, "With a cowboy-hatted Mike Love fronting the band and singing most of the leads, the group returned to the days when it sang about sixteen-year-old girls in bikinis . . . Al Jardine is still singing harmony and playing guitar, Carl Wilson maintains lead guitar duties, and yes, even Brian was there, seated at the piano and occasionally taking a chorus or two, as he did with 'Sloop John B.'"

FRIDAY, NOVEMBER 16, 1979: Colorado State University, Fort Collins, CO, with John Stewart (8:00 p.m. show)
A small but enthusiastic crowd turned out at Colorado State. Mitch Little of the *Rocky Mountain Collegian* reported, "Mike Love proved to be the catalyst of their show as he continually moved about the stage and identified upcoming songs with witty one-liners. Carl Wilson and Bruce Johnston seemed amazed at the crowd reaction and voiced the Beach Boys' thanks many times."

SATURDAY, NOVEMBER 17, 1979: University of Utah, Salt Lake City, UT, with John Stewart
The Salt Lake City show was a nostalgic occasion. KNAK DJ Bill Hesterman, who'd emceed the band's 1960s appearances at the Lagoon, introduced them. All six Beach Boys were present, though Dennis had injured his arm the previous night and played with one arm in a cast. Tom Wharton of the *Salt Lake Tribune* noted, "The Beach Boys sounded good Saturday night, much better than the first time I saw them in 1968 at Lagoon's Patio Gardens. Love . . . still has the same energy he had then, although his beard is graying a bit. Carl Wilson and Al Jardine both sounded good on the vocals, as did Bruce Johnston . . . Brian Wilson was very aloof, as befits his image as the brain behind the group. And Dennis Wilson, the drummer, was his old zany self."

The Beach Boys, minus Dennis, spent the end of the year finishing their upcoming album, to be titled *Keepin' the Summer Alive.*

CONCERTS NOT PLAYED

An appearance at the Music Inn in Lenox, Massachusetts, scheduled for September 2, was canceled.

1980

THINGS SEEMED to be back on relatively stable ground in the early months of 1980. As Carl remarked in a press release, "The last two years have been the most important and difficult time of our career ... We had to decide whether what we had been involved in since we were teenagers had lost its meaning. We asked ourselves, and each other, the difficult questions we'd often avoided in the past. We stopped fighting and started talking. In the end, it all came together again. Now as we enter this new decade, we're as excited and committed and dedicated to our music and our ideals as we've ever been." Whether or not Carl truly believed that, the band was in better shape than they'd been in awhile. They had a new album to promote as they prepared to embark on their first European tour since 1972.

The album *Keepin' the Summer Alive*, released in spring 1980, featured contributions from everyone except Dennis. CBS was intent on marketing it as if Brian had been heavily involved. He went along with the charade, telling one reporter, "Michael and I wrote five songs for the new album . . . really nice songs I think. He said 'We're going to Hawaii and write songs.' I said, 'Write songs—ugh.' But we went, Michael and Carl and myself, and it really worked." In reality, with the exception of the single "Goin' On," the songs composed by Brian and Mike were eminently forgettable. Neither the faux-reggae "Sunshine," nor the tired ballad "Oh Darlin'," suggested inspiration had been found in Hawaii. The truth was that Brian had quickly lost interest, forcing the band to raid the vaults to make it look like he was more active. Of the other songs for which Brian was listed as a composer, "When Girls Get Together" was a dreary *Sunflower* outtake, while "Santa Ana Winds" was considered for *LA (Light Album)* and rejected in 1978. The album did feature some workmanlike contributions from Carl, in collaboration with Randy Bachman, including the title song and the country-inspired "Living with a Heartache," but neither song could push the album out of the pedestrian. Bruce handled production duties and the result was a bland overall sound. *Keepin' the Summer Alive* was released to indifference in March, reaching a disappointing number seventy-five on the *Billboard* album charts.

The failure of the album placed the band at a crossroads. Marc Zakem of the *Louisville Courier Journal* put his finger on the issues facing them in an August concert review. He asked, "Is the continued success of the Beach Boys entirely due to nostalgia? If not, why did Al Jardine practically apologize for playing three newer numbers by confessing, 'We don't want to load you down with too much new stuff'? . . . In connection with that, if the band is not simply concerned with regurgitating the past, what are its goals? Between Mike Love's nightclub prancing and Bruce Johnston's cocktail lounge piano, it seems apparent that the Beach Boys aren't striving to be the world's greatest rock 'n' roll band.

CONCERTS PLAYED IN
1980

SUNDAY, JANUARY 13, 1980: Oakland Coliseum, Oakland, CA, with the Grateful Dead, Jefferson Starship, Joan Baez, and Santana (7:00 p.m. show)
Surrounded by Bay area favorites, the Beach Boys were odd men out at this event organized to aid the people of Cambodia. Peter Stack of the *San Francisco Chronicle* argued that they gave an uneven performance, though he admitted, "Halfway through their set [they] suddenly pounced on 'Surfer Girl' and went on a splurge of energy with a handful of favorites, finally reaching a peak with tight harmonies in 'Good Vibrations.'"

TUESDAY, JANUARY 15 TO SUNDAY, JANUARY 20, 1980: Sahara Tahoe, Stateline, NV, with Glenn Super

FRIDAY, FEBRUARY 22, 1980: Memorial Coliseum, Fort Wayne, IN (8:00 p.m. show)
In Fort Wayne, where the group hadn't appeared in many years, 10,000 turned out. Connie Trexler of the *News Sentinel* noted that the Beach Boys "built the concert out of 'California Girls,' 'Sloop John B,' 'Little Deuce Coupe,' 'In My Room,' 'Be True To Your School,' 'Little Surfer Girl,' 'Help Me Rhonda,' 'Wouldn't It Be Nice,' 'I Get Around,' and 'Surfin' USA,' every one a hit beloved by hundreds if not thousands of individuals in the audience."

SATURDAY, FEBRUARY 23, 1980: Joe Louis Arena, Detroit, MI (8:00 p.m. show)

SUNDAY, FEBRUARY 24, 1980: Wings Stadium, Kalamazoo, MI
Tom Thinnes of the *Kalamazoo Gazette* reported, "The Beach Boys really jacked up the audience with 'Be True To Your School' with Love prancing all over the stage like a frenzied cheerleader trying to pump up the crowd to root for the winning touchdown . . . Meanwhile with the audience going absolutely bananas, there's Brian Wilson . . . calmly playing the piano, a cigarette jutting out of his mouth. He could have been playing 'As Time Goes By' in Humphrey Bogart's joint in Casablanca."

TUESDAY, FEBRUARY 26, TO SUNDAY, MARCH 2, 1980: Palace Theater, Cleveland, OH, with Glenn Super (One show each night at 8:00 p.m. Tuesday to Friday and two shows at 7:00 and 10:30 p.m. on Saturday and Sunday)
The group performed at the tiny Palace Theater, which seated 2700 and mainly hosted cabaret acts. Anastasia Pantsios of the *Cleveland Plains Dealer* was troubled by what she saw as the Beach Boys' "segue into nightclub act status." She noted that a Vegas comedian (Glenn Super) opened and that they played nothing but oldies. Bruno Bornino of the *Cleveland Press* was more enthusiastic, gushing, "The Beach Boys not only delivered, but got stronger with each song. By the time the band completed the last song—'Fun, Fun, Fun'—the fans were standing on chairs, climbing on stage, and getting crazy."

SUNDAY, MARCH 9, 1980: Sunrise Music Theatre, Sunrise, FL
This was a fundraiser for Republican presidential candidate George Bush Sr. Carl told a reporter from the *BBFun Newsletter* they didn't play the show for political reasons, but instead "It was more of a human thing on our side. He took several hours out of a really busy schedule and came to see us in a city we were playing one Sunday morning. We spent about three hours with him, and he's just a nice fella, a nice man, and we did it on that basis."

WEDNESDAY, MARCH 19, 1980: Civic Centre, Ottawa, ON, Canada
The band had expunged concert staples of the past few years like "It's OK" and "Roller Skating Child," though "Long Tall Texan," was back for the first time since the sixties. Backing musicians consisted of Mike Meros, Bobby Figueroa, and Joe Chemay.

THURSDAY, MARCH 20, 1980: Civic Center, Hartford, CT
Almost 14,000 fans attended this show. An amusing moment occurred when Brian announced after Mike's performance of "Long Tall Texan," "Now listen, who's better, Mick Jagger or Mike Love?" Before the audience could answer, Mike asked, "Who's better at songwriting, Paul McCartney or Brian Wilson?" The audience yelled Brian's name, as Brian humbly exclaimed, "McCartney!"

FRIDAY, MARCH 21, 1980: Cumberland County Civic Center, Portland, ME, with John Hall (8:00 p.m. show)

SATURDAY, MARCH 22, 1980: Boston Garden, Boston, MA, with John Hall (8:00 p.m. show)

FRIDAY, APRIL 18, 1980: Spectrum, Philadelphia, PA, with Brewer and Shipley (9:30 p.m. show)
In addition to Joe Chemay, Bobby Figueroa, and Mike Meros, Ed Carter accompanied the band on this tour. In an interview on WIOQ, which broadcast the Philadelphia show, Bruce mentioned that Carter had been added as third guitarist at the request of the record label, to beef up their sound.

SATURDAY, APRIL 19, 1980: University of North Carolina, Chapel Hill, NC (Afternoon) and U.S. Naval Academy, Annapolis, MD, with Brewer and Shipley
The Beach Boys flew to North Carolina for an outdoor appearance at UNC. ABC TV filmed it as part of a *20/20* segment and brief clips of the group performing their hits, including "Be True to Your School" and "California Girls," were used in the piece.

The appearance in Annapolis that night was enthusiastically received. Jack Daniel of the *Georgetown Hoya* noted, "Aside from a few mellow numbers, the crowd remained on its feet for the entire show . . . Signing off with an encore which included 'Good Vibrations,' 'Barbara Ann,' and 'Fun, Fun, Fun,' the Beach Boys reminded their fans that no new wave can take the place of good ol' rock 'n' roll."

SUNDAY, APRIL 20, 1980: Market Square Arena, Indianapolis, IN, with Brewer and Shipley (8:30 p.m. show)
This concert was attended by 12,000 fans. Zach Dunkin of the *Indianapolis News* reported, "Love encouraged the music mania with his nonsensical chatter and free movement around the stage with a wireless microphone, while Carl Wilson, Al Jardine, and 'honorary' Beach Boy Bruce Johnston concentrated more on the vocals . . . Brian sat at the piano, puffing like a locomotive and played or sang whenever the mood struck him . . . It was sad to see the chain-smoking Wilson destroy what was once an incredible set of vocal chords."

MONDAY, APRIL 21, 1980: Michigan State University, East Lansing, MI, with Brewer and Shipley (8:00 p.m. show)

TUESDAY, APRIL 22, 1980: Wendler Arena, Saginaw, MI, with Brewer and Shipley (8:00 p.m. show)
The group worked several new numbers into their set but Nancy Kuharevicz of the *Saginaw News* commented, "The Beach Boys are legendary for their surfin' sound, something they perfected about fifteen years ago. When they attempt to introduce new material, which deviates from their well-established standard, they sound like museum pieces shallowly imitating themselves. On the other hand, when they're playing old favorites, they don't just capture an audience's attention, they control it."

WEDNESDAY, APRIL 23, 1980: UD Arena, University of Dayton, Dayton, OH, with Brewer and Shipley (8:00 p.m. show)

THURSDAY, APRIL 24, 1980: Kingston Armory, Kingston, PA, with Brewer and Shipley (8:00 p.m. show)

FRIDAY, APRIL 25, 1980: Memorial Auditorium, Buffalo, NY, with Brewer and Shipley (8:00 p.m. show)

But can any band continue to satisfy and be satisfied simply replaying past hits?" The failure of *Keepin' the Summer Alive* suggested, once again, that the public wasn't interested in new Beach Boys music. Soon the group would be resigned to a career as an oldies act. When they went on the road in October, the set consisted of sixties hits, period.

"The last two years have been the most important and difficult time of our career . . . We had to decide whether what we had been involved in since we were teenagers had lost its meaning."

Carl later depicted the period as the nadir of the band. He told reporter Marc Shapiro in 1983, "We weren't really taking care of things onstage. We weren't rehearsing that much and there was just no energy in our live shows at all. There were nights when I'd be onstage and thinking to myself, 'What the fuck! There's no mystery or excitement to this anymore.'" It didn't help that the best songwriters in the group were in terrible shape. Brian's presence was on and off, but even when he was there he wasn't. Dennis remained *persona non grata* in early 1980. It wasn't until the European tour in June that he returned on a regular basis. Unfortunately,

> "We weren't rehearsing that much and there was just no energy in our live shows at all. There were nights when I'd be onstage and thinking to myself, 'What the fuck! There's no mystery or excitement to this anymore.'"
>
> —Carl Wilson

he hadn't used the layoff to clean up his act. If anything, his addictions had grown much worse and his once-handsome face showed disturbing evidence of disintegration.

The continuing problems within the group cast a shadow over their approaching twentieth anniversary. The

SUNDAY, APRIL 27, 1980: Maple Leaf Gardens, Toronto, ON, Canada, with Brewer and Shipley (8:00 p.m. show)

MONDAY, JUNE 2, 1980: Ekeberghallen, Oslo, Norway

On May 30 the Beach Boys landed in Oslo to begin their first European tour since 1972. Due to promoters' demands, Dennis was with the group for the first time since 1979. The group played the same set they'd been performing in the states but added "Cotton Fields," which was a hit in Europe in 1970. Bobby Figueroa recalled, "That was a real fun tour . . . what blew my mind was that people actually knew who I was. They knew the names of everyone in the band. The crowds that came out in Holland and Denmark and Norway were very good."

The group held a press conference at the Hotel Ambassadeur on June 1. The Oslo show marked their first appearance in Norway. The show wasn't a sellout. Norwegian journalist Lars Keilhau reported in *BBFun*, "It was not their best performance, but being the first date of the European tour, it was not to be expected . . . Dennis was the one who in a way came to the 'rescue.' Halfway through the concert, after 'Long Tall Texan,' he walked to the front of the stage and 'commanded' everyone to stand up and come up front. Although it irritated the front row ticket holders, it raised the spirits both on and offstage. From 'Cotton Fields' and onwards the excitement just got bigger and bigger . . . The rest of the concert was just plain fun."

TUESDAY, JUNE 3, 1980: Grona Lund, Stockholm, Sweden

The group flew to Stockholm, where they gave an afternoon press conference. Asked if they still had fun, Mike replied, "For nineteen years the Beach Boys have toured, and we still think it's fun. Compared to in the beginning, it's actually even more fun now when we make lots of money even though we play shorter sets." Brian sat silently but coughed up "Paul McCartney and Elton John" when asked who influenced him. After the conference, the group played an evening concert at Grona Lund. Gunner Salander of *Svenska Dagbladet* had attended their 1967 appearance and reported, "Thirteen years have past since I last saw the Beach Boys, but I can't say that there was something particularly different back then. There has of course been some new material . . . But the highlights are the same as back then, "Good Vibrations," "Help Me Rhonda," "Be True to Your School," and so on. Sure, the harmonies aren't as tight as they used to be, but it's good enough to initiate a certain nostalgic happiness in the old folks who were there when it happened."

WEDNESDAY, JUNE 4, 1980: Tivoli Gardens, Copenhagen, Denmark

The group was greeted enthusiastically in Denmark, where they'd last played in 1966. The concert at the outdoor Tivoli Gardens drew 50,000 fans. Ebbe Iverson of *Berlingske Tidende* commented, "The huge crowd sent recurring waves of good vibrations up to the group, which blew away some of the weariness of travel in the music, which consisted of a pleasant mix of new songs and such old hits as 'California Girls' and 'Barbara Ann.' Those last songs got the loudest cheering from the crowd, since everyone who grew up in the sixties knows them."

FRIDAY, JUNE 6, 1980, AND SATURDAY, JUNE 7, 1980: Wembley Arena, London, England, with Chris Rea

The Beach Boys' first U.K. appearances since 1977 brought out the fans and critics. Richard Williams of the *London Times* noted, "Within eighty minutes they gave us twenty-five songs, mostly from their golden age in the sixties, yet only towards the end did a partisan crowd display the anticipated fervor, responding wholeheartedly to the surges of 'Help Me Rhonda' and 'Fun, Fun, Fun.' Before that epiphany they were forced to endure the tiresome antics of singer Michael Love and several passages of distinctly substandard harmonies." Andrew G. Doe in *Add Some Music* reported all eyes were on Brian, who frequently missed instrumental and vocal cues, but "it was obvious to all there that if Brian had just stood center stage and done nothing, the crowd would have applauded. Every note, however hoarse, and each half formed gesture were greeted with rapturous applause. The rest of the band willingly accepted their subsidiary roles with good humor, all of which added to the general bonhomie."

~~~~~~

1980

SUNDAY, JUNE 8, 1980: Palais Des Sports, Paris, France

MONDAY, JUNE 9, 1980: Congresgebouw, The Hague, Holland
A fan filmed this appearance and a video makes the rounds.

SATURDAY, JUNE 21, 1980: Knebworth Festival, Knebworth, England, with Mike Oldfield, Elkie Brooks, Lindisfarne, the Blues Band, and Santana (12:00 p.m. to 11:00 p.m.)
After a break, the group returned to the road to headline the Knebworth Festival, a massive outdoor event sponsored by Capital Radio, which broadcast it live. Over 40,000 fans camped out in the rain, the majority to see the Beach Boys. The show took place the day after Brian's thirty-eighth birthday and a cake was wheeled out so he could blow out the candles. He did little else during the show, but looked striking, having shaved his beard for the first time since the early seventies. The set consisted of "California Girls," "Sloop John B," "Darlin'," "School Days," "In My Room," "Good Timin'," "God Only Knows," "Be True To Your School," "Do It Again," "Little Deuce Coupe," "Catch a Wave," "Cotton Fields," "Heroes and Villains," "Some of Your Love," "Keepin' the Summer Alive," "Lady Lynda," "Surfer Girl," "I Write the Songs," "Santa Ana Winds," "Help Me Rhonda," "Wouldn't It Be Nice," "Rock and Roll Music," "I Get Around," "Surfin' USA," "You Are So Beautiful," "Good Vibrations," "Barbara Ann," and "Fun, Fun, Fun."

The concert was professionally filmed and recorded but the band felt the tapes weren't up to snuff and held a session in November to "sweeten" them. Backing vocals were added and some guitar and keyboard parts were redone before they shelved the tapes. A DVD and CD were released years later, once the performance had taken on significant historical importance. It was the last appearance of the original lineup of the Beach Boys in Europe. Bobby Figueroa commented, "I thought it was a good show but I think we've been much, much better. But, considering all the things we were going through it was pretty good. And it was one of the last times that the original band was together."

THURSDAY, JULY 3, 1980: Hampton Coliseum, Hampton, VA, with Le Roux (8:00 p.m. show)
Over 7,000 people attended this show. Eric Feber of the *Virginian Pilot* was unimpressed and commented, "If they weren't so damned legendary they would be playing supper clubs and Holiday Inns instead of packing them in at stadiums like they did in Hampton Thursday night . . . Their new albums don't sell well and I defy anyone to name a new Beach Boys tune that anyone could recognize or even hum. The group, with their drained leader helplessly looking on, is now nothing more than a hollow impression."

FRIDAY, JULY 4, 1980: Washington Monument, Washington, DC (4:00 p.m. show)
The Beach Boys had ambitious plans for July 4. Mike told reporters, "We wanted to have a worldwide July 4 celebration. We were going to begin the day with a show in Copenhagen, Denmark, then fly to London for another show, then on to Washington for a concert on the mall, then to Southern California for another concert, and finish off the night with a show in Hawaii. It would have been billed as a worldwide California surf party." Logistics and reality put an end to those plans, and the group settled for a massive free show in front of the Washington Monument.

Over 500,000 people attended, the largest crowd the group had ever played for. The concert was broadcast on WRQX radio in D.C. and WABC in New York. In addition, it was videotaped, and an edited, "sweetened" version aired on HBO as The *Beach Boys in Concert.* The band arrived at 2:00 p.m. and spent two hours milling about backstage. A freshly shaved Dennis, who'd also significantly shortened his hair, spent his downtime drinking and was in poor shape when an interviewer caught up with him. He seemed dazed, barely able to string his thoughts together. Nevertheless, he attacked the drums with gusto when the band took the stage. Charles McCollum of the *Washington Star* noted, "For the most part the Beach Boys stuck to the music that made them famous—songs like 'California Girls,' 'Surfin' USA,' 'Sloop John B,' 'Good Vibrations,' and 'Fun, Fun, Fun.' The soaring harmonies and good cheer created moments that were as purely American as . . . well, the Fourth of July."

situation was evident to all who viewed the group's *Good Morning America TV* appearance on December 5. The Beach Boys were there to promote an upcoming anniversary show at the L.A. Forum, but there was no enthusiasm evident. Dennis, strung out and unsteady, could barely manage to keep his head up to answer questions. Brian stared at the camera in terror. Mike, Carl, and Al looked uncomfortable and annoyed. Although the Forum show was a success, no one in the band looked as though they could stomach another twenty years.

THE BEACH BOYS IN CONCERT

"The list of hits they played was impressive— 'Sloop John B,' 'Little Deuce Coupe,' 'Help Me Rhonda,' 'God Only Knows,' 'Be True To Your School,' 'I Get Around'—the memories kept flooding forth with no hint that the band was interested in playing, or the audience in hearing, any new music. Brian Wilson . . . sat impassively at the piano, looking on as the songs he created ignited the audience."

SATURDAY, JULY 5, 1980: Nassau Coliseum, Uniondale, NY (8:00 p.m. show)

FRIDAY, JULY 25, 1980: Rushmore Plaza Civic Center, Rapid City, SD, with the Tremblers
The group began a two-week tour with the Tremblers, led by Peter Noone of Herman's Hermits fame. Brian wasn't on the tour. The group put out a statement that he was in the hospital but a roadie told a reporter from the *Grand Rapids Press*, "He's not in a hospital. He just didn't feel like coming. And he's got the money to do anything he wants." Mike Meros, Ed Carter, and Bobby Figueroa rounded out the backing band.

SATURDAY, JULY 26, 1980: Civic Center, Bismarck, ND, with the Tremblers (8:00 p.m. show)

SUNDAY, JULY 27, 1980: Duluth Arena, Duluth, MN, with the Tremblers (8:00 p.m. show)
Rick Shefchick of the *Duluth News-Tribune*, declared this a fun show because "The Beach Boys don't condescend to their material. The closing third of the show began with "Help Me Rhonda" and continued through "Be True To Your School," "Wouldn't It Be Nice," "Rock and Roll Music," "I Get Around," "Surfin' USA," "Good Vibrations," "Barbara Ann," and "Fun, Fun, Fun" all in their full versions. No medleys, no clowning with the lyrics, and no indifferent performances."

MONDAY, JULY 28, 1980, Met Stadium, Bloomington, MN, with the Tremblers (8:00 p.m. show)

TUESDAY, JULY 29, 1980: City Auditorium, Omaha, NE, with the Tremblers (8:00 p.m. show)
Steve Millburg of the *Omaha World Herald* reported, "The last half hour or so, starting with 'Help Me Rhonda' and Dennis Wilson's order 'Everybody up!' was bedlam. Practically everyone was standing, clapping, and singing along from that point through . . . 'Surfin' USA,' which ended the main set. After a thunderous ovation . . . Wilson sang 'You Are So Beautiful' to the crowd. Then everyone came back to sing 'Good Vibrations,' 'Barbara Ann,' and 'Fun, Fun, Fun.'"

WEDNESDAY, JULY 30, 1980: Five Seasons Center, Cedar Rapids, IA, with the Tremblers (8:00 p.m. show)

THURSDAY, JULY 31, 1980: Wisconsin State Fair, West Allis, WI (7:30 p.m. show)

FRIDAY, AUGUST 1, TO SUNDAY, AUGUST 3, 1980: Pine Knob Music Theater, Clarkston, MI, with the Tremblers (One show each night at 7:30 p.m.)

MONDAY, AUGUST 4, AND TUESDAY, AUGUST 5, 1980: Poplar Creek Music Theater, Hoffman Estates, IL, with the Tremblers
The Beach Boys were one of the first bands to appear at this outdoor facility near Chicago. Eric Zorn of the *Chicago Tribune* condemned them as "a self-made anachronism, buried helplessly in the sand of their former success" and argued they had nothing relevant to say. However, he declared the show a success as an "exercise in greatness revisited."

THURSDAY, AUGUST 7, 1980: Mississippi River Festival, Edwardsville, IL, with the Tremblers

FRIDAY, AUGUST 8, 1980: Ionia Free Fair, Ionia, MI (Two shows at 6:30 and 9:00 p.m.)
Mary Kramer of the *Grand Rapids Press* commented that the concerts "were an easygoing nostalgia trip with the Beach Boys planted firmly behind the wheel. They played nothing that hadn't been recorded before 1970; the people came to hear the oldies and oldies are what they heard . . . the band worked about two dozen ghostly hits from summers past into a seventy-minute set."

One amusing moment occurred when Bruce announced that a couple in the audience had gotten engaged and joked, "I hope it works out at least to the combined length of time Mike has been married to all of his wives."

SATURDAY, AUGUST 9, 1980: Community War Memorial, Rochester, NY, with the Tremblers

SUNDAY, AUGUST 10, 1980: State Fairgrounds, Louisville, KY, with the Tremblers
Laurice Niemtus of the *Louisville Times* reported, "The Beach Boys . . . came to the Fairgrounds Stadium last night and filled it with fun and sun and visions of simpler days. Their special magic showered the crowd with 'Good Vibrations' despite the wretched heat and humidity and the potent smells of animals and sweat."

FRIDAY, OCTOBER 17, TO WEDNESDAY, OCTOBER 22, 1980: Caesars Tahoe, Stateline, NV
The full lineup was present in Tahoe, and a TV crew from *World of People* filmed them hanging out in their suite as well as onstage. The backstage footage showed the group compiling a list of acts that had opened for them, so they could invite them all to their upcoming anniversary show at the Forum.

FRIDAY, OCTOBER 24, 1980: Brigham Young University, Provo, UT, with Hi-Fi (7:30 p.m. show)
The group was thrown for a loop when their sound and lighting system got lost en route from Reno, but the show still went on. Kim Kaatman of the *Daily Universe* noted, "The energy level of the band tripled as they sensed the enthusiasm of the crowd . . . The enthusiasm peaked as the words of 'Help Me Rhonda' filled the Marriott Center. Arms waved in time with the music all around the stage, setting the entire Center in motion. The audience was carried back in time despite changes in the Beach Boys."

SATURDAY, OCTOBER 25, 1980: University of Montana, Missoula, MT

FRIDAY, NOVEMBER 7, 1980: La Crosse Center, La Crosse, WI
All six Beach Boys were present for the first of several November dates. Geri Parlin, of the *La Crosse Tribune*, raved, "Each golden oldie brought cheers, clapping, stomping feet and a frenzy of singing voices joining in."

SATURDAY, NOVEMBER 8, 1980: University of Toledo, Toledo, OH, with the Barooga Bandits (8:00 p.m. show)
Richard Paton of the *Toledo Blade* noted that the group played nothing from their recent albums, "but that was just fine as far as the fans were concerned . . . The list of hits they played was impressive—'Sloop John B,' 'Little Deuce Coupe,' 'Help Me Rhonda,' 'God Only Knows,' 'Be True To Your School,' 'I Get Around'—the memories kept flooding forth with no hint that the band was interested in playing, or the audience in hearing, any new music. Brian Wilson . . . sat impassively at the piano, looking on as the songs he created ignited the audience."

THURSDAY, NOVEMBER 13, 1980: Dane County Coliseum, Madison, WI, with Off Broadway (8:00 p.m. show)

FRIDAY, NOVEMBER 14, 1980: Hammons Center, SW Missouri State University, Springfield, MO, with Off Broadway (8:00 p.m.)
Around 5,000 fans attended this show. Susan Lyle of the *Southwest Standard* reported, "The crowd, though they might not have always known the words or the titles, recognized every tune and responded accordingly. The encore was also typical of the Beach Boys' crowd-pleasing ways. 'Good Vibrations' were felt throughout the student center as the nine-member band held out for close to five minutes of 'we want more' before going back on stage."

SATURDAY, NOVEMBER 15, 1980: Lloyd Noble Center, University of Oklahoma, Norman, OK, with Off Broadway

FRIDAY, DECEMBER 12, 1980: Mini Dome, Pocatello, ID with the Professional Band
The group flew to Idaho from Hawaii, where they'd filmed an appearance on *The Mike Douglas*

Don't Get Left Out In The Cold...
Come To The Beach Party

Schon Productions present:

The
BEACH BOYS
Nov. 14 8 p.m.
Hammons Student Center
Tickets $10.50 and on Sale at

Heers	Kaleidoscope
Mercantile Bank	All Great Southern
House of Sound	Savings & Loan
Empire Bank	Locations

Hammons Student Center Box Office

Advertisement for a 1980 appearance in Missouri.
Courtesy of Missouri State University

Dennis performing "You Are So Beautiful" at the group's Twentieth Anniversary Show, L.A. Forum, New Year's Eve, 1980. *Courtesy of Ben Valley*

Show. The band played a mini concert on the beach for the TV cameras on December 10. Appropriately, they performed "Hawaii" as well as "California Girls," "School Days," "I Get Around," "Catch a Wave," "Fun, Fun, Fun," "Surfin' USA," and "Help Me Rhonda". Dennis commented that this was the first time the Beach Boys had actually performed "on the beach."

The Idaho show was attended by 3,000 fans. Jill Small of the *Idaho State Journal* commented, "Vocalist Mike Love . . . was as crazy as ever, stocking-footed on the white-carpeted stage. Dennis Wilson played hard driving drums. Carl and Al sang and played guitar through the twenty Beach Boy hits and Brian Wilson accompanied on piano. The only shortcoming to develop in twenty years, except weaker voices, seems to be the missing high-pitched, fill in vocals, the 'oo oo's,' I assume used to flow from Brian. They could vaguely be heard, but I wasn't sure if they were coming from the stage or the audience."

SATURDAY, DECEMBER 13, 1980: Washington State University, Pullman, WA

SUNDAY, DECEMBER 14, 1980: Hec Edmunson Pavilion, University of Washington, Seattle, WA, with Walter Egan (7:30 p.m. show)

MONDAY, DECEMBER 15, 1980: Pacific Coliseum, Vancouver, BC, Canada, with Jerry Doucette (8:00 p.m. show)
Fiona McQuarrie of the *Vancouver Sun* reported, "Although a band that's been together almost twenty years should be able to present a more unified image on stage, those sunny harmonies are still intact and most of the band seemed to have fun singing them . . . you could almost believe it was the early sixties all over again."

WEDNESDAY, DECEMBER 31, 1980: L.A. Forum, Inglewood, CA
The year 1981 would mark the group's twentieth year in the music business. On December 30, a star was dedicated to the Beach Boys on the Hollywood Boulevard Walk of Fame. Everyone was present at the afternoon ceremony except for Dennis. To mark the occasion of their anniversary, the group played a sold-out show at the L.A. Forum. Al was dressed in one of the old striped shirts and Bruce put one on for the encore. They included numbers they hadn't played in years, including "Surfin," "Surfin' Safari," "Shut Down" (with Mike on sax), and "Don't Worry Baby" (with Brian singing a passable but weak lead). For the encore, Jan and Dean joined them for "Little Old Lady from Pasadena" and "Barbara Ann" with the Honeys on backing vocals. Following the show, the band and friends headed to the Berwin Entertainment Center for a private party, held at the bottom of a drained swimming pool.

The Beach Boys with guests Jan and Dean, L.A. Forum New Years Eve 1980. *Courtesy of Ben Valley*

Courtesy of Ben Valley

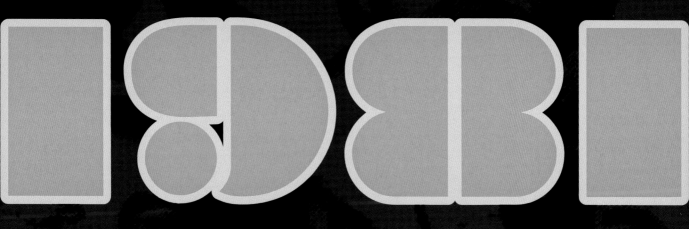

NINETEEN EIGHTY-ONE was a difficult year for the Beach Boys. Carl was dissatisfied with the group's effort and left the band in April to pursue a solo career. He felt his creativity was being stifled inside the Beach Boys bubble. Ron Altbach commented, "I always felt Carl wanted to be a rock 'n' roll guy. He wanted to be able to play rock 'n' roll and be able to improvise. But playing in the Beach Boys is like playing in an orchestra: you have a part." Carl was particularly annoyed by the oldies-only sets. He told *Washington Post* reporter Geoffrey Himes, "I'd like to see a variety of the later, more artistic

this album would encourage the guys to get off their butts and really want to make some great records." He added, "It's gotten so the act really hasn't changed—our in-person act really hasn't changed in three or four years. It's time we did something different and maybe this album will be the spark that leads to that."

When his album was

> "I always felt Carl wanted to be a rock 'n' roll guy. He wanted to be able to play rock 'n' roll and be able to improvise. But playing in the Beach Boys is like playing in an orchestra: you have a part."

released in March, Carl toured with a band that included Billy Hinsche and Myrna Smith of the Sweet Inspirations. Those that attended hoping to hear favorite Beach Boys tunes were disappointed. They were treated to an uncompromising set that included only one Beach Boys song, "Long Promised Road." Carl was excited to try something different, but going

CONCERTS PLAYED IN
1981

FRIDAY, JANUARY 16, 1981: Sports Arena, San Diego, CA, with American Spring (8:00 p.m. show)
The Beach Boys' first show of 1981 was a family affair: American Spring, featuring Brian's ex-wife and ex-sister in law, opened. Dean Torrence joined the band for encores of "Barbara Ann" and "Fun, Fun, Fun." Bob Laurence of the *San Diego Union* noted that Dennis was "quite disoriented, carrying on with inappropriate clowning, and in 'Wouldn't It Be Nice,' bashing the drums with considerably more abandon then the song called for." He was replaced midway through the show by Bobby Figueroa.

SATURDAY, JANUARY 17, 1981: University of California, Davis, CA, with American Spring (8:00 p.m. show)
A near-sell-out crowd attended this show. Duncan Strauss, of the *Davis Enterprise*, noted, "The group played mostly early hits like 'Surfer Girl,' 'Help Me Rhonda,' 'Surfin',' 'Wouldn't It Be Nice,' and 'Surfin' USA.' The strong sense of nostalgia and the infectious rhythms of most of these classics—and the large number of people onstage contributing vocals—helped to obscure the fact that many voices in the band, most noticeably Love's and Brian Wilson's, have seriously deteriorated."

MONDAY, JANUARY 19, 1981: DAR Constitution Hall, Washington, DC
The group took part in the inaugural festivities for President Reagan. The group's "Concert for Youth" was attended by 3,000 young Republicans, including two of Vice President Bush's sons. In addition to the concert, the Beach Boys served as honorary chairmen of the entertainment committee at the Vice President's reception Monday afternoon at the Smithsonian.

THURSDAY, FEBRUARY 12, 1981: Summit, Houston, TX, with Randy Meisner and the Silverados (8:00 p.m. show)
The group began a twelve-day tour with Randy Meisner, formerly of the Eagles. Sterling Smith was in Meisner's band and the Beach Boys invited him to guest on "Lady Lynda."

Bob Claypool of the *Houston Post* lambasted the group's performance. He opined that "The Beach Boys have finally crossed the line that separates strong, continuously creative rock groups from the so-so oldies bands . . . These days the group doesn't even try to do new material . . . Nope, they just trot out the oldies, the surf music that made them famous in the sixties . . . Trouble is they can't even do those warhorses the way they used to."

FRIDAY, FEBRUARY 13, 1981: University of Texas, Austin, TX, with Randy Meisner and the Silverados

SATURDAY, FEBRUARY 14, 1981: Assembly Center, Louisiana State University, Baton Rouge, LA, with Randy Meisner and the Silverados (8:00 p.m. show)

SUNDAY, FEBRUARY 15, 1981: Reunion Arena, Dallas, TX, with Randy Meisner and the Silverados (8:00 p.m. show)
The set for this show consisted of "California Girls," "Sloop John B," "Darlin'," "School Days," "In My Room," "God Only Knows," "Do It Again," "Surfer Girl," "Surfin'," "Surfin' Safari," "Catch a Wave," "Long Tall Texan," "I Write the Songs," "Lady Lynda," "Don't Worry Baby," "409," "Shut Down," "Little Deuce Coupe," "Help Me Rhonda," "Be True to Your School," "Wouldn't It Be Nice," "Rock and Roll Music," "I Get Around," "Surfin' USA," "Good Vibrations," "Barbara Ann," and "Fun, Fun, Fun."

MONDAY, FEBRUARY 16, 1981: Bicentennial Center, Salina, KS, with Randy Meisner and the Silverados
A sellout crowd of 7,600 attended this show. The *Salina Journal* declared, "Playing all the hits that

made the Beach Boys famous during the 1960s, the rock 'n' roll band had the audience on its feet a large part of the evening." Fans were so enthusiastic that they literally brought the house down, as frenzied stomping caused part of the ceiling to collapse.

WEDNESDAY, FEBRUARY 18, 1981: Hilton Coliseum, Iowa State University, Ames, IA, with Randy Meisner and the Silverados (8:00 p.m. show)
The Beach Boys' appearance at Iowa State in 1972 was one of the most poorly received shows of their career, as they refused to play the oldies that the crowd wanted to hear. By 1981, however, things had changed. Bob Steenson of the *Iowa State Daily* noted, "Most of the concert was devoted to a medley of early BB hits, with very few selections from more recent albums. There were only minor problems with the performance, including occasional mixing problems, feedback squeals, and a coughing attack by a morose Brian Wilson during his falsetto solo in 'Don't Worry Baby.'"

THURSDAY, FEBRUARY 19, 1981: Kemper Arena, Kansas City, MO, with Randy Meisner and the Silverados
Al put the 8,500 fans at this show at ease right away by announcing, "We'll play all the old stuff. That's what we're all here for anyway." Leland Rucker of the *Kansas City Star* reported, "The group has given up trying to do anything else, of course. Nobody listened when the Beach Boys tried to say something besides 'Fun, Fun, Fun.' Except for 'Lady Lynda' from the LA Light album, all the material was pre-1966."

FRIDAY, FEBRUARY 20, 1981: Barton Coliseum, Little Rock, AR, with Randy Meisner and the Silverados (8:00 p.m. show)

SATURDAY, FEBRUARY 21, 1981: Gulf Coast Coliseum, Biloxi, MS, with Randy Meisner and the Silverados

SUNDAY, FEBRUARY 22, 1981: Mabee Center, Tulsa, OK, with Randy Meisner and the Silverados

MONDAY, FEBRUARY 23, 1981: Eastern New Mexico University, Portales, NM, with Randy Meisner and the Silverados (8:00 p.m. show)
This concert was a disappointment for the activities committee that organized it. It cost $47,000 to stage but only 1868 tickets were sold, bringing in barely $19,000.

TUESDAY, FEBRUARY 24, 1981: University of New Mexico, Albuquerque, NM, with Randy Meisner and the Silverados (8:00 p.m. show)
A moment occurred at this show that provided evidence of Dennis' big heart. Sterling Smith recalled, "The Beach Boys were in the middle of their show and the Randy Meisner Band was leaving. Dennis saw that I was waving goodbye and he stopped playing the drums and came over and gave me a big hug and said, 'It was an honor to be on the same stage with you.' That was nice."

FRIDAY, MAY 1, AND SATURDAY, MAY 2, 1981: Valley Forge Music Fair, Devon, PA (Two shows on Friday at 7:00 and 11:00 p.m. and Saturday at 8:00 and 10:00 p.m.)
These shows were the first played without Carl, who left to pursue solo work. Ed Carter moved to guitar and Ernie Knapp was added on bass. Bobby Figueroa recalled: "I felt a tremendous loss when Carl left because he was the trail boss. He's the one who kept everyone together on the road and at the shows. So it was up to us to maintain that and I just felt like there was big piece missing. It wasn't the same."

SUNDAY, MAY 3, 1981: Stanley Theater, Pittsburgh, PA (Two shows at 8:00 and 10:00 p.m.)
With Carl absent, Brian was called upon to sing more. As he was singing "God Only Knows," Mike interrupted to ask the crowd, "Can he sing or what?" Bill Stieg of the *Pittsburgh Post Gazette* reported that the group "didn't do a single song post-1966 and the sellout crowd loved every

solo proved difficult. Lynn Van Matre of the *Chicago Tribune* noted, "The songs . . . aren't awful by any means . . . but most are pedestrian and totally unmemorable. So is Wilson's stage presence, which works fine as a part of the Beach Boys but comes off as woefully lackluster for someone fronting a band."

The Beach Boys were initially charitable towards Carl's solo aspirations. When they hit the road in May, Mike told reporters they were playing without Carl because they didn't want to sit at home but he'd be back soon. However, when the next tour rolled around, Carl wasn't back. He decided to spend the summer opening for the Doobie Brothers. Carl told the *Omaha World Herald*, "I haven't quit the Beach Boys but I do not plan on touring with them until they decide that 1981 means as much to them as 1961. The making of the album and the first tour were scheduled around the Beach Boys' activity . . . But by the time my tour ended in late April it was becoming clear that things weren't going to work out the way I hoped. Three issues I have raised remained unchanged." The group continued to be resistant to rehearsing and showed no interest in going into the studio. Carl was also at odds with the band over the decision to play in Lake Tahoe and Las Vegas, which he felt was "un-rock 'n' roll." He told *Hartford Courant* reporter Colin McEnroe, "The trouble with those places is that you go down to the showroom around nine each night and you do a real short set because they want to get the crowd out and bring the next group in. It means doing a lot of the old meat and potatoes numbers and you can wind up going through the motions."

Some of the other Beach Boys saw things differently. Mike responded to Carl's complaints about Vegas gigs by noting to reporter Jack Garner, "The big hockey rinks are fun. The concerts are big events. But some of our older fans don't like the hassle of going to the municipal halls. We want to go where the audiences are." He also added, "I disagree with what Carl says about the band. I think that people that come to see the Beach Boys want to hear our old stuff. I think you're doing them and yourself a really big disservice if you kid yourself into thinking they don't want to hear those songs."

The group soldiered on without Carl. The concerts, however, often lacked the spirit of fun. Without his steadying influence the band was completely divided. It was a difficult time, with bitter arguments taking place on airplanes and backstage. Bobby Figueroa recalled, "Dennis had problems and was in a really pissed-off state a lot. And a lot of his anger was directed at his partners, the other original Beach Boys. They would actually get into brawls backstage. I mean, knockdown drag-out fights. So it was a tense situation on stage because you never knew what was going to happen. You didn't know what Dennis was going to do, say, or throw. So I had to be ready at a moment's notice to go out there if something happened or they dragged him offstage. So it wasn't as much fun as it had

minute. From the opening 'California Girls' to the triple encore of 'Good Vibrations,' 'Barbara Ann,' and 'Fun, Fun, Fun,' the theater was one big happy summertime party."

MONDAY, MAY 4, 1981: Hershey Park Arena, Hershey, PA

WEDNESDAY, MAY 6, 1981: Lee County Civic Center, Fort Myers, FL
In their first Fort Myers appearance, the group played for 7,300 people.

THURSDAY, MAY 7, 1981: Lakeland Civic Center, Lakeland, FL (8:00 p.m. show)

FRIDAY, MAY 8, AND SATURDAY, MAY 9, 1981: Sunrise Musical Theatre, Sunrise, FL, with John Day (Two shows on Friday at 8:00 and 11:00 p.m. and Saturday at 7:00 and 10:30 p.m.)

SUNDAY, MAY 10, 1981: University of Florida, Gainesville, FL (8:00 p.m. show)

FRIDAY, MAY 15, 1981: Anaheim Stadium, Anaheim, CA (5:30 p.m. show)
This show took place prior to a game by the California Surf. C.P. Smith of the *Orange County Register* reported that they "turned in a generally mediocre performance. Those harmonies aren't so easy to achieve anymore and cracked, off-key renditions of 'Don't Worry Baby' and 'God Only Knows' were particular low points Friday night."

SATURDAY, MAY 16, 1981: County Bowl, Santa Barbara, CA (Two shows)

SUNDAY, MAY 17, 1981: Concord Pavilion, Concord, CA (Two shows at 2:00 and 8:00 p.m.)
Playing five shows in one weekend took a toll. There were plenty of bad notes and cracked voices during the Concord shows. Bruce called out, "Where's Carl?" in mock desperation while he struggled to handle the lead on "God Only Knows." Brian took a more active role, but Joel Selvin of the *San Francisco Chronicle* reported he wasn't up to the challenge. "The eldest Wilson grinned a lot. Sang very little and badly, played inaudible cling-cling-cling on piano and obliviously performed yoga neck-rolls. Vocalist Mike Love explained that Wilson suffered from a sore throat, but neglected to mention that the condition has apparently lasted almost ten years now."

TUESDAY, MAY 26, 1981: Fourth Annual National Cheerleading Championships, Fontainebleau Hilton, Miami, FL
The group (minus Brian) performed on the beach for this live televised event hosted by Victoria Principal and Andy Gibb. They sang "Be True to Your School" and appeared during the closing credits to sing "Surfin' USA."

FRIDAY, MAY 29, 1981: Cumberland County Civic Center, Portland, ME, with Frankie and the Knockouts (8:00 p.m. show)
Bobby Figueroa, Ed Carter, Ernie Knapp, and Mike Meros accompanied the group on this ten-day tour, which garnered the Beach Boys some of the worst reviews of their career.

SATURDAY, MAY 30, 1981: Civic Center, Hartford, CT, with Frankie and the Knockouts
A disappointed Colin McEnroe of the *Hartford Courant* noted that "Brian . . . spent most of the evening in a zombie-like state puffing a succession of cigarettes while absentmindedly playing the piano and gazing off into the wings." Nor did the band get much help from Dennis. He spent most of the show "hurling cups of water and verbal abuse at the roadies, throwing his drumsticks to the floor in disgust, and generally suggesting, through his angry and rather bizarre behavior, that his brief association with Charles Manson was not an entirely isolated phenomenon."

SUNDAY, MAY 31, 1981: Memorial Auditorium, Buffalo, NY, with Frankie and the Knockouts (8:00 p.m. show)
Jim Bisco of the *Buffalo News* compared this performance unfavorably to one he'd witnessed the

previous April and placed the blame on Brian. He noted that he "didn't come anywhere near the melody of 'Little Surfer Girl.' He butchered brother Carl's big song 'God Only Knows.' He sounded like the worst *Gong Show* contestant trying to hit the high notes on 'Don't Worry Baby,' a little-sung hit in concerts. And 'Wouldn't It Be Nice' wasn't by the time he plowed through that beloved opening."

MONDAY, JUNE 1, 1981: Civic Center, Providence, RI, with Frankie and the Knockouts

---

TUESDAY, JUNE 2, 1981: Community War Memorial, Rochester, NY, with Frankie and the Knockouts (8:00 p.m. show)
About 7,000 fans turned out at the 10,000-seat venue. Jack Garner of the *Democrat and Chronicle* reported, "Those famous and intricate Beach Boy harmonies were missed more than they were made and some of the lead vocals were thin or downright flat . . . Drummer Dennis Wilson . . . didn't even try to sing onstage. Though his drumming was strong and contemporary, he also acted a bit erratic by throwing down his sticks and quitting in the middle of 'Surfin' USA.'"

THURSDAY, JUNE 4 TO SUNDAY, JUNE 7, 1981: Westbury Music Fair, Westbury, NY (One show Thursday and Friday at 8:30 p.m. and two shows Saturday and Sunday)
The group played six shows at Westbury. British guitarist Adrian Baker sat in with them. He'd recorded a medley called "Beach Boys Gold" with his band Gidea Park that became a U.K. hit. When Roger Scott of Capitol Radio interviewed the Beach Boys that spring, he played them a "Happy Birthday Brian Wilson" recording Baker had made. The group was impressed and invited him to Westbury. Baker recalled, "Bruce told me to watch out for the song 'Don't Worry Baby' because Brian might not be able to sing it . . . Normally he would sing 'Don't Worry Baby' but that's what

been. Nobody likes to play under those circumstances or situations."

With the band crumbling, Mike tried to build a solo identity. His album *Looking Back with Love* was released in the fall and Mike toured the clubs with his Endless Summer Beach Band. However, the album sold poorly and many dates were canceled due to poor attendance. Mike quickly realized he needed the group as much as they needed him.

THE BEACH BOYS IN CONCERT

Meanwhile, the band's shows had become so erratic that critics and even some fans suggested they call it a day. The Beach Boys, however, seemed immune to criticism and uninterested in public opinion. 1981 signaled a low point for a band with a long history of ups and downs.

"All we have to do is show up. We can do a real turkey of a set, and people will come back and say, 'That's the greatest show I've ever seen.'"

—Carl Wilson

Bruce was getting at! He wanted me to sing it . . . I jumped to my microphone as fast as I could and sang the song. Mike Love congratulated me and the audience was quite appreciative. The show came to an end and I was feeling pretty strange but it was a fantastic experience!" It was an audition, and Baker was invited to join the group for their next tour.

SATURDAY, JUNE 20, 1981: Poplar Creek Music Theater, Hoffman Estates, IL, with Glen Super
The group started a two-week tour with Adrian Baker. Bobby Figueroa recalled, "Adrian was a cool guy to play with. He had a [Beach Boys] medley thing out and I was amazed at how well he did it. He toured with us for a while and did a great job."

SUNDAY, JUNE 21, TO TUESDAY, JUNE 23, 1981: Pine Knob Music Theatre, Clarkston, MI, with Glen Super (One show each night at 7:30 p.m.)

WEDNESDAY, JUNE 24,1981: Six Flags Over Georgia, Atlanta, GA, with Glen Super (Two shows at 7:00 and 10:00 p.m.)

THURSDAY, JUNE 25, 1981: H. U. Brown Theater, Indianapolis, IN, with Glen Super (Two shows at 6:30 and 9:30 p.m.)
The Beach Boys' management booked them into this small outdoor Brown Theater. Attendance was good, but the shows were disappointing. Bruce commented that the audience "sat on its hands." *The Indianapolis Star* blamed the group, noting, "There was no production. They simply came out and did their thing. Little fanfare, little talk, and no attempt to establish rapport with the overflowing crowd—they do that with their music."

FRIDAY, JUNE 26, 1981: Blossom Music Center, Cuyahoga Falls, OH, with Glen Super
A capacity crowd attended but only came to life when Dennis claimed the piano and the band leapt into "Be True To Your School." Jane Scott of the *Plains-Dealer* blamed audience coolness on the band. She commented, "Love moved more or less like an older man and the overall effect was stilted . . . A big drawback, ironically, was the mastermind of the group, Brian Wilson. He sat glumly at the piano, almost as if hypnotized . . . When he did sing a song, God only knows it was a mistake. His voice was rough and tuneless."

SATURDAY, JUNE 27, 1981: Municipal Auditorium, Nashville, TN, with Glen Super (8:00 p.m. show)

SUNDAY, JUNE 28, 1981: Carowinds Palladium, Charlotte, NC, with Glen Super (Two shows at 3:00 and 7:00 p.m.)
An SRO crowd filled the 9000-seat Palladium for both shows.

TUESDAY, JUNE 30, 1981: Gaillard Municipal Auditorium, Charleston, SC, with Glen Super (Two shows)

WEDNESDAY, JULY 1, 1981: Civic Center, Huntington, WV, with Glen Super (8:00 p.m. show)

SATURDAY, JULY 4, 1981: Washington Mall, Washington, DC (6:00 p.m. show)
For the second year in a row, the group played a free concert in Washington. Prior to the gig, Mike made the rounds, speaking to the press and promoting Hawaiian Tropic Suntan Oil. He told reporter Lloyd Grove: "This is not a flag-waving thing. Its just summertime, that's all, and that's a natural time for the Beach Boys . . . People like to have a good time and forget about their troubles. That explains the whole show . . . What Bob Hope was to his generation, I hope the Beach Boys will become to this generation . . . We want to create an atmosphere of positivity."

Over 400,000 people were present when the group took the stage. Geoffrey Himes of the *Washington Post* admired the spectacle but was less impressed with the event as a musical performance. He noted that they only played two songs recorded after 1968 ("Lady Lynda" and "I Write the Songs") and that with Carl gone, Dennis mute on drums, and Brian banging inaudibly on piano and only occasionally singing an off-key vocal, "this left the show in the hands of Al Jardine, Mike Love, and Bruce Johnston, who seemed to have little feel for a great musical legacy. They cloaked around and undermined beautiful songs like 'Wouldn't It Be Nice' with sloppy arrangements. They also passed over a long list of superlative songs to sing such weak selections as 'Long Tall Texan.'"

SUNDAY, JULY 5, 1981: Queen Mary, Long Beach, CA, with Rick Springfield, Three Dog Night, Jan and Dean, Pablo Cruise, and John Sebastian
The group flew across the country to take part in another free concert. Marty Pasetta (whose credits included *Elvis: Aloha from Hawaii*) filmed the event for a TV special titled *Good Vibrations over America*. Fifty-one television stations and numerous radio stations across the country broadcast the Mike Love–organized concert live. Mike told the *Los Angeles Times*, "We want to give something back to the people." Unfortunately, a long flight from Washington and hours backstage in the hot sun took a toll. Many fans remember this concert as the band's all-time worst performance. Carl, watching on TV while on tour with the Doobie Brothers in Michigan, called it "painful" and commented to the *Baltimore Sun*, "It made me feel real bad to see the guys, because they looked like they'd been on a plane all night. But I think it's inexcusable to not communicate the song as best you can. When you're a professional musician and people have learned to love what you do and have paid money to come see you, I think you're obliged to make a real good delivery." Brian's horrific vocals on "Don't Worry Baby" created a wince-inducing moment broadcast to thousands around the U.S. Jan and Dean joined the band for "Barbara Ann" and hosts Wolfman Jack and Charlie Tuna sang along for closer "Fun, Fun, Fun."

THURSDAY, JULY 9, TO WEDNESDAY, JULY 15, 1981: Caesars Tahoe, Stateline, NV, with Glen Super

FRIDAY, JULY 17, AND SATURDAY, JULY 18, 1981: Greek Theatre, Los Angeles, CA, with Glenn Super
The Beach Boys shows at the Greek Theatre were unmitigated disasters. There were tensions emanating from the stage for the entire performance on Friday. Brian was frustrated by problems with his microphone and raced offstage after singing a few lines of "God Only Knows." Al had to coax him back out to finish the song. As soon as it was over Brian tried to leave again, but was blocked by Dennis. Richard Cromelin of the *Los Angeles Times* reported that once seated back at the piano, Brian punched his microphone stand in frustration, knocking it on the floor, and then disappeared after playing one more number. Cromelin noted that Dennis strode "to the rim of the stage and graciously waved his rear end to the crowd." Mike was allegedly so incensed by his behavior that he confronted Dennis backstage. According to *Creem* magazine, they "had a bloody fistfight" that resulted in Dennis again being temporarily suspended. Despite the drama, Daryl Dragon and Toni Tennille joined in for the encore of "Fun, Fun, Fun."

SUNDAY, JULY 19, 1981: Park West, Salt Lake City, UT
With Dennis gone, the 9000 that attended were treated to a drama-free show. Tom Wharton of the *Salt Lake Tribune* declared "This was a great concert that was fun for everyone. Mike Love, gray beard and all, was there to sing all the oldies. Al Jardine was there to play the rhythm guitar. And Bruce Johnston was around to play the keyboard and add some fine vocals."

FRIDAY, AUGUST 14, 1981: Rosenblatt Stadium, Omaha, NE, with Little River Band and Hit and Run (5:00 p.m.)
A crowd estimated at 20,843 attended this show. Dennis remained absent (the reason given was that he was suffering from an abscessed tooth).

SATURDAY, AUGUST 15, 1981: Illinois State Fair, Springfield, IL (Two shows at 7:00 and 9:30 p.m.)

SUNDAY, AUGUST 16, 1981: Wisconsin State Fair, West Allis, WI (4:00 p.m. show)
Dennis was back and Duane Dudek of the *Milwaukee Sentinel* singled him out as "the only member

to work up a sweat." He noted that Brian "was planted in front of a white piano, and he scowled and chain-smoked his way through the show. His one solo, 'Wouldn't It Be Nice,' was delivered in a clear, nasal voice and was a surprise to those who thought he could no longer speak . . . Al Jardine barely earned his paycheck with 'School Days.'"

MONDAY, AUGUST 17, 1981: Holiday Star Theatre, Merrillville, IN

TUESDAY, AUGUST 18, 1981: Six Flags Over Mid-America, St. Louis, MO (Two shows at 7:00 and 10:00 p.m.)

WEDNESDAY, AUGUST 19, AND THURSDAY, AUGUST 20, 1981: Red Rocks Amphitheater, Morrison, CO, with Jim Photoglo (One show per night at 7:30 p.m.)
Opening act Jim Photoglo, then on the charts with "Fool in Love with You," recalled, "I grew up in Inglewood, California, which is next to Hawthorne, where the Wilsons lived. The Love family was also from Inglewood. Stan Love, Mike's brother, was a basketball star at our high school and went on to play for the L.A. Lakers. Stephanie Love, Mike's sister, and I were classmates in junior and senior high school. I was a fan of the Beach Boys from the first time I heard 'Surfin'.' [By 1981] I'd had a couple hit singles out and had some name recognition and my manager secured the opening slot for me. The Beach Boys and their crew treated my band and me very well. They were very supportive. I don't think The Beach Boys were at their best during this time. Carl was not on the tour. Dennis was in pretty rough shape, and Brian wasn't doing so well. But the fans loved them. From the moment the opening song began, the audience would be up and dancing."

FRIDAY, AUGUST 21, 1981: Colorado State Fair, Pueblo, CO, with Jim Photoglo (7:30 p.m. show)

SATURDAY, AUGUST 22, 1981: Zoo Amphitheater, Oklahoma City, OK, with Jim Photoglo
Dennis was absent and the rest of the band may have wished they'd skipped this show too. Charles Jones of the *Oklahoman* reported that audience members "hurled beer, Frisbees, food, ice, toilet paper, and even one soft drink bottle at the stage . . . During the group's second offering, 'Sloop John B,' . . . a gallon jug partially full of beer smashed against Brian Wilson's baby grand piano, spraying the reclusive artist with the sticky brew. During the next tune, 'Surfin',' a cup of ice hurled from the crowd soaked Al Jardine's right arm."

MONDAY, AUGUST 24, 1981: Freedom Hall Civic Center, Johnson City, TN, with Jim Photoglo (8:00 p.m. show)

TUESDAY, AUGUST 25, 1981: Merriweather Post Pavilion, Columbia, MD, with Jim Photoglo (7:30 p.m. show)
Dennis was absent again.

WEDNESDAY, AUGUST 26, 1981: Mann Music Center, Philadelphia, PA, with Jim Photoglo

THURSDAY, AUGUST 27, 1981: Tanglewood Music Festival, Lenox, MA, with Jim Photoglo (Three shows)

FRIDAY, AUGUST 28, 1981: Brendan Byrne Arena, East Rutherford, NJ, with Jim Photoglo (8:00 p.m. show)

SATURDAY, AUGUST 29, 1981: Exhibition Grandstand, Lansdowne Park, Ottawa, ON, Canada (7:30 p.m. show)
While admitting the capacity crowd had a great time, Richard Labonte of the *Ottawa Citizen* took the Beach Boys to task for sliding "steadily into dotage . . . The band has become the Elvis Presley of the 1980s, trading without shame on the fact that people are in the habit of remembering once-great music, of remembering that they were once excited by it, of enjoying the experience re-lived."

"I disagree with what Carl says about the band. I think that people that come to see the Beach Boys want to hear our old stuff. I think you're doing them and yourself a really big disservice if you kid yourself into thinking they don't want to hear those songs."

—Mike Love

SUNDAY, AUGUST 30, AND MONDAY, AUGUST 31, 1981: CNE Grandstand, Toronto, ON, Canada, with Ian Thomas

The Beach Boys remained popular in Toronto. Over 22,000 fans showed up on Sunday alone. Dennis played the first night but was absent on Monday. Mike commented to the crowd, "Dennis is back at the hotel incapacitated."

TUESDAY, SEPTEMBER 1, 1981: SPAC, Saratoga, NY, with Jim Photoglo (7:00 p.m. show)

Over 9,300 fans turned out at SPAC. Mike Hochanadel of the *Schenectady Gazette* declared it "a lackluster greatest hits show" and commented, "Now a musical period piece, with no new material for years, the Beach Boys are losing even their longstanding appeal as a living pop music museum through poor performances. Unless they come up with new songs and dramatically improve their performance quality, they have no future and should quit exploiting their past."

WEDNESDAY, SEPTEMBER 2, 1981: NY State Fairgrounds, Syracuse, NY, with Jim Photoglo

A crowd of 15,000 braved torrential downpours to watch the group. John Bonfatti of the *Post Standard* complained that they put on a sloppy, indifferent performance and criticized the audience for not minding. He asked, "Is it important that the band's musical medley about automobiles . . . came to an abrupt halt when lead singer Mike Love apparently forgot the simple chorus to '409'? Or that Brian Wilson hacked out some raspy coughs during several songs, including the dreamy introduction to the band's first encore, 'Good Vibrations'? . . . Probably not."

THURSDAY, OCTOBER 8, 1981: U.S. Air Force Academy, Colorado Springs, CO (8:00 p.m. show)

This was the opening date of the band's fall tour. Mike Meros, Adrian Baker, Bobby Figueroa, Ernie Knapp, and Ed Carter accompanied them.

FRIDAY, OCTOBER 9, 1981: University of Notre Dame, South Bend, IN, with Red Rider

SATURDAY, OCTOBER 10, 1981: Indiana State University, Terre Haute, IN, with Red Rider

The group's jet had engine trouble in South Bend and they chartered two small planes to get them to Terre Haute. They arrived at the venue considerably late and were greeted with hisses and boos by the restless crowd. Some of the backup musicians were on a slower plane and missed the show altogether, including Bobby Figueroa. The drummer from Red Rider filled in. The *Sycamore Yearbook* declared the show hardly worth the wait: "For those expecting good sound and solid musicianship, this performance was just short of tragic. 'California Girls,' the opening number of the Quasi-Beach Boys, was predictably shaky as were most of the remaining songs."

SUNDAY, OCTOBER 11, 1981: Civic Center, St. Paul, MN (8:00 p.m. show)

MONDAY, OCTOBER 12, 1981: Robertson Fieldhouse, Bradley University, Peoria, IL (7:30 p.m. show)

TUESDAY, OCTOBER 13, 1981: Coliseum, Fort Wayne, IN

WEDNESDAY, OCTOBER 14, 1981: Joe Louis Arena, Detroit, MI

THURSDAY, OCTOBER 15, 1981: Civic Center, La Crosse, WI (Canceled)

FRIDAY, OCTOBER 16, 1981: Riverfront Coliseum, Cincinnati, OH (8:00 p.m. show)

SATURDAY, OCTOBER 17, 1981: Indiana University, Bloomington, IN, with Red Rider (8:00 p.m. show)

The Beach Boys played at IU's homecoming celebration. The *Arbutus Yearbook* reported, "A wave of exhilaration splashed over the audience as the Beach Boys took the stage following the warmup act Red Rider. Beginning the show with 'California Girls,' the band managed to keep the crowd on its feet, dancing and clapping throughout the evening."

THE BEACH BOYS IN CONCERT

SUNDAY, OCTOBER 18, 1981: Civic Center, Wheeling, WV

MONDAY, OCTOBER 19, 1981: Coliseum, Knoxville, TN

TUESDAY, OCTOBER 20, 1981: Jacksonville State University, Jacksonville, AL
This show was scheduled for the Huntsville Civic Center but the venue was switched. Dennis was absent.

WEDNESDAY, OCTOBER 21, 1981: Civic Center, Savannah, GA, with Red Rider
While many reviewers were critical of the 1981 Beach Boys, Hank Orberg of the *Savannah Morning News* reported, "Lead singer Mike Love was battling a sore throat and didn't have his usual range. But no matter, halfway through their performance, Love's vocals evened out as he belted out 'Be True To Your School.' By then, the audience was on its feet clapping and singing along to 'Help Me Rhonda' and 'Barbara Ann' . . . After they finished their regular set, the audience, now nearing hysteria, demanded an encore, which consisted of 'Good Vibrations' and 'Rock and Roll Music.'"

THURSDAY, OCTOBER 22, 1981: Augusta-Richmond County Civic Center, Augusta, GA, with Red Rider

FRIDAY, OCTOBER 23, 1981: Virginia Tech University, Blacksburg, VA, with Red Rider (8:00 p.m. show)

SATURDAY, OCTOBER 24, 1981: Clemson University, Clemson, SC, with Red Rider

SUNDAY, OCTOBER 25, 1981: Duke University, Durham, NC, with Red Rider (8:00 p.m. show)
Once again Dennis was absent. But despite the presence of only one Wilson, Kathy Geier of the *Chronicle* called the show "energetic, exciting and, most important of all, fun . . . Their harmonies were as magical as ever." Geier declared Brian's performance of 'God Only Knows' a highlight. "He did a good job on the song and the others which he sang, revealing his voice to be in fine shape."

TUESDAY, OCTOBER 27, 1981: Saenger Theater, New Orleans, LA, with Red Rider (Two shows at 8:00 and 11:00 p.m.)

WEDNESDAY, OCTOBER 28, 1981: Louisiana State University, Baton Rouge, LA (8:00 p.m. show)

THURSDAY, OCTOBER 29, 1981: Leon County Civic Center, Tallahassee, FL

FRIDAY, OCTOBER 30, 1981: Orange Bowl, Miami, FL, with the Commodores (6:30 p.m. show)
The Beach Boys performed at a pep rally prior to the UM-Penn State football game. During "Be True To Your School," they were joined by UM cheerleaders. They excited Mike and cheerleaders became a fixture during this song in the 1980s. Ronnie Ramos of the *Miami Hurricane* commented, "Their background harmony and lead vocals were surprisingly good compared to their Long Beach performance. The only disappointment was Brian Wilson's 'God Only Knows.' His voice no longer has what it takes to make this song the soft swaying classic that it became when he first wrote and performed it."

SATURDAY, OCTOBER 31, 1981: University of Alabama, Tuscaloosa, AL, with Tom Chapin

SUNDAY, NOVEMBER 1, 1981: Rupp Arena, Lexington, KY, with Tom Chapin (8:00 p.m. show)

FRIDAY, NOVEMBER 27, 1981: Memorial Coliseum, Portland, OR (8:00 p.m. show)
Ed Carter, Mike Meros, and Ernie Knapp accompanied the group on this tour, but Bobby Figueroa was absent. His back gave out, forcing him to quit, and Mike Kowalski replaced him. Adrian Baker was also gone, but returned the following summer.

"I haven't quit the Beach Boys but I do not plan on touring with them until they decide that 1981 means as much to them as 1961."

—Carl Wilson

Alex Cooley Presents

BEACH BOYS
IN CONCERT

LEXINGTON CENTER'S RUPP ARENA
TONIGHT 8:00 P.M.
GOOD SEATS STILL AVAILABLE
TICKETS: $10.50, $9.50 ALL SEATS RESERVED
ON SALE: At The Lexington Center Ticket Office,
For Information Call: 233-3565

Ad for an appearance minus Carl in Lexington, Kentucky, on November 1, 1981. Ian Rusten Collection

THE BEACH BOYS IN CONCERT

> "I don't think
> The Beach
> Boys were
> at their best
> during this
> time. Carl was
> not on the
> tour. Dennis
> was in pretty
> rough shape,
> and Brian
> wasn't doing
> so well. But
> the fans loved
> them. From
> the moment
> the opening
> song began, the
> audience would
> be up and
> dancing."

Tour program for the group's ill-timed appearance in Sun City in December 1981.
Collection of Chris Woods

The show in Portland was marred by an ugly incident involving the group's security and three sheriff's deputies from Clark County, Washington. When the off-duty deputies tried to take photos, they were allegedly physically assaulted and "falsely imprisoned" by security, which claimed the men were "violating the Beach Boys' copyrights." The case went to trial in 1985 and the deputies were awarded 5.4 million dollars by an Oregon judge.

SATURDAY, NOVEMBER 28, 1981: Paramount Theater, Seattle, WA, with the Pamela Moore Band (Two shows at 7:00 and 10:00 p.m.)

SUNDAY, NOVEMBER 29, 1981: McArthur Court, University of Oregon, Eugene, OR, with Joe Erickson (8:00 p.m. show)
Fred Crafts of the *Eugene Register Guard* commented, "Mike Love . . . pranced and danced and shook green and yellow University of Oregon pompons in time to 'Be True To Your School.' The rest of the band was more businesslike. Chubby Brian Wilson sat stolidly at the piano, Al Jardine worked seriously on his rhythm guitar, and Dennis Wilson did his best to beat his drums into pieces."

THURSDAY, DECEMBER 3, 1981: SEMA Awards Banquet, Hilton Hotel, Las Vegas, NV

FRIDAY, DECEMBER 4, AND SATURDAY, DECEMBER 5, 1981: Circle Star Theater, San Carlos, CA (Two shows per night at 7:30 and 11:00 p.m.)
Dennis missed these shows.

THURSDAY, DECEMBER 24, TO SUNDAY, DECEMBER 27, 1981, AND WEDNESDAY, DECEMBER 30, TO SUNDAY, JANUARY 3, 1982: Superbowl, Sun City, South Africa, with Lulu (One show per night)
The group played Sun City, despite the fact that the U.N. had asked entertainers to boycott the country to help end apartheid. Mike offered no apologies. He crassly commented to Gene Triplett of the *Oklahoman*, "It's nice money. The U.N. can go screw themselves. They never buy tickets to Beach Boys concerts." Fortunately for the band, they'd sunk so far off the public radar that there was no public outcry.

Ernie Knapp, Mike Meros, Mike Kowalski, and guitarist Jeff Foskett accompanied them. Foskett recalled in the fanzine *Add Some Music*, "Eddie Carter had a hernia, so Michael called me, much to the dismay of Alan Jardine. Alan didn't know me, but it was just the first time Michael had ever invited anybody into the band . . . So South Africa, December '81, they call me. I say, 'Yeah, love to. Are you kidding?' My dreams come true, right? So I did the gig."

Peter Feldman of the *Johannesburg Star* reported, "The group did an adroit job but sadly the members had nothing new to offer in the field of experimentation. There were no clever interludes to break this surfin' safari, nor did they bother to unveil any new facets to the Beach Boys of the 80s . . . The songs of their creative years, 'Barbara Ann,' 'In My Room,' 'Help Me Rhonda,' 'Surfin' USA,' and 'California Girls,' were all executed with some flourish. They rounded off the evening's wallow in the past with the ambitious breakthrough 'Good Vibrations,' but devoid here of the vocal and musical crispness inherent on the recording. It was nevertheless exciting in its intensity . . . All in all a lively musical mix for this time of the year at Surf (sorry, *Sun*) City."

1982

NINETEEN EIGHTY-TWO started off darkly. Carl was absent and every story that appeared about the Beach Boys was negative. The two remaining Wilson brothers were in bad shape and concerts were usually erratic affairs. Brian's chain-smoking ravaged his voice, which only magnified Carl's absence. When Carl finally returned to the Beach Boys in May, he insisted on changes.

Carl quickly dismissed bassist Ernie Knapp and brought back Ed Carter. Jeffrey Foskett assumed he'd be out of a job, but Carl asked him to stay. Also remaining were Mike Kowalski on drums, Mike Meros on keyboards, and Adrian Baker. However, as a fourth guitarist in the band would be superfluous, Baker moved to piano. The group tightened up their set to one hour and a single encore. After a month of rehearsals, a revitalized Beach Boys hit the road for their summer tour. Critics noticed the heightened energy within the group. The tour garnered better reviews than the previous year. There seemed to be a renewed *esprit de corps*. Carl remarked to a reporter, "We're having a better time than we've had in quite a while."

The band's shows were certainly more professional, but many felt there was still a lack of ambition. The set remained strictly oldies. The group seemed determined to blot out all traces of their early-seventies recordings. Long gone were "Sail on Sailor," "Feel Flows," and "The Trader." Every song played came from the "sun and fun" years. When they did add new material to the set list it was usually their versions of other people's oldie hits like Del Shannon's 'Runaway' and Jan and Dean's "Little Old Lady from Pasadena."

CONCERTS PLAYED IN
1982

Carl's behest, the band added classics to the set that they'd not played in years, such as "I Can Hear Music" and "Dance, Dance, Dance," but the group only played excerpts. As Jill Warren of the *Indianapolis Star* commented, "just about everything the band played was a medley of old hits. It just seems like a cheap way of trying to please everybody while exerting only as much energy as is absolutely required." The group would open shows with a "dance" medley, and then play a "girls" medley, before cranking out "car" and "surf" medleys. It was the only way to play all the hits in a one-hour show, but it meant the integrity of individual songs was lost. Still, most fans walked away happy. Ron Altbach commented, "The car songs are cool and people loved them. You have to appreciate the fact that sometimes they'd play for as many as 50,000 people singing along, having a great time. So you can't replace that. The energy that comes out of that is just unbelievable."

One thing that made the summer tour run smoother was the absence of Dennis and Brian. Mike explained somewhat uncharitably to *The Oklahoman*, "Brian is sitting it out. We're trying to encourage him to get more into the positive therapy thing he was in a few years ago. He was doing better for a while, but lately he's been backsliding, getting fatter and fatter . . . acting weirder all the time. We're hopeful that he gets himself together. Dennis is currently drunk. He's battling alcoholism. I don't know if he'll make it or not (on this tour). He hasn't shown up yet."

FRIDAY, JANUARY 15, TO MONDAY, JANUARY 18, 1982: Harrah's Tahoe, Stateline, NV, with Stoddard and Cole (Two shows per day at 8:00 and 11:30 p.m.)
The group kicked off the year with another Tahoe residency. Ernie Knapp, Mike Kowalski, and Mike Meros accompanied them. Jeff Foskett was also along, much to his surprise. He recalled in the *Add Some Music* fanzine, "I came back from South Africa, twenty days with the Beach Boys. I thought, well that's it. But they kept me in the band. Jardine, for some reason was very impressed, which impressed me, 'cause I thought that he would be the hardest to get along with."

FRIDAY, FEBRUARY 19, 1982: Ricks College, Rexburg, ID (Two shows at 7:00 and 10:00 p.m.)

SATURDAY, FEBRUARY 20, 1982: Brigham Young University, Provo, UT (7:30 p.m. show)
This appearance was marred by Brian's blasé behavior. The University had a no-smoking policy, which Brian ignored. He sat glumly at the piano, occasionally playing along while chain-smoking. The *Deseret News* reported, "BYU spokesman Paul Richards said other members of the Beach Boys group tried to get Wilson to stop smoking during the concert and even took his cigarettes away from him. But he said the piano player found more cigarettes during a break and continued smoking in front of the 17,000 students and others who attended the concert." The group apologized for his behavior.

SUNDAY, FEBRUARY 21, 1982: Selland Arena, Fresno, CA, with Sneaker

TUESDAY, FEBRUARY 23, TO FRIDAY, FEBRUARY 26, 1982: Harrah's Tahoe, Stateline, NV

SATURDAY, FEBRUARY 27, 1982: Compton Terrace, Phoenix, AZ (2:00 p.m. show)

SUNDAY, FEBRUARY 28, 1982: New Mexico State University, Las Cruces, NM
The Beach Boys' appearance at NMSU attracted 7,000 fans. The audience had a good time, though there were technical problems. They had to restart "God Only Knows" twice. Michelle Stephens of the *Round Up* commented, "One couldn't help but realize that the Beach Boys are getting old. It was very noticeable, especially with Brian Wilson, who never seemed to move except on or off stage and to puff a cigarette. He seemed to choke out the lyrics to 'Good Vibrations.' All of their songs were several years old—nothing new . . . They're burnt out."

WEDNESDAY, MARCH 17, 1982: Summit, Houston, TX, with Delbert McClinton and the Fabulous Thunderbirds
The group embarked on a three-week tour, still without Carl, who was completing his album.

THURSDAY, MARCH 18, 1982: Tarrant County Convention Center, Fort Worth, TX, with Delbert McClinton and the Fabulous Thunderbirds (8:00 p.m. show)
This was a busy day for Mike. In the afternoon, he played with Dean Torrence in Florida. Then he joined the group in Texas. Pete Oppel of the *Dallas News* felt they "seemed more self assured" and praised Dennis, who "attacked the drums with bravado, playing as though he was a closet maniac in a family of well-respected Southern Californians."

FRIDAY, MARCH 19, TO SUNDAY, MARCH 21, 1982: Sunrise Musical Theatre, Sunrise, FL (One show on Friday at 8:00 p.m., two on Saturday at 8:00 and 11:00 p.m., and one on Sunday at 7:00 p.m.)

TUESDAY, MARCH 23, 1982: Lee Civic Center, Fort Myers, FL
The Beach Boys' stay in Fort Myers was marred by the arrest of Brian's girlfriend Carolyn Williams. Brian missed the next night's show in St. Petersburg.

WEDNESDAY, MARCH 24, 1982: Bayfront Center Arena, St. Petersburg, FL, with Bertie Higgins (8:00 p.m. show)

THURSDAY, MARCH 25, 1982: Stanley Theater, Pittsburgh, PA, with John Moran
Brian was back for this show, though Bill Stieg of the *Pittsburgh Post-Gazette* argued it might've been better without him. He commented, "He had few songs to himself, a wise move in retrospect. His verses on 'Sloop John B' were barely passable: he missed the high notes on the difficult 'God Only Knows,' and the ending was botched, and on 'Surfer Girl' he showed little control of his voice or breathing." Stieg did, however, have kind words for Dennis. "Dennis Wilson was a marvelous madman on the drums. He gave new, faster finishes to 'Sloop John B' and 'I Get Around,' and by the final encore ('Fun, Fun, Fun') had shaken his kit loose from its moorings."

FRIDAY, MARCH 26, TO SUNDAY, MARCH 28, 1982: Westbury Music Fair, Westbury, NY, with Glenn Super (One show on Friday at 8:30 p.m., two on Saturday at 6:30 and 10:30 p.m., and two on Sunday at 3:00 and 7:30 p.m.)
The Beach Boys sold out four shows at Westbury, necessitating a fifth be added. Dennis was absent on Sunday. The set on Friday consisted of "California Girls," "Sloop John B," "Do It Again," "Heroes and Villains/Cotton Fields" (medley), "In My Room," "Come Go with Me," "409/Shut Down/Little Old Lady from Pasadena/Little Deuce Coupe" (medley), "I Get Around," "Long Tall Texan," "I Write the Songs," "Lady Lynda," "Be My Baby," "God Only Knows," "Help Me Rhonda," "Be True To Your School," "Graduation Day," "Rock and Roll Music," "Wouldn't It Be Nice," "Darlin'," "Surfer Girl," "Surfin' Safari/Surf City/Surfin' USA" (medley), "Good Vibrations," "Barbara Ann," and "Fun, Fun, Fun."

The performance of "Graduation Day" was to fulfill a request. The group took requests at a number of shows on the tour, though they didn't always play what was asked. Mike refused a request for "Wendy" in St. Petersburg with the remark "Nobody's heard that one in years!"

MONDAY, MARCH 29, 1982: Kleinhans Music Hall, Buffalo, NY (Two shows at 7:00 and 10:00 p.m.)
Dale Anderson, of the *Buffalo News*, was disappointed by the conservative set list. He commented, "With Carl away, the remaining Beach Boys have regressed so deeply that they barely acknowledged anything newer than their 1968 hit 'Do It Again' . . . All the surf songs and the car songs were condensed into medleys, a bit like Stars on 45. For new material, they went for stuff as old as their own—the Del Vikings' 1957 'Come Go with Me,' the Ronettes' 1963 'Be My Baby,' and Murry Kellum's 1963 'Long Tall Texan.'"

TUESDAY, MARCH 30, 1982: Ocean State PAC, Providence, RI (7:00 p.m. show)
Poor sales led to the cancelation of a 10:00 p.m. concert.

WEDNESDAY, MARCH 31, 1982: Coliseum, Moncton, NB, Canada (8:00 p.m. show)
The Beach Boys' appearance in Moncton attracted 9,000 fans. Much to the audience's delight, Carl joined them, remaining for the next three nights. However, he wasn't satisfied with the experience. He commented to Geoffrey Himes of *Musician*, "Everything was rushed; it was very mechanical. There was resistance to rehearsing out of habit. But it all finally came together at the last minute."

THURSDAY, APRIL 1, 1982: Metro Centre, Halifax, NS, Canada, with Sam Moon and the Universal Power (8:00 p.m. show)
The group's first Halifax appearance since 1968 drew 10,000 fans. Nancy MacDonald of the *Chronicle-Herald* commented, "The concert quickly evolved into a musical experience, with the surprisingly young audience clapping, swaying, and singing. Some even formed a conga line, which snaked its way around the mezzanine . . . Early in the performance their voices were strained and hoarse, either from age or fatigue, but as the show progressed, grew stronger. Carl Wilson was the one whose singing ability seemed the least affected by time."

FRIDAY, APRIL 2, AND SATURDAY, APRIL 3, 1982: Holiday Star Theater, Merrillville, IN
Carl was present both nights. However, he left the tour on Sunday to work on his second solo album, *Youngblood*.

Brian, especially, was an impediment to the band onstage. When he returned in August, he weighed 310 pounds and was completely out of it. Manager Tom Hulett recalled, "I got very scared. I worked with Elvis and saw what he went through . . . I told the other guys in the band if we don't do something Brian was going to be the next headline [death] . . . I heard rumors of drug

> "Dennis is currently drunk. He's battling alcoholism. I don't know if he'll make it or not (on this tour). He hasn't shown up yet."
>
> **—Mike Love**

dealers showing up and I knew we had to take action." The Beach Boys made a fateful decision. Although they had little love for Dr. Landy, he'd gotten Brian back on his feet in 1976. Brian resisted going back into his care, so the band gave him an ultimatum. On November 5, Brian was fired from the Beach Boys and told he wouldn't be allowed back until he entered treatment with Landy. Brian relented and was spirited away to Landy's compound in Hawaii.

As the year progressed, Brian showed signs of improvement. However, Dennis was spiraling down at an alarming rate, and no one knew how to deal with that problem.

"I told the other guys in the band if we don't do something Brian was going to be the next headline [death] . . . I heard rumors of drug dealers showing up and I knew we had to take action."

—Tom Hulett

SUNDAY, APRIL 4, TO TUESDAY, APRIL 6, 1982: Chateau De Ville, Framingham, MA
Promoters booked the group into this small club, which attracted an older crowd. It was probably a smart move, as the band was in poor shape. Jeff Foskett told writer Brad Elliot that he considered the April 5 show their all-time worst performance. "Bruce and I had the flu. Michael had such severe congestion he really could not sing. I was dualing every one of his leads. Jardine was so upset with the fact that he couldn't even see the first person in the row because the smoke was so thick. And Brian was off in his own world. Dennis was there and doing a damn good job that night because no one else was."

Foskett certainly proved his worth at the engagement. When Mike declared Brian would sing "God Only Knows," Don Cunningham of *Add Some Music* reported, "From his throat emerged a choking 'I may not always love you, but long as there are stars . . . aaarrrghhh . . . stop . . . stop . . . Bruce, you sing it. I'm too hoarse.' They began again with Bruce taking up the lead . . . But Bruce also quit due to a cold in his throat . . . As Bruce's voice faded, the lead was assumed quietly by Jeff Foskett . . . A fantasy emerged: a single spotlight shone on Jeff, who gave it all he had . . . 'God Only Knows' came alive, and the strength of the song itself took over, to the immediate pleasure of both the audience and the Beach Boys."

THURSDAY, APRIL 8, TO SUNDAY, APRIL 11, 1982: Harrah's Marina Hotel and Casino, Atlantic City, NJ, with Glenn Super (Two shows per night at 8:00 and 11:00 p.m.)

SUNDAY, MAY 2, 1982: Jack Murphy Stadium, San Diego, CA
With Carl back, the group played for over 50,000 after a Padres game. The show was promoted by radio station KFMB and Pax Productions. The Beach Boys drove onto the field in a Woody and were introduced by 100 cheerleaders, who clustered around the stage. Dennis disappeared backstage with a young woman and didn't take the stage until midway through the show. Matt Damsker of the *San Diego Union* commented that the group looked like "grizzled veterans" (though Mike actually looked years younger, having shaved off his beard) but argued, "Their music holds up, catchy and buoyant as ever. They proved that yesterday from the opening song, 'California Girls,' through the final rave-up of 'Good Vibrations' and 'Barbara Ann.'"

FRIDAY, MAY 14, 1982: Ector County Coliseum, Odessa, TX
While rehearsing for their summer tour, the group played a few dates, minus Brian and Dennis.

SATURDAY, MAY 15, 1982: Free Coliseum Grounds, San Antonio, TX, with Flash Cadillac and Jerry Jeff Walker (3:30 p.m. show)

FRIDAY, MAY 28, TO SUNDAY, MAY 30, 1982: Pine Knob Music Theater, Clarkston, MI (One show each night at 7:30 p.m.)
The Beach Boys' 1982 summer tour was one of the biggest they'd ever done, with over seventy concerts between June and September. Brian and Dennis were absent for the first leg. Adrian Baker, Mike Meros, Jeff Foskett, Mike Kowalski, and Ed Carter filled out the band.

The tour opened with three nights at Pine Knob. The set for the May 29 show consisted of "It's OK/I Can Hear Music/Sloop John B/Darlin'/Dance, Dance, Dance/Wouldn't It Be Nice" (medley), "In My Room," "Good Timin'," "409/Shut Down/The Little Old Lady from Pasadena/Little Deuce Coupe" (medley), "I Get Around," "Runaway," "Do It Again," "Come Go with Me," "Be True To Your School," "Surfer Girl," "God Only Knows," "Disney Girls," "I Write the Songs," "All Summer Long," "Help Me Rhonda," "Rock and Roll Music," "Surfin' Safari/Surf City/Surfin' USA" (medley), "California Girls," "Good Vibrations," "Barbara Ann," and "Fun, Fun, Fun."

Jim McFarlin of the *Detroit News* admitted he'd written off the group after years of subpar performances, but reported that they played "with renewed spirit and energy . . . Carl Wilson, who vowed never to return unless the Beach Boys modernized their act, was back and frisky . . . And no, that was not Mike Love's little brother cavorting and posturing like some musclebound beach god. It was brother Love himself, shorn of the beard he's worn for fifteen years, looking twenty years younger and acting like the take-charge frontman he hasn't been in a decade."

MONDAY, MAY 31, 1982: Riverfront, Paducah, KY (9:30 p.m. show)
An afternoon concert was called off due to foul weather and the evening show took place later than scheduled. Despite the rain, 4,000 fans remained and were treated to an hour of hits.

WEDNESDAY, JUNE 2, 1982: Greensboro Coliseum, Greensboro, NC, with Alliance (8:00 p.m. show)
Malcolm Jones of the *Greensboro Daily News* reported, "It was lovely to hear such beautiful songs as 'God Only Knows' done with deep and impressive sincerity. It was downright fun to hear just plain excellent rock 'n' roll in such songs as 'Do It Again' . . . But still. The medleys of old hits came and went a little quick for my taste—if a song is worth doing, it's worth doing with relish. Too many tunes got no more than a tip of the hat."

THURSDAY, JUNE 3, 1982: Cumberland County Memorial Auditorium, Fayetteville, NC, with Alliance

FRIDAY, JUNE 4, 1982: Six Flags, Jackson, NJ (Two shows at 7:00 and 11:00 p.m.)

SATURDAY, JUNE 5, AND SUNDAY, JUNE 6, 1982: Valley Forge Music Fair, Devon, PA (Two shows on Saturday at 6:00 and 10:00 p.m. and Sunday at 3:00 and 7:30 p.m.)

TUESDAY, JUNE 8, 1982: Hampton Coliseum, Hampton, VA, with Le Roux (8:00 p.m. show)

WEDNESDAY, JUNE 9, 1982: Civic Center, Charleston, WV, with Le Roux

THURSDAY, JUNE 10, 1982: University of Toledo, Toledo, OH, with Paul Davis

FRIDAY, JUNE 11, 1982: Blossom Music Center, Cuyahoga Falls, OH
A live version of "Runaway" recorded at this show was considered for single release. It ultimately remained in the vault, but was made available on a hard-to-obtain LP put out in 1986 by the Sunkist corporation. Fans had to collect and mail in proof-of-purchase tokens to get it.

The band picked a good show to tape. Anastasia Pantsios of the *Cleveland Plains Dealer* declared it "one of the most satisfying they have done here in a long time . . . Currently the band has no new product it feels obligated to promote. So it gave the audience a brisk, solid hour plus of what it really wanted to hear: the Beach Boys oldies from 'Catch a Wave' to 'I Get Around' to 'Dance, Dance, Dance' to 'God Only Knows.'" A local TV crew filmed performances of "Darlin'" and "Wouldn't It Be Nice" for a short segment, though they used audio from *Live in London* rather than the actual show.

SATURDAY, JUNE 12, 1982: Mesker Music Theatre, Evansville, IN (Postponed), and Poplar Creek Music Theatre, Hoffman Estates, IL
Due to bad weather, the Evansville show was postponed until June 26. Over 25,000 turned out at Poplar Creek. Tom Valeo of the *Daily Herald* commented, "Starting with a rapid fire recital of some of their most popular songs, including 'I Can Hear Music,' 'Sloop John B' and 'Wouldn't It Be Nice,' the band played their hits continuously for nearly twenty-five minutes. Then came sets neatly packaged into car songs . . . girl songs (including 'Little Surfer Girl' and 'California Girls') and surfing songs . . . . The Beach Boys have all grown far beyond the concerns expressed in these songs and their performance was automatic and uninspired."

TUESDAY, JUNE 15, 1982: Coliseum, Jackson, MS (8:00 p.m. show)

WEDNESDAY, JUNE 16, 1982: Six Flags, Eureka, MO (Two shows at 6:00 and 9:00 p.m.)

THURSDAY, JUNE 17, 1982: Mabee Center, Tulsa, OK, with Poco (8:00 p.m. show)

FRIDAY, JUNE 18, 1982: Lloyd Noble Center, University of Oklahoma, Norman, OK, with Poco

THE BEACH BOYS IN CONCERT

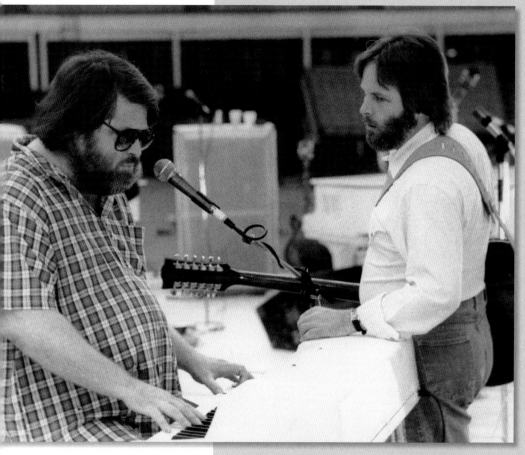

An extremely overweight Brian and his brother Carl rehearsing for a gig in late 1982. Keith Reeves Collection

This concert was scheduled for the Zoo Amphitheater but moved indoors because of rain. The band encountered the boisterous crowds they were used to in Oklahoma. At one point, a plastic beer-can holder thrown from the audience narrowly missed Mike's head and several women thought they were at a Tom Jones show and threw their bras onstage.

SATURDAY, JUNE 19, 1982: Astro World, Houston, TX, and Civic Center, Amarillo, TX, with Poco

SUNDAY, JUNE 20, 1982: Six Flags Over Texas, Arlington, TX (Two shows at 6:00 and 9:00 p.m.)
Pete Oppel of the *Dallas News* noted the difference in the group since Carl's return. He commented, "The lineup was much stronger than the one that came through in March . . . The Beach Boys that played Fort Worth in March were fun, but they weren't too cohesive. This time the boys were fun and a lot tighter."

MONDAY, JUNE 21, 1982: Mississippi Coast Coliseum, Biloxi, MS (8:00 p.m. show)

TUESDAY, JUNE 22, 1982: Von Braun Civic Center, Huntsville, AL, with Frankie and the Knockouts (8:00 p.m. show)

WEDNESDAY, JUNE 23, 1982: Six Flags Over Georgia, Atlanta, GA (Two shows at 7:00 and 10:00 p.m.)

THURSDAY, JUNE 24, 1982: Engel Stadium, Chattanooga, TN, with Frankie and the Knockouts (8:00 p.m. show)
Over 11,000 fans filled Engel Stadium. David Jenkins of the *News-Free Press* reported, "The opening six-song medley got the good-natured crowd in the right frame of mind with 'Sloop John B' bringing the tempo up. And although missing Brian's usual high-end harmonies, the band . . . was able to reach out for the smooth studio-polished harmonies, especially on 'Wouldn't It Be Nice' and later 'California Girls,' that hasn't always been attained by the band on stage . . . A high energy version of 'Help Me Rhonda,' spurred by what could only be called 10,000-part harmony, and a surfing medley apparently brought the show to a close, but the band surprised once again with a three-song encore."

FRIDAY, JUNE 25, 1982: King's Dominion, Doswell, VA (Two shows at 6:00 and 10:00 p.m.)

SATURDAY, JUNE 26, 1982: Mesker Music Theatre, Evansville, IN

SUNDAY, JUNE 27, 1982: Carowinds Amusement Park, Charlotte, NC (Two shows at 3:00 and 8:00 p.m.)

SATURDAY, JULY 3, 1982: Mann Music Theatre, Philadelphia, PA
Dennis was back for the second leg of the tour, while Brian remained MIA. The group was scheduled

to appear at the Philadelphia Art Museum but bad weather forced a change to this theatre in Fairmount Park. The concert attracted over 40,000 people.

SUNDAY, JULY 4, 1982: Veil of the Prophet Fair, St. Louis, MO, with Bob Hope (4:30 p.m. show)

MONDAY, JULY 5, 1982: Winnipeg Arena, Winnipeg, MB, Canada, with the Terry Crawford Band (8:00 p.m. show)

The group's first Winnipeg appearance since 1969 was attended by 7,500. While many came for nostalgic reasons, Glen Gore-Smith of the *Winnipeg Free Press* declared that the Beach Boys showed "a new crew how vibrant its music is *now*, from the opening number to an encore played to a tidal wave of cheers that almost drowned out the group. The band set the theme with the first song, 'It's OK' . . . and piled on hit after hit, overflowing with uncontrived, endless summers and eternal youth—like 'Wouldn't It Be Nice,' 'Little Deuce Coupe,' 'I Get Around,' 'God Only Knows,' 'Do It Again,' 'California Girls,' and 'Good Vibrations.'"

TUESDAY, JULY 6, 1982: Agridome, Regina, SK, Canada, with the Terry Crawford Band (8:00 p.m. show)

WEDNESDAY, JULY 7, 1982: Northlands Coliseum, Edmonton, AB, Canada, with the Terry Crawford Band (8:00 p.m. show)

THURSDAY, JULY 8, 1982: Sportsplex, Lethbridge, AB, Canada, with the Terry Crawford Band (8:00 p.m. show)

The Beach Boys' first appearance in Lethbridge attracted a capacity crowd. Dave Obee of the *Lethbridge Herald* declared the show "the best to hit Lethbridge in years . . . The music of the Beach Boys seems just as fresh as the day it first came over a tinny transistor radio."

FRIDAY, JULY 9, 1982: Boise State University, Boise, ID, with the Greg Kihn Band (8:00 p.m. show)

SATURDAY, JULY 10, 1982: "Can Am Jam," Joe Albi Stadium, Spokane, WA, with Rail and the Greg Kihn Band (2:30 p.m. show)

This show was attended by 14,000 fans. One amusing moment occurred prior to the car medley when Mike told the crowd, "These songs are getting raggedly and old. I'll bet you don't know what I mean when I say '409.' I bet some of you think 'Little Deuce Coupe' is a fruit dessert."

TUESDAY, JULY 13, 1982: Concord Pavilion, Concord, CA, with Dr. Gonzo (8:00 p.m. show)

THURSDAY, JULY 15, TO WEDNESDAY, JULY 21, 1982: MGM Grand, Las Vegas, NV (Two shows each night)

Interviewed around this time, Carl commented that he was pleased with the band's improvement since his return. "There's a give and take without compromising the quality, which is the big thing with me. I still want to see the guys record, and there are some gigs that I would choose not to do—for instance, there's a Las Vegas thing coming up that . . . oh, yikes. But we're working on it." The "Las Vegas thing" was a weeklong residency at the MGM Grand. He later commented, "It was really difficult going down those stairs twice a night to put on the same cookie-cutter show, and it didn't take too long before the group started going to sleep again. We had to revert to some really silly stage antics to keep ourselves awake." Brian was present for the engagement, though he missed the first two nights.

SUNDAY, JULY 25, 1982: Irvine Meadows Amphitheater, Los Angeles, CA, with Glenn Super

Barry Koltnow of the *Orange County Register* praised the group for delivering "what a Beach Boys concert promises—lots of old hits. And more importantly, they delivered them as if they cared . . . Carl has always held the key to this group and when Carl is happy, which he seemed to be Sunday with this ninety-minute set, the audience can feel the excitement."

THE BEACH BOYS IN CONCERT

WEDNESDAY, AUGUST 11, 1982: La Crosse Center, La Crosse, WI (8:00 p.m. show)
The group began another month of dates. The set remained mostly oldies, but Carl explained to reporter Lynn Van Matre, "What we're doing now is new. If you keep putting new energy into something and doing it maybe a bit different that keeps it new. And you know, this tour is so darned much fun. There's no question but what we all had our disagreements last year but I really feel close to all the guys now."

Brian joined the band for the opener in La Crosse, a makeup for a show canceled the previous October. Geri Parlin of the *La Crosse Tribune* reported, "Brian joined in on a few of the famous Beach Boys harmonies, but he mainly sat on the side and plunked away at the piano, every once in a while beaming a smile towards the others in the group as if to say, 'I made them what they are today. Aren't they wonderful' . . . They are the old men of the sea and surf, gurus of harmony who can still blend their voices into a distillation of magical mergence."

THURSDAY, AUGUST 12, 1982: "Chicago-Fest," Navy Pier, Chicago, IL, with Cheap Trick
Rock fans that attended this event were faced with a difficult choice. The Beach Boys played simultaneously with Cheap Trick on separate stages on the Navy Pier. However, the *Chicago Tribune* reported both bands attracted large and satisfied crowds.

FRIDAY, AUGUST 13, 1982: Illinois State Fair, Springfield, IL (Two shows at 7:00 and 9:30 p.m.)
Close-to-capacity crowds attended both concerts. Bob Mahlburg of the *State Journal Register* noted Brian, "looking haggard and very overweight," departed after only a few songs, but reported that the "crowd danced and screamed as the Beach Boys wound their way through 'Wouldn't It Be Nice,' 'Help Me Rhonda,' 'California Girls,' and more than a dozen other classics."

SATURDAY, AUGUST 14, 1982: Wisconsin State Fair, West Allis, WI (Two shows at 3:00 and 7:00 p.m.)

SUNDAY, AUGUST 15, 1982: Cardinal Stadium, Louisville, KY, with the Epics
Brian was absent and Carl's voice was giving out, but the crowd didn't care. John Herzfeld of the *Courier Journal* reported, "They played sun and fun standards such as 'Dance, Dance, Dance,' 'Surfin' Safari,' 'Surfer Girl,' and 'California Girls.' During 'Barbara Ann' Mike Love, Al Jardine, and Carl Wilson danced together. During 'Fun, Fun, Fun,' Love leaped atop the piano to deliver his vocal."

TUESDAY, AUGUST 17, 1982: Timber Wolf Amphitheater, King's Island, OH (7:00 p.m. show)

WEDNESDAY, AUGUST 18, 1982: Mud Island Amphitheater, Memphis, TN (Two shows at 2:00 and 8:00 p.m.)
In between shows, the group visited Graceland, the former home of Elvis Presley. At that night's show, Dennis dedicated "You Are So Beautiful" to the King. John Belfuss of the *Memphis Press Scimitar* commented, "Though the Beach Boys have lost the endearing, rough garage-band edge of their early recordings, their unique harmonies and the vocals of Mike Love sound practically unchanged. And original member Carl Wilson let loose some sharp Chuck Berry riffs. The crowd especially appreciated the 'car medley' . . . the 'girls medley' . . . and the 'surfin' medley.'"

THURSDAY, AUGUST 19, 1982: Ohio State Fair, Columbus, OH (Two shows at 3:30 and 7:30 p.m.)

FRIDAY, AUGUST 20, 1982: Missouri State Fair, Sedalia, MO (Two shows)

SATURDAY, AUGUST 21, AND SUNDAY, AUGUST 22, 1982: San Destin Resort, Destin, FL
These shows in the Florida panhandle drew 12,000 fans.

TUESDAY, AUGUST 24, 1982: Astrodome, Houston, TX
The group played after an Astros game.

WEDNESDAY, AUGUST 25, 1982: North Carolina State Fair, Asheville, NC

THURSDAY, AUGUST 26, 1982: State Fairgrounds, Indianapolis, IN (Two shows at 7:00 and 9:30 p.m.)

The Beach Boys arrived forty-five minutes late for the first of two shows and had to combat a faulty sound system. Jill Warren of the *Indianapolis Star* commented that both the audience and band seemed bored, especially "a rotund" Brian (whom she misidentified as Dennis), "who was clearly more interested in keeping a fresh cigarette going than in entertaining the audience."

FRIDAY, AUGUST 27, 1982: Michigan State Fair, Detroit, MI (Two shows at 3:30 and 8:30 p.m.)

SATURDAY, AUGUST 28, 1982: Minnesota State Fair, St. Paul, MN (Two shows at 6:00 and 9:00 p.m.)

SUNDAY, AUGUST 29, 1982: Lansdowne Park, Ottawa, ON, Canada, with Minglewood Band (7:30 p.m. show)

MONDAY, AUGUST 30, 1982: J.W. Little Stadium, London, ON, Canada, with Del Shannon and John Cougar

The group's performance was overshadowed by drama prior to their set. John Cougar was booked to play before them and he became angry when promoters insisted he wrap up early. He told the press, "Before I got on the bill, the Beach Boys had sold 2,000 tickets. So here are the kids paying fifteen dollars a ticket to see me play thirty-five minutes." He launched into an onstage tirade against the promoters and threw the rented instruments provided for him into the audience, before kicking in one of the Beach Boys' monitors.

Carl Wilson performing in 1982. Courtesy of Ben Valley

TUESDAY, AUGUST 31, 1982: NY State Fairgrounds, Syracuse, NY, with the Rockets

Dennis was absent for the rest of the tour. The group put out a statement that he'd returned home for the delivery of his first child with new wife Shawn. However, they'd used the same explanation for his absence in June.

Reviewers were unanimous in their praise for the group. Dale Kasler of the *Syracuse Herald Journal* declared the show "about a hundred times better than the sloppy concert they gave here a year ago," while John Bonfatti of the *Post Standard* called it "everything last year's show wasn't: tight, error-free and very entertaining . . . Carl Wilson's splitting of the lead vocal chores with Love was a double treat in that it showcased Wilson's supple baritone and kept Love from straining too much from overwork . . . Fortunately Brian, who looked lost on the stage and is now merely a shell of his former self, was limited to singing a couple of verses of 'Sloop John B.'"

WEDNESDAY, SEPTEMBER 1, 1982: SPAC, Saratoga, NY

FRIDAY, SEPTEMBER 3, 1982: CNE Grandstand, Toronto, ON, Canada, with Minglewood Band (8:30 p.m. show)

Mike played an afternoon solo show in Massachusetts and then traveled to Toronto to appear with the group. Brian was present but according to Liam Lacey of the *Globe and Mail*, other than singing one verse of "Sloop John B" he spent the night "on the side of the stage, occasionally playing, more often just watching or banging his hands to the music, less a musical force than an exhibit."

SATURDAY, SEPTEMBER 4, 1982: Canfield Fair, Canfield, OH

SUNDAY, SEPTEMBER 5, 1982: Allentown Fair, Allentown, PA (Two shows at 3:00 and 8:00 p.m.)

MONDAY, SEPTEMBER 6, 1982: Cleveland Stadium, Cleveland, OH (5:00 p.m. show)

This concert took place after an Indians game attended by 40,000. Brian was absent.

THE BEACH BOYS IN CONCERT

WEDNESDAY, SEPTEMBER 8, AND THURSDAY, SEPTEMBER 9, 1982: Resorts International Casino, Atlantic City, NJ (Two shows a night at 7:30 and 11:00 p.m.)

The contract for this engagement reveals that the group was promised $40,000 versus ninety percent of the gross, whichever was greater. As seating capacity was 1,650 and the group played four shows, they had the potential to make far more than $40,000. However, expenses were high. The group needed seven one-bedroom suites and sixteen rooms in the hotel to accommodate them.

FRIDAY, SEPTEMBER 10, 1982: Kansas State Fair, Hutchinson, KS (Two shows at 6:00 and 8:30 p.m.)

The Beach Boys concerts in Hutchinson were special for the Wilsons, since their father's family had lived there for generations. Charles Wilson, brother of their grandfather Buddy, visited Carl backstage. Brian was present for the concert but didn't take part in the meeting.

SATURDAY, SEPTEMBER 11, 1982: Nebraska State Fair, Lincoln, NE (Two shows at 5:30 and 8:30 p.m.)

Brian missed both state fair shows.

SUNDAY, SEPTEMBER 12, 1982: Red Rocks Amphitheater, Morrison, CO

SATURDAY, SEPTEMBER 18, 1982: Candlestick Park, San Francisco, CA

SUNDAY, SEPTEMBER 19, 1982: Hollywood Bowl, Los Angeles, CA (7:30 p.m. show)

MONDAY, SEPTEMBER 20, 1982: Puyallup Fair, Puyallup, WA (Two shows at 5:00 and 8:00 p.m.)

WEDNESDAY, OCTOBER 6, 1982: Ventura County Fair, Ventura, CA (8:00 p.m. show)

SUNDAY, NOVEMBER 7, 1982: Arizona State Fair, Phoenix, AZ (7:00 p.m. show)

Brian was absent, having been "fired." He didn't play another show until February 1983.

FRIDAY, NOVEMBER 19, AND SATURDAY, NOVEMBER 20, 1982: Billy Bob's Texas, Fort Worth, TX, with the Juke Jumpers (Friday) and Turnabout (Saturday) (One show a night at 8:00 p.m.)

Joining the group on tour were Jeff Foskett, Mike Kowalski, Ed Carter, Mike Meros and, for the first time since 1977, Billy Hinsche. He recalled that fitting back in took time, since "I returned to a band of musicians I didn't know, including Jeff Foskett, Adrian Baker, and Mike Meros whom had all been recruited during my absence from the group . . . " Hinsche remained with the band until 1996.

SUNDAY, NOVEMBER 21, 1982: Centrum, Worcester, MA, with Gary U.S. Bonds

MONDAY, NOVEMBER 22, 1982: Civic Center, Hartford, CT, with Gary U.S. Bonds

FRIDAY, NOVEMBER 26, 1982: Jamaica Music Festival, Bob Marley Entertainment Center, Montego Bay, Jamaica, with Aretha Franklin, Rita Marley, the English Beat, the Clash, the Grateful Dead, Skeeter Davis, Black Uhuru, Jimmy Cliff, Gladys Knight and the Pips, the B-52s, Joe Jackson, Stacy Lattishaw, Squeeze, and Toots and the Maytals

The Beach Boys played on the second night of this three-day music festival in Montego Bay. The group had flown to Jamaica on Tuesday but despite ample rehearsal, their performance was underwhelming due to unforeseen circumstances. Billy Hinsche recalled, "The hotel the Beach Boys stayed at in Jamaica was located quite a great distance from the venue, so it took a long time to drive there. Once we got on site, there was an element of disorganization and we were not able to take the stage until something like 3:00 a.m.—it was tough to stay alert and focused since we were all half-asleep."

MONDAY, DECEMBER 27, 1982, TO SUNDAY, JANUARY 2, 1983: Harrah's Tahoe, Stateline, NV, with Carol Leifer

1983

NINETEEN EIGHTY-THREE was ultimately a year of triumph and tragedy for the Beach Boys. It began as another lost year for the group's creative process. While there was nothing new from the Beach Boys record-wise, Carl and Mike each released solo product. Carl's second LP *Youngblood* was recorded in spring 1982 under the tutelage of guitarist Jeff Baxter. Carl met Baxter in 1974 when the Beach Boys shared a bill with Steely Dan and the two became friends. The LP included the upbeat dance-pop of "What You Do to Me" and a cover of John Fogerty's "Rockin' All over the World," both of which Carl performed during Beach Boys shows. He also played a solo tour in support of *Youngblood* in June. Mike countered with a cassette-only release called *Rock 'N' Roll City* in tandem with Dean Torrence. Mike and Dean performed "My Boyfriend's Back" and Mike sang "The Locomotion." The tape was only available at Radio Shack. It sold a respectable 100,000 copies and Mike followed it up with a seasonal cassette titled *Christmas Party*.

The big story of early 1983 was the remarkable transformation of Brian. In late 1982, when he arrived in Hawaii to begin treatments with Dr. Landy, he weighed 320 lbs. By mid-February he'd kicked drugs and had lost sixty pounds. The Beach Boys were thrilled and expressed confidence that Brian's

CONCERTS PLAYED IN
1983

improved health would lead to more participation. However, his involvement with Landy ultimately pulled him further away from the group. Brian's treatment involved "Twenty-Four-Hour Therapy," in which Dr. Landy had total control over the patient and every aspect of his life. Landy told a reporter from the *Milwaukee Journal*, "I'm the good father. I'm re-parenting the way he perceives life. Children are born and are dependent. They know nothing. And you teach them. It's the same with him. That's why it's re-parenting." He saw his mission to re-educate Brian about everything, from table manners to driving. Brian played only a handful of Beach Boys concerts in 1983.

The group's fortunes took an unexpected turn when U.S. Secretary of the Interior James Watt announced he was banning them from playing at the Washington Monument on July 4 because rock bands attracted "the wrong element." Watt ludicrously referred to the group as "hard rock" and argued many people that attended their shows were drug and alcohol abusers. Watt opted for "patriotic, family-based entertainment" to be provided by singer Wayne Newton and the U.S. Army Blues Band. The Beach Boys held a press conference to denounce the decision. Al commented, "It's really none of his business. You can't legislate morality." Carl told the press, "Beach Boys music represents joy of life and joy of living. I don't think it [Watt's judgement] applies to us."

As the story gathered momentum, President Reagan and members of his cabinet

THURSDAY, FEBRUARY 17, 1983: Stampede Corral, Calgary, AB, Canada (7:30 p.m. show)

FRIDAY, FEBRUARY 18, 1983: Memorial Arena, Victoria, BC, Canada (8:00 p.m. show)

SATURDAY, FEBRUARY 19, 1983: Paramount Theatre, Portland, OR (Two shows at 7:00 and 10:00 p.m.)
John Wendeborn of the *Oregonian* found little to be enthusiastic about at the first of two Portland shows. He commented, "Hearing those dozens of oldies for the umpteenth time wasn't really that much fun, and the band (ten musicians) looked as close to bored as the guy in the balcony loge with his kids who kept nodding off in the first thirty minutes . . . Of course the Boys perked up and managed to do a concert of the music the folks paid to hear: nostalgia."

SUNDAY, FEBRUARY 20, 1983: University of Oregon, Eugene, OR (Canceled)

TUESDAY, FEBRUARY 22, 1983: Sullivan Sports Arena, Anchorage, AK
Although they'd planned to play there in 1968, this concert marked the group's first Alaskan appearance. Peter Porco of the *Anchorage Daily News* declared, "The Beach Boys performed as expected. For more than a decade, this band of perennial youthful and fun loving musicians has been locked into a typical concert repertoire. It was no different Tuesday night."

FRIDAY, FEBRUARY 25, 1983: NBC Arena, Honolulu, HI (8:00 p.m. show)
The Hawaii shows were overshadowed by the media circus surrounding Brian. He remained under Landy's care, but played the Hawaii dates. He took part in band rehearsals on Thursday and Bruce told the press that Brian "was the sharpest I've seen him in a long time." At the Honolulu show, Brian, dressed in a Hawaiian shirt, played piano and took his old leads on "Sloop John B" and "Surfer Girl."

SUNDAY, FEBRUARY 27, 1983: Maui Football Stadium, Maui, HI (3:00 p.m. show)
Brian played this show. However, he didn't take part in March or April dates.

SUNDAY, MARCH 6, 1983: Sun Devil Stadium, Tempe, AZ (1:00 p.m. show)
The group, including Dennis, played prior to an Arizona Wranglers football game.

FRIDAY, MARCH 25, 1983: Metro Centre, Rockford, IL, with Big Twist and the Mellow Fellows (8:00 p.m. show)
This show drew 8,400 fans. Mike Meros, Billy Hinsche, Jeff Foskett, Ed Carter, and Mike Kowalski accompanied the group on their sixteen-day tour. There were a few new tunes in the set: Mike performed John Lennon's "Imagine" and Carl sang two numbers from *Youngblood*. He told a reporter, "The guys are doing a good job on the tunes. Michael has gotten a kick out of 'What You Do to Me,' the single, because I do it with a hand mike and that's usually his trip."

SATURDAY, MARCH 26, 1983: Palace Theatre, Louisville, KY (Two shows at 7:00 and 10:30 p.m.)
Near-capacity crowds turned out in Louisville. Michael Quinlan of the *Journal-Courier* reported, "There were a few lulls, several songs that didn't jell, and a couple of times when Dennis Wilson, who was chugging beer with abandon, played too loud. But the pure 'Fun, Fun, Fun' of the last half of the show made up for all the miscues."

SUNDAY, MARCH 27, 1983: UD Arena, University of Dayton, Dayton, OH (7:30 p.m. show)

TUESDAY, MARCH 29, 1983: Augusta Richmond County Civic Center, Augusta, GA, with La Roux

1983

This show was marred by Dennis' behavior. He continually wandered offstage, only occasionally taking the drums. However, Mike Kowalski picked up the slack.

WEDNESDAY, MARCH 30, 1983: West Mississippi Coliseum, Jackson, MS, with Windows (7:30 p.m. show)
This was a benefit for DREAM and its anti-drug abuse programs.

THURSDAY, MARCH 31, 1983: Florida State University, Tallahassee, FL

FRIDAY, APRIL 1, 1983: Bayfront Center Arena, St. Petersburg, FL, with Pizazz
The Beach Boys met with a tepid response for the first half of this concert. Drew Rashbaum of the Times argued the fault lay with the band, which performed the two opening medleys as if they were "playing by rote." He commented, "The most satisfying moments came when rich-voiced guitarist Carl Wilson took over lead vocals from Mike Love. While performing his new solo single 'What You Do to Me,' however, Wilson was drowned out by the musical accompaniment."

SATURDAY, APRIL 2, 1983: Memorial Stadium, Daytona Beach, FL
Over 15,000 spring breakers came out for this afternoon show.

SUNDAY, APRIL 3, 1983: Sunrise Musical Theater, Sunrise, FL (Two shows at 7:00 and 10:30 p.m.)

TUESDAY, APRIL 5, 1983: Metro Center, Halifax, NS, Canada, with Luba (8:00 p.m. show)

WEDNESDAY, APRIL 6, 1983: Coliseum, Moncton, NB, Canada, with the Nylons (8:00 p.m. show)
While in Moncton, James Watt's announcement hit the press and the group held a news conference before the show to respond.

THURSDAY, APRIL 7, 1983: University of New Brunswick, Fredericton, NB, Canada, with the Nylons (8:00 p.m. show)
The Beach Boys' appearance in Fredericton attracted a large, excited crowd. Bruce Oliver of the *Daily Gleaner* reported, "The band showed a lot of spirit and did not seem to be at all bored with their material. They were well rehearsed and in complete control as they presented hit after hit. Front man Mike Love was personable and entertaining as he led the band. All the musicians had a few golden moments during the set, with drummer Dennis Wilson showing particular verve and taste."

FRIDAY, APRIL 8, 1983: Brendan Byrne Arena, East Rutherford, NJ, with the Greg Kihn Band
Dean Torrence and Billy Joel made surprise appearances at this show.

SATURDAY, APRIL 9, 1983: Stanley Theater, Pittsburgh, PA (Two shows at 7:30 and 10:00 p.m.)

SATURDAY, MAY 7, 1983: County Bowl, Santa Barbara, CA, with Pablo Cruise (2:00 p.m. show)
This show marked Brian's first appearance with the group since Hawaii. Seated behind a white piano, he looked slimmer than he had in years and seemed to enjoy himself. However, the rest of the band hadn't played in a month and Tom Bolton of the *Santa Barbara News-Press* reported, "Flaws in the performance included a miscue on the words to 'Sloop John B,' sloppy harmonies on 'Wouldn't It Be Nice,' and a sluggish version of 'Surfer Girl' that was saved only by the enthusiastic vocal support of the crowd. Drummer Dennis Wilson—shirtless and scruffy-looking—spent the afternoon distracting his colleagues and crowd. He added nothing to the day."

SUNDAY, MAY 8, 1983: Jack Murphy Stadium, San Diego, CA
The group took the stage after a Padres game. In the wake of James Watt's comments, fans expressed solidarity with the band. One audience member told Joe Gandelman of the *San Diego Union*, "Contrary to what he [James Watt] thinks, the Beach Boys are not a hard rock group. They're very mellow. They represent most of California—the sun and the surf."

made it clear that they didn't share Watt's views. Deputy Chief of Staff Michael Deaver announced, "There are a lot of us who think they are a national institution. Anybody that thinks that the Beach Boys are hard rock must think Mantovani plays jazz." First

> "The Beach Boys haven't had so much media attention since our first trip to England. The press followed us all the way to New Brunswick to get our comments and then Mrs. Reagan called us there to apologize."

Lady Nancy Reagan declared she was a Beach Boys fan, as did Vice President George Bush. In front of the national press, the President presented Watt with a plaster foot with a hole in it to teasingly admonish him for shooting himself in the foot. Watt apologized and, while stating it was too late to reschedule the entertainment for that year, commented, "The President is a friend of the Beach Boys and likes them and I'm sure when I get to meet them, I'll like them." Interestingly, the Beach Boys' connection to Ronald and Nancy Reagan began a decade earlier when, while Reagan was Governor of California, Dennis had a romantic relationship with their daughter Patti.

Ultimately, the July 4

"That's what we had to tell Dennis from time to time. Take some time off and get yourself together. But he never did."

—Mike Love

controversy was a godsend for the group. The incident catapulted them back into the spotlight. As Carl commented to a reporter from the *Philadelphia Daily News*, the outcry against Watt did "great things for our spirit. The Beach Boys haven't had so much media attention since our first trip to England. The press followed us all the way to New Brunswick to get our comments and then Mrs. Reagan called us there to apologize. A DJ locked himself into a radio station

THE BEACH BOYS IN CONCERT

SATURDAY, MAY 21, 1983: SARA Park, Lake Havasu, AZ, with Charlie Daniels, Dave Mason, and Greg Allman

SUNDAY, MAY 22, 1983: Kingdome, Seattle, WA
This show took place after a 1:30 p.m. Mariners game. It featured all six Beach Boys and was filmed for the Jumbotron screens. It was a fun, if sloppy, show, though it's hard to watch today without wincing at Dennis's physical deterioration. Nevertheless, even if he looked terrible, Dennis pounded the drums with gusto. Brian, dressed in a yellow space-needle T-shirt and blue jeans, was more involved than he'd been in years, singing "Sloop John B" and dancing onstage (awkwardly) to "Runaway."

FRIDAY, MAY 27, TO SUNDAY, MAY 29, 1983: Pine Knob Music Theater, Clarkston, MI (One show each night at 7:30 p.m.)
These were the opening shows of a twenty-four-day tour. Brian played only a few dates, but Dennis was present for most.

TUESDAY, MAY 31, 1983: Mid South Fairgrounds, Memphis, TN, with Firefall and Rick Christian

WEDNESDAY, JUNE 1, 1983: Norfolk Scope, Norfolk, VA, with Firefall (8:00 p.m. show)
This show was attended by 6,000 fans. Dennis was absent "with the flu," but Eric Feber of the *Virginian-Pilot* still declared the show "much better than their recent Tidewater appearance. Sure their rock 'n' roll is totally anemic, but those white-boy high vocal harmonies came through like shootin'-a-curl."

THURSDAY, JUNE 2, 1983: Colt State Park, Bristol, RI

FRIDAY, JUNE 3, 1983: Six Flags, Jackson, NJ

SATURDAY, JUNE 4, 1983: University of Toledo, Toledo, OH, with Firefall

SUNDAY, JUNE 5, 1983: Poplar Creek Music Theatre, Hoffman Estates, IL, with Firefall
Despite lousy weather, the Beach Boys played to over 15,000 fans.

TUESDAY, JUNE 7, 1983: Bicentennial Center, Salina, KS, with Firefall (8:00 p.m. show)

WEDNESDAY, JUNE 8, 1983: Starlight Theatre, Kansas City, MO, with Firefall (8:00 p.m. show)

THURSDAY, JUNE 9, 1983: Five Seasons Center, Cedar Rapids, IA, with Firefall
Roxanne Mueller of the *Cedar Rapids Gazette* reported, "While the performance as a whole was upbeat and lively, there were occasional signs of boredom, and worse, injections of a Las Vegas slickness that made your jaw drop. Carl Wilson's turn at 'What You Do to Me' lacked only kisses blown to the audience at the end. Where it counted most, though, the show moved to the best of the Beach Boys."

FRIDAY, JUNE 10, 1983: Memorial Stadium, Charlotte, NC (9:30 p.m. show)
The group performed after a Carolina Lightnin' game.

SATURDAY, JUNE 11, 1983: Lanierland Music Park, Cummings, GA (Two shows at 7:30 and 10:30 p.m.)

SUNDAY, JUNE 12, 1983: RFK Stadium, Washington, DC, and South Lawn, White House, Washington, DC
This Beach Boys concert, after a soccer game, was attended by 50,000 people. Barbara Feinman of the *Washington Post* reported that they sounded better than they had in years. She credited the improvement to the fact that all three Wilsons were present: "A healthier, livelier Brian Wilson . . . contributed more to the show than he had in the past. Drummer Dennis Wilson gave the music a kick it had been lacking. Carl Wilson led the tightly packed harmony vocals, which once

again sounded well rehearsed and accordingly gorgeous."

The afternoon concert at RFK was overshadowed by the band's second gig that day. The group performed a fundraiser on behalf of Special Olympics on the south lawn of the White House. Warner Brothers, who premiered their new film *Superman III* as part of the entertainment, sponsored the event. However, in light of the controversy with James Watt, media attention was focused on the Beach Boys. Watt abstained from attending rather than deal with an awkward encounter. However, President Reagan and first lady Nancy Reagan made their feelings clear by dancing along to the music. At the end of the show, the 1,000 guests in attendance shouted for more. President Reagan whispered conspiratorially with Mike and told the crowd, "You know, this is a democracy. Therefore, the Beach Boys have said they'll do another number or two if you want." The crowd applauded and danced to the encores. Reagan then thanked the band for coming and quipped, "We were looking forward to seeing them on the Fourth of July. I'm glad they got here earlier." Later, the group helped George Bush celebrate his fifty-ninth birthday at a party in his honor.

This June 3, 1983, press conference in New York announcing the group's Fourth of July show in Atlantic City revealed a badly deteriorating Dennis (top center). Photo: Chuck Pulin.com

TUESDAY, JUNE 14, 1983: Mann Music Center, Philadelphia, PA, with Firefall (8:00 p.m. show)

WEDNESDAY, JUNE 15, 1983: Broome County Veteran's Memorial, Binghamton, NY, with Firefall (8:00 p.m. show)
Mike came down with strep throat and missed all the remaining June dates. Only four Beach Boys were present: Carl, Dennis, Bruce, and Al. But David Maney of the *Binghamton Press* reported the audience didn't seem to mind Mike's absence, though he noted that as a result, "for a good deal of the show the band sounded weak, especially in the vocal department." Jeff Foskett handled most of Mike's leads.

THURSDAY, JUNE 16, 1983: Tullio Convention Center, Erie, PA, with Firefall (8:00 p.m. show)
Pat Howard of the *Erie Times* reported, "From the opener 'California Girls,' to encores including 'Good Vibrations' and 'Barbara Ann,' the rest of the Beach Boys captivated the audience. People of all ages knew the words to the songs and didn't hesitate to sing along. The songs, some of them twenty years old, sounded bouncy and fresh."

FRIDAY, JUNE 17, 1983: Timber Wolf Amphitheater, King's Island, OH, with Firefall

SATURDAY, JUNE 18, 1983: Blossom Music Center, Cuyahoga Falls, OH, with Firefall
Dennis didn't appear at this show, but Al's son Matt came out to sing "Runaway."

SUNDAY, JUNE 19, 1983: SPAC, Saratoga Springs, NY, with Firefall (8:15 p.m. show)

SATURDAY, JULY 2, 1983: Summerfest, Milwaukee, WI, with the Nylons (8:00 p.m. show)
The group launched the second leg of their tour. Joining them were Mike Meros, Billy Hinsche, Jeff Foskett, Ed Carter, Mike Kowalski, and (for the first time since 1981) Bobby Figueroa. Brian was also present and remained on the road for the rest of the tour.

in Washington, DC, as a protest." The public rallied to the Beach Boys' defense in an unexpectedly passionate way. Although the group ultimately spent the Fourth of July performing in Atlantic City, they were invited to the White House to visit the President and entertained at Vice President's Bush's birthday party. The whole matter became a great triumph in the Beach Boys saga. From this time forward, the Beach Boys were forever known as "America's Band."

The great tragedy of 1983 was the death of

"He was just so sweet, but he looked like somebody's grandpa. And then he said, 'I'm going to go rest up.' He went back in the trailer and fell asleep and the rest of the band came out and did the show. And about six or eight songs into the show, here comes Dennis. He comes walking onstage, just in these shorts like he was when we saw him backstage! And he couldn't even talk because of his voice (problems) but he still stole the show from

---

THE BEACH BOYS IN CONCERT

SUNDAY, JULY 3, 1983: "Veil of the Prophet Fair," Busch Stadium, St. Louis, MO, with Sheriff, Foghat, and the Charlie Daniels Band

MONDAY, JULY 4, 1983: Boardwalk, Atlantic City, NJ (8:00 p.m. show)
An audience of 200,000 attended the band's most anticipated concert of the year. The group played on a ten-foot-high stage set up between the boardwalk and the water's edge. The set consisted of "California Girls/I Can Hear Music/Sloop John B/Darlin'/Dance, Dance, Dance/ Wouldn't It Be Nice" (medley), "You're So Good to Me," "The Warmth of the Sun," "Imagine," "God Only Knows," "What You Do to Me," "409/Shut Down/The Little Old Lady from Pasadena/Little Deuce Coupe/I Get Around" (medley), "Runaway," "Surfer Girl," "Come Go with Me," "Rockin' All Over the World," "Help Me Rhonda," "Rock and Roll Music," "Surfin' Safari/Surf City/Surfin' USA" (medley), "Good Vibrations," "Barbara Ann," and "Fun, Fun, Fun."
    Making fun of the circumstances that led to them playing Atlantic City instead of Washington, DC, Mike announced to the crowd, "It's good to see not everyone went to the Wayne Newton show!" The full group was in attendance, including Brian and Dennis, who thrashed away on drums and hoarsely sang a sad version of "You Are So Beautiful."

THURSDAY, JULY 7, 1983: Jones Beach, Wantaugh, NY (8:00 p.m. show)

FRIDAY, JULY 8, 1983: Pier 44, New York, NY (7:30 p.m. show)
In between Jones Beach shows, the group played on the water in Manhattan. Stephen Holden of the *New York Times* reported that "though the group's close three- and four-part harmonies were far from smooth, they were seldom gratingly out of tune."

SATURDAY, JULY 9, 1983: Jones Beach, Wantaugh, NY (8:00 p.m. show)
Brian Donlon of the *Gannett Westchester* papers reported, "the California-based band proved once again why they are masters of four-part harmony and America's premiere party band with rousing renditions of their classic tunes: 'Sloop John B,' 'California Girls,' 'I Get Around,' and 'Good Vibrations' . . . Brian Wilson sat at the keyboards and joined in on vocals much to the joy of the audience."

SUNDAY, JULY 10, 1983: Mt. Cranmore Stadium, North Conway, NH

SATURDAY, JULY 16, 1983: Candlestick Park, San Francisco, CA
The group played after a Giants game. Brian was present, but missed the remaining July shows.

SUNDAY, JULY 17, 1983: Plateau Pavilion Site, Chico, CA, with America (6:00 p.m. show)

WEDNESDAY, JULY 20, 1983: B.C. Place Stadium, Vancouver, BC, Canada
The show followed a Vancouver Whitecaps' game. Burton Cummings of the Guess Who came out during the encore for "Barbara Ann" and "Fun, Fun, Fun." Marke Andrews of the *Vancouver Sun* reported, "Mike Love and Carl Wilson and the rest of the middle-aged California sextet . . . did the big hits . . . Cars, girls, surf and sand, that's the world of the Beach Boys. No wonder I felt some trepidation when Mike Love began singing John Lennon's 'Imagine' . . . but the group did the song justice. Unfortunately the sound did not do the Beach Boys justice . . . What reached the folks in the blue seats was a muddy aural porridge."

FRIDAY, JULY 22, 1983: Events Center, Casper, WY (8:00 p.m. show)
This concert marked the Beach Boys' first appearance in Wyoming.

SATURDAY, JULY 23, 1983: North Dakota State Fair, Minot, ND (Two shows at 7:00 and 9:30 p.m.)

SUNDAY, JULY 24, 1983: Mile High Stadium, Denver, CO
The group played after a Denver Bears game.

1983

FRIDAY, JULY 29, AND SATURDAY, JULY 30, 1983: "Starfest," Park Central, Dallas, TX, with the Planets (One show each night at 8:15 p.m.)

WEDNESDAY, AUGUST 3, 1983: Pacific Amphitheatre, Costa Mesa, CA, with Jack Mack and the Heart Attack (8:00 p.m. show)
This show was filmed and portions were used in the 1985 film *The Beach Boys: American Band*. It's the last filmed record of the Beach Boys with Dennis. He sang a painfully raspy version of "You Are So Beautiful," which he dedicated to Brian and Eugene Landy. For the 15,000 in attendance, it was Brian's return that captured most of the attention. He joined the group for opener "California Girls," and remained onstage the rest of the night. Brian even played a solo version of a new song called "It's Just a Matter of Time." However, he still exhibited eccentric behavior. Randy Lewis of the *Los Angeles Times* reported that during "Wouldn't It Be Nice," Brian "ripped off his shirt and cavorted bare-chested around the stage. At the end of the song, he quickly re-donned his shirt and calmly sat back down at the electric piano he played most of the night. In other songs he abruptly walked off and wandered behind the band at the rear of the stage."

THURSDAY, AUGUST 4, 1983: "Napa Town and Country Fair," Napa, CA (Two shows at 6:30 and 9:00 p.m.)
Dennis was present for this show, but Brian was absent. Panyiotis Bagdanos, a regular contributor to *Beach Boys Stomp* fanzine, was backstage. He recalled, "Dennis was sleeping but he got up and came out, just in a pair of shorts that looked wrinkled and old. He looked so tired. He was real puffy and hyper and looked like he'd got hit by a bus. But he was such sweet man! I had that old (concert) program from 1964, the aqua-colored one. And he goes 'Oh Wow! My dad put that together for us way back in 1964. Wow, I haven't seen this in years!' And he autographed it for me. He was just so sweet, but he looked like somebody's grandpa. And then he said, 'I'm going to go rest up.' He went back in the trailer and fell asleep and the rest of the band came out and did the show. And about six or eight songs into the show, here comes Dennis. He comes walking onstage, just in these shorts like he was when we saw him backstage! And he couldn't even talk because of his voice (problems) but he still stole the show from everybody else! But I could clearly see that he was just a thorn in the side of the band."

FRIDAY, AUGUST 5, 1983: Park West, Salt Lake City, UT (7:00 p.m. show)
The group played outdoors before thousands of fans. Jo-Ann Wong of the *Deseret News* reported, "Love and Johnston were joined by guitarist Al Jardine, the Wilson brothers, Dennis on drums and Carl. Carl, who has several independent projects to his credit, contributed 'What You Do to Me' from his *Youngblood* album. With his adventuresome attitude, Carl added some enjoyable and necessary new material to the Beach Boys show."

SATURDAY, AUGUST 6, 1983: Caesars Palace, Las Vegas, NV (10:00 p.m. show)

SUNDAY, AUGUST 7, 1983: San Luis Obispo County Mid-State Fair, Paso Robles, CA (Two shows)

FRIDAY, AUGUST 12, 1983: Wisconsin State Fair, West Allis, WI
Brian and Dennis were absent from this show and the remaining dates of the tour. Jim Higgins of the *Milwaukee Sentinel* complained that the group sounded sluggish and pointedly asked "why a group with such a rich legacy played so much obvious filler. Lackluster covers of 'Rockin' All over the World,' Del Shannon's 'Runaway,' and Chuck Berry's 'Rock and Roll Music' were time extenders and little more."

SATURDAY, AUGUST 13, 1983: "Chicago Fest VI," Soldier Field, Chicago, IL

Dennis singing "You Are So Beautiful" for one of the last few times at Costa Mesa on **August 3, 1983.** Courtesy of Ben Valley

everybody else! But I could clearly see that he was just a thorn in the side of the band."

SUNDAY, AUGUST 14, 1983: Hermitage Landing, Nashville, TN (Afternoon) and Giants Stadium, East Rutherford, NJ (Post-game)

MONDAY, AUGUST 15, AND TUESDAY, AUGUST 16, 1983: Ohio State Fair, Columbus, OH (Two shows each day at 3:30 and 8:00 p.m.)
When the group showed up in their van at 3:30 p.m. for their Monday appearance at the fair, the security guard at the gate didn't recognize them and refused to let them in until they paid the $4.00 admission price. The Beach Boys said it was the first time they ever had to pay to get into their own show!

WEDNESDAY, AUGUST 17, 1983: Indiana State Fair, Indianapolis, IN (Two shows at 7:00 and 9:30 p.m.)
Zach Dunkin of the *Indianapolis News* reported that after a few years of substandard shows the band was back in fine form. Carl credited the improvement to rehearsal. He told Dunkin, "You would think that by rehearsing the same tunes they would absolutely drive you mad. But it works the opposite way. If you don't rehearse you go out and do them and they'll run you into the ground."

THURSDAY, AUGUST 18, 1983: Auditorium, Sioux City, IA, with Bitter Sweet (8:00 p.m. show)

FRIDAY, AUGUST 19, 1983: Mississippi Valley Fairgrounds, Davenport, IA

SATURDAY, AUGUST 20, 1983: Illinois State Fair, Springfield, IL (8:00 p.m. show)
Bob Mahlburg of the *Journal Register* reported, "The group opened with 'California Girls' and 'I Can Hear Music' and wound their way through nearly two dozen other vintage hits before returning for their killer standard encore set of 'Good Vibrations,' 'Barbara Ann,' and 'Fun, Fun, Fun.' Other highlights included a nice remake of the Del Shannon hit 'Runaway' and 'Surf City.'"

SUNDAY, AUGUST 21, 1983: CNE Grandstand, Toronto, ON, Canada (8:00 p.m. show)

TUESDAY, AUGUST 23, 1983: Central Canada Exhibition, Lansdowne Park, Ottawa, ON, Canada (7:30 p.m. show)
Despite a small turnout, Bill Provick of the *Ottawa Citizen* commented, "This is the best I've seen the Beach Boys play in a good many years. Minus Brian and Dennis Wilson, the band was surprisingly tight, displaying great energy and efficiency in cranking out a delightfully crisp and clean sound. Even the trademark vocal harmony was more than a mere approximation of past greatness."

THURSDAY, AUGUST 25, 1983: Windsor Stadium, Windsor, ON, Canada
A power outage threatened to prevent the show and the opening acts were canceled. However, the problem was fixed in time for the group to take the stage.

FRIDAY, AUGUST 26, 1983: Swan Valley High School, Saginaw, MI

SATURDAY, AUGUST 27, 1983: Holiday Star Theater, Merrillville, IN (Two shows at 7:00 and 10:30 p.m.)
Wryly commenting on the Watt controversy, Chris Isidore of the *Gary Post Tribune* noted, "The Beach Boys classic hits, like 'Help Me Rhonda' and '409,' prompted even the older members of the crowd into such 'undesirable' behavior as clapping, tossing a four-foot beach ball, and dancing in the aisles."

SUNDAY, AUGUST 28, 1983: Orange County Fairgrounds, Middletown, NY, with the John Hall Band (5:30 p.m. show)

TUESDAY, AUGUST 30, 1983: Du Quoin Fair, Du Quoin, IL (Two shows at 6:30 and 9:00 p.m.)

WEDNESDAY, AUGUST 31, 1983: Minnesota State Fair, St. Paul, MN (Two shows at 6:00 and 9:00 p.m.)

Ian Rusten Collection

Dennis. He had become an erratic presence at concerts. When he showed up, it was often depressing for fans. The sex symbol of the group had worn out his body from years of substance abuse, and by 1983 he looked older than his thirty-nine years. His once soulful voice had deteriorated into a pathetic rasp. The Beach Boys were extremely concerned about his health, but felt powerless to do anything. Dennis couldn't be manipulated into getting well like Brian. No one could control Dennis—especially Dennis. Mike told a reporter in 1984, "It was a stress on the whole group. Of course we had a difference of opinion. It's like, if you're a corporation,

THURSDAY, SEPTEMBER 1, 1983: Boston Common, Boston, MA (8:00 p.m. show)

FRIDAY, SEPTEMBER 2, 1983: NY State Fairgrounds, Syracuse, NY (8:00 p.m. show)
Russ Donahue of the *Post Standard* commented, "Friday night's show was long on imagination, full of rock 'n' roll but lacking the vocal spark that once made such a difference on the radio . . . Fortunately Carl Wilson sang most of the ballads and slower numbers. 'God Only Knows' proved how much of a savior he really is to the band. Of the original members he is the only one whose voice has maintained any of its original ability." Penny Sori of the *Syracuse Herald Journal* reported Dennis wasn't present because he was "recovering from minor surgery."

SATURDAY, SEPTEMBER 3, 1983: State Fair, Allentown, PA (Two shows at 3:00 and 8:00 p.m.)
These shows took place on Al's birthday and Bruce dedicated "Disney Girls" to him. Prior to playing it, he commented, "I think it's really great a guy can be in a band twenty-one years and grow up not being a drug addict in rock 'n' roll or an alcoholic." Mike replied, "We can't all be Wilsons!" How Carl, the only Wilson present, felt about that remark is not recorded.

SUNDAY, SEPTEMBER 4, 1983: Garden State Arts Center, Holmdel, NJ

MONDAY, SEPTEMBER 5, 1983: "River Fest," Harrisburg, PA

TUESDAY, SEPTEMBER 6, 1983: Bowman Field, Williamsport, PA

FRIDAY, SEPTEMBER 16, 1983: National Cattle Congress, Waterloo, IA (Two shows at 6:30 and 9:00 p.m.)
The Beach Boys were scheduled to play in Waterloo on September 24 but the concerts were rescheduled so the group would be free to tape a TV appearance.

SATURDAY, SEPTEMBER 17, 1983: New Mexico State Fair, Albuquerque, NM, with Lee Greenwood
About 15,000 fans attended this show. The following morning, the group traveled to Santa Fe as guests of Governor Toney Anaya and attended an afternoon party at the executive residence.

SUNDAY, SEPTEMBER 18, 1983: Boise State University Pavilion, Boise, ID (7:30 p.m. show)

MONDAY, SEPTEMBER 19, AND TUESDAY, SEPTEMBER 20, 1983: Puyallup Fair, Puyallup, WA (Two shows each day at 5:00 and 8:00 p.m.)

MONDAY, SEPTEMBER 26, AND TUESDAY, SEPTEMBER 27, 1983: Pomona Fair, L.A. County Fairgrounds, Pomona, CA (One show each night at 8:30 p.m.)
The group's Pomona Fair appearances attracted little media attention. However, these shows have taken on great significance in retrospect because they marked the last-ever appearances of Dennis onstage. He showed up unexpectedly on the first night and was invited to play. Photographs make clear that he was on drums through most of the show. He also got onstage briefly on Tuesday, but his drunken behavior was allegedly so disruptive that he wasn't allowed back again.

THURSDAY, SEPTEMBER 29, 1983: Kern County Fair, Bakersfield, CA

SATURDAY, OCTOBER 1, 1983: Frost Amphitheatre, Stanford University, Palo Alto, CA

SUNDAY, OCTOBER 2, 1983: Cal-Expo Amphitheater, Sacramento, CA, with the Edge and Pablo Cruise

THURSDAY, OCTOBER 13, 1983: Grand Plaza Hotel, Grand Rapids, MI, with Skiles and Henderson and Pearl Bailey
This was a benefit emceed by former President Ford to raise money for the Grand Rapids

like General Motors, and some key management guy is drunk all the time, you tell him either straighten up and get help or you're fired. Or take some time

"When the group showed up in their van at 3:30 p.m. for their Monday appearance at the fair, the security guard at the gate didn't recognize them and refused to let them in until they paid the $4.00 admission price. The Beach Boys said it was the first time they ever had to pay to get into their own show!"

off to get yourself together. That's what we had to tell Dennis from time to time. Take some time off and get yourself together. But he never did."

~~~~~~

THE BEACH BOYS IN CONCERT

Dennis made his last appearances with the group in September. He attempted detox and rehab programs several times but never lasted beyond a day or two before fleeing. Ultimately homeless, and directionless, he drowned on December 28 while diving from a friend's boat in Marina Del Rey. Carl told Zach Dunkin of the *Indianapolis News*, "The family was devastated by Dennis' loss. My mother was with us at my home in the mountains [in Colorado] over the Christmas holidays when it happened. I had to be the one to tell her and it wasn't easy. It wasn't easy on any of us. Although we were all very aware of Dennis' problems for years, we never expected this to happen. He was working real hard on it [the alcoholism]. He'd fall off the wagon and get back on it again. His spirit will always be with us."

Foundation, the Gerald R. Ford Museum, and the Arts Council of Greater Grand Rapids. The event came on the heels of James Watt's announcement that he was resigning. Ford commented, "He finally made the right decision." Mike also made reference to Watt when he told the crowd that he observed some "undesirables" in the audience.

FRIDAY, OCTOBER 14, 1983: Kentucky King Warehouse, Maysville, KY

SATURDAY, OCTOBER 15, 1983: Roberts Stadium, Evansville, IN (8:00 p.m. show)
The group played at homecoming celebrations for the University of Evansville.

SUNDAY, OCTOBER 16, 1983: Six Flags Over Texas, Arlington, TX (6:00 p.m. show)

MONDAY, OCTOBER 17, 1983: Gable Field, Northeastern State University, Tahlequah, OK (7:30 p.m.)
This show was attended by 5,000 people. Mike kept things light. Before the car medley he announced, "We're getting ready to do some very moving songs—so moving they have wheels on them. Except here we are in Oklahoma and you folks might not like car songs like 'I Get Around,' so we're going to do country songs instead. We're ready to do 'On the Road Again' or how about some of Dolly Parton's biggest . . . biggest hits that is!" The band than performed an abbreviated version of "Okie from Muskogee."

SATURDAY, NOVEMBER 5, 1983: Dee Events Center, Weber State College, Ogden, UT, with the Greg Kihn Band (8:00 p.m. show)
The group made a brief two-day swing through the Southwest. Neither Brian nor Dennis took part. Van N. Williams of the *Signpost* reported, "The band performed so many songs from their numerous albums that it was hard to keep track, but as a whole the audience seemed to remember most of the words. At one point in the program, the Beach Boys sang a John Lennon hit, 'Imagine,' and a hush fell over the concert hall."

SUNDAY, NOVEMBER 6, 1983: Arizona State Fair, Phoenix, AZ (7:00 p.m. show), Benefit for Hacienda de Los Angeles, Private Home, Phoenix, AZ (2:00 PM Show), and Arizona State Fair, Phoenix, AZ (7:00 PM Show)

SUNDAY, NOVEMBER 13, 1983: Jack Murphy Stadium, San Diego, CA

THURSDAY, NOVEMBER 17, TO SATURDAY, NOVEMBER 19, 1983: Universal Amphitheatre, Los Angeles, CA (One show each night at 8:00 p.m.)
All three nights at Universal Amphitheatre sold out. For the occasion, a five-piece horn section accompanied the group. Richard Cromelin of the *Los Angeles Times* reported that the most striking aspect of the shows was their sheer "uneventfulness." Indeed, with Dennis absent and Mike "more subdued than usual," the most notable event was the appearance of a trim Brian. He sang strong leads on "Sloop John B" and "Wouldn't It Be Nice" and even took over bass duties on "Good Vibrations." He also played two recent compositions, "It's Just a Matter of Time" and "The Boogie's Back in Town."

WEDNESDAY, NOVEMBER 30, 1983: Aladdin Hotel, Las Vegas, NV
This show took place at a computer dealer's exposition. Franklin Computer Corporation paid the group $100,000 to perform. Manager Tom Hulett commented in *Forbes* magazine, "This is an easy way for a company to say 'thank you' to its people and give them something they'll remember for a long time to come." A crowd of 7,500 heard an hour and a half of hits, as well as a few new tunes by Brian.

The year ended with the group spending the holiday season with their respective families, a peaceful time marred by the news of Dennis' death on December 28.

1984

I N THE AFTERMATH of Dennis's death, the group made the decision to keep going. There was little chance they'd disband. Dennis had been only a part-time presence during the previous three years. Despite his once-formidable talent and charisma, at this stage Dennis' passing meant little to the potential commerce of future Beach Boys tours. However, the band needed time to mourn and regroup. Bruce commented to Randy Alexander of the *Trenton Times*, "It's a personal adjustment for all of us. When you lose one of your friends, you don't recover in two weeks. I know Dennis would have wanted us to jump right back on the road. But I think about him every day. You're not supposed to lose friends when they're young." The band didn't play a concert until February 15.

By the summer the Beach Boys were back on the road and running like a well-oiled machine. Bruce commented to reporter Randy Alexander of the *Trenton Times*, "When you've got touring down blindfolded and you

CONCERTS PLAYED IN
1984

love Dodger Stadium in Los Angeles."

The postgame shows compounded the idea of the Beach Boys as an all-American, wholesome attraction. It was an identification the band shied away from in the 1970s, but now embraced with some caveats. Carl took umbrage with the idea that they were "the Republicans' pet band," as many people termed them. He told the *Oklahoman*, "The President and Mrs. Reagan were as nice as they could possibly be about it and even if I would disagree with them politically—and I certainly do on some things—personally I support them. I'd say the group is pretty varied, politically."

The group's patriotic image lent itself well to corporate sponsorship. They began playing private parties and lucrative corporate events. Bruce explained to writer Mark Misercola, "Corporate concerts are really kind of new to us. But a lot of companies are doing it. Many want to reward their employees with a private concert. So at sales shows or incentive trips they'll hide us right up through the show, bring all the employees into an auditorium and raise the curtain." Corporations regularly hired the group because they were a known entity. By 1984 you knew exactly what you'd get at a Beach Boys show. No one expected or wanted many new sounds. The band, including Carl, came to terms with the fact that they'd always be Beach Boys. And they'd have to play the car and surf songs that made them famous.

However, the group still had a desire to record. Al remarked, "I'm glad to

JANUARY 24, 1984: Troy State University, Troy, AL (Canceled)
This was supposed to be the opening date of the Beach Boys' first 1984 tour. It had been booked in late 1983 and Tom Hulett told *Amusement Business*, soon after Dennis's death, that the group would fulfill their commitments. However, they clearly had a change of heart, because at a press conference on January 9 they announced they were canceling all pending shows. Other canceled dates were: Civic Center, Albany, GA (January 25); University of New Orleans, LA (January 26); Civic Center, Shreveport, LA (January 27); University of Oklahoma, Norman, OK (January 28); University of Texas, Austin, TX (January 29); Hemisfair Arena, San Antonio, TX (January 30); Civic Center, Lubbock, TX (January 31); Civic Center, Beaumont, TX (February 1); Harrah's Lake Tahoe (February 3 to 6); Ft. Collins, CO (February 7); and Rapid City, SD (February 9).

WEDNESDAY, FEBRUARY 15, TO MONDAY, FEBRUARY 20, 1984: Harrah's Tahoe, Stateline, NV, with Gary Mule Deer (Two shows each night)
These were the first concerts played following Dennis's death. According to *Add Some Music*, Brian played some shows, though he was absent on the night a *Rolling Stone* reporter attended. In addition to Ed Carter, Mike Meros, Billy Hinsche, Jeff Foskett, Mike Kowalski, and Bobby Figueroa, the group brought along the five-piece horn section they'd utilized at the Universal shows in November. The set remained the same as the previous year, but "Runaway" was dropped and Carl's "Heaven" added as a tribute to Dennis.

SATURDAY, MARCH 3, 1984: Reunion Arena, Dallas, TX, with Lynn Anderson
Braniff Airlines sponsored this show and the proceeds were donated to the March of Dimes. Airline workers received free tickets as a reward for hard work.

FRIDAY, MARCH 16, 1984: Savannah, GA (Canceled)

SATURDAY, MARCH 17, 1984: Guidry Stadium, Nicholls State University, Thibodaux, LA (2:00 p.m. show), and Civic Center, Albany, GA

THURSDAY, APRIL 5, 1984: Maui, Hawaii
This was a private show for employees of the Union Mutual Insurance Co. Mike told a reporter, "We did this private little party for 300-400 people. We fly over to one of our favorite spots, we play for an hour or so, hang out for a week and have a good time and talk and write music and see the sights."

FRIDAY, APRIL 13, 1984: Market Square Arena, Indianapolis, IN
This show took place after a Pacers basketball game. Zach Dunkin of the *Indianapolis News* reported, "Mixed with the usual offering of 'Barbara Ann,' 'Good Vibrations' and the surf and car medleys, were a few oldies the band hadn't done in a while such as 'Wendy,' 'Do It Again' and 'Don't Worry Baby.' New in the Beach Boys repertoire was an interesting interpretation of the 1957 hit by the Hollywood Flames, 'Buzz, Buzz, Buzz.'"

SATURDAY, APRIL 14, 1984: University of Texas, Austin, TX
The band opened with "Rock and Roll Music" and the crowd shot out of their seats to dance. This infuriated security, which continually ordered them to sit. Mike finally weighed in, announcing, "The security people are a little over zealous tonight-it isn't a Frank Sinatra concert. If you want to dance, then dance."

SUNDAY, APRIL 15, 1984: Astrodome, Houston, TX

MONDAY, APRIL 16, 1984: Municipal Auditorium, Mobile, AL (8:00 p.m. show)
This show was a disappointment for promoters. A small crowd of just over 5,000 turned out, which was less than half the seating capacity of the venue.

TUESDAY, APRIL 17, 1984: Flowers Hall, University of North Alabama, Florence, AL
Judy S. Carle of the *Tuscaloosa Times Daily* reported, "The Tuesday concert proved that the Beach Boys still have the same gusto and audience appeal that made them famous more than twenty years ago. They opened their show with 'Barbara Ann' and followed up with all their major hits including 'Surfer Girl,' 'Good Vibrations,' 'Fun, Fun, Fun,' and 'I Get Around.' The fans loved it and most sang along."

WEDNESDAY, APRIL 18, 1984: Knoxville Festival, Knoxville, TN

FRIDAY, APRIL 20, 1984: USF Sun Dome, Tampa, FL, with Mick Fleetwood's Zoo

SATURDAY, APRIL 21, 1984: Coliseum, Jacksonville, FL

MONDAY, MAY 7, 1984: Radio City Music Hall, New York, NY, with George Burns, America, Doc Severinsen and Emcee Susan Anton (7:30 p.m. show)
This was a benefit for the National Fitness Foundation.

SATURDAY, MAY 12 1984: Laguna Seca Raceway, Monterey, CA, with the Greg Kihn Band

SUNDAY, MAY 13, 1984: Jack Murphy Stadium, San Diego, CA (3:50 p.m. show)
The show took place after a Padres game. Brian wasn't present.

THURSDAY, MAY 24, 1984: United World College of the American West, Montezuma, NM
The Beach Boys began their summer tour with a commencement appearance at this IB School. Brian wasn't on the tour. The reason given was that he needed time to write and arrange songs for the group's upcoming album. Billy Hinsche, Mike Meros, Ed Carter, Jeff Foskett, Mike Kowalski and Bobby Figueroa accompanied them.

FRIDAY, MAY 25, TO SUNDAY, MAY 27, 1984: Pine Knob Music Theater, Clarkston, MI (with Warren Zevon)
Gary Graff of the *Detroit Free Press* reported, "The group . . . has become an oldies show of inconsistent quality. Friday's concert was plagued by a relatively poor sound mix . . . Add to that watered down renditions of favorites like 'Barbara Ann,' 'Rock and Roll Music,' 'Good Vibrations' and 'Help Me Rhonda' and you're talking about a band that's dangerously close to becoming a caricature of itself."

MONDAY, MAY 28, 1984: Metrodome, Minneapolis, MN

WEDNESDAY, MAY 30, 1984: Augusta Center, Augusta, ME
The set consisted of: "Rock and Roll Music," "Darlin'," "Do It Again," "Little Deuce Coupe," "Help Me Rhonda," "I Get Around," "Warmth of the Sun," "God Only Knows," "Come Go with Me," "Buzz, Buzz, Buzz," "Wendy," "Little Surfer Girl," "Heaven," "Don't Worry Baby," "Sloop John B," "California Girls," "Dance, Dance,Dance," "Wouldn't It Be Nice," "Good Vibrations," "Surf City," "Surfin' Safari," "Surfin' USA," "Barbara Ann," "Rockin' All Over the World" and "Fun, Fun, Fun."

THURSDAY, MAY 31, 1984: Stabler Arena, Lehigh University, Bethlehem, PA, with the Limits

FRIDAY, JUNE 1, 1984: Garden State Arts Center, Jackson, NJ

SATURDAY, JUNE 2, 1984: War Memorial Stadium, Buffalo, NY
The Beach Boys played following a 2 p.m. Bison's game.

do new songs. It's a burnout to do those old things over and over." In early 1984 the group teamed up with Latin phenomenon Julio Iglesias on a remake of the Hollies' "The

"It's a personal adjustment for all of us. When you lose one of your friends, you don't recover in two weeks. I know Dennis would have wanted us to jump right back on the road. But I think about him every day. You're not supposed to lose friends when they're young."

—Bruce Johnston

Air That I Breathe." They also agreed that, with Brian on the mend, it was time to consider a new album. Mike told a reporter for the *St. Petersburg Times* in April, "We've got lots and lots of new songs. Brian's got about thirty finished songs and I've got about ten. Let's

Carl leading the band at Laguna Seca Raceway, May 12, 1984. Photo: Panayiotis Bagdanos

SUNDAY, JUNE 3, 1984: Blossom Music Center, Cuyahoga Falls, OH (8:00 p.m. show)
Scott Stephens of the *Elyria Chronicle Telegram* commented, "The Beach Boys are seasoned pros by now, and save a shortened, lifeless reading of 'California Girls,' all of the old hits clicked Sunday. The only question is whether the group has anything new to offer, or if they are instead caught frozen in a past they'll never escape or improve upon."

TUESDAY, JUNE 5, 1984: Sandstone Amphitheater, Bonner Springs, KS, with Steve, Bob, and Rich (7:30 p.m. show)
John Hughes of the *Kansas City Star* admitted the audience was in "surf heaven" but criticized the band for a lack of ambition, noting, "Other bands that have had equal or more success than the Beach Boys have been able to sustain long careers by constantly offering the fans something new. The Beach Boys owe it to their very loyal and energetic fans to do the same."

WEDNESDAY, JUNE 6, 1984: Memorial Coliseum, Fort Wayne, IN (8:00 p.m. show)

THURSDAY, JUNE 7, 1984: Metro Centre, Rockford, IL

1984

FRIDAY, JUNE 8, 1984: Musicland, Calhoun, GA (Two shows at 8:00 and 10:00 p.m.)

SATURDAY, JUNE 9, 1984: Arie Crown Theatre, Chicago, IL, with America and emcee Susan Anton (7:30 p.m. show)
This was a benefit for the National Fitness Foundation.

SUNDAY, JUNE 10, 1984: Outagamie County Fair, Seymour, WI

TUESDAY, JUNE 12, 1984: Civic Center, Wheeling, WV (8:00 p.m. show)
Prior to this show, Mike, Bruce, and Al held a press conference in Miami to announce they'd be playing a free show there on July 4.

WEDNESDAY, JUNE 13, 1984: Civic Center, Huntington, WV
A small crowd of 3,700 (less than half of capacity) turned out. Dave Peyton of the *Herald Dispatch* reported, "The Beach Boys did them all last night, from the slow, moody 'God Only Knows' to the light and rhythmic 'Help Me Rhonda.'"

THURSDAY, JUNE 14, AND FRIDAY, JUNE 15, 1984: Mud Island Amphitheater, Memphis, TN (One show each night at 8:00 p.m.)

SATURDAY, JUNE 16, 1984: Six Flags Over Mid-America, Eureka, MO

SUNDAY, JUNE 17, 1984: Mile High Stadium, Denver, CO, with the Denver Symphony Orchestra (8:40 p.m. show)
This was a special Father's Day show billed as "a salute to dad." The group were backed by the Denver Symphony on five numbers: "God Only Knows," "California Girls," "Good Vibrations," "Wouldn't It Be Nice," and "Fun, Fun, Fun."

FRIDAY, JUNE 29, 1984: Pacific Amphitheatre, Costa Mesa, CA, with the Busboys
The Beach Boys, without Brian, played for a near-capacity crowd. Jim Washburn of the *Orange County Register* singled out Carl's vocal contributions as "the only proof that the group is still capable of being more than just human jukeboxes. His hauntingly beautiful ballad 'Heaven,' dedicated to his brother Dennis, carried an emotional spark the Beach Boys could certainly use more of."

The day before this show, the Beach Boys (with Brian) appeared on the NBC TV *Tonight Show*, with guest host Joan Rivers. They performed "Graduation Day," backed by the *Tonight Show* Orchestra.

SATURDAY, JUNE 30, 1984: Candlestick Park, San Francisco, CA
The group performed before 26,990 after a Giants game. Brian was absent.

MONDAY, JULY 2, 1984: Six Flags Over Georgia, Atlanta, GA (9:00 p.m. show)

WEDNESDAY, JULY 4, 1984: Washington Monument, Washington, DC, with Idle Tears, Hank Williams Jr., Three Dog Night, America, Lynn Anderson, Latoya Jackson, and the O'Jays (Afternoon) and "Miami Beach Party," Lummus Park, Miami, FL, with Idle Tears and Three Dog Night (Evening)
On July 3 the group attended a D.C. party hosted by corporate sponsors. They were also interviewed for inclusion in the upcoming documentary *The Beach Boys: American Band*. Brian spoke optimistically about the band's future, while Mike joked, "I don't think the Watt thing hurt us too much." Indeed, it could be argued the incident had resuscitated their career.

The Fourth of July show attracted 565,000 people and tremendous media attention. A number of guest stars took part. Latoya Jackson and Julio Inglesias joined the Beach Boys for a performance of "Surfer Girl." Ringo Starr played drums for the last twenty minutes of the set,

303

face it, we haven't produced any new music in a few years, so we've got quite a stockpile between us." The group was not without trepidation. As Carl admitted to writer Gary

By 1984 you knew exactly what you'd get at a Beach Boys show. No one expected or wanted many new sounds. The band, including Carl, came to terms with the fact that they'd always be Beach Boys. And they'd have to play the car and surf songs that made them famous.

Graff, "We're damned if we do and damned if we don't. If we do a record that sounds like the others, it's the same old thing. And if we do something new, we'll be attacked because it doesn't sound like us."

Nevertheless, they began work on a new LP that

Performing at Candlestick Park in San Francisco on June 30, 1984. Photo: Panayiotis Bagdanos

summer. They were reluctant, however, to take any breaks from the cash cow of touring, so the album wasn't completed until 1985.

including a performance of "Back in the USSR." Justin Hayward and John Lodge of the Moody Blues also made appearances.

Mike made light of the fact that the Beach Boys had been banned the previous year, by thanking "all you undesirable elements" for coming. The concert was filmed and recorded. An album called *Fourth of July: A Rockin' Celebration of America*, which contained live recordings from this show, as well as the band's 1985 July 4 shows, received limited release. The film footage was edited into a TV special titled *D.C. Beach Party* that aired in syndication.

Following the show, the group and many of their guests (including Three Dog Night, Julio Inglesias, and Ringo) flew to Miami for another free show, attended by over 100,000 people. The Beach Boys took the stage at 9:40 p.m. Brian, however, was absent. He flew back to California and soon afterwards traveled to London to work on the next LP. He wasn't present at any other July shows.

FRIDAY, JULY 6, 1984: Riverside-Brookfield HS Stadium, Chicago, IL (8:00 p.m. show)
This was a special concert to celebrate the fiftieth anniversary of the Brookfield Zoo.

SATURDAY, JULY 7, 1984: All-Iowa Fair, Cedar Rapids, IA (8:00 p.m. show)

SUNDAY, JULY 8, 1984: Wade Stadium, Duluth, MN, with Dakota Crossing and Three Dog Night
A crowd of 5,860 turned out. Bob Ashenmacher of the *News Tribune* commented, "It's difficult for some of us to be comfortable with the band presenting itself as merely an oldies act—there's no emphasis on new material, nor any interpretation put into the old stuff. Finally it's painful to the point of grotesque to hear 'Good Vibrations' made into a sing-a-long . . . All that said, it was a good oldies show."

The group remained in Duluth overnight so they could take part in a charity softball game against Three Dog Night on Monday.

WEDNESDAY, JULY 11, 1984: Six Flags Over Texas, Arlington, TX

THURSDAY, JULY 12, 1984: All Sports Stadium, Oklahoma City, OK
The group played following an Oklahoma 89ers game.

FRIDAY, JULY 13, 1984: Swiss Valley Amphitheater, Lampe, MO, with the Lefty Brothers (Two shows)

SATURDAY, JULY 14, 1984: Skelly Stadium, Tulsa, OK
This concert took place after a Cosmos-Roughnecks soccer game.

SUNDAY, JULY 15, 1984: Sec Taylor Stadium, Des Moines, IA
Ken Fuson of the *Des Moines Register* criticized the group for racing through their hits in quick medleys. "There is, of course, nothing wrong with a fast paced concert, but it would have been much sweeter had the group caught their breath between classics. Great songs, like great meals, are meant to be savored."

MONDAY, JULY 16, 1984: Red River Valley Fair, Fargo, ND

TUESDAY, JULY 17, 1984: John O'Donnell Stadium, Davenport, IA (8:00 p.m. show)
The day after this concert, group members appeared at the Quad City Open Celebrity Pro-Am golf tournament.

WEDNESDAY, JULY 25, 1984: Olympic Gala, Greek Theater, Los Angeles, CA, with Neil Diamond, Peggy Fleming, Tammy Wynette, Olivia Newton John, Willie Nelson, Placido Domingo, and others
The Beach Boys took part in this ABC TV Olympic celebration hosted by Jane Fonda and Robert Wagner. They performed "Surfin' USA."

SATURDAY, JULY 28, 1984: Civic Stadium, Portland, OR
This concert followed a Portland Beavers game.

SUNDAY, JULY 29, 1984: Montana State Fair, Great Falls, MT

THURSDAY, AUGUST 2, 1984: University of Utah, Salt Lake City, UT
This appearance was marred by sound problems. The volume from the microphones was so low that it was difficult to hear the vocalists if you were not seated near the stage. Jerry Spangler of the *Deseret News* reported that the sound system "was not just bad. It was terrible. A $69 Sears ghetto blaster would have put out a more distinguishable sound."

FRIDAY, AUGUST 3, 1984: Great America, Santa Clara, CA

SATURDAY, AUGUST 4, AND SUNDAY, AUGUST 5, 1984: Caesars Palace, Las Vegas, NV

"We're damned if we do and damned if we don't. If we do a record that sounds like the others, it's the same old thing. And if we do something new, we'll be attacked because it doesn't sound like us."

—Carl Wilson

THE BEACH BOYS IN CONCERT

MONDAY, AUGUST 6, 1984: Hilton Hotel, Beverly Hills, CA
This was a private show for ABC TV staff covering the 1984 Olympics.

TUESDAY, AUGUST 7, 1984: UCLA Village, Los Angeles, CA
The group performed for 3,400 Olympic athletes quartered at the UCLA Village.

THURSDAY, AUGUST 9, 1984; Oakwood Lake Resort, Manteca, CA (8:00 p.m. show)

SATURDAY, AUGUST 18, 1984: Apparel Mart, Dallas, TX
The Beach Boys, accompanied by Brian, performed at a fashion show and reception, for which guests paid $100 each. The concert was one of many events set up to coincide with the 1984 Republican Convention.

The show was overshadowed by Brian's arrest the next day. He and two other men wandered into the Republican Convention at the Dallas Convention Center without proper credentials and were seized by security. Drugs were allegedly found on the men with Brian, though he had none himself. Brian was detained for three hours on criminal trespassing charges but released when the Republican National Committee declined to press charges. He returned to California and wasn't on the rest of the tour.

SUNDAY, AUGUST 19, 1984: Riverfront Stadium, Cincinnati, OH
This show took place following a Cincinnati Reds game.

MONDAY, AUGUST 20, 1984: CNE Grandstand, Toronto, ON, Canada, with Poco
The Beach Boys performed at the CNE for the umpteenth time, but Liam Lacey of the *Globe and Mail* noted, "Each time the Beach Boys come out, they tinker slightly with the basic format of the show; Carl Wilson offered a pretty ballad, 'Heaven,' which was dedicated to Dennis Wilson. But even in the middle, slower portion of the show, the band basically stuck to the hits—'In My Room,' 'God Only Knows,' 'Wouldn't It Be Nice,' and a slightly unusual choice, the minor 1964 hit, 'Wendy.'"

TUESDAY, AUGUST 21, 1984: Sherkston Beach, Fort Erie, ON, Canada, with Poco

FRIDAY, AUGUST 24, AND SATURDAY, AUGUST 25, 1984: Jones Beach, Wantagh, NY, with Poco (One show each night at 8:00 p.m.)
Stephen Williams of *Newsday* reported, "Some of the famous Beach Boys harmonies were rather gritty early on; they sounded like a 33rpm record played at 30rpm. But (Carl) Wilson, Al Jardine, and Love were terrific together on 'Wendy'—Love especially—and Wilson's guitar bridge on 'I Get Around' was, like most of his practiced work, strong and consistent."

SUNDAY, AUGUST 26, 1984: Garden State Arts Center, Holmdel, NJ, with Poco (7:30 p.m. show)
The set for this show consisted of "California Girls," "I Can Hear Music," "Sloop John B," "Darlin'," "Dance, Dance, Dance," "Wouldn't It Be Nice," "In My Room," "Do It Again," "409/Little Deuce Coupe/I Get Around" (medley), "The Warmth of the Sun" (sung by Jeff), "God Only Knows," "Come Go with Me," "Buzz, Buzz, Buzz," "Be True to Your School," "Wendy" (sung by Jeff), "Surfer Girl," "Heaven," "Disney Girls," "Don't Worry Baby," "Help Me Rhonda," "Rockin' All Over the World," "Rock and Roll Music," "Surfin' Safari/Surf City/Surfin' USA" (medley), "Good Vibrations," "Barbara Ann," and "Fun, Fun, Fun."

MONDAY, AUGUST 27, 1984: RFK Stadium, Bridgeport, CT, with Poco (7:00 p.m. show)

WEDNESDAY, AUGUST 29, 1984: Bradner Stadium, Olean, NY, with Poco (7:00 p.m. show)
Bob Schnettler of the *Times-Herald* noted, "From the opener 'California Girls' to their closing 'Good Vibrations,' the group had control of the situation, working the crowd like the pros they are. They blended the harmonies in the sound they forged oh so many years ago, and if at times the lyrics were unintelligible because of the louder music, no one seemed to mind. The audience knew what they were and often sang right along."

THURSDAY, AUGUST 30, 1984: SPAC, Saratoga Springs, NY, with Poco
Michael Hochandel of the *Schenectady Gazette*, who'd described their 1983 appearance as "embarrassing," was pleasantly surprised at this show. He reported, "They were tight, spirited, clearly committed to the music and each other. At its best, the show was inspiring for its musicianship and its feeling . . . The talented Jeff Foskett . . . sang Brian's high vocal parts . . . Carl Wilson delivered the show's most touching moment, with 'Heaven,' an eloquent ballad dedicated to Dennis."

FRIDAY, AUGUST 31, 1984: NY State Fairgrounds, Syracuse, NY, with Charlie Slavin

---

SATURDAY, SEPTEMBER 1, 1984: Dunn Field, Elmira, NY, with Poco

---

SUNDAY, SEPTEMBER 2, 1984: Canfield Fair, Canfield, OH (Two shows at 6:30 and 9:00 p.m.)

MONDAY, SEPTEMBER 3, 1984: Busch Gardens, Williamsburg, VA (Two shows at 5:00 and 8:00 p.m.)

THURSDAY, SEPTEMBER 6, 1984: Five Flags Center, Dubuque, IA
A capacity crowd of 5,000 attended. David Fryxell of the *Telegraph Herald* reported, "The Beach Boys segued from one hit into another as smoothly as waves breaking on the beach. Each familiar song fit like a pair of old sandals. 'Some things get better with age, don't they?' Love hollered, discarding his jacket and getting down to business. He asked 'Is everybody ready to go surfing?' Everybody was."

FRIDAY, SEPTEMBER 7, 1984: Kansas State Fair, Hutchinson, KS (Two shows at 5:30 and 8:30 p.m.)
Eighty-four-year-old Charles Wilson, brother of the Wilsons' grandfather Buddy, attended with his nephew Phil McCrory.

SATURDAY, SEPTEMBER 8, 1984: Nebraska State Fair, Lincoln, NE
A capacity crowd of 13,870 attended and the group delivered a sparkling show. One audience member commented, "I haven't heard these guys sound so good in a long time." Kent Warneke of the *Omaha World-Herald* reported, "Over the years the voices of Mike Love, Carl Wilson, Al Jardine, and Bruce Johnston, the main Beach Boys, haven't always been in great shape . . . But only a few times during Carl Wilson's solo on 'Don't Worry Baby' did any voice falter Saturday night. The rest of the ninety-minute show that included one encore was right on target."

SUNDAY, SEPTEMBER 9, 1984: Bismarck Arena, Bismarck, ND

MONDAY, SEPTEMBER 10, 1984: Puyallup Fair, Puyallup, WA (Two shows at 5:00 and 8:00 p.m.)

SATURDAY, SEPTEMBER 22, 1984: Veteran's Stadium, Philadelphia, PA
This show took place following a noon Temple-Pittsburgh football game.

SUNDAY, SEPTEMBER 23, 1984: Fraser Field, Lynn, MA, with the Stompers and the Gesh Group (2:00 p.m. show)
This show in the field adjacent to the Manning Bowl drew 10,000 fans. Steve Morse of the *Boston Globe* commented, "Minus only Brian Wilson . . . the Boys blazed through their timeless surf anthems . . . Vocals were crystalline despite a needlessly over-miked sound system, and they reached an exalted height on an encore of 'Good Vibrations.'"

TUESDAY, SEPTEMBER 25, 1984: Bloomsburg Fair, Bloomsburg, PA

THURSDAY, SEPTEMBER 27, 1984: Civic Center, Lansing, MI, with Flash Kahan (8:00 p.m. show)
David Winkelstern of the *State Journal* reported, "From 'California Girls' to 'Help Me Rhonda' to 'Fun, Fun, Fun,' the Beach Boys played music with few surprises. Most of their songs heard in the

"From the opener 'California Girls' to their closing 'Good Vibrations,' the group had control of the situation, working the crowd like the pros they are. They blended the harmonies in the sound they forged oh so many years ago."

Civic Center were classics from the sixties and early seventies. And it seemed to be just what the crowd of about 4,200 wanted."

FRIDAY, SEPTEMBER 28, 1984: Civic Center, Peoria, IL

SATURDAY, SEPTEMBER 29, 1984: Waldo Stadium, Western Michigan University, Kalamazoo, MI
The group played after a WMU-Marshall football game.

SUNDAY, SEPTEMBER 30, 1984: Oil Palace, Tyler, TX, with the Gatlin Brothers

TUESDAY, OCTOBER 2, 1984: Louisiana World Expo Amphitheater, New Orleans, LA (8:00 p.m. show)

SATURDAY, OCTOBER 6, 1984: Ventura County Fair, Los Angeles, CA
The largest crowd ever at the Ventura Fair, 11,140 people attended. Steve Chaikin of the *Press Courier* reported, "The band performed for more than an hour and a half, playing the 'California sound' surfing songs that made them famous, and the crowd seemed to enjoy every minute of it, asking for three encores."

SUNDAY, NOVEMBER 4, 1984: Veterans Memorial Coliseum, Phoenix, AZ
While recording their new album, the group played an afternoon show. Their current producer, Steve Levine, performed with them.

THURSDAY, DECEMBER 6, 1984: Riverside Theater, Milwaukee, WI, with Flash Kahan (Two shows at 7:00 and 10:00 p.m.)
The first of two shows at the Riverside Theater drew 2,400 people. There were problems with the sound that rendered the piano inaudible, but Jim Ohlschmidt of the *Milwaukee Journal* reported, "regardless of those technical flaws, the crowd was immediately in the grasp of what has been called 'America's Band' from the moment it opened with the ever popular 'California Girls' to the last chorus of 'Fun, Fun, Fun,' which closed a ten-minute encore."

FRIDAY, DECEMBER 7, 1984: Ohio Theatre, Columbus, OH (Two shows)

SATURDAY, DECEMBER 8, 1984: Hulman Center, Indiana State University, Terre Haute, IN
Sheila Hoffman reported in the *Sycamore Yearbook*, "Singing the ballad 'God Only Knows,' guitarist Carl Wilson brought tears to the eyes of many. Each song was more intense than the last. 'Wouldn't It Be Nice,' 'Little Surfer,' 'Don't Worry Baby,' and 'Help Me Rhonda' all continuously brought fans to their feet clapping and singing."

SUNDAY, DECEMBER 9, 1984: Holiday Star Theatre, Merrillville, IN (Two shows at 4:00 and 7:30 p.m.)

TUESDAY, DECEMBER 11, 1984: Civic Center, Baltimore, MD

THURSDAY, DECEMBER 13, 1984: Memorial Auditorium, Greenville, SC

SATURDAY, DECEMBER 15, 1984: Auditorium Theatre, Rochester, NY, with Henry Gross (Two shows at 7:00 and 10:30 p.m.)

1985

THE BEACH BOYS maintained a very high profile in 1985. That spring a documentary film titled *The Beach Boys: An American Band* was released. It featured footage culled from TV appearances, concerts, and the band's personal archive, as well as new framing sequences filmed in 1984. While the film dealt in large measure with the travails of Brian and Dennis, it ended on an up note with the group's triumphant July 4, 1984, appearance in Washington. The film suggested the Beach Boys had triumphed over adversity and were back on top.

In 1985 the group also released their first album in five years. Steve Levine, who'd produced hits for Culture Club, oversaw the record, which was simply titled *The Beach Boys*. Sessions began in London in the summer of 1984 and stretched until March 1985. Brian contributed more than he had in years. "I'm So Lonely," "Crack at Your Love," "It's Just a Matter of Time" and the CD bonus track "Male Ego" were all composed by him in collaboration with Dr. Landy, who'd deemed himself qualified to be a songwriter. None of the songs were egregious. However, none had that old Brian magic, perhaps because he didn't produce them. His strongest composition was "California Calling," a perky surf number co-written with Al. Also on the album was "Getcha Back," a catchy single composed by Mike and Terry Melcher and enlivened by Brian's best falsetto in years. Carl's charming ballad "Where I Belong" may have been the album's high point.

The album suffered from Levine's decision to record digitally with vocal sampling, programmed drums, and techno-cheese keyboards. It gave the LP a cold and sterile feel. Al expressed reservations over Levine's decision to include songs by Boy George ("Passing Friend") and Stevie Wonder

"Anybody seen David Lee Roth around here? I'm looking for that sucker. He ripped off 'California Girls,' if you know what I mean? I told the other guys in the group I'm going to get a fright wig and do 'Jump' during our show.'"

—Mike Love

("I Do Love You"). He commented to Cliff Radel of the *Cincinnati Enquirer*, "That was the producer's idea . . . No one asked us about putting those tunes on the album. They just did it. Now, no one is going to complain about a Stevie Wonder song . . . But I was hoping to have his person

CONCERTS PLAYED IN
1985

SATURDAY, JANUARY 19, 1985: Presidential Inauguration, Convention Center, Washington, DC
The group, dressed in tuxedos, performed at President Reagan's televised second inaugural gala, including an a cappella "Their Hearts Were Full of Spring."

THURSDAY, JANUARY 31, 1985: Northlands Coliseum, Edmonton, AL, Canada, with K.D. Lang

FRIDAY, FEBRUARY 1, 1985: Olympic Saddledome, Calgary, AL, Canada, with America
Prior to performing "California Girls," Mike joked, "Anybody seen David Lee Roth around here? I'm looking for that sucker. He ripped off 'California Girls,' if you know what I mean? I told the other guys in the group I'm going to get a fright wig and do 'Jump' during our show.'" James Muretich of the *Calgary Herald* reported, "The sound wasn't the greatest, the band was sloppy at times and they're certainly not showmen of the year. Yet nobody cared. They were there for the hits and they got them: 'Sloop John B,' 'Wouldn't It Be Nice,' 'Little Deuce Coupe,' 'Do It Again,' 'Help Me Rhonda' and far too many more to mention without the *Herald* putting out a special supplement."

SATURDAY, FEBRUARY 2, 1985: Utah State University, Logan, UT

SUNDAY, FEBRUARY 3, 1985: Colorado State University, Fort Collins, CO, with America
Mike Kontrelos reported in the *Silver Spruce Yearbook*, "The Beach Boys echoed their sound throughout Moby Gym for nearly two hours; yet, the concert seemed to have lasted only minutes. After playing a two song encore accompanied by America, the Beach Boys bid farewell with their final song 'Good Vibrations' and good vibes are exactly what the concert participants left with."

MONDAY, FEBRUARY 4, TO THURSDAY, FEBRUARY 7, AND TUESDAY, FEBRUARY 12, TO THURSDAY, FEBRUARY 14, 1985: Harrah's Tahoe, Stateline, NV

CIRCA MARCH 16, 1985: Marriot Hotel, Maui, HI
The group performed at the Kemper Open Golf festivities.

WEDNESDAY, MARCH 20, 1985: Symphony Hall, Salt Lake City, UT
This was a benefit to raise money for the Special Olympics. The Beach Boys dedicated the concert to Dennis. Mike told reporters, "Dennis had a lot of personal problems but the very best thing about him was his compassion. We're doing this for him."

FRIDAY, MARCH 22, 1985: Bonaventure Hotel, Los Angeles, CA (Private show for IBM)

SUNDAY, MARCH 24, 1985: Rushmore Plaza Civic Center, Rapid City, SD, with Dee Dee and the Pharaohs

FRIDAY, APRIL 5, 1985: West Palm Beach Auditorium, Palm Beach, FL, with America (8:00 p.m. show)
Jim Presnell of the *Palm Beach Post* reported, "Dennis Wilson has died and Brian Wilson didn't perform but the Beach Boys have been around a quarter century, almost, and still can thrill an audience with their skilled ten-piece ensemble . . . The music remained excellent throughout the night . . . From 'Help Me Rhonda' to 'Don't Worry Baby,' it definitely was all-classic rock night."

SATURDAY, APRIL 6, 1985: "Spring Music Festival," Metropolitan Park, Jacksonville, FL, with the Platters, the Four Tops, and the Association (4:00 p.m. show) and Civic Center, Pensacola, FL (9:00 p.m. show)

The group played an afternoon show in Jacksonville, and then headed to Pensacola to play a benefit for the Sacred Heart Foundation. Lou Elliot of the *Pensacola Journal News* reported, "While the group did not perform any songs on their new album due out in June, their old songs were a siren for the audience. The group's sound was the same one that made them famous with the harmonies and soft rolls in all the right places."

SUNDAY, APRIL 14 1985: "Sixty-Third Convention of National Association of Broadcasters," Convention Center, Las Vegas, NV

MONDAY, APRIL 29, 1985: "Second Genesis Benefit," Marriot Hotel, Washington DC

FRIDAY, MAY 3, 1985: Municipal Stadium, Phoenix, AZ (9:00 p.m. show)
This show took place following a Phoenix Giants game. It was the opening date of a forty-city tour sponsored by Jeep. At each show, a pickup truck was given away to a lucky fan. Mike Meros, Ed Carter, Billy Hinsche, Bobby Figueroa, Mike Kowalski, and Jeff Foskett accompanied the group.

SATURDAY, MAY 4, 1985: Hi-Corbett Field, Tucson, AZ
The group appeared after a Tucson Toros game.

THURSDAY, MAY 16, 1985: Eisenhower Hall, West Point, NY

FRIDAY, MAY 17, 1985: Rensselaer Polytechnic Institute, Troy, NY (8:30 p.m. show)

SATURDAY, MAY 18, 1985: New York Hilton, New York, NY
The group performed at the Tenth Anniversary Humanitarian Awards Dinner for the T.J. Martell Foundation for Leukemia and Cancer Research.

FRIDAY, JUNE 21, 1985: Montgomery Civic Center, Montgomery, AL

SATURDAY, JUNE 22, 1985: Mississippi Coast Coliseum, Biloxi, MS, with America

SUNDAY, JUNE 23, AND MONDAY, JUNE 24, 1985: Mud Island Amphitheatre, Memphis, TN, with America (One show each night at 8:00 p.m.)
Michael Donahue of the *Commercial Appeal* reported, "The Beach Boys aren't content to rest on their numerous hits of the past. They recently showed that they could still make hits with 'Getcha Back.' They performed this song, which has the Beach Boys ingredients including the wailing vocals. It would have been hard for a Beach Boys fan to walk away unsatisfied."

THURSDAY, JUNE 27, 1985: "Summer Fest," Marcus Amphitheatre, Milwaukee, WI
At "Summer Fest" the set was heavy on oldies, but the band played a few new songs, including "California Calling" and "Getcha Back." Jim Higgins of the *Milwaukee Sentinel* reported, "The band played with consistent grace and charm . . . Concert highlights included a slinky version of 'Do It Again,' a revved up 'Help Me Rhonda,' and the encore triumvirate of 'Good Vibrations,' 'Barbara Ann,' and 'Fun, Fun, Fun.'"

FRIDAY, JUNE 28, 1985: Cardinal Stadium, Lamar University, Beaumont, TX, with Joan Jett and the Blackhearts

SATURDAY, JUNE 29, 1985: All Sports Stadium, Oklahoma City, OK

SUNDAY, JUNE 30, 1985: Rangers Stadium, Arlington, TX
The group played after a Rangers game.

THURSDAY, JULY 4, 1985: Philadelphia Art Museum, Philadelphia, PA, with Robert Hazard,

on the record as well. But the producer didn't think it was appropriate to have him sing, which is stupid."

Nevertheless, Carl was excited by it. He told Gene Triplett of *The Oklahoman*, "We haven't really done our best work in the recent past. It just feels really good to do a good job and we put a lot of work into it. It just takes a lot of time to care."

CBS had high hopes for the album. Early signs were positive as the single "Getcha Back" managed a respectable number twenty-six on the *Billboard* charts, while its video received some MTV airplay. Carl told a Milwaukee reporter, "The video is a lot of fun . . . real fun, good natured, good hearted fun. It's not a traditional video. I loved it. I'm looking forward to doing more, you bet." *The Beach Boys*, however, peaked at a disappointing number fifty-two on the *Billboard* charts. It was another commercial failure for the group and marked the end of their time at CBS. They wouldn't release another LP until 1989.

Typically, the Beach Boys received a bigger boost by the release of a cover of one of their old songs than from anything new. David Lee Roth of Van Halen released a solo EP titled *Crazy from the Heat*, which contained a version of "California Girls" with backing vocals by Carl. The song rocketed to the top of the charts, largely on the strength of a video that received constant airplay on MTV. Like the *Endless Summer* LP, the Roth cover boosted interest in the music of the Beach Boys among a younger generation. Young people continued to flock to Beach Boys concerts to hear Brian's 1960s songs.

Those that came out to see Brian were usually disappointed. Other than

"It's his choice not to be here. We ask him to play all the time: saying if he's going to come to the really big shows then he should come to the more normal dates. Come into the trenches; don't just go for the easy glory. It's been that way since 1963; this isn't anything new."

—Bruce Johnston on Brian Wilson

appearances on July 4 and at Live Aid, he played no shows on the summer tour. Bruce commented to the *Toronto Globe*, "It's his choice not to be here. We ask him to play all the

Joan Jett and the Blackhearts, the Oak Ridge Boys, Joe Ely, the Sons of the Beach, the Neville Brothers, Frank Stallone, and Katrina and the Waves (2:30 p.m. show) and Washington Memorial, Washington, DC, with Radiant, Katrina and the Waves, the Bellamy Brothers, New Edition, Southern Pacific, the Four Tops, the Oak Ridge Boys, and Joan Jett and the Blackhearts (4:00 p.m. show)

The Beach Boys performed in two different cities for a TV special titled *Bring on the Summer with the Beach Boys*. Both shows featured guest stars, running the gamut from the sublime to the ridiculous. Flamboyant *A Team* actor Mr. T played drums on "Rock and Roll Music." Guitar legend Jimmy Page led the band on a fun version of Little Richard's "Lucille." New Edition sang harmonies in Philadelphia on "Help Me Rhonda." Christopher Cross joined the group on "Good Vibrations." The Oak Ridge Boys collaborated with the Beach Boys on "Come Go with Me" and Joan Jett helped sing a sloppy but fun "Barbara Ann." Also present was actor John Stamos, who sat in on drums. A huge Beach Boys fan, he would end up having a long association with them. He continues to occasionally perform with the group to this day.

Although he didn't play in Philadelphia, Brian joined the band for the evening performance in Washington. Geoffrey Himes of the *Washington Post* declared the highlight of the day "a gorgeous version of 'Wouldn't It Be Nice' by a trim, beardless Brian Wilson, who sounded better than he had onstage in two decades."

Recordings of "Barbara Ann" and "Come Go with Me" were included on *Fourth of July: A Rockin' Celebration of America*, a limited-release LP issued on Mike's Love Foundation label.

SATURDAY, JULY 6, 1985: War Memorial Stadium, Buffalo, NY
The show took place following a Bisons game.

SUNDAY, JULY 7, AND MONDAY, JULY 8, 1985: Pine Knob Music Theater, Clarkston, MI, with Flash Kahan (Two shows on Sunday at 1:00 and 7:30 p.m. and one show on Monday at 7:30 p.m.)
Gary Graff of the *Detroit Free Press* attended the first of three Pine Knob concerts and commented that the group seemed rejuvenated by the injection of new songs into the set (they played "California Calling," "Crack At Your Love," and "Getcha Back") and "came up with a brisk twenty-three-song, sixty-five-minute show that was tighter and more energetic than their concerts have been in many a year."

SATURDAY, JULY 13, 1985: "Live Aid," JFK Stadium, Philadelphia, PA, with REO Speedwagon, Joan Baez, Bob Dylan, Mick Jagger, Phil Collins, Tina Turner, CSNY, Madonna, and many others.
The Beach Boys were one of numerous acts that took part in this massive benefit (one of two simultaneous concerts—the other was held in London) organized by rocker Bob Geldof to aid African hunger relief efforts.

Brian joined the group for their set, which is available as part of the *Live Aid* DVD. They performed "California Girls," "Help Me Rhonda," "Wouldn't It Be Nice," "Good Vibrations," and "Surfin' USA." Members of the group also sang backing vocals on "Roll with the Changes" during REO Speedwagon's set.

WEDNESDAY, JULY 17, 1985: Doyle Field, Bangor, ME

THURSDAY, JULY 18, AND FRIDAY, JULY 19, 1985: Jones Beach, Wantagh, NY, with Flash Kahan (One show each night at 8:00 p.m.)
The set for the first of two Jones Beach shows consisted of "California Girls," "Sloop John B," "Darlin'," "Wouldn't It Be Nice," "Getcha Back," "Do It Again," "Little Deuce Coupe," "I Get Around," "God Only Knows," "Heaven," "It's Gettin' Late," "She Believes in Love Again," "Crack at Your Love," "Help Me Rhonda," "Rockin' All over the World," "Come Go with Me," "Rock and Roll Music," "Surfin' Safari/Surf City/Surfin' USA," "California Calling," "Good Vibrations," "Barbara Ann," and "Fun, Fun, Fun." As the list makes evident, the group hadn't completely given in to the crowd's desire for oldies. They played five songs from their new album.

~~~~~~

1985

SATURDAY, JULY 20, 1985: Memorial Stadium, Scranton, PA, with Krysti Rose and the Midnight Walkers

SUNDAY, JULY 21, 1985: Riverfront Stadium, Cincinnati, OH
The group played after a Reds game.

MONDAY, JULY 22, 1985: Rickwood Field, Birmingham, AL
This concert was rescheduled from July 11.

WEDNESDAY, JULY 24, 1985: "Eleventh National Scout Jamboree," Bowling Green, VA
The Beach Boys took part in celebrations marking the opening of the National Scout Jamboree.

FRIDAY, JULY 26, 1985: Kingswood Music Theater, Vaughan, ON, Canada

SATURDAY, JULY 27, 1985: Legend Valley, Columbus, OH, with Flash Kahan, John Cafferty and the Beaver Brown Band, and Phil Dirt and the Dozers (2:00 p.m. show)

SUNDAY, JULY 28, 1985: Civic Arena, Pittsburgh, PA, with Flash Kahan and John Cafferty and the Beaver Brown Band
The set included "Getcha Back," "California Calling," "It's Gettin' Late," and "She Believes in Love Again" from the new album. Pete Bishop of the *Pittsburgh Press* commented, "the Beach Boys are getting better with age. They played and sang all their songs—and they did a pile of 'em, twenty-two songs in sixty-eight minutes—very well, and the sound system was terrific. Every nuance from the four Beach Boys themselves (Brian Wilson was absent) and their six sidemen came through."

MONDAY, JULY 29, 1985: Hershey Park, Hershey, PA (7:00 p.m. show)

WEDNESDAY, JULY 31, 1985: Ionia Fair, Ionia, MI (2 shows)

FRIDAY AUGUST 2, 1985: Metro Centre, Rockford, IL, with Flash Kahan and John Cafferty and the Beaver Brown Band
Gail Baruch of the *Register Star* reported, "'California Girls,' 'Sloop John B,' and 'Wouldn't It Be Nice' led an evening of mostly golden oldies. Sprinkled here and there were songs from their first new album in five years, *The Beach Boys*. The new stuff sounds—surprise—like their old stuff, which suited the audience. That's what they came for."

SATURDAY, AUGUST 3, 1985: Muni Opera, St. Louis, MO, with Flash Kahan and John Cafferty and the Beaver Brown Band

SUNDAY, AUGUST 4, 1985: Poplar Creek, Hoffman Estates, IL, with Flash Kahan and John Cafferty and the Beaver Brown Band (Two shows)
The group's Chicago concerts attracted capacity crowds. Ruth Silverman of the *Daily Herald* noted, "In the performance were old favorites, numbers from their new album, *The Beach Boys*, and plenty of good natured hijinks, including Bruce Johnston abandoning his keyboard to 'surf' on an onstage ramp. Mike Love lived up to his name, blowing fingertip kisses to starry-eyed fans and beckoning Sandie Castagno of Palestine from her seat to help her up to the stage. After an impromptu boogie, he planted a well-placed kiss and sent her back to the audience, weak-kneed but happy."

WEDNESDAY, AUGUST 7, 1985: Blossom Music Center, Cuyahoga Falls, OH, with Flash Kahan and John Cafferty and the Beaver Brown Band (8:00 p.m. show)

FRIDAY, AUGUST 9, 1985: Sports Center, Indianapolis, IN, with Flash Kahan and John Cafferty and the Beaver Brown Band

time: saying if he's going to come to the really big shows then he should come to the more normal dates. Come into the trenches; don't just go for the easy glory. It's been that way since 1963; this isn't anything new."

Though Brian was seldom around, touring was profitable. The band continued to be a popular concert draw. While some critics charged there was something soulless about the oldies shows they performed, fans walked away happy. The Beach Boys were an institution and they cruised along despite criticism and middle age.

THE BEACH BOYS IN CONCERT

SATURDAY, AUGUST 10, 1985: Starlight Theater, Kansas City, MO, with Flash Kahan and John Cafferty and the Beaver Brown Band (8:00 p.m. show)

SUNDAY, AUGUST 11, 1985: Mohawk Park, Tulsa, OK (3:00 p.m. show)

TUESDAY, AUGUST 13, 1985: Swiss Villa Amphitheater, Lampe, MO

WEDNESDAY, AUGUST 14, 1985: Illinois State Fair, Springfield, IL

THURSDAY, AUGUST 15, 1985: Iowa State Fair, Des Moines, IA
The group played before a crowd of 10,000. Looking out at the happy throng, Al commented, "Look at this. I love to do state fairs. It's an attitude. People are here to have fun." Mike interjected, "Everyone is in such a good mood." Bob Shaw of the *Des Moines Register* noted, "Thursday night everyone was a surfer. There wasn't an un-tapping foot in the house when the Hawaiian-shirted band opened with 'California Girls,' not a unsmiling face when they crooned 'Little Deuce Coupe,' not a seat filled—everyone was standing—when they closed with 'Fun, Fun, Fun.'"

SUNDAY, AUGUST 18, 1985: Thomas and Mack Center, Las Vegas, NV

WEDNESDAY, AUGUST 21, 1985: Pacific Coliseum, Vancouver, BC, Canada
John Mackie of the *Vancouver Sun* noted, "The highlight of the evening was Carl singing 'God Only Knows:' there was a moment at the song's end when he and Bruce Johnston sang 'God only knows what I'd be without you' one after the other, followed by a little drum roll, that was divine."

THURSDAY, AUGUST 22, 1985: Civic Stadium, Portland, OR
The show took place after a Portland Beavers game.

FRIDAY, AUGUST 23, 1985: Red Rocks Amphitheatre, Morrison, CO, with Diane Brown

SUNDAY, AUGUST 25, 1985: Lawrence Dumont Stadium, Wichita, KS, with John Cafferty and the Beaver Brown Band

WEDNESDAY, AUGUST 28, 1985: University of North Dakota, Grand Forks, ND, with the Rockin' Hollywoods

THURSDAY, AUGUST 29, 1985: South Dakota State Fair, Huron, SD (Two shows at 7:00 and 930 p.m.)

FRIDAY, AUGUST 30, 1985: Nebraska State Fair, Lincoln, NE

SATURDAY, AUGUST 31, 1985: Riverfront Amphitheater, Hannibal, MO, with Stagefright (8:00 p.m. show)
This show on the banks of the Mississippi was attended by 8,000 fans. Beverly Darr of the *Courier Post* reported, "The California group . . . proved that talent, energy, and performing ability need not decrease with age . . . The Beach Boys seemed to grow more energetic as they sang 'Rockin' All over the World,' 'Rock and Roll Music,' and 'Surfin' Safari.' They appeared just as excited as their audience, jumping, dancing or shifting from foot to foot during the rest of the concert."

SUNDAY, SEPTEMBER 1, 1985: Albi Stadium, Spokane, WA, with the Greg Kihn Band, Quarterflash, Rendezvous, All Fall Down, and Mynx
At this show, technical problems with the sound played havoc with the set. The group briefly left the stage while technicians tried to repair it. They carried on with the show, but without the aid of monitors. Kevin Baxter of the *Spokane Chronicle* reported, "Faced with such insurmountable odds, the group switched on the automatic pilot, completing the seventy-one-minute performance without much of the verve and spontaneity that has marked its twenty-five-year career."

MONDAY, SEPTEMBER 2, 1985: Pacific Amphitheater, Costa Mesa, CA, with Quarterflash (8:00 p.m. show)

SATURDAY, SEPTEMBER 14, AND SUNDAY, SEPTEMBER 15, 1985: Puyallup Fair, Puyallup, WA

SUNDAY, SEPTEMBER 22, 1985: "Farm Aid," University of Illinois, Champaign, IL
The Beach Boys took part in this star-studded concert organized by Willie Nelson to raise money for America's struggling farmers. The entire show was televised on the Nashville Network. The group, minus Brian, performed a similar set to the one they played at Live Aid.

FRIDAY, SEPTEMBER 27, 1985: Southern Star Amphitheater, Houston, TX
A crowd of 10,000 turned out for the first date of the fall tour. Marty Racine of the *Houston Chronicle* reported, "The brand new audience of teenagers and a few of their parents, neither of whom were really around when Brian, Carl, and Dennis Wilson; Al Jardine, Mike Love and Bruce Johnston elevated California dreamin' to American pop reality, was standing in appreciation Friday night and clapping along to a medley of hits: 'I Get Around,' 'California Girls,' 'Sloop John B,' and all the others."

SATURDAY SEPTEMBER 28, 1985: UNO Baseball Field, New Orleans, LA, with John Cafferty and the Beaver Brown Band (1:00 p.m. show) and Arkansas State Fair, Little Rock, AR, with Michael Martin Murphy

SUNDAY, SEPTEMBER 29, 1985: Auditorium Shores, Austin, TX

TUESDAY, OCTOBER 1, 1985: University of Virginia, Charlottesville, VA

WEDNESDAY, OCTOBER 2, 1985: Civic Center, Charleston, WV, with Three Dog Night

THURSDAY, OCTOBER 3, 1985: Coliseum, Charlotte, NC, with Three Dog Night (8:00 p.m. show)

FRIDAY, OCTOBER 4, 1985: University of Tennessee, Chattanooga, TN, with Three Dog Night (8:00 p.m. show)

SATURDAY, OCTOBER 5, 1985: Hampton Coliseum, Hampton, VA, with Three Dog Night

SUNDAY, OCTOBER 6, 1985: George Mason University, Fairfax, VA, with Three Dog Night

TUESDAY, OCTOBER 8, 1985: Ocean Center, Daytona Beach, FL, with Three Dog Night

WEDNESDAY, OCTOBER 9, 1985: USF Sun Dome, Tampa, FL, with Three Dog Night

THURSDAY, OCTOBER 10, 1985: Carolina Coliseum, Columbia, SC, with Three Dog Night (Two shows)

FRIDAY, OCTOBER 11, 1985: Fox Theater, Atlanta, GA, with Three Dog Night (Two shows)

SATURDAY, OCTOBER 12, 1985: Middle Tennessee State University, Murfreesboro, TN, with Three Dog Night (8:00 p.m. show)
Keyboardist Jimmy Greenspan of Three Dog Night joined the band for "Fun, Fun, Fun."

SUNDAY, OCTOBER 13, 1985: Purdue University, Lafayette, IN, with Three Dog Night

THURSDAY, OCTOBER 24, 1985: Coast Guard Hangar, San Diego, CA
This was a private show for the Young President's Organization.

"Mike Love lived up to his name, blowing fingertip kisses to starry-eyed fans and beckoning Sandie Castagno of Palestine from her seat to help her up to the stage. After an impromptu boogie, he planted a well-placed kiss and sent her back to the audience, weak-kneed but happy."

THE BEACH BOYS IN CONCERT

FRIDAY, NOVEMBER 1, 1985: Concord Pavilion, Concord, CA, with Trak (8:00 p.m. show)
The set consisted of "California Girls/Sloop John B/Darlin'/Dance, Dance, Dance/Wouldn't It Be Nice" (medley), "Do It Again," "Little Deuce Coupe," "I Get Around," "God Only Knows," "Heaven," "Come Go with Me," "Getcha Back," "She Believes In Love Again," "Help Me Rhonda," "Be True to Your School," "Rockin' All Over the World," "Rock and Roll Music," "Surfin' Safari/Surf City/Surfin' USA" (medley), "Good Vibrations," "Barbara Ann," and "Fun, Fun, Fun."

SATURDAY, NOVEMBER 2, 1985: Arizona State Fair, Phoenix, AZ

SUNDAY, NOVEMBER 10, 1985: University of Arizona, Tucson, AZ (7:00 p.m. show)
The group played as part of UA's centennial celebration. The 5,000 fans that attended had a blast, but M. Scot Skinner of the Arizona Daily Star declared the band boring and noted they played the exact same show he'd witnessed at Hi Corbett Field in May. "The Beach Boys have become the George Burns of rock 'n' roll. They have been playing their sunny surfin' tunes for twenty-five years and the pumped up reaction to their concert last night would indicate many more happy years in the sand."

WEDNESDAY, NOVEMBER 13, 1985: Centrum, Worcester, MA

SATURDAY, NOVEMBER 16, 1985: Olympic Center, Lake Placid, NY, with Todd Hobin and the Heat
Ron Landfried of the *Lake Placid News* reported, "Group leader Mike Love led the band, with six vocalists and two drummers, through renditions of all the good old songs, including 'Surfin' USA,' 'Little Deuce Coupe,' and 'Help Me Rhonda.' The band's encore was three great oldies— 'Good Vibrations,' 'Barbara Ann,' and 'Fun, Fun, Fun' . . . My only criticism of the concert was that it wasn't longer and there was only one encore."

"The Beach Boys have become the George Burns of rock 'n' roll. They have been playing their sunny surfin' tunes for twenty-five years and the pumped up reaction to their concert last night would indicate many more happy years in the sand."

1986

NINETEEN EIGHTY-SIX was a busy year, including a summer tour sponsored by Sunkist. Brian took part in some TV shoots but played only a few concerts. The group spent little time in the studio, but put out two singles, "Rock and Roll to the Rescue" and "California Dreamin'," both of which appeared on the compilation *Made in the USA* released that year.

CONCERTS PLAYED IN
1986

MONDAY, JANUARY 27, TO WEDNESDAY, JANUARY 29, 1986: Harrah's Tahoe, Stateline, NV

FRIDAY, JANUARY 31, 1986: Civic Center, Hartford, CT

SATURDAY, FEBRUARY 1, 1986: Copps Coliseum, Hamilton, ON, Canada

FRIDAY, MARCH 28, 1986: West Palm Beach Auditorium, FL, with Firefall

SATURDAY, MARCH 29, 1986: John L. Knight Center, Miami, FL

SATURDAY, MAY 3, 1986: Metro Center, Halifax, NS, Canada, with Cats Can Fly

SUNDAY, MAY 4, 1986: Coliseum, Moncton, NB, Canada

MONDAY, MAY 5, 1986: Aitken Center, Fredericton, NB, Canada

WEDNESDAY, MAY 7, 1986: Memorial Stadium, St. John, NB, Canada (Two shows)

SUNDAY, MAY 18, 1986: Jack Murphy Stadium, San Diego, CA
Portions of this show were filmed for a video for "Rock and Roll to the Rescue."

SATURDAY, MAY 31, 1986: Metropolitan Stadium, Jacksonville, FL
The group's tour was to start May 29, but the schedule was adjusted so they could complete the "Rock and Roll to the Rescue" video at Venice Beach that day. Brian took part, as did a young Drew Barrymore.

SUNDAY, JUNE 1, 1986: Gulf Coast Coliseum, Biloxi, MI

MONDAY, JUNE 2, 1986: Greer Stadium, Nashville, TN

WEDNESDAY, JUNE 4, AND THURSDAY, JUNE 5, 1986: Mud Island Amphitheater, Memphis, TN

FRIDAY, JUNE 6, 1986: Joe Davis Stadium, Huntsville, AL

SATURDAY, JUNE 7, 1986: Muni, St. Louis, MO, with Roger McGuinn

SUNDAY, JUNE 8, 1986: Texas Stadium, Dallas, TX

MONDAY, JUNE 9, 1986: All Sport Stadium, Oklahoma City, OK

WEDNESDAY, JUNE 11, 1986: Lakeview Arena, Marquette, MI

THURSDAY, JUNE 12, 1986: Metro Center, Rockford, IL, with Roger McGuinn

FRIDAY, JUNE 13, 1986: Timber Wolf Amphitheater, King's Island, OH, with Roger McGuinn

SATURDAY, JUNE 14, 1986: Sports Center, Indianapolis, IN, with Roger McGuinn

SUNDAY, JUNE 15, AND MONDAY, JUNE 16, 1986: Blossom Music Center, Cuyahoga Falls, OH, with John Cafferty and the Beaver Brown Band

1986

TUESDAY, JUNE 17, 1986: Broome County Veterans Arena, Binghamton, NY

WEDNESDAY, JUNE 18, 1986: Civic Center, Erie, PA

THURSDAY, JUNE 19, AND FRIDAY, JUNE 20, 1986: Pine Knob Music Theater, Clarkston, MI, with Roger McGuinn

SATURDAY, JUNE 21, 1986: Fairgrounds, York, PA, with Roger McGuinn (Two shows)

SUNDAY, JUNE 22, 1986: War Memorial Arena, Rochester, NY, with Roger McGuinn

MONDAY, JUNE 23, 1986: SPAC, Saratoga, NY, with Todd Hobin and the Heat

WEDNESDAY, JUNE 25, 1986: Arms Park, Manchester, NH, with America

Onstage in Sacramento on July 18, 1986. Panayiotis Bagdanos

THURSDAY, JUNE 26, 1986: La Ronde, Montreal, QB, Canada

FRIDAY, JUNE 27, 1986: Molson Park, Barrie, ON, Canada

SATURDAY, JUNE 28, 1986: War Memorial Stadium, Buffalo, NY

SUNDAY, JUNE 29, 1986: Lumberton Music Festival, Muskegon, MI and Castle Farms, Charlevoix, MI

TUESDAY, JULY 1, 1986: Roberts Stadium, Sioux City, IA, with the Moody Blues

WEDNESDAY, JULY 2, 1986: Sandstone Amphitheater, Bonner Springs, KS, with the Fixx and the Moody Blues

THURSDAY, JULY 3, 1986: Rosenblatt Stadium, Omaha, NE, with the Moody Blues and the Fixx
The set for this show consisted of: "Rock and Roll to the Rescue," "Rock and Roll Music," "Good Vibrations," "Getcha Back," "Darlin'," "Dance, Dance, Dance," "Wouldn't It Be Nice," "God Only Knows," "Sloop John B," "Come Go with Me," "Little Deuce Coupe/Little Old Lady from Pasadena/Hey Little Cobra/Shut Down/409/Little GTO/I Get Around," "Surfer Girl," "Do It Again," "Help Me Rhonda," "Surfin' Safari/Hawaii/Catch a Wave/Surf City/Surfin' USA," "Lady Liberty," "California Girls," "Barbara Ann," and "Fun, Fun, Fun."

FRIDAY, JULY 4, 1986: "Farm Aid," Manor, TX, and U.S.S. Iowa, NY
The Beach Boys took part in the second Farm Aid benefit, televised on TNN. The set included "Rock and Roll to The Rescue" and a reworked version of "Lady Lynda" called "Lady Liberty." They then flew to New York for a show aboard the U.S.S. Iowa near the Statue of Liberty.

TUESDAY, JULY 15, 1986: Oasis Water Park, Palm Springs, CA

WEDNESDAY, JULY 16, 1986: Pacific Amphitheater, Costa Mesa, CA, with Southside Johnny and the Asbury Jukes

THURSDAY, JULY 17, 1986: Shoreline Amphitheater, Mountain View, CA, with Southside Johnny and the Asbury Jukes

THE BEACH BOYS IN CONCERT

FRIDAY, JULY 18, 1986: Cal-Expo Amphitheater, Sacramento, CA, with Southside Johnny and the Asbury Jukes

SATURDAY, JULY 19, 1986: Silver Dollar Fairgrounds, Chico, CA and Park West, Salt Lake City, UT, with Southside Johnny and the Asbury Jukes

SUNDAY, JULY 20, 1986: Red Rocks Amphitheater, Morrison, CO

MONDAY, JULY 21, 1986: Fairgrounds, Minot, ND

TUESDAY, JULY 22, 1986: Rushmore Plaza Civic Center, Rapid City, SD

THURSDAY, JULY 24, 1986: Alpine Valley Music Theater, East Troy, WI, with the Moody Blues

FRIDAY, JULY 25, 1986: Astrodome, Houston, TX, with Jose Feliciano and Otis Day and the Knights
The group took part in the opening ceremonies for the U.S. Olympic Festival.

SATURDAY, JULY 26, 1986: Harper Stadium, Ft. Smith, AR, with Three Dog Night

SUNDAY, JULY 27, 1986: Dumont Stadium, Wichita, KS

MONDAY, JULY 28, 1986: Swiss Villa Amphitheater, Lampe, MO

WEDNESDAY, JULY 30, 1986: Mesker Theater, Evansville, IN

THURSDAY, JULY 31, 1986: Hara Arena, Dayton, OH, with Roger McGuinn

FRIDAY, AUGUST 1, 1986: Civic Arena, Pittsburgh, PA, with Katrina and the Waves

SATURDAY, AUGUST 2, 1986: Fair, Clearfield, PA (Two shows)

SUNDAY, AUGUST 3, 1986: Coliseum, Fort Wayne, IN

MONDAY, AUGUST 4, 1986: State Fair, Columbus, OH

WEDNESDAY, AUGUST 6, 1986: Great Woods, Mansfield, MA, with Katrina and the Waves

THURSDAY, AUGUST 7, 1986: Cayuga County Fair, Weedsport, NY, with Katrina and the Waves

FRIDAY, AUGUST 8, 1986: Monroe County Fair, Monroe, MI

MONDAY, AUGUST 11, AND TUESDAY, AUGUST 12, 1986: Garden State Arts Center, Holmdel, NJ

THURSDAY, AUGUST 14, AND FRIDAY, AUGUST 15, 1986: Jones Beach, Wantagh, NY

SATURDAY, AUGUST 16, 1986: JFK Stadium, Bridgeport, CT and Civic Center, Springfield, MA, with John Cafferty and the Beaver Brown Band

SUNDAY, AUGUST 17, 1986: Merriweather Post Pavilion, Columbia, MD, with Roger McGuinn

TUESDAY, AUGUST 19, 1986: Broome County Veterans Arena, Binghamton, NY, with Katrina and the Waves

WEDNESDAY, AUGUST 20, 1986: Mann Music Center, Philadelphia, PA, with Katrina and the Waves

The Beach Boys (including a trimmed-down Brian) pose with actor John Stamos in September 1986. Ian Rusten Collection

FRIDAY, AUGUST 22, 1986: Kentucky State Fair, Louisville, KY

SATURDAY, AUGUST 23, 1986: Du Quoin Fair, Du Quoin, IL

SUNDAY, AUGUST 24, 1986: Iowa State Fair, Des Moines, IA

MONDAY, AUGUST 25, 1986: Minnesota State Fair, St. Paul, MN

THE BEACH BOYS IN CONCERT

TUESDAY, AUGUST 26, 1986: South Dakota State Fair, Huron, SD

WEDNESDAY, AUGUST 27, 1986: Poplar Creek, Hoffman Estates, IL, with Roger McGuinn

FRIDAY, AUGUST 29, 1986: Chastain Park, Atlanta, GA, with Roger McGuinn

SATURDAY, AUGUST 30, 1986: Riverfront Stadium, Charleston, WV

SUNDAY, AUGUST 31, 1986: State Fair, Allentown, PA, with Pretty Poison (Two shows)

MONDAY, SEPTEMBER 1, 1986: Busch Gardens, Williamsburg, VA (Two shows)

FRIDAY, SEPTEMBER 12, 1986: Expo Theatre, Vancouver, BC, Canada

SATURDAY, SEPTEMBER 13, AND SUNDAY, SEPTEMBER 14, 1986: Puyallup Fair, Puyallup, WA (Two shows each day)

MONDAY, SEPTEMBER 29, 1986: Kern County Fair, Bakersfield, CA
On September 26 the group (including Brian) taped an appearance on NBC TV's *You Again* with John Stamos. They performed "California Girls," "Surfin' USA," and "California Dreamin'" before a live audience.

THURSDAY, OCTOBER 2, 1986: Ventura County Fair, Ventura, CA

SATURDAY, OCTOBER 4, 1986: Central Washington State Fair, Yakima, WA

MONDAY, OCTOBER 6, 1986: Odeum Expo, Villa Park, IL (Private)

SATURDAY, OCTOBER 18, 1986: Rice Stadium, Houston, TX

FRIDAY, OCTOBER 24, 1986: Oak Mountain Amphitheater, Pelham, AL, with Roger McGuinn

SATURDAY, OCTOBER 25, 1986: Orlando Stadium, Orlando, FL

SUNDAY, OCTOBER 26, 1986: Civic Center, Pensacola, FL, with Roger McGuinn

MONDAY, OCTOBER 27, 1986: Manatee Civic Center, Palmetto, FL

THURSDAY, OCTOBER 30, 1986: University of Florida, Gainesville, FL

FRIDAY, OCTOBER 31, 1986: Valdosta State University, Valdosta, GA

SATURDAY, NOVEMBER 1, 1986: Superdome, New Orleans, LA

FRIDAY, DECEMBER 12, 1986: Royal Hawaiian Hotel, Waikiki, HI, with Ray Charles, Belinda Carlisle, Jeffrey Osborne, Three Dog Night, the Everly Brothers, Joe Piscopo, Glen Campbell, Patrick Duffy, the Fabulous Thunderbirds, Paul Shaffer, and Gloria Loring
The Beach Boys taped their twenty-fifth anniversary show before a live audience. It aired in early 1987 on ABC TV. The show featured numerous guest stars, including Ray Charles on "Sail on Sailor" and the Everly Brothers on "Don't Worry Baby." It was most notable for the closing performance by Brian of his new song, "Spirit of Rock and Roll."

WEDNESDAY, DECEMBER 17, 1986: Sullivan Arena, Anchorage, AK, with Razar
Mike was ill, so Brian filled in at this show.

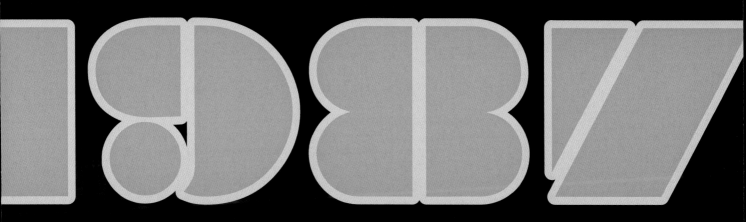

NINETEEN EIGHTY-SEVEN was another hectic year, with numerous concerts, including a summer tour sponsored by Chevrolet and European dates in July. Other than collaborating with the Fat Boys on "Wipe Out" and Little Richard on "Happy Endings," the band stayed out of the studio. At this point they lacked a recording contract. Carl expressed an interest in making a deal, but Mike told a reporter that he preferred having the freedom to work for whomever they pleased. Brian was busy working on a solo album for Sire Records. He played a handful of dates, including a week

THE BEACH BOYS IN CONCERT

CONCERTS PLAYED IN
1987

FRIDAY, JANUARY 23, 1987: Celebrity Theater, Phoenix, AZ

SUNDAY, JANUARY 25, 1987: Super Bowl XXI Pre-Game, Rose Bowl, Pasadena, CA
The day before this appearance, the group appeared on "Super Night at the Super Bowl" on CBS TV. They performed "The Little Old Lady from Pasadena" with Brian.

MONDAY, JANUARY 26, 1987: Universal Sheraton Hotel, Los Angeles, CA (private)

THURSDAY, JANUARY 29, 1987: Dane County Coliseum, Madison, WI

FRIDAY, JANUARY 30, 1987: Masonic Auditorium, Toledo, OH (Two shows)

SATURDAY, JANUARY 31, 1987: Embassy Theater, Fort Wayne, IN (Two shows)

TUESDAY, FEBRUARY 3, 1987: Memorial War Arena, Johnstown, PA

WEDNESDAY, FEBRUARY 4, 1987: Memorial Auditorium, Utica, NY, with Joan Jett

THURSDAY, FEBRUARY 5, 1987: Civic Center, Providence, RI, with Roger McGuinn

FRIDAY, FEBRUARY 6, 1987: Civic Center, Hartford, CT

SATURDAY, FEBRUARY 7, 1987: Sands, Atlantic City, NJ (Two shows)

SUNDAY, FEBRUARY 8, 1987: Coliseum, Richmond, VA

MONDAY, FEBRUARY 9, 1987: Morehead University, Morehead, KY

TUESDAY, FEBRUARY 10, 1987: University of Notre Dame, South Bend, IN, with Joan Jett

THURSDAY, FEBRUARY 12, TO SUNDAY, FEBRUARY 15, 1987: Caesars Tahoe, Stateline, NV

WEDNESDAY, FEBRUARY 18, TO MONDAY, FEBRUARY 23, 1987: Caesars Palace, Las Vegas, NV
Brian played several of these shows.

FRIDAY, MARCH 27, 1987: Clarendon Plaza Hotel, Daytona Beach, FL (Free show)

FRIDAY, APRIL 3, 1987: West Palm Beach Auditorium, West Palm Beach, FL

SATURDAY, APRIL 4, 1987: Hiram Bithorn Stadium, San Juan, Puerto Rico

SUNDAY, APRIL 5, 1987: Miami Marine Stadium, Miami, FL

WEDNESDAY, APRIL 8, 1987: University of Louisiana, Monroe, LA

THURSDAY, APRIL 9, 1987: Audubon Zoo, New Orleans, LA

FRIDAY, APRIL 10, 1987: UNC, Wilmington, NC (Two shows)

SATURDAY, APRIL 11, 1987: Memorial Stadium, Charlotte, NC, with the Fantastic Shakers

SUNDAY, APRIL 12, 1987: Civic Center, Tallahassee, FL

FRIDAY, APRIL 17, AND SATURDAY, APRIL 18, 1987: Universal Amphitheater, Los Angeles, CA
Brian played in place of Al.

SUNDAY, APRIL 26, 1987: Hi Corbett Field, Tucson, AZ

WEDNESDAY, APRIL 29, 1987: Sportsplex, Lethbridge, AB, Canada

THURSDAY, APRIL 30, 1987: Northlands Coliseum, Edmonton, AB, Canada

SATURDAY, MAY 2, 1987: Olympic Saddledome, Calgary, AB, Canada

SUNDAY, MAY 3, 1987: Agridome, Regina, SK, Canada

MONDAY, MAY 4, 1987: Arena, Winnipeg, MB, Canada, with the Terry Crawford Band

WEDNESDAY, MAY 6, 1987: Green Bay, WI

THURSDAY, MAY 7, 1987: Arena, Sudbury, ON, Canada, with the Terry Crawford Band
Over 7,000 people attended this show. Sheri Haigh of the *Sudbury Star* reported, "The group cranked out all its hits, including 'Surfer Girl,' 'Good Vibrations,' and 'Fun, Fun, Fun' . . . Things really seemed to pick up when Love encouraged the audience to stand for 'Help Me Rhonda.' It seemed as though every single member of the audience clapped or danced to the song."

FRIDAY, MAY 8, 1987: Copps Coliseum, Hamilton, ON, Canada

SATURDAY, MAY 9, 1987: Quebec Coliseum, Quebec City, QB, Canada

SUNDAY, MAY 10, 1987: Civic Centre, Ottawa, ON, Canada

MONDAY, MAY 11, 1987: Forum, Montreal, QB, Canada

SATURDAY, MAY 23, 1987: Metropolitan Park, Jacksonville, FL

SUNDAY, MAY 24, 1987: Cramton Bowl, Montgomery, AL, and Municipal Auditorium, Mobile, AL

MONDAY, MAY 25, 1987: Tanglewood Park, Clemmons, NC, with Chairmen of the Board and Smylie (6:00 p.m.)

THURSDAY, MAY 28, 1987: Chastain Park, Atlanta, GA

FRIDAY, MAY 29, 1987: Oak Mountain Amphitheater, Pelham, AL

SATURDAY, MAY 30, 1987: Centroplex, Baton Rouge, LA, and "The Cenlebration Festival," Alexandria, LA

SUNDAY, MAY 31, 1987: Mud Island Amphitheatre, Memphis, TN (two shows)

THURSDAY, JUNE 4, 1987: Timber Wolf Amphitheatre, King's Island, OH

FRIDAY, JUNE 5, 1987: Van Braun Center, Huntsville, AL

THE BEACH BOYS IN CONCERT

SATURDAY, JUNE 6, 1987: Starwood Amphitheater, Nashville, TN, with Mel and the Party Hats

SUNDAY, JUNE 7, 1987: Wolf Trap Farm, Vienna, VA

TUESDAY, JUNE 9, 1987: "Digital Communications Associates for Comdex Trade Show," Atlanta, GA (Private)

WEDNESDAY, JUNE 10, 1987: Sunken Garden, San Antonio, TX, with Omar and the Howlers

THURSDAY, JUNE 11, 1987: Sunland Race Track, El Paso, TX (Canceled)

FRIDAY, JUNE 12, 1987: Zoo Amphitheatre, Oklahoma City, OK

SATURDAY, JUNE 13, 1987: Rosenblatt Stadium, Omaha, NE

SUNDAY, JUNE 14, 1987: Arlington Stadium, Arlington, TX

MONDAY, JUNE 15, 1987: Miller Outdoor Stage, Burlington, IA

TUESDAY, JUNE 16, 1987: Sandstone Amphitheatre, Bonner Springs, KS

THURSDAY, JUNE 18, 1987: State Fairgrounds, Columbus, OH

FRIDAY, JUNE 19, 1987: Auditorium Theater, Chicago, IL (Benefit)

SATURDAY, JUNE 20, 1987: Pine Knob Music Theater, Clarkston, MI

SUNDAY, JUNE 21, 1987: Val Du Lakes Music Theater, Silver Lake, MI, and Pine Knob Music Theater, Clarkston, MI

MONDAY, JUNE 22, 1987: Community College of the Finger Lakes, Canandaigua, NY
On June 23, the Beach Boys filmed the "Wipe Out" video in New York City with the Fat Boys. Brian was present, but Carl didn't participate.

WEDNESDAY, JUNE 24, 1987: Civic Arena, Pittsburgh, PA, with the Washington Squares
Brian filled in for Al for a week of dates. Terry Hazlett of the *Observer Reporter* commented, "Looking out of place in an oversized suit, he sang off-key versions of 'Don't Worry Baby' and 'In My Room' and seemed to think he was part of a Vegas act instead of a rock show. He waltzed across the stage and gestured to the audience as if he were a lounge singer."

THURSDAY, JUNE 25, 1987: Marcus Amphitheater, Milwaukee, WI, with the Washington Squares

FRIDAY, JUNE 26, 1987: Blossom Music Center, Cuyahoga Falls, OH, with the Washington Squares
Commenting on Brian's presence, Jane Scott of the *Plains-Dealer* noted, "Wilson crisscrossed the stage, singing lead on 'Help Me Rhonda.' He wasn't actually spontaneous—there was the feeling his moves had been carefully rehearsed—but he danced as he moved, sometimes backwards . . . His voice may be a little colorless and he has no facial expressions but the joy was in knowing that he could do this."

SATURDAY, JUNE 27, 1987: Molson Park, Barrie, ON, Canada

SUNDAY, JUNE 28, 1987: Turn Road Stadium, Old Orchard Beach, ME

MONDAY, JUNE 29, AND TUESDAY, JUNE 30, 1987: Great Woods Center, Mansfield, MA, with Mason Ruffner

1 JAHR **RSH** -WIR FEIERN!

Good Vibrations over Germany

the BEACH BOYS

Open Air

BRIAN WILSON, CARL WILSON,
MIKE LOVE, AL JARDINE,
BRUCE JOHNSTON
& Supporting Musicians

+Opening Act

Mittwoch
22. Juli 87
Bad Segeberg
Freilichtbühne

Einlaß 18 Uhr
Beginn
20 Uhr

Verb. Vorverkauf:
38,- DM zzgl.
10% Vvk. Geb.
Tageskasse: 45,-

Vorverkauf an allen bekannten Vorverkaufsstellen
in Norddeutschland, schriftl. Bestellung an
Karsten Jahnke Konzertdirektion Hallerstr. 72, 2000 Hamburg 13,
tel. Bestellung über den Sunrise Kartenservice 04158/ 275.

GAULOISES
Drehtabak
Würzig und
rund im
Geschmack.

Cooperation:
Sunrise /
Karsten Jahnke
Konzertdirektion

SUNRISE

THE BEACH BOYS IN CONCERT

WEDNESDAY, JULY 1, 1987: Garden State Arts Center, Holmdel, NJ, with Mason Ruffner
Al returned for this show, but Brian remained for the remaining tour dates.

THURSDAY, JULY 2, 1987: High School Stadium, Parkersburg, WV

SATURDAY, JULY 4, 1987: Tampa Stadium, Tampa, FL, with Starship, Roger McGuinn, and Whitney Houston and Zilker Park, Austin, TX
Brian took part in both shows, singing lead on "Don't Worry Baby" and "Surfer Girl."

SUNDAY, JULY 19, 1987: Wembley Arena, London, England, with Taj Mahal
This was the opening date of the Beach Boys' first European tour since 1980. It was a truncated four-day affair, with Carl the only Wilson present. Jeff Foskett, Billy Hinsche, Ed Carter, Bobby Figueroa, Mike Kowalski, and Mike Meros accompanied them.

U.K. fans expressed disappointment that they played only one British date. However, most agreed it was a good show. Paul Young and Katrina and the Waves joined in on "Barbara Ann." The full set consisted of "California Girls," "I Can Hear Music," "Sloop John B," "Darlin'," "Dance, Dance, Dance," "Wouldn't It Be Nice," "Do It Again," "Then I Kissed Her," "Don't Worry Baby," "In My Room," God Only Knows," "Cotton Fields," "Okie from Muskogee" (one verse), "Little Deuce Coupe/Little Old Lady from Pasadena/Shut Down/409/GTO/I Get Around" (medley), "Surfer Girl," "Heaven," "Getcha Back," "California Dreamin'," "Come Go with Me," "Disney Girls," Good Vibrations," "Rock and Roll Music," "Help Me Rhonda," "Barbara Ann," "Wipe Out" (instrumental), "Surfin' Safari/Surf City/Surfin' USA," and "Fun, Fun, Fun."

TUESDAY, JULY 21, 1987: "Windsurf Festival," Knokke Heist, Belgium
WEDNESDAY, Belgian TV filmed this show.

WEDNESDAY, JULY 22, 1987: Bad Segerberg, Germany

THURSDAY, JULY 23, 1987: Paleo Folk Festival, Nylon, Switzerland, with Blow Monkeys and Carmel

SUNDAY, JULY 26, 1987: War Memorial Stadium, Buffalo, NY

MONDAY, JULY 27, 1987: Tanglewood Festival, Lennox, MA, with the Partland Brothers

WEDNESDAY, JULY 29, AND THURSDAY, JULY 30, 1987: Jones Beach, Wantagh, NY

FRIDAY, JULY 31, 1987: U.S. Submarine Base, Groton, CT

SATURDAY, AUGUST 1, 1987: The Pier, New York, NY

SUNDAY, AUGUST 2, 1987: Waterloo Festival of the Arts, Stanhope, NJ, and Memorial Stadium, Scranton, PA

MONDAY, AUGUST 3, 1987: Garden State Arts Center, Holmdel, NJ, with the Partland Brothers

TUESDAY, AUGUST 4, 1987: County Fair, Clearfield, PA

WEDNESDAY, AUGUST 5, TO MONDAY, AUGUST 10, 1987: Caesars Palace, Las Vegas, NV
Jan Berry appeared at one show to sing "Little Old Lady from Pasadena."

THURSDAY, AUGUST 13, 1987: California Mid-State Fair, Paso Robles, CA

FRIDAY, AUGUST 14, 1987: Pacific Amphitheater, Costa Mesa, CA

Receiving an award backstage at the Shoreline Amphitheater, August 16, 1987. Photo: Panayiotis Bagdanos

SATURDAY, AUGUST 15, 1987: Sonoma County Fairgrounds, Santa Rosa, CA

SUNDAY, AUGUST 16, 1987: Shoreline Amphitheater, Mountain View, CA

MONDAY, AUGUST 17, TO THURSDAY, AUGUST 20, 1987: Caesars Tahoe, Stateline, NV

SATURDAY, AUGUST 22, 1987: Civic Auditorium, Portland, OR

SUNDAY, AUGUST 23, 1987: Pacific Coliseum, Vancouver, BC, with Tangerine
While in Vancouver, the group also played a private show for L-M dealers.

SATURDAY, AUGUST 29, 1987: Colorado State Fair, Pueblo, CO

WEDNESDAY, SEPTEMBER 2, 1987: Du Quoin Fair, Du Quoin, IL, with Three Dog Night

THURSDAY, SEPTEMBER 3, 1987: Poplar Creek, Hoffman Estates, IL, with Marshall Crenshaw

FRIDAY, SEPTEMBER 4, 1987: Allentown Fair, Allentown, PA

SATURDAY, SEPTEMBER 5, 1987: SPAC, Saratoga, NY, with Marshall Crenshaw and The Sands, Atlantic City, NJ

THE BEACH BOYS IN CONCERT

SUNDAY, SEPTEMBER 6, 1987: The Sands, Atlantic City, NJ

MONDAY, SEPTEMBER 7, 1987: Cawley Memorial Stadium, Lowell, RI, with Michael McDonald and Merriweather Post Pavilion, Columbia, MD, with Marshall Crenshaw

FRIDAY, SEPTEMBER 18, 1987: Boise State University, Boise, ID

SATURDAY, SEPTEMBER 19, AND SUNDAY, SEPTEMBER 20, 1987: Puyallup Fair, Puyallup, WA (Three shows)

WEDNESDAY, SEPTEMBER 23, 1987: Northrop Auditorium, Minneapolis, MN

THURSDAY, SEPTEMBER 24, 1987: University of Iowa, Iowa City, IA, with Sawyer Brown

FRIDAY, SEPTEMBER 25, 1987: Oklahoma State Fair, Oklahoma City, OK

SATURDAY, SEPTEMBER 26, 1987: Astrodome, Houston, TX, and Six Flags Over Texas, Arlington, TX

TUESDAY, SEPTEMBER 29, 1987: New Mexico State University, Las Cruces, NM

WEDNESDAY, SEPTEMBER 30, 1987: BYU, Provo, UT, with the Kingsmen

THURSDAY, OCTOBER 1, 1987: Kern County Fair, Bakersfield, CA

FRIDAY, OCTOBER 2, 1987: Concord Pavilion, Concord, CA

SATURDAY, OCTOBER 3, 1987: Cal-Expo Amphitheater, Sacramento, CA

SUNDAY, OCTOBER 4, 1987: Jack Murphy Stadium, San Diego, CA

WEDNESDAY, OCTOBER 7, TO MONDAY, 12, 1987: Caesars Palace, Las Vegas, NV

WEDNESDAY, OCTOBER 14, 1987: Fox Theater, St. Louis, MO

THURSDAY, OCTOBER 15, 1987: La Crosse, WI

FRIDAY, OCTOBER 16, 1987: Grand Valley State College, Grand Rapids, MI, with Mitch Ryder

SATURDAY, OCTOBER 17, 1987: University of Michigan, Ann Arbor, MI

SUNDAY, OCTOBER 18, 1987: Western Illinois University, Macomb, IL

TUESDAY, OCTOBER 20, 1987: Civic Center, Huntington, WV

WEDNESDAY, OCTOBER 21, 1987: William and Mary, Williamsburg, VA, with Sawyer Brown

FRIDAY, OCTOBER 23, 1987: University of Georgia, Athens, GA, with Greg Allman
Carl was absent from this show and the next two, due to his upcoming wedding.

SUNDAY, OCTOBER 25, 1987: Louisville Gardens, Louisville, KY, with Sawyer Brown

TUESDAY, OCTOBER 27, 1987: Greenville, SC

N 1988, the Beach Boys' legendary status was affirmed by their induction into the Rock and Roll Hall of Fame. They also received the award of merit at the American Music Awards. In addition, they snagged their first number one single since 1966 with "Kokomo," which took the public by storm. The song's massive success overshadowed Brian's first solo LP, *Brian Wilson*, which despite good reviews peaked at a disappointing number fifty-four on the *Billboard* charts. However, promoting his new album kept him busy and he made few concert appearances with the Beach Boys.

CONCERTS PLAYED IN
1988

WEDNESDAY, JANUARY 6, 1988: Salt Palace, Salt Lake City, UT

TUESDAY, JANUARY 12, 1988: Orange Bowl, Miami, FL

SATURDAY, JANUARY 16, 1988: Hula Bowl, Aloha Stadium, Oahu, HI

SUNDAY, JANUARY 17, 1988: Scopus Awards Dinner, Los Angeles, CA

WEDNESDAY, JANUARY 20, 1988: Rock and Roll Hall of Fame Dinner, Waldorf-Astoria, NY
The celebratory nature of the Beach Boys' induction into to the Rock and Roll Hall of Fame was overshadowed by Mike Love's speech in which he managed to offend nearly everyone in the room. Among Mike's comments was, "I know Mick Jagger won't be here tonight . . . he's always been chickenshit to get on stage with the Beach Boys."

SATURDAY, JANUARY 23, 1988: Caesars Palace, Atlantic City, NJ (Two shows)

FRIDAY, FEBRUARY 19, TO SUNDAY, FEBRUARY 21, 1988: Caesars Tahoe, Stateline, NV
Brian was present for the February 21 show, where he replaced Al. Robert Tunick reported for *Beach Boys Stomp* that "he gave the best performance of 'In My Room' I have ever heard . . . I almost wept with joy when I heard his powerful lead vocal in 'Surfer Girl,' his evocative rendering of 'Wouldn't It Be Nice,' and sprang to my feet (along with the audience) when he launched into 'Help Me Rhonda,' with a zest for performing."

WEDNESDAY, FEBRUARY 24, TO MONDAY, FEBRUARY 29, 1988: Caesars Palace, Las Vegas, NV

WEDNESDAY, APRIL 13, TO TUESDAY, APRIL 19, 1988: Caesars Palace, Las Vegas, NV
Brian was present for some shows.

SUNDAY, MAY 15, 1988: Rangers Stadium, Arlington, TX
This was the opening show of the Beach Boys' "Chevy Heartbeat of America" tour. University of Nevada-Las Vegas cheerleaders accompanied them. Other than Bobby Figueroa's departure, the backing musicians remained unchanged from the last several years.

FRIDAY, MAY 20, 1988: Mesa Amphitheater, Gilbert, AZ
A fan filmed this show. It included rare performances of "Forever" (sung by Carl) and "This Whole World."

SATURDAY, MAY 21, 1988: Candlestick Park, San Francisco, CA, and Pacific Amphitheater, Costa Mesa, CA, with Gallagher

SUNDAY, MAY 22, 1988: Jack Murphy Stadium, San Diego, CA

FRIDAY, MAY 27, 1988: Chicago, IL (Private)

SATURDAY, MAY 28, 1988: Riverfront Stadium, Cincinnati, OH, and Crampton Bowl, Montgomery, AL (Benefit)

SUNDAY, MAY 29, 1988: Atlanta Fulton County Stadium, Atlanta, GA, and Starwood Amphitheater, Nashville, TN with Miami Sound Machine

"I know Mick Jagger won't be here tonight . . . he's always been chickenshit to get on stage with the Beach Boys."

—Mike Love

OFFICIAL PROGRAM

CHEVY'S Heartbeat OF AMERICA

The Beach Boys TOUR

Delco Electronics
Subsidiary of GM Hughes Electronics

SATURDAY, AUGUST 20, 1988
AT PILOT PARK

WBUF
fm 93

GOOD
NEIGHBOR
Chevy
DEALERS

THE BEACH BOYS IN CONCERT

MONDAY, MAY 30, 1988: USF Stadium, Tampa, FL, with Miami Sound Machine and Mississippi Coast Coliseum, Biloxi, MS, with America

WEDNESDAY, JUNE 1, 1988: Von Braun Center, Huntsville, AL, and Oak Mountain Amphitheater, Birmingham, AL

THURSDAY, JUNE 2, 1988: Civic Center, Augusta, GA

FRIDAY, JUNE 3, 1988: Cardinal Stadium, Louisville, KY

SATURDAY, JUNE 4, 1988: Mud Island Amphitheatre, Memphis, TN, with Southern Pacific (Two shows)

SUNDAY, JUNE 5, 1988: Carrowinds Palladium, Charlotte, NC, and Kings Dominion, Doswell, VA

MONDAY, JUNE 6, 1988: Wilcomico Youth and Civic Center, Salisbury, MD

WEDNESDAY, JUNE 8, 1988: J. Edgar Hoover Building, Washington, DC (Benefit for the FBI)

FRIDAY, JUNE 10, 1988: Blossom Music Center, Cuyahoga Falls, OH, with Roy Orbison and John Cafferty and the Beaver Brown Band

SATURDAY, JUNE 11, 1988: Blossom Music Center, Cuyahoga Falls, OH, with Roy Orbison and John Cafferty and the Beaver Brown Band and Pine Knob Music Theater, Clarkston, MI, with John Cafferty and the Beaver Brown Band

SUNDAY, JUNE 12, 1988: Pine Knob Music Theater, Clarkston, MI, with John Cafferty and the Beaver Brown Band

MONDAY, JUNE 13, AND TUESDAY, JUNE 14, 1988: Valley Forge Music Fair, Devon, PA (One show each night)

WEDNESDAY, JUNE 15, 1988: Columbus, OH (benefit)

FRIDAY, JUNE 17, 1988: Great Woods, Mansfield, MA, with Roy Orbison

SATURDAY, JUNE 18, 1988: Old Orchard Beach Ballpark, ME, with Roy Orbison and Great Woods, Mansfield, MA, with Roy Orbison

SUNDAY, JUNE 19, 1988: U.S. Submarine Base, Groton, CT, and Cambria County War Memorial, Johnstown, PA, with Todd Hobin and the Heat
Following these shows, the Beach Boys taped a TV special at Disney World on June 22 (it aired July 4).

THURSDAY, JUNE 23, 1988: Niagara Falls, NY

FRIDAY, JUNE 24, 1988: Tanglewood Festival, Lennox, MA, with John Cafferty and the Beaver Brown Band
Shel Horowitz of the *Union News* declared this show before 7,000 fans deserving of an award for "Most Unsatisfying Rehash." He reported, "Their music deserves better than this treatment. The group . . . was so lifeless that it seemed like someone had handed out guitars to a bunch of robots, wound them up, and told them to play. There was not an ounce of creativity: not in the song selection and order, not in the wooden performance and certainly not in the way they chose to massacre their own creative work. The show was a collection of medleys that completely buried each individual song."

1988

SATURDAY, JUNE 25, 1988: Wonderland, Maple, ON, Canada (Two shows)

SUNDAY, JUNE 26, 1988: Cheshire Fairgrounds, Keene, NH, with America, Three Dog Night, the Four Seasons, and the Mamas and the Papas and Yankee Stadium, Bronx, NY
The set list included "California Girls," "Sloop John B," "Wouldn't It Be Nice," "Dance, Dance, Dance," "Do You Wanna Dance," "Rock and Roll Music," "Surfer Girl," "California Dreamin'," "This Whole World," "Don't Worry Baby," "Little Deuce Coupe/Little Old Lady From Pasadena/Shut Down/409/ Little GTO/I Get Around" (medley), "God Only Knows," "Kokomo," "Good Vibrations," "Be True to Your School," "All Summer Long," "Help Me Rhonda," "Surfin' Safari/Surf City/Surfin' USA" (medley), "Wipe Out" (instrumental), "Barbara Ann," and "Fun, Fun, Fun."

MONDAY, JUNE 27, 1988: Champlain Valley Fairgrounds, Essex Junction, VT

TUESDAY, JUNE 28, 1988: Forum, Montreal, QB, Canada, with Roy Orbison

THURSDAY, JUNE 30, 1988: Edmonton, AL, Canada

FRIDAY, JULY 1, 1988: Toronto, ON, Canada (Private) and Laurentian University, Sudbury, ON, Canada, with Linden and Roy Orbison

SATURDAY, JULY 2, 1988: Waterloo Festival of the Arts, Stanhope, NJ, and Civic Arena, Pittsburgh, PA

SUNDAY, JULY 3, 1988: Six Flags, Jackson, NJ, and Bally's, Atlantic City, NJ

MONDAY, JULY 4, 1988: Bally's, Atlantic City, NJ

FRIDAY, JULY 15, 1988: Mackay Stadium, Reno, NV

SATURDAY, JULY 16, 1988: Fiddler's Green, Denver, CO

SUNDAY, JULY 17, 1988: Beaver Creek, Vail, CO

MONDAY, JULY 18, 1988: Civic Center, Casper, WY

TUESDAY, JULY 19, 1988: Auditorium, Sioux City, IA, with Three Dog Night and Bicentennial Center, Salina, KS, with Three Dog Night

WEDNESDAY, JULY 20, 1988: Missoula, MT, with Three Dog Night and America and Montana State Fair, Great Falls, MT, with Three Dog Night and America

THURSDAY, JULY 21, 1988: Billings, MT, with Three Dog Night and America and Rushmore Plaza Civic Center, Rapid City, SD, with Three Dog Night and America

FRIDAY, JULY 22, 1988: Civic Center, Cheyenne, WY

SATURDAY, JULY 23, 1988: Central Washington Fair, Yakima, WA, with Three Dog Night and America and Civic Stadium, Portland, OR

SUNDAY, JULY 24, 1988: Victoria, BC, Canada and Expo Theatre, Vancouver, BC, Canada

TUESDAY, JULY 26, 1988: Sportsplex, Lethbridge, AB, Canada, with Three Dog Night and America

WEDNESDAY, JULY 27, 1988: Edmonton, AL, Canada

"Their music deserves better than this treatment. The group . . . was so lifeless that it seemed like someone had handed out guitars to a bunch of robots, wound them up, and told them to play."

~~~~

THE BEACH BOYS IN CONCERT

THURSDAY, JULY 28, 1988: Sask Place, Saskatoon, SK, Canada, with Three Dog Night and America

FRIDAY, JULY 29, 1988: Keystone Centre, Brandon, MN, Canada, with the Razorbacks and Arena, Winnipeg, MN, Canada, with America and Three Dog Night

SATURDAY, JULY 30, 1988: North Dakota State Fair, Minot, ND, and Detroit Lakes, MI

SUNDAY, JULY 31, 1988: Rhinelander, WI, and Lakeview Arena, Marquette, MI

TUESDAY, AUGUST 2, 1988: Kearney, NE

THURSDAY, AUGUST 4, 1988: Clearfield Fair, Clearfield, PA (Two shows)

FRIDAY, AUGUST 5, 1988: Stabler Arena, Bethlehem, PA, and Erie, PA

SATURDAY, AUGUST 6, 1988: Lakeland Community College, Kirtland, OH

SUNDAY, AUGUST 7, 1988: Ionia Fair, Ionia, MI, and Poplar Creek, Hoffman Estates, IL

TUESDAY, AUGUST 9, 1988: Ohio State Fair, Columbus, OH

THURSDAY, AUGUST 11, 1988: Ozark Mountain Amphitheatre, Springfield, MO

FRIDAY, AUGUST 12, 1988: Sandstone Amphitheater, Bonner Springs, KS, with Southern Pacific

SATURDAY, AUGUST 13, 1988: Illinois State Fair, Springfield, IL, with Southern Pacific and Jackson, MO

SUNDAY, AUGUST 14, 1988: Wisconsin State Fair, West Allis, WI, and Six Flags Over Mid-America, Eureka, Mo (Two shows)

MONDAY, AUGUST 15, 1988: Castle Farms Music Theatre, Charlevoix, MI

WEDNESDAY, AUGUST 17, 1988: Lake Compounce, Bristol, CT, and Rockland County Fair, Rockland, NY

THURSDAY, AUGUST 18, AND FRIDAY, AUGUST 19, 1988: Jones Beach, Wantagh, NY

SATURDAY, AUGUST 20, 1988: Pilot Field, Buffalo, NY, and Walpack Inn, Walpack, NJ

SUNDAY, AUGUST 21, 1988: Wolf Trap, Vienna, VA (Two shows)

MONDAY, AUGUST 22, AND TUESDAY, AUGUST 23, 1988: Garden State Arts Center, Holmdel, NJ

WEDNESDAY, AUGUST 24, 1988: Lansdowne Park, Ottawa, ON, Canada, with the Four Seasons

FRIDAY, AUGUST 26, 1988: Indiana State Fair, Indianapolis, IN

SATURDAY, AUGUST 27, 1988: Minnesota State Fair, St. Paul, MN (Two shows)

SUNDAY, AUGUST 28, 1988: Rosenblatt Stadium, Omaha, NE, and Iowa State Fair, Des Moines, IA, with Sawyer Brown

MONDAY, AUGUST 29, 1988: Du Quoin Fair, Du Quoin, IL

WEDNESDAY, AUGUST 31, 1988: Missouri State Fair, Sedalia, MO

THURSDAY, SEPTEMBER 1, 1988: Metro Centre, Rockford, IL, with Barry's Truckers

FRIDAY, SEPTEMBER 2, 1988: NY State Fair, Syracuse, NY, with Exile

SATURDAY, SEPTEMBER 3, 1988: SPAC, Saratoga, NY, with Greg Allman and Canfield Fair, Canfield, OH

SUNDAY, SEPTEMBER 4, 1988: Quonset Point Naval Base, Providence, RI, with John Cafferty and the Beaver Brown Band and Roomful of Blues and Finger Lakes PAC, Canandaigua, NY

MONDAY, SEPTEMBER 5, 1988: Bradner Stadium, Olean, NY

WEDNESDAY, SEPTEMBER 7, 1988: "Hampton Bays Day" Festival, Hampton Bay, VA

FRIDAY, SEPTEMBER 9, 1988: Expo Centre, Topeka, KS

SATURDAY, SEPTEMBER 10 1988: McNichols Arena, Denver, CO (Two shows)
These were private shows for Martin Marietta Astronautics Group.

SATURDAY, SEPTEMBER 17, AND SUNDAY, SEPTEMBER 18, 1988: Puyallup Fair, Puyallup, WA, with Three Dog Night (Two shows on September 17 and one on September 18)

FRIDAY, SEPTEMBER 23, 1988: Cal Expo Amphitheater, Sacramento, CA
On this same day, an episode of the soap opera *One Life to Live* aired featuring Mike, Al, Bruce, and Jeff playing "Kokomo" at a high-school reunion.

SATURDAY, SEPTEMBER 24, AND SUNDAY, SEPTEMBER 25, 1988: Great America, Santa Clara, CA
Alan Boyd reported in *Beach Boys Stomp*, "I have never heard the Beach Boys so tight, so well rehearsed, so professional. The arrangements were fresh . . . the harmonies impeccable, and the choice of songs showed a self-confidence in the band that I hadn't seen in their live act before. When they took a deep breath and plunged into the opening of 'Hushabye,' chills went up and down my spine."

SATURDAY, OCTOBER 1, 1988: Jaycee Park, Wichita Falls, TX, with the Fabulous Thunderbirds and Bramlage Coliseum, Kansas State College, Manhattan, KS

THURSDAY, OCTOBER 6, 1988: Memorial Coliseum, Jacksonville, FL

FRIDAY, OCTOBER 7, 1988: Marine Center, Miami, FL

SATURDAY, OCTOBER 8, 1988: Nassau, Bahamas (Private)
A U.S. corporation booked the band to play one show for 800 lucky employees.

SUNDAY, OCTOBER 9, 1988: Boscobel Beach Hotel, Kingston, Jamaica
The Beach Boys flew to Jamaica with the Fabulous Thunderbirds as part of a prize package given away in promotion of the movie *Cocktail*.

WEDNESDAY, OCTOBER 19, TO MONDAY, OCTOBER 24, 1988: Caesars Palace, Las Vegas, NV

FRIDAY, OCTOBER 28, TO SUNDAY, OCTOBER 30, 1988: Caesars Tahoe, Stateline, NV

SATURDAY, NOVEMBER 5, 1988: Memorial Coliseum, Los Angeles, CA

THE BEACH BOYS IN CONCERT

The Beach Boys appeared with Brian following a USC football game. The appearance was partly seen in the episode of John Stamos' sitcom *Full House* that aired on November 18.

SUNDAY, NOVEMBER 6, 1988: Arizona State Fair, Phoenix, AZ

FRIDAY, DECEMBER 2, 1988: Palladium, New York, NY (Without Al)

MONDAY, DECEMBER 5, 1988: Warner Theatre, Washington, DC

FRIDAY, DECEMBER 9, 1988: Civic Center, Hartford, CT

SATURDAY, DECEMBER 10, 1988: Patriot Center, Washington, DC (Private)

"I have never heard the Beach Boys so tight, so well rehearsed, so professional. The arrangements were fresh . . . the harmonies impeccable, and the choice of songs showed a self-confidence in the band that I hadn't seen in their live act before. When they took a deep breath and plunged into the opening of 'Hushabye,' chills went up and down my spine."

—Alan Boyd

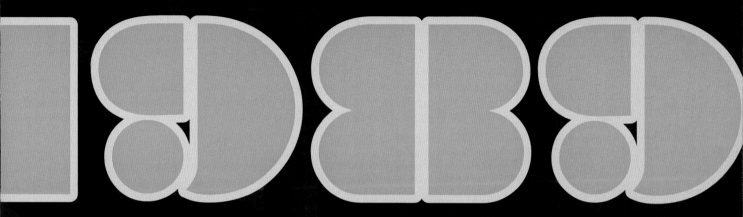

1988

THE SUCCESS OF "Kokomo" led to the Beach Boys starring in a summer TV show called *Endless Summer*. The show featured clips of the group in concert and performances by guest stars. The most interesting part of the show was the legendary "campfire" segments. The group, with Brian and assorted wives and friends, were filmed performing on the beach while sitting around a campfire. Brian was in great form and the group got into the spirit of the occasion, playing oldies and their own songs. The TV show aired while the band was on a reunion tour with Chicago, which was highly profitable if not as earth-shattering an event as the 1975 tour. Brian appeared at some shows to play a short solo set. The

CONCERTS PLAYED IN
1989

SATURDAY, JANUARY 7, 1989: Aloha Stadium, Honolulu, HI
The group performed with Brian after the Hula Bowl game.

WEDNESDAY, JANUARY 18, 1989: George Bush Inaugural, Lincoln Memorial, Washington, DC

TUESDAY, JANUARY 24, 1989: Spectrum, Philadelphia, PA, with Chicago
This was the first of three warmup "Beachago" shows to gear up for their big reunion tour. All three shows featured special appearances by Brian—he played "Surfer Girl" with the Beach Boys, and then performed solo sets with Andy Paley and Michael Bernard. They played "Love and Mercy," "Melt Away," and "Walking the Line." Brian returned for the Beachago encore. Both bands played "Kokomo," "In the Midnight Hour," "Dancing in the Streets," "Feelin' Stronger Every Day," and "Fun, Fun, Fun."

WEDNESDAY, JANUARY 25, 1989: Centrum, Worcester, MA, with Chicago

FRIDAY, JANUARY 27, 1989: Nassau Coliseum, Uniondale, NY, with Chicago

FRIDAY, FEBRUARY 10, AND SATURDAY, FEBRUARY 11, 1989: Circle Star Theater, San Carlos, CA (Two shows each day)

SUNDAY, APRIL 16, 1989: "Sports Kids Nominees Party," Irvine Marriot, Los Angeles, CA (Private)

FRIDAY, MAY 19, 1989: Cardinal Stadium, Louisville, KY

SATURDAY, MAY 20, 1989: Riverfront Stadium, Cincinnati, OH

SUNDAY, MAY 21, 1989: Atlanta Fulton County Stadium, Atlanta, GA

FRIDAY, MAY 26, 1989: Oakland Coliseum, Oakland, CA, with Chicago

SATURDAY, MAY 27, 1989: Pacific Amphitheater, Costa Mesa, CA, with Chicago
This show was filmed and used in the *Endless Summer* TV show. Brian performed a short solo set that included "Country Feeling," "In My Car," and "Love and Mercy." The group's set consisted of "California Girls," "Sloop John B," "Wouldn't It Be Nice," "Be True to Your School," "Surfer Girl," "Little Deuce Coupe/Little Old Lady from Pasadena/Shut Down/Little GTO/I Get Around" (medley), "God Only Knows," "Kokomo," "Good Vibrations," "Help Me Rhonda," "Wipe Out" (instrumental), "Barbara Ann," and "Surfin' Safari/Surf City/Surfin' USA" (medley). The encore with Chicago consisted of: "Darlin'," "Does Anybody Know What Time It Is?" "You're the Inspiration," "Rock and Roll of Music," "In the Midnight Hour," "Dancing in the Street," "Feelin' Stronger Every Day," and "Fun, Fun, Fun."

SUNDAY, MAY 28, 1989: Jack Murphy Stadium, San Diego, CA (Post-game), and Hollywood Bowl, Los Angeles, CA, with Chicago
Brian took part in the Hollywood Bowl show.

TUESDAY, MAY 30, 1989: Universal Studios, Los Angeles, CA
Filming took place for the *Endless Summer* TV show, including the sublime campfire segments (with fun performances of "Surfin'," "Smoky Joe's Café," "Be My Baby," "All I Have to Do Is Dream," "Graduation Day," and others).

1989

WEDNESDAY, MAY 31, 1989: Park West, Salt Lake City, UT, with Chicago

THURSDAY, JUNE 1, 1989: Fiddler's Green Amphitheater, Denver, CO, with Chicago

FRIDAY, JUNE 2, 1989: Eagle Raceways, Lincoln, NE, with Chicago
Heavy rains marred this show. The Beach Boys played but Chicago had to stop after three songs. The stage set was heavily damaged. A June 3 show in Davenport, IA, and June 4 show in Milwaukee were postponed.

TUESDAY, JUNE 6, 1989: Deer Creek, Noblesville, IN, with Chicago

WEDNESDAY, JUNE 7, 1989: Columbus, OH

THURSDAY, JUNE 8, AND FRIDAY, JUNE 9, 1989: Blossom Music Center, Cuyahoga Falls, OH, with Chicago

SATURDAY, JUNE 10, AND SUNDAY, JUNE 11, 1989: Poplar Creek, Hoffman Estates, IL, with Chicago

TUESDAY, JUNE 13, AND WEDNESDAY, JUNE 14, 1989: Lake Compounce, Bristol, CT, with Chicago

FRIDAY, JUNE 16, AND SATURDAY, JUNE 17, 1989: Great Woods, Mansfield, MA, with Chicago

SUNDAY, JUNE 18, 1989: Lackawanna County Stadium, Montage Mountain, PA, with Chicago

TUESDAY, JUNE 20, AND WEDNESDAY, JUNE 21, 1989: Merriweather Post Pavilion, Columbia, MD, with Chicago
Carl was not present at these shows due to "family matters."

FRIDAY, JUNE 23, AND SATURDAY, JUNE 24, 1989: Brendan Byrne Arena, East Rutherford, NJ, with Chicago

SUNDAY, JUNE 25, 1989: SPAC, Saratoga, NY, with Chicago
Michael Hochandel of the *Schenectady Gazette* reported that touring with Chicago seemed to give the Beach Boys renewed energy. He commented, "The harmonies were sharp last night and the show overall was above average for them . . . After the Beach Boys finished with signature surfing songs, Chicago returned and the two bands . . . crooned 'Wishing You Were Here,' then alternated Chicago and Beach Boys tunes deep into oldies land with 'Rock and Roll Music,' 'Midnight Hour,' and 'Dancing In the Street.'"

TUESDAY, JUNE 27, TO FRIDAY, JUNE 30, 1989: Jones Beach, Wantagh, NY, with Chicago

SUNDAY, JULY 2, 1989: Parlee Beach, Shediac, NB, Canada

MONDAY, JULY 3, 1989: Pilot Field, Buffalo, NY

TUESDAY, JULY 4, 1989: Yankee Stadium, Bronx, NY, and "Save the Bay," Norfolk, VA

FRIDAY, JULY 14, TO SUNDAY, JULY 16, 1989: Pine Knob Music Theater, Clarkston, MI, with Chicago

TUESDAY, JULY 18, 1989: Riverbend, Cincinnati, OH, with Chicago

WEDNESDAY, JULY 19, 1989: Civic Arena, Pittsburgh, PA, with Chicago

FRIDAY, JULY 21, 1989: Seashore PAC, Old Orchard Beach, ME, with Chicago

"They may look long in the tooth but vocal quality is unimpaired and much in evidence, especially when Carl Wilson launches 'God Only Knows' to the heavens."

THE BEACH BOYS IN CONCERT

SATURDAY, JULY 22, 1989: Riverside, Manchester, NH, with Chicago

SUNDAY, JULY 23, 1989: City Island, Harrisburg, PA, with Chicago

TUESDAY, JULY 25, 1989: Orange County Fairgrounds, Middletown, NY, with Chicago

WEDNESDAY, JULY 26, 1989: Cayuga County Fairgrounds, Weedsport, NY, with Chicago

FRIDAY, JULY 28, 1989: Starwood Amphitheater, Nashville, TN, with Chicago

SATURDAY, JULY 29, 1989: Lakewood Amphitheater, Atlanta, GA, with Chicago

SUNDAY, JULY 30, 1989: Greensboro Coliseum, Greensboro, NC, with Chicago

TUESDAY, AUGUST 1, 1989: Marcus Amphitheatre, Milwaukee, WI, with Chicago

WEDNESDAY, AUGUST 2, 1989: Davenport, IA, with Chicago

THURSDAY, AUGUST 3, 1989: Sandstone Amphitheatre, Bonner Springs, KS, with Chicago

FRIDAY, AUGUST 4, 1989: Starplex Amphitheatre, Dallas, TX, with Chicago

SATURDAY, AUGUST 5, 1989: Southern Star Amphitheatre, Houston, TX, with Chicago

SUNDAY, AUGUST 6, 1989: Corpus Christi, TX (Private)

TUESDAY, AUGUST 8, 1989: Hilton Head, SC

WEDNESDAY, AUGUST 9, 1989: King's Dominion, Doswell, VA

THURSDAY, AUGUST 10, 1989: Myrtle Beach, SC

FRIDAY, AUGUST 11, 1989: Greenville, SC

SATURDAY, AUGUST 12, 1989: Mud Island Amphitheater, Memphis, TN (Two shows)

MONDAY. AUGUST 14, AND TUESDAY, AUGUST 15, 1989: Garden State Arts Center, Holmdel, NJ, with Chicago

THURSDAY, AUGUST 17, 1989: Erie Stadium, Erie, PA, with Chicago

FRIDAY, AUGUST 18, 1989: CNE Grandstand, Toronto, ON, Canada, with Chicago

SATURDAY, AUGUST 19, 1989: Castle Farms Music Theatre, Charlevoix, MI

SUNDAY, AUGUST 20, 1989: Avilla Speedway, Avilla, IN and Shelbyville, IL
Glen Campbell joined the group in Indiana for "Barbara Ann." The Kokomo High School Cheerleaders also appeared. It was proclaimed "Beach Boys Day" in nearby Kokomo, Indiana.

THURSDAY, AUGUST 24, 1989: Minnesota State Fair (Canceled)

SUNDAY, AUGUST 27, 1989: Neundorf-Egerkingen, Switzerland, with Asia, It Bites, and King Creole
This was the opening date of another European tour. An August 26 show in Munich was canceled.

Courtesy of Michael Osterkamp

FRIDAY, SEPTEMBER 1, 1989: Waldbuhne, Berlin, Germany, with Asia, It Bites, and King Creole

SATURDAY, SEPTEMBER 2, 1989: Sport Park, Hannover, Germany, with Asia, It Bites, and King Creole

SUNDAY, SEPTEMBER 3, 1989: Loreley, St. Goarshausen, Germany, with Asia, It Bites, and King Creole

WEDNESDAY, SEPTEMBER 6, 1989: NEC, Birmingham, England

THURSDAY, SEPTEMBER 7, AND FRIDAY, SEPTEMBER 8, 1989: Wembley Arena, London, England (One show each night)

The Beach Boys packed Wembley Arena both nights. Max Bell of the *Evening Standard* reported, "They may look long in the tooth but vocal quality is unimpaired and much in evidence, especially when Carl Wilson launches 'God Only Knows' to the heavens. Even Mike Love, the leader elect, was less oafish than usual, restraining himself to one swipe at Mick Jagger before cranking up the ultimate car, surf, and male-bonding fantasy of 'I Get Around.' Mercifully there were no medleys but lots of crowd pleasing and enough good vibrations to set the usually sterile arena throbbing."

SUNDAY, SEPTEMBER 10, 1989: The Point, Dublin, Ireland, with the Flame

THURSDAY, SEPTEMBER 14, 1989: Schleyerhalle, Stuttgart, Germany

SATURDAY, SEPTEMBER 16, 1989: Prater Stadium, Vienna, Austria

TUESDAY, SEPTEMBER 19, 1989: Monaco (Benefit)

THURSDAY, SEPTEMBER 21, 1989: Marseilles, France (Canceled)

FRIDAY, SEPTEMBER 22, 1989: Paris, France (Canceled)

THE BEACH BOYS IN CONCERT

FRIDAY, OCTOBER 6, 1989: St. Lucie County Sports Complex, Port St. Lucie, FL, with Chicago
The Beachago tour resumed for sixteen dates.

SATURDAY, OCTOBER 7, 1989: Arena, Miami, FL, with Chicago

SUNDAY, OCTOBER 8, 1989: Sundome, Tampa, FL, with Chicago

TUESDAY, OCTOBER 10, 1989: Rupp Arena, Lexington, KY, with Chicago

---

WEDNESDAY, OCTOBER 11, 1989: Chattanooga, TN, with Chicago

THURSDAY, OCTOBER 12, 1989: University of Tennessee, Knoxville, TN, with Chicago

---

FRIDAY, OCTOBER 13, 1989: Carolina Coliseum, Columbia, SC, with Chicago

---

SATURDAY, OCTOBER 14, 1989: Clemson University, Clemson, SC, with Chicago

---

SUNDAY, OCTOBER 15, 1989: Charlotte, NC, with Chicago

TUESDAY, OCTOBER 17, 1989: Spectrum, Philadelphia, PA, with Chicago

---

WEDNESDAY, OCTOBER 18, 1989: William and Mary University, Williamsburg, VA, with Chicago

---

FRIDAY, OCTOBER 20, 1989: University of Notre Dame, South Bend, IN, with Chicago

---

SATURDAY, OCTOBER 21, 1989: University of Illinois, Champaign, IL, with Chicago

---

SUNDAY, OCTOBER 22, 1989: Hilton Coliseum, Iowa State University, Ames, IA, with Chicago

---

MONDAY, OCTOBER 23, 1989: Marine Stadium, Miami, FL (Private)

WEDNESDAY, OCTOBER 25, 1989: Arena, St. Louis, MO, with Chicago

---

THURSDAY, OCTOBER 26, 1989: Roberts Stadium, Evansville, IN, with Chicago

---

FRIDAY, OCTOBER 27, 1989: University of Toledo, Toledo, OH, with Chicago

---

SATURDAY, OCTOBER 28, 1989: Rosemont Horizon, Chicago, IL, with Chicago

---

SATURDAY, NOVEMBER 4, 1989: Coliseum, Los Angeles, CA

TUESDAY, NOVEMBER 14, TO FRIDAY, NOVEMBER 17, 1989: Caesars Palace, Las Vegas, NV

FRIDAY, NOVEMBER 24, TO SUNDAY, NOVEMBER 26, 1989: Atlantic City, NJ

1990

THE BEACH BOYS continued their relentless touring, including a profitable summer tour sponsored by Texaco. Brian took part in some shows, including subbing for Mike while he was ill. The group recorded "Problem Child" for the John Ritter film of the same name. Brian spent time in the studio recording a follow-up to his 1988 LP. The label rejected the album known as *Sweet Insanity*, and it remains unreleased.

CONCERTS PLAYED IN
1990

Brian
responded
to the fans
asking where
Mike was by
informing
them that he
was "near
death." The
audience was
understandably
shaken and
Al had to
step in and
inform them
Mike was just
"taking care of
business."

WEDNESDAY, MARCH 21, TO MONDAY, MARCH 26, 1990: Caesars Palace, Las Vegas, NV
Al didn't play any of these shows. Brian filled in.

WEDNESDAY, MARCH 28, 1990: Caesars Tahoe, Stateline, NV

TUESDAY, MAY 1, 1990: Sports Arena, San Diego, CA, with Three Dog Night and America

WEDNESDAY, MAY 2, 1990: Arizona State University, Phoenix, AZ

FRIDAY, MAY 4, 1990: Hemet, CA (Private)

SATURDAY, MAY 5, AND SUNDAY, MAY 6, 1990: Circle Star Theatre, San Carlos, CA, with Foster and Lloyd (Two shows each day)
Brian appeared with the group. He took the lead on "In My Room," "Surfer Girl," and "Wouldn't It Be Nice." The full set consisted of "California Girls," "Sloop John B," "Wouldn't It Be Nice," "California Saga," "Be True to Your School," "Surfer Girl," "Somewhere Near Japan," "Please Let Me Wonder," "Don't Worry Baby," "Still Cruisin'," "Little Deuce Coupe/Little Old Lady from Pasadena/Shut Down/Little GTO/I Get Around" (medley), "In My Room," "God Only Knows," "Good Vibrations," "Kokomo," "Help Me Rhonda," "Surfin' Safari/Surf City/Surfin' USA" (medley), "Wipe Out" (instrumental), "Barbara Ann," and "Fun, Fun, Fun."

THURSDAY, MAY 10, 1990: Myriad Arena, Oklahoma City, OK, with America and Three Dog Night

FRIDAY, MAY 11, 1990: Lawrence-Dumont Stadium, Wichita, KS

SATURDAY, MAY 12, 1990: Driller's Stadium, Tulsa, OK, and Starplex Amphitheatre, Dallas, TX, with Three Dog Night and America
Mike was absent from Tulsa. He may have missed the two previous dates as well.

SUNDAY, MAY 13, 1990: Sea World, San Antonio, TX, with Three Dog Night and America

MONDAY, MAY 14, 1990: Summit, Houston, TX, with Three Dog Night and America

TUESDAY, MAY 15, 1990: Will Rogers Memorial Court Theatre, Fort Worth, TX, with Three Dog Night and America

FRIDAY, MAY 25, 1990: Mile High Stadium, Denver, CO
The backing musicians for the 1990 summer tour consisted of mainstays Ed Carter, Mike Meros, Billy Hinsche, Mike Kowalski, and Jeff Foskett plus newcomer Matt Jardine (Al's son), who played congas and sang. John Stamos also appeared at many shows.

MONDAY, MAY 28, 1990: Atlanta Fulton Stadium, Atlanta, GA, and Hoover Stadium, Hoover, AL
Mike missed the May 28 through June 3 dates because he was in Japan playing solo gigs. Gerry Beckley of America filled in.

THURSDAY, MAY 31, 1990: Timber Wolf Amphitheater, Kings Island, OH, and Clipper's Stadium, Columbus, OH

FRIDAY, JUNE 1, 1990: Cardinal Stadium, Louisville, KY

~~~~~

1990

SATURDAY, JUNE 2, 1990: Molson Park, Barrie, ON, Canada and Cleveland Stadium, Cleveland, OH

SUNDAY, JUNE 3, 1990: Pilot Field, Buffalo, NY

FRIDAY, JUNE 29, 1990: Olympic Park, Calgary, AB, Canada, with Crash Vegas, Northern Pikes, the Band, and Luba

Mike was apparently ill and Brian filled in for him on this short tour. In Calgary, Brian responded to the fans asking where Mike was by informing them that he was "near death." The audience was understandably shaken and Al had to step in and inform them Mike was just "taking care of business."

SATURDAY, JUNE 30, 1990: Evergreen Park, Saskatoon, SK, Canada, with Northern Pikes, Trooper, and Blue Rodeo

Terry Craig of the *Star Phoenix* reported, "Unlike the previous time the group performed in Saskatoon, the reclusive Brian Wilson joined the band on stage. However, singer Mike Love was noticeably absent. According to one backstage observer, Love and Wilson are in the middle of an acrimonious battle over control of the group . . . The four original band members—Al Jardine, Brian and Carl Wilson, and Bruce Johnston—were augmented by a seven-piece backing band including television celebrity John Stamos."

SUNDAY, JULY 1, 1990: Centennial Park, Grand Falls, NL, Canada, with Rawlins Cross, Stogger Tight, Five Alive, Sideline, and Alibi

---

MONDAY, JULY 2, 1990: Montreal, QB, Canada

There's a video circulating of Brian, John Stamos, Jeff, and Bruce fooling around at the piano in a hotel from this day.

WEDNESDAY, JULY 4, 1990: Otis Air Force Base, Falmouth, MA, with John Cafferty and the Beaver Brown Band and Northern Maine Fairgrounds, Presque Isle, ME, with Wrecking Crew

Mike was back for these shows, but Brian also remained. These were Jeff Foskett's last shows with the Beach Boys until 2012. Adrian Baker returned to the group in August.

THURSDAY, AUGUST 2, 1990: Allentown Fair, Allentown, PA

FRIDAY, AUGUST 3, 1990: Lake Compounce, Bristol, CT, with the Moody Blues and Kingston Fairgrounds, Kingston, NH

SATURDAY, AUGUST 4, 1990: Garden State Arts Center, Holmdel, NJ (Two shows)

SUNDAY, AUGUST 5, 1990: Little Creek Naval Amphitheater, Norfolk, VA, and Carrowinds Palladium, Charlotte, NC

TUESDAY, AUGUST 7, 1990: King's Dominion, Doswell, VA, and Merriweather Post Pavilion, Columbia, MD

WEDNESDAY, AUGUST 8, 1990: Fairgrounds, Hagerstown, MD, and Star Lake Amphitheater, Burgettstown, PA, with the Moody Blues

---

THURSDAY, AUGUST 9, 1990: Deer Creek Music Center, Noblesville, IN

FRIDAY, AUGUST 10, 1990: Riverfront Stadium, Cincinnati, OH

SATURDAY, AUGUST 11, 1990: Walker Arena, Muskegon, MI, with Da Yoopers and the Beach Bashers and Pine Knob Music Theater, Clarkston, MI

Tour patch. Collection of Chris Woods

SUNDAY, AUGUST 12, 1990: Wisconsin State Fair, West Allis, WI

MONDAY, AUGUST 13, 1990: Illinois State Fair, Springfield, IL, with the Marshall Tucker Band

WEDNESDAY, AUGUST 15, 1990: Poplar Creek, Hoffman Estates, IL

THURSDAY, AUGUST 16, 1990: University of Toledo, Toledo, OH, with Dailey and the Marshall Tucker Band

FRIDAY, AUGUST 17, 1990: Blossom Music Center, Cuyahoga Falls, OH, with the Marshall Tucker Band

SATURDAY, AUGUST 18, 1990: Lansdowne Park, Ottawa, ON, Canada

1990

SUNDAY, AUGUST 19, 1990: London, ON, Canada and CNE Grandstand, Toronto, ON, Canada

TUESDAY, AUGUST 21, AND WEDNESDAY, AUGUST 22, 1990: Jones Beach, Wantagh, NY

THURSDAY, AUGUST 23, 1990: NY State Fair, Syracuse, NY, with the Marshall Tucker Band
Mary Fran Gleason of the *Syracuse Herald Journal* reported, "The Beach Boys showed that despite some grey hair and more than a few wrinkles they can carry off tunes that once enthralled teens of the sixties . . . The Beach Boys added a troupe of bikini clad dancers, who brought sizzle to pop tunes such as the trio, 'Surfin Safari,' 'Surf City,' and 'Surfin' USA' . . . The group's softer ballads, such as 'Please Let Me Wonder' sung by Johnston, carried a convincing Beach Boys trademark harmony."

SATURDAY, AUGUST 25, 1990: Mud Island Amphitheater, Memphis, TN (Two shows)

SUNDAY, AUGUST 26, 1990: Exchange Park, Ladson, SC (Benefit)

TUESDAY, AUGUST 28, 1990: Von Braun Center, Huntsville, AL, and King's Dominion, Doswell, VA

WEDNESDAY, AUGUST 29, 1990: Chastain Park, Atlanta, GA

THURSDAY, AUGUST 30, 1990: Muni, St. Louis, MO

FRIDAY, AUGUST 31, 1990: Sandstone Amphitheater, Bonner Springs, KS, with the Marshall Tucker Band

SATURDAY, SEPTEMBER 1, 1990: Minnesota State Fair, St. Paul, MN (Two shows)

SUNDAY, SEPTEMBER 2, 1990: Sioux City, IA, and Sec Taylor Stadium, Des Moines, IA, and Nebraska State Fair, Lincoln, NE

MONDAY, SEPTEMBER 3, 1990: Memorial Park, Appleton, WI, and Fargo, ND, and Husett Speedway, Sioux Falls, SD

WEDNESDAY, SEPTEMBER 5, 1990: Seattle Coliseum, Seattle, WA

THURSDAY, SEPTEMBER 6, 1990: Civic Stadium, Portland, OR

SATURDAY, SEPTEMBER 8, 1990: USU Romney Stadium, Logan, UT

SUNDAY, SEPTEMBER 9, 1990: Jack Murphy Stadium, San Diego, CA, and Pacific Amphitheater, Costa Mesa, CA

TUESDAY, SEPTEMBER 11, 1990: Universal City Hilton, Los Angeles, CA (Benefit)

FRIDAY, SEPTEMBER 28, TO SUNDAY, SEPTEMBER 30, 1990: Caesars Tahoe, Stateline, NV
Carl wasn't present, as he was recovering from appendicitis surgery.

SATURDAY, SEPTEMBER 29, 1990: Stanford University, Palo Alto, CA
Between Lake Tahoe shows, the group played an afternoon concert at Stanford.

FRIDAY, OCTOBER 5, 1990: Estadio Carlos Tartiere, Oviedo, Spain, with Jerry Lee Lewis
Due to the success of a recent compilation album release, the group embarked on their first-ever tour of Spain. Carl was absent.

SUNDAY, OCTOBER 7, 1990: Paseo De La Alameda, Valencia, Spain

THE BEACH BOYS IN CONCERT

TUESDAY, OCTOBER 9, 1990: Rockodromo de la Casa del Campo, Madrid, Spain

SATURDAY, OCTOBER 13, 1990: County Bowl, Santa Barbara, CA, with Jesse Colin Young (Benefit)

SATURDAY, NOVEMBER 3, 1990: Rocky Mountain Adoption Exchange Fantasy Ball, Denver, CO

SUNDAY, NOVEMBER 4, TO THURSDAY, NOVEMBER, 15, 1990: Caesars Palace, Las Vegas, NV

THURSDAY, NOVEMBER 29, 1990: White House, Washington, DC
The group appeared at the White House with President Bush to help launch the Star Serve Program for kids. They sang "Kokomo" and "Barbara Ann."

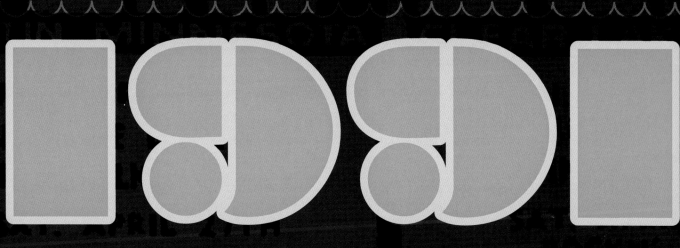

1991

THE GROUP TOURED mostly county fairs and baseball stadiums. They again toured in Europe and were well received, though some were disappointed by the "just the hits" sets and occasionally lackluster performances. The group spent little time in the studio, but did record a new version of "Crocodile Rock" for an Elton John tribute album. Brian was a no-show at Beach Boys concerts but released a very controversial autobiography, *Wouldn't It Be Nice*, which he allegedly had little involvement in writing. Nevertheless, he went on a promo tour to promote it. The year 1991 marked the end of his relationship with Dr. Landy. Early the following year, Landy was ordered by a judge to stop treating Brian after allegations of misconduct.

CONCERTS PLAYED IN
1991

FRIDAY, JANUARY 11, 1991: Governor Pete Wilson's Inaugural, Convention Center, San Diego, CA

THURSDAY, FEBRUARY 7, 1991: Wright State University, Dayton, OH

FRIDAY, FEBRUARY 8, AND SATURDAY, FEBRUARY 9, 1991: Fox Theatre, Detroit, MI (Two shows on the February 8 and one on February 9)

SUNDAY, FEBRUARY 10, 1991: Front Row Theater, Highland Heights, OH, with Nicolette Larson (Two shows)

MONDAY, FEBRUARY 11, 1991: Wisconsin State Fairgrounds, West Allis, WI and Riverside Theater, Milwaukee, WI, with Nicolette Larson

MONDAY, MARCH 4, 1991: Spectrum, Philadelphia, PA
Daryl Dragon played this show in place of Mike Meros.

TUESDAY, MARCH 5, 1991: Central Park Conservancy Dinner, Plaza Hotel, New York, NY

WEDNESDAY, MARCH 6, 1991: Madison Square Garden, New York, NY (USO Benefit)

FRIDAY, MARCH 8, 1991: Naples, FL

SATURDAY, MARCH 9, AND SUNDAY, MARCH 10, 1991: Sunrise Musical Theatre, Sunrise, FL, with Stu Moss (Two shows on the March 9 and one on March 10)

THURSDAY, APRIL 25, 1991: Waco, TX

SATURDAY, APRIL 27, 1991: Sports Stadium, Albuquerque, NM

SUNDAY, APRIL 28, 1991: Cohen Stadium, El Paso, TX

SATURDAY, MAY 4, 1991: Riverfront Stadium, Cincinnati, OH

SUNDAY, MAY 5, 1991: Fulton County Stadium, Atlanta, GA (Canceled)

MONDAY, MAY 6, 1991: Gym, East Burke HS, Icar, NC

FRIDAY, MAY 10, 1991: Regions Park, Birmingham, AL
The backing band at most summer 1991 dates consisted of Adrian Baker, Ed Carter, Mike Meros, Mike Kowalski, and Billy Hinsche.

SATURDAY, MAY 11, 1991: Riverfront Amphitheater, Little Rock, AR (Day) and Starplex Amphitheater, Dallas, TX (Night), with Mitch Ryder, Alex Chilton, and the Turtles

SUNDAY, MAY 12, 1991: All Sports Stadium, Oklahoma City, OK and Drillers Stadium, Tulsa, OK

THURSDAY, MAY 16, 1991: Standley Lake HS, Denver, CO

FRIDAY, MAY 17, 1991: Desert Sky Pavilion, Phoenix, AZ

"The band's live set is moving ever closer towards one block of medleys . . . The combined effect is like being force fed your favorite food."

〰〰〰

1991

SATURDAY, MAY 18, 1991: Temecula Valley Balloon and Wine Festival, Temecula, CA, and Pacific Amphitheater, Costa Mesa, CA, with Terrell

SUNDAY, MAY 19, 1991: Great American, Santa Clara, CA (Two shows)

SATURDAY, MAY 25 1991: Welcome Home Celebration for Desert Storm troops, Houston, TX

SUNDAY, MAY 26, 1991: Plaza Hotel, New York, NY (Private)

FRIDAY, MAY 31, 1991: Pilot Field, Buffalo, NY

SATURDAY, JUNE 1, 1991: Cleveland Stadium, Cleveland, OH

SUNDAY, JUNE 2, 1991: Yankee Stadium, Bronx, NY, and Lake Compounce, Bristol, CT

SATURDAY, JUNE 15, 1991: BIC, Bournemouth, England
This was the first date of the 1991 European tour.

SUNDAY, JUNE 16, 1991: Brighton Centre, Brighton, England

MONDAY, JUNE 17, 1991: G-Mex, Manchester, England

TUESDAY, JUNE 18, 1991: SECC, Glasgow, Scotland

WEDNESDAY, JUNE 19, 1991: King's Hall, Belfast, Ireland

SATURDAY, JUNE 22, 1991: Greve Stadium, Copenhagen, Denmark

SUNDAY, JUNE 23, 1991: NEC, Birmingham, England

MONDAY, JUNE 24, AND TUESDAY, JUNE 25, 1991: Wembley Arena, London, England
Andrew Doe reported in *Beach Boys Stomp* fanzine that the Wembley show "was a surprisingly accomplished concert: granted there were no great surprises, but it was all well done, with the exception of 'Kokomo'—and, though little more than a succession of medleys, satisfying enough. The inclusion and excellent performance of 'Please Let Me Wonder' was my high spot, just edging out the *Pet Sounds* sequence."

THURSDAY, JUNE 27, 1991: Grugahalle, Essen, Germany, with the Little River Band

FRIDAY, JUNE 28, 1991: Waldbuhne, Berlin, Germany, with the Allman Brothers, Manfred Mann and the Little River Band

SATURDAY, JUNE 29, 1991: Inselwiese, Dinklesbuhl, Germany, with Manfred Mann, the Little River Band, and the Allman Brothers

SUNDAY, JUNE 30, 1991: Jahnstadion, Gottingen, Germany, with the Little River Band, Manfred Mann, and the Allman Brothers

TUESDAY, JULY 2, 1991: Nya Ullevi, Gothenburg, Sweden, with Manfred Mann, the Little River Band, and the Allman Brothers

FRIDAY, JULY 5, 1991: Fussballstadion, Aue, Germany, with Manfred Mann, the Little River Band, and the Allman Brothers

THE BEACH BOYS IN CONCERT

SATURDAY, JULY 6, 1991: VFB Waldstadion, Giessen, Germany, with the Allman Brothers, Manfred Mann, and the Little River Band (3:00 p.m. show)

SUNDAY, JULY 7, 1991: Pferderennbahn, Frauenfeld, Switzerland

TUESDAY, JULY 9, 1991: Urfahrer Festival, Linz, Austria

TUESDAY, JULY 23, 1991: Walnut Creek Amphitheatre, Raleigh, NC, with the Everly Brothers

WEDNESDAY, JULY 24, 1991: Carowinds Palladium, Charlotte, NC, with the Everly Brothers

THURSDAY, JULY 25, 1991: King's Dominion, Doswell, VA, with the Everly Brothers

FRIDAY, JULY 26, 1991: Norfolk, VA, with the Everly Brothers

SATURDAY, JULY 27, 1991: Garden State Arts Center, Holmdel, NJ (Two shows)

SUNDAY, JULY 28, 1991: Hershey Park, Hershey, PA, and Merriweather Post Pavilion, Columbia, MD, with the Everly Brothers

MONDAY, JULY 29, 1991: Merriweather Post Pavilion, Columbia, MD, with the Everly Brothers

TUESDAY, JULY 30, 1991: Holman Stadium, Nashua, NH, with the Everly Brothers

WEDNESDAY, JULY 31, 1991: Great Woods, Mansfield, MA, with the Everly Brothers

THURSDAY, AUGUST 1, AND FRIDAY, AUGUST 2, 1991: Jones Beach, Wantagh, NY, with the Everly Brothers (One show each night)

SATURDAY, AUGUST 3, 1991: Montgomery Avenue Beach, Wildwood, NJ, with Tommy Conwell and the Rumblers and John Cafferty and the Beaver Brown Band and Coliseum, Moncton, NB, Canada

SUNDAY, AUGUST 4, 1991: Metro Center, Halifax, NS, Canada

MONDAY, AUGUST 5, 1991: Sydney, NS, Canada

WEDNESDAY, AUGUST 7, 1991: "Locomotive Works Heritage Benefit," Allen County Fairgrounds, Lima, OH, with the Danger Brothers and Capital Music Center, Grove City, OH
August 7 was declared "Al Jardine Day" in his hometown of Lima and he was presented with the key to the city.

THURSDAY, AUGUST 8, 1991: Timber Wolf Amphitheatre, King's Island, OH, with the Everly Brothers

FRIDAY, AUGUST 9, 1991: Grand Rapids, MI

SATURDAY, AUGUST 10, 1991: Jackson Fairgrounds, Jackson, MI and Deer Creek Music Center, Noblesville, IN

SUNDAY, AUGUST 11, 1991: Wisconsin State Fair, West Allis, WI and Poplar Creek, Hoffman Estates, IL, with the Everly Brothers

WEDNESDAY, AUGUST 14, 1991: Illinois State Fair, Springfield, IL, with the Everly Brothers

1991

THURSDAY, AUGUST 15, 1991: Starwood Amphitheater, Nashville, TN, with the Everly Brothers and the Y-107 Band

FRIDAY, AUGUST 16, 1991: Riverport Amphitheater, Maryland Heights, MO, with Everly Brothers

SATURDAY, AUGUST 17, 1991: Springfield, MO, and Sandstone Amphitheatre, Bonner Springs, KS, with Alabama and Shelby Lynne

SUNDAY, AUGUST 18, 1991: Missouri State Fair, Sedalia, MO, with Alabama and Mud Island Amphitheater, Memphis, TN

WEDNESDAY, AUGUST 21, 1991: Six Flags, Agawam, MA, with the Everly Brothers and Knickerbocker Arena, Albany, NY, with the Everly Brothers

THURSDAY, AUGUST 22, 1991: Lansdowne Park, Ottawa, ON, Canada, with the Everly Brothers

FRIDAY, AUGUST 23, 1991: NY State Fairgrounds, Syracuse, NY, with the Everly Brothers

Jon Stebbins Collection

SATURDAY, AUGUST 24, 1991: Pine Knob Music Theater, Clarkston, MI and Star Lake Amphitheater, Burgettstown, PA, with the Turtles

SUNDAY, AUGUST 25, 1991: Kingswood Music Theater, Vaughan, ON, Canada (Two shows)

WEDNESDAY, AUGUST 28, 1991: King's Dominion, Doswell, VA, and Louisville, KY

THURSDAY, AUGUST 29, 1991: Davenport, IA

FRIDAY, AUGUST 30, 1991: Nebraska State Fair, Lincoln, NE

SATURDAY, AUGUST 31, 1991: Clearwater Beach, Des Moines, IA and South Dakota State Fair, Huron, SD

SUNDAY, SEPTEMBER 1, 1991: Minnesota State Fair, St. Paul, MN (Two shows)

MONDAY, SEPTEMBER 2, 1991: Colorado State Fair, Pueblo, CO

FRIDAY, SEPTEMBER 13, AND SATURDAY, SEPTEMBER 14 1991: Puyallup Fair, Puyallup, WA (Two shows each day)

FRIDAY, SEPTEMBER 20, 1991: Tulare County Fair, Tulare, CA

SATURDAY, SEPTEMBER 21, 1991: L.A. Coliseum, Los Angeles, CA

SUNDAY, SEPTEMBER 22, 1991: Jack Murphy Stadium, San Diego, CA

THURSDAY, SEPTEMBER 26, TO SUNDAY, SEPTEMBER 29, AND THURSDAY, OCTOBER 3, TO SUNDAY, OCTOBER 6, 1991: Caesars Palace, Las Vegas, NV

THE BEACH BOYS IN CONCERT

SUNDAY, OCTOBER 27, 1991: Veterans Memorial Coliseum, Phoenix, AZ (Two shows)

FRIDAY, NOVEMBER 1, AND SATURDAY, NOVEMBER 2, 1991: Nippon Budokan, Tokyo, Japan (One show each night)

The Beach Boys flew to Tokyo on October 28 to begin their third Japanese tour. Adrian Baker, Matt Jardine, Ritchie Cannata, Ed Carter, Mike Kowalski, Billy Hinsche, and Mike Meros accompanied them. The show on November 2 was filmed for TV.

The opening show featured the now-usual elements, including cheerleaders. Sean Macreavy reported in *Beach Boys Stomp*, "The band's live set is moving ever closer towards one block of medleys . . . The combined effect is like being force fed your favorite food . . . For some time now, the group has been a mere commercial bandwagon, parading the songs they believe the punters want. The alarming fact is that the current set contains not one song written by the group in the twenty years between 1968 and 1988."

MONDAY, NOVEMBER 4, 1991: Century Hall, Nagoya, Japan

TUESDAY, NOVEMBER 5, 1991: Kobe Kokusai Kaikan, Kobe, Japan

SATURDAY, NOVEMBER 16, 1991: Brevard County Fair, Cocoa, FL

SUNDAY, NOVEMBER 17, 1991: Sun Dome, Tampa, FL (Benefit)

FRIDAY, NOVEMBER 15, 1991: Orlando, FL

The group played a concert for Dick Clark's National Music Foundation

TUESDAY, DECEMBER 31, 1991: New Year's Eve Ball, Arvada, CO

1992

THE YEAR 1992 saw the release of the Beach Boys' first full album of new music since 1985. *Summer in Paradise* wasn't a return to form and received generally negative reviews. Neither the album nor the single, "Hot Fun in the Summertime," charted in the U.S. It is the only Beach Boys album to feature no involvement from Brian. Although

CONCERTS PLAYED IN
1992

FRIDAY, JANUARY 31, AND SATURDAY, FEBRUARY 1, 1992: Caesars Circus Maximus, Stateline, NV
Al was absent from most early 1992 shows.

SUNDAY, FEBRUARY 2, 1992: "Rocky Mountain Adoption Exchange Fantasy Ball," Stouffer Concourse Hotel, Denver, CO

WEDNESDAY, FEBRUARY 5, 1992: Roseland Ballroom, New York, NY (Private)

SATURDAY, APRIL 25, 1992: Balboa Park, San Diego, CA

SATURDAY, MAY 2, 1992: Ohio Stadium, Columbus, OH
Al was back for this show.

FRIDAY, MAY 22, TO SUNDAY, MAY 24, 1992: Auditorio Nacional, Mexico City, Mexico

MONDAY, MAY 25, 1992: Centro de Convenciones, Acapulco, Mexico

SATURDAY, MAY 30, 1992: Marine World, Vallejo, CA, and Mervyn's Riverfront Amphitheatre, Marysville, CA, with America
The backing band for the summer tour consisted of Adrian Baker, Ed Carter, Billy Hinsche, Mike Meros, Mike Kowalski, Matt Jardine, and Ritchie Cannata.

SUNDAY, MAY 31, 1992: Concord Pavilion, Concord, CA

WEDNESDAY, JUNE 3, 1992: "One to One Benefit," New York, NY
Soon after this, the Beach Boys attended the Earth Summit in Rio de Janeiro.

WEDNESDAY, JUNE 10, 1992: Marriot, Orlando, FL

THURSDAY, JUNE 11, 1992: Ft. Meyers, FL

FRIDAY, JUNE 12, 1992: Vinoy Park, St. Petersburg, FL

SATURDAY, JUNE 13, 1992: Bayfront Park Amphitheatre, West Palm Beach, FL, with America

SUNDAY, JUNE 14, 1992: South Florida Fairgrounds, Palm Beach, FL, with America
The next day the group filmed a video for the single "Hot Fun in the Summertime" in Orlando.

WEDNESDAY, JUNE 17, 1992: Walnut Creek Amphitheatre, Raleigh, NC, with America

THURSDAY, JUNE 18, 1992: King's Dominion, Doswell, VA

FRIDAY, JUNE 19, 1992: Lakewood Amphitheater, Atlanta, GA

SATURDAY, JUNE 20, 1992: Mud Island Amphitheater, Memphis, TN

SUNDAY, JUNE 21, 1992: Texas Stadium, Dallas, TX

WEDNESDAY, JUNE 24, 1992: Mid-Hudson Civic Center, Poughkeepsie, NY

THURSDAY, JUNE 25, 1992: Finger Lakes PAC, Canandaigua, NY

Jon Stebbins
Collection

~~~~
1992

FRIDAY, JUNE 26, 1992: Brendan Byrne Arena, East Rutherford, NY (Canceled)

SATURDAY, JUNE 27, 1992: Merriweather Post Pavilion, Columbia, MD, with America

SUNDAY, JUNE 28, 1992: Riverside Park, Hartford, CT, and Six Flags, Agawam, MA, with John Cafferty and the Beaver Brown Band

FRIDAY, JULY 3, 1992: "Veil of the Prophet Fair," St. Louis, MO

SATURDAY, JULY 4, 1992: Cougar Stadium, Provo, UT

FRIDAY, JULY 31, 1992: Great Woods, Mansfield, MA, with David Cassidy

SATURDAY AUGUST 1, 1992: Olympic Center, Lake Placid, NY

SUNDAY, AUGUST 2, 1992: Kingswood Theater, Vaughan, ON, Canada (Two shows)

MONDAY, AUGUST 3, 1992: National Governor's Conference, Princeton, NJ

WEDNESDAY, AUGUST 5, 1992: Mansion Park, Altoona, PA

THURSDAY, AUGUST 6, 1992: Municipal Stadium, Binghamton, NY

FRIDAY, AUGUST 7, 1992: Poplar Creek, Hoffman Estates, IL

SATURDAY, AUGUST 8, 1992: Blossom Music Center, Cuyahoga Falls, OH, with David Cassidy

SUNDAY, AUGUST 9, 1992: Timberwolf Amphitheater, King's Island, OH

TUESDAY, AUGUST 11, 1992: Interlochen Center for the Arts, Traverse City, MI

WEDNESDAY, AUGUST 12, 1992: Sec Taylor Stadium, Des Moines, IA

THURSDAY, AUGUST 13, 1992: Rosenblatt Stadium, Omaha, NE

FRIDAY, AUGUST 14, 1992: Kansas City, MO (Canceled)

SATURDAY, AUGUST 15, 1992: Sioux Empire Fair, Sioux Falls, SD

SUNDAY, AUGUST 16, 1992: Wisconsin State Fair, West Allis, WI, with Poco and Deer Creek Music Center, Noblesville, IN, with David Cassidy

TUESDAY, AUGUST 18, 1992: Illinois State Fair, Springfield, IL

WEDNESDAY, AUGUST 19, 1992: Cooper Stadium, Columbus, OH

THURSDAY, AUGUST 20, 1992: Garden State Race Track, Cherry Hill, NJ

FRIDAY, AUGUST 21, 1992: Star Lake Amphitheatre, Burgettstown, PA

SATURDAY, AUGUST 22, 1992: Convention Center, Wildwood, NJ, and Pilot Field, Buffalo, NY

TUESDAY, AUGUST 25, 1992: Lansdowne Park, Ottawa, ON, Canada, with Southside Johnny and the Asbury Jukes

"'Surfer Girl,' 'In My Room,' and 'God Only Knows' showed that although the Beach Boys have aged, like good wine, they have only gotten better."

THE BEACH BOYS IN CONCERT

WEDNESDAY, AUGUST 26, AND THURSDAY, AUGUST 27, 1992: Garden State Arts Center, Holmdel, NJ (One show each night)

FRIDAY, AUGUST 28, 1992: Jones Beach, Wantagh, NY

SATURDAY, AUGUST 29, 1992: SPAC, Saratoga, NY, and Jones Beach, Wantagh, NY

SUNDAY, AUGUST 30, 1992: North Woods at Cranmore, Conway, NH and Holman Stadium, Nashua, NH, with David Cassidy

Jan Bennicoff of the *Telegraph* reviewed the Holman Stadium show and reported, "Although it's been a few years since their first release, you wouldn't know it. They had the same tight harmonies, and their voices, if anything, have improved . . . 'Surfer Girl,' 'In My Room,' and 'God Only Knows' showed that although the Beach Boys have aged, like good wine, they have only gotten better. One of the most outstanding songs was their rendition of 'Under the Boardwalk' from their new album *Summer in Paradise*."

WEDNESDAY, SEPTEMBER 2, 1992: Allentown Fair, Allentown, PA

THURSDAY, SEPTEMBER 3, 1992: Champlain Valley Exposition, Essex Junction, VT

FRIDAY, SEPTEMBER 4, 1992: NY State Fairgrounds, Syracuse, NY, with David Cassidy

---

SATURDAY, SEPTEMBER 5, 1992: Pine Knob Music Theater, Clarkston, MI

SUNDAY, SEPTEMBER 6, 1992: Minnesota State Fair, St. Paul, MN, with David Cassidy (Two shows)

SATURDAY, SEPTEMBER 12, 1992: Pacific Amphitheater, Costa Mesa, CA

SUNDAY, SEPTEMBER 13, 1992: Shoreline Amphitheater, Mountain View, CA

SATURDAY, SEPTEMBER 19, 1992: Hospital, Lake Forest, IL (Benefit)

SATURDAY, SEPTEMBER 26, AND SUNDAY, SEPTEMBER 27, 1992: Puyallup Fair, Puyallup, WA, with America (Two shows each day)

WEDNESDAY, OCTOBER 21, AND THURSDAY, OCTOBER 22, 1992: Veterans Memorial Coliseum, Phoenix, AZ

FRIDAY, OCTOBER 30, 1992: Greek Theater, Los Angeles, CA (a show on October 31 was canceled)

THURSDAY, NOVEMBER 19, AND FRIDAY, NOVEMBER 20, 1992: Entertainment Centre, Brisbane, QLD, Australia

The group landed in Sydney on November 16 to begin their fourth tour of Australia.

SUNDAY, NOVEMBER 22, 1992: Olympic Park, Melbourne, VIC, Australia

---

MONDAY, NOVEMBER 23, 1992: Newcastle, NSW, Australia

WEDNESDAY, NOVEMBER 25, 1992: Bruce Stadium, Canberra, ACT, Australia

---

THURSDAY, NOVEMBER 26, AND FRIDAY, NOVEMBER 27, 1992: Adelaide Entertainment Centre, Adelaide, SA, Australia

---

SATURDAY, NOVEMBER 28, 1992: North Narrabeen Reserve, Sydney, NSW, Australia

---

SUNDAY, NOVEMBER 29, 1992: The Esplanade, Perth, WA, Australia

---

WEDNESDAY, DECEMBER 30, AND THURSDAY, DECEMBER 31, 1992: Las Vegas Hilton, Las Vegas, NV

1993

THIS YEAR SAW little recording by the group, but quite a bit of touring, including another European trip. Capitol Records released a boxed set, *Good Vibrations: 30 Years of the Beach Boys*, containing material from the group's entire career as well as many unreleased tracks. To promote the release, the group played a special tour in November. Fans fondly recall these shows because the band played two-hour sets for the first time since the 1970s and included rarely played songs, such as "Take a Load off Your Feet" and "Vegetables." Brian played no shows with the group in 1993, but was busy. He recorded new versions of a number of his classic songs for a documentary film by Don Was titled *I Just Wasn't Made for These Times*, released in January 1995.

CONCERTS PLAYED IN
1993

FRIDAY, JANUARY 1, 1993: Blockbuster Bowl, Ft Lauderdale, FL

TUESDAY, FEBRUARY 16, 1993: Freeman Coliseum, San Antonio, TX

THURSDAY, FEBRUARY 18, 1993: Civic Center Coliseum, Amarillo, TX

SATURDAY, FEBRUARY 20, 1993: Superdome, New Orleans, LA

SUNDAY, FEBRUARY 21, 1993: Civic Center, Pensacola, FL

WEDNESDAY, FEBRUARY 24, TO SATURDAY, FEBRUARY 27, 1993: Fox Theater, Detroit, MI (One show each night and two shows on February 27)

TUESDAY, MARCH 9, 1993: National Association of Recording Merchandisers Convention, Orlando, FL

MONDAY, MARCH 22, 1993: Kellogg Arena, Battle Creek, MI

TUESDAY, MARCH 23, 1993: Breslin Center, Lansing, MI

WEDNESDAY, MARCH 24, 1993: Wright State University, Dayton, OH

THURSDAY, MARCH 25, 1993: Memorial Coliseum, Fort Wayne, IN, with Henry Gross

FRIDAY, MARCH 26, 1993: War Memorial Arena, Johnstown, PA
Rebecca Cochran of the *Indiana Gazette* reported, "It's hard to believe the Beach Boys have been blending their harmonies for more than thirty years, but they haven't sounded better, especially on the ballad 'In My Room' . . . The band encouraged the fans to sing along with them throughout the evening and the crowd happily joined in during 'Good Vibrations,' 'Help Me Rhonda,' and 'Fun, Fun, Fun.'"

SATURDAY, MARCH 27, 1993: Star Plaza, Merrillville, IN (Two shows)

SUNDAY, MARCH 28, 1993: Princess Hotel, Phoenix, AZ (Private)

FRIDAY, APRIL 16, 1993: Baylor University, Waco, TX

SATURDAY, APRIL 17, 1993: Six Flags Over Texas, Arlington, TX

SUNDAY, APRIL 18, 1993: Mohawk Park, Tulsa, OK, with Paul Revere and the Raiders

TUESDAY, APRIL 20, 1993: Ft. Myers, FL

WEDNESDAY, APRIL 21, 1993: Palm Beach, FL

THURSDAY, APRIL 22, AND FRIDAY, APRIL 23, 1993: Sunrise Musical Theatre, Sunrise, FL

SATURDAY, MAY 1, 1993: Boonesfield College of the Desert, Palm Springs, CA
This was probably Adrian Baker's last show until 1998.

"The Boys were enthusiastic; smiling at each other and actually acknowledging each other's presence!"

1993

SUNDAY, JUNE 6, 1993: Kaivopuisto, Helsinki, Finland
The group embarked on another European tour with Matt Jardine, Mike Kowalski, Mike Meros, Billy Hinsche, Ed Carter, and Richie Cannata.

SATURDAY, JUNE 12, 1993: Middlefart Festival, Aarhus, Denmark

SUNDAY, JUNE 13, 1993: Sporthalle, Hamburg, Germany

TUESDAY, JUNE 15, 1993: Frankenhalle, Nurnberg, Germany

WEDNESDAY, JUNE 16, 1993: Schleyerhalle, Stuttgart, Germany

THURSDAY, JUNE 17, 1993: Rudi-Sedlmayer Halle, Munich, Germany

FRIDAY, JUNE 18, 1993: Strandbad, Neusiedler See, Austria

SATURDAY, JUNE 19, 1993: Freilichtbuhne, Loreley, Germany, with the Hollies

MONDAY, JUNE 21, 1993: Dusseldorf, Germany (Canceled)

TUESDAY, JUNE 22, 1993: Unterfrankenhalle, Aschaffenburg, Germany (Originally scheduled for June 9)

WEDNESDAY, JUNE 23, 1993: Hanover, Germany (Canceled)

FRIDAY, JUNE 25, 1993: Arena, Sheffield, England

SATURDAY, JUNE 26, 1993: G-Mex, Manchester, England

SUNDAY, JUNE 27, 1993: NEC, Birmingham, England

TUESDAY, JUNE 29, AND WEDNESDAY, JUNE 30, 1993: Wembley Arena, London, England

SATURDAY, JULY 3, 1993: Pinneviken, Lysekil, Sweden

SUNDAY, JULY 4, 1993: Bryggeparken, Skien, Norway

TUESDAY, JULY 6, 1993: Christinehof, Sweden

FRIDAY, JULY 9, 1993: Leysin, Switzerland

SATURDAY, JULY 10, 1993: Frauenfeld, Switzerland

MONDAY, JULY 12, 1993: Rock Under Broen, Funen, Denmark

SATURDAY, JULY 31, 1993: Portland Meadows Race Track, Portland, OR, and The Gorge, George, WA, with America

SUNDAY, AUGUST 1, 1993: Blue Ridge Bluff, Kelowna, BC, with America and Valdy and Royal Athletic Park, Victoria, BC, with America

MONDAY, AUGUST 2, 1993: Deer Lake Park, Burnaby, BC

TUESDAY, AUGUST 3, 1993: Las Vegas, NV (Private)

THE BEACH BOYS IN CONCERT

WEDNESDAY, AUGUST 4, 1993: California Mid-State Fair, Paso Robles, CA

THURSDAY, AUGUST 5, 1993: Beach Party, Capitol Records, Los Angeles, CA
The Beach Boys performed outside the Capitol Tower to celebrate the release of the *Good Vibrations: 30 Years of the Beach Boys* Box Set. *Entertainment Tonight* filmed part of the event.

FRIDAY, AUGUST 6, 1993: Concord Pavilion, Concord, CA
Footage from this appearance was used in the video for "Summer in Paradise."

SATURDAY, AUGUST 7, 1993: Reno Hilton Amphitheater, NV, with America

SUNDAY, AUGUST 8, 1993: Shoreline Amphitheater, Mountain View, CA

TUESDAY, AUGUST 10, 1993: Park West, Salt Lake City, UT

THURSDAY, AUGUST 12, 1993: Mark of the Quad Cities, Moline, IA (Benefit) and Sec Taylor Stadium, Des Moines, IA

FRIDAY, AUGUST 13, 1993: Illinois State Fair, Springfield, IL, with America

SATURDAY, AUGUST 14, 1993: Festival, Little Rock, AR, and Stoneridge Amphitheatre, Camdenton, MO

SUNDAY, AUGUST 15, 1993: Mud Island Amphitheater, Memphis, TN, and Riverport Amphitheatre, Maryland Heights, MO, with K.C. and the Sunshine Band

TUESDAY, AUGUST 17, 1993: Merriweather Post Pavilion, Columbia, MD, with America

WEDNESDAY, AUGUST 18, 1993: Kings Dominion, Doswell, VA

THURSDAY, AUGUST 19, 1993: Timber Wolf Amphitheater, Kings Island, OH

SATURDAY, AUGUST 21, 1993: Kingswood Music Theater, Vaughan, ON, Canada (Two shows)

SUNDAY, AUGUST 22, 1993: Pilot Field, Buffalo, NY, and Pine Knob Music Theater, Clarkston, MI

TUESDAY, AUGUST 24, 1993: Great Woods, Mansfield, MA, with America

WEDNESDAY, AUGUST 25, 1993: SPAC, Saratoga, NY

FRIDAY, AUGUST 27, 1993: Garden State Arts Center, Holmdel, NJ

SATURDAY, AUGUST 28, 1993: NY State Fairgrounds, Syracuse, NY, and Jones Beach, Wantagh, NY, with America

SUNDAY, AUGUST 29, 1993: Beach Stage, Ocean City, MD, and Jones Beach, Wantagh, NY, with America

MONDAY, AUGUST 30, 1993: Champlain Valley Fair, Essex Junction, VT

TUESDAY, AUGUST 31, 1993: Oakdale Theater, Wallingford, CT (Two shows)

THURSDAY, SEPTEMBER 2, 1993: Blossom Music Center, Cuyahoga Falls, OH, with America

FRIDAY, SEPTEMBER 3, 1993: Du Quoin Fair, Du Quoin, IL, with America

SATURDAY, SEPTEMBER 4, 1993: Boblo Island Amusement Park, Amherstburg, ON, Canada and Great Lakes Concert, Spirit Lake, IA, with Dion

SUNDAY, SEPTEMBER 5, 1993: Minnesota State Fair, St. Paul, MN, with America (Two shows)

MONDAY, SEPTEMBER 6, 1993: Poplar Creek, Hoffman Estates, IL, with America

FRIDAY, SEPTEMBER 17 1993: Marriot Center, Salt Lake City, UT (Private)
Carl was absent.

FRIDAY, SEPTEMBER 24, 1993: Starlight Amphitheater, Burgettstown, PA
Carl was absent.

SUNDAY, SEPTEMBER 26, 1993: Valley Forge Music Fair, Devon, PA (Two shows)

FRIDAY, OCTOBER 1, 1993: Fresno Fair, Fresno, CA

SATURDAY, OCTOBER 2, 1993: Mesa Amphitheater, Mesa, AZ and Arizona State Fair, Phoenix, AZ

SUNDAY, OCTOBER 3, 1993: Santa Rosa, CA (Canceled)

SATURDAY, OCTOBER 9, 1993: Sea World, San Antonio, TX

SUNDAY, OCTOBER 10, 1993: Celebrity Theater, Anaheim, CA

THURSDAY, NOVEMBER 18, 1993: Oven's Auditorium, Charlotte, NC
This was the first show of the short but memorable "Box Set Tour."

FRIDAY, NOVEMBER 19, 1993: Center Stage Theater, Atlanta, GA

SUNDAY, NOVEMBER 21, 1993: Valley Forge Music Fair, Devon, PA
A contributor to *Beach Boys Stomp* who'd witnessed a lackluster performance by the group at Valley Forge on September 26 was stunned by the difference at this show. He reported, "The Boys were enthusiastic; smiling at each other and actually acknowledging each other's presence! . . . About forty-five minutes into the show, Mike mentioned the success of the box set and announced, 'For those who saw us here a few weeks ago; well, you're in for a treat tonight! . . . What followed for the next hour was incredible music, well performed and obviously well rehearsed . . . A capella 'Their Hearts Were Full of Spring' . . . 'I Just Wasn't Made for These Times,' with Al really putting out the lead vocal; 'Heroes and Villains'; a fabulous Carl lead on 'It's Over Now' and 'Caroline, No'; a wonderful 'Wonderful'; 'All This Is That'; 'You Still Believe In Me'; 'The Night Was So Young' with Carl's shattering lead; 'Vegetables' with box set ending . . . on and on it went."

MONDAY, NOVEMBER 22, 1993: Palace of Auburn Hills, Auburn Hills, MI

TUESDAY, NOVEMBER 23, 1993: Princeton University, Princeton, NJ

WEDNESDAY, NOVEMBER 24, 1993: Holiday Star Theatre, Merrillville, IN

FRIDAY, NOVEMBER 26, 1993: Paramount Theater, New York, NY

SATURDAY, NOVEMBER 27, 1993: Brandeis University, Waltham, MA

BUSTER CONCERTS

HANSJÖRG FUNCK + MATTHIAS GEBHARDT PRESENT:

Mittwoch, 9. Juni 1993, 21 Uhr
Aschaffenburg · Unterfrankenhalle

präsentiert von:

RADIO
Primavera
IHRE SYMPATHISCHE WELLE

ENDLESS SUMMER '93

The Beach Boys

Veranstalter: **BUSTER CONCERTS Konzertagentur GmbH**, Babenhausen
Tourneeleitung: **Concertbüro Hänsel GmbH**

Keine Haftung für Sach- und Körperschäden. Zurücknahme der Karten
nur bei genereller Absage der Veranstaltung gegen Rückgabe der Ein-
trittskarte an der entsprechenden Vorverkaufsstelle, bis 1 Woche nach
Veranstaltungsdatum. Keine Zurückerstattung der Vorverkaufsgebühr.
Das Mitbringen von Tonband-, Film-, Foto- und Videokameras sowie
von Glasbehältern/Dosen, Waffen oder waffenähnlichen Gegenstän-
den ist untersagt.

Vorverkauf: DM 48,–   zuzügl.
Abendkasse: DM 55,–   Vorverkaufsgebühr
                                          incl. 7% Mwst.

Tribüne   690 ✻   Tribüne

Ian Rusten Collection

SUNDAY, NOVEMBER 28, 1993: Massey Hall, Toronto, ON, Canada

MONDAY, NOVEMBER 29, 1993: Baltimore, MD (Private)

FRIDAY, DECEMBER 31, 1993: Las Vegas, NV (Private)

1984

THIS WAS AN uneventful year filled with touring, but no recording. Brian played no shows, and he was locked in a painful lawsuit with Mike over songwriting credits. Mike eventually was awarded co-writing credit on over thirty songs and a five million dollar settlement. Much to the surprise of observers, Brian and Mike reconciled by the end of the year.

CONCERTS PLAYED IN
1994

> "Opening
> the set with
> 'California
> Girls,' the
> Beach Boys
> hit a groove,
> following
> with pristine
> versions of
> 'Rock and Roll
> Music,' 'Do
> You Wanna
> Dance?' and
> a harmony
> soaked read of
> 'In My Room'
> that sent chills
> down the
> spine."
>
> —Alan Boyd

SATURDAY, JANUARY 1, 1994: Las Vegas Hilton, Las Vegas, NV (Two shows)

THURSDAY, MAY 12, 1994: "The Farewell Party," Olympic Stadium, Berlin, Germany, with Charles Aznavour and Status Quo
This was a huge show to celebrate the withdrawal of allied troops from Berlin following the collapse of communism. Over 150,000 people attended.

THURSDAY, MAY 26, 1994: Starplex Amphitheater, Dallas, TX

SATURDAY, MAY 28, 1994: Sea World, San Antonio, TX

MONDAY, MAY 30, 1994: Mississippi Coast Fair and Expo 94, Biloxi, MS

SATURDAY, JUNE 4, 1994: Holiday Star Theatre, Merrillville, IN

SUNDAY, JUNE 5, 1994: Riverbend Music Center, Cincinnati, OH

FRIDAY, JUNE 10, 1994: Wolf Mountain, Salt Lake City, UT, with America

SATURDAY, JUNE 11, 1994: Mile High Stadium, Denver, CO, with Jan and Dean, the Mamas and Papas, and Martha Reeves and the Vandellas

TUESDAY, JUNE 14, 1994: Joe Davis Stadium, Huntsville, AL

WEDNESDAY, JUNE 15, 1994: Mesker Amphitheater, Evansville IN, with America

THURSDAY, JUNE 16, 1994: Deer Creek Music Center, Noblesville, IN, with America

FRIDAY, JUNE 17, 1994: Blossom Music Center, Cuyahoga Falls, OH, with America

SATURDAY, JUNE 18, 1994: Starlite Music Theatre, Latham, NY
Michael Lisi of the *Daily Gazette* reported, "Opening the set with 'California Girls,' the Beach Boys hit a groove, following with pristine versions of 'Rock and Roll Music,' 'Do You Wanna Dance?' and a harmony soaked read of 'In My Room' that sent chills down the spine. Vocally the band was right on target, its patented three- and four-part harmonies absolutely shimmering on songs like 'All Summer Long' and the a cappella 'Their Hearts Were Full of Spring.'"

SUNDAY, JUNE 19, 1994: Fairgrounds Arena, Watertown, NY

WEDNESDAY, JUNE 22, 1994: Chastain Park, Atlanta, GA

FRIDAY, JUNE 24, 1994: Walnut Creek Amphitheater, Raleigh, NC, with America and Carowinds Palladium, Charlotte, NC, with the Bishop Brothers

SATURDAY, JUNE 25, 1994: Star Lake Amphitheater, Burgettstown, PA, with America

SUNDAY, JUNE 26, 1994: Pilot Field, Buffalo, NY

WEDNESDAY, JUNE 29, 1994: Finger Lakes PAC, Canandaigua, NY, with America

THURSDAY, JUNE 30, 1994: Merriweather Post Pavilion, Columbia, MD, with America

FRIDAY, JULY 1, 1994: University of Toledo, Toledo, OH

SATURDAY, JULY 2, 1994: Veil of the Prophet Fair, St. Louis, MO

SUNDAY, JULY 3, 1994: Hyannis Village Green, Cape Cod, MA

MONDAY, JULY 4, 1994: Six Flags, Jackson, NJ

WEDNESDAY, JULY 6, 1994: Oakdale Theatre, Wallingford, CT (Two shows)

THURSDAY, JULY 7, 1994: Warwick Music Theater Warwick, RI

FRIDAY, JULY 8, TO SUNDAY, JULY 10, 1994: Trump Castle, Atlantic City, NJ

Bruce, Carl, and Al backstage in 1994. Jon Stebbins Collection

THURSDAY, JULY 28, 1994: Starplex Amphitheatre, Dallas, TX, with America

FRIDAY, JULY 29, 1994: Cashman Field, Las Vegas, NV

SATURDAY, JULY 30, 1994: Epicenter, Rancho Cucamunga, CA, with John Sebastian

SUNDAY, JULY 31, 1994: Jack Murphy Stadium, San Diego, CA

FRIDAY, AUGUST 5, 1994: Sun Devil Stadium, Phoenix, AZ

SATURDAY, AUGUST 6, 1994: El Camino College, Torrance, CA and Reno Hilton Amphitheater, Reno, NV, with America
Brian attended the El Camino show but didn't perform.

SUNDAY, AUGUST 7, 1994: Concord Pavilion, Concord, CA, with America

TUESDAY, AUGUST 9, 1994: Kresge Auditorium, Interlochen, MI (Two shows)

WEDNESDAY, AUGUST 10, 1994: Wisconsin State Fair, West Allis, WI, with America

FRIDAY, AUGUST 12, 1994: Poplar Creek, Hoffman Estates, IL, with America

SATURDAY, AUGUST 13, 1994: Red Wings Stadium, St. Johns, MI and Pine Knob Music Theater, Clarkston, MI, with America

THE BEACH BOYS IN CONCERT

SUNDAY, AUGUST 14, 1994: Kingswood Theater, Vaughan, ON, Canada (Two shows)

WEDNESDAY, AUGUST 17, 1994: Illinois State Fair, Springfield, IL, with America

THURSDAY, AUGUST 18, 1994: Missouri State Fair, Sedalia, MO, with America

FRIDAY, AUGUST 19, 1994: Cleveland Stadium, Cleveland, OH

SATURDAY, AUGUST 20, 1994: Waterpark, Conneaut, PA

SUNDAY, AUGUST 21, 1994: Great Woods, Mansfield, MA, with America

WEDNESDAY, AUGUST 24, 1994: Oakdale Theatre, Wallingford, CT, with Mark Verselli (Two shows)

THURSDAY, AUGUST 25, 1994: Scranton, PA

FRIDAY, AUGUST 26, AND SATURDAY, AUGUST 27, 1994: Jones Beach, Wantagh, NY, with America

SUNDAY, AUGUST 28, 1994: Ted Forstmann's House, Watermill, NY (Private), and Garden State Arts Center, Holmdel, NJ, with America
The Beach Boys made a guest appearance on *The David Letterman Show*, singing his Top Ten list on August 30.

WEDNESDAY, AUGUST 31, 1994: Minnesota State Fair, St. Paul, MN, with America

THURSDAY, SEPTEMBER 1, 1994: Du Quoin Fair, Du Quoin, IL and Allentown Fair, Allentown, PA, with Fabulous Thunderbirds

FRIDAY, SEPTEMBER 2, 1994: Naval Academy Alumni Hall, Annapolis, MD

SATURDAY, SEPTEMBER 3, 1994: Virginia Beach Amphitheater, VA and Beach Concert, Ocean City, MD with Jefferson Starship

SUNDAY, SEPTEMBER 4, AND MONDAY, SEPTEMBER 5, 1994: National Corvette Convention, Smith Stadium, Bowling Green, KY

TUESDAY, SEPTEMBER 13, 1994: Bismarck, ND, with America

THURSDAY, SEPTEMBER 15, 1994: Fargodome, Fargo, ND, with America

FRIDAY, SEPTEMBER 16, 1994: Caesars Tahoe, Stateline, NV

SATURDAY, SEPTEMBER 17, 1994: Puyallup Fair, Puyallup, WA

SUNDAY, SEPTEMBER 18, 1994: Twisp, WA

SATURDAY, SEPTEMBER 24, 1994: Tustin Ranch, Tustin, CA

SATURDAY, DECEMBER 31, 1994, TO SUNDAY, JANUARY 1, 1995: Caesars Tahoe, Stateline, NV (Three shows)

1995

I N 1995, Brian made his first appearances with the Beach Boys since 1990 and agreed to record with them. Initially the band gathered to record songs for a proposed *Baywatch Nights* TV show, which led to an agreement to make an album of all-new music under Brian and Don Was' direction. After a few sessions the project ran aground, allegedly due to Carl's displeasure with the material. Instead, they re-recorded a selection of their old songs with C&W artists like Willie Nelson and Tammy Wynette. Brian Wilson and Joe Thomas served as producers for what became the *Stars and Stripes* album. Brian also sang on Van Dyke Parks' album *Orange Crate Art*.

CONCERTS PLAYED IN
1995

WEDNESDAY, JANUARY 18, 1995: Folsom Auto Mall, Folsom, CA

WEDNESDAY, APRIL 5, TO SUNDAY, APRIL 9, 1995: Superstar Theater, Atlantic City, NJ

FRIDAY, APRIL 28, AND SATURDAY, APRIL 29, 1995: Riviera, Las Vegas, NV
Brian appeared with the group.

SATURDAY, MAY 13, 1995: Amphitheater, Pompano Beach, FL, with Bertie Higgins (Two shows)

TUESDAY, MAY 16, 1995: Prince George Wharf, Nassau, Bahamas
This was part of a special cruise promotion.

SATURDAY, MAY 20, 1995: Georgia Dome, Atlanta, GA, with Paul Revere and the Raiders

SUNDAY, MAY 21, 1995: Callaway Gardens, Pine Mountain, GA, with Bertie Higgins

TUESDAY, MAY 23, 1995: Ritz Carlton, Maui, HI

FRIDAY, MAY 26, 1995: Cohen Stadium, El Paso, TX

SATURDAY, MAY 27, 1995: Sea World, San Antonio, TX

SUNDAY, MAY 28, 1995: Astroworld, Houston, TX

MONDAY, MAY 29, 1995: Six Flags Over Texas, Arlington, TX

SATURDAY, JUNE 10, 1995: Dixie Center/Burns Arena, St. George, UT

SUNDAY, JUNE 11, 1995: Mirage, Las Vegas, NV

WEDNESDAY, JUNE 14, 1995: Arena, Sioux Falls, SD, with Christopher Cross

THURSDAY, JUNE 15, 1995: Pinewood Bowl, Lincoln, NE, with Christopher Cross

FRIDAY, JUNE 16, 1995: Sec Taylor Stadium, Des Moines, IA

SATURDAY, JUNE 17, 1995: Riverport Amphitheater, Maryland Heights, MO, with Christopher Cross

SUNDAY, JUNE 18, 1995: Mark of the Quad Cities, Moline, IL, with Christopher Cross

WEDNESDAY, JUNE 21, 1995: Merriweather Post, Columbia, MD, with Christopher Cross

THURSDAY, JUNE 22, 1995: King's Dominion, Doswell, VA

JUNE 23, 1995: Knight's Castle, Fort Mill, SC

JUNE 24, 1995: Riverfront Stadium, Cincinnati, OH

~~~~~

1995

SATURDAY, JUNE 25, 1995: Silver Stadium, Rochester, NY

TUESDAY, JUNE 27, 1995: Civic Center, Mankato, MN

THURSDAY, JUNE 29, 1995: Edmonton Stadium, Edmonton, AB, Canada

FRIDAY, JUNE 30, 1995: Rocky Mountain Music Fest, Calgary, AB, Canada, with Toby Keith

SATURDAY, JULY 1, 1995: Rocky Mountain Music Fest, Calgary, AB, Canada, with Riders in the Sky and Waylon Jennings and Community Auditorium, Thunder Bay, ON, Canada
Carolin Veseley of the *Lethbridge Herald* attended the Calgary show and reported: "The greying foursome—ages forty-eight to fifty-four—crooned and harmonized their way through more than twenty songs with the same brightness and charm of their classic recordings. Also vying for attention on stage were the Beach Boys Cheerleaders—four bikini clad dancers (obviously not the originals) and a few of the band members' tousled haired tykes."

SUNDAY, JULY 2, 1995: Fox City Stadium, Appleton, WI

MONDAY, JULY 3, 1995: Mall of America, Bloomington, MN

TUESDAY, JULY 4, 1995: Six Flags, Jackson, NJ, and Ben Franklin Parkway Arts Museum, Philadelphia, PA

THURSDAY, JULY 6, TO SUNDAY, 9, 1995: Trump Castle, Atlantic City, NJ (Five shows, two on July 8)

WEDNESDAY, JULY 19, 1995: Santa Monica Pier, Santa Monica, CA
The Beach Boys, joined by David Marks, performed a concert on the Santa Monica Pier filmed for the *Baywatch* TV show.

FRIDAY, JULY 21, 1995: Cashman Field, Las Vegas, NV

SATURDAY, JULY 22, 1995: Wolf Mountain Amphitheatre, Park City, UT

SUNDAY, JULY 23, 1995: Boise, ID

TUESDAY, JULY 25, 1995: Billings, MT

WEDNESDAY, JULY 26, 1995: Butte, MT

THURSDAY, JULY 27, 1995: Festival, Sandpoint, WA

FRIDAY, JULY 28, 1995: Portland, OR

SATURDAY, JULY 29, 1995: Gorge Amphitheater, George, WA

WEDNESDAY, AUGUST 3, 1995: California Mid-State Fair, Paso Robles, CA

THURSDAY, AUGUST 4, 1995: Epicenter, Rancho Cucamonga, CA, and Blockbuster Pavilion, Devore, CA, with Christopher Cross

FRIDAY, AUGUST 5, 1995: Hilton Amphitheater, Reno, NV

SATURDAY, AUGUST 6, 1995: Concord Pavilion, Concord, CA

"The greying foursome—ages forty-eight to fifty-four—crooned and harmonized their way through more than twenty songs with the same brightness and charm of their classic recordings."

featuring . . .

Lorrie Morgan

James House

Junior Brown

Doug Supernaw

Sawyer Brown

Toby Keith

Ricky Van Shelton

T. Graham Brown

Willie Nelson

Collin Raye

Kathy Troccoli

Timothy B. Schmit

Jon Stebbins Collection

TUESDAY, AUGUST 9, 1995: Connors Pointe Festival Park, Superior, WI, with Mark Rubin

WEDNESDAY, AUGUST 10, 1995: Wisconsin State Fair, Allis, WI

THURSDAY, AUGUST 11, 1995: New World Theater, Chicago, IL

FRIDAY, AUGUST 12, 1995: Pine Knob Music Theater, Clarkston, MI

SATURDAY, AUGUST 13, 1995: Kingswood Theater, Vaughan, ON, Canada

MONDAY, AUGUST 15, 1995: Three Rivers Stadium, Pittsburgh, PA, with Eddie Money

WEDNESDAY, AUGUST 17, TO FRIDAY, AUGUST 19, 1995: Center for the Performing Arts, Cerritos, CA

SATURDAY, AUGUST 20, 1995: Desert Sky Pavilion, Phoenix, AZ

TUESDAY, AUGUST 22, 1995: Theatre du Forum, Montreal, QB, Canada, with Christopher Cross

WEDNESDAY, AUGUST 23, 1995: Super Ex Grandstand, Ottawa, ON, Canada, with Christopher Cross

THURSDAY, AUGUST 24, 1995: NY State Fair, Syracuse, NY, with Christopher Cross
Mark Bialczak of the *Syracuse Post-Standard* reported, "To ward off the crags of age, they've assembled a fine band of musicians around them. And for one touching portion of the show, they brought out the clear-voiced son of Al, Matt Jardine, for spine tingling five-part harmony on 'Surfer Girl,' 'Hushabye,' and 'Wendy' . . . Other high points were a funky surf version of Brian Wilson's cranky 'Do It Again' and a harmonious version of 'California Dreamin.'"

SATURDAY, AUGUST 26, 1995: Pilot Field, Buffalo, NY, and Jones Beach, Wantagh, NY, with Christopher Cross

SUNDAY, AUGUST 27, 1995: Maryland National Guard, Havre de Grace, MD, and Garden State Arts Center, Holmdel, NJ, with Christopher Cross
Blondie Chaplin guested on "Sail on Sailor."

MONDAY, AUGUST 28, 1995: Harborlights, Boston, MA, with Paul Wayne

TUESDAY, AUGUST 29, 1995: Oakdale Theater, Wallingford, CT (Two shows)

FRIDAY, SEPTEMBER 1, 1995: Metropolitan Park, Jacksonville, FL, with America

SATURDAY, SEPTEMBER 2, 1995: Amphitheater, Virginia Beach, VA

SUNDAY, SEPTEMBER 3, 1995: Jackson Airport, Jackson, MS

SATURDAY, SEPTEMBER 9, 1995: Belleview Mido, Bellair, FL, with the Kingsmen (Benefit)

SATURDAY, SEPTEMBER 30, 1995: Prado Regional Park, Chino, CA
Brian appeared with the group.

MONDAY, OCTOBER 2, 1995: Hoffman Center, Walnut Creek, CA

THURSDAY, OCTOBER 5, 1995: State Fair of Texas, Dallas, TX
The group was in Texas to begin recording sessions for Stars and Stripes. Brian replaced Carl at this show. Chris Farmer, who stayed until 2007, replaced Ed Carter.

THURSDAY, OCTOBER 19, 1995: Chattanooga, TN
Carl was again absent.

THE BEACH BOYS IN CONCERT

SUNDAY, OCTOBER 22, 1995: Laguna Seca, Monterey, CA

FRIDAY, NOVEMBER 3, AND SATURDAY, NOVEMBER 4, 1995: Eastern Illinois University, Charleston, IL

MONDAY, NOVEMBER 6, 1995: Paradice Riverboat Casino, East Peoria, IL

WEDNESDAY, NOVEMBER 29, TO SUNDAY, DECEMBER 3, 1995: TropWorld Casino, Atlantic City, NJ

1996

THE GROUP FINISHED work on *Stars and Stripes* and appeared at the Nashville Fan Fair in June (with Brian) to promote it. The LP was not a big success, though a DVD documenting the sessions, titled *Nashville Sounds*, was also released. The failure of *Stars and Stripes* led to a split with Brian, who played his last gig with them (until 2012) in September. The group continued touring without him. They also contributed interviews for a documentary by Alan Boyd. The film aired on VH1 in 1998 as *Endless Harmony*.

CONCERTS PLAYED IN
1996

SUNDAY, JANUARY 28, 1996: Brixton Academy, London, England
The group (with Brian) appeared at a Status Quo concert to perform "Fun, Fun, Fun," which Status Quo had covered on a recent album. The Beach Boys remained in the U.K. to promote the track, including an appearance on *The Des O'Connor Tonight Show* on February 7.

FRIDAY, FEBRUARY 23, 1996: Abravanel Hall, Salt Lake City, UT (Benefit)

FRIDAY, MARCH 29, AND SATURDAY, MARCH 30, 1996: Riviera Casino, Las Vegas, NV
Billy Hinsche left at this time and was replaced by Tim Bonhomme.

THURSDAY, APRIL 11, 1996: UNC, Wilmington, NC (Two shows)

THURSDAY, APRIL 25, 1996: Presbyterian Hospital Dinner, Waldorf-Astoria, New York, NY

SATURDAY, APRIL 27, 1996: Valley Forge Music Fair, Devon, PA (Two shows)

THURSDAY, MAY 30, 1996: Chastain Park, Atlanta, GA

FRIDAY, MAY 31, 1996: McCarver Park, Memphis, TN

SATURDAY, JUNE 1, 1996: Knights Castle, Charlotte, NC

FRIDAY, JUNE 14, 1996: Fan Fair, Nashville, TN
The Beach Boys spent a week in Nashville, promoting *Stars and Stripes*. In addition to this special concert with Brian, which was filmed for an accompanying DVD, the group performed "I Get Around" with Sawyer Brown at the Music City News Awards on June 10.

SATURDAY, JUNE 15, 1996: Six Flags Over Texas, Arlington, TX

THURSDAY, JUNE 27, 1996: Santa Fe Springs, CA

WEDNESDAY, JULY 3, AND THURSDAY, JULY 4, 1996: Six Flags, Jackson, NJ

THURSDAY, JULY 11, 1996: Frontier Field, Rochester, NY

FRIDAY, JULY 12, 1996: Montage Mountain PAC, Scranton, PA

SUNDAY, JULY 14, 1996: Palace Theater, Myrtle Beach, SC

FRIDAY, JULY 26, 1996: Paramount Arts Center, Aurora, IL

SATURDAY, JULY 27, 1996: Convention Center, Minneapolis, MN (Private)

SUNDAY, JULY 28, 1996: Mystic Lakes Casino, Shakopee, MN

TUESDAY, JULY 30, 1996: Kingswood Music Theater, Vaughan, ON, Canada

WEDNESDAY, JULY 31, 1996: Ionia Fair, Ionia, MI

THURSDAY, AUGUST 1, 1996: Dane County Coliseum, Madison, WI, with Robert J
Natasha Kassulke of the *Wisconsin State Journal* reported, "Some fans wondered what happened to the women in bikinis and the cheerleaders who have paraded on stage at past shows. But they were treated instead to some songs off a soon to be released album, *Stars and Stripes*. Even the ice-lovers had to smile through sun-inspired hits such as 'Good Vibrations,' 'I Get Around,' and 'Help Me Rhonda.'"

FRIDAY, AUGUST 2, 1996: "WE Fest," Soo Pass Ranch, Detroit Lakes, MN

SATURDAY, AUGUST 3, 1996: Reno Hilton Amphitheater, Reno, NV

SUNDAY, AUGUST 4, 1996: Concord Pavilion, Concord, CA

FRIDAY, AUGUST 9, 1996: Riverfront Stadium, Cincinnati, OH

SATURDAY, AUGUST 10, 1996: Columbus Zoo, Columbus, OH

SUNDAY, AUGUST 11, 1996: Illinois State Fair, Springfield, IL

TUESDAY, AUGUST 13, 1996: Starlight Amphitheater, Kansas City, MO, with James House

WEDNESDAY, AUGUST 14, 1996: Westfair Amphitheater, Council Bluffs, IA

THURSDAY, AUGUST 15, 1996: Riverport Amphitheater, Maryland Heights, MO

FRIDAY, AUGUST 16, 1996: Pine Knob Music Theater, Clarkston, MI

SATURDAY, AUGUST 17, 1996: RCA Dome, Indianapolis, IN

TUESDAY, AUGUST 20, 1996: Mid-Hudson Civic Center, Poughkeepsie, NY

WEDNESDAY, AUGUST 21, 1996: Oakdale Theater, Wallingford, CT
Brian joined the group for a *David Letterman* TV taping in New York. They sang "Little Deuce Coupe" with James House.

THURSDAY, AUGUST 22, 1996: Dodd Stadium, Norwich, CT

FRIDAY, AUGUST 23, 1996: Harbor Lights Pavilion, Boston, MA

SATURDAY, AUGUST 24, 1996: Jones Beach, Wantagh, NY

SUNDAY, AUGUST 25, 1996: Garden State Arts Center, Holmdel, NJ

TUESSAY, AUGUST 27, TO SUNDAY, SEPTEMBER 1, 1996: Merv Griffin's Resort Casino, Atlantic City, NJ

THURSDAY, SEPTEMBER 5, 1996: Memphis, TN (Canceled)

FRIDAY, SEPTEMBER 6, 1996: Casino, Evansville, IN

SATURDAY, SEPTEMBER 7, 1996: Roberts Stadium, Evansville, IN

SUNDAY, SEPTEMBER 8, 1996: Navy Pier, Chicago, IL (Two shows)
Brian played both shows, his last concerts with the Beach Boys until 2012.

"Even the ice-lovers had to smile through sun-inspired hits such as 'Good Vibrations,' 'I Get Around,' and 'Help Me Rhonda.'"

THE BEACH BOYS IN CONCERT

THURSDAY, SEPTEMBER 26, TO WEDNESDAY, OCTOBER 2, 1996: Rio, Las Vegas, NV
During this Vegas stand, the group played an afternoon show on September 27 at Town Center Plaza in Santa Fe Springs, California, and a private Vegas show on October 1.

THURSDAY, OCTOBER 3, 1996: Amarillo, TX

FRIDAY, OCTOBER 4, 1996: State Fair, Tulsa, OK

SATURDAY, OCTOBER 5, 1996: Texas State Fair, Dallas, TX

TUESDAY, OCTOBER 8, 1996: Tyler, TX

THURSDAY, OCTOBER 10, 1996: Alexandria, VA

SATURDAY, OCTOBER 12, 1996: "Farm Aid," Columbia, SC

SUNDAY, OCTOBER 13, 1996: Veterans Memorial Coliseum, Winston Salem, NC

SATURDAY, OCTOBER 19, 1996: Country Music People's Choice Awards, San Diego, CA

SUNDAY, OCTOBER 20, 1996: Konocti Resort, Kelseyville, CA

SATURDAY, OCTOBER 26, 1996: Delta Center, Salt Lake City, UT

SUNDAY, OCTOBER 27, 1996: Arizona State Fair, Phoenix, AZ

SATURDAY, DECEMBER 14, 1996: Lakeland Center, Lakeland, FL

SUNDAY, DECEMBER 15, 1996: Amphitheater, Pompano Beach, FL

FRIDAY, DECEMBER 27, TO TUESDAY, DECEMBER 31, 1996: Rio, Las Vegas, NV

1987

CAPITOL RELEASED a box set of *The Pet Sounds Sessions*, featuring new mixes, outtakes, and session tapes. The release was overshadowed by more troubling developments. In 1996 there'd been signs something was wrong with Carl, and by 1997 he'd been diagnosed with cancer. The initial prognosis for recovery was promising, although his treatment forced him to miss a number of shows. By August it was evident he'd have to leave the band and David Marks returned as his replacement. The relationship between Mike and Al became increasingly fraught and the year ended with doubts about the future of the group.

CONCERTS PLAYED IN
1997

SATURDAY, MARCH 1, 1997: Mar-A-Lago Club, Palm Beach, FL

THURSDAY, MARCH 20, 1997: Centroplex Exhibition Hall, Baton Rouge, LA (Benefit)

THURSDAY, APRIL 17, 1997: Helsinki, Finland, with Jormas
Carl didn't make the trip to Europe. Phil Bardowell filled in.

SATURDAY, MAY 24, AND SUNDAY, MAY 25, 1997: Harrah's, Laughlin, NV (One show each night)
Carl was absent from these shows.

FRIDAY, MAY 30, 1997: Riverport Amphitheater, Maryland Heights, MO, with Chicago

SATURDAY, MAY 31, 1997: Polaris Amphitheater, Columbus, OH, with Chicago

SUNDAY, JUNE 1, 1997: Deer Creek Music Center, Noblesville, IN, with Chicago

TUESDAY, JUNE 3, 1997: Marcus Amphitheater, Milwaukee, WI, with Chicago

THURSDAY, JUNE 5, 1997: Stadium, Sioux City, IA, with Chicago

FRIDAY, JUNE 6, 1997: Sandstone Amphitheater, Bonner Springs, KS, with Chicago

SATURDAY, JUNE 7, 1997: Starplex Amphitheater, Dallas, TX

SUNDAY, JUNE 8, 1997: Woodlands Amphitheater, Houston, TX, with Chicago

TUESDAY, JUNE 10, 1997: Chastain Park, Atlanta, GA, with Chicago

THURSDAY, JUNE 12, 1997: Coliseum, Charleston, SC, with Chicago

FRIDAY, JUNE 13, 1997: Walnut Creek, Raleigh, NC, with Chicago

SATURDAY, JUNE 14, 1997: Amphitheater, Virginia Beach, VA, with Chicago

SUNDAY, JUNE 15, 1997: Blossom Music Center, Cuyahoga Falls, OH, with Chicago

TUESDAY, JUNE 17, 1997: Merriweather Post Pavilion, Columbia, MD, with Chicago

WEDNESDAY, JUNE 18, 1997: Star Pavilion, Hershey, PA, with Chicago

FRIDAY, JUNE 20, 1997: Hartford, CT, with Chicago

SATURDAY, JUNE 21, 1997: World Scholar Athlete Games, University of Rhode Island, RI, and Harbor Lights, Boston, MA, with Chicago

MONDAY, JUNE 30, TO WEDNESDAY, JULY 2, 1997: House of Blues, North Myrtle Beach, SC

THURSDAY, JULY 3, 1997: Richmond, VA

Carl Wilson performing at one of his last shows with the Beach Boys, August 19, 1997, at the Rosemont Theater in Rosemont, Illinois. Courtesy of Rob Kenny

FRIDAY, JULY 4, 1997: Six Flags, Jackson, NJ

SATURDAY, JULY 5, 1997: Eagle Crest Aerodrome, Lewes, DE

SATURDAY, JULY 19, 1997: A&P Tennis Tournament, Mahwah, NJ

SUNDAY, JULY 20, 1997: Star Lake Amphitheater, Burgettstown, PA

SATURDAY, AUGUST 2, 1997: Concord Pavilion, Concord, CA

SUNDAY, AUGUST 3, 1997: Blockbuster Pavilion, Devore, CA

SATURDAY, AUGUST 9, 1997: Reno Hilton Amphitheater, Reno, NV

SUNDAY, AUGUST 10, 1997: Reno Hilton Amphitheater, Reno, NV, and Cashman Stadium, Las Vegas, NV

TUESDAY, AUGUST 19, 1997: Rosemont Theater, Rosemont, IL
This was Carl's last tour with the group. He spent much of his time playing guitar while seated on a stool.

WEDNESDAY, AUGUST 20, 1997: Pine Knob Music Theater, Clarkston, MI

THURSDAY, AUGUST 21, 1997: NY State Fair, Syracuse, NY, with America
Mark Bialczak of the *Syracuse Herald Journal* reported that the group's umpteenth appearance at the New York State Fair was enlivened by the presence of Carl, who despite sitting on a stool, still delivered a "stand up" performance, and by the aid of Matt Jardine. "The son of longtime Beach Boy Al not only pounded on percussion, but he took the high vocal parts originally written for Brian Wilson."

THE BEACH BOYS IN CONCERT

Jon Stebbins Collection

SATURDAY, AUGUST 23, 1997: Jones Beach, Wantagh, NY

SUNDAY, AUGUST 24, 1997: Garden State Arts Center, Holmdel, NJ, and Jones Beach, Wantagh, NY

TUESDAY, AUGUST 26, TO SUNDAY, 31, 1997: Resorts Casino, Atlantic City, NJ

Sadly, this residency marked Carl's last shows with the Beach Boys. His final concert took place on August 29, after which he headed home to rest. Despite high hopes for recovery, he died in February 1998.

FRIDAY, SEPTEMBER 12, 1997: Branson, MO

SATURDAY, SEPTEMBER 13, 1997: Memphis, TN

THURSDAY, SEPTEMBER 25, 1997: Miami, FL

David Marks returned to the band as lead guitarist.

THURSDAY, OCTOBER 9, TO SATURDAY, OCTOBER 11, 1997: The Orleans, Las Vegas, NV

SUNDAY, OCTOBER 12, 1997: Charles Probst Center, Thousand Oaks, CA

FRIDAY, OCTOBER 24, 1997: Dee Events Center, Ogden, UT, with Jerry Lee Lewis and BTO

WEDNESDAY, OCTOBER 29, 1997: Bryce Jordan Center, State College, PA, with Chicago

THURSDAY, OCTOBER 30, 1997: Centrum, Worcester, MA, with Chicago

FRIDAY, OCTOBER 31, 1997: Pepsi Arena, Albany, NY, with Chicago

SUNDAY, NOVEMBER 2, 1997: Meadows, Hartford, CT, with Chicago

WEDNESDAY, NOVEMBER 5, 1997: Coliseum, Fort Wayne, IN, with Chicago

THURSDAY, NOVEMBER 6, 1997: Van Endel, Grand Rapids, MI, with Chicago

FRIDAY, NOVEMBER 7, 1997: Heritage Theatre, Saginaw, MI, with Chicago

SATURDAY, NOVEMBER 8, 1997: The Palace, Auburn Hills, MI, with Chicago

SUNDAY, NOVEMBER 9, 1997: Roberts Stadium, Evansville, IN, with Chicago

TUESDAY, NOVEMBER 11, 1997: Metro Center, Rockford, IL, with Chicago

WEDNESDAY, NOVEMBER 12, 1997: Wright State University, Dayton, OH, with Chicago

THURSDAY, NOVEMBER 13, 1997: SW Missouri State University, Springfield, MO, with Chicago

FRIDAY, NOVEMBER 14, 1997: Arie Crown Theatre, Chicago, IL, with Chicago

SATURDAY, NOVEMBER 15, 1997: University of Notre Dame, South Bend, IN, with Chicago

SUNDAY, NOVEMBER 16, 1997: Target Center, Minneapolis, MN

1998–2011

AFTER CARL'S TRAGIC death at age fifty-one on February 6, the band frayed. By late May, Al and Mike had gone their separate ways. Having won the rights to use the name "the Beach Boys," Mike, Bruce, and David (who left again in 1999) continued to tour, while Al headed a group billed as "the Beach Boys Family and Friends," which included Brian's daughters Carnie and Wendy. Brian released a long-awaited second solo album, *Imagination*, and began touring with his own band. Thus, at times there were three competing Beach Boys–related bands vying for concert bookings. The three entities wouldn't come together again until 2012.

ITINERARY
DECEMBER 6 - 20, 1998
AUSTRALIA

SUN.	DEC. 06	TRAVEL TO AUSTRALIA
MON.	DEC. 07	FLYING
TUE.	DEC. 08	ARRIVE and DAY OFF IN BRISBANE
WED.	DEC. 09	PLAY BRISBANE
THU.	DEC. 10	TRAVEL TO and DAY OFF IN MELBOURNE
FRI.	DEC. 11	PLAY MELBOURNE
SAT.	DEC. 12	TRAVEL TO and PLAY ADELAIDE
SUN.	DEC. 13	TRAVEL TO and DAY OFF IN SYDNEY
MON.	DEC. 14	DAY OFF IN SYDNEY
TUE.	DEC. 15	PLAY SYDNEY
WED.	DEC. 16	TRAVEL TO and PLAY CANBERRA
THU.	DEC. 17	TRAVEL TO and DAY OFF IN SYDNEY
FRI.	DEC. 18	PLAY NEWCASTLE
SAT.	DEC. 19	PLAY WOLLONGONG
SUN.	DEC. 20	TRAVEL HOME

Jon Stebbins Collection

Bruce Johnston and David Marks performing in 1998.
Marks Family Archive

SELECTED CONCERTS PLAYED IN
1998

SUNDAY, JANUARY 25, 1998: Super Bowl Pre-Game Show, San Diego, CA
Mike, Bruce, David Marks, and Glen Campbell performed on NBC TV. Al wasn't informed of the show and only became aware as he viewed it on TV.

SUNDAY, MAY 3, 1998: Ritz Carlton Buckhead, Atlanta, GA (Private)

WEDNESDAY, MAY 6, 1998: Kentucky Horse Park, Lexington, KY (private)

SATURDAY, MAY 9, 1998: American Cancer Society Benefit, Detroit, MI
This was the last show Mike and Al played together until 2011.

SELECTED BEACH BOYS SHOWS PERFORMED AFTER CARL WILSON'S DEATH

The Beach Boys continued to perform a full slate of concert dates despite only featuring one founding member. We have chosen to list only a sampling of representative or important shows rather than a complete list of dates.

FRIDAY, JUNE 20, AND SATURDAY, JUNE 21, 1998: Fiddler's Green, Denver, CO

FRIDAY, JULY 4, AND SATURDAY, JULY 5, 1998: Trump Marina Casino, Atlantic City, NJ, with KC and the Sunshine Band

FRIDAY, SEPTEMBER 11, AND SATURDAY, SEPTEMBER 12, 1998: Macomb University, Clinton Township, MI

THURSDAY, NOVEMBER 12, AND FRIDAY, NOVEMBER 13, 1998: Grand Theatre, Biloxi, MS

THURSDAY, DECEMBER 3, AND FRIDAY, DECEMBER 4, 1998: Horseshoe Casino, Tunica, MS

WEDNESDAY, DECEMBER 9, 1998: Entertainment Centre, Brisbane, QLD, Australia, with America

TUESDAY, DECEMBER 15, 1998: Sydney, NSW, Australia, with Richard Clapton and America

SATURDAY, DECEMBER 19, 1998: Newcastle, NSW, Australia, with America

TUESDAY, DECEMBER 29, TO THURSDAY, DECEMBER 31, 1998: Orleans, Las Vegas, NV (Two shows)

SELECTED CONCERTS PLAYED IN 1999

SATURDAY, FEBRUARY 13, AND SUNDAY, FEBRUARY 14, 1999: Konocti Harbor Resort, Kelseyville, CA

SATURDAY, FEBRUARY 27, 1999: Napier, North Island, New Zealand

SUNDAY FEBRUARY 28, 1999: Queenstown, South Island, New Zealand

FRIDAY, APRIL 9, AND SATURDAY, APRIL 10, 1999: Trump Marina, Atlantic City, NJ

SUNDAY, MAY 16, 1999: Starplex Amphitheatre, Nashville, TN, with Creedence Clearwater Revisited

FRIDAY, JUNE 11, 1999: Kanalbuhne, Gelsenkirchen, Germany

MONDAY, JUNE 14, 1999: Freilichtbuhne, Stuttgart, Germany

TUESDAY, JUNE 15, 1999: Forest National, Brussels, Belgium

FRIDAY, JUNE 25, 1999: Stadtpark, Hamburg, Germany

SUNDAY, JUNE 27, 1999: Donauinselfest, Vienna, Austria

TUESDAY, JUNE 29, 1999: Les Palais Des Congres, Paris, France

SUNDAY, JULY 4, 1999: Konocti Harbor Resort, Kelseyville, CA, with Dick Dale
David Marks left the Beach Boys again following this concert. He would often guest with them

David Marks performing with the Beach Boys in Germany 1999. Marks Family Archive

The
Beach
Boys
Foxwoods
Resort Casino

Backstage Access

February 5 - 6, 1999

Backstage pass. Marks Family Archive

THE BEACH BOYS IN CONCERT

during the 2000s, but would not return as a full-time member until the 2012 reunion.

SATURDAY, JULY 17, 1999: Yasgur's Farm, Bethel, NY and A&P Tennis Classic, Mahwah, NJ

FRIDAY, AUGUST 13, 1999: Shasta Fairgrounds, Anderson, CA, with Jesse Colin Young

MONDAY, AUGUST 30, 1999: Hampton Beach Casino, Hampton Beach, NH

SUNDAY, SEPTEMBER 12, 1999: Pendleton Round Up Stadium, Pendleton, OR

SUNDAY, SEPTEMBER 19, 1999: Crystal Grand Music Theater, Wisconsin Dells, WI (Two shows)

TUESDAY, OCTOBER 5, 1999: University of Illinois, Champaign, IL

THURSDAY, DECEMBER 2, 1999: University of Indiana, Indiana, PA

MONDAY, DECEMBER 6, 1999: Hammerstein Ballroom, New York, NY (Private benefit show)

WEDNESDAY, DECEMBER 29, 1999: El Bajio, Guadalajara, Mexico

SELECTED CONCERTS PLAYED IN
2000

SATURDAY, FEBRUARY 26, 2000: Westbury Music Center, NY, with Glen Super

SATURDAY, APRIL 22, 2000: Earth Day, Washington DC

FRIDAY, APRIL 28, 2000: Arbor Daze, Euless, TX

SATURDAY, JUNE 10, 2000: Chastain Park, Atlanta, GA

TUESDAY, JULY 4, 2000: Festival, Buffalo Bayou Park, Houston, TX

TUESDAY, JULY 11, 2000: Jackpot Junction Casino, Morton, MN, with Dean Torrence and the Surfaris

TUESDAY, AUGUST 1, 2000: Stanislaus County Fair, Turlock, CA, with Nelson

SUNDAY, AUGUST 13, 2000: Skyline Stage, Navy Pier, Chicago, IL

TUESDAY, AUGUST 15, 2000: Illinois State Fair, Springfield, IL, with Johnny Rivers

MONDAY, SEPTEMBER 4, 2000: Nebraska State Fair, Lincoln, NE

SATURDAY, OCTOBER 14, 2000: George Washington University, Washington DC

WEDNESDAY, DECEMBER 13, 2000: Mann Hall, Fort Meyers, FL

THURSDAY, DECEMBER 28, TO SATURDAY, DECEMBER 30, 2000: B.B. King Blues Club, New York, NY

SELECTED CONCERTS PLAYED IN
2001

FRIDAY, JANUARY 19, 2001: Inaugural Gala, Washington DC

TUESDAY, MARCH 27, 2001: John Philips Memorial Concert, Los Angeles, CA

WEDNESDAY, MAY 16, 2001: Rock and Roll Hall of Fame Concert, Cleveland, OH

SATURDAY, JULY 14, 2001: Auditorio Del Parque De Castrelos, Vigo, Spain

SUNDAY, JULY 15, 2001; Orange Biarritz Surf Festival, Stade Aguilera, Biarritz, France

THURSDAY, JULY 19, 2001: Edinburgh Castle, Edinburgh, Scotland, with Status Quo

SATURDAY, JULY 21, 2001: Liverpool Docks, Liverpool, England, with Status Quo

SUNDAY, JULY 22, 2001: Hyde Park, London, England, with Status Quo

TUESDAY, JULY 24, 2001: Tivoli Gardens, Copenhagen, Denmark

THURSDAY, JULY 26, 2001: Borgholm Slottsruin, Borgholm, Sweden

TUESDAY, JULY 31, 2001: Sammilsdal, Leksand, Sweden

WEDNESDAY, SEPTEMBER 5, 2001: LSU Assembly Center, Baton Rouge, LA

SATURDAY, OCTOBER 20, 2001: County Stadium, Charlotte, NC

SATURDAY, NOVEMBER 3, 2001: Stratosphere Hotel, Las Vegas, NV

SUNDAY, DECEMBER 30, 2001: Tropicana Casino, Atlantic City, NJ

SELECTED CONCERTS PLAYED IN
2002

SATURDAY, APRIL 13, AND SUNDAY, APRIL 14, 2002: Stratosphere Hotel, Las Vegas, NV

THURSDAY, MAY 16, 2002: Fundraiser for Governor Rendell, Philadelphia, PA

MONDAY, JULY 1, 2002: Molson Amphitheater, Toronto, ON, Canada

TUESDAY, JULY 23, 2002: Mark of the Quad, Moline, IL

FRIDAY, NOVEMBER 29, 2002: Adrian Phillips Hall, Atlantic City, NJ

WEDNESDAY, DECEMBER 27, TO FRIDAY, DECEMBER 29, 2002: Harrah's Lake Tahoe, Stateline, NV

THE BEACH BOYS IN CONCERT

SELECTED CONCERTS PLAYED IN
2003

TUESDAY, MAY 6, 2003: Oven's Auditorium, Charlotte, NC

SATURDAY, JUNE 7, 2003: Konocti Harbor Resort, Kelseyville, CA, with the Kingsmen

SUNDAY, JULY 13, 2003: Tollwood Summer Festival, Munich, Germany

SATURDAY, JULY 19, 2003: Le Sporting Monte Carlo, Monaco

FRIDAY, JULY 25, 2003: Thetford Forest, Suffolk, England

SATURDAY, AUGUST 30, TO MONDAY, SEPTEMBER 1, 2003: Caesars Palace, Atlantic City, NJ

THURSDAY, OCTOBER 4, 2003: Dalewood Wyndham Winery, Hunter Valley Estates, NSW, Australia

FRIDAY, NOVEMBER 7, 2003: AVO Sessions Festival, Basel, Switzerland

SUNDAY, NOVEMBER 9, 2003: Filaforum, Milan, Italy

SELECTED CONCERTS PLAYED IN
2004

FRIDAY, MAY 21, AND SATURDAY, MAY 22, 2004: Brown Amphitheater, Peachtree City, GA

MONDAY, JUNE 14, 2004: Ravinia Festival, Highland Park, IL

SATURDAY, JULY 2, 2004: Tivoli Stadium, Innsbruck, Austria

SUNDAY, JULY 10, 2004: Faenol Festival, Bangor, Wales

SUNDAY, AUGUST 2, 2004: Harris Park, London, ON, Canada

WEDNESDAY, AUGUST 18, 2004: Hampton Beach Casino, Hampton Beach, NH

FRIDAY, NOVEMBER 6, 2004: Opera Hall, Blackpool, England

SATURDAY, NOVEMBER 7, 2004: Royal Centre, Nottingham, England

FRIDAY, NOVEMBER 13, 2004: Carling Apollo, Hammersmith, London, England

MONDAY, NOVEMBER 16, 2004: Guildhall, Portsmouth, England

THURSDAY, NOVEMBER 19, 2004: Clyde Hall, Glasgow, Scotland

FRIDAY, NOVEMBER 20, 2004: Metro Radio Arena, Newcastle, England

SELECTED CONCERTS PLAYED IN
2005

MONDAY, JANUARY 8, 2005: Hyatt, Maui, HI

FRIDAY, APRIL 22, 2005: Gran Rex Theatre, Buenos Aires, Argentina

THURSDAY, JULY 4, 2005: West Lawn, U.S. Capitol, Washington DC, with the National Symphony Orchestra

SUNDAY, JULY 31, 2005: Fuji Rock Festival, Naeba, Nigata, Japan

SUNDAY, SEPTEMBER 25, 2005: Greek Theater, Los Angeles, CA

MONDAY, DECEMBER 19, 2005: Philharmonic Center for the Arts, Naples, FL

SELECTED CONCERTS PLAYED IN
2006

FRIDAY, JANUARY 13, 2006: Tim Kaine's Inaugural, Kaplan Hall, Williamsburg, VA

THURSDAY, MARCH 30, TO SATURDAY, APRIL 1, 2006: River Rock Casino, Vancouver, BC, Canada

MONDAY, JULY 8, 2006: Waikiki Shell, Honolulu, HI

FRIDAY, AUGUST 9, 2006: Mohegan Sun, Uncasville, CT

SATURDAY, NOVEMBER 3, 2006: Riverwind Casino, Norman, OK

THURSDAY, NOVEMBER 23, 2006: Helsinki Ice Hall, Helsinki, Finland

SUNDAY, DECEMBER 31, 2006: Luxor, Las Vegas, NV

SELECTED CONCERTS PLAYED IN
2007

SATURDAY, MARCH 24, 2007: Paramount Theater, Rosemont, IL

SATURDAY, JULY 4, AND SUNDAY, JULY 5, 2007: RFD-TV Theatre, Branson, MO

SATURDAY, AUGUST 3, TO MONDAY, AUGUST 5, 2007: The Orleans, Las Vegas, NV

SUNDAY, NOVEMBER 2, 2007: Palise Theatre, Melbourne, Australia, with Christopher Cross

SATURDAY, NOVEMBER 15, 2007: Harbor Theatre, Sydney, NSW, Australia

SELECTED CONCERTS PLAYED IN 2008

TUESDAY, APRIL 3, 2008: Brighton Centre, Brighton, England

David Marks joined Mike and Bruce for the entire British tour.

WEDNESDAY, APRIL 4, 2008: Hammersmith Apollo, London, England

THURSDAY, APRIL 12, 2008: Manchester Apollo, Manchester, England

MONDAY, JULY 4, 2008: Atlantic City Hilton, Atlantic City, NJ

TUESDAY, AUGUST 4, 2008: Ventura County Fair, Ventura, CA

TUESDAY, SEPTEMBER 16, 2008: Safeco Field, Seattle, WA

THURSDAY, DECEMBER 6, 2008: Hanover PAC, Worcester, MA

SELECTED CONCERTS PLAYED IN 2009

FRIDAY, MARCH 27, TO SUNDAY, MARCH 29, 2009: Kiewit Concert Hall, Holland PAC, Omaha, NE

TUESDAY, JULY 4, 2009: Pitea Havsbad, Sweden

WEDNESDAY, SEPTEMBER 23, TO FRIDAY, SEPTEMBER 25, 2009: Humphrey's by the Bay, San Diego, CA

David Marks, Scott Totten, and Mike Love performing on the Beach Boys U.K. tour in 2008. Marks Family Archive

THE BEACH BOYS IN CONCERT

SELECTED CONCERTS PLAYED IN
2010

Pictured left to right—John Cowsill, Christian Love, Bruce Johnston, Randell Kirsch, Mike Love, Scott Totten, and Tim Bonhomme. Ian Rusten Collection

WEDNESDAY, JANUARY 27, 2010: Araneta Coliseum, Quezon City, Philippines

SUNDAY, FEBRUARY 7, 2010: King's Park, Perth, WA, Australia

FRIDAY, JUNE 25, 2010: Waterfront Hall, Belfast, Ireland

FRIDAY, JULY 2, 2010: Mariebergsskogen, Karlstad, Sweden

SUNDAY, JULY 18, 2010: Mountain Winery, Saratoga, CA

THURSDAY, JULY 22, 2010: Asser Levy Park, Brooklyn, NY

THURSDAY, SEPTEMBER 30, 2010: Jubilee Auditorium, Calgary, AB, Canada

MONDAY, DECEMBER 6, AND TUESDAY, DECEMBER 7, 2010: Grand West's Grand Arena, Cape Town, South Africa

SELECTED CONCERTS PLAYED IN
2011

FEBRUARY 5, 2011: Ronald Reagan Centennial Birthday Celebration, Reagan Library, Simi Valley, CA
Al Jardine appeared with the Beach Boys for the first time since 1998.

SATURDAY, MARCH 5, 2011: Seawell Ballroom, Denver, CO

THURSDAY, APRIL 7, 2011: Niagara Fallsview Casino, Niagara Falls, ON, Canada

FRIDAY, MAY 13, 2011: Von Braun Center, Huntsville, AL

THURSDAY, JULY 7, 2011: Epsom Downs Race Course, Epsom Downs, England

FRIDAY, JULY 15, 2011: Escenario Puerta Del Angel, Madrid, Spain

SATURDAY, AUGUST 27, 2011: Biltmore House, Asheville, NC

FRIDAY, SEPTEMBER 9, 2011: Cobb Energy PAC, Atlanta, GA

SUNDAY, DECEMBER 4, 2011: St. George Theater, Staten Island, NY

SATURDAY, DECEMBER 31, 2011: Thunder Valley Casino, Lincoln, CA

THE BEACH BOYS' SOLO CONCERTS

VARIOUS MEMBERS of the Beach Boys have performed as solo acts, or individually with bands other than the Beach Boys. The following is a selected overview of their solo endeavors.

DAVE AND THE MARKSMEN (1963-1965)

David Marks performed with his band the Marksmen upon leaving the Beach Boys in late 1963. As A&M and Warner Brothers recording artists, the Marksmen performed around California during 1964 and 1965, including concerts at the Memorial Coliseum in Sacramento, the San Jose County Fairgrounds, and Veterans Memorial Hall in Santa Rosa.

DENNIS WILSON (1977-1978)

Dennis scheduled a solo tour to promote his 1977 solo LP *Pacific Ocean Blue*. Venues booked included the Dorothy Chandler Pavilion in L.A., Avery Fisher Hall in New York, and the Pine Knob Music Theater in Michigan. Although Dennis played a few solo sets during the intermission of Beach Boys concerts, his planned solo tour was ultimately canceled.

DENNIS WILSON AND CHRISTINE MCVIE (1980)

The duo of Dennis and Christine were advertised as one of the acts scheduled to perform at a January 29, 1980, benefit for Cambodian Relief at the Dorothy Chandler Pavilion. Also on the bill were the Jacksons and John Travolta. It's not known if Dennis actually played this show.

MIKE LOVE SOLO CONCERTS (1974-1998)

THURSDAY, MAY 9, 1974: "An Evening with Salvador Allende," Madison Square Garden, New York, NY, with Bob Dylan, Arlo Guthrie, and Phil Ochs
Mike performed a solo version of "California Girls," backed by Charles Lloyd on flute and John McLaughlin on guitar.

FRIDAY, SEPTEMBER 12, 1975: Freedom Train Event, Sioux City, IA
With 1976 approaching, the Bicentennial Commission created the American Freedom Train. Mike appeared for free at some towns where the train stopped. He also appeared with the train at the Union Pacific Railroad Shop, Omaha, Nebraska, with King Harvest on September 23, 1975.

SUNDAY, MARCH 28, 1976: Lakeland Civic Center, Lakeland, FL, with Tom Paxton, Hickory Wind, Paul Winter Consort, and others (6:00 p.m. show)
Mike acted as emcee at this benefit sponsored by the Cousteau Society.

WAVES

OCTOBER 1977

In October 1977, Mike played several shows with a band he put together called Waves. Ron Altbach recalled, "When we finished up in Switzerland in 1977, Mike, Charles, and I went to see Maharishi and [magician] Doug Henning was there. And we made a promise that we'd tour with Henning to raise awareness and money for TM." The group organized a series of benefits to fund the creation

Mike performing at USC with Celebration on April 28, 1978.
Jon Stebbins Collection

of "Age of Enlightenment" TM facilities. Mike's band Waves included Charles Lloyd, Ron Altbach, Ed Carter, Rusty Ford (on bass), Ernie Rodriguez (on guitar), Gary Griffin, and Mike Kowalski. Al also played with them. The dates were: Berkeley Community Theater, Berkeley, California (October 17); Music Hall, Houston, Texas (October 19); El Camino College Auditorium, El Camino, California (October 21); Wilshire Ebell Theater, Los Angeles, California (circa October 22); and California Theater, San Diego, California (two shows on October 23).

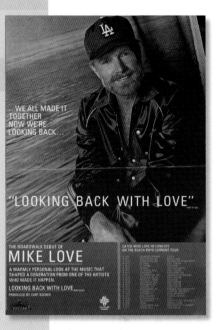

Nineteen eighty-one tour poster advertising Mike's solo album *Looking Back with Love.* Ian Rusten Collection

MIKE LOVE AND CELEBRATION

APRIL TO JUNE 1978

On April 15, 1978, Mike made an appearance outside Peaches Records in Dallas, Texas, with his side project Celebration. This was the first of several free concerts the group played to promote the film *Almost Summer*.

On April 28, 1978, Celebration played at USC in Los Angeles. The musicians that played this show were Ed Carter, Mike Kowalski, Charles Lloyd, Ron Altbach, Dave Robinson, Wells Kelly, and Gary Griffin. They were joined by emcee Wolfman Jack, a reunited Jan and Dean, Carl Wilson, and an extremely animated Brian. Ron Altbach recalled, "Brian, every once in a while, would chip in. At that particular show I remember that Brian was just fantastic! I mean he was really into it. He was digging it. He was having a good time."

On April 29, 1978, Celebration performed at UC Santa Barbara, California. The show was filmed for promo purposes. Mike was quite taken with opening act the Reverie Rhythm Rockers, who included Jeffrey Foskett (guitar), Randall Kirsch (bass), and Bo Fox (drums). All three would later be part of Mike's Endless Summer Beach Band.

Further Celebration shows took place at: Shaw Park, Marietta, GA on May 6 (with Dean Torrence and bassist Ed Carter); the Swiss Embassy in Washington, DC, on May 21; Volunteer Park in Seattle, Washington, on May 27; and in the San Fernando Valley, California, on the morning of May 28, and on June 4 at Blossom Music Center, Cuyahoga Falls, Ohio (with Alex Bevan). At the Blossom show, 2,000 fans attended and the group played Beach Boys songs, including "Little Deuce Coupe," "Fun, Fun, Fun," "Surfin' USA," and "Barbara Ann." They also performed "Country Pie" and their three songs from the film *Almost Summer*.

MIKE LOVE AND THE ENDLESS SUMMER BEACH BAND

1981 TO 1996

On Saturday, May 23, 1981, at the Presentation Point Amphitheater in Lake Lanier Islands, Georgia, Mike played the first of numerous solo shows with his own band. Sunkist sponsored this show. The Beach Boys were asked, but were unwilling to do it for the amount offered. Mike put together a group he dubbed "the Endless Summer Beach Band." It consisted of Jeff Foskett on guitar, Randall Kirsch on bass, Bo Fox on drums, and Jim Studer, who'd helped produce *Looking Back with Love*, on keyboards.

In August 1981, Mike played dates with this band (with Bobby Figueroa in place of Bo Fox on drums) at Hobey Baker's, Goleta, California (with the Dreamers on Tuesday and the Snapshots on Wednesday) on Tuesday, August 4 and Wednesday, August 5; at the Bodega, Campbell, California, (two shows) on Thursday, August 7; and at the Country Club in Los Angeles, California (with Soldier) on Friday, August 8. David Marks sat in with Mike and his band at the Country Club show.

In September 1981 Mike played another short tour with the Endless Summer Beach Band (Jeff Foskett, Jim Studer, Bobby Figueroa, and Randall Kirsch). The dates were Nepenthe Club, Fort Lauderdale, Florida (two shows each night) on September 4 and September 5; Brassy's Nightclub, Cocoa Beach, Florida, on September 6; Knott's Berry Farms, Buena Park, California (with the Surfaris, Tweed Sneakers, Surf Raiders, King Neptune, Malibooz, and the Surf City Boys) on September 11; and Disney World, Orlando, Florida (with Jim Photoglo) on September 12. Mike also played at Club Foot in Austin, Texas, at some point during this period.

Mike tied the knot with Kathy Martinez on September 17. The Endless Summer Beach Band played the wedding and accompanied Mike on his honeymoon on the Princess Cruise Line to Acapulco, Mexico. While onboard, they played one show on Saturday, September 26, 1981.

In November–December 1981, to promote his solo LP *Looking Back with Love*, Mike and the Endless Summer Beach Band (Jeff Foskett, Randall Kirsch, either Jim Studer or Mike Meros on keyboards, and Mike Kowalski on drums) played more shows. The dates were Gainesville, Florida (November 2); Agora Ballroom, Atlanta, Georgia (November 4); The Bayou, Washington, DC, (November 5); Brandywine Club, Chadd's Ford, Pennsylvania, and Left Bank Club, Mount Vernon, New York (November 6); Philadelphia, Pennsylvania (Canceled) and North Stage, Glen Cove, New York, with Broken Arrow (November 7); Savoy Club, New York, New York (November 8); Toad's Place, New Haven, Connecticut (November 9, canceled); Channel Club, Boston, Masschusetts (November 13, canceled); Harpo's Club, Detroit, Michigan (November 20, canceled); Showplace Lounge, Sheraton Airport, Portland, Oregon (December 10, two shows); and Astor Park, Seattle, Washington (December 13, canceled).

In March 1982 Mike teamed up with Dean Torrence. The duo performed a series of free shows, in between Beach Boys tours, with the Endless Summer Beach Band sponsored by the Anheuser-Busch Corporation. The dates were South Padre Island, Texas (March 18); Bandshell, Daytona Beach, Florida (March 22); Presentation Point Amphitheater, Lake Lanier Islands, Georgia (May 8); Ontario Place Forum, Toronto, ON, Canada (May 26); Knott's Berry Farm, Buena Park, California (July 30, two shows without Dean); and Hollywood HS Homecoming Hop, Los Angeles, California (October 22). The latter show was filmed for an episode of the TV series *Hart To Hart*.

In October—November 1982 Mike and Dean and the Endless Summer Beach Band played a series of shows at universities sponsored by Budweiser and billed as "Be True To Your School" events. Chris Farmer played bass, Gary Griffin played keyboards, and Mike Kowalski played drums. Also along were Jeff Foskett and Adrian Baker, who sang lead on "Don't Worry Baby" and the Four Seasons' "Sherri." The dates were Coliseum, North Texas State University, Denton, Texas (October 28); South Houston State University, Huntsville, Texas (November 8); Texas Tech, Lubbock, Texas (November 12); UNO Baseball Field, New Orleans, Louisiana (November 14); University of Louisiana, Monroe, Louisiana (November 16); and University of Texas, El Paso, Texas (November 18).

In March 1983, Mike and Dean and the Endless Summer Beach Band again teamed up for more spring break concerts sponsored by Anheuser Busch. The dates were Jetty's Beach, South Padre Island, Texas (March 15); Bandshell, Daytona Beach, Florida (March 17); Ft. Lauderdale Beach, Florida (March 23); Bandshell, Daytona Beach, Florida (March 24); and Wayside Park, Fort Walton Beach, Florida (March 31).

In April–May 1983, Mike and Dean played gigs to promote their cassette release *Rock 'N' Roll City*. The band consisted of Jeff Foskett (guitar), Adrian Baker (guitar), Randall Kirsch (bass), John Cowsill (drums), and Gary Griffin (keyboards). The dates were: Rockefeller's, Houston, Texas (April 21); Radio Shack Convention in Dallas, Texas (mid-May); Adventure Island Park, Tampa, Florida (May 26); and Tulane University, New Orleans, Louisiana (May 30).

Some shows without Dean Torrence were Hyannis Village Green, South Yarmouth, Massachusetts (September 3, 1983), and Orange Bowl Parade, Miami, Florida, canceled, (January 2, 1984).

On Tuesday, March 20, and Wednesday, March, 21, 1984, in Ft. Lauderdale, Florida, Mike and Dean played for spring breakers for the third year in a row.

In 1988 Mike reformed the Endless Summer Beach Band and began playing occasional solo dates. Dates included: Continental Airlines Christmas Party, Effingham Park Hotel, Copthorne, West Sussex, England (December 20, 1988); Embassy Suites Resort at Kaanapali, Maui, Hawaii (March 1989); America's Bar, Chicago, Illinois (October 30, 1989); Jeff's Pirate Cove, Guam (December 7, 1989); Dreamworld, QLD, Australia (December 15 and 16, 1989); Daytona Beach Marriott, Florida (March 16 and 17, 1990); Flower Expo, Osaka, Japan (early June 1990); and the Nineteenth Tokyo Music Festival, Tokyo, Japan (early June 1990). At the latter televised event, Mike and the ESBB performed "California Girls," "Surfin' Safari," "Surf City," "Surfin' USA," "Barbara Ann," "I Get Around," "Fun, Fun, Fun," "Good Vibrations," and "Kokomo." Mike also presented an award to Wilson Phillips.

After a four-year lull, Mike played some sporadic dates with a reformed Endless Summer Band, including the Grand Hyatt Hotel, Hong Kong on June 8, 1994; and the Alexandra Palace, London, England, on October 30, 1994. The latter was a private show for employees of Northwest Airlines at which Bruce Johnston and Matt Jardine participated. Mike and the ESSB also played on February 26, 1995, at Welleby Park, Sunrise, Florida; and on August 8, 1996, at Asser Levy Seaside Park, Brooklyn, New York.

MIKE LOVE AND THE CALIFORNIA BEACH BAND

1997

Planting the seeds for what became the modern-age Beach Boys (aka the Mike and Bruce band), a number of shows took place in late 1997 without Al. David Marks also was absent. The act was billed as the "California Beach Band." The dates were San Bernardino, California (September 20 or 21); Studio 21, Hilversum, Netherlands (September 30); American Embassy, New Delhi, India (October 3); Regal Ballroom, Mumbai, India (October 6); and Grand ballroom, San Diego, California (October 7).

CARL WILSON SOLO CONCERTS (1980–1995)

MONDAY, JULY 7, 1980: Sheraton Universal Hotel, Los Angeles (Private)

Carl's first solo gig (other than some undocumented prison and hospital appearances in the early seventies) was on behalf of the Movement of Inner Spiritual Awareness, a religious organization founded by John-Roger in 1968.

SUNDAY, APRIL 5, 1981: Park West, Chicago, IL

This was the opening date of Carl's tour in support of his debut album. For the tour he assembled his own band, composed of Billy Hinsche on guitar and keyboards, John Daley on lead guitar, Myrna Smith on vocals, Gerald Johnson on bass, and Alan Krigger on drums.

MONDAY, APRIL 6, 1981: Center Stage, Detroit, MI

TUESDAY, APRIL 7, 1981: Agora, Cleveland, OH (9:00 p.m. show)

WEDNESDAY, APRIL 8, 1981: El Mocambo Club, Toronto, ON, Canada (Two shows at 7:00 and 11:00 p.m.)

FRIDAY, APRIL 10, 1981: Paradise Club, Boston, MA

SATURDAY, APRIL 11, 1981: My Father's Place, Roslyn, NY

SUNDAY, APRIL 12, 1981: Emerald City, Cherry Hill, NJ (9:00 p.m. show)

MONDAY, APRIL 13, 1981: Bottom Line, New York, NY

Stephen Holden of the *New York Times* attended Carl's appearance at the Bottom Line. He commented, "Though he is a passable rock crooner, Mr. Wilson's hard rock singing is sloppy and lackadaisical," and added that Carl's five-piece band "was also disappointing as it plodded clumsily through a rehash of the Beach Boys' familiar motorized sound." While in New York, Carl taped an appearance on the NBC TV *Tomorrow Show*.

MIKE LOVE
AND
THE CALIFORNIA BEACH BAND

ITINERARY
MAY 10 - 24, 1998

NAGOYA
HONG KONG
MANILA
TAIPEI
SINGAPORE
BANGKOK
HAWAII

Itinerary for Mike's May 1998 Asian tour with the California Beach Band. Jon Stebbins Collection

Carl goes solo with Myrna Smith and guitarist John Daley at the Roxy on April 23, 1981. Photo: Ed Roach ©1981, 2012

Ad for Carl's solo show in Indiana on September 5, 1981. Ian Rusten Collection

WEDNESDAY, APRIL 15, 1981: Bayou Club, Washington, DC, with the Bob Duncan Band (Two shows)

THURSDAY, APRIL 16, 1981: Agora, Atlanta, GA

FRIDAY, APRIL 17, 1981: The Poet's Club, Memphis, TN

SUNDAY, APRIL 19, 1981: The Agora, Dallas, TX

Dallas News reporter Pete Oppel complained that the set was short and should have featured more than one Beach Boys song, but still declared, "His performance, as brief as it was, was superior to the one the Beach Boys gave in Reunion Arena earlier this year. He relied almost exclusively on hard-driving, upbeat numbers, even increasing the tempo of the Beach Boys–flavored songs from his solo album."

MONDAY, APRIL 20, 1981: Agora Ballroom, Houston, TX, with the Sirens

THURSDAY, APRIL 23, 1981: The Roxy, Los Angeles, CA (Two shows)

Carl's hometown appearance brought out friends and relations. Amongst those in attendance were Brian, Dennis, Mike, Bruce, Ricci Martin, and Marilyn and Diane Rovell. Betty Collignon reported in the *BBFun* newsletter that at the early show "Carl seemed a little nervous performing in his hometown and in front of his family. By the second show he warmed up, relaxed and really enjoyed himself . . . He sang selections from his album including his single 'Hold Me,' two R&B tunes, 'Too Early To Tell' and 'I Wanna Thank You;' and a special touch of his first song he ever wrote, 'Feel Flows.'"

SATURDAY, APRIL 25, 1981: Old Waldorf Club, San Francisco, CA

Carl concluded his tour with a Bay Area show that attracted a modest crowd. Joel Selvin of the *San Francisco Chronicle* remarked, "On his solo outing, Carl Wilson showed himself to be the craftsman one would expect from a Beach Boy. His band smoothly wrapped swinging little instrumental figures . . . Wilson's singing, as always, was exquisite."

TUESDAY, JUNE 16, 1981: Salt Palace, Salt Lake City, UT

This was the first date of the Doobie Brothers tour, with Carl as opener. Other dates Carl appeared at were Red Rocks Amphitheater, Morrison, Colorado (June 18–20); Zoo Amphitheater, Oklahoma City, Oklahoma (June 22); Bicentennial Center, Salina, Kansas (June 23); Kemper Arena, Kansas City, Missouri (June 24); Five Seasons Center, Cedar Rapids, Iowa (June 25); Alpine Valley Music Theatre, East Troy, Wisconsin (June 27–28); Pine Knob Music Theatre, Clarkston, Michigan (June 30–July 5); Convention Center, Myrtle Beach, South Carolina (July 7); Pavilion, Virginia Beach, Virginia (July 8); Mann Music Center, Philadelphia, Pennsylvania (July 10); Music Mountain, South Fallsburg, New York (July 11); Hartford Civic Center, Hartford, Connecticut (July 12); Blossom Music Center, Cuyahoga Falls, Ohio (July 14–15); War Memorial Auditorium, Rochester, New York (July 16); Merriweather Post Pavilion, Columbia, Maryland (July 17); and SPAC, Saratoga Springs, New York (July 19). According to *Amusement Business*, Carl wasn't present for the Doobies gigs in West Orange, NJ on July 9 or Belmont, New York, on July 18.

Carl updated his show to generate more excitement, adding some Beach Boys songs, including "Darlin'." However, opening for the Doobies proved to be humbling. Reviewers praised his singing but noted the same thing: Carl just didn't have the charisma or energy to be a frontman like Mike. Carl told a reporter, "Now that I'm alone, I really respect the hell out of what Michael does for the Beach Boys, what all the guys do. It's like–what's wrong with this picture? The guys aren't there, that's what."

SATURDAY, JULY 18, 1981: Bottom Line, New York, NY (Two shows at 9:00 p.m. and 12:00 a.m.)

While touring with the Doobies, Carl found time to play some club dates.

THE BEACH BOYS' SOLO CONCERTS

MONDAY, JULY 20, 1981: Toad's Place, New Haven CT

TUESDAY, AUGUST 25, 1981: Bismarck Arena, Bismarck, ND
This was the opening date of the second leg of the Doobie Brothers tour. The other shows Carl played were Sioux Falls Arena, Sioux Falls, South Dakota (August 26); Rushmore Plaza Civic center, Rapid City, South Dakota (August 27); Civic Auditorium, Omaha, Nebraska (August 28); Hilton Coliseum, Ames, Iowa (August 29); Poplar Creek, Chicago, Illinois (September 1); Green Bay, Wisconsin (September 3); and La Crosse, Wisconsin (September 4).

SATURDAY, SEPTEMBER 5, 1981: "Third Rock 'N' Picnic Jam," Marion County Fairgrounds, Indianapolis, Indiana, with Rick Springfield (12:00 p.m. show)
Carl embarked on another short solo tour. The other dates were: Mabel's, Champaign, Illinois (September 6); Ontario Place Forum, Toronto (September 9); Le Club Montreal, Montreal (September 10); Hampton Beach, New Hampshire (September 11); Willimantic, Connecticut (September 12); Fountain Casino, Aberdeen, New Jerseay (September 13); and the Stone Balloon, Newark, Deleware (September 14).

WEDNESDAY, JUNE 22, 1983: Parker's, Seattle, WA
This was the first concert of a short tour Carl played in support of *Youngblood*. The same musicians that backed him in 1981 were present, including Myrna Smith and Billy Hinsche.

FRIDAY, JUNE 24, AND SATURDAY, JUNE 25, 1983: Greek Theatre, Los Angeles, CA, with America
Carl opened for America on three successive nights. In addition to playing a solo set, he joined America for their encore of "A Horse with No Name." Apparently, the first show was marred by the surprise appearance of Dennis. Drunk and disorderly, he commandeered a microphone and started yelling to the crowd, before being hustled off stage. Gerry Beckley warned Carl not to let such unprofessional incidents happen again.

SUNDAY, JUNE 26, 1983: Irvine Meadows Amphitheatre, Los Angeles, CA, with America (8:00 p.m. show)
Veronica Young of the *Orange County Register* commented that Carl "appeared to be having more fun than he has at most Beach Boys concerts."

WEDNESDAY, JUNE 29, 1983: Old Waldorf Club, San Francisco, CA, with Metro (8:00 p.m. show)
The set for this show consisted of: "Too Early Too Tell," "Darlin'," "What You Gonna Do About Me," "Youngblood," "Givin' You Up," "What More Can I Say," "Long Promised Road," "Heaven," "What You Do to Me," "Treat Me Right" (sung by Myrna Smith), "I'm Not Dreaming" (sung by Myrna Smith), "Hold Me," "The Right Lane," "Rockin' All Over the World" and "Thank You."

SATURDAY, JANUARY 21, 1995: Little America Hotel, Salt Lake City, UT
Carl played a benefit with Billy Hinsche, Gerry Beckley, and Robert Lamm.

BRIAN WILSON SOLO CONCERTS (1979–1997)

THURSDAY, JULY 19, 1979, TO SATURDAY, JULY 28, 1979: Disneyland, Anaheim, CA
While the Beach Boys were off the road, Brian joined Papa-Doo-Run-Run at Disneyland. Papa-Doo-Run Run, created as a tribute to the surf bands of the 1960s, was composed of Jim Armstrong, Don Zarilli, Jim Rush, Mark Ward, and Jim Shippey. Jim Armstrong told Paula Perrin of *BBFUN*, "The first night he came out on his own. Every night after that we invited him and he just wanted to go. He played with us. Brian was having such a good time I could tell that he wanted to come back, so I

said 'Just come on back.' Sometimes the guy is so humble and so modest that you've got to force something on him for him to do it."

SUNDAY, MARCH 10, 1985: Palace Theater, Los Angeles, CA, with Jackson Browne, the Bangles, and Belinda Carlisle
A trimmed-down Brian performed at a benefit for L.A.'s homeless.

SUNDAY, MAY 12, 1985: Malibu Emergency Room Benefit, Pepperdine University, Los Angeles, California, with Stephen Stills, the Bangles, and John Stewart
Brian, now beardless, played a short set, which was filmed. He sang "Da Doo Run Run," "I'm So Lonely," "Male Ego," and encores of "California Girls" and "Sloop John B."

MONDAY, FEBRUARY 24, 1986: Forum, Los Angeles, CA
Brian appeared at a Vietnam Veterans benefit.

FRIDAY, DECEMBER 5, 1986: Wembley Arena, London, England
This was a Moody Blues show at which Brian sang "Sloop John B" and "Help Me Rhonda." He also came out at the end to "shake a tambourine" on "Ride My See-Saw."

SATURDAY, DECEMBER 6, 1986: NAS Tribute Show, Beverly Theater, Beverly Hills, CA

THURSDAY, JANUARY 22, 1987: Rock and Roll Hall of Fame dinner, Waldorf Astoria, NY
As part of a Lieber-Stoller tribute, Brian performed "On Broadway." An impressed Seymour Stein of Sire Records offered him a contract.

SATURDAY, SEPTEMBER 24, 1988: STOMP Convention, Visitation Parish Centre, Greenford, Middlesex, England
Brian made a surprise appearance at the *Beach Boys Stomp* convention. He sang three songs, "Night Time," "Surfer Girl," and "Love and Mercy." Most people in the room had no idea he was going to appear. Michael Grant, editor of *Beach Boys Stomp*, recalled, "I will never forget that moment when the curtains opened up and I saw the faces of all the fans who continually support us at our conventions. The looks of surprise, disbelief, and sheer pleasure (along with a few tears) were fantastic."

SATURDAY, OCTOBER 1, 1988: Ibiza 92 Festival, Ibiza, Spain
At this televised event, Brian mimed to two songs.

SATURDAY, DECEMBER 3, 1988: NAS Fourth Annual Tribute Show, Los Angeles, CA
Brian sang "God Only Knows" and "I Sleep Alone" at this televised ceremony.

SUNDAY, NOVEMBER 12, 1989: Pro-Choice Rally, Los Angeles, CA

SATURDAY, JULY 28, 1990: Endless Summer Quarterly Beach Boys Convention, Handlery Hotel, San Diego, CA
Dressed in a blue and white striped shirt, Brian made a surprise performance at this videotaped ESQ event. He sang four songs: "God Only Knows," "California Girls," "The Spirit of Rock and Roll," and "Good Vibrations."

SATURDAY, DECEMBER 1, 1990: Heal the Bay Benefit, Santa Monica, CA
Brian performed "California Girls," "Love and Mercy," "Water Builds Up," "Make A Wish," "God Only Knows," and "The Spirit of Rock and Roll."

FRIDAY, DECEMBER 6, 1990: AIDS Fundraiser, San Francisco, CA
Brian appeared with cartoonist Gary Trudeau at a private fundraiser. He performed "California Girls," "Love and Mercy," "Water Builds Up," "Make a Wish," "God Only Knows," and other songs.

MONDAY, JANUARY 28, 1991: China Club, Los Angeles, CA
Accompanied by Don Was and a small band led by guitarist Kal David, Brian played an eleven-song set. They played "Sloop John B," "In My Room," "Help Me Rhonda," "Be My Baby," "You've Lost That Loving Feeling," "Melt Away," "Johnny B. Goode," "Spirit of Rock and Roll," "Good Vibrations," "California Girls," and "Surfer Girl."

SUNDAY, JUNE 9, 1991: Pediatric AIDS Benefit, Yosemite National Park, CA

THURSDAY, FEBRUARY 20, 1992: Pro-Set L.A. Music Awards, Los Angeles, CA
Brian received a Lifetime Achievement Award and performed his unreleased rap song "Brian" and "California Girls." His band featured Don Was and Gregg Allman.

MONDAY, MARCH 14, 1994: Algonquin Hotel, New York, NY
Brian appeared as part of "East Meets West: The Musical Legacy of Both Coasts." Ronnie Spector was also there.

JULY 1994: Japan Music Festival
Brian appeared with Don Was.

TUESDAY, OCTOBER 25, 1994: House of Blues, Los Angeles, CA
Brian performed with frequent collaborator Andy Paley.

THURSDAY, NOVEMBER 3, 1994: "Tribute to Brian Wilson," Morgan-Wixson Theater, Santa Monica, CA
Brian performed a few songs at this show in his honor. Amongst the participants were the Wondermints, who later became Brian's backing band on his solo tours.

MONDAY, JANUARY 1, 1995: Sundance Film Festival, Park City, UT
To promote *I Just Wasn't Made for These Times*, Brian performed with Don Was.

WEDNESDAY, AUGUST 16, 1995: SOB Club, New York, NY
Brian performed with his daughters after a showing of *I Just Wasn't Made for These Times*.

THURSDAY, SEPTEMBER 7, 1995: Walter Reade Theater, New York, NY
To promote *I Just Wasn't Made for These Times*, Brian sang "California Girls," "Warmth of the Sun," "God Only Knows," "409," and "Do It Again."

SATURDAY, JUNE 8, 1996: Will Geer Theater, Topanga, CA
Brian appeared with Van Dyke Parks at a songwriters' symposium.

NOTABLE BRIAN WILSON SOLO SHOWS (1998–2011)

Beginning in 1999, Brian toured semi-regularly with his backing band the Wondermints and Jeffrey Foskett. The following is a selected list of his post-1997 concerts.

SATURDAY, MAY 9, 1998: Norris Cultural Center, St. Charles, IL
This was a special show filmed for VH1 to help promote the *Imagination* album.

SATURDAY, OCTOBER 3, 1998: "Farm Aid," Tinley Park, IL

WEDNESDAY, SEPTEMBER 16, 1998: Norris Cultural Center, St. Charles, IL
Brian taped an episode of *Front Row Center* with Deana Carter for TNN TV.

THE BEACH BOYS IN CONCERT

Jon Stebbins Collection

TUESDAY, MARCH 9, 1999: Michigan Theatre, Ann Arbor, MI
This was the opening date of Brian's first solo tour, portions of which were filmed for the DVD *Brian Wilson on Tour*. Other March dates were Rosemont, Illinois (March 10), Milwaukee (March 12), and Minneapolis (March 14). The tour resumed in June with East Coast shows, including New York (June 18) and Boston (June 21).

FRIDAY, JULY 9, 1999: Festival Hall, Osaka, Japan

MONDAY, JULY 12, TO WEDNESDAY, JULY 14, 1999: International Forum, Tokyo, Japan
Brian played his first Japanese tour dates.

FRIDAY, OCTOBER 15, 1999: Moore Theatre, Seattle, WA
Opening date of the Pacific Northwest portion of the tour. Dates included Portland (October 17 and 18), San Francisco (October 20), and Los Angeles (October 23).

SATURDAY, OCTOBER 30, AND SUNDAY, OCTOBER 31, 1999: Bridge School Benefit, Shoreline Amphitheater, Mountain View, CA

FRIDAY, APRIL 7, AND SATURDAY, APRIL 8, 2000: Roxy Theater, Los Angeles, CA
These shows were recorded for the live album *Live at the Roxy*.

FRIDAY, JULY 7, 2000: State Theater, Easton, PA
This was the first date of the forty-three-show *Pet Sounds* tour. Notable dates included: Boston (July 18), Chicago (July 22), Los Angeles (September 24), and New York (November 17–19).

THURSDAY, MARCH 29, 2001: *Tribute to Brian Wilson*, Radio City Music Hall, New York, NY
This show was filmed for a TNT TV special.

SATURDAY, JUNE 9, 2001: Gorge Amphitheater, George, WA
This was the first show of a twenty-nine-date tour with Brian opening for Paul Simon. Dates included Los Angeles (June 12 and 13); Denver (June 24); and Indianapolis (July 4).

SUNDAY, JANUARY 20, 2002: Annexet, Stockholm, Sweden
Brian took *Pet Sounds* to Europe, including four nights at the Royal Festival Hall in London (January 27 to 30), filmed to make the *Pet Sounds Live* DVD.

MONDAY, JUNE 3, 2002: Buckingham Palace, London, England
Brian and his band played at the Queen's Golden Jubilee.

WEDNESDAY, JUNE 5, 2002: Brighton Centre, Brighton, England
Brian played a short U.K.-only *Pet Sounds* tour. Other dates included London (June 9 and 10), Edinburgh (June 12), and Manchester (June 13).

Jon Stebbins Collection

TUESDAY, DECEMBER 10, 2002: Entertainment Centre, Brisbane, QLD, Australia
This was the opening date of the Australian *Pet Sounds* tour, which included gigs in Sydney (December 12 to 14), Canberra (December 16), and Melbourne (December 17 and 18).

SATURDAY, JUNE 14, 2003: Hatch Memorial Shell, Boston, MA
This is one of only three shows Brian played in 2003. He also played at the Beacon in New York on June 16 and at a Carl Wilson benefit at UCLA on October 16.

Brian signing autographs in Portland, Oregon, October 1999. Photo: David Lee Higginbotham

FRIDAY, FEBRUARY 20, TO FEBRUARY 27, 2004: Royal Festival Hall, London, England
Brian debuted *Smile* during a six-day residency in London (no shows on February 23 or 25).

MONDAY, MARCH 1, TO SUNDAY, MARCH 14: European Tour
He toured *Smile* all over Europe, including dates in Frankfurt (March 10), Amsterdam (March 13), and Paris (March 14).

TUESDAY, JULY 13, TO SUNDAY, AUGUST 7: European Tour
This tour includes Stockholm as well as a second Festival Hall residency in July.

SUNDAY, SEPTEMBER 26, 2004: Center Staging, Burbank, CA
Brian played two shows, which were filmed for the *Beautiful Dreamer* DVD.

RX0408F GA GA8 32 ADULT
EVENT CODE · SECTION/AISLE · ROW/BOX · SEAT · ADMISSION
$37.50 GENERAL ADMISSN 37.50
SECTION/AISLE
GA AN EVENING WITH
BRIAN WILSON
PF 1X ALL AGES
GA8 SEAT 32 R O X Y T H E A T R E
500ATMC 9009 W.SUNSET, HOLLYWOOD
2MAR00 SAT APRIL 8 2000 DRS@8PM

Ticket for one of Brian's solo shows at the Roxy Theatre in Los Angeles, April 2000. Jon Stebbins Collection

~~~~~

THE BEACH BOYS IN CONCERT

THURSDAY, SEPTEMBER 30, 2004: Orpheum Theatre, Minneapolis, MN
This was the opening date of the first North American *Smile* tour. Dates included: Chicago (October 2); New York (October 12 and 13), Dallas (October 25), and Los Angeles (November 2 and 3).

TUESDAY, NOVEMBER 30, 2004: Opera House, Sydney, NSW, Australia
Brian took the *Smile* tour to Australia and New Zealand. Other dates included: Melbourne (December 8 and 9), Brisbane (December 15), Wellington (December 18), and Auckland (December 19).

SUNDAY, JANUARY 30, 2005: Nakano Sun Plaza, Tokyo, Japan
This was the opening show of a four-date Japanese *Smile* tour.

WEDNESDAY, JUNE 22, 2005: Hampton Court Festival, Surrey, England
This was the opening show of a twenty-two-date European "Greatest Hits" tour. Other dates included: Glastonbury (June 26), Live 8 in Berlin (July 2), the Roskilde Festival in Denmark (July 3), the Montreux Festival (July 10), Brighton Dome (July 14), and Rome (July 22).

TUESDAY, AUGUST 9, 2005: Bank of America Pavilion, Boston, MA
Brian embarked on another North American *Smile* tour. Dates included: Jones Beach (August 13), Philadelphia (August 16), Vancouver (August 29), Portland (August 31), and L.A. (September 4).

WEDNESDAY, NOVEMBER 1, 2006: Royce Hall, UCLA, Los Angeles, CA
This was the first of eleven "*Pet Sounds*/Fortieth Anniversary" shows. Al Jardine guested at ten shows, including Boston (November 17), New York (November 21 and 22), and Long Beach (January 27, 2007).

SATURDAY, JUNE 16, 2007: Skovdalen, Aalborg, Denmark
Another European "greatest hits" tour; dates included: Brussels (June 20), Paris (June 26), Vienna (July 3), and Dublin (July 8).

MONDAY, SEPTEMBER 10, TO SEPTEMBER 16, 2007: Royal Festival Hall, London, England
Brian premiered *That Lucky Old Sun*. Shows also took place in Bristol (September 18), Bournemouth (September 20), Edinburgh (September 22), Manchester (September 23), and Birmingham (September 24).

SATURDAY, JANUARY 5, 2008: The Domain, Sydney, NSW, Australia
This was the first of four Sydney shows. Brian played his greatest hits on this night, and then played *That Lucky Old Sun* (January 7 and 8) and *Pet Sounds* (January 9).

THURSDAY, MAY 8, 2008: Carnegie Hall, New York, NY (Rainforest benefit)

SATURDAY, JUNE 28, 2008: Kenwood House, London, England
This was the first date of a three-date U.K. "greatest hits" tour. The other dates were: Regents Theatre, Ipswich (June 29) and the Royal Albert Hall in London (July 1).

FRIDAY, SEPTEMBER 5, 2008: Paramount Theater, Oakland, CA
Brian began his North American *That Lucky Old Sun* tour. Other dates included Portland (September 7), Chicago (November 16), Boston (November 19), New York (November 21), and L.A. (January 28, 2009).

SATURDAY, JULY 4, 2009: Deutsches Theatre, Munich, Germany
This was the opening date of another European tour. Other dates included Amsterdam (July 6), Gothenburg, Sweden (August 30), Glasgow (September 1), and London (September 3).

THURSDAY, OCTOBER 22, 2009: Sangamon Auditorium, Springfield, IL
Brian opened his 2009 North American tour, playing twenty-one dates between October and December, including Milwaukee (October 24), Providence (November 4), and Boston (November 12).

FRIDAY, OCTOBER 29, 2010: Entertainment Centre, Wollongong, NSW, Australia

This was the first date of a short Australian tour. Chicago, America, and Peter Frampton appeared with Brian here and at shows in Brisbane (October 30), Melbourne (November 1), and Hunter Valley (November 6).

Brian performing at the Zelt festival in Mainz, Germany, on June 28, 2007. Photo: Michael OsterKamp

MONDAY, JUNE 6, 2011: Filene Center, Wolf Trap, Vienna, VA

Brian performed *Brian Wilson Reimagines Gershwin* on this fifteen-date North American tour. Dates included New York (June 11 to 13), Montreal (June 17), and Vancouver (June 28).

FRIDAY, JULY 29, 2011: Frederik Meijer Gardens, Grand Rapids, MI

Brian launched a short eleven-date "greatest hits" tour of the states. Dates included Atlanta (August 3), Saratoga (August 24), and Napa, California (August 25).

WEDNESDAY, SEPTEMBER 7, 2011: Grand Canal Theatre, Dublin, Ireland

Brian played twelve dates in Europe, including shows in Glasgow (September 11), London (September 16 to 18), and Paris (September 20). The tour concluded in Brussels, Belgium on September 22.

SELECTED AL JARDINE SOLO SHOWS (1998–2011)

Al performed under the banner "Beach Boys Family and Friends," as well as other solo entities and offshoots. The following is a selected list of the shows Al performed.

OCTOBER 18, 1998: Carl Wilson Benefit Concert, Roxy Theater, Los Angeles, CA

FEBRUARY 28, 1999: Strawberry Festival, Plant City, FL (Two shows)

AUGUST 26, 1999: NY State Fair, Syracuse, NY, with the Turtles and Herman's Hermits

THE BEACH BOYS IN CONCERT

NOVEMBER 18, TO DECEMBER 1, 1999: MGM Grand, Las Vegas, NV

MAY 28, 2000: Great America, Santa Clara, CA

OCTOBER 8, 2000: Third Carl Wilson Benefit, Malibu, CA

MAY 19, 2001: Georgia Dome, Atlanta, GA

JULY 4, 2002: Fort Stewart, Hinesville, GA

AUGUST 24, 2002: NY State Fair, Syracuse, NY (Two shows)

JULY 25, 2003: Harborfest, Oswego, NY

OCTOBER 4, 2003: Tuscany Hotel and Casino, Las Vegas, NV

NOVEMBER 10, 2004: Hammerstein Ballroom, New York, NY

DECEMBER 16, 2004: Red Barn Holiday Jam, Red Barn Studios, Big Sur, CA

APRIL 19, 2005: Fairmont Hotel, San Francisco, CA

SEPTEMBER 2, 2005: Caesars Palace, Las Vegas, NV

MARCH 17, 2006: Cerritos Center for the Performing Arts, Cerritos, CA

JULY 4, 2006: "The Taste of Minnesota," St. Paul, MN

JULY 28, 2007: Westhampton Beach PAC, Westhampton, NY

APRIL 4, AND 5, 2008: Suncoast Hotel and Casino, Las Vegas, NV

JULY 4, 2008: Tanner Park, Babylon, NY

JULY 24, 2009: New Jersey Festival of Ballooning, Readington, NJ

SEPTEMBER 19, 2009: Newport Beach, CA

JULY 13, 2010: John J. Burns Town Park, Massapequa, NY

OCTOBER 8, 2010: Henry Miller Memorial Library, Big Sur, CA

FEBRUARY 18, 2011: Tokyo, Japan

MAY 7, 2011: Mayfest, North Myrtle Beach, SC, with Surf City All Stars

JUNE 18, 2011: Coliseum, Hamilton, ON, Canada, with Surf City All Stars

SEPTEMBER 17, 2011: Lakeside Theater, East Meadow, NY

THE 2012 REUNION

FOLLOWING THE death of Carl in February 1998, as well as an acrimonious lawsuit between Mike and Al over the rights to use the Beach Boys name and Brian Wilson's resurrection as a solo performer, it seemed highly unlikely that the surviving Beach Boys would ever reunite. However, as the fiftieth anniversary of the group's formation approached, there were signs of a thaw in the relations between former members. In March 2011, Al joined Mike and Bruce onstage for the first time since 1998. And although 2011 passed without a full reunion, members made it clear that 2012 would see major developments.

The year 2012 turned out to be an incredible year for fans of the band. Brian Wilson, Mike Love, Al Jardine, Bruce Johnston, and David Marks reunited in the studio to record a brand new album, titled *That's Why God Made the Radio*, and announced a major world tour. Backed by heavy promotion, including appearances on PBS' *Front Row Center*, *Late Night with Jimmy Fallon*, *The Tonight Show*, and *Good Morning America*, the album sold surprisingly well. It debuted at an impressive number three on the *Billboard* album charts, making it their highest charting album of new material since 1965. Fans and critics were unanimous in their praise of the three-song suite composed by Brian that concludes the album. If "From There to Back Again," "Pacific Coast Highway," and "Summer's Gone" turn out to be the last recorded works of the Beach Boys as a group, they can walk away with their heads held high.

The tour announcement was also extremely well received. Over seventy dates were booked and shows sold out at major venues across the country. The tour kicked off in Tucson on April 24 and from the start received great critical buzz. It was clear that the five surviving Beach Boys were determined to make the reunion a special event. The shows were longer than they'd played in some time, and they continually added songs to the set as the tour progressed, including rarely played gems like "Marcella" and "Add Some Music to Your Day." As of this writing it is not known whether the surviving Beach Boys will continue beyond the 2012 reunion or resume their individual careers. Either way, the group's 2012 success marks an unexpected crescendo to their story.

2012 REUNION CONCERTS

TUESDAY, APRIL 10: Dodgers Stadium, Los Angeles, CA

TUESDAY, APRIL 24: Anselmo Valencia Amphitheater, Tucson, AZ

THURSDAY, APRIL 26: Verizon Amphitheater, Grand Prairie, TX

FRIDAY, APRIL 27: New Orleans Jazz and Heritage Festival, New Orleans, LA

SATURDAY, APRIL 28: Chastain Amphitheater, Atlanta, GA

SUNDAY, APRIL 29: Raleigh Amphitheater, Raleigh, NC

WEDNESDAY, MAY 2: Amphitheater, St. Augustine, FL

FRIDAY, MAY 4: Seminole Hard Rock Hotel and Casino, Hollywood, FL

SATURDAY, MAY 5: Stratz Center for the Performing Arts, Tampa, FL

TUESDAY, MAY 8, AND WEDNESDAY, MAY 9: Beacon Theater, New York, NY

FRIDAY, MAY 11: Benedum Hall, Pittsburgh, PA

SATURDAY, MAY 12, AND SUNDAY, MAY 13: Mohegan Sun, Uncasville, CT

TUESDAY, MAY 15: Westchester County Center, Westchester, NY

THURSDAY, MAY 17: Sands Bethlehem Events Center, Bethlehem, PA

SATURDAY, MAY 19: Borgata Hotel and Casino, Atlantic City, NJ

MONDAY, MAY 21, AND TUESDAY, MAY 22: Chicago Theater, Chicago, IL

FRIDAY, MAY 25: Cricket Wireless Amphitheater, Chula Vista, CA

SATURDAY, MAY 26: Fantasy Springs Special Events Center, Indio, CA

SUNDAY, MAY 27: Red Rocks Casino, Las Vegas, NV

MONDAY, MAY 28: Santa Barbara Bowl, Santa Barbara, CA

FRIDAY, JUNE 1: Greek Theater, Berkeley, CA

SATURDAY, JUNE 2: Hollywood Bowl, Los Angeles, CA

SUNDAY, JUNE 3: Verizon Wireless Amphitheater, Irvine, CA

FRIDAY, JUNE 8: Cynthia Woods Mitchell Pavilion, The Woodlands, TX

THE 2012 REUNION

Author Jon Stebbins with the reunited Beach Boys, September 2013. Jon Stebbins Collection

SUNDAY, JUNE 10: Bonnaroo Festival, Manchester, TN

TUESDAY, JUNE 12: Riverbend Music Center, Cincinnati, OH

WEDNESDAY, JUNE 13: Blossom Music Center, Cuyahoga Falls, OH

FRIDAY, JUNE 15: Central Park, New York, NY (for *Good Morning America*'s summer concert series), and Merriweather
Post Pavilion, Columbia, MD

SATURDAY, JUNE 16: Susquahanna Bank Center, Camden, NJ

SUNDAY, JUNE 17: Bethel Woods Center for the Arts, Bethel Woods, NY

TUESDAY, JUNE 19: Molson Amphitheater, Toronto, ON, Canada

WEDNESDAY, JUNE 20: Bell Center, Montreal, QB, Canada

The reunited Beach Boys performing in New Orleans on April 27, 2012.
Photo: Jon Stebbins

THE 2012 REUNION

FRIDAY, JUNE 22: Waterfront Center, Bangor, ME

SATURDAY, JUNE 23: SPAC, Saratoga Springs, NY

SUNDAY, JUNE 24: Jones Beach, Wantagh, NY

TUESDAY, JUNE 26: Bank of America Pavilion, Boston, MA

WEDNESDAY, JUNE 27: PNC Bank Arts Center, Holmdel, NJ

FRIDAY, JUNE 29: Performing Arts Center, Darien Lakes, NY

SATURDAY, JUNE 30: DTE Energy Music Theater, Clarkston, MI

SUNDAY, JULY 1: Summerfest, Marcus Amphitheater, Milwaukee, WI

TUESDAY, JULY 3: Farm Bureau Live at Virginia Beach, Virginia Beach, VA

WEDNESDAY, JULY 4: Lavell Edwards Stadium, BYU, Provo, UT

FRIDAY, JULY 6: Sandia Casino, Albuquerque, NM

SATURDAY, JULY 7: Grand Canyon University Arena, Phoenix, AZ

TUESDAY, JULY 10: Red Rocks Amphitheater, Morrison, CO

WEDNESDAY, JULY 11: Saddledome, Calgary, AB, Canada

FRIDAY, JULY 13: Chateau Ste. Michelle Winery, Woodinville, WA

SATURDAY, JULY 14: Cuthbert Amphitheater, Eugene, OR

SUNDAY, JULY 15: Harvey's Lake Tahoe Amphitheater, Stateline, NV

SATURDAY, JULY 21: Hoyos del Espino, Avila, Spain

MONDAY, JULY 23: Pobles Espanyol, Barcelona, Spain

THURSDAY, JULY 26: Ippodromo delle Capannelle, Rome, Italy

FRIDAY, JULY 27: Civic Arena, Milan, Italy

SUNDAY, JULY 29: Tradgaardsforeningen, Gothenburg, Sweden

TUESDAY, JULY 31: Spektrum, Oslo, Norway

WEDNESDAY, AUGUST 1: Musikhuset Aarhus Amfiscenen, Aarhus, Denmark

FRIDAY, AUGUST 3: O2 World Arena, Berlin, Germany

SATURDAY, AUGUST 4: Hanns Martin Schleyerhalle, Stuttgart, Germany

SUNDAY, AUGUST 5: Hockey Park, Monchengladbach, Germany

THE BEACH BOYS IN CONCERT

TUESDAY, AUGUST 7: Lokerse Festival, Lokeren, Belgium

THURSDAY, AUGUST 16: QVC Marine Field, Tokyo, Japan

FRIDAY, AUGUST 17: Osaka Prefectural Gym, Osaka, Japan

SUNDAY, AUGUST 19: Gaishi Hall, Nagoya, Japan

WEDNESDAY, AUGUST 22: Singapore Indoor Stadium, Kallang, Singapore

TUESDAY, AUGUST 28: Entertainment Centre, Brisbane, Australia

THURSDAY, AUGUST 30: Allphones Arena, Sydney, Australia

FRIDAY, AUGUST 31: Rod Laver Arena, Melbourne, Australia

SUNDAY, SEPTEMBER 2: Entertainment Centre, Adelaide, Australia

THURSDAY, SEPTEMBER 6: Burswood Dome, Perth, Australia

THURSDAY, SEPTEMBER 27: Royal Albert Hall, London, England

FRIDAY, SEPTEMBER 28: Wembley Arena, London, England

Jon Stebbins Collection

BIBLIOGRAPHY
BOOKS

Abbott, Kingsley. *Back to the Beach: Brian Wilson and the Beach Boys Reader.* London: Helter Skelter Publishing, 1999.

Badman, Keith. *The Beach Boys: The Definitive Diary of America's Greatest Band on Stage and in the Studio.* San Francisco: Backbeat, 2004.

Carlin, Peter Ames. *Catch a Wave: The Rise, Fall & Redemption of the Beach Boys' Brian Wilson.* Emmaus, Pennsylvania: Rodale, 2006.

Dalley, Robert J. *Surfin' Guitars.* Ann Arbor: Popular Culture, Ink, 1996.

Doe, Andrew, and John Tobler. *The Complete Guide to the Music of the Beach Boys.* London: Omnibus, 1997.

Einarson, John, and Richie Furay. *For What It's Worth: The Story of Buffalo Springfield.* New York: Cooper Square Press, 2004.

Feran, Tom, and John Gorman. *The Buzzard: Inside the Glory Days of WMMS and Cleveland Rock Radio.* Cleveland: Gray and Company, 2007.

Gaines, Steven. *Heroes and Villains: The True Story of the Beach Boys.* New York: New American Library, 1986.

Heyman, Richard. *Boom Harangue.* New York: iUniverse, 2002.

Hinman, Doug. *The Kinks: All Day and All of the Night.* London: Backbeat Books, 2004.

Lambert, Philip. *Inside the Music of Brian Wilson.* New York: The Continuum International Publishing Group, 2007.

Leaf, David. *The Beach Boys and the California Myth.* New York: Grosset, 1978.

Lloyd, Jack. *Endless Summer: My Life with the Beach Boys.* Albany, GA: Bear Manor Media, 2010.

Loudenback, Douglas. *Springlake Amusement Park.* Charleston: Arcadia Publishing, 2008.

McParland, Stephen J. *Our Favorite Recording Sessions.* North Stratfield: California Music, 2000.

———. *The California Sound: An Insider's Story, Volume 1.* North Stratfield: California Music, 2000.

———. *Smile, Sun, Sand & Pet Sounds.* North Strathfield: California Music, 1999.

Priore, Domenic. *Look! Listen! Vibrate! Smile!* Surfin' Colours Productions, 1988.

Stebbins, Jon. *The Real Beach Boy: Dennis Wilson.* Toronto: ECW Press, 1999.

Stebbins, Jon with David Marks. *The Lost Beach Boy.* London: Virgin Books, 2007.

Webb, Adam. *Dumb Angel: The Life and Music of Dennis Wilson.* Creation Books, 2001.

White, Timothy. *The Nearest Faraway Place: Brian Wilson, the Beach Boys and the Southern California Experience.* New York: Holt, 1994.

Wyman, Bill. *Stone Alone.* New York: Viking Press, 1990.

ARTICLES

In researching and writing this book we used articles that appeared throughout the years in the U.K. music publications *Melody Maker, Rave, Fabulous 208, Record Mirror, Top Pops, New Musical Express, Sounds,* and *Disc & Music Echo.* We also referred to articles that appeared in the American trade publications *Billboard, Amusement Business,* and *Variety.* Articles from the Beach Boys fanzines *Add Some Music, Beach Boys Stomp,* and *BBFUN* were also consulted. In addition, we scoured countless newspapers and university publications looking for advertisements and reviews. We have referred to the authors and publications in the text.

Information from the following sources was also used:

"At Home With the Beach Boys' Brian Wilson." *Teenset,* June 1966.

Bartlett, Rob. "Holland: An Expensive Way to Kill a 'Damned Surfing Image.'" *Beat Instrumental,* April 1973.

"Beach Boys." *Beat Instrumental,* February 1971.

"Beach Boy Wedding." *Tiger Beat,* November 1966.

"Carl Wilson: The Press Has Been Writing the Most Wicked Nonsense About Us For Years." *MuziekKrant OOR,* July 5, 1972.

BIBLIOGRAPHY

Catlin, Roger. "Carl Wilson's Departure Strikes Sour Note in 'Good Vibrations.'" *Omaha World Herald*, August 9, 1981.

Crawford, Linda, and Howard Bloom. "Are the New Beach Boys For Real?" *Circus*, December 1971.

Cohen, Scott. "The Dennis Wilson Interview." *Circus*, October 26, 1976.

"Dennis Wilson: The Prince of Pop." *Phonograph Magazine*, August 1972.

Felton, David. "The Healing of Brother Bri." *Rolling Stone*, November 4, 1976.

Forlenza, Richard. "Interview with Carl and Dennis." *NY Rocker*, April–May 1979.

Gabler, Neil. "The Beach Boys: Riding a New Wave." *New Times*, April 2, 1976.

Gollan, Jean. 1970. "Beach Boys." *Go-Set*, May 2, 1970.

Goodman, Pete. "Brian: Heavyweight Genius of the Beach Boys." *Beat Instrumental*, September 1966.

Graham, Samuel. "Beach Boys Bounce Back." *Record World*, June 1979.

Guidi, Federico. "Hanno Gia Venduto 100 Milioni di Dischi." *Bolero Teletutto*, January 12, 1969.

Helinski, Jack. "New Beach Boy Vibes." *Music World and Record Digest*, June 27, 1979.

Himes, Geoffrey. "The Beach Boys: High Times and Ebb Tides." *Musician*, September 1983.

Lambert, Glenn. "Beach Boys In NY: A Taste of Cool Water." *Rock*, April 12, 1971.

Leaf, David. "Beach Boys Rock L.A. Forum." *Pet Sounds*, Vol. 1, No. 1., February 1977.

———. "Bruce Johnston: A Voice from the Past Helps With Tomorrow." *Pet Sounds. Vol. 2*, November 1978.

Leaf, Earl. "BBs Adventures in Europe." *Teen Set*, Vol. 2., 1965.

———. "Beach Boys Battle in Britain." *Teen Screen*, February 1965.

———. *Beach Boys Scene*, June 1965.

———. "My Fair and Frantic Hollywood." *Teen Magazine*, March 1965.

———. "Treks, Trips & Travels." *Teenset*, October 1964.

Mamis, Toby. "Beach Boys Hang Ten in Hotel Lobby." *Creem*, October 1971.

McVeigh, Linda. "Surfs Out for the Beach Boys." *The Harvard Crimson*, November 30, 1965.

Miller, Jim. "Holland." *Rolling Stone*, March 1, 1973.

"Mike Love Talks About The Beach Boys' Early Days." *Flip Magazine*, January 1967.

Moss, Rick. "The Beach Boys and the Maharishi." *Circus*, December 1971.

Nash, Robert, and Mike Sigman. "A Conversation with Brian Wilson." *Record World*, July 28, 1973.

Newman, Ralph, and Jeff Tamarkin. "The Beach Boys: From the Beginning." *Time Barrier Express*, April–May 1979.

Nolan, Tom. "The Beach Boys: A California Saga, Part One: Mr. Everything." *Rolling Stone*, October 28, 1971.

Nolan, Tom. "The Beach Boys: Tales of Hawthorne." *Rolling Stone*, November 11, 1971.

Nolan, Tom. "The Frenzied Frontier of Pop Music." *LA Times West Magazine*, November 27, 1966.

"One Nighter with the Beach Boys." *Beat Instrumental*, January 1967.

Paulsen, Don. "Backstage With the Beach Boys." *Hit Parader*, September 1965.

Quigley, Mike. "The Beach Boys: Vancouver 1969." *The Georgia Straight*, July 30, 1971.

Reed, Bill. "The Beach Boys." *Rock*, November 30, 1970.

Rieley, Jack. "Frank Words from Brian Wilson." *Rolling Stone*, September 17, 1970.

Rodriguez, Juan. "An Interview with Carl Wilson." *Hit Parader*, March 1969.

Schroder, Peter. "Beach Boys on Holiday in the Netherlands." *Hit Week*, May 18, 1967.

Shapiro, Marc. "Beach Boy Carl Wilson's Solo Toy." *BAM*, May 20, 1983.

Sharp, Ken. "Al Jardine, A Beach Boy Still Riding the Waves." *Goldmine*, July 28, 2000.

Sharp, Ken. "Mike Love." *Goldmine*, September 18, 1992.

Siegel, Jules. "The Religious Conversion of Brian Wilson: Goodbye Surfing, Hello God." *Cheetah Magazine*, October 1967.

Snyder, Patrick. "Beach Boys: Ten Years After." *Crawdaddy*, June 20, 1971.

"Some Producers' Hints from Beach Boy Brian." *KRLA Beat*, April 30, 1966.

Soocher, Stan. "Beach Boys Harmonize." *Circus*, November 21, 1978.

Swenson, John. "Beach Boys: No More *Fun, Fun, Fun*." *Rolling Stone*, October 20, 1977.

Tobler, John. "Return of the Beach Blanket." *New Music News*, June 1980.

Wenner, Jann. "Rock and Roll Music." *Rolling Stone*, December 14, 1967.

"We Travel with the Beach Boys." *Flip Magazine*, September 1966.

Wilson, Carl. "My Brothers: The Beach Boys." *Tiger Beat*, February 1966.

Young, Charles. "Music: Beach Boys Still Feuding." *Rolling Stone*, October 20, 1977.

WEBSITES AND OTHER MEDIA

ESQ's Beach Boys Archives. http://www.beachboysarchives.com

Jeff Griffin, producer. *The Beach Boys Story*. 1974. BBC radio documentary narrated by Bob Harris.

Dick Clark, host. *Dick Clark Presents the Beach Boys: A 20th Anniversary Tribute to the Great American Band.* 1981.

Bellagio 10452. http://www.esquarterly.com/bellagio

Wilson, Brian. Radio interview by Jack Wagner. September 1967.

————. Radio interview by Jamake Highwater. January 11, 1968.

Carl Wilson: Here and Now. 2011. A film by Billy Hinsche.

Endless Harmony. Delilah Films, 1998.

Eric Anniversario's Beach Boys Set List Archive. http://members.tripod.com/~fun_fun_fun/setlists.html

Smiley Smile Dot Net. http://www.smileysmile.net